THE LEAGUE

THE CHEERS . . .

THE PLAYERS . . .

COMMISSIONER PETE ROZELLE—The "Boy Czar" who transformed a floundering giant into a billion-dollar gold mine . . . only to watch his empire disintegrate into chaos before his eyes.

CARROLL ROSENBLOOM—The shrewd, charming yet totally unscrupulous team owner who swapped the Baltimore Colts for the L.A. Rams, he spent his final years obsessed with one goal: the complete ruination of Commissioner Rozelle.

THE LEAGUE

THE CHEERS ...

"HARRIS HAS REPORTED ONE OF THE STUNNING STORIES OF THE DECADE, A BOOK EPIC IN ITS SWEEP, THRILLING IN THE INTENSITY OF ITS HUMAN DRAMA, COMIC IN ITS COLLECTION OF BIZARRE BUFFOONS AND LOUTS, REMORSELESS IN ITS ANALYSIS OF UN-CHECKED GREED AND POWER RUN AMOK ... EVEN TRAGIC IN ITS IMPLICATIONS FOR THE FUTURE OF THE SPORT."
—*Los Angeles Herald-Examiner*

"THE MOST COMPREHENSIVE—AND DAMAGING—BOOK EVER PUBLISHED ABOUT PRO FOOTBALL. THE GOOD, THE BAD, THE RICH AND THE POWERFUL—IT'S ALL HERE."
—*Detroit News*

"ZANY OWNERSHIP. FINANCIAL TURMOIL. FRANCHISE SKULDUGGERY. PASSIONS AND HATREDS. LAWSUITS AND MULTIMILLION-DOLLAR JUDGMENTS. IT'S WON-DERFUL STUFF ... HARRIS'S BOOK IS A REMINDER THAT VERY OFTEN, WHAT GOES ON OFF THE FIELD IN THE NFL IS A LOT MORE INTERESTING THAN THE GAMES."
—*St. Louis Post-Dispatch*

THE PLAYERS ...

AL DAVIS—One of the most despised yet respected owners in the game, he challenged Rozelle's authority, moving his Raiders from Oakland to L.A. and won—almost single-handedly ending the "golden days" of the NFL.

GEORGIA ROSENBLOOM FRONTIERE—CR's glamorous wife, she took control of the Rams after her husband's tragic drowning—and a storm of controversy followed.

THE LEAGUE

THE CHEERS ...

"HARRIS HAS WRITTEN A POWERFUL EXPOSÉ OF THE INNER WORKINGS OF PRO FOOTBALL, FROM 1960 TO THE PRESENT . . . HARRIS HAS BROUGHT OFF A FORMIDABLE UNDERTAKING."   —*Publishers Weekly*

"DEFINITIVE . . . AMAZING . . . ABSORBING . . . EVERY CLUB AND EVERY OWNER, INDEED, EVERY EXECUTIVE IN THE WORLD OF PROFESSIONAL FOOTBALL FROM 1974 TO THE PRESENT DAY, IS GIVEN A COMPLETE DOSSIER. THEIR MACHINATIONS, BOTH PUBLIC AND PRIVATE, ALSO UNDERGO THE SCRUTINY OF THE AUTHOR WHO HAS OBVIOUSLY PRODUCED A BOOK TO STAND THE TEST OF HISTORICAL REVIEW . . . HARRIS GIVES US MORE THAN WE REALLY HAD A RIGHT TO EXPECT TO KNOW. A MONUMENTAL EFFORT HAS BEEN REWARDED BY A MONUMENTAL BOOK."
—*The West Coast Review of Books*

THE PLAYERS ...

BILLY SULLIVAN—The feisty owner of the New England Patriots, he was a Boston battler whose team was pulled out from under him, yet whose fierce pride and tenacity enabled him to win it back.

LEONARD TOSE—The flamboyant, extravagant owner of the Philadelphia Eagles whose scandalous life-style and uncanny ability for losing money threatened to cost him his franchise on more than one occasion.

NOW, ENTER THE HARD-HITTING TRUE STORY OF *THE LEAGUE* . . .

By David Harris

I SHOULDA BEEN HOME YESTERDAY
THE LAST SCAM
DREAMS DIE HARD
THE LEAGUE

THE
LEAGUE
THE RISE AND DECLINE
OF THE
NFL

DAVID HARRIS

BANTAM BOOKS
TORONTO · NEW YORK · LONDON · SYDNEY · AUCKLAND

THE LEAGUE

A Bantam Book

Bantam hardcover edition / October 1986
Bantam revised paperback edition / November 1987

Photo credits (inside back cover):
1st row—UPI/Bettmann Newsphotos, UPI/Bettmann Newsphotos,
UPI/Bettmann Newsphotos
2nd row—UPI/Bettmann Newsphotos, Fred Kaplan/Sports
Illustrated
3rd row—Craig Molenhouse/Sports Illustrated, AP/Wide World
Photos, UPI/Bettmann Newsphotos
4th row—Phil Huber/Sports Illustrated, UPI/Bettmann
Newsphotos

The song "Hoosier Heartland" is by James Irsay.
Vice-President and General Manager of the Indianapolis Colts.

Library of Congress Cataloging-in-Publication Data

Harris, David, 1946–
The League: the rise and decline of the NFL.

Includes index.
1. National Football League—History. I. Title.
GV955.5.N35H37 1986   796.332'64'0973   86-47575
ISBN 0-553-26516-4

Published simultaneously in the United States and Canada

Bantam Books are published by Bantam Books, Inc. Its trade-
mark, consisting of the words "Bantam Books" and the por-
trayal of a rooster, is Registered in U.S. Patent and Trademark
Office and in other countries. Marca Registrada. Bantam
Books, Inc., 666 Fifth Avenue, New York, New York 10103.

PRINTED IN THE UNITED STATES OF AMERICA

O   0 9 8 7 6 5 4 3 2 1

for Martin Arnold, a friend indeed.

ACKNOWLEDGMENTS

The information I have used to construct this book was obtained along four principal avenues of reporting.

The first was a series of interviews with the principal characters conducted between 1983 and 1986. Most were on an attributable basis. Included among these were Joe Alioto, Jack Kent Cooke, Hugh Culverhouse, Jack Donlan, Keith Fahnhorst, Ed Garvey, Robert Gries, Jr., Lamar Hunt, Jim Kensil, Gene Klein, Don Klosterman, Wellington Mara, Bob Marr, Bill McPhail, Art Modell, Bob Moore, Jay Moyer, Stephen Reinhardt, Joe Robbie, Bill Robertson, Art Rooney, Dan Rooney, Steve Rosenbloom, George Ross, Pete Rozelle, Tex Schramm, Billy Sullivan, Chuck Sullivan, Paul Tagliabue, Leonard Tose, and Wayne Valley. Al Davis refused to respond to two letters and some three dozen phone calls, but his version of events was available in great detail through court records, testimony, and depositions. While Georgia and Dominic Frontiere would not consent to a formal interview, they, too, were available through court records and did allow me some off the record contact that helped me to understand them better. In addition, I conducted some thirty other interviews with individuals who directly observed the principals or the events I have chronicled but were themselves either unimportant or tangential to the story I've told. I thank them all for their cooperation.

The second large body of information was provided by the testimony of a number of the principals under oath both before the United States Congress and in a succession of court cases that have spanned more than a decade. The congressional testimony included *Oversight Hearings on National Football League Labor-Management Dispute, Rights of Professional Athletes, TV Blackout of Sporting Events, Inquiry into Professional Sports, Labor Reform Act of 1977, Sports Anti-Blackout Legislation, Oversight Hearings on Equal Employment Opportunities in the National Football League, Professional Sports Anti-Trust Immunity.* The court testimony was available either from courtroom transcripts, deposition sessions conducted under oath, or affidavits, again submitted under oath. Among the court cases were *LAMCC v. NFL, NASL v. NFL, Mackey v. NFL, Gries Sports Enterprises v. Cleveland Browns, Valley v. Davis, Barrero v. Davis, Coggins v. New England Patriots, Tose v. First Pennsylvania Bank, City of Oakland v. Oakland Raiders,* and *Philadelphia Eagles et al v. Oakland Raiders.* In total, this avenue of research yielded tens of thousands of pages of direct examination on the subjects I have explored. In most cases, the materials were loaned me by various law firms involved and I thank them all very much for their cooperation, but will refrain from naming them lest they be held responsible for what I've written.

The third pillar upon which this book was constructed was an immense store of documentary information made available either through the cooperation of the National Football League, the cooperation of individual owners, or through the evidence process in the above-mentioned legal actions. Again, this avenue yielded thousands of pages of valuable material whose validity was either without question or attested to under oath. Among those materials were the complete National Football League minutes between 1972 and 1984, the SRI Report on Expansion, the letters between Pete Rozelle and Lamar Hunt on the subject of ownership policy, the communications between the commissioner's office and the rest of the League on the same subject, the letters between Pete Rozelle and Al Davis on the subject of Davis's move to Los Angeles, portions of the minutes of the Los Angeles Memorial Coliseum Commission, the internal memos of the banks involved in the restructuring of the New England Patriots, the communications between Carroll Rosenbloom and Cabot, Cabot & Forbes on the subject of Anaheim Stadium Associates and their mutual communications with the city of Anaheim, and the communications between Robert Gries and Art Modell concerning Cleveland Stadium Corp.

The fourth and final informational base was the enormous body of reporting done over the last twenty years by more than 150 newspapers, magazines, and authors. In collecting this reservoir of fact and anecdote, I was aided immeasurably by the cooperation of a number of institutions who opened their facilities or clipping files to my purposes. Among them were the Stanford University libraries, the University of California libraries, the Cleveland Public Library, the Miami Public Library, the Data Center, the National Football League, *The New York Times,* the *Los Angeles Times,* the *San Diego Union* and the *San Diego*

Tribune, The Dallas Morning News, The [Baltimore] *Sun, The Boston Globe, The* [Philadelphia] *Inquirer, The* [Oakland] *Tribune,* the *San Francisco Chronicle, The Washington Post, The Indianapolis Star* and *The Indianapolis News,* the *Kansas City Times, The Phoenix Gazette,* and the *Miami News.* The reportage assembled along this avenue was a critical element in nailing down this story and for that I wish to thank the thousands of reporters who had covered this ground before I reached it. While I didn't necessarily follow their footsteps, knowing where they'd been was of great use.

I also wish to credit the people who assisted me in assembling this body of information. My personal research assistant, Ted Tyson, was invaluable for his insights as well as his research. In addition, a number of other individual researchers aided me in this task: Mary Louise Madigan, Brad Kava, Will Brults, Maria Newman, Chris Wolff, Mel Greenberg, Craig Smith, Virginia Baker, Lucy Anderson-Morshead, Louise Beale, and Liz Davis. My computer services were provided by Peter Golitzen and PKG Systems.

The people who made all this effort worthwhile were my agent, Kathy Robbins, her agency, the Robbins Office, and my publisher, Linda Grey.

Finally, I must thank my wife, Lacey Fosburgh, my son, Gabe, and my daughter, Sophie. This book took me away from our mutual life at critical moments for all of them and they welcomed me back nonetheless. On numerous occasions they were forced to cover my act as a husband and father, so I could pursue this project. In all circumstances, they endured my obsession and comforted me when I needed comfort badly. It all would have been impossible without their support.
—D.H.
    April 1986

PART ONE

STATUS
QUO
ANTE

1
The Good Old Days Begin to End

The 1974 annual meeting of the National Football League convened behind closed doors at the Americana Hotel in Bal Harbour, Florida, on February 25 at 10:00 A.M. Scheduled to last a week, this yearly gathering was traditionally the longest and most significant of the NFL's business year, and the lobby outside was swarming with reporters.

By 1974 the long and costly war with the American Football League had been officially over for four years, and the twenty-six-team professional football monopoly that had emerged from the conflict was the ranking success story of the sports/entertainment industry. Super Bowl VIII, climaxing the NFL's season just a month before, had been the third most watched sporting event in American television history, topped only by the two preceding Super Bowls. Those events' audience included more Americans than had voted in any presidential election in the nation's history. *Christian Century* called it "America's new religion." To most of those who watched, football, as presented to the public by the NFL, was simply "America's game."

Its constitution and bylaws defined the NFL as an "unincorporated association, not for profit," organized "to promote and foster the primary business of League members, each member being an owner of a professional football club located in the United States." Membership was limited to twenty-six franchises, each of whom granted the League "exclusive control of the exhibition of football games in the home territory of each member" in exchange for one vote in the League's innermost councils. All the League's decisions required at least a three quarters majority. Overseeing this process for the League was "a person of unquestioned integrity"—the commissioner—who was granted "full, complete, and final jurisdiction and authority" over "any dispute involving a member or members in the League."

Pete Rozelle had been the commissioner for the last fourteen years—an unprecedented reign in the more than fifty years of

3

NFL history. By the time the League met in Bal Harbour, the position and Rozelle's persona were virtually synonymous. At forty-seven years old, Rozelle looked tan and fit. Six feet two inches tall, he managed to seem smaller. His dark hair was receding and long cheeks gave Rozelle's face a hound-dog look that made him seem easygoing and appealing. It was difficult to find a hard edge anywhere in his demeanor. Rozelle was, everyone agreed, "a nice guy," and his plain vanilla style made him an easy man to underestimate. To do so was, of course, a mistake.

At the time, the commissioner seemed without challenge. Leonard Tose, majority owner of the Philadelphia Eagles, observed, "It's more like we work for him than he works for us." Jack Kent Cooke, part owner of the Washington Redskins, called Rozelle "as skillful a politician as I have met in my life." Al Davis, managing general partner of the Oakland Raiders, summed it up. "Rozelle," he claimed, "is the most powerful man in professional sports." When the League met in Bal Harbour, it seemed Pete Rozelle's dominance would last forever.

It would not.

That no one in Bal Harbour noticed what was in store for Pete Rozelle and the National Football League was understandable. In those days, it was hard for anyone to look at the League and see much besides unmitigated success, and no single individual was given more credit for that success than Rozelle. Comprised of just twelve teams when he took office in 1960, most of them confined to the northern industrial belt, the League's current twenty-six were spread among each of the nation's major areas, with the sole exception of the Pacific Northwest. The biggest membership jump had come in 1966, when the upstart rival American Football League merged into the NFL. After this merger, the football business entered the golden years of "the Rozelle era." In the year before Rozelle was hired, the NFL had staged seventy-two games in front of 3,140,000 paid spectators; in 1973 the League presented 182 games cheered from the stands by 10,731,000 fans. The first League-wide TV contract negotiated by Rozelle in 1962 had been worth $326,000 a year to each franchise. The contract completed with the 1973 season was worth $1.7 million a year to each of twice as many teams.

As a matter of policy, Pete Rozelle attempted to underplay such business matters whenever he could. "The strong public view that professional football is more business than sport," he explained, "can only hurt the game." Instead, Rozelle's League was marketed on another plane altogether. "We sell an experience," he explained. To an audience whose own five-day-a-week struggles were generally confused, mundane, restrained, and without resolution, the weekend battles staged by the League were clear, heroic, uninhibited, decisive, and, at times, even noble. In 1961, after Pete Rozelle's first year, thirty-four percent of the nation told the Gallup Poll they considered baseball their favorite sport and only twenty-one percent named football. By 1972, thirty-six percent named football and only twenty-one percent baseball. Along the way, Rozelle became the only sports executive ever to be named Sportsman of the Year by *Sports Illustrated*, an honor otherwise reserved for athletes and coaches. Rozelle, the magazine pointed out, was "perfectly cast in the role of a modern executive" and had "decisively and brilliantly guided a great and growing sport." Art Rooney, owner of the Pittsburgh Steelers, called Rozelle "a gift from the hand of Providence." By 1974, his skill at handling his employers was legendary. "He lets the owners talk unchecked," one NFL executive noted, "and wear themselves down. By the end of the meeting, he railroads what he wants through when everyone is tired and wants to go home. His patience is infinite."

As was his tradition, Rozelle opened the 1974 annual meeting with his "Annual Report and Review," delivered with an earnest touch in typical low-key manner.

A great deal of his report this year was devoted to public relations. Though confident, Pete Rozelle was not sanguine about the future and repeated a somewhat ritualized warning. At the 1972 annual meeting, he had "again emphasized that self-discipline . . . and strong internal discipline . . . could help avoid problems." In 1973, he said that "although the NFL was widely respected for its harmony and togetherness, cooperation and interchange was more important than ever because internal disputes had increased in the past year." Now, at Bal Harbour, he struck the same note again. Nineteen seventy-three had been a record year for club fines, and he said that, members could look for an escalation of disciplinary action should violations continue. Commissioner Rozelle urged each organization to stress that public statements by any NFL members about League matters could have serious legal and public relations consequences

The minutes made no record of how Rozelle's twenty-six employers responded to his lecture. A number of them no doubt had been distracted by the first item on the agenda: new four-year television contracts with CBS, NBC, and ABC. It was news the twenty-six had been awaiting eagerly, and Pete Rozelle, as usual, did nothing to disappoint them.

Rozelle had spent the last few months in face-to-face negotiations with the networks as the NFL's sole bargaining agent, empowered to make whatever deal he chose. "As a negotiator," one of the network representatives remembered, "Rozelle was cool as a cucumber and very definitive on the things he wanted. He appreciated what TV could do and had mastered its demographics." Those demographics gave the commissioner enormous leverage over networks in the business of selling advertising time. "With the networks," Rozelle remembered, "we were able to stay very close to the numbers we walked in with."

Over the next four years, he announced, the three networks would collectively pay the NFL $60 million a year. Split twenty-six ways, that was $2.3 million per franchise per year, an increase of some $600,000 each. "They were pleasantly surprised," Rozelle remembered. "They always were." At the time, the deal seemed enormous.

Several of those listening to the commissioner's annual report remembered a lot of self-congratulatory chuckles and suckings of breath. In 1974, it was widely assumed his twenty-six employers were putty in Pete Rozelle's hands.

2
Pete Rozelle Rises from Obscurity

Few had expected such singular achievement from Pete Rozelle when he assumed the commissionership at age thirty-three. He was a man whose pervasive ordinariness masked what would later prove to be extraordinary talents.

Born outside Los Angeles in 1926, Pete Rozelle's given name was Alvin Ray. Neither of his parents liked the name Alvin, and in the years immediately after his birth, each blamed the other for choosing it. Finally a kindly uncle supplied the nickname "Pete" and it stuck. Most of Pete's early life was spent in Lynwood, California, then a small town southwest of Los Angeles. Pete's father, Ray Rozelle, owned a small grocery store that went belly-up during the Depression. Ray started over as a shipping clerk, then purchasing agent, at the nearby Alcoa aluminum plant.

Pete was the older of Ray's two sons, and his father was the biggest single influence in his life. "He was my role model," Pete remembered. "I got my temperament from him. He in particular was a calm person. I got his patience probably. He had a lot of friends and was regarded as a good guy." The best piece of advice Pete Rozelle can remember from his early days is from a summer day camp counselor: "Character is what you are and reputation is what people think you are. If your reputation is bad, you might as well have bad character."

"Whether it's right or wrong," Rozelle remembers, "this is the standard you have when you exist in the limelight. Your reputation is valuable. You might as well have bad character if people think you do."

In Lynwood, much of Rozelle's time was spent in sports. Pete attended Methodist Sunday school until age twelve, but dropped out to play touch football instead. The world he occupied was "middle class or lower middle class," long on wholesomeness and short on glitter. At nearby Compton High School, Rozelle was a six-foot forward on the varsity basketball team and played doubles on the tennis squad. His first contact with the strata of money and power came when the Compton basketball squad was bused up to Beverly Hills High School for a game. "Beverly Hills High School had an oil well on its grounds," he remembered, "and I'd never seen anything quite so plush before. Their gym had glass backboards. At halftime, the gym floor parted to reveal a swimming pool, and they had an aquatic exhibition instead of song girls. My eyes were like saucers."

Immediately after finishing high school in 1944, Rozelle enlisted in the navy. In 1946, he mustered out, returned home, and enrolled at Compton Junior College. There he worked as the college's athletic news director, and was a stringer covering high school games for the Long Beach and Los Angeles papers. He was paid fifty cents a game.

Pete Rozelle's return from the war also coincided with the arrival of professional football in Los Angeles. That year, the NFL's Cleveland Rams moved to Los Angeles to establish the League's first foothold on the Pacific Coast. It was fortuitous that the Rams chose Compton Junior College as a training camp. Rozelle quickly made contact and was hired as a gofer for Maxwell Stiles, the franchise's public relations director. In his first encounter with the NFL, he made a good impression, and he continued to work for the Rams until he left town to finish college at the University of San Franscisco.

Rozelle also obtained the athletic news director position at USF as a part-time job. When he graduated in 1950, his news director position became full-time. Again luck was with him. Those were the glory years of USF athletics. The football team was undefeated and nine of its eleven starting players made successful careers in the NFL. The basketball team won the National Invitational Tournament, then the college sport's most prestigious post-season event. "It was a chance to meet a lot of people," Rozelle said.

One of those he met was Tex Schramm, then general manager of Rozelle's hometown Rams. "USF had a very good football team," Schramm remembered, "and I started working with Pete, getting information about their players. He was a very bright young man. I was very impressed with the way he picked things up." In 1952, when the Rams public relations director left, Schramm offered Rozelle the job. Rozelle served with the Rams from 1952 to 1955, then went back to San Francisco to join a PR firm run by Ken Macker, a New York expatriate Rozelle had first met at USF. Macker was Rozelle's best man at his first marriage and godfather to his only child, Anne Marie. "I've never met anybody that has more captivated me," Macker remembered, "then or since. Pete was a bright, interesting young man. I was extraordinarily impressed by him. I needed a strong partner and I talked him into joining." Macker could not have been more pleased with his new partner.

Rozelle's biggest account in his years with Macker belonged to Australia. The country was preparing for the 1956 Olympics at Melbourne and was receiving so much bad press that the International Olympics Committee threatened to move the games. "Rozelle immediately took the mayor of Melbourne around the country," Macker remembered, "and within two weeks, the feeling was totally reversed." Next, Rozelle took the *Time, Newsweek, Sports Illustrated,* AP, and UPI sports editors to Melbourne for an on-site inspection. Afterward, he was asked to handle the world press for the Melbourne Olympics. In 1957, the NFL began trying to lure Rozelle back. The League's commissioner, Bert Bell, took a personal interest in recruiting Rozelle to rejoin the Rams, largely because the Rams had a problem he thought only Rozelle might be able to solve. In the years since Rozelle had left them, the Rams had been almost paralyzed by

inner turmoil. The difficulties grew out of the club's ownership
arrangement. Fifty percent of the club was owned by Dan Reeves,
and fifty percent by two other partners who could not stand
Reeves. The result was total impasse. By 1957, it had reached
the point where Tex Schramm, fed up with civil war around him,
resigned his general manager's job to join CBS Sports. Bell
wanted someone who could get along with the two warring
factions well enough to get the Rams moving again. Bell thought
Pete Rozelle was exactly what Los Angeles needed.

At first, Rozelle wasn't going for the change. "I'm doing
what I want to do," he told Bell. Bell, however, did not give up,
and before 1957 was over, Rozelle had signed a contract as
general manager of the Los Angeles Rams.

Rozelle was indeed able to bring relative peace to the franchise, making the Rams at least operational. Otherwise, Pete
Rozelle was no great shakes as a general manager. As a judge of
player personnel, he was too inherently sentimental to excel. His
strong suit was marketing. And though he now had access to the
League's top echelons, he was by no means an NFL power. "I
didn't know the big boys very well," he recalled.

That all began to change on October 11, 1959. That Sunday,
while attending a Philadelphia Eagles game, Bert Bell dropped
dead from a heart attack. The commissioner's job remained
vacant for the remainder of the season. The League's 1960
annual meeting took up the issue of Bell's successor at the top
of its agenda. Rozelle, now thirty-three years old, was in attendance to help out his boss, Dan Reeves. Rozelle was not considered a likely candidate; in fact, his name did not even come up
until the meeting was a week under way and a dozen other
candidates had been considered.

Over ten days the owners had cast twenty-three ballots and
gotten nowhere. The leading candidate through most of the
balloting was Marshall Leahy, the San Francisco attorney who
was the NFL's legal counsel. Leahy, however, had made himself
enormously controversial by insisting that, if chosen, he would
move League headquarters from Pennsylvania to San Francisco.
The anti-Leahy faction was led by Art Rooney of the Pittsburgh
Steelers and Carroll Rosenbloom of Baltimore's Colts. The leaders of the pro-Leahy group were Paul Brown of the Cleveland
Browns, Wellington Mara of the New York Giants, and Rozelle's
boss, Dan Reeves. After ten days of deadlock, however, it was,
according to Mara, obvious to the Leahy forces that they couldn't
have their man without "seriously dividing the League." It was

at that point that Pete Rozelle's name first arose. Reeves suggested his General Manager as a compromise candidate. "Few of us knew Rozelle," Mara remembered, "but Reeves's recommendation was high."

"Rozelle?" Frank McNamee of the Philadelphia Eagles blurted out when he heard the news. "Who's he?"

Rozelle learned he was being considered after the January twenty-sixth afternoon session was adjourned. "I was quite surprised," Rozelle recalled, "because of my age." He nonetheless knew he had a significant advantage. "I was the only candidate," he pointed out, "who hadn't already alienated most of the people in that meeting." At the evening session, Rozelle was asked to leave the room while he was being considered. He waited, chain-smoking, in the men's room. To camouflage his reasons for being there, Rozelle washed his hands every time one of the waiting reporters came in to use the facilities.

Back in the room where the League was meeting, *Sports Illustrated* reported, the owners were sunk in "stalemate and despair." The tide was turned when Art Rooney declared that if Rozelle was good enough for Mara and Reeves, he was good enough for Rooney. On a motion by Carroll Rosenbloom, seconded by Paul Brown, at 10:35 P.M., the National Football League voted eight for Rozelle, three abstentions, and one for Leahy. Carroll Rosenbloom was asked to fetch Rozelle from the bathroom, and found him at the sink. By then the future commissioner's hands were soggy.

"Well," Pete Rozelle quipped upon rejoining the meeting, "I can honestly say I come to you with clean hands."

Pencil-necked, skinny, and dog-jowled, Rozelle was also young, relatively inexperienced, and certainly untested. The sports press quickly dubbed him "the boy czar" and, within the hour, bets were being made that it would be only a matter of months before Rozelle's notoriously irascible employers had cut their new boy to shreds and proceeded to find more seasoned help.

3
Rozelle Introduces League Think and Remakes the NFL

The League Pete Rozelle inherited had been founded in 1920, in a Canton, Ohio, Hupmobile showroom. "It was hit or miss," Rozelle explained. "It wasn't very organized. Teams came and they went." In 1926, the League included twenty-two franchises, but by 1931, it was down to ten. Bert Bell became commissioner in 1946, and simple financial survival remained the League's paramount issue until well into his term. As late as 1952, NFL franchises were still going bankrupt and having to be reorganized. The possibility of actually making considerable sums of money out of their teams became an issue of discussion among owners only shortly before Bell's death. Most still found such an eventuality hard to imagine.

Pete Rozelle's first step was to move the League offices from Bala Cynwyd, Pennsylvania, to New York City. Relocating in Manhattan was a move into the Madison Avenue mainstream of American culture. In that same spirit, the young Pete Rozelle recognized football's potential future in television and threw himself into the medium.

"When I came to CBS," remembered Bill McPhail, then President of CBS Sports, "college football was the big package. The NFL was just a blue-collar thing, for guys with no college to root for. The first year we decided to go with it, the rights were all scattered around. Pete changed all that. He understood the industry almost immediately. He would go to affiliate meetings and got to know the big stations. It was hard at first. Local stations made more money then by showing old movies than they did showing professional football games. Pete got friendly with the affiliates and was willing to do things for CBS to help sell them on NFL broadcasts. It was a very smart attitude. At the beginning, people didn't even know about the NFL. Television lifted the League out of the boondocks."

Pete Rozelle knew a good thing when he saw it, and the

11

advent of big-time sports television was the single most fortuitous coincidence of his commissionership. That the NFL had a
genuine national audience was discovered when CBS broadcast
the 1958 Baltimore Colts–New York Giants NFL championship
game, which went into sudden death overtime and became the
talk of the nation for several weeks afterward. At that time, only
a little more than half the nation's households owned TV sets.
Within two years the "boy czar" had used the issue of TV to
remake the League after his own design. "Pete," Dan Rooney,
Pittsburgh Steelers president, observed, "thought League from
his first day on the job."

"League Think" soon was to become the central ideology of
the Rozelle era. "One of the key things that a sports league
needs," Rozelle would point out over and over, "is unity of
purpose. When you have unity and harmony and can move
basically as one, you can have a successful sports league." For
Rozelle, "the basic objective of the League rules is to reverse
the process by which the weak clubs get weaker and the strong
clubs get stronger. . . . The entire history of professional football supports the importance of these rules. Leagues do not come
and go, and one sport does not gain on another because of the
superiority of their stronger teams. Favorable results are a product of the degree to which each league can stabilize itself through
its own competitive balance and leaguewide income potential."
It was a simple premise: "When we stay together on something,
we're normally successful and we grow. When we're going to
splinter off, we're not as successful." The object of the approach
was to transform what had been a feudal organization into a
modern corporate combine, "a single entity, like Sears or
McDonald's."

League Think was introduced into the NFL through Rozelle's
TV policy. He proposed that the League sell its collective TV
rights as a single package and share its broadcast revenues
equally among all franchises. If each franchise were left to shift
for itself, he argued, the ensuing division into rich and poor
would give a few big market franchises enormous advantages as
television grew. This would cause a corresponding imbalance on
the field, greatly lessening the marketability of the League as a
whole and costing everybody money in the long run.

The commissioner's argument was underlined by the policy of
the recently organized rival American Football League which, in
1960, incorporated leaguewide pooling of television rights and
revenues in its first broadcast contract with ABC. The arrange-

ment was an idea Lamar Hunt, the AFL's founder, had borrowed from Branch Rickey, the legendary baseball entrepreneur. In addition to that AFL precedent, CBS was also pressuring the League to adopt Rozelle's proposal because that network was forced to watch NBC compete with it by paying for only two of the League's teams while it paid for nine and got the same thing.

Pete Rozelle credited the League's owners for the innovation. "We were able to do it," he remembered, "because the owners thought League. The Maras in New York, Dan Reeves in L.A., and George Halas in Chicago—the three dominant markets— agreed to share TV equally with the others, which was a major concession. They were wise enough to see the long term and they've been rewarded. All the franchises have seen their money increase from TV as a consequence and the League as a whole has remained strong. All of the franchises have remained viable and have the means to compete with the rest of the League. That's what I think sports should be."

Getting his employers to accept the arrangement was, however, only part of the problem Rozelle faced. He also had to secure a limited antitrust exemption from Congress in order to put the agreement into practice. Apprehensive that such sharing might be considered an illegal monopoly under the Sherman Act, Rozelle had first had the League attorneys pursue a declaratory judgment from the federal courts to the contrary. When the Court ruled against the League, Pete Rozelle spent the summer of 1961 in Washington, D.C., lobbying for legislative help. In September 1961, Congress finally passed a Sports Antitrust Broadcast Act, allowing sports leagues to pool and sell their TV rights. The bright, earnest, vanilla young commissioner had proved one of the better outside operators Capitol Hill had seen in a while and his work began to pay off immediately. The first Leaguewide TV contract Rozelle negotiated was with CBS Sports for the years 1962 and 1963. It paid the League $4,650,000 a year, some $330,000 per franchise. League Think hit high gear in 1964 when the next contract came up for bids, this time from all three networks in a highly publicized bidding contest. The winning offer was $14.1 million a year from CBS. Per franchise that was $1 million a year—ten times more than any team had made from TV under Bert Bell. The sum was considered so astounding that William Paley, CBS's founder and chairman, worried to Bill McPhail that the contract "appears irresponsible to stockholders, worse than Hollywood."

That contract confirmed Pete Rozelle's claim to power within the League. With this kind of money to share, sharing was easy. In truth, the financial escalation, like League Think, had only just begun. Henceforth, League Think would become manifest in virtually every economic aspect of the football business, starting with the gate. Rozelle explained, "After direct game expenses, [the NFL] splits the gate receipts of each game on a sixty-forty basis—sixty percent to the home team and forty percent to the visiting team. . . . Every NFL club is thus economically dependent on the sucessful home business operations of every other NFL club." Ed Garvey, executive director of the League's player's union, described the arrangement as "socialism for management." Rozelle preferred "one for all and all for one." By whatever name, League Think was the lynchpin of the Rozelle era.

If they underestimated his vision, those who doubted the choice of Rozelle as commissioner in 1960 also underestimated the toughness he would employ to implement that vision. Rozelle, one owner later noted, "can be cold as a whore's heart, all the while flashing that PR smile." The "boy czar's" conflict with George Preston Marshall, then owner of the Washington Redskins, came during the campaign for a new TV policy and educated the doubters. Early on, Rozelle took Bill McPhail along to Washington, D.C., to bring Marshall around. "Marshall was a real character," McPhail remembered. "He had his own individual network around the country and thought of himself as a TV visionary. He was resentful of Rozelle. . . . Pete would ask him a question and Marshall would scream, lecture, and shake his finger. Pete sat there and took it all, and when Marshall finished screaming, took up where he left off. 'Mr. Marshall,' Pete said, 'you still haven't answered my question.' My mind was blown." Rozelle and McPhail left Marshall's office with exactly the agreement Rozelle had set out to get from him.

George Halas's turn came in 1964. The Chicago Bears owner was the only surviving League member who had actually been a participant in the 1920 meeting in the Canton Hupmobile dealership. He was not used to being messed with by anyone, especially not a commissioner half his age. During the 1964 season, Halas made bitter public complaints about the officiating after a game in San Francisco. Such public complaining was a violation of League rules and Rozelle ordered the League's patriarch to New York for a disciplinary hearing. Halas responded that if the commissioner wanted to come to Chicago to see him, he would make time on his schedule. Rozelle said come to New York.

Halas offered to fly into LaGuardia Airport and meet Rozelle there. The commissioner said come to my office in Manhattan. Halas appeared at Rozelle's office as ordered, was fined, and left with his mouth shut.

Perhaps most important, the new commissioner was proving that when he needed to, Pete Rozelle was very good at getting things done. The merger with the AFL in 1966 was the climactic act in forming the League's modern incarnation, and Rozelle's role was central. Once agreed to, the merger required Congressional permission and Pete Rozelle delivered it.

Rozelle received Congressional assistance by dangling an NFL expansion team for New Orleans in front of Louisiana's Senator Russell Long and Representative Hale Boggs. The specific legislation Rozelle sought was attached as a rider on a Johnson Administration anti-inflation bill. An hour before the final House vote on the rider, Rozelle and Hale Boggs met to touch base a final time.

"Well, Pete," Boggs offered, "it looks great."

"Great, Hale," Rozelle answered, "that's great."

"Just for the record," Boggs continued, "I assume we can say the franchise for New Orleans is firm?"

"Well," Rozelle hedged, "it looks good, of course, Hale, but you know it still has to be approved by the owners. I can't make any promises on my own."

Boggs said nothing for a moment, just staring at Rozelle. "Well, Pete," he finally answered, "why don't you just go back and check with the owners. I'll hold things up here until you get back."

Now it was Rozelle's turn to go silent for a moment. "That's all right, Hale," he finally offered. "You can count on their approval."

Less than an hour later, the NFL had its merger exemption.

Three weeks later, the freshly merged football business added its first expansion franchise, the New Orleans Saints.

Pete Rozelle was not yet forty years old when New Orleans joined the League, but all references to the "boy czar" had ceased for good.

4

The NFL Becomes America's Game and Rozelle Finally Finds Company in His Life at the Top

Thereafter, Rozelle's luck continued to hold. Among other things, the peace that now descended on the football business transformed the war that had preceded it into an asset. The rival AFL had been with NBC since 1964 and its competition with the NFL had also become a struggle between the nation's two major networks. The merger left the new NFL on both networks and took advantage of the burgeoning interest in the twin rivalry. TV, entering its color era, had uncovered a seemingly unquenchable appetite for what the football business had to offer.

The League finally invaded prime time in 1970 when CBS broadcast on a few Monday nights as an experiment. "The ratings were very good," Rozelle remembered, but CBS declined to make a bid on weeknight games. At the time, CBS's Monday night prime time was locked up with *I Love Lucy*, and Bill McPhail was told that football would never make it during the week because housewives would not tolerate it. NBC was unwilling to drop *Laugh-In*, its top of the line Monday offering. Monday Night Football went to ABC by default, then dominated its time slot and was an integral factor in turning ABC into a true major network. "What we were after," Rozelle remembered, "was not just the football fans, but the other people." That was, of course, exactly what the League got.

"I was lucky," Rozelle said of his success, "and in the beginning, because of my youth, the owners were very kind to me. . . . I've seen it written occasionally that I'm slick, but I don't think I'm slick. I believe in advance preparation. . . . In everything I do, I work better by trying to work out of the limelight and behind the scenes. My public relations background was helpful. All I had to do in the public relations business was get along with people, which isn't difficult and is fun. The tough part has been the difficult decisions you have to make. I found out early on that you're not going to make everybody happy. There were many times . . . that as many as ten or twelve clubs might be upset with me. Fortunately, there's a turnover on it all the time. You make up with someone and then someone else gets mad at you. . . . You've got to stay cool and get as much information on the subject as you can and try to convince them with logic. . . . It's mainly just patience, calm, preparation, and, I guess, a degree of political persuasion." This professional recipe took Pete Rozelle higher in life than anyone had ever imagined he might rise.

Pete Rozelle's personal journey had been a long one as well. His first marriage had been, according to a Rozelle intimate, an early casualty of his wife's reported alcoholism and the strains of his commissionership. While his divorce was being worked out, he shared a Manhattan apartment with Bill McPhail. With the exception of his responsibilities to the League, Rozelle was unencumbered during that period. That footloose quality diminished after Rozelle's divorce came through and he assumed custody of his daughter, Anne Marie.

He was, all his friends agree, a "conscientious" father. Rozelle set up house on exclusive Sutton Place. During football season, he often spent the weekends on the road but still made a point of taking time to raise his only child. Rozelle was by then a recognizable face to a lot of people. Though he accepted it as a "price" of the NFL's success, he found his own celebrity somewhat confining. Not long after the merger, for example, he took his daughter to the circus in Madison Square Garden. To escape recognition, the commissioner wore dark glasses. His disguise lasted about a minute until "some kid" walked by and said, "Hi, Pete." His daughter laughed. "Daddy," she pointed out, "you just look like Pete Rozelle in sunglasses."

To get away from it all, Rozelle sought out "warm-weather spots where you could both fish and play tennis." He sometimes went to the horse races with Bill McPhail but, for years, he refused to place any kind of bet at all. When he finally did, he insisted McPhail go to the window for him. "For Pete," one of his friends noted, "his reputation for honesty was everything; he cherished his credibility." His only vices were cigarettes and his predilection for relaxing after work with a couple of Rusty Nails.

Rozelle was acquainted with an enormous number of people, but close to only a few. "Despite his coolness on the outside," a friend noted, "he's a lot more sensitive than people realize. He can laugh at himself and . . . he doesn't take himself seriously. Pete likes things to be easy. He hates conflict but isn't afraid of it. He sees the humor in a lot of things. If he were in private business and accomplished what he had with the NFL, he'd be worth one hundred million dollars.''

As football's Rozelle era entered its golden years, the only noticeable deficiency in Pete Rozelle's life was a certain personal loneliness. That vacuum, however, began to be filled at Super Bowl VII in early 1973. There, at one of the League's many parties leading up to the championship game, he was introduced to one Carrie Cooke, an attractive blond divorcee. Her previous husband had been John Cooke, the son of Jack Kent Cooke, a partner in the Washington Redskins. When the party was over, Rozelle asked one of his friends who she was. He next saw her after the Super Bowl game while he was having a drink with one of his close friends. Carrie Cooke came by their table. ''Mr. Rozelle,'' she challenged him, ''I'll bet I can beat you at tennis.'' They were married within the year.

The new Mrs. Rozelle was outgoing and social and she would soon become a factor in both her husband's life and the League. ''She has more influence on him than anybody,'' one of Rozelle's friends explained. ''Their relationship is one of the warmest I've ever observed. They are very close, virtually inseparable.'' In truth, once married, they would never spend a night apart. ''They weren't wedded,'' another friend observed, ''they were welded.''

The big change in Rozelle's life did not go unnoticed inside the League. At Bal Harbour in 1974, his contract was altered so that the League paid for him to take Carrie along on NFL business. One NFL executive observed that ''. . . when Carrie entered the picture, she organized a lot of tennis tournament kind of things to entertain the wives at League meetings. She was a little overbearing and more attractive than most NFL wives. She might be a bit of a phony, it's hard to tell.'' One of Rozelle's future critics went further on the subject: ''She comes on so strong that a lot of owners' wives eventually came to dislike her intensely. She's a great charmer and Rozelle was crazy about her. She wanted power through him. There was a distinct personality change when he married Carrie. Before, he was gentle and diplomatic. . . . She changed him a lot.''

Rozelle himself considered Carrie ''the best thing that ever happened to me.'' They renovated a five-bedroom home in Westchester County, New York, and moved there with their

combined brood. The commissioner commuted to work in a Ford
station wagon provided gratis to the League by the Ford Motor
Company and driven by a League chauffeur. The Rozelles did
most of their personal entertaining at home on the evenings they
weren't in Manhattan for charity events.

The wedding had taken place in December 1973, some two
months before the 1974 annual meeting. It was a private affair to
which just twenty couples were invited. The only League members there were Tex Schramm, Art Modell, and Dan Rooney. All
were close Rozelle friends.

While still honeymooning, the Rozelles flew to Dallas to
watch Schramm's Cowboys battle Max Winter's Minnesota Vikings for one of the two slots in Super Bowl VIII. The commissioner, Carrie, and Marty Schramm, Tex's wife, sat together in
one of the stadium owner's boxes. Tex, as was his habit, watched
the game by himself from the press box. Thinking she would be
gracious with one of Pete's best friends, Carrie arranged with
Marty Schramm for the two couples to have dinner together after
the game. When Rozelle was informed, he winced. A commissioner's wife, he pointed out, must never ask an owner to
socialize after a game. She saw why when the Rozelles and the
Schramms met after the Cowboys had lost, 27 to 10. Schramm
was a figure of somewhat legendary temper, and he was fuming.
He thought the officiating had cost the Cowboys the game and
his comments were, Rozelle remembered, "dramatic, very emotional, and very personal." Carrie was stunned.

"If he's one of your good friends in the League," she gasped,
"what are the rest like?"

5

A Roomful of Egotists—the Owners

The twenty-six men with whom Pete Rozelle's future rested were
often referred to collectively as the most exclusive club in the
United States. Each had his own way of explaining what brought
him to the football business. "It's every sports fan's dream,"
Art Modell, owner of Cleveland Browns, offered, "and I was a
fan." Gene Klein, owner of the San Diego Chargers, pointed out:

"It's different from any other business. It's a disease. You've got to be a little crazy to get into it. There's a great deal of ego involved." Leonard Tose owner of the Philadelphia Eagles, agreed: "Every man wants to own a football team. . . . It's an ego trip and anyone who says it isn't is not telling the truth." Carroll Rosenbloom, owner of the Los Angeles Rams, summed it up succinctly: "When I was just rich, nobody knew me. . . . Now that I own the Rams, everybody knows me." All twenty-six men Gene Klein observed, were "obsessed with the need to win."

"My life and my existence are tied up with the NFL," Tex Schramm admitted. "I get demonstrative." Carroll Rosenbloom ranked near the top on the League's scale of obsessive behavior. One observer noted, "At Rams home games, Rosenbloom doesn't even let the demands of his bladder interrupt his concentration. . . . When nature can no longer be denied Rosenbloom picks up the nearest empty cup and uses it as a urinal."

Most owners characterized their obsession as a public trust. "Nobody really owns an NFL franchise," Gene Klein claimed. "The community owns it—it's a cultural asset of the city." Billy Sullivan, president of the New England Patriots, agreed: "I look on sports as a quasi-civic enterprise and with that comes the responsibility to be good public citizens." Rarely mentioned by any of them was the business behind it all. While the NFL itself was not for profit, its individual members were decidedly *for* profit. For many of the League's more influential members, the football business was their principal means of support. Some were independently wealthy but all twenty-six were fond of talking in private about the bottom line.

During 1973, that bottom line had averaged $6.2 million in gross receipts per franchise—"a gross about the size," one League attorney pointed out, "of a large supermarket." Sixty-one percent of that gross was generated by ticket sales and twenty-seven percent from broadcast rights. According to Arthur Andersen & Company, the League's accountants, the average franchise's total operating expenses totaled $5.3 million. That left more than $900,000 in average operating profit. Collectively, the League's $163 million gross put it $250 million short of ranking in the *Fortune* 500. Any given franchise's tangible assets usually included little more than an NFL membership certificate, a lease on a stadium, and contracts with some fifty players. That relative intangibility had not, however, suppressed those assets' value. A franchise worth $1 million when Pete

Rozelle assumed the commissionership in 1960 was worth in the neighborhood of $15 million in 1974. As a business, Al Davis of the Oakland Raiders observed, any of those franchises was "a very simple operation to run." According to Edward Bennett Williams of the Washington Redskins, "any bright, reasonable person could assimilate" everything needed to run such an enterprise "in two days."

While close to ninety-five percent of the NFL's gross receipts were subject to League Think sharing formulas, profits and losses were not. Each of the League's franchises was a separate legal entity, keeping its own books, and making its own decisions about how its money was spent. The forms of ownership were varied, ranging from sole proprietorships to limited partnerships to private stock syndicates. Each franchise was required to designate one individual to act on its behalf in the conduct of League business. Those twenty-six "owners" met in either a general session, when each owner could be accompanied by two front office employees, or in an executive session, when the owners and the commissioner met alone.

While Rozelle's League Think had centralized much of the NFL's power, there remained large pockets of business activity which were each owner's alone to control. One of the most significant was each franchise's stadium arrangements. All relations between owners and their landlords was franchise business, and the owners had no League obligations other than to file a copy of their lease with the League office. Those leases, unfortunately for Rozelle, remained the nuts and bolts of the football business. Stadiums were still the League's principal financial underpinning. Even with the raises in the new contract, TV would account for only some thirty-four percent of the League's gross revenues. "If you can't fill the stadium," Tex Schramm explained, "none of the rest of it works." In the Rozelle era, of course, filling stadiums had already become the NFL's forte. "Of all professional sports," a Brookings Institution study observed, "football is the one with the most obvious excess demand for its product. . . . The size of stadium capacity comes very close to predicting the size of attendance."

That land office ticket sale business was split according to League Think's universal sixty-forty ratio with some significant variables. One was the lease. According to League rules, the home team could take a fifteen percent deduction off the top for rent and game expenses. While the rent allowance was uniform and Leaguewide, the leases governing the rents were not. The

difference between actual rent and the League's rent allowance
was considered found money, the home team's to keep. Stadium
leases were generally longterm but of varying duration, so only a
few leases were ever up for negotiation at any given time. After
1974, many franchises would be involved in their first lease
negotiations since the emergence of football as America's Game.
The leverage thus afforded each football baron over his respective landlord was large and growing steadily.

The most obvious evidence of that leverage in 1974 was an
escalating scale of commitments by stadium authorities to finance and construct new, "modern" stadiums. This construction
boom was such that the NFL, as part of the AFL merger agreement, made a home stadium with a minimum seating capacity of
fifty-five thousand a condition of membership. By the time the
Rozelle era was well on its way to falling apart, twenty-three
franchises would play in new or remodeled stadiums. *Fortune*
called it all "Promoters v. Taxpayers in the Super Stadium Game."

Houston had pioneered the Super Stadium Game in 1962 with
the $43 million Astrodome, the nation's first domed stadium and
home field to the Houston Oilers. The construction boom took
off in the early 1970s. In Michigan, $126 million was committed
to build the Silverdome in suburban Pontiac, home field of
William Clay Ford's Detroit Lions. New Jersey committed $300
million to erect a marshlands sports complex with a seventy-five-
thousand-seat stadium for Wellington Mara's New York Giants.
The state of the art superstadium circa 1974 was New Orleans's
Superdome, the largest fully enclosed stadium in the world, with
seats for nearly seventy-five thousand football fans. Originally
scheduled to cost $35 million, the Superdome eventually cost
almost five times that much. Faced with this monumental over-
run, a Louisiana official responded by reassuring the citizenry
that "we are not going to let a couple of million dollars stop
us."

Still relatively fresh to the big time in 1974, Pete Rozelle's
twenty-six employers had yet to take such inflated treatment for
granted or realize just how far their leverage might carry them.
Most were still just marveling at how the rising tide of superstadia
was transforming the game. What was once played in the mud or
trampled sod was now staged on artificial carpets that remained
green, clean, and intact whatever season of the year. Where
ticket purchasers had once huddled along splintered wood benches,
more and more watched from the snug comfort of molded plastic
seats totally removed from the weather. Giant television screens

offered the crowd instant replays, commentary, and advertise-
ments—just like TV.

With the superstadium came the "luxury box." Completely
enclosed, these boxes usually held anywhere from eight to twenty
people and were generally located along the stadium's best sight
lines. The occupants of luxury boxes watched the game below
through giant Plexiglas windows, entered their boxes on private
elevators, and had their own private bars, kitchenettes, and rest
rooms. While only a minority of franchises had such accommo-
dations in 1974, all the League's owners wanted them. They
added a new, privileged upper echelon to the swarming crowds.
Proprietorship of those boxes could be had for $15,000 to $30,000
per box per year. And luxury-box income was not covered by
any of League Think's sharing formulas. Any owner who could
get luxury-box income could keep it all.

None of these changes in the football business seemed a
significant threat to League Think when the NFL gathered at Bal
Harbour, yet stadiums would easily prove the most volatile
element in the League's coming destabilization, embroiling each
of the football barons in his own local war. Some years down the
road, the stadium issue would also provide the staging ground
for the decisive assault on Pete Rozelle's commissionership.

6
Tex Schramm—
"Mr. Vice-Commissioner"

While the stability that reigned in the NFL was identified with
Pete Rozelle, it was by no means a single-handed accomplishment. Perhaps the most helpful figure to the commissioner in
effecting his agenda was his old friend Tex Schramm, president
of the Dallas Cowboys, and sometimes jokingly referred to as
"Mr. Vice-Commissioner."

Technically, Schramm was not an owner at all. The Dallas
Cowboys were actually owned by a partnership dominated by
Clint Murchison Jr., an heir to the legendary Texas oil fortune
amassed by his father and namesake. In 1982, Clint Jr. and his

brother, John, were worth $260 million and owned ninety per-
cent of the Cowboys. Clint handled the football interest for the
family.

Nevertheless, it was Tex Schramm's team. He had run the
entire operation since its founding in 1960. Clint Murchison
attended only two meetings during his entire ownership and,
unlike most owners, never meddled. "I'd rather let the people
who know what they are doing run things," he observed. "Besides, I'm shy."

It was the kind of relationship Rozelle held up to the public
and the rest of the League as the model NFL ownership. Ideally,
an owner "has plenty of money outside of football and [leaves]
the running of the team to a competent football man," he said.

Tex Schramm's acknowledged expertise as a "football man"
was the basis of his NFL stature as well as his control of the
Cowboys. "He's the best," one owner acknowledged. "He's
the most knowledgeable football man in the League. . . . He's a
no bullshit kind of guy." Another reason for Schramm's influence inside the NFL was, of course, that he and Pete Rozelle
went back a long way.

Texas Schramm Jr. was born in 1920 in Los Angeles. He
enrolled as a journalism student at the University of Texas
shortly before the outbreak of World War II. There he played on
the freshman football team and worked on the student newspaper.
After the Japanese attack on Pearl Harbor, Schramm joined the
Army Air Corps and was discharged at war's end with the rank
of captain. He finished his studies, then worked as a sports editor
for two years before abandoning journalism for good. His got his
first job in football in 1947 when he learned that the Rams
managing owner, Dan Reeves, was looking for a new publicity
director. As the Rams' general manager in the early 1950s,
Schramm first met Pete Rozelle. It would prove a long association.

Tex Schramm stayed with the Rams for ten years until driven
out by the disorder inside the franchise. When the opportunity to
go to New York and join CBS Sports arose, he jumped at the
chance and was eventually replaced by his friend Pete Rozelle.
At CBS Schramm worked under Bill McPhail as assistant director of sports, obtaining events to televise. Among the contracts
he handled were those with the network's assortment of NFL
teams.

Tex Schramm's path finally merged with Rozelle's at the 1960
League meeting at which Rozelle was chosen commissioner. The
other hot issue that winter was the prospect of expanding the

League by two more franchises, one to be located in Dallas. Schramm was recommended to its prospective owner, Clint Murchison, by George Halas and Murchison hired Schramm as general manager of a franchise that did not yet exist. CBS let him resign contingent upon Murchison actually securing the franchise he sought.

The primary roadblock to NFL expansion into Dallas in 1960 was George Preston Marshall, then owner of the Washington Redskins and one of the most powerful figures in the League. Marshall's television holdings were largely in stations around the South, and he thought of the entire area as Redskins home turf. He had steadfastly opposed any invasion of the region by another football team. In addition, there was no love lost between Marshall and the rich young Texan, Murchison. During the 1950s, Murchison had sought unsuccessfully to buy Marshall's franchise with the idea of selling it should the NFL expand into his hometown, but the deal fell apart because Marshall insisted on being kept on by the new ownership in a management position and Murchison did not want him. Marshall led the fight to keep the NFL from expanding into Dallas.

Then Murchison played his hole card.

Marshall loved band music at football games and in particular loved his team's fight song, "Hail to the Redskins." He had, however, fired the song's composer, and in a fit of pique the bandleader had sold the rights to the tune to a Murchison crony. When Murchison threatened to deny the Redskins the use of their theme song, Marshall relented and the Dallas Cowboys were born on January 28, 1960. Not counting the price of the song, the franchise cost Murchison $600,000.

As the new franchise's general manager, Tex Schramm immediately set about building his reputation as a "football man." Though starting an NFL team from scratch was no small task, the Cowboys would soon be identified by Rozelle as "the most successful modern expansion team in the NFL." At the fore in that rise was Schramm, "one of the game's great innovators."

In 1962, for example, an IBM subsidiary approached the fledgling franchise seeking to sell it computers to handle its accounting problems. Instead, Schramm challenged them to develop a system to handle the task of choosing which football players to hire. Within a few years, the Cowboys' computerized system was acknowledged as the premier scouting apparatus in the League.

In 1964, Murchison named Schramm president and gave him

the option to buy twenty percent of the team at its 1960 price. In the early 1970s, Schramm exercised that right and then quickly retired his stock for what the *Dallas Morning News* described as "a huge profit."

Though long acknowledged as "a driving force" inside the League, Schramm confirmed his central role in 1966, when the war with the American Football League had been going on for six long and expensive years. Several different informal contacts between owners of the two leagues had gone nowhere. The contact that finally led to peace took place between Tex Schramm and Lamar Hunt at Dallas's Love Field airport on April 6, 1966. The two men knew each other from the early days in Dallas, when Hunt's AFL franchise was located there.

At the time of their meeting, Hunt was headed to the AFL gathering in Houston, where Al Davis would be appointed AFL commissioner. Hunt and Schramm's first conversation about merger took place inside a parked car at the airport. "At this point," Schramm remembered, "we did not want to be seen together." Hunt was noncommittal about the plan presented to him, but agreed with Schramm's proposal that the two act as the leagues' intermediaries. A month later, the two met again at Hunt's home and then again the following week. At that point, Hunt was finally convinced that "any problems could be solved." That conclusion was followed by another month of frantic negotiations between Schramm, Rozelle, and the rest of the NFL owners on the one hand, and Hunt and the rest of the AFL on the other. All of it was cloaked in secrecy so intense that at one point, Schramm and Rozelle registered under assumed names in a Washington, D.C., hotel in order to meet with Hunt and then forgot to tell Hunt what name they had registered under. As a consequence, the AFL representative spent two hours in the lobby trying to locate them.

On June 8, 1966, the agreement for merging the two leagues was announced. Its three key provisions were the payment of $18 million in indemnities by the AFL, a four-year interim period before commencing business as a single organization, and the retention of Rozelle as the merged NFL's commissioner. In all accounts of the process, Tex Schramm was described as its "architect."

7

Schramm Builds the Cowboys ...
and Murchison Plays
the Superstadium Game

At the heart of Tex Schramm's first-among-equals stature inside the League was the success of the franchise he built. Football was America's Game, but Schramm's Cowboys alone were "America's team"—the most visible and prestigious of the League's franchises. As a history of the franchise noted, "the Cowboys have more avid fans coast to coast than any other athletic team in our history." Among the thousands of T-shirts, mugs, pennants, and ashtrays embossed with team decals licensed by NFL Properties, close to half the annual sales were Dallas Cowboy items.

The Dallas franchise was predicated upon stability. Starting from the ground up in 1960, Schramm had installed a system and stuck with it. The front office he assembled was recognized as "the ablest in the League" and every person in it, from owner to head coach, had remained unchanged throughout the franchise's fourteen-year history.

Schramm's goal had been to build a model modern football organization and he had been enormously successful. In addition to pioneering the uses of computers in its talent search, Schramm's Cowboys were also the first to make all its prospective employees take tests measuring intelligence as well as personality and character traits. Schramm was looking for people who, in his words, are "really hurt when they lose or are embarrassed publicly." To find such people, he needed as much information as possible. "Nothing escapes us," one Cowboy assistant coach bragged. By 1974, Schramm's approach had made the Dallas franchise into what *Esquire* called "the playing field apotheosis of America's twentieth-century corporate technology."

The Cowboys were among the first to win big in the Super Stadium Game. Real estate was a subject about which Clint

Murchison did not claim ignorance, and securing a new stadium for his team's home games would be his principal personal contribution to the franchise's ongoing operation. He wanted Dallas to build a downtown sports entertainment complex, but in spring 1966 the city government instead committed themselves to refurbishing the existing Cotton Bowl. Murchison called it throwing good money after bad and decided to pursue his other option.

That other option was land Murchison had purchased in the Dallas suburb of Irving, Texas. Murchison was an NFL pioneer in his choice of locations. He was the first to discover the leverage afforded by playing the suburbs off against the cities they surrounded. "As I see the situation," Clint later explained, "Irving would like to build the stadium and the city of Dallas wouldn't."

The deal Murchison cut in Irving influenced the standards of reward and control in the Super Stadium Game for years to come. Under its terms, Irving financed the $25 million project through the sale of thirty-five-year bonds, but management of the stadium during the life of those bonds was the sole responsibility of Texas Stadium Corporation, a wholly owned subsidiary of the Dallas Cowboys. The contract for constructing the stadium went to J. W. Bateson Co., Inc., owned by the Murchison brothers. The contract to sell concessions at the stadium went to Cebe Corporation, a subsidiary of the Dallas Cowboys. The exclusive right to sell liquor at the stadium went to the Cowboys' Stadium Club. The insurance contract was given to Kenneth Murchison Co., the insurance agency that had belonged to Clint's late uncle and of which Clint owned eight percent. As one critic of the deal put it, "if you mailed a letter to the mayor of Murchison, Texas, it would be delivered to the City Hall in Irving."

Though the rest of the NFL admired Murchison's favorable terms, the most acclaimed aspect of the Cowboys' new stadium was its accoutrements. Texas Stadium dubbed their 158 luxury boxes "the circle suites." In addition to its purchase price, a circle suite required the purchase of $50,000 in stadium bonds, the purchase of twelve season tickets at $1300 per ticket per season for thirty-two of the next thirty-five years, and the purchase of twelve memberships in the $300-per-season Stadium Club. The luxury boxes sold like hotcakes, half of them purchased by Dallas-based corporations for expense account entertaining. The circle suite owner received a sixteen foot by sixteen foot bare concrete shell. Decor varied with the individual taste and bank accounts of the owners, but perhaps the top of the line was a suite described in the *Dallas Morning News:* "blue velvet Louis XIV couches, gilt armchairs, blue velvet draperies, miniature bar with leather armrests, tufted velvet love seats, crystal chandelier hanging from a vaulted gold ceiling, and hand-painted French panels concealing closed-circuit television sets for instant replays." Within ten years of Texas Stadium's opening, circle suites would be moving on the resale market for as much as $600,000 apiece—$2,343 a square foot.

Murchison applied his financing plan to the rest of the seats in the house as well. Seating between the thirty yard lines required the purchase of one one-thousand-dollar bond per seat and seats outside the thirties and into the end zones went for a $250 bond. The scheme soon led to impassioned newspaper editorials "on behalf of the tens of thousands of fans who dearly loved their Cowboys and now possibly can't afford them." Murchison was unmoved. "What could be fairer than having the stadium financed by the fans who use it?" he asked. The explanation failed to stem the criticism, but Murchison did not have to deal with it. That was Tex Schramm's job. All the bonds were sold on schedule, and Schramm also raised the price of season tickets after the bonds had been sold.

Though he did a credible job of insulating Murchison from the heat over Texas Stadium, Tex Schramm was not nearly as emotionally suited to the demands of public relations as his friend Pete Rozelle. "He makes enemies," one NFL executive observed. "Tex burns fast," another friend explained.

Over six feet tall, Schramm had a thick neck, thinning hair, heavy German cheeks, and very cold eyes. He also had a tendency to flush when angry. Schramm was his most notoriously bellicose when dealing with players. In 1970, he served on the NFL's committee charged with negotiating a new contract with the National Football Players Association. In their most intense phase, the talks lasted through an entire night, hashing over the issue of travel expenses for players who were forced to relocate when traded between teams. At five A.M. one of the player representatives expressed his frustration.

"I don't give a damn about all that crap," the player snapped. "What I want to know plainly is how much money I'll get if I'm traded from say, Green Bay to the Dallas Cowboys."

At this, Schramm exploded out of his seat, almost flying across the table. "That's one goddamn thing you don't have to worry about," the president of the Dallas Cowboys screamed.

Tex Schramm was a man for whom football was just about everything and who was constantly at the mercy of his obsession. His only releases were gardening and deep sea fishing. In his neat and orderly vegetable patch, each row of plants was labeled and obviously well tended. His attachment to working in his garden was, however, strictly therapeutic. "I have to do something when I'm away from football," he explained, "or I'd go crazy." Tex Schramm's taste for salt water angling was a hobby he shared with Pete Rozelle. Their trips to the islands to relax were a way for Schramm to "get away from football" without ever leaving it. Even on vacation in the tropics Tex Schramm was Tex Schramm. Once, he and one of his fishing parties were walking along the shore in the Bahamas when someone spotted a shark cruising in the shallows nearby. Incensed by its lurking, Schramm immediately grabbed a stick, waded into the water, and beat the man-eater over the head.

While Tex Schramm's relentless drive no doubt took its toll on the rest of his life, it made him an effective whip for Rozelle's NFL agenda. Schramm said what he meant, rarely backed off, and the rest of the League listened to Schramm. Where football was concerned, he was right a lot more often than not, largely because he thought about little else. Rozelle counted on Schramm to further League Think, and Schramm did, even when Rozelle's agenda was in such bad shape that Schramm would make no difference.

8
The Rise of Art Modell

If an election had been held among the twenty-six men at Bal Harbour for the title of second most powerful man in the NFL, Tex Schramm's only competition would have been Art Modell, majority owner of the Cleveland Browns.

Modell had little of Schramm's stature as a "football man"; his influence was a function of style and personality. Modell's presence in the League was rooted in his attitude toward the football business as an exclusive club to which he was thrilled to belong. "Art Modell is part of a power clique within the NFL,"

Al Davis pointed out. "He runs in the pack. He has to because he can't operate if he didn't run in the pack." Belonging was a big thing for Modell, and League Think was simply an extension of what any club ought to be. "He enjoys it," one NFL executive observed. "He doesn't have disputes with other people. He's good at League meetings because he has a great sense of humor."

For those owners uncomfortable with Rozelle's starched-collar henpecking about the League's image, Art Modell was enough of a "sportsman" in the nineteenth-century barroom sense to put them at ease. Five feet eight inches tall, dark-haired, hawk-nosed, and built like a stump, Modell was, one sportswriter noted, "a hustler kind of guy," easy to have a drink with, jovial, but always playing the angles. Having friends on both sides of most issues, Modell took the camaraderie approach to League Think. He could bridge divisions in a way Schramm's stubborn advocacy and Rozelle's moralizing could not. Like Schramm, Modell was an unflagging booster of Rozelle's commissionership. The two had been close friends ever since Modell bought into the NFL in 1961. During Rozelle's bachelor years, the two did, Modell recalled, "a lot of crazy stuff" together.

Ironically, Art Modell was far from the commissioner's abstract concept of the ideal owner. He had come to the football business with relatively nothing in the bank and, by 1974, football had made him rich. Far from retreating offstage like Clint Murchison, Modell assumed the foreground in his franchise whenever possible. He enjoyed the attention. The same age as Rozelle, he had not started life anywhere near the top of the ladder. "I went to the school of hard knocks," Modell said of himself. "I worked my ass off for what I got today. I didn't have anything handed to me."

Indeed, Modell's childhood had been a searing experience. He grew up "poor" in Brooklyn, while his father "worked his butt off trying to keep the family going." Art Modell remembered his father as, "a great man. He had a great sense of humor. He was handsome, a wonderful, wonderful father. I loved him dearly." Their relationship was terminated abruptly when Art was fourteen years old. While on a trip to Austin, Texas, George Modell, a traveling wine salesman, was found unconscious and partially clothed in a local hotel and died eight hours later. A woman with whom he had reportedly spent the night had disappeared. "It was," as Modell remembered it, "a terrible blow." The circumstances also mingled embarrassment and scandal with grief. To console his mother, Modell promised her that he would never marry in her lifetime. In the meantime, George Modell's death left his family "devastated financially."

Art Modell stayed in high school until age fifteen and then dropped out to work as an electrician's helper for less than a dollar an hour. He supplemented his income shooting billiards. Modell enlisted during World War II, and was discharged in 1945, a man with few prospects but enormous dreams. Art Modell's dreams started coming true when he returned to New York and cast his lot with the then newborn television industry. After attending the American Theatre Wing on the G.I. Bill, Modell and another student started a production company. Their first break was a contract with ABC in 1948 that led to *Market Melodies,* New York's first daytime television show. "That started the postwar career of Art Modell," Art Modell later recalled.

In 1948, Modell, twenty-three years old, began "knocking on doors at Grand Union with a novel marketing idea"—erecting television sets in the supermarkets and broadcasting twelve hours a day of *Market Melodies.* Modell would supply the television sets and the programming, ABC would broadcast, the sales of advertising would generate revenues to pay for it all, and Grand Union would sell more groceries as a result. Grand Union went for it and *Market Melodies* went on the air in 1949. It was, as one reviewer described it, "twelve hours of solid commercial, uninterrupted by entertainment."

The only part of Modell's daytime television scheme that didn't pan out was Grand Union's. The delicate televisions sets lost their tuning whenever a subway train passed and had to be constantly readjusted. Within four months, Grand Union had removed most of them. The failure did not, however, sour Grand Union on Modell. Grand Union's advertising director remembered, "When he got out of television and into advertising, we stayed with him. Art was a poor boy from Brooklyn and he was going to make it. . . . This guy was a wonder. He always got along. He always had an angle."

Modell got out of television and into advertising in 1954 and stayed there for seven years. His opportunity to move on to the football business came in September 1960. It was a lucky break and Modell made the most of it.

At the time, the Browns were about to be sold but the deal fell apart three days before the contract of sale was to be signed. The franchise's representative called New York theatrical agent Vinnie

Andrews looking for someone to pick up the deal. "I know a guy who's a client of mine," Andrews told him, "and a friend. He's a real football nut, Art Modell." Modell jumped at the opportunity. "I wanted it," he later remembered with great understatement. Within the day, he had committed himself to putting together an offer and immediately began serious negotiations with the sellers. They settled with Modell at $3,925,000, then a record for NFL franchises.

Setting the price was a lot easier than paying it. No bank would loan Modell more than $250,000 on his personal assets, leaving him $3,675,000 short. Cleveland's Union Commerce Bank committed to loaning an additional $2,500,000 against the franchise itself. Modell's plan for the rest had two stages. The first was to find another major partner to provide the additional $250,000 necessary to make a nonrefundable $500,000 deposit in order to seal the deal. The remaining $900,000 Modell figured to raise in a second stage by selling minority partnerships.

Modell's original candidate for the other major partner was Vinnie Andrews, the agent who had turned him on to the deal. Andrews agreed and then, the night before a party Modell was throwing to celebrate his ascension to the NFL, backed out. Modell immediately called his attorney, who, within twenty-four hours, found brewery heir Donald Schaeffer to take Andrews's place.

On January 25, 1961, Modell and Schaeffer bought the Cleveland Browns and began issuing stock. Modell maintained control, and sold off the remaining fifty percent to eight different minority partners. The most significant of those was the Robert Gries family of Cleveland, whose participation in the new ownership had been a condition of sale. Gries bought twenty-eight percent of the stock. Eventually the Gries family's involvement would come back to haunt Art Modell. In the beginning, however, "I was a stranger in town and they introduced me to many people and made me very welcome," he remembered. Nevertheless, Modell was "young and didn't know Cleveland" and, to many, was little more than a carpetbagger from New York. It wasn't until 1964, when the Browns won the NFL championship, that he finally turned the corner on his road to civic elevation. "Winning," Modell pointed out, "changes everything."

From then on, Modell's rise in the eyes of Cleveland was steady. Once he established himself as a winner, Modell fit in easily. During the day, he could be seen driving his maroon-and-black Cadillac with classical music playing on the stereo at top volume. His home was a five-room twenty-fourth-floor apartment on "swanky" Winton Place with a "spectacular" view of Lake Erie. "Art Modell," *The* [Cleveland] *Plain Dealer* pointed out, "is an intense, successful man who can rarely be found at ease. He is static tension, three packs of half-smoked cigarettes and a peripatetic schedule." Throughout the 1960s, he was also considered Cleveland's most eligible bachelor.

Modell's bachelorhood ended in the summer of 1969, some eighteen months after his mother died. Modell was forty-four. His bride, Patricia, was a soap opera actress. Their marriage took place in Las Vegas, at the home of "a top official" of Caesars Palace hotel and casino. Patricia had two sons from a previous marriage whom Modell quickly adopted. The Modells replaced the apartment on Winton Place with a Tudor mansion in the exclusive suburb of Waite Hill.

Waite Hill was a long way from Brooklyn and the childhood terror of financial collapse. In his fifth decade of life, Art Modell was finally rich and he owed it all to the National Football League. Modell got into the football business when the getting was good. Once the Rozelle era of television contracts began, the Browns' receipts skyrocketed, as did the value of the franchise.

Modell used his newfound leverage to consolidate his control over the Cleveland Browns. His first step was to buy Schaeffer out for $1,500,000 in 1965. To raise the capital, Modell wanted the Browns to borrow another $3 million and then pay it out in dividends. His fifty percent share in that dividend would be used to pay off Schaeffer. The only stumbling block to Modell's plan was the Gries family. By now, Robert Gries Sr., who had treated the young Modell "like one of the family," was on his death bed and the rest of the family balked at the arrangement. It was, as one of the Grieses remembered, "the first real hassle" inside the franchise. To convince them, Modell signed an agreement guaranteeing the family two seats on the Browns' seven-man board of directors.

One of the odd aspects of the Browns franchise was that throughout it all, few in Cleveland even knew Art Modell had a partner, and even fewer knew his name. One sportswriter who noticed Robert Gries Jr. riding the Browns plane to road games assumed he was "an auto salesman on a promotional junket." No one informed the reporter otherwise and Art Modell liked it that way. Modell, according to one of his former employees, "wanted to be the Browns and he wanted his name to be associated with the Browns and his name only."

Ignorance about the true state of the Browns' ownership would
continue unchecked until League Think started coming apart.
Then the complaints of Modell's partner would finally become a
source of public embarrassment that Art Modell could not escape. Until then, however, even most of the men meeting in Bal
Harbour assumed their friend Art owned his franchise lock,
stock, and barrel. In 1974, Art Modell was still the Browns, the
Browns were Cleveland, and Art Modell played the role to the
hilt.

9
Modell Plays the Superstadium Game and Cleveland Goes for It

Art Modell's proficiency at pack-running had made him a principal Rozelle lieutenant, serving as the NFL's president during the
merger's transition period. The financial splendors of America's
Game had also made the fatherless hustler from Pacey's Pool
Hall in Brooklyn into an Ohio dignitary of the first order.
Eventually, he would even be mentioned as a possible candidate
for governor. For Modell, his most precious possession was his
"good name" which also translated into dollars and cents. As
much was apparent in the Superstadium Game Modell played
shortly before the 1974 annual meeting.

Cleveland Municipal Stadium was built in 1931 as part of a
plan to attract the 1932 Olympic Games to Cleveland, but the
games went to Los Angeles instead. The eighty-thousand-seat
stadium sat vacant until the Browns finally occupied it in 1946.
Even with tenants, the stadium fared poorly, and, the facility
was "deteriorating at a rapid rate." By 1972, it was a certifiable
shambles. "The electrical system," Modell later testified, "was
in utter chaos and hadn't been touched in years. Every expansion
joint in the stadium was in need of repair . . . chunks of concrete
were falling from the ramps to the concourse . . . and the
plumbing was in disarray. The main structural beam [supporting
the stadium's entire upper deck] . . . had corroded . . . to a size
slightly larger than a pen."

Modell demanded that Cleveland rehabilitate the structure. "I could not get their attention, let alone get any money for such a rehabilitation program," said Modell. In 1972, the Browns' lease with Cleveland came up for renewal and Modell's venture into the Superstadium Game began. At first *The* [Cleveland] *Plain Dealer* reported "Browns, City Agree." At six percent of gross receipts, less the city's three percent admissions tax, the lease Modell "agreed" to was one of the ten best in the NFL. Modell would operate under the terms of this agreement over the next two years, but would never actually sign a lease.

The most significant signal of Modell's intentions in that unsigned lease was the provision allowing the Browns to "abandon the stadium if the team, a private developer, or the city builds a new stadium." Modell proceeded to buy up some two hundred acres in the vicinity of Strongsville, Ohio, eighteen miles from downtown Cleveland, for some $800,000. Eventually, he had a "secret" model of a stadium built in Strongsville kept on display in his office at Browns' headquarters.

Robert Gries Jr., Modell's anonymous partner, saw the model there on several occasions. To Gries, Modell implied that his intention was "to shake up the city of Cleveland," not actually to build in the suburbs. Modell promised to keep him informed, but remained uncommunicative. Ten years later Gries learned that Modell knew "that the stadium couldn't be done cheaply . . . In addition, there was city council opposition in Strongsville. At best, it would have been a battle all the way." None of that was public knowledge at the time.

All the public knew in January 1973 was that Art Modell had bought Strongsville land and appeared well on his way toward building a new stadium outside the Cleveland city limits. Then, said Robert Gries Jr., "Cleveland got panicky." According to Art Modell, "it hit the newspapers like war headlines," and he was approached by two of the city's most prominent bankers and the head of the Greater Cleveland Growth Association and asked to "reconsider" his apparent move. Modell agreed to reconsider if he could put the same monies into Cleveland Stadium as he planned to put into Strongsville.

City Hall was ready. The committee appointed to make recommendations about the "immediate and long-range future of the stadium" was headed by George Steinbrenner III, Modell's friend who would later purchase the New York Yankees. The Steinbrenner committee's thrust was that Cleveland Stadium had to be improved and that the city of Cleveland ought to get out of the stadium business. The blue ribbon report urged renovation and "private professional management" as cures to the city's dilemma. The committee advised Cleveland "that the chances of long-term success would be greatly enhanced if the operation of Cleveland Stadium could be removed from political considerations and placed in the hands of business-oriented management . . . to take over the existing stadium on a long-term lease."

That Art Modell saw himself as that "business-oriented management" and hence his own landlord, was not immediately obvious. Modell's only public hint in early 1973 was his offer to take over Cleveland Stadium's concession contract. In private, however, his plan was much more defined. It was called Cleveland Stadium Corporation, and was originally envisioned as a joint venture with the other major Stadium tenant, the Cleveland Indians. This idea went nowhere. The baseball franchise was in no position to commit itself to any new financial enterprises. As Modell later testified, "the Indians had more financial problems than even the city of Cleveland . . . bank debts up to their eyeballs." Modell then proceeded to develop Cleveland Stadium Corp. as a corporate entity completely separate from the Browns, which would hold a "net operating type lease" with the city of Cleveland, allowing it to treat the stadium as its own for the next twenty-five years.

Modell's first partner in this enterprise was Shelly Guren; Modell would own "a shade better" than fifty percent of Cleveland Stadium Corp. and Guren and several other partners would hold the rest. Modell's proposal was to "invest $10 million in stadium improvements and provide the city with an additional $10 million in revenue" in return for a twenty-five-year lease. In July of 1973, Modell and Mayor Ralph Perk reached an "agreement" that would take another six months of negotiations before being finalized. In the meantime, Shelly Guren brought in as an investor George Steinbrenner III, the man whose blue ribbon committee report had started Cleveland Stadium Corp.'s ball rolling.

To finance the corporation's $10 million in stadium improvements, Modell's plan was what Robert Gries Jr. would later describe as a "win/win" deal. After arranging what was planned to be a shortterm bridge loan secured by the partners' personal assets and a new twenty-five-year lease that Cleveland Stadium Corp.'s Modell negotiated with his own Cleveland Browns, Guren created a real estate investment trust to assume permanent financing. REITs were a Guren specialty and once such an instrument assumed responsibility, "Modell and Guren wouldn't be risking a cent." Art Modell officially became his own landlord on the evening of October 29, 1973, and by January 1974 Cleveland Stadium Corp. was in business.

Though his fellow NFL owners considered Art Modell a "good businessman" as well as a "good guy," Cleveland Stadium Corp. would become a financial disaster, precipitating the crash of Art Modell's civic reputation and the savaging of his hardwon wealth. But like the dismemberment of League Think and the problems that would beset his friend, the commissioner, Art Modell's decline seemed unthinkable in February 1974, when he arrived in Bal Harbour to meet with the rest of the League.

10
Carroll Rosenbloom—"A Prince in His Domain"

Carroll Rosenbloom, owner of the Los Angeles Rams, had begun life with all the things to which Art Modell spent most of his life aspiring. The youngest of eight children, Carroll had been rich since the day he was born in 1907. "I've just been fortunate—I don't think I ever worked that hard," he explained. Carroll Rosenbloom was nonetheless good enough at what he did to turn the significant inheritance from his father into a positive fortune. After his death, his holdings in "land, stock, and oil leases" were worth at least $300 million.

Whereas Modell was driven to wealth by the memory of privation, "C.R."—as Rosenbloom was called by those who worked for him—seemed to be driven simply by the competition of it all. "He liked to win," the Oakland Raiders' Al Davis noted, "and he liked to be number one and he wasn't going to do anything based on just pure emotion or an altruistic experience." C.R. was also vain. "Carroll liked to have things his own way," Wellington Mara of the New York Giants remembered. "He wanted to be deferred to and he didn't like to be told he was wrong. He had a very big ego." When the Rams played at home, *Esquire* noted, "their owner enters the L.A. Coliseum like a head of state: fans calling out his name, Coliseum employees rushing up to wish him their best. Once inside, as the crowd starts to swell, Rosenbloom tours the field, chatting with his players. Shouts of 'Carroll' or 'Mr. R' ring out from the stands and friends try to get his attention. The spotlight is on and Carroll Rosenbloom loves it. He is a prince surveying his domain, a star onstage.''

Carroll Rosenbloom could also be an unscrupulous son of a bitch if the urge struck him. During the 1960s, four insurance companies sued him for making a false fire insurance claim and his sister sued him for breach of trust in the administration of their father's estate, claiming he "favored his own interests at the expense of the other beneficiaries." When he bought out his last remaining minority partners in the Baltimore Colts, his first franchise, in 1964, C.R. neglected to mention to them that the NFL was about to announce a new television contract that would double the value of their shares. "He took advantage of me," one of those partners remembered. "He gave us a sob story . . . He pleaded . . . that he wanted the team for his boy [Steve]. The day after we signed the contract, I saw the headlines that the $14 million CBS contract had been announced. We knew nothing. . . . There isn't any question he let us have it with both barrels right between the eyes."

While all these traits were often cloaked by "the horsepower of his unusual charm," Carroll Rosenbloom stepped on people's toes and enjoyed it. "He didn't like things settled," Steve Rosenbloom, his oldest son, explained. "He liked to stir things up."

Rosenbloom's relationships inside the League were always on-again off-again depending on the state of his itch for combat. Pete Rozelle would later joke about the time when one of C.R.'s fellow owners asked Rosenbloom if he would get six or seven friends together to vote a certain way. Before Rosenbloom could answer, one of them pointed out to him that he would have trouble finding that many friends. Rozelle no doubt chuckled nervously when he told the story. Carroll Rosenbloom feuded with everybody, but the feuds he waged with Pete Rozelle would become his greatest obsession.

The amiability Carroll Rosenbloom first displayed toward the new commissioner in 1960 lasted roughly three years, and was replaced with a resentment that would never quite recede. The collapse of their relationship came about out of the League crisis in which Rozelle went a long way toward winning his spurs as commissioner.

The crisis began with the new year in 1963 when reports of betting on NFL games by the League's players were confirmed and, as *Sports Illustrated* observed, "rumors of fix and other folly flamed across the land." At issue was the influence of gamblers over NFL games, and, ultimately, the NFL's credibility as a legitimate sporting event. Rozelle investigated the charges for 102 days, despite a public outcry for speedier action. On the 103rd day, Rozelle convened a press conference and announced there was "no evidence that any NFL player has given less than his best in playing any game" and "no evidence that any player has ever bet against his own team" or "sold information to gamblers." Rozelle then suspended the star halfback of the Green Bay Packers and the star defensive tackle of the Detroit Lions indefinitely for having placed bets on NFL games in which they were not involved. Five players on the Detroit Lions were fined two thousand dollars apiece for having bet on the NFL championship game and the Lions franchise was fined four thousand because its head coach "ignored a police tip that some players had been seen with undesirable characters."

The posture Rozelle assumed, standing slim and solemn before the assembled press, was an overwhelming success. His employers appreciated the performance. "Pete Rozelle's handling of the investigations," Tex Schramm observed, "was the thing that made everybody accept him as commissioner and no longer a boy playing the part. He gained once and for all everybody's complete respect." It had been a masterful display of crisis management.

The aspect of the 1963 gambling crisis that required the most dexterity from the commissioner was how to treat his employers under the guidelines he had invoked at his press conference. In particular, Carroll Rosenbloom loved to gamble and most everybody knew it. The C.R. betting legend dated from the December 1958 NFL championship game between Rosenbloom's Baltimore Colts and the New York Giants—the exciting sudden-death game that had established NFL football as a television attraction with enormous audience potential. Rosenbloom attended the game with his "sidekick" Louis Chesler, the man author Bernie Parrish credited with being "the front" for Mafia boss Meyer Lansky in the Bahamas. Chesler was also described as a "compulsive gambler." As the story went, Rosenbloom and Chesler had together wagered "a bundle" on the Colts. Some placed the figure at $1 million, but no one really knew. Supposedly the bet was the Colts minus three and a half points, meaning Chesler

and Rosenbloom won if the Colts' margin of victory was four
points or more. The Colts' margin of victory would indeed be
one of the game's most memorable aspects. The Colts surprised
everyone by passing up the opportunity to kick an easy field goal
and win the game by three points. Instead, they risked everything, scored a touchdown, and won by six. Some insisted that
C.R. himself got on the press box phone to his team's coach and
ordered him to go for broke, but there was no evidence of such a
phone call on the public record. In any case, the Colts won by
six instead of three and Rosenbloom and Chesler were "ecstatic."

In early January 1963, Rozelle had just begun waiting out the
gambling crisis's first hundred days. The League was meeting in
Miami, the commissioner recalled, when a bellhop entered the
meeting room with a stack of envelopes and handed them to an
NFL official. Thinking it was something the group had sent out
to be copied, the official automatically passed them around the
room. The envelopes contained four affidavits from friends and
employees of Rosenbloom's, alleging that C.R. not only bet on
NFL games but also even bet against his own team, all in
complete violation of NFL rules. With them was a cover letter
from a Miami private detective stating he had delivered copies of
this information to Rozelle's office the previous fall but no
action had been taken. The first owner to open his envelope and
read the contents suggested they throw it all away.

The affidavits were a heretofore secret outgrowth of a lawsuit
against Carroll Rosenbloom filed by one Mike McLaney in
1960. The private eye who revealed these affidavits felt it was
his "patriotic duty" to do so despite a judge's order sealing the
suit's records. McLaney framed the new charges in a deposition:
"[Due to] my betting knowledge and background . . . a betting
partnership was formed for the purpose of betting large sums of
money on football games. It was Mr. Rosenbloom and myself. . . . On one occasion . . . he bet as high as $55,000 against
his own team." There were three additional affidavits. Robert J.
McGarvey, a former Philadelphia policeman swore that "Mr.
Rosenbloom bet frequently in large amounts on professional
football games. A friend of McGarvey's swore that C.R. "bet a
large amount of money against his own team," and a Rosenbloom
golfing partner swore that "during one professional football
season, [Rosenbloom] made nine straight winning bets on professional football games." Coming when it did, the new information complicated Rozelle's problems enormously.

Rosenbloom denied all the charges, but Rozelle contended he

had no choice but to investigate, as he was doing in the other, player-related gambling charges. To do otherwise, Rozelle pointed out to Rosenbloom, would be to admit to a double standard.

Rozelle's investigation lasted until well after his Rockefeller Center press conference, when most of the press were busy praising the commissioner for having saved the NFL's integrity. Rosenbloom, Rozelle remembered, was "upset about the delay and thought he was being left on the hook." The investigation finally reached its conclusion in the summer of 1963, when Mike McLaney called Rozelle and said he wanted to talk. McLaney gave the commissioner an envelope containing retractions to the previous charges. Rozelle looked surprised and McLaney "muttered something about the Irish Mafia being after him." Rozelle knew that Rosenbloom was a good friend of both Joe Kennedy, the clan's patriarch, and Jack Kennedy, the President. "Apparently the IRS was after McLaney," Rozelle concluded. In any case, the retractions ended Carroll Rosenbloom's role in the 1963 gambling scandals. "The charges were unfounded," Rozelle reported.

By then it was far too late for Pete Rozelle to salvage his relationship with Carroll Rosenbloom. As part of the commissioner's final report, Rosenbloom "freely admitted that he has bet substantial sums on activities other than professional football" but "stated that he has ceased such practices." It no doubt galled Carroll Rosenbloom to have to make such a claim. He did not take being jacked around lightly and he had a reputation for holding his grudges a long time. When the NFL met in Bal Harbour almost eleven years later, there was no active issue in his feud with Rozelle, and Rosenbloom was content to put a lot of public distance between himself and those League members who were preparing to canonize the man already being called "the best commissioner in the history of professional sports."

"Hell," C.R. was fond of telling people, "with the game we've got, my grandmother could have negotiated those TV contracts."

11

C.R. Solves his "Baltimore Problem"

In 1974, Carroll Rosenbloom was sixty-seven years old, one of only four NFL members who predated Rozelle's commissionership. To Rosenbloom, "the commissioner" would always be Bert Bell, "a great man," Rosenbloom's college football coach, and a good friend.

Bert Bell brought Rosenbloom into the NFL in 1953 to solve "the Baltimore problem." Professional football first came to Baltimore in 1947 as the All-America Football Conference's franchise called the Colts. The Colts and several other All-America Conference survivors joined the NFL in 1950. In 1951, after losing money hand over fist, the Colts folded. The following year a new NFL team, the Texans, started in Dallas, but halfway through the 1952 season, it, too, went broke. Bell's solution was to take the Texans franchise, transplant it to Baltimore as the reborn Colts, and this time do it right. The key was to find an owner with plenty of money to lose and enough Baltimore roots to make the franchise a genuine hometown team.

Carroll Rosenbloom had an abundance of both. Born in Baltimore, Rosenbloom grew up near the home of journalist H. L. Mencken. "He didn't like kids as a rule," Rosenbloom remembered about Mencken, "but he liked me because I was a mean little so-and-so." Rosenbloom attended public schools and then Baltimore City College, where he was a football and baseball standout. He finished his education at the University of Pennsylvania, playing halfback for Bert Bell. After college, he tried the family business and spent his first year on the job cleaning lavatories in one of his father's buildings, making $3.50 a week.

The next year, Carroll began making his own fortune. Dispatched to one of his father's denim mills with orders to close it down, Rosenbloom instead borrowed money and purchased the mill himself. A firm of eighty employees and annual revenues of $350,000 when he purchased it, sixteen years later it employed 20,000 and had revenues of $175 million. At age thirty-three, he turned the running of his business over to others and "retired" to a 480-acre farm on Maryland's Eastern Shore. "I don't know why anyone would work if they didn't have to," C.R. explained. Carroll Rosenbloom's retirement ended when his father died in 1942 and Carroll merged his father's holdings with his own.

During World War II, the Rosenbloom mills churned out uniforms and parachutes. After the war, he merged the family business into the Philadelphia and Reading Corp., one of the nation's first conglomerates, and "walked away with a fortune." By the time Bert Bell approached him with his idea of restarting the Colts, Carroll Rosenbloom was "bored with conventional business" and looking for excitement.

Rosenbloom paid $250,000 for Baltimore's new NFL franchise and upon becoming majority owner, put another $1.5 million in the bank. "That was how much I was willing to lose," he explained. "After that, I'd get out." Rosenbloom never had a money-losing season and at the end of the 1950s, his Colts were considered the NFL's premier franchise.

At the same time, Carroll Rosenbloom became a significant power inside the NFL. His closeness with Bell lent him influence in the beginning and his teams' successes enhanced it. Rosenbloom was instrumental in getting the League to accept a players' union. He was also the first to approach the AFL, though unsuccessfully, about a possible merger. While always a man to chart his own course, Rosenbloom wasn't isolated. His relationships with other owners were inevitably there to retrieve when he decided to turn them on rather than off. All of them considered him "cunning." Rosenbloom's habit at Rozelle's League conclaves was to have his son Steve sit through the "bullshit" and "only come in if it was something of significance."

According to Steve, Carroll Rosenbloom kept his own counsel and usually acted on his own. He was in many respects a mystery to the rest of the League. "He was an odd person," his friend Art Modell remembered. "His temperament was really even and level. He was very shrewd. I still can't figure him out. He was a team player to a certain point. Al Davis was always the Lone Ranger, but Carroll invoked the League. He gave speech after speech about unity. He looked for an edge but he was fundamentally an NFL man. Except for his vendetta against Rozelle. That was unconscionable."

Ironically, in 1971, it seemed doubtful that Rosenbloom would play much, if any, of a role at all in the coming NFL decade. He seemed bored with the business. For the last eight years he had been living, for all intents and purposes, in Florida. He traveled to New York a lot and as a rule, he appeared in Baltimore only for home games. In early 1971, C.R. made his boredom official. "Steve Rosenbloom Replaces Dad As President of Colts," *The* [Baltimore] *Sun* announced in March. C.R. continued as owner and chairman of the Colts' board.

Needless to say, the retirement was an illusion. "I ran all the daily stuff," Steve Rosenbloom remembered, "but Carroll never withdrew. All he needed was a phone and we talked every day." Rosenbloom was indeed bored, but he was, as it turned out, bored with Baltimore, not with football. "Carroll got disgusted," Steve noted. "People began to expect a world championship every year. My father finally said 'Jesus Christ, all we've done is win. What the hell do they want?' "

In July 1972, Rosenbloom announced a surprise solution to his "Baltimore problem." Instead of moving the Colts, he traded the franchise in toto for the Los Angeles Rams. It was the first and only such franchise trade in NFL history, and with it Carroll Rosenbloom began a second life in the League.

According to Rosenbloom, the idea of taking over the Rams was first suggested to him by Dan Reeves, then the Rams' owner, in 1968. Reeves was suffering from terminal cancer. "My number can come up any time now," Reeves told C.R. "I don't think my family will keep the club after I'm gone. If I go before you do, I hope you'll give serious thought to acquiring this franchise."

Reeves finally died in 1971, the year C.R. "retired." Rosenbloom's initial idea was simply to give the Colts to Steve and buy the Rams himself. The NFL constitution however, prohibited any individual from owning more than one franchise, and two members of the same immediate family owning separate franchises was too close for Rozelle's comfort. Rozelle suggested that Rosenbloom instead sell the Colts and buy the Rams.

The principal argument against that option from Rosenbloom's point of view was the tax consequences. A straight cash sale of a property that had increased close to $20 million in value during the term of his ownership would have left C.R. with a $4.4 million tax bill for capital gains. Trading was a way around the tax law. C.R.'s first candidate for a swap was Willard Keland, a former partner in the Miami Dolphins who, according to *Sports Illustrated*, had been squeezed out of the franchise by owner Joe Robbie. Keland agreed to buy the Rams from Dan Reeves's estate for $19 million and trade the franchise straight across for the Colts. The Keland deal fell apart because Keland couldn't raise enough money. A second buyer for the Colts was found, Chicago heating contractor, Robert J. Irsay. The deal received formal approval by League vote and C.R. began looking for a place to live in L.A.

As deals go, Carroll Rosenbloom's swap of the Baltimore Colts for the Los Angeles Rams was a prime candidate for shrewdest in the history of the NFL. He had paid not a cent in taxes while managing to convert $20 million of accrued franchise value into another franchise, worth potentially a great deal more. Carroll Rosenbloom had also managed to trade one of the League's lesser media markets for a market second only to New York City in size and visibility. "Owning the Colts is like owning a local brewery," one observer commented. "Owning the Rams is like owning Twentieth Century Fox."

Rosenbloom left his old hometown on a final note of on-the-field triumph. In their last season before his "retirement" and subsequent exit, Carroll Rosenbloom's Colts finally triumphed in a Super Bowl, defeating Tex Schramm's Dallas Cowboys 16 to 13 in Miami's Orange Bowl, where he had been humiliated two years earlier when his Colts were whipped by Sonny Werblin's New York Jets and became the first team in the old NFL to lose a Super Bowl to a former member of the AFL. When that embarrassing situation was finally rectified, it no doubt added to Rosenbloom's sense that it was time to leave Baltimore.

The first Super Bowl after his history-making swap was in the Los Angeles Memorial Coliseum, C.R.'s new home field. As host owner, Rosenbloom was planning a party at his new Bel-Air home and "borrowed" his Super Bowl trophy from the Colts to use as a centerpiece for the affair. The sterling silver football was hand delivered by Rosenbloom's nephew, who had stayed on as the Colts' business manager. Once it was in C.R.'s hands, he simply kept it.

Rosenbloom displayed "his" trophy in his den. Several years after C.R.'s Super Bowl party, the Colts' assistant general manager saw it there during a visit with Rosenbloom. Not wanting to get mixed up in the controversy, he commented on what a remarkable "replica" it was. "You're a smart kid," Rosenbloom chuckled.

In 1982, Robert Irsay finally stopped waiting for the trophy to be returned and purchased an $11,000 copy from Tiffany and Company in New York.

12
C.R. Versus the LAMCC—A Running Battle Begins

C.R. loved L.A. "Carroll Rosenbloom became an instant celebrity," an acquaintance observed. "He's part of the Hollywood–Beverly Hills–Malibu axis. He and his business are the talk of the town."

C.R. lived in a luxurious estate on five wooded acres in Bel-Air with a swimming pool, tennis courts, and sprawling formal gardens. The house staff numbered seven or eight. Rosenbloom's "place in the country" was a house at exclusive Trancas Beach, north of Malibu. He entertained the likes of Kirk Douglas, Warren Beatty, Jack Lemmon, Walter Matthau, and Dinah Shore. Whenever Ted Kennedy was in Los Angeles, he stayed in Rosenbloom's guest quarters.

In his second hometown with his second NFL franchise, Carroll Rosenbloom was also raising his second family. His marriage to his first wife, Velma, ended in the mid-sixties after some twenty-five years. Of their four children, only Steve was in the football business. In settlement discussions with Velma, Rosenbloom warned her he would not part with any portion of the Colts. "I would never do that," he admonished her. "Especially I'd never give them up to a woman."

C.R. remarried almost immediately. By then his second wife, Georgia, had been his behind-the-scenes companion for a number of years. She was a former lounge singer, musical comedy performer, and TV weather girl. Carroll Rosenbloom was Georgia's sixth husband. Georgia contended they were introduced by Joseph Kennedy, patriarch of the Kennedy clan and the only man Rosenbloom's friends ever remembered him addressing as "sir." In any case, the effect was immediate. "She was a dynamite chick," her fifth husband recalled. "She was very much a knockout. Being so attractive, she always had people hitting on her." Carroll Rosenbloom reportedly "hit" on her immediately. "She had the catnip," Georgia's agent remembered. "Men just

47

dribbled over her. [Rosenbloom] was mad about her. He didn't like anything or anyone who took Georgia away from him. He didn't want her out in public with those kind of people looking at her. I got her married. I kept booking her out of the country until Carroll couldn't stand it.''

Carroll and Georgia were married less than a month after his divorce from Velma was final. Georgia was then thirty-eight years old, Carroll, fifty-nine. According to later published reports, at the time of their marriage, the younger of the two children C.R. fathered by Georgia was already two years old. When the Rosenblooms entertained, Georgia sometimes offered their guests a rendition of songs. "Georgia would get up," a frequent visitor remembered, "and sing to his [Rosenbloom's] eyes. He was like a little boy when she did that. He loved it.''

Despite his continuing infatuation with his second wife, Carroll Rosenbloom's Los Angeles obsession was the Rams, and for him football was strictly a male enterprise. Georgia was invited to the Rams' offices only once. The only other time she showed up at headquarters was to deliver some papers Carroll had left home and then he wouldn't let her past the receptionist in the lobby. Steve was sent down to fetch what she'd brought. Women, Rosenbloom lectured his son, should not be meddling in the football business. Wives of the Colts' front office personnel were allowed to sit with the men in C.R.'s owner's box only if the weather was wet or freezing. Otherwise, they sat in a separate section a good distance away.

In Los Angeles, Rosenbloom devoted himself to his team with renewed energy. Every Thursday during football season he was either flown by helicopter or driven by Mercedes to the Rams' training facility in Long Beach to watch his team's final intense practice and huddle with his coaches. While watching, he sat in a Hollywood director's chair with "C. Rosenbloom" stitched on the back. C.R. left the daily details of the club to his son Steve, now installed as Rams' executive vice-president.

In Baltimore, C.R. had spent several years haggling with city and state authorities over the possibility of a "modern" facility to replace Baltimore's Memorial Stadium. None was ever constructed. It was Rosenbloom's frustration with that inaction that reinforced his desire to leave Baltimore any way possible. In Los Angeles, C.R. inherited a lease that had only two years left to run for the "Grand Duchess" of American stadiums. Built in 1923 and then remodeled for the 1932 Olympics, the L.A. Coliseum could seat as many as ninety-five thousand. C.R.

targeted the "Grand Duchess" for mothballs shortly after arriving in L.A.

Whatever Rosenbloom's intentions, the L.A. Coliseum proved to have remarkable staying power. A quasi-independent enterprise, it was governed by the Los Angeles Memorial Coliseum Commission, a nine-member board appointed by three different governmental entities. At the time C.R. showed up in Los Angeles, the LAMCC's members were, according to one former member, "usually big political contributors who wanted the glory" of association with the stadium's tenants. Their association with Carroll Rosenbloom, however, would prove considerably less than glorious.

C.R.'s immediate problem was what to do when his current lease ran out after the 1973 season. Neither Dodger Stadium nor Anaheim's Big A Stadium was then a suitable option. Building his own stadium was also impossible due to the high price of land and construction. "There was," Rosenbloom noted, "no place else to go." The paucity of options placed him under stringent restrictions in his bargaining, but didn't make him any easier for the LAMCC to deal with. "His sport was hassling with stadiums," his son Steve remembered.

For its part, the LAMCC was under severe financial restrictions as well. They had little money to spend on Carroll Rosenbloom and even less desire to spend it. The LAMCC's difficulties were a function of its disastrous decision in the late 1960s to build the Los Angeles Sports Arena, a companion indoor arena to the Coliseum which was continuously vacant except for an occasional rock concert. It had become a white elephant, kept solvent only by the income generated by the "Grand Duchess of Stadiums." There was no money to spare once the Sports Arena's bills were paid.

Rosenbloom opened his negotiations by announcing in August 1973 that he was prepared to "wholly underwrite" a $7 million bond for improvements in the Coliseum. At the top of his suggested improvement list was the construction of luxury boxes and a stadium club for the box holders' entertainment. By November, the LAMCC had rejected C.R.'s offer and accused him of using "pressure tactics." Instead of yielding, the Coliseum Commission was insisting the Rams' rent be raised. "Negotiations" on the issues were at best a distant proposition for C.R. For his part, C.R. accused the LAMCC of trying to "paint me as the bad boy and I'm not. They have to have more revenue because they have done a bad job of operating the Sports Arena

. . . I could accept their thinking if they came to me with their cards up. I'd even be willing to assist them out of my charity fund. But they're using a new lease to cover up a losing operation—a mishandled operation.'' A month after his complaint, Rosenbloom gave in and signed a three-year lease with an option to renew. The new deal required him to pay twice his previous rent and to assume the janitorial expenses previously borne by the LAMCC. In Rosenbloom's mind, it was a stopgap solution only.

Already past normal retirement age, Carroll Rosenbloom operated with a constant apprehension that his time might well be running out. "Some people say I'm too mean to die," he told the *Los Angeles Times*, "but I guess I'll probably die anyway." In the meantime, he made a point of not letting his age diminish his vigor. Over six feet tall, fit, square-jawed, and handsome, he wore a custom-made gray-blond toupee, played tennis with ferocity, if not skill, and maintained a hectic daily schedule.

When C.R. announced "I don't ever want this football team to leave my family," everyone assumed he meant Steve, his heir apparent and proxy at many of the 1974 annual meeting's "bullshit" sessions. Outside the meeting rooms, Rosenbloom "complained bitterly about how arrogantly the L.A. Coliseum had dealt with him.'' Most owners assumed it would not be the last they would hear about the LAMCC. No one, however, anticipated that, thanks to Carroll Rosenbloom, the "Grand Duchess of Stadiums'' would become the decisive battleground in the civil war that would be League Think's undoing.

13
Saving Football for Oakland—Al Davis

The man who would eventually triumph in that climactic battle, Al Davis, managing general partner of the Oakland Raiders, was one of the few people in the NFL whose relationship with Carroll Rosenbloom was perpetually on rather than on-again off-again. "I like Al Davis because he is a mean, conniving s.o.b.," C.R. explained, "just like I am." Eventually the two men talked "every day or every other day" on the telephone. "I was very fond of Mr. Rosenbloom," Davis would later testify. One of the traits C.R. and Davis shared was their estimate of themselves. Like Carroll Rosenbloom, Al Davis was not the kind to hide his light under a basket.

When the AFL asked Davis to be commissioner, he was thirty-seven years old. Unaware that Lamar Hunt had met with Tex Schramm just the day before and begun to make peace, the choice of Davis by the AFL was a choice to prosecute their war with the NFL to the fullest extent. Later that day, Davis and an AFL publicist prepared the AFL's announcement of Davis's selection. The publicist typed while Al Davis read over his shoulder. When he got to the part describing Davis, the new AFL commissioner leaned forward and penciled the words *dynamic* and *genius* on the top of the page. "Think you can work these in?" Al asked.

Al Davis was widely identified as "the most hated man in professional football." The reputation didn't bother Davis a bit. "He's the kind of guy you can't insult," his archenemy, Gene Klein, noted. "You spit in his eye and he says it's raining." While his mentor, Carroll Rosenbloom, often rubbed people both ways, Davis usually settled for the wrong way only. "He has himself paged when he comes into a hotel," one of his fellow owners said derisively, "and he's the kind of man who never passes a mirror without combing his hair. He always was an arrogant son of a bitch and nothing will change until he finally gets his ass whipped."

Whipping Al Davis's ass was a tall order. After the 1966 merger, no one's teams won more games than his. "He is a genius in terms of football," one NFL executive noted. "Very few others understand either the game or the business as well as he does. He's like a hawk who can pick on other birds of prey. Most of the others were just not capable of competing with him."

"He has a remarkable capacity for seeing himself as a victor in confrontations," one of Davis's friends observed. "He likes to walk away chuckling and tell his friends, 'I sure jerked the rug out from under that guy but he doesn't even know it yet.' " As another NFL executive complained to *The Saturday Evening Post,* "He'd do anything to win, even if it meant stepping on his mother. He's a ruthless, persistent cuss, full of chicanery. Yet you have to give the devil his due. He's nothing but successful."

In compiling Davis's due, one of the first entries that must be credited to him is the city of Oakland's place on the national map. Few in the NFL doubted that, without Davis, Oakland's tenuous grasp on big league stature might well have been lost in its infancy. San Francisco's less glamorous neighbor was not an automatic selection, even to the fledgling AFL in 1959, and the league's original list of eight franchises did not include it. Until the rise of the Raiders, the city was most famous for Gertrude Stein's description of it as having "no there, there." Oakland's chance finally came at the infant league's first official meeting when Max Winter's Minnesota franchise withdrew and announced it was expecting to join the NFL, precipitating the first skirmish of the AFL war.

Lamar Hunt was desperate after Winter's defection. He had put the league together and now he had to fill the hole in its lineup fast. To do so, he floated a rumor that a group in Oakland was interested. An [Oakland] *Tribune* sportswriter, Scotty Stirling, picked the story up and ran it. "Hunt was on a fishing expedition," Stirling later remembered. "He wanted to see whether a group would surface . . . three groups popped up and expressed interest." The group that won the franchise was a limited partnership run by Wayne Valley, a millionaire California home builder.

Wayne Valley got into football because, as one of his friends put it, he "was a football nut." Valley had been an offensive lineman at Oregon State during the Depression, and until he bought into the Oakland franchise, held forty season tickets to the NFL's San Francisco 49er games. Their first year, the Raiders played their games in San Francisco, lost $500,000, and one of Valley's two other general partners dropped out. After the 1961 season in Oakland's tiny Frank Youell Field, the losses were even bigger and Valley had to reorganize again to insulate himself from some of the red ink. By the end of 1962, the situation was desperate and there was talk that the Raiders might soon move. At that point, Wayne Valley found Al Davis and saved Oakland for the big leagues.

At the time, Davis was an assistant coach for the AFL's San Diego Chargers. He would eventually be one of only two men ever to rise out of the coaching ranks to ownership. Asked when in his life he first knew he was going to run a football team for a living, Davis answered, "When I was six."

The son of a successful clothing merchant, Al Davis grew up in Brooklyn. "I really wasn't much of an athlete," he recalled. "I played a little football and baseball, but it would be inaccu-

rate to say I starred or anything like that. I didn't get along with
the coaches. You follow me?"

"He wants to be thought of as an athlete," one of Al Davis's
former employees told *Sports Illustrated*, "but he isn't even particularly well coordinated. And he may have the skinniest pair of
wheels in America, which is why he never takes off his pants
where anyone can see. Then there's the Al Davis handshake. It's
done with the fingers held apart and rigid so his little hand will
seem bigger." But no one in the NFL ever questioned Davis's
grasp of the game they all owned. "If I said Al Davis is
lovable," Wayne Valley pointed out, "I'd be a liar. But you don't
have to love him, just turn him loose."

After he'd graduated from Syracuse University, Davis's knack
took him to Adelphi College as football coach, but his first
significant coaching success came in the army as a coach for the
Fort Belvoir, Virginia, football team. "He was a private," *Look*
magazine observed of Davis's army career, "but he had a car
and driver and was the only enlisted man who always wore an
officer-type peaked hat." Davis explained, "You know how
generals are. They want to win. This general gave me carte
blanche. I also had very good contacts in the Pentagon that could
move people. You follow me?" According to *Look*, "Davis left
Fort Belvoir . . . only a step ahead of a congressional investigation into the coddling of athletes."

After the army, Davis was a scout for the Baltimore Colts,
assistant coach at The Citadel, and at the University of Southern
California, and then landed with the Chargers. He and Valley
first made contact in 1962. By early 1963, Davis, Valley, and
the other Raider general partner, Ed McGah, met for a formal
job interview. Davis showed none of the humility or intimidation
one might have expected from an assistant coach seeking his first
professional head coaching position. Valley invited two Oakland
reporters to sit in on the hotel room session. "Al considered
owners to be dilettantes," one of the reporters said, "playing
with their new toy. The real pros needed to shove them aside,
and the sooner they did, the sooner the AFL would be a real
league." When Valley and McGah left the room at one point,
Davis turned to the press and began making fun of the men who
were interviewing him. "They don't even know what questions
to ask," he said, smirking.

After turning Valley down twice, Davis accepted the Raider
job. "I would have sole and complete control of the operation of

the football team,'' is the way the new head coach and general
manager later summarized his contract.

One of the noncontractual assurances Davis had insisted upon
from Valley was that Oakland would soon provide a better
stadium for the Raiders' home field. Valley had been working
feverishly for such a stadium since his entry into the football
business. In 1960, Coliseum, Inc., a private nonprofit corporation, offered to sell bonds to finance construction of a stadium
and then lease the facility back to the city and county for
$750,000 apiece per year. The stadium Coliseum, Inc., proposed
would cost somewhere between $17 and $21 million. County
approval finally came in late 1963, during Davis's phenomenally
successful first year on the job.

One of the sticking points in the stadium's development was
the question of whether the Raiders would sign a twenty year
lease. Valley refused. At the time, the AFL was hip-deep in the
very expensive war with the NFL, and, as Valley put it, ''I was
losing my ass. It was not at all clear we were going to succeed.''
The negotiations over lease terms lasted two years. Coliseum,
Inc., finally settled for a five-year lease with five three-year
options. They agreed because Valley made ''a handshake deal''
that he would never leave Oakland as long as the club was
successful. At the time the discussions began, such ''success''
was, of course, highly problematical.

Making success real was Al Davis's job and he did it like a
whirlwind. Inheriting a team that had won one game and lost
thirteen the year before, Davis immediately bettered the record to
ten and four. *Sports Illustrated* described his arrival on the AFL
scene: ''In flew Al Davis, big-shouldered, with half a scowl . . .
eyes that seemed to be reflecting some hidden joke, a kidding
voice . . . and with his fingernails mostly bitten off.'' Before
Davis took over, according to one Raider player, ''it was terrible. We practiced on lots with rocks and broken glass. There was
no organization, no leadership. Then Davis came in and he went
out and got it done, all of it, the whole shebang.'' By 1965, the
Raiders were regular contenders for the AFL's Western Division
championship and Oakland had begun to fall in love with them.

The rest of the AFL, however, had something of the opposite
reaction. ''It is not at all certain,'' *Sports Illustrated* noted,
''where Al Davis would finish in a popularity contest among
sharks, the mumps, the income tax, and himself.'' The source of
Davis's unpopularity was his reputation for doing whatever it
took to win, no holds barred—the stuff of legend itself. As

people came to believe Davis capable of anything, they spent a
lot of time looking over their shoulders to see what he was up to.
After Coliseum, Inc.'s stadium had been built, the Raiders were
hosting their archrival, the San Diego Chargers. Just before the
start of the game, when his team was making its way out into the
stadium, the Chargers' coach sat in his team's locker room,
alone and apparently deep in thought. When shouts reached him
that it was time to take the field, the San Diego coach leaped to
his feet and began shouting into the light fixture, convinced there
was a listening device hidden in it. "Fuck you, Al Davis! Fuck
you! I know you're up there. Fuck you!"

Almost everyone in the football business agreed that Al Davis
would be a considerable asset for any franchise for whom he
might work. By 1965, he had turned down several offers to leave
Oakland and coach elsewhere in both the AFL and NFL. He
approached his task with single-mindedness, and his need to win
seemed to provide endless energy. Even after he ascended to the
ranks of ownership, he would still spend his evenings during football season studying films of the opposition, looking for cracks
in their armor. "Al Davis is a very smart guy who works overtime," Wayne Valley observed. "This is his life, his whole life."

What life Davis actually had outside football was centered on his
home, where he lived with his wife, Carol, and his son, Mark Clark
Davis. "When we were married," Davis explained, "I said the only
thing that would take me away from football was life or death."

Once, after a marathon film study session in the Raiders'
offices, Davis returned to Piedmont very late. While Al was
undressing, Carol woke up.

"Good God, you're late," she complained groggily.

"You can call me Al," Davis answered.

14

Davis and Rozelle—the Disloyal Opposition

Davis emerged from the AFL war looking like a cross between
Robert E. Lee and Genghis Khan. He made that reputation
during the four months he spent as the American Football League's
commissioner. When Valley suggested Davis for the job, "ev-

erybody hated his aggressiveness. They said he'd do anything to win. 'That's fine,' I said. 'We need aggressiveness and we sure as hell need a winner.' '' Valley's attitude took hold. ''Davis would be the perfect choice,'' another AFL executive agreed. ''He'll sit up all night scheming and conniving . . . he's just the kind of man we need to compete with Pete Rozelle.''

Al Davis lived up to all those expectations and more. Entering a conflict that seemed locked in costly stalemate, his response was blitzkrieg. Davis set about raiding the NFL's prize quarterbacks, signing them to record-setting contracts and bonuses to induce them to jump leagues. By June, Davis had seven of the NFL's fourteen best quarterbacks prepared to switch. On June 8, 1966, Pete Rozelle announced the merger. One of the people from whom much of the negotiations leading to that announcement had been kept secret was Davis. ''He didn't learn about it until it was announced,'' Tex Schramm remembered. ''Al was displeased, to put it mildly.''

When Billy Sullivan, president of the New England Patriots broke the news to Davis, Davis told him ''. . . I thought he had abandoned me and personally had sold me out and that we had the thing won and I thought they gave it away.'' ''I was the general who won the war,'' Davis later complained, ''but the politicians lost the peace. . . . We knocked the hell out of the NFL. . . . We didn't have to give them nothin'.'' Davis would ever after describe the merger as football's Yalta. Perhaps the bitterest pill for him to swallow was Rozelle's retention as commissioner of the merged league. One of his Oakland friends commented, ''He thought he'd showed up Rozelle as an ineffective leader. He expected to be offered the combined commissionership. He didn't recognize then that his methods had offended some of the owners. Even some in his own league were shocked by his piracy. The upshot was that he was so successful, he frightened the owners and ended any possibility of remaining as commissioner.''

Davis did not stay unemployed for long. Wayne Valley and his partners wanted him back badly. Davis told Valley he could ''relate to'' becoming a general partner with ''managing control.'' Valley soon agreed to such an arrangement. ''My philosophy,'' he explained, ''is that key men should own a piece of the business.'' Davis was given ten percent, second only to Valley's in size. To make acquiring it easy, the book value of the franchise was listed as $185,000 and Davis was sold his share for $18,500, in effect buying a million dollars of franchise for $18,500.

Davis was also named managing general partner under a ten-year employment contract which specified, according to Davis, that "I would have total and complete operational control. I could do as I see fit." When that contract was signed, Al Davis left the ranks of coaching forever. According to Valley, Davis's elevation changed him. "I thought he was aggressive," Valley remembered bitterly, "but if I had thought he was a crook, I would never have brought him back. Within that first year, he was a changed man. He gradually drew away from me, our discussions became limited, and he didn't want to talk about things . . . he built a wall between us."

While walling off Valley, Davis put the finishing touches on the organization he had been molding in his own image since 1963. He selected the Raiders' silver and black color scheme and he provided their motto, "Pride and Poise." Davis "coaxed first-rate performances out of players who had been given up on." The Raiders' game day agendas listed starting time as *"We go to war!"* The emblem on the side of Raiders' helmets was a man wearing an eyepatch with a knife clenched in his teeth. Davis cherished that outlaw image. "I don't want to be the most respected team in the League," he explained. "I want to be the most feared."

There was no doubt that the organization behind the team was all his. "In order to run an efficient organization," he argued, "there has to be a dictator. People in an organization have to have the feeling that there's someone there who, if they don't move in the right direction, will chop." Davis acquired a reputation for going through public relations men at a rapid rate. "I used to go to work every morning with a knot in my stomach," one former employee told *Look*. "I never knew when the next attack was coming." Another former employee explained, "Davis thinks people perform better if they are afraid."

"The goal," Al Davis pointed out, "isn't to be a topflight football team. The goal is to be the number-one football team." Davis's own singleness of purpose was profound. "The real thrill of life comes from setting goals, from meeting challenges, from overcoming adversity. . . . Singleness of purpose, a rational approach to all emotional situations, sound judgment . . . more than make up for huge staffs and computers."

Davis didn't drink or smoke, and lifted weights to keep fit. When offered coffee, he asked for water. He dressed habitually in his team's colors and when he went out to dinner, he inevitably ended up diagramming plays on the tablecloth. "Tell him a joke," one former employee pointed out, "and you'll get a blank look. But if a general manager on another club calls him up and congratulates him on some fast deal he put over, he'll laugh like hell."

Though his style was diametrically different from Tex Schramm's at the Cowboys, the success of Al Davis's system was predicated on information, just like Schramm's. "Davis always acts like he's got some kind of secret information nobody else knows about," one former AFL coach pointed out, "and much of the time it's true."

While the computer was at the heart of Schramm's information-gathering, the telephone was at the heart of Davis's. He spent no less than five hours a day glued to a receiver. "Al has an amazing information system working for him," a friend commented. "He always knew what was happening. He stayed close to the sportswriter network in the NFL by phone and he had a network of friendly helpers who would go watch teams practice and other things. He always laughed at scouting combines. He learned more over the phone."

"Davis Sees Continued Raider Success" was the headline that announced Al Davis's return to Oakland, and he lived up to it. His Raiders were the old AFL's representative in the second Super Bowl, losing to the Green Bay Packers, 33 to 10. Though the merged NFL had no taste for him as a commissioner, Davis was a man of influence among the old AFL faction and played a central role in the drawn-out process of trying to make the peace final, helping lead one final successful charge by the old AFL during the final moments of separation. The issue was how to align the new twenty-six-team league. It was agreed that the merged NFL would have two conferences, the National and American, but which teams to put where was a matter of intense disagreement. The NFL wanted to continue to play as separate entities with a minimum of games between what were once different leagues. This diehard position was the conclusion of a joint AFL/NFL Committee report given to the combined owners at their meeting in March 1969. The loudest opposition to the idea came from Carroll Rosenbloom. He was trying unsuccessfully to move three old NFL teams over to the AFL, his own included. "Behind the scenes," The [Oakland] Tribune reported, "Davis was steering strategy. He held the AFL together." A source The Tribune would only identify as "one AFL owner" bragged, "The NFL couldn't handle us. We surprised them."

The issue of alignment remained unresolved until January

1970, the year the transition period was scheduled to end. Finally Rozelle kept the League convened for a marathon session, which culminated in a lottery in which three NFL teams were picked to join the old AFL. It was, in essence, Carroll Rosenbloom's original plan and his Colts were also one of the franchises to switch. The others were Art Modell's Cleveland Browns and the Rooney family's Pittsburgh Steelers. Each of the three was compensated with a $3 million payment to ease the transition. With that, the merged NFL became official and the AFL was dead.

By then, however, it was also apparent that the best of its commissioners was not. Al Davis might not be running a league now, but by no means was anyone rid of him.

15

Controlling the Raiders

Despite having joined their ranks, Al Davis's opinion of football owners had changed little from his assistant coach days. "Not all of them are the brightest of human beings," he pointed out

In League meetings, Davis quickly developed a reputation for obscure statements in pursuit of strategies he rarely chose to reveal. "Mr. Davis is a clever man," Gene Klein complained. "Mr. Davis can talk in half sentences. He can say several things in one sentence. Personally, I think that is by design." Al Davis also had several voices in which he delivered his statements. One sounded as though he hailed from Brooklyn, one sounded as though he were from South Carolina, and another sounded as though he'd moved to California early in life.

Al Davis did have some friends in the NFL, but his relationship with Pete Rozelle could at best be described as uneasy. Modell blamed Davis's animosity toward Rozelle on Rozelle's selection over Davis as the merged League's commissioner. "That gnawed at him," Modell claimed. Davis denied all such claims. "I didn't want to be commissioner," he told *Look*. "No way. It's a desk job."

Whatever the reason, his lack of deference to Rozelle was a mainstay of League meetings. "Where others tended to tiptoe around Rozelle," one owner remembered, "Davis didn't even try to adopt social graces. When he disagreed, he'd just snap 'that's bullshit' or 'that won't fly.' That there was little respect was obvious." Rozelle remembered, "The antagonism was under the surface, but I knew it was there. I thought Al Davis was a good football man but that was as much as I could say for him."

An even greater difference was the two men's contrary visions of the NFL. To Davis, League Think sounded like " 'my league right or wrong' and I don't believe in that." Also at issue between them was an entity called NFL Properties, the League's independent "marketing and promotional company." As a condition of the merger agreement, all clubs were required to grant it control of NFL copyright privileges. It also printed all the League's game programs and developed "other self-liquidating premium items they would work out with advertisers and sponsors designed to promote the League." NFL Properties generated a relatively small income. NFL Charities had been developed in 1972 to distribute those revenues. "It was," one NFL executive commented, "a good PR gesture."

It was also Pete Rozelle's pet project and during the first two years of NFL Charities' existence, all National Football League teams were members of it.

Then Al Davis withdrew. "I don't like the reason why Charities was formed," Davis pointed out. "If we wanted to give to charity, we would do it on our own." From 1974 on, Al Davis demanded the Raiders' one twenty-sixth share in NFL Properties' revenue and got it. Rozelle was powerless to force Davis but the incident grated on him.

Al Davis was not the kind of man to share power if he could figure out a way to corner it for himself—and he usually could. With the Raiders, that opportunity arose in 1972, during the seventh year of his ten-year contract. Davis wanted to insure his control of the franchise and the organization of the Oakland Raiders Ltd. made his move possible. Under the terms of the franchise's limited partnership, it was necessary only for two of the three general partners to agree in order for the franchise to assume financial obligations such as a contract. As a consequence, Davis didn't need Wayne Valley's approval as long as he had Ed McGah's, and Davis had McGah in his pocket. "Al stroked McGah," one of Davis's friends recalled. "He made Ed think he was the best friend Al had. Ed swallowed it." Prior to the contract discussions he had with Davis, McGah "had no interest in the way the club was run. He was almost a silent partner. As long as the team played, he didn't care."

Davis later claimed he informed Valley of his intention to sign a new contract with McGah in the course of a meeting of the general partners on July 6, 1972. "I told Mr. Valley," Davis testified, "that I was going to sign the ten-year agreement that Ed was offering. . . . Mr. Valley went on as to how happy he was with the way things were going and wasn't concerned about it [the contract] . . . and just expressed great enthusiasm about the way the Oakland Raiders were going, that he didn't want any operational control, that he had his own business."

Four days later, Al Davis and Ed McGah signed a ten-page employment agreement. Davis had to have been pleased with its terms. According to one NFL attorney, "it so broadened Al Davis's control as to not just involve the football operation but also all the business and financial parts of the partnership as well. It virtually relegated Valley and McGah to the status of limited partners." Ed McGah later admitted, first to Valley and then to *The* [Oakland] *Tribune*, that he had never read the document.

For his part, Wayne Valley never saw a copy of the contract until late November 1972. At that point, Valley's auditor was starting the year's audit and Valley got an unexpected phone call from him. The auditor said he had been shown a copy of a new contract for Al Davis by the Raiders' bookkeeper. "You better do something about it," the auditor advised. After reading it, Valley called Rozelle.

Rozelle's meeting with the Raider general partners finally took place in February 1973. Valley, Davis, McGah, Rozelle and two attorneys convened the meeting to discuss a suit against the franchise by one of the limited partners. Then "out of left field," Valley announced his grievance. "Very dramatically," Davis later testified, "Valley pulled from a briefcase a newspaper and threw it on the table." The current issue of *Sporting News* contained an item about Davis signing a new contract with McGah.

"Is this true?" Valley demanded of Davis.

Caught unprepared, Rozelle and the NFL counsel Jay Moyer watched with "our jaws going slack." At the time, they had no idea to what Valley was referring.

When Davis answered that it was true, Valley roared, "How can you do this without me even being aware of it?"

According to Moyer, Davis responded by saying, " 'I can d
any damn thing I want,' or words to that effect." According t
Davis, "I told him that I had told him about it two differen
times. . . . McGah reiterated that he had told him about it . . .
said 'You knew about it and I don't know what the hell i
bugging you.' "

"I am not going along with this contract," Valley fumed.

"What the hell do you mean, you are not going along wit
this contract?" Davis demanded.

"I'm not going for it," Valley repeated.

At this point, according to Davis, Valley "challenged McGa
for taking such a big interest in football all of a sudden." McGa
responded by asking Valley "what the hell he was pulling this i
front of the commissioner for."

Finally, Rozelle stopped the meeting and all the parties left th
room. Valley cornered McGah outside in the hall.

"Why the hell did you sign it?" Valley demanded. "You
never signed a fucking contract in your life."

According to Valley, McGah told him that Davis would have
left for another team and he didn't want to lose him.

Valley then asked if McGah had read the damn thing before he
signed it and McGah told him no.

Before leaving, Valley informed Rozelle that he didn't desire
any intervention by the commissioner's office in the issue. This
he said, "is between me and Davis."

A month after that meeting, the NFL convened its 1973 annual
meeting. As usual, both Valley and Davis were in attendance.
Both men represented the club during the League's general
sessions, and when the League went into executive session in
which each franchise was limited to one representative, Davis sa
in for the Raiders.

Valley used the forum of that annual meeting to announce tha
he was suing Davis in California Superior Court. As one NFL
attorney described the action, "Valley sought two things. The
first was recision or at least amendment of Davis's contract
so it at least didn't abrogate the authority of the general
partners. Then he went the second mile and said, 'I want A
Davis out of this organization entirely because he's not fit to
live with.' "

At the time of the Bal Harbour annual meeting in 1974, the
lawsuit was still awaiting a court date. According to one NFL
executive, the owners' reactions varied: "If you were a football

person, you picked Davis. If you were an owner, you picked Valley.''

While the war he was fighting with Wayne Valley added to the edginess the rest of the League felt about Al Davis, there were still no signs of the outright hatred Davis would generate when he later told the League to go to hell and went for Rozelle's throat.

16
The Brilliant Businessman Comes to Football—Gene Klein

At the 1974 annual meeting in Bal Harbour, Gene Klein, despite having been in the League for eight years, had yet to really emerge as a figure inside the NFL and lacked a firm place in the League's pecking order. Only during the previous year had Gene Klein decided to devote himself exclusively to the business of football, abandoning a meteoric career in the world of big money conglomerates. The career he abandoned had made him one of the richer men in the NFL.

Like Art Modell, Gene Klein had started life in New York City with relatively nothing. After graduating from high school, Klein could not afford to go to college full-time so he sold encyclopedias door-to-door and studied electrical engineering at NYU night school. Six feet five inches tall, Gene Klein played end on NYU's varsity between his encyclopedia rounds. Klein was in the stands at a New York Giants game on December 7, 1941, when the bombing of Pearl Harbor was announced. The man in the seat next to him asked Klein where Pearl Harbor was and Klein didn't know. The next day, Gene Klein enlisted in the Army Air Corps. He spent the war as a pilot ferrying bombers to various fronts. At the end of the war, he was stationed in Long Beach, had a wife and baby daughter, and, using two thousand dollars borrowed from his father, purchased a used car lot in the San Fernando Valley. Gene Klein had a genuine knack for selling things. Named ''Quality Motors,'' his first used car lot started with four cars, three of which he sold during his first day

in business. "I had a buyer for the fourth," Klein recalled, "but
I turned him down. I needed something to drive home." It
proved to be the opening round in a somewhat legendary rise to
the upper echelons of American enterprise. The gimmick that got
Gene Klein started in the used car business grew out of his
wife's 1946 complaints about the cost of hamburger. Inspired,
Klein began weighing his cars and selling them by the pound.
"Cheaper Than Hamburger," he advertised. He soon added
more lots and then jumped into the new car business when he
bought the western states' Volvo distributorship in the early
1950s. The Volvo distributorship made him wealthy. His next
step made him rich.

At a friend's behest, he bought some shares in National Theatres and Television Corp., then just a chain of aging movie
houses saddled with a money-losing television production arm.
Klein was soon invited onto National Theatres' board and named
to a committee to find a new chief executive officer. The committee ended up asking Klein to take the job and he agreed on
what he called "a temporary basis." Soon after, the corporation
was involved in a proxy fight that Klein's side won. "I get my
dander up when I'm attacked," Klein explained with great understatement, "and I decided to stay on."

One of Gene Klein's first steps was to change its name to
National General Corporation and write off the television production part of the business. At the time, National General had
net profits of minus $8 million; a dozen years later, the company
had a net profit of $48 million.

Klein's success had two distinct stages. The first involved
making a success out of his firm's movie houses. To do so, he
lengthened the intermissions from five to twelve minutes and
instructed his employees to put extra salt on the popcorn to sell
more drinks as well. He also expanded National General's theater holdings by persuading "shopping centers to build theaters
for him with money *they* could borrow on the strength of twenty-
year leases with National General." With the credit afforded by
his movie houses' success, Klein launched his second stage and
began making National General Corp. into one of America's first
conglomerates, having interests in moviemaking, savings and
loans, insurance, book publishing, fruit distribution, and mobile
home manufacture.

At the apex of the pyramid was Gene Klein, reviewing as
many as five to ten possible acquisitions a day. Later he would
regret that he hadn't "spent more time with Fran and the kids

when they were growing up. Every day was a highly organized experience. My time was broken down to fifteen-minute segments. There were always thirty or forty calls backed up, always meetings to attend. . . . I was always under pressure to make decisions at what seemed like supersonic speed. . . . Late every afternoon my secretary made up a full agenda of the next day's appointments and I'd take it home and study it at night.''

Conglomerates were a controversial development in American business and Gene Klein's conglomerate was among the more controversial. In 1970, one of his insurance companies was fined for alleged instances of self-dealing. *Business Week* noted Wall Street's ''distinct coolness towards Klein's succession of complicated deals. The deals smacked more of 'cronyism and self-aggrandizement,' as one broker puts it, than of real interest in the stockholders.''

But one facet of Gene Klein's business career that was not in dispute was the wealth it had brought him. Klein traveled in a chauffeured Rolls-Royce originally built for Queen Elizabeth and a Grumman Gulfstream private jet. In the late sixties Klein lived with his wife, Frances, in a twenty-room house, worth some $3.5 million, on six and a half acres in Beverly Hills. His country house in Palm Springs cost $500,000. He and Frances belonged to Beverly Hills's exclusive Hillcrest Country Club, where he played tennis with Debbie Reynolds or James Garner and socialized with Bob Hope and George Burns. When National General's stock began to sink somewhat in 1970, Klein convinced Frank Sinatra to buy in and stabilize the price. ''The list of his business associates and friends,'' *Business Week* noted, ''reads like a Who's Who of Southern California.''

Among all Gene Klein's assets, the San Diego Chargers were closest to his heart. For years he flew his family and friends into town on game days and was, by his own admission, a man obsessed. Given the choice, he once admitted, ''I would rather be in the NFL than the [U.S.] Senate.'' He bought into the AFL Chargers in 1966 for a purchase price of $10 million which was, at the time, a record for NFL franchises.

A hearty, bluff personality, Klein looked ''like a man who trims his hair with a lawnmower.'' He drew mixed reviews when he arrived on the scene in the League. ''When he came in, he didn't understand the business,'' one owner remembered. ''The guys who have the trouble in the NFL,'' another owner pointed out, ''are those who think that because they've made it in the construction business or something, they can make it in pro football. It is not a particularly difficult business, but it's different. I'm not sure that Gene wants to put in the time to learn it.'' In his early days in the football business, it was not at all clear Klein thought he had anything to learn. "He's an authority on everything," one owner said privately, offering the opinion that "he doesn't know a fucking thing."

Gene Klein demonstrated his capacity to rub people the wrong way at his first AFL meeting. The decision to merge with the NFL had been announced, and the two leagues were working out the specifics. It was a tense time. In one discussion, Klein began to lecture one of his fellow owners. "Look, you son of a bitch," Klein began, "let me tell you about limited partnerships . . ." Klein got no further in his advice because the other owner jumped to his feet and "hit him in the chops."

Prior to his notorious hatred of Al Davis, the most public of Klein's disagreements was with his own partner, Sam Shulman. Originally Shulman and Klein had each bought 24.5 percent in the franchise, with Klein acting as the club's president and Shulman as chairman of its board. When still on good terms, the two men also bought a share in the Seattle Supersonics professional basketball team, only this time Shulman managed their interests. Their falling out came in 1972 when, according to *The* [San Diego] *Tribune,* "Klein's leadership of National General had been challenged by some of the corporation's officers." Shulman was among the dissidents whom Klein then "fired." As part of the breakup of their relationship, Klein bought Shulman's share of the Chargers and Shulman Klein's share in their basketball enterprise.

The split with Shulman marked the beginning of the end for Gene Klein at National General. "The heavy pace was getting to me," he later explained, "I grew tired of life at the top." When Frances died unexpectedly in March 1973, Klein decided to get out of the corporate life for good. "It was time to slow down and enjoy what I had," he said.

By fall 1973, Gene Klein had sold all his National General holdings. "I'll never run another business," he told the *Los Angeles Times.* "I've won that game." His only remaining active interest was his NFL franchise and soon he upped his share in it to fifty-six percent. He had his Chargers' office done over and the walls papered with what his decorator described as "a fabric with the color and texture of pigskin." He added a four-foot-wide and eight-foot-long burl elm desk and a carpet in a geometric design of white and rust. "Mr. Klein is not an informal person," the decorator observed. "He likes quiet elegance. He is very European, very high style." Klein sported a mustache and muttonchops and kept a complete wardrobe at each of his three houses, all of it cut in the fashion then known as "mod."

A little more than a year after Frances's death, he remarried. His birthday present to the second Mrs. Klein was a Mercedes wrapped in a pink bow and his engagement ring a thirteen-karat square cut emerald surrounded by diamonds. "Now," Klein pointed out, "for the first time in many years, I am getting to know myself. . . . Instead of prowling around relentlessly in the jungle of business . . . I revel in my own discoveries of happiness. . . . The frantic pace is gone. There are no must-do appointments. . . . I just want to be truly free. My obsession is relaxing and avoiding tension."

As a prediction of the actual agenda lurking in Gene Klein's future, "relaxing and avoiding tension" could not have been further from the mark. When later asked to explain the discrepancy, Gene Klein would answer, "Al Davis."

17
Disciplining Klein

Gene Klein came to the 1974 annual meeting in the commissioner's doghouse.

The incident that clouded Klein's relationship with Rozelle grew out of Klein's extreme frustration with his team's performance. After winning seasons in his first four years as an owner, the Chargers had nosedived to one of the worst teams in the NFL and Klein was frantic. He was being booed unmercifully by the San Diego crowds. "What the fuck am I going to do?" Klein roared at one of his employees in the team's locker room after a particularly galling loss. "That was the worst sixty minutes of football that the Chargers have ever played, and I've owned this goddamned organization for . . . years. The fans are rioting out there. I'm not sure it's safe to leave the stadium."

The Chargers then hired Dr. Arnold Mandell, chairman of the psychiatry department at the University of California at San Diego's School of Medicine. The idea was to see if he could discover an edge that might turn losers into winners. Mandell also had a particular interest in pharmacological research, and Mandell encountered a pharmacological nightmare on the team. "A drug agony rages, silently as the plague, through the body of professional football," Mandell later wrote. "It is likely that half the players [in the NFL] are using stimulant drugs to play. . . . Athletes stoked themselves with club-supplied uppers, usually Dexedrine and Benzedrine."

Mandell's discovery was not exactly a secret prior to his arrival at the Chargers for the 1973 season. In the 1960s, the St. Louis Cardinals had been sued by a former player for causing him to take "potent, harmful, illegal, and dangerous drugs . . . so that he would perform more violently." During the 1972 season, one former Oakland Raider player charged in an Oakland damage suit that the Raiders spent some $6000 on Daprisal and biphetamine that were administered by the club's trainer. By 1973, the issue had become what Rozelle considered a "problem."

The League's "problem" became apparent when, "Congress got all excited about it," and held a set of hearings about rampant drug use among athletes. At a League executive session in June 1973, Rozelle took steps to "bring the situation under control." According to Rozelle, "I announced to the clubs, this is the way it's going to be." Henceforth, he declared, all clubs would have to file an inventory of "prescription drugs" with the League office, report "immediately any situation wherein . . . personnel reportedly are involved in a drug incident," and participate in an expansion of League "educational programs, particularly in the ghetto area, designed to discourage drug use."

"The commissioner," the meeting minutes reported, "will take disciplinary action, up to and including suspension from the NFL . . . against team personnel for improper disposition or use of drugs."

Dr. Arnold Mandell's style of dealing with the same problem insured that the commissioner's new policy would soon have an object lesson. After the fourth game of the 1973 season, the San Diego Chargers' psychiatrist had concluded "there was no way to discuss or manipulate the psychological aspects of pro football without grappling with the pervasive, systematic use of mood-altering drugs." Mandell's approach was to counsel players on the subject and prescribe the drugs people needed "so that they wouldn't go to Tijuana and get the bad stuff."

Rozelle first got hints of what Mandell was doing through the NFL's director of security. According to Mandell, NFL Security soon "had copies of some of my prescriptions, [and] confidential medical records . . . The commissioner was sounding more and more like Big Brother." At the end of the 1973 season, Klein's team, despite the edge they hoped Mandell would give them, had finished with 2 wins, 11 losses, and 1 tie. For his part, the commissioner was now ready to act.

Rozelle dispatched a letter to Klein. Mandell, reconstructing the text of the letter in his book, recalls:

> The time has come when we must have a definitive resolution of the drug problems on your team. We have completed our investigations . . . [and] it is clear that you have not acted on warnings that were sent you. . . . You have either disregarded these warnings or have been inept in handling the problems. This situation cannot be allowed to continue. . . . My information indicates that Dr. Arnold Mandell, whom you state you have consulted in these matters, instead of helping may be contributing to the difficulties. . . . It threatens to soil the good name of professional football in this country. Significant punitive measures must be taken. . . .

The letter invited Klein to a disciplinary hearing at League headquarters.

One action Rozelle proposed taking was banning Klein's general manager, the man responsible for Mandell, from the NFL for life. The proposal made Klein furious. He threatened to sell his franchise immediately if Rozelle did it. Had he been willing to even go so far as to fire the general manager, Klein might have escaped a fine, but he wasn't. "I wouldn't make him the scapegoat," Klein explained. According to Rozelle, Klein's worry wasn't about the money a fine would entail but about bad press.

Their meeting was followed by a press release from the League office. "Players and management of the San Diego Chargers were disciplined today for violations of the National Football League drug policies," it announced. "The discipline . . . consisted of fines totalling $40,000 plus probationary action." Rozelle remembered, "Gene was angry at the time, but it didn't last too long. . . . once the commissioner had acted, he accepted it and let it drop." The incident did not damage the two men's relationship. In truth, they would just get closer with this behind them. "Rozelle did what he thought he had to do," Klein explained. "We had our differences, but I'll tell you what, I always knew where he stood."

The fines themselves were hailed as precedent-setting, and some even predicted the action would turn the corner on athletic drug abuse once and for all. That, too, was an illusion.

18
Is the NFL Legal? Ed Garvey and the Players Union

Virtually all of the National Football League's serious legal dilemmas had their roots in the Sherman Anti-Trust Act. Passed in 1890, the Sherman Act declared "every contract, combination . . . or conspiracy in restraint of trade or commerce to be illegal." In the hands of the Supreme Court, that stricture was made significantly more vague by the interpretation that all such proscribed combinations and conspiracies had to be "unreasonable." Vague or not, the dilemma such a law posed for the sports business was obvious. The business's basic form, the league, was on its face exactly such a monopoly to restrain and control the commerce of staging games. The open question of whether or not all its arrangements for doing so were "reasonable" insured a potentially perpetual state of litigation once lawsuits had become a relatively mass American practice.

Professional baseball escaped the dilemma in 1922, when the Supreme Court ruled that professional baseball was not interstate commerce and hence was exempt from the Sherman Act. The NFL later argued that the Federal Baseball Club exemption ought to cover football as well. The Supreme Court did not agree. It may be inconsistent to include football and not baseball under the Sherman Act, the Court ruled, but it was up to Congress, not the Court, to remedy the situation. Henceforth, the Sherman Act was a fact of life in the football business.

Then commissioner Bert Bell immediately began approaching Congress in search of a blanket exemption from antitrust law. Though he came close, Bell was unsuccessful. Rozelle took up the cause upon Bell's death. After securing a limited exemption to allow League Think to be applied to television revenues in 1961, Rozelle went back to Congress in 1964 and 1965 in search of something more comprehensive. Like Bell, Rozelle came close, getting bills through different houses in different sessions, but got no closer. Since securing another limited exemption to allow the 1966 merger, Rozelle had not been back to ask for more.

That inaction was a recognition of legislative realities rather than a quiescence on Rozelle's part about the potential dangers posed by the Sherman Act. Given the wrong ruling, he noted, "our whole League and everything it does could be found illegal." In 1974 Rozelle was concerned only about the Sherman Act being used against the League by "outsiders." It was still unthinkable then that any member of the League might use the statute against the League itself.

The principal Sherman Act "outsider" Rozelle worried about was the National Football League Players Association and by 1974, these worries were anything but abstract. *John Mackey, et al. v. National Football League* filed by the union in 1972 challenged what the League called "the Rozelle Rule." Under this rule, any franchise whose contract with a player expired had the right to compensation from the player's new employer should that player subsequently work for another franchise. The compensation was to be a player of equal caliber, selected by the commissioner. The effect of the Rozelle Rule was to make competition between franchises for experienced talent virtually nonexistent, thereby suppressing player salaries. Mackey wanted the Court to award free agency, allowing players to sell their services without the penalty of compensation. Anything less, Mackey contended, was a violation of the Sherman Act.

Most agreed that the man behind the suit was Ed Garvey, NFLPA executive director. In 1974, Garvey had been with the union for barely three years. Already most of the League considered him anything from an obnoxious nuisance to a dire threat. Even when they could agree on little else, the mention of Garvey's name alone was enough to turn most NFL conversations unanimously ugly.

The owners of football first crossed paths with Garvey during negotiations in 1970 for a new four-year union contract. At the time, Ed Garvey was fresh from law school. John Mackey brought in his law firm to help write the contract once general agreement on terms had been reached. The owners first heard about him from the players. During contract negotiations one of the conditions was that no attorneys be present, just owners and players. Rozelle was present, but he was "impartial," looking out for the interests of football itself. When the players wanted to consult their lawyer, they left negotiations and huddled in a room where Garvey was waiting. "You think we're radical," they told the owners back in negotiations, "you should hear what Garvey is saying in the back room."

Garvey was hired to be the union's new executive director once the contract was signed. His selection was confirmed by vote of the union's executive committee in May 1971. The only owner to congratulate Garvey on his new job was Al Davis. "The whole philosophy changed with Garvey's arrival," Lamar Hunt would later complain. "Now anything management did had to be negative." From Garvey's perspective, the union he inherited was weak and matched against people who "played for keeps." It was that weakness that led him to the Sherman Act. "Without the Mackey case," he later pointed out, "we would have been lost."

While the threat *Mackey v. NFL* posed to the Rozelle era's "all for one, one for all" economics would no doubt have been sufficient to make the owners gathered at Bal Harbour antagonistic to Garvey, the manner in which the case had been filed turned that antagonism vicious. Even Garvey would later call the timing of it all an "unfortunate coincidence."

Immediately before the filing, the League's relations with Garvey had seemed to be on an upswing. Garvey agreed to talk to the owners in an olive branch discussion. "He was a bright young man," Wellington Mara described Garvey, "and he was extremely conciliatory." Garvey himself considered the session "fun. . . . I talked about the union and how I hoped relations would improve. They hollered about the union's newsletter. I enjoyed it tremendously." There was no mention in the discussions of the Sherman Act or any possible lawsuit. The next day, the NFLPA filed *Mackey v. NFL*. By then Garvey was out of the country on vacation. "It was," Rozelle noted, "a gesture of absolute disdain. The owners were furious."

When League Think started coming apart, Ed Garvey would hound the League's flanks, smudging its image, costing it money, and providing the owners with someone besides each other to hate. His decision to pursue *Mackey v. NFL* also presaged the form of the civil war to come. The Sherman Act would be the weapon of choice.

"Garvey is interested in breaking the NFL," Gene Klein pointed out, "making it impossible for us to exist."

19
The Giants' Patriarch Makes a Killing

The League discussed its labor relations as the Management Council, strictly an owners group. The Management Council in turn hired professional negotiators, who were overseen by an elected Management Council executive committee. In 1974, its chairman was Wellington Mara of the New York Giants.

The New York Giants were a family business, and Wellington, like all the Maras before him, treated it that way. "Next to my own family," Wellington, fifty-eight years old and father of ten children, once told a friend, "I care most about the Giant family."

When Wellington was nine years old, his father, Tim, a bookmaker, bought the Giants for $500. One of Mara's earliest football memories was of standing outside church after a Sunday Mass and hearing his father tell a friend, "Today's the day we see if football can go over in New York." It did, and Wellington Mara had been an officer of the franchise since he was twelve years old. Wellington's favorite team was the 1938 Giants. At the time he had just graduated from Fordham with a degree in philosophy and was resisting his father's demands that he follow his brother, Jack, on to law school. Instead, he wanted to spend a year in the football business.

That year turned into a lifetime. During it, Wellington chased balls at practice and roomed with the team's starting halfback. "All the fellows were my age," he remembered. "I was close to them, a part of them. There was an entirely different atmosphere in pro football in those days." The team all lived together and when they traveled, it was by train with plenty of time for banter and cards and "getting to know a man's character." The average Giant earned $2500 a season and most players worked in construction during the off season. Wellington was smitten by it all and, except for three years during World War II, had been nestled in the Giant family ever since, most of that time acting as the club's general manager.

His father died in 1959, leaving equal shares in the franchise to his two sons, and Wellington's brother, Jack, took over the Giants' reins. Jack died in 1965, and in the family's order of succession, the club was now Wellington's to run. His sense of his role and the franchise were still rooted largely in that first 1938 season. By the time of the Bal Harbour annual meeting, that made him decidedly "old-fashioned"—a poor candidate for dealing with Ed Garvey.

The trouble he would have with that role was obvious to his players in 1971 when Mara became worried that he had gotten out of touch with the team's players and approached the Giants' union representative, a defensive end, with his problem. He wanted a survey of the team's opinions of Mara's rapport with them and what they thought of the Giant family. "He asked for an honest report," the end later told *Sports Illustrated,* "and I gave it to him both barrels. I told him, 'You have no rapport with the players and the Giant family image is not there.' He was crushed . . . I wasn't trying to hurt the guy, but to tell him the truth he asked for. He shook my hand and said, 'At least you gave me an honest answer.' " By the end of that day, the defensive end had been cut from the Giants' roster and was out of the family for good.

Wellington Mara's life-style was also old-fashioned. He lived in Westchester County and commuted to the Giants' Manhattan offices every day after first attending Mass. He had met his wife, Ann, in church, when they both rushed to help an old woman who had fainted. The Maras had four sons and six daughters. Most of their friends were Catholic doctors, and at Wellington's instigation, a priest was appointed the Giants' honorary chaplain. Mara also sent tickets for every game to the rector of St. Ignatius and the faculty at Fordham. One section of seats for Giants games was known as "Jesuit Row."

Giants tickets were perhaps the most sought after in the business and the franchise was always a League leader in attendance receipts, giving Wellington stature inside the NFL. Despite his lack of flash, Mara, as perhaps the most successful player ever in the Superstadium Game, was the object of no small amount of envy from his peers.

Mara's opponent was the city of New York, until 1972 his landlord at Yankee Stadium. At the time, John Lindsay was mayor. The wild card in the contest was Sonny Werblin, head of the New Jersey Sports Authority, the guiding light in plans for a new sports complex to be located in the as yet undeveloped marshland just across the Hudson from lower Manhattan. One of the first people Werblin approached was Wellington Mara, who said he was "receptive to a possible move."

Mara's receptiveness was a function of his dissatisfaction with both his stadium and his landlord. "Yankee Stadium was built for baseball," he pointed out. Mayor Lindsay insisted that a remodeling job was the answer. Mara disagreed. "It's just a new coat of paint on an old lady," he said of the mayor's plan. Mara liked what he heard from New Jersey much better. Werblin's plans called for a seventy-five-thousand-seat outdoor football stadium with a racetrack next door. "Giants Stadium" would also feature theater-style seats, two instant replay scoreboards, a two-story press box, and seventy-two luxury boxes. The luxury boxes would be financed separately by the Giants and would become their private property, initially rented out, mostly to corporations and banks, for $16,000 a year each.

Wellington Mara signed a lease on the as yet unbuilt and unfinanced Giants Stadium in September 1971. It was a generous deal. According to *Sports Illustrated,* the Giants "get free office space, free watchmen, free maintenance staff, free cops, free scoreboard crew, free insurance, free water, free heating, free electricity, free sewage and waste disposal, and free transportation for all fans who have to park more than a quarter of a mile away. The Giants pay only for the PA announcer and their phone calls. The Giants also get twenty-five percent of parking fees, 400 free parking spaces, fifty percent of concessions, all advertising in programs and souvenir books . . . all membership fees in the stadium club, all radio and TV revenue, and up to 2,700 free tickets per game." The rent was fifteen percent of gross receipts.

Newsweek renamed Mara's franchise "the Hackensack Giants." Mara protested: "New York is not losing a team, but gaining a sports complex." The new Giants' home field was just seven miles from midtown Manhattan, he pointed out, only a mile more than Yankee Stadium. The explanation made little headway with the city of New York. The city's first response was to evict the Giants from Yankee Stadium, even though their lease had another three years to run. "If they want to play in a swamp," one city politician snorted, "let them play in a swamp right now." As a consequence, the Giants spent the three years they had to wait for their new stadium as vagabonds.

In the meantime Lindsay threatened "to seek another NFL franchise" to play inside the city limits. For an NFL member to make such a move would require unanimous approval of all member clubs, giving Mara a crucial veto. Lindsay warned that if the League did block such a move, he would sue under the Sherman Act.

In retrospect, all the rhetoric surrounding the Giants' move sounded like premonition. Seven years later the language would all be repeated virtually verbatim in Los Angeles when Carroll Rosenbloom finally decided to give "the Grand Duchess of Stadiums" what he thought she deserved. The difference between New York in 1971 and Los Angeles in 1978 was that New York did nothing to back up its threat.

Other than vituperation of Mara, New York's only other serious response was to fight a rear guard action, hoping to derail Werblin's nascent plans and leave Mara nowhere to go. To actually build Giants Stadium, New Jersey had first to sell several hundred million dollars' worth of construction bonds. According to Mara, "New York bankers were told quietly that if they bought bonds, they would no longer receive any city or state business. . . . Fortunately, the banks and businesses of New Jersey stepped in." It was a close fight and the New Jersey Sports Authority almost didn't make it, but finally, the New Jersey's Meadowlands sports complex became a financial reality. "No public money was spent," Mara would later brag, "and the investment made out like gangbusters."

20
Irsay

At the Bal Harbour General Sessions, the newest member of the nation's most exclusive club, was Robert Irsay of the Baltimore Colts. Most viewed Irsay as the creature of his general manager, Joe Thomas. Thomas himself shared that view and was not reluctant to say so. Shortly after becoming general manager for the Colts' new ownership, Thomas hosted a pre-game dinner.

"Where's Mr. Irsay tonight?" a reporter asked. "If I were he, picking up the tab for this wonderful dinner, I'd want to be here to enjoy it."

"Forget him," Joe Thomas replied. "You guys are still living in the Carroll Rosenbloom era, where the owner took you by the hand. The owner counts for nothing. Just don't worry about him."

"Well, he hired you," the reporter pointed out, "so he counts for something."

"Get this straight," Thomas snarled. "He didn't hire me. I hired him. I could have had six guys for that job and I picked him. He's in the League because I brought him in."

The last statement was accurate. Irsay would likely never have entered the NFL had not Thomas found him for Carroll Rosenbloom at the last minute, when Rosenbloom was desperate to head off a competing bid for the Rams. At the press conference announcing his entrance into the NFL, Robert Irsay proclaimed, "Pro football is one of the most exciting things in my life. . . . I think all the owners are great guys," the Chicago air-conditioning millionaire added.

The response of the Baltimore press corps, Carroll Rosenbloom's old bugaboo, was enthusiastic. "New Colt Owner's Approach Refreshing" the News-American headlined. ". . . He is as naive and enthusiastic about owning a NFL team as Rosenbloom has become jaded." Robert Irsay was seen, in The Sun's words, as "a sturdily-built, chesty man. . . . He looks fit for anything, somewhat along the lines of an archetypal military officer. . . . He has a firm handshake and you soon gather . . . that his word is his bond. He's honest they say. For a millionaire, they say, he's a helluva guy."

For Baltimore newspapers, it was a gushy reception. They took Robert Irsay at face value and, indeed, as Irsay described himself, there were a lot of attractive features. "Amazing accomplishments," the Colts' new game programs declared, "are nothing new to Irsay." Irsay had started life poor in the rough section of Chicago. Through hard work, the profile Irsay commissioned about himself claimed, he "enrolled in the University of Illinois, where he received a mechanical engineering degree and played 'fourth or fifth or sixth string quarterback.' From 1941 to 1945, he served in the U.S. Marine Corps." Most of Irsay's military career, he claimed, had been spent in combat and he was wounded once pretty badly in the leg.

The money Irsay used to buy the Colts came from an airconditioning firm he had founded with "an initial investment of $800" borrowed from his wife in 1951. "In twenty years, he expanded that investment into one of the world's most famous heating, ventilating, and air-conditioning firms," which he sold for $8.5 million the year before the Colts purchase.

Certainly Robert Irsay arrived in Baltimore with all the accoutrements of wealth: an $800,000 home, a Learjet in which to commute to Colts games, a retreat in Florida, and a sixty-five-foot yacht. Eventually he would also buy a condominium, another house in Dallas, and a Lockheed Jetstar aircraft to replace the Lear. Normally the wealthy weren't accorded a lot of gratuitous sympathy in Baltimore, but in Irsay's case there was enough visible human pain in his life to make him appear sympathetic.

A devoted family man, Irsay and his wife, Harriet, had three children, and by the time Irsay joined the football business, tragedy had overtaken two of them. His oldest son, Tommy, had been born mentally retarded and, at age eight, placed in an institution in Florida. In 1971, Irsay's daughter, Roberta, was killed in an automobile accident outside of Chicago. For years afterward, the Irsays would keep Roberta's room intact, "full of pictures of Roberta riding horses" and "rows of ribbons she won." Irsay never got over the loss. "I can't say I have everything I want," the new Colts owner told *The Sun*. "If I could, I would want my daughter back, but that's impossible. They caught the kids who ran her car off the road. They were on drugs when it happened. They got ten to twenty years, but the way things are today they'll probably be out in five. I felt like killing them myself, but that wouldn't help anything."

No one bothered to check the facts of Robert Irsay's life for another ten years. By then, the picture of Robert Irsay had grown decidedly more negative. "The Colts owner is," *The Baltimore Sun* wrote in 1984, "an insecure man who deeply desires to be courted, a man given to royal tantrums when he doesn't get his way, a man prone to titanic swings in behavior. . . . There has been widespread speculation that Mr. Irsay drinks heavily. . . . [He is] a loud, brutish, erratic man who cannot be taken at his word . . . an interfering, miserly, incompetent manager . . . a man who thrives on turmoil no matter the cost." In that mood, *The Sun* finally set out to find if Robert Isray really was the man he claimed to be and came up with a history significantly at odds with the one Isray had commissioned.

The registrar's office at the University of Illinois had records of him attending only from the fall of 1940 to the summer of 1942 and leaving without a degree. The Marine Corps "records show a man with same name, birth date, and father's first name enlisted as a staff sergeant in October 1942." That "Robert J. Irsay" had been demoted for taking a jeep without permission and "getting into a minor accident." A year after he entered the

Corps and without ever having seen duty overseas, this Irsay was discharged. The "$800" of his wife's money Robert Irsay claimed he had used to start his business "was really a lot more money than that," Harriet Irsay admitted, and it didn't come from her. Even his story of Roberta's death turned out to have been significantly embellished.

Robert Irsay would continue to distribute the same biography even after everyone knew it was considerably short of accurate. By then, his reputation inside the NFL was also suffering. One fellow owner defended him. "He makes irresponsible statements and he drinks a lot, but he's not a bad guy. He's just a little crazy and off the wall sometimes." An NFL executive offered an even more blunt opinion: "His brain is baked." He continued, "He's a jerk who says the dumbest goddamn things. You have to talk to him early in the morning or he's unintelligible."

In 1974, the Colts "war hero" owner came off as little more than eccentric to the rest of the owners. One owner noted, ". . . you couldn't shut him up. It was all heated participation with no substance. You had to suspect whether he knew his ass from a hole in the ground but, like I said, nobody paid much attention to him." All anyone in the NFL knew for certain about Robert Irsay in 1974 was that he had a profound dislike for Carroll Rosenbloom.

Some observers claimed Irsay felt C.R. had misled him about the stadium possibilities in Baltimore and others pointed out how upset Irsay had been about the details of the player contracts he inherited from Rosenbloom. The most obvious reason was the swap that had brought the two men together in the first place. While Rosenbloom was applauded as slick for having pulled it off, Irsay was the sucker who had made it all possible. "He was pissed at my father because the media wrote that Carroll had made a brilliant move," Steve Rosenbloom remembered. "He began to resent it after the fact and couldn't see that it was in fact the only way he could ever have got into this closed fraternity." For his part, C.R. considered Irsay "a fool."

Carroll Rosenbloom kept his distance from the man he'd brought into the NFL. At one of the annual meetings, however, Irsay cornered Carroll and Steve at the hotel elevator. Irsay reportedly smelled of liquor and that, in itself, turned C.R.'s stomach because Carroll didn't drink. While Rosenbloom waited uncomfortably for the elevator, trying not to get queasy, Irsay ranted in his face. "You couldn't even understand what he was talking about," Steve remembered. "He was literally unintelligible."

C.R. shook his head. "Jesus Christ," he muttered to Steve, inside the elevator. "Do you believe that guy?"

21
A Stalemate for Rozelle

The executive sessions in which Irsay was fast making his reputation were reserved for the League's most sensitive discussions. Closeted by themselves with Pete Rozelle in the chair, the owners attended to the business at the heart of their business: selection of Super Bowl sites, reports from the finance committee, the most sensitive discussions with attorneys, and tinkering with the structure and composition of the League itself.

In the years between the 1966 merger and the 1974 annual meeting, the hottest executive session issue was "ownership policy," the League's standards for membership. Prior to 1966, those standards were little more than a loosely enforced, informal, and largely unarticulated understanding. "Just having a policy was enough in those days," Rozelle said. "On important matters, people just didn't violate them." By 1966, however, Rozelle concluded that "it was important that it be specifically reduced to writing." In so doing, he hoped to standardize the character of the League's ownership, much as he had already standardized its marketing and internal economics. While described by Rozelle as no more than an articulation of what was already a Leaguewide understanding, the attempt to formalize an ownership policy was unprecedented and authorship was for the most part ascribed to Rozelle alone.

Rozelle's first such attempt was to have his ownership policy formalized as part of the NFL/AFL merger agreement. The ownership policy was a further elaboration on League Think, containing four principal provisions.

The first prohibited "corporate ownership." While entities like Anheuser-Busch, Ralston Purina Corp., and CBS owned franchises in other sports leagues, such were not allowed in the NFL. "A corporation engaged in other business activities owning or controlling one of our football teams would make it impossible for us to control ownership in our League,'' Rozelle explained.

The second provision prohibited public ownership of NFL franchises. Again the issue was control. Public ownership, Rozelle noted, deprived the League of its ability to regulate both who owned a franchise and those owners' other activities. "You would [also] be required to make more disclosures of your business through stockholder reports . . . [and] the stockholders of a public company might well have different views than what might be prudent in operating a football team."

The third provision, "the fifty-one percent rule," required all franchises' ownership to include someone with at least a bare majority, so that franchise control was vested in a single individual. "Virtually in every instance where a team has not had a fifty-one percent rule," Rozelle pointed out, "there has been a problem. . . . There's been disharmony, there have been disputes, and there's been several cases of litigation where clubs did not have one firm, controlling entity."

The final provision dealing with "cross-ownership" was by far the most controversial. At issue was the ownership of other sports businesses by NFL members. The League's "traditional position" was that "no person having an operating control of a franchise in the NFL may acquire control of, directly or indirectly, any other team sports enterprise or business."

Rozelle's 1966 attempt to reduce ownership policy to constitutional League Think didn't work. Instead of a constitutional amendment containing the explicit details of ownership policy, the Supplementary Merger Agreement dated December 1, 1966, bound "all present franchises of the NFL and the AFL" to "present NFL [ownership] policies" but only "with respect to changes of club ownership after February 1, 1967."

Had Rozelle not been willing to settle for the continuance of a vague informality which exempted all violations by those who were members prior to 1967, it is doubtful he would have gotten any written ownership policy at all. A number of the new NFL's members were in violation of one or more of Rozelle's ownership standards and in no mood to force the issue:

• Lamar Hunt was an original investor in the Dallas franchise of the North American Soccer League, a founder and fifty percent owner of the WCT professional tennis tour, "indirectly" the sponsor of a professional bowling team, owner of a large piece of a Dallas minor league baseball franchise, and eventually a ten percent partner in the Chicago Bulls professional basketball franchise.

• The Rooney family had "significant" horse racing and race-track interests and briefly bought into a Pennsylvania soccer franchise.

• Gene Klein shared control of the Seattle basketball franchise with Sam Shulman for several years.

• The New England Patriots NFL franchise had no fifty-one percent owner and had issued publicly traded stock.

• The Green Bay Packers were owned by a quasi-public civic group and no fifty-one percent owner.

• Neither the New York Giants nor the Dallas Cowboys had a fifty-one percent owner.

• Art Modell briefly dipped below fifty-one percent control of the Cleveland Browns and had also sponsored a golfer and dabbled in horse racing.

• Bill Bidwill, the Bidwill brother who would eventually control the St. Louis Cardinals NFL team, also owned a piece of a soccer franchise.

• Jack Kent Cooke, a partner in the Washington Redskins, also owned the professional basketball and hockey franchises in Los Angeles.

While accepting the political impasse created by those realities, Pete Rozelle considered the 1967 solution to the ownership issue to be stopgap at best. He resumed his quest to make ownership policy both formal and comprehensive again in 1970. His opportunity to do so arose at the annual meeting and the discussion "was prompted by concern about estate sales. . . . Some of the clubs felt that such restrictions as the fifty-one percent requirement and no public stock issuance and no corporate ownership . . . were too restrictive and would hurt the sale of a franchise."

Pete Rozelle's appointed an intraleague "special committee on membership rules and ownership policy" to study these objections. Tex Schramm's boss, Clint Murchison, chaired the committee, which also included Gerald Phipps, owner of the Denver Broncos, and Edward Bennett Williams, president of the Washington Redskins and the most vocal internal critic of the commissioner's proposed ownership policy. "It was quite clear I was outmanned two to one on the committee at every stage," Williams remembered.

The report of the special committee "constituted a consensus of the three" and was presented to the membership in May of

1970. Its League Think premise was apparent in the first paragraph: "It is the view of the committee that the information [given] most consideration should be the effect the League's rule would have on the League and professional football rather than on the interest of those presently having ownership positions."

The report's principal proposed policy modifications were to the fifty-one percent and cross-ownership provisions. The fifty-one percent rule was loosened to permit "fragmentation" as long as one person still had the right to make a franchise's decisions. The cross-ownership provision, however, emerged in an even more restrictive form. The special committee's proposal would have refused approval of "any future transfers of interests in member clubs" to anyone with "either a majority or minority interest in other professional sports organizations."

The committee's recommendations were tabled pending unspecified further discussions, but the issue of ownership policy did not stay tabled for long. In February 1971, Art Modell opened the issue again by circulating his own memo on ownership policy, proposing changes in both the public stock prohibition and the cross-ownership policy. The idea went nowhere when it was discussed by the League in March. "My plan failed for lack of a second," its author remembered. "I had no support in the League."

The same could not be said for his idea on cross-ownership. It amounted to the most serious assault yet, not only on future cross-ownership, but on the heretofore sacrosanct grandfather provisions as well. After discussing a "proposed rule that no controlling stockholder, voting trustee, officer, or employee of a member club may own an interest in any other major sports teams or enterprise," Modell proposed that "a period of three years shall be allowed for disposal of present interests inconsistent with this policy." While the Browns' owner considered his proposal "generous and fair in giving people a chance to divest," to its more flagrant violators it was remarkable for even raising divestiture at all.

Art Modell's cross-ownership proposal was not immediately accepted, but it raised the ownership policy stakes geometrically, and in so doing, initiated a new era of internal conflict in the NFL. It also narrowed the issue. Henceforth, discussions of ownership policy would focus virtually exclusively on cross-ownership and so would Rozelle's quest for a constitutional amendment. In the immediate moment, the commissioner suc-

ceeded in galvanizing the majority behind his policy and they
made their weight felt when the League met in May 1971.

Ownership policy was a principal part of that meeting's agenda.
Rozelle himself considered such cross-ownership a "conflict of
interest," but as usual said little in the official discussion. The
majority who supported his position were not yet prepared to
demand as stringent a solution as Modell's, but demanded formal
action of some sort soon. At this stage, the discussion "centered
on no one acquiring a new interest or increasing a present interest.
They," Rozelle noted of the owners, "were satisfied with holding
the line while they attempted to work out the other guidelines."

The agreement was, Rozelle pointed out, "another stopgap,"
and the commissioner's attitude insured that the truce it signaled
was only momentary.

.22
Ownership Policy—Conflict of Interest?

Pete Rozelle needed three quarters agreement in order to pass a
constitutional amendment and marshaling that agreement would
prove no small task. He included an amendment on ownership
policy in the 1972 annual meeting's March agenda. This measure
"would have clarified constitutional language concerning possible conflict of interest resulting from ownership in other team
sports." Discussion of this amendment was delayed until May,
when the League met again in New York City.

The case in favor of prohibition was framed by Rozelle's
concern over "conflict of interest." Among the majority propo-
nents of the commissioner's proposal were a good portion of the
remaining roster of past, current, or potential violators. While
the intensity with which each individual in the majority made his
particular argument varied, "everyone," according to Tex
Schramm, "felt a strong necessity to do something about it."

The premise of the commissioner and his majority was that the
football business was in competition with all other sports businesses for a limited pool of "sports spectator dollars." To
promote other sports was therefore automatically stripping the
NFL of potential revenues. It was a situation that bred conflicts

of interest at every turn. What if an NFL owner is involved in another league and the other league takes a position in "our relations with Congress" contrary to the NFL's? What if an owner of another sports franchise uses the health and profitability of his NFL holdings to maintain a floundering investment in another league, thereby ruining them both? Were that to happen, everyone in the NFL would suffer. Just as worrisome as the potential dilution of capital was the dilution of operational talent. An owner who had to divide his attention, it was argued, robbed the League of his fullest effort. If that same owner also "leaked things said at NFL meetings" to his other sports business, the outcome would be "a damaging cross-pollination of confidences."

The proposition's critics included Lamar Hunt and Joe Robbie, but chief among them continued to be Edward Bennett Williams. Already a legendary courtroom attorney, Williams was, as a maker of speeches, easily the most persuasive voice in the NFL. He was also, as one of his fellow owners described him, "one of the brightest men in the League."

"I always got along well with Williams," Rozelle remembered. "He was a very authoritative speaker and very helpful at the League meetings. . . . He's a charming guy. But over this issue we had differences."

"I begged the owners of the NFL to abandon this thing, this folly, as being prospectively outlandishly costly, and all for nothing," Williams recalled. "It's just burning the barn down to roast the pig." He agreed with none of Rozelle's arguments to the contrary. "There was no other major sport that could enforce such a proscription," he pointed out. "The same know-how that helps you run one sports franchise will help you run the other. . . . I don't think there is a dilution of talent or resources or energies. . . . It's been proven time and again that it's great for Lord and Taylor to have a Neiman-Marcus in the same shopping center because they both benefit. I believe the same thing holds in sports. . . . I thought it was an imprudent rule [and] that it was not in the interests of the League. . . . To have such a rule would circumscribe the prospective pool of owners of NFL franchises . . . and it was in [the League's] economic interest to have the largest prospective pool of owners that there could be. Furthermore . . . there were all sorts of people in the NFL who had other sports interests, then, now, and at all times."

Key to Rozelle's strategy was narrowing the number of those interests covered by the prohibition, thereby minimizing personalized opposition. To do so, he had confined his proposed amendment to "major sports." Said Williams, "I never understood it. . . . If the rule had validity . . . if there was a sound basis for it, then it would be equally applicable to all sports, but it was never proposed in that form." Though he found any cross-ownership proposal abhorrent, Williams's riposte in this instance was to unsuccessfully demand the widest and most comprehensive prohibition possible.

Another key to Rozelle's strategy was to gather sufficient momentum to enter his prohibition in the constitution itself rather than settle for one of the lesser levels of legality. On that front, Williams's counter arguments made headway. Rather than such a constitutional amendment, Williams endorsed a resolution expressing "the will of the majority" that would "obtain for the ensuing year." The attorney explained, "A bylaw has a certain permanence about it. . . . To be in breach of a bylaw would carry disciplinary consequences," whereas "breaching a resolution" was a matter Williams thought considerably more "amorphous."

Amorphousness was still attractive among the majority in 1972, and Rozelle fell short once again. His amendment "was withdrawn, and in its place, this resolution was unanimously adopted to be effective through the 1973 NFL Spring Meeting:

> RESOLVED, that no person owning a majority interest in or direct or indirect operational control of a member club may acquire any interest in another major team sport. Additionally, any person holding such financial interest at the time this Resolution is adopted will in no case increase his percentage of such interest."

While a lot less than he ultimately intended to get, this resolution was nonetheless a victory in Rozelle's political ledger. For six years he had sought at least "something in writing" and now he had it. The resolution secured the major team sports limitation essential to maintaining and motivating his majority, and in the course of discussing it, Rozelle had also won a remarkable concession on the issue of divestiture. "All agreed," according to the official record of the discussion, "that there would be a best effort made to dispose of current holdings," tightening the pressure on the grandfathered interests and insuring that divestiture would henceforth be discussed by the majority as a matter of when to do it rather than whether or not it should be done.

When the 1972 resolution came up for renewal in 1973, a new

element of personal animosity entered the discussion, introduced
by Leonard Tose of the Philadelphia Eagles. He was furious with
Lamar Hunt because Hunt had recently journeyed to Philadelphia
and held a press conference announcing the formation of a
Philadelphia franchise of the North American Soccer League.
The front of *The Philadelphia Inquirer*'s sports page showed a
picture of Hunt accepting a check from Tom McCloskey, a
friend of Tose's and the new Philadelphia soccer entrepreneur.
The gesture infuriated the Eagles owner. "Leonard Tose," Joe
Robbie remembered, "was miffed that another owner would
come into his city and attend a press conference for another
sport."

"I was indignant," Tose admitted. "I confronted [Hunt] personally and tried to stand up close to him so he would get my
message. . . . Mr. Hunt is not that big a man alone, but what he
has done is taken the prestige of the NFL and turned it into
bringing a team into Philadelphia to compete . . . rather than
coming into Philadelphia to help me. . . . The mere fact that
[Hunt] sits in our meetings and [then reports] whatever we do to
the soccer league to me is reprehensible. . . . It turns my stomach. It is against everything I have been taught. It is un-
American. . . . I don't have the vocabulary to tell you how
disgusting that is to me."

Hunt remained unruffled by the attack. "Lamar is a very laid
back seeming guy" an NFL executive noted. "He's hard to get
excited." When Tose demanded a report about the state of
Hunt's agreed upon "best efforts" to divest himself, Hunt simply offered that he was working on it.

In fact, no one had sold off anything during 1972. Instead, the
ranks of cross-owners had indirectly grown. The addition was
Joe Robbie of the Miami Dolphins and his cross-ownership was
indirect because the soccer interest with which he had recently
become associated had been purchased by his wife and not
himself. Nonetheless, Robbie would personally serve as an ex-
officio member on two of the NASL's internal committees.
"The Robbie situation" was nonetheless outside the ownership
policy's control. And Joe Robbie had been a vocal opponent of
Rozelle's policy even before his wife's purchase.

"This policy through the years has been more honored by
ignoring it than enforcing it," Robbie complained. "I haven't
gone trumpeting soccer around the country. And. . . . I don't
consider soccer that highly competitive to professional football."
Robbie also scoffed at Rozelle's "selective" notion of conflict

of interest. He pointed out that the same law firm was advising the NFL and the NASL on the same subjects. Robbie offered that if the League's lawyers didn't consider the two in conflict, there was hardly much case for the owners treating it any differently.

Despite Joe Robbie's new status, Lamar Hunt's lagging "best efforts," and Leonard Tose's outrage, Rozelle didn't force the issue in June 1973. The expiration of the 1972 resolution itself provoked only a short discussion. "The question simply came up that the one-year resolution was expiring," Joe Robbie remembered, "and it was agreed that the policy be extended for two more years." This time the vote to do so was twenty-one yes, one no, and four abstentions. Edward Bennett Williams cast the one no. The Bal Harbour annual meeting in 1974 was the first one in five years at which ownership policy was not the subject of belabored discussion.

23

The Boy Wonder of the Football Business—Lamar Hunt

In 1974, Pete Rozelle accepted the "limitations" of the League's continuing resolution and, for the moment, considered ownership policy a dormant issue. The presence of Lamar Hunt in the opposition likely had more to do with the League's "unreadiness" than any other single factor. Forty-two years old at the time of Bal Harbour, Hunt was already enshrined in the Pro Football Hall of Fame and was a legend in the business of staging games for profit.

The first thing anyone ever noticed about Lamar Hunt was his last name. "Hunt" and "wealth" were already synonymous when Lamar entered the football business in 1959. *Texas Monthly* described his father, Texas oilman H. L. Hunt, as "the richest man in America," worth "around $2 billion" in 1954. Lamar was the sixth and youngest child. When it was later revealed that H.L. had secretly fathered eight more children by two other women, Lamar and his five siblings were henceforth referred to

as Hunt's "first family." They all started wealthy and, for most
of their lives, got only more so. Asked on the witness stand to
state his occupation, Lamar Hunt, then worth "over $500 mil-
lion," would find himself momentarily at a loss. "I guess the
way you describe it," he finally answered, is "self-employed."

Specifically, the root of Lamar's fortune was the trust established by his father in 1935. Each of H.L.'s first family received
a similar arrangement, and together they controlled Placid Oil
Company, "reputedly the world's largest privately held company." In 1978, the worth of Placid's reserves would be estimated at "in excess of $2 billion" with "a gross annual income
of $300 million." "The most significant thing" about according
to *Texas Monthly*, "is their cohesiveness."

Margaret, the first family's firstborn, was seventeen years
older than Lamar and "reigned as queen bee." Haroldson Lafay-
ette Hunt III, the second born, had suffered a nervous breakdown and been institutionalized since Lamar was in junior high
school. Caroline, the second sister, "impressed everybody with
the gentleness of her disposition." Bunker, born fourth, became
a legendary oilman in his own right. At age thirty-five, he was
"at least on paper, the world's richest man." Herbert, the next
brother, was considered "the steadying force of the family" and
was a partner in a number of Bunker's oil deals. Together with
Lamar, Herbert and Bunker also owned Penrod Drilling, one of
the world's largest drilling contractors. Both Lamar and Herbert
were dedicated joggers. Bunker, on the other hand, was a habitual eater and would eventually balloon to three hundred pounds.
Lamar was considered by *Texas Monthly* as "the most preoccupied of the Hunt brothers, the one . . . determined to make a
name for himself apart from the family."

That he chose the football business to do so no doubt came as
little surprise to his brothers. As youngsters, he and Bunker went
over the small print at the back of the sports page together,
discussing what all the numbers meant. "I read the box scores
and the attendance figures," Lamar recalled. "I was always
interested in attendance at sporting events." Lamar also "grew
up playing football." Despite being under six feet, thin, and
wearing glasses with thick plastic frames, Hunt went out for
football all four of his years at Southern Methodist University in
Dallas. Lamar started his first successful sports business while
still an undergraduate. It was a batting cage complete with
watermelon concession. After that came a miniature golf course,
but it failed. "We expanded too fast," Hunt explained. Two

years later, Lamar decided to get into professional football. "I just felt I had a good understanding of the entertainment world," he explained. "It was a challenge and I think I had some good ideas."

Lamar and Bunker both agreed that Dallas could support a pro football business despite the failed 1951 franchise which had fled east and become Carroll Rosenbloom's Baltimore Colts. In 1958, Lamar called NFL Commissioner Bert Bell with the idea of expanding into Dallas but Bell said "the League was not interested." In 1959, Hunt tried to buy an existing NFL franchise with the idea of moving it to Dallas. The franchise was the Chicago Cardinals, and the attempt was unsuccessful. Though the League wanted the Cardinals to leave Chicago, the then owners, the Wolfson family, wanted to stay. The Wolfsons would not agree to sell more than forty-nine percent and that was of no interest to Hunt. In the course of those negotiations, he learned that three other parties had approached the Wolfsons, and all had been run through the same routine as Lamar.

On Lamar Hunt's flight back from his final meeting with the Wolfsons, the American Football League was born. "It was just like one of those cartoons, where the light bulb goes off over the character's head," Hunt remembered. "That is one of the few times in my life that I felt something like that. I just thought, 'Why not start another professional football league?' " Hunt elaborated: "Why wouldn't a second league work? All the basic information I needed had been supplied by the Wolfsons. . . . They had dropped the names of . . . a bunch of people on the outside wanting in. . . . Why not start a new league? . . . It was all very simple, which is one of the big reasons I think it worked. There were no studies, no marketing reports. . . . Like all successful products, there must be a need, or you must create one. We did not have to create one."

After returning to Dallas, Lamar immediately put in a call to Houston's Bud Adams, a Texas oil scion like himself, and found that Adams was still sore from his treatment by the Wolfsons. He agreed to Hunt's proposal. "From that point on," Hunt remembered, "I was trying to recruit people. I went to Denver and Minneapolis. Nobody turned us down, so now we had four cities. The original thought was to field a six-team league and include New York and Los Angeles." Hunt then sent an emissary to Bert Bell, "to inform him there was going to be a new league and that we wanted him to be the commissioner of both. I told myself I didn't want to go into this if it meant some kind of battle. Of course," Hunt admitted, "this was one of the more naive thoughts in the history of sports." Bell refused. He thought the new league would fail but wished them luck.

In July 1959, Hunt received an unexpected phone call from Bell. As part of his continuing effort to secure NFL exemption from the Sherman Act, the commissioner was due to testify in front of Congress. According to Hunt, Bell "wanted permission to mention our league. I'm sure he felt it would be helpful to him if he could. I agreed, but asked that he not mention any names or cities." Hunt sat unrecognized in the back of the hearing room when Bell testified. Prior to that hearing, the public knew nothing of Hunt's new league. Bell changed all that. "I want to tell you about this new league," he volunteered to the congressmen. "I can't tell you any of the details, but there are going to be eight or nine cities." Bell promised the NFL would "foster and nourish" its new competition. "The news created an incredible stir," Hunt remembered. "No one had put up a penny and I had no commitments from anybody in New York or Los Angeles, but Bert Bell, the NFL commissioner, had announced it, had said we were in business."

Less than a week later, Lamar Hunt and Bud Adams made Bell's announcement official at a press conference in Adams's oil-company office in Houston. Adams's office was "the biggest in a business known for offices the size of football fields" and "complete with barbecue pit, lily pond, and a desk as long as a bowling alley." Lamar Hunt's style could not have seemed more different: he was "shy, quiet, and frugal, in appearance almost a ringer for Wally Cox," the star of a 1950s television series called *Mr. Peepers*. The two Texans announced that they were the first of the league's franchise holders and that others would be identified soon.

Over the next few months, Hunt collected six more teams to go along with his Dallas Texans and Adams's Houston Oilers. Bob Howsam took the Denver Broncos and Max Winter the Minnesota Vikings. For the Los Angeles Chargers, Hunt found hotel heir Barron Hilton, whose chief claim to notoriety was having once had Zsa Zsa Gabor for his stepmother and Elizabeth Taylor as his sister-in-law. The hotel heir "really didn't know a lot about football," according to Hunt, "but he enjoyed himself." The New York Titans franchise was sold to Harry Wismer, "a lovable rogue who spent everything he had to make his team successful, but he finally ran out of money. He ran his team out of his apartment.'' Ralph Wilson wanted a team in Miami, where he kept a winter home. Miami refused and Wilson settled for Buffalo and named his team the Bills. The last addition to the original AFL roster were the Boston Patriots. Hunt offered the opportunity to Billy Sullivan one Sunday if Sullivan could raise $25,000 by the next day. "At that time," Sullivan remembered, "I had eight thousand dollars to my name, not all of it in cash." By Monday, however, he transferred $25,000 to the AFL's account.

The whole group met for the first time in November 1959. For Sullivan, it was the first time he had laid eyes on the league's prodigy founder. "I walked into the meeting," he recalled, "and I sat down next to a mild-looking man who turns out to be Lamar Hunt. He was not at all what I pictured. He has one shoe up on the table and there is a hole in the bottom of it. He couldn't help but notice I was staring at it. He raises his other leg and crosses his ankle and this shoe has a hole in it too. He looks at me and says, 'I do twice as well as Adlai.' . . . I wasn't sure how to take it. Stevenson had lost in a landslide.''

Everyone in the room knew that they were in for a war with the NFL. Bert Bell's promise to "foster and nourish" had not lasted a month and he soon reversed the position he had taken the previous year and announced that the NFL wanted to expand. That "expand" translated as "raiding the AFL" was apparent when Max Winter opened the meeting with the announcement that his Vikings were joining the other league. At that point, Billy Sullivan wondered "if he had spent a lifetime of scrambling and scratching to climb aboard a sinking ship." Hunt, however, didn't panic.

Hunt turned to Oakland's Wayne Valley to fill the hole left by Winter's defection, and bring the infant league's membership back to eight. By then, Pete Rozelle was the new NFL commissioner and announced the NFL was expanding into Dallas to slug it out with Hunt himself. Before doing so, they had offered Lamar the opportunity to defect, leaving the AFL stillborn. Hunt himself was somewhat angered at the offer. The AFL "was darn important to me," he explained. "I had a lot of money in it. Emotionally, I spent a lot of time, effort, and energy on it. I felt an obligation. A guy like Billy Sullivan had everything he had in it. [Taking the offer of an NFL franchise] wouldn't have been the right thing to do." When Hunt refused, the NFL awarded the Dallas Cowboys to Clint Murchison Jr., and the war was on.

The NFL and AFL competed head to head in three cities and

in all three the AFL came out second best. By 1963, Harry
Wismer's New York Titans had been driven bankrupt and had to
be restarted as the Jets by Sonny Werblin. Bud Adams visited
Wismer as his string was running out. "The heat was turned
off," Adams remembered. "It was cold and drafty and the floor
was uncarpeted. I stood there in my overcoat and I reached into
my pocket and handed Harry ten thousand-dollar bills . . . to
use . . . whatever way he needed. Harry could be very dramatic.
He looked at me and said, 'The ship is sinking.' . . . Then he
put his arms around me and started to cry." In order to avoid a
similar fate in Los Angeles, Barron Hilton had already moved
his Chargers south to San Diego. The third head-to-head contest
was in Dallas, where the Texans and Cowboys were fighting
over a town where one pro football business had gone belly-up
all by itself less than a decade before. Their struggle had national
visibility and was billed as the battle of Texas millionaires. In
their first year, Clint Murchison lost $700,000; Lamar Hunt
reportedly lost $1,000,000. Lamar's father reacted that at this
rate, "the boy only has 123 years to go."

After three of those years, Lamar recognized the handwriting
on the wall. Dallas would not support two football franchises.
Hunt decided to move. Renamed the Chiefs, Hunt's AFL franchise left Dallas for Kansas City in May 1963. To induce him
there, Kansas City had offered free use of a stadium for two
years and a guaranteed sale of twenty-five thousand season
tickets. Murchison and Schramm were "elated" to have Hunt in
Missouri rather than Texas, but the AFL's retreat from Dallas
"did not end the problems of uncontrolled competition." The
war would last another three years.

By the time Tex Schramm and Lamar Hunt began talking
peace in 1966, the AFL had come of age. "We had the right
product at the right time," Hunt explained. "We helped make
pro football a national game. . . . The battle caught public imagination." Along the way, the men Lamar had ushered into the
football business formed what NFL Properties' *Pro* magazine
called "a bonding, a fellowship, that may have been unique in
professional sports." Lamar Hunt was at the heart of that bond.
"Lamar was always the guy who kept his temper," Bud Adams
pointed out, "who, when things would get out of hand, would
bring everybody back around to making a decision. He was a
quiet, quiet force, but it was his baby, and he cared deeply about
it."

The merger secured Hunt's stature as the nation's premier

sports entrepreneur. "The AFL was an astonishing success," the *Kansas City Times* pointed out, "becoming the first sports league to reach parity with its more established rival." The success of Hunt's league was also "the forerunner of an explosion in sports teams, leagues, and interest that gripped this country from the late 1960s to the middle 1970s." Had Hunt not been in the forefront of that explosion, it is doubtful Lamar and the commissioner would ever have crossed swords.

24
Hunt and Rozelle—Collision Course

As a rule, Lamar never flaunted his name or his money. While a number of the owners prided themselves on personal jets and slick wardrobes, Hunt, by far the wealthiest, wore old clothes and flew commercial coach. One of his fellow owners described him as "cheap." Though such habits led to jokes when he was out of earshot, the effect of Hunt's style on the other members was by and large positive. "He's almost too good to be true," one owner noted. "He's as regular as an old shoe. He's soft-spoken, sincere. He was looked upon as a leader. Not a forceful, abrasive leader, but leadership by example." Hunt exercised less of that leadership inside the NFL after the merger. Now that his league had been a success and was under Rozelle's stewardship, he was content simply to manage his own franchise and turn the rest of his attention elsewhere.

Among Lamar's new preoccupations was family business. During the sixties, the Hunt family financial picture had doubled in complexity. Lamar's widowed father married Ruth Ray, a woman by whom he had already fathered a son and three daughters. The instant establishment of a second official Hunt family complete with offspring apparently "had a powerful effect on the sons and daughters of the first family," *Texas Monthly* reported, ". . . the first family apparently saw the second replacing them in the hierarchy of their father's affections."

In 1968, that "replacement" had become a financial concern as well. H.L. was now "older and dottier" and rumors began to circulate that two of the old man's most trusted Hunt Oil execu-

tives "were allied with Ruth in advising H.L. to leave the bulk
of his estate to his second family." According to *Texas Monthly*,
when those rumors were followed in early 1969 by evidence that
those same executives had embezzled an estimated $50 million,
Lamar's brothers, Bunker and Herbert, decided to act. They
tapped the suspects' phones and were eventually indicted for
illegal wiretapping. The suspect Hunt Oil executives were indicted for mail fraud and one "acknowledged using his influence
on Mr. Hunt to get H.L. to change his will in favor of the second
family." In 1974, H.L. was eighty-five, still living with Ruth,
and reportedly "fond of munching on nuts spread out on a
newspaper and doing 'creeping' exercises on the floor."

None of those events, however, was sufficient to keep Lamar's energies out of sports. He had been, as he put it, "bitten
by the entertainment business bug." Once his league merged
with the NFL, he immediately began diversifying his sports
entertainment interests. By 1974, only about twenty percent of
Hunt's working time was spent on football. An equal percentage
was now devoted to his other sports businesses. As one friend
put it, "Lamar can take care of things."

In 1966, Lamar bought an 11.25 percent interest in the Chicago Bulls professional basketball team and founded the Dallas
Tornado North American Soccer League franchise. In 1967, he
founded the World Championship Tennis tour. Of the three, the
tennis tour was the most successful. It was actually the beginning
of the pro tennis circuit.

This tennis venture, flying in the teeth of what had been a
monopoly, the International Lawn Tennis Federation, bore the
closest resemblance to his AFL assault on the football market.
Both led immediately to promotion wars and in both, Lamar
Hunt eventually won parity. In tennis, it would take ten years.
By the time of Bal Harbour, Lamar's share of WCT was up to
ninety-five percent.

The least successful of Lamar's sports diversifications was
professional soccer. "It has been a very broadening experience
from the standpoint of business knowledge," he later said of his
North American Soccer League investment. In 1966, soccer
looked like a growth industry. The televised final of international
soccer's World Cup between England and West Germany had
created a sudden surge of American interest in this "foreign"
game and some thought that the 1966 World Cup would surely
prove analogous to the Giants-Bears 1958 NFL Championship
that birthed the televised football juggernaut. Lamar bought in by

patching together commitments from friends and family, with the Hunt family having eighty-three percent control. As Lamar's share grew, professional soccer nosedived. The stampede to get in on the sport's ground floor was so heavy that the soccer market was glutted from birth. Twenty-two teams in two rival leagues emerged for the 1967 season; the two leagues merged into the NASL for the 1968 season. By the time the 1968 season was over, financial losses had reduced professional soccer to five teams.

It was after that disastrous 1968 soccer season that Lamar Hunt made the decision that put him on a collision course with Pete Rozelle. "The losses were considerably higher than some of the partners had expected," Hunt remembered, and "they didn't want to continue. . . . Rather than let the thing fold, I did take over a larger ownership interest. . . . I felt I had a commitment," Lamar explained, "which I had made publicly—to attempt to build and help develop a team in Dallas and I didn't feel that two years was a fair trial. I guess I am a little hardheaded from that standpoint and I don't want to be known as a quitter."

Henceforth, Lamar devoted a great deal of time promoting soccer. He served on the NASL planning committee and, without consulting the NFL, provided soccer with the names of "people who were interested in . . . an NFL team in their cities." Lamar also became a visible spokesman for soccer as "the sport of the future." Lamar and his wife frequently told how even their eight-year-old son was "a total soccer convert." Lamar was fond of repeating the boy's words: "No, Daddy, I am not going to play football. It might ruin me for soccer."

With Lamar Hunt's shoulder to the wheel, the NASL eventually grew as large as twenty-four teams. Along the way, Hunt located investors in whatever way he could. The Philadelphia NASL franchise which so infuriated Leonard Tose was a case in point. Tom McCloskey, the Philadelphia contractor who bought it from Hunt, according to *Sports Illustrated,* was "in Los Angeles for the Super Bowl . . . with eight friends and no tickets. He was standing in a hotel lobby when Lamar Hunt . . . learned of his problem. Lamar pulled nine tickets out of his pocket, fanned himself with them and said, 'How would you like to have a soccer franchise in Philadelphia?' "

Hunt's soccer role generated irritation in the football business even before Leonard Tose blew his top in 1973. Lamar tried to deal with that irritation by participating in the ownership policy debate as little as possible. Edward Bennett Williams later complained, "When I would make statements against the policy, I would have expected Mr. Hunt to support my statements by saying that he disagreed with the policy. He didn't do that. . . . What he did was pass whenever this subject came up and retained a very, very strong silence on the subject. . . ."

Despite his silence, Lamar recognized that the anger coming his way over the issue had "damaged my capacity to work inside the League." In 1972, he agreed to make his "best efforts" to divest all his sports holdings other than football. Hunt claimed to be responding to "pressure from individuals within the League." To the rest of the NFL, however, the "football Hunt" seemed to take that pressure in stride. "Lamar got used to being yelled at," one owner observed. "He didn't really seem to pay much attention to it all."

Hunt was somewhat more attentive in his direct dealings with the commissioner's office and, from 1972 on, Rozelle and Lamar conducted what would become a six-year correspondence on the subject of Lamar's cross-ownerships. Rozelle was annoyed with Hunt's soccer promotion. The 1968 and 1970 increases in Hunt's soccer ownership were the only violations of the League ownership policy between 1967 and 1972. Once the 1972 ownership policy resolution was in effect, Rozelle began their exchange of letters by inquiring about Hunt's basketball holdings. In the recent sale of the National Basketball Association Chicago Bulls, rather than divesting himself of basketball as part of that sale, Hunt had renewed his interest in the new ownership. Rozelle reminded Hunt that "minority ownership in other teams" was included in ownership policy prohibitions. Lamar Hunt had decided to hold on to his basketball interest because he "didn't think that the price was a favorable price." In responding to Rozelle, he acknowledged, "I am aware of the best efforts to divest situation. However, I believe the feeling was that no such sale should be [made] under less than desirable circumstances. I hope I am correct in that interpretation."

The correspondence of the two men then ebbed for a year until Hunt was provoked by a phone call from Lou Spadia, president of the NFL San Francisco 49ers. Hunt had recently met "with a number of prospective people relative to a soccer franchise in the Bay Area" and Spadia was furious. Hunt vented his own frustration in a long letter to the commissioner dated November 12, 1973.

"Dear Pete," Lamar began. "A recent call from a professional football club official prompts me to put some thoughts down concerning the question of my investments in other team sports.'' In defense of himself, Hunt pointed out that he had disposed of his minor league baseball team and had resisted ''several offers and even community pressure to invest'' in the major league baseball franchise recently arrived in Dallas. ''The apparent position of some,'' he complained, ''is that if Hunt has his picture taken with a basketball or if he talks to someone about a promotion of ownership, et cetera, in soccer, he is doing something illegal. . . .''

''Dear Lamar,'' Pete answered. ''The points you make are very valid and I do not feel anyone should expect a rapid sale that would involve a sacrifice.''

Sensing that Rozelle was backing off a bit, Hunt's next letter in 1974 was conciliatory and optimistic. ''Frankly,'' Lamar admitted, ''I think I blew it not selling my interest in the [basketball] Bulls a year or so ago. . . . The soccer interest is tougher [to sell] because there really are essentially no buyers for existing teams. . . . I personally, [however], think I see the light at the end of the tunnel and have some ideas that could conceivably accomplish it at the right time.''

''That was,'' Pete Rozelle would point out when reminded of Hunt's letter six years later, ''a long tunnel.''

25
The NFL's Truckdriver Prince—Leonard Tose

In the struggle over ownership policy, Leonard Tose's posture as Lamar Hunt's loudest critic was a confrontation of opposites. Where Hunt was quiet, shy, and unobtrusive, Tose was loud, profane, and pushy. Hunt, astride one of America's greatest fortunes, was frugal. Tose was profligate to the extreme. ''He thought wealth should always be seen,'' a fellow owner noted about Tose. ''He loved the trappings and was extremely arrogant. He tried to be debonair, like an Italian count, but it didn't quite come off. He was still a Philadelphia truck driver's son.''

When Leonard Tose was born in 1915, his father had recently

purchased his first truck. Thousands more would follow. "My father couldn't read or write," Tose remembered, but before long, Tose Trucking Company was one of the largest common carriers in the midatlantic states. After college, Leonard went to work in the family business, first as a truck driver, then as a salesman of trailer rigs, then as the company's chief labor negotiator.

The Teamsters Union with whom Tose bargained was by no means easy to deal with, and Tose bragged of his "close relationship" with the Teamsters. Some of his favorite stories were about sitting across the table from Jimmy Hoffa. "At the risk of sounding egotistical," Tose pointed out, "I think I am an expert on labor and labor relations and dealing with union contracts."

Leonard Tose's principal reputation as he approached the age of forty was as the Tose family's wild hare. After his first marriage failed, according to *Philadelphia* magazine, "Tose was one of Philadelphia's more playful residents. . . . Handsome, sharply dressed (he favors continental suits, brightly striped shirts, and shoes with brass buckles) . . . he escorted beautiful and famous women. . . . Tose was quite a swinger . . . [then] . . . there was some difficulty between Leonard Tose and his father," and Leonard left the trucking business for a soft-drink packager. He eventually returned to Tose Trucking when his older brother died, and when his father died two years later, Tose Trucking was Leonard's alone. Remarried, Tose now "settled down to a life of hard work."

His career as a Tose Trucking Company chief executive was considerably less than distinguished and the company lost money under his stewardship. He also established a less than favorable reputation; as *Philadelphia* magazine put it, "he seems to have cultivated more than his share of ex-friends." The magazine quoted one ex-friend: "Leonard has an ego problem. If he thought he could get away with it, he'd have a big picture of himself on every one of his trucks. You can never convince me that Leonard Tose has partners. He may have other people's money, but they aren't his partners. . . . He's always telling people that other people love him."

Leonard Tose's reputation was more elevated in Philadelphia's sporting circles where he "always hobnobbed with the famous of sport" and was known as someone "anxious to be associated with a sports franchise." From 1949 to 1963, Tose had owned one percent of the NFL's Philadelphia Eagles in a partnership known as "the 100 brothers." In 1963, they were all bought out

by Chicago construction phenom Jerry Wolman. Leonard Tose's
$3000 1949 investment was by then worth $60,500. Tose wanted
to buy the club himself but his bid fell far short of Wolman's and
he was instead momentarily out of the football business.

Leonard Tose's chance to get back in again in a big way came
when disaster overtook Wolman's construction empire in late
1968 and his holdings ended up in the hands of a federal
bankruptcy judge. Rozelle was shocked when he found out.
Before approving Wolman's ownership, the commissioner's office had spent "more time and money" checking out Jerry
Wolman "than any other prospective owner we've had. . . . We
retained the right through the judge of approving someone that
[sic] would be developed as a potential buyer." Among those
potential buyers were known to be at least four "combines of
millionaires." The two most prominent were headed by Leonard
Tose and Tom McCloskey, the Philadelphia contractor Lamar
Hunt would later induce into the soccer business. Despite his
bankruptcy, Wolman remained the wild card in the situation and
he still had a lot of say in who would buy the team.

Through a mutual friend, Tose arranged to meet with Wolman
at Super Bowl III in January 1969. The two men discussed
possible prices and Wolman's plans. Tose's tone was described
as that of "a generous businessman coming to the aid of a less
fortunate fellow businessman in a time of crisis." Wolman was
"heartbroken to sell the club" and "pursuing every conceivable
avenue to avoid losing the team." At the moment, Wolman told
Tose, he was attempting to float his assets in a new company for
which he intended to sell $36 million in public stock. If he was
successful in doing so, he wanted the right to buy the Eagles
back. Leonard Tose wished Jerry Wolman luck and even offered
to purchase the last million of Wolman's new stock offering
himself. He also said a ninety-day buy-back agreement was
acceptable and could be included in the contract of sale. Because
of that agreement, the bankruptcy judge gave Leonard Tose the
right to top the highest bid. Not surprisingly, his final offer of
$16,055,000 was $5000 more than Tom McCloskey's. The price
was then an NFL record but Tose was eager to spend the money.
"I'm fifty-three," he said. "I don't think there will be another
chance in my lifetime. I know I can afford it. What am I
supposed to do, wait until I'm eighty?"

Despite Tose's assurances that he could "afford it," most of
the $16 million price tag would be paid with other people's
money. Such was his partners' eagerness to join Leonard Tose's

football venture, that the men all put up their money without a formal partnership agreement. The understanding was that Tose "would manage the day to day operations" and that "the role of the backers, other than Tose, would temporarily be kept quiet." That silence, Tose assured them, would be only momentary. "We'll all drive down Broad Street when we win," he pledged, "we'll all get the calls from the fans when we lose. It's your money and you'll have as much say as anybody."

For the first six months of 1969, however, Leonard Tose kept a strict silence about his combine's existence. When he delivered a certified check for $1.5 million to the bankruptcy court to seal the purchase, he made no mention that it had been drawn by John Connelly. He took a similar approach when he went to New York to be interviewed by Rozelle, Art Modell, and the NFL attorneys. Although the League required all of a franchise's ownership interests, both majority and minority, to be formally approved by them, the only name Leonard Tose submitted was his own. Consequently, the only name presented to the NFL as a whole for final approval was, once again, Leonard Tose.

Though Tose was granted NFL membership as a matter of course, some owners were less than enthusiastic about the development. After the vote, Vince Lombardi, then president of the Green Bay Packers, and two other owners were out in the anteroom getting a helping of coffee and doughnuts. Lombardi was obviously bothered and started to talk.

"I'll tell ya," he offered, "this is the last goddamn Jew I'm going to vote for. And only because he's replacing another Jew. You get too many of those sons of bitches and you got a problem."

The other two men, both gentiles, agreed.

Had the rest of the NFL's Jews known that Leonard Tose was the standard by which they were all being judged, they no doubt would have been appalled. "He's a weirdo," one of the Jewish owners later observed. "He's been in money trouble since the day he was born. He's a habitual gambler. He's got a big mouth and no sense at all. On top of that, you can't take his word for a damn thing."

That owner's opinion would eventually be shared by virtually everyone who participated in the purchase that brought Leonard Tose into the football business.

The first to be disillusioned was Jerry Wolman, who had come up with $16 million and wanted his team back. The deadline on his buy-back agreement was August 1, 1969, and in June, little

more than a month after Tose entered the NFL, Wolman notified
the new Eagles owner that he intended to buy him out in two
months, as per the terms of their agreement. Tose refused to sell.
Wolman appealed to the bankruptcy court, but his appeal was
rejected. He then filed two different lawsuits. After losing both
of them, Jerry Wolman faded from the sports pages forever.

Wolman's disgust with Tose was next echoed by the faction of
Eagles investors led by John Connelly. One of them later testified that they had expected "we would all be partners and we
would all share in it. We'd all have fun in it and our friends
would have fun in it." At the time they had bought in, Tose had
told them a written agreement was to follow, confirming their
oral understanding. Instead, "the various agreements given to
them by Tose over the next year were greatly at variance with
that understanding." All of them proposed that Tose would have
"eighty percent of the team and complete authority." Tose also
promised repeatedly to submit their names for approval to the
League but never did so. "Tose changed," a source close to
Connelly told *Philadelphia* magazine. "When you get to own
the Eagles and people recognize you in restaurants, you start
getting the feeling people love you and you stop being the
considerate person you used to be. . . . The publicity went to
Tose's head."

The Connelly faction eventually appealed to the commissioner's office to force the Eagles "owner" to recognize their full
partnership rights. By then, "at least one very prominent football
man had raised hell with [the commissioner] for permitting the
Philadelphia franchise to get out of joint again." Rozelle applied
catch-22 to the situation and ruled the Connelly group was "not
considered partners because this only occurs when they are
formally submitted to the League for approval."

The Connelly group's next step was a lawsuit in the Philadelphia Court of Common Pleas. charging that Tose had "refused
to honor [their] oral agreement," that he "had represented himself as the sole owner of the Philadelphia Eagles," and had
"refused to consult them." Tose defended himself by claiming
the $1.5 million supplied by the three men was simply "a
friendly loan" and pointing out that the partnership agreement
they had refused to sign had been accepted by the rest of the men
involved. Their suit was heard in June 1970. On his way into the
courtroom, Tose pronounced the threat it posed was "no sweat
at all."

Once inside, Leonard Tose was the first witness called by the defense. *Philadelphia* magazine evaluated him as "far and away the worst witness of the case. He came off as either a reckless liar or an incredibly inept businessman. . . . He proclaimed that he, and he alone, ran the Eagles and made the important decisions [then] proceeded to confess ignorance of various basic phases of the Eagles business. . . . He projected arrogance. He attempted sarcasm. Every time [the plaintiffs' attorney] cornered Tose, which he did frequently, Tose either couldn't remember details or claimed the matter had been handled by somebody else. He was, in short, unbelievable."

Despite himself, Tose won the suit. The court did order him, however, to repay the men's "friendly loan" with interest. Tose was more than happy to do so. On receipt of the court's decision, the Eagles owner launched a round of celebration in Philadelphia's night spots. When those closed, he moved on to South Jersey, where he was seen at 5 A.M., reading the court's decision for the fifth time that evening.

"This gives me complete vindication as far as my integrity," he crowed to *The* [Philadelphia] *Bulletin* the next day. "As far as my reputation is concerned, I've always been a man of my word." Short and dressed to the nines, the silver-haired Tose puffed confidently on a cigarette and couldn't stop smiling. When asked if he was going to have any trouble raising the money to pay the Connelly faction off, Leonard Tose dismissed it as an issue. "The bank," he pointed out, "only says good things about us."

The bank in question was First Pennsylvania and, in truth, it already had its collective doubts about Leonard Tose. Even before the trial with Connelly, the bank had demanded he recollateralize his loan. To oblige, Tose pledged part of the Eagles. "We were disturbed by the suit," said one of First Pennsylvania's officers, but their shakiness was mitigated by the Eagles' profitability. The Eagles' revenues "were pouring in so swiftly" that the original $8 million loan had been paid down to $6.5 million and was ahead of schedule. In the end, the bank agreed to enlarge the original loan to $9 million, providing Tose with enough to buy out the three Connelly plaintiffs. After a three-year struggle, Tose now owned a clear majority interest in the NFL franchise he had coveted for most of his adult life. "I've got it," Tose exulted to *The Bulletin*. "I've got it!"

While certainly now the clear owner of record, what Leonard Tose had exactly "got" was extraordinarily compromised by prevailing NFL standards. The terms of the bank loan specified controls on players' salaries, the hiring of coaches, and included a stipulation that Tose could not draw more than $25,000 in salary and $10,000 in expenses. According to Tose's financial adviser, "the loan is designed so that, for all purposes, the bank gets all the money." In the case of the Eagles, in 1972 that amounted to net profits of more than $1 million a year. A copy of Tose's loan was filed with the commissioner's office. When he learned what was in it, Rozelle could not have been pleased. After carefully working the "Philadelphia situation" through the bankruptcy court so that the NFL didn't lose control over its membership process, he was now stuck with an arrangement in which First Pennsylvania Bank, a corporation and nonmember, had "the final word in running the Eagles' business office."

Leonard Tose, on the other hand, at last both "vindicated" and refinanced, couldn't have been more pleased. "Now," he announced, "all my problems are solved."

26
Leonard Lives It Up

Refinanced or not, Leonard Tose still remained a risky investment. The problem, from a banker's point of view, was his life-style, which only seemed to be escalating. "My rule," Tose explained, "is if you can't go first class, stay home." It was the kind of rule that gave bankers nightmares. Tose never considered changing. "The jackals have been at my heels all my life," he shrugged. "They will be until the day I die. They're jealous. Big fucking deal."

He and his second wife lived in a mansion, complete with cook, houseman, and driver for their Cadillac, Lincoln, and Mercedes-Benz. He often chartered planes at $1000 an hour. Tose bought his suits twenty at a time and, insistent that his wife never wear the same dress twice, sent her up to New York on weekly shopping trips. On cold days, Andrea wore sable. "My husband always had to have the finest, the biggest, the best, and the most of everything," Andrea Tose noted. "Len's philosophy in life is that nothing is to be banked. Money is to be spent."

In Philadelphia, Tose enjoyed casting himself as a philanthro-

pist as well as sportsman, giving to his alma mater, to his synagogue, and to the United Jewish Appeal. The Toses journeyed to
Miami four times a year, to Acapulco regularly, to Europe at
least once a year, and to the Caribbean when it struck their
fancy. At the airport, they were met by two limousines, one for
them and the other for their luggage. At their hotel, the Toses
took the penthouse suite. In order to have transportation immediately available, Tose sometimes put the chauffeur in a suite as
well. When on the town, he handed one-hundred-dollar bills to
bartenders and piano players.

Leonard Tose was a man of numerous indulgences, but perhaps his greatest was gambling. It was not uncommon for him to
bet $10,000 on a gin game or a round of golf. At the racetrack,
the Eagles owner was known to lose money hand over fist, often
wagering as much as $5000 on a single race. "He bets five
horses at a time," his wife explained, "[so] even when he wins,
he loses. . . , Leonard doesn't know what a two-dollar window
is. . . . Leonard was an inveterate gambler who never won."
Tose's time at the track decreased greatly when he took over the
Eagles. "He got bored with it," Andrea remembered. He also
stopped betting on NFL games, thereby saving himself "between
$200,000 and $300,000 a year." The rest of the gambling
continued apace.

Tose's life-style stopped being private in spring 1971, when
Andrea started proceedings for divorce. She charged her husband
with "having committed adultery repeatedly and continuously."
The "other woman" was identified as one Betsy Rubin, a
former Miss U.S.A. contestant and wife of Philadelphia "furniture and carpeting tycoon" Mickey Rubin. According to the
Philadelphia Daily News, "Betsy's big attraction to Len—who
is almost thirty years her senior—is the Eagles franchise." One
of her friends pointed out, "Betsy likes to sit in the main box.
That's the kind of life that impressed her. Football games,
yachts, trips to Europe. I think Mickey lost Betsy by spending
too much time at the stores." Betsy and Tose became "inseparable." When the NFL held its 1971 annual meeting in Palm
Beach, Tose took Betsy along, renting not only a hotel suite, but
also a yacht. In May 1971, two months after that meeting, it
seemed that Leonard Tose had settled with Andrea amicably.
Her lawyers agreed to settle for $1.8 million paid out in annual
installments of $100,000. Had Tose then signed the papers her
lawyers drew up, it is likely the details of his life-style would

have stayed private. Instead, he refused and offered a substitute arrangement for far less money. Andrea struck back quickly.

In June, the still Mrs. Leonard Tose asked the Philadelphia Court of Common Pleas to take the extraordinary step of declaring her husband "incompetent" to handle his own affairs and appointing a receivership to handle his estate. Andrea claimed any settlement she might eventually receive was in danger of being "dissipated" because "he habitually and compulsively engages in illegal and incompetent gambling, incurring losses of very large sums of money, and makes reckless, ostentatious, and lavish expenditures far beyond his means, without any consideration for the proper payment therefor." In addition to his First Pennsylvania debt, she pointed out, he was also floating $6 million in short term notes, most from friends and payable on demand. He was, she claimed, "liable . . . to become insolvent or bankrupt unless a receiver is appointed." Andrea's action set the stage for what was to be a rancorous divorce trial. Ultimately, the scandalous divorce trial was suspended and a settlement announced. "Len Tose Pays Off Wife with 400 G's" the *Philadelphia Daily News* headlined its sports page. Outside the courtroom, the former couple were now all smiles. "See you in Acapulco," Andrea told Leonard as she left. "It's been such an ordeal for the Toses," the *Daily News* explained, "that both are going to Acapulco to rest at separate hotels."

Leonard Tose ran his football team as an adjunct of his now highly public life-style and had little inclination to change, whatever he had promised the bank. To celebrate his new loan following the Connelly suit, Tose bought a $150,000 helicopter in which to commute to the Eagles' suburban training facility. The aircraft was painted in the Eagles' colors and had a team emblem painted on the side. The first day he owned it, an Eagles practice session was halted while the boss landed in a rush of wind on the twenty-yard line. When he went to leave after the practice was over, the helicopter developed engine trouble and another had to be dispatched to ferry him home. Tose had established a definite reputation among the League's football playing employees. "I'll never complain again," one New York Giants player told the *Philadelphia Daily News*. "Those poor Eagles really know what it's like to work for a slapped ass."

During the first five years of Tose's stewardship, his Eagles won 20 games, lost 45, and tied 5. At one low point, Tose stormed into the team's locker room and berated them personally. Despite Tose's lavish buffets with free drinks on game days, the Philadelphia press corps tended to locate the Eagles' problems in the franchise's front office. "Is Tose Hurting Eagles?" *The* [Philadelphia] *Bulletin* asked. Yes, the *Daily News* answered. "Leonard Tose bought a sagging franchise to finance his own ego trips. He deserves what he's getting. . . . Pete Rozelle . . . must have some kind of secret grudge against Philadelphia. . . . A man like Leonard Tose does not belong in the National Football League."

Belong or not, Leonard Tose was in the NFL and intended to stay there a long time. Until he attacked Lamar Hunt in 1973, Tose was most conspicuous inside the League for his flair for spending money. "He's the kind of guy," one owner noted, "who, if we're having an all-day meeting at the League offices, will hire a limo to take him the four blocks from his hotel. Then, instead of having it come back, he has it wait at the curb all day."

Tose considered the years before 1973 to have been a kind of apprenticeship in League politics. "When you come into this League," Tose pointed out, "you come in as a rookie and you don't say a hell of a lot . . . the first couple years until you get to think you know what you are saying." Once he broke that silence, however, Leonard Tose made a definite impression. "He doesn't pull any punches," one NFL executive noted. "When Leonard came in, there was no longer any reverence. He was very outspoken and would get aggravated. We heard more four-letter words at his first meeting than in the whole previous ten years. I always liked him. He spiced up our meetings."

27
By the Skin of His Teeth—Billy Sullivan Comes to Football

Though Billy Sullivan of the New England Patriots was, in his own way, as significant a violator of Rozelle's ownership policy as Lamar Hunt, nonetheless, Sullivan took little personal abuse for the violations. Leonard Tose, uncompromisingly shrill on the subject, was fond of Billy Sullivan and considered him one of his favorite owners. Tose was by no means alone. With the exception of Al Davis, just about everyone in the NFL liked "Old Billy." Sullivan was the prototype Irish hale-fellow-well-met: short, white-haired, and quick with a funny story or a slap on the back. "He's not smart," one owner noted, "but he is positively the most verbose man you'll ever meet. You ask him for the time and he'll tell you how to make a watch."

Despite that tendency to run at the mouth, Sullivan was a man of no small influence inside the League, a stature first confirmed by his crucial role in the agreement to merge. Sullivan's affability helped make the AFL acceptable to its rivals and put the NFL at ease. Throughout that process, the president of the Patriots had been an outspoken backer of Rozelle's ownership policy, despite the fact that his franchise lacked both a fifty-one percent owner and traded its stock publicly. Sullivan consistently pledged to bring the Patriots franchise in line with policy and asked only that he be given time to do so. One result of Sullivan's plea was the specific grandfathering of the Patriots' violations as part of the final merger agreement exempting the franchise from forced compliance. Another was the development of a close relationship between Billy and Pete Rozelle. "Never was I refused when I went to Pete," Sullivan remembered. "There were times when I felt he couldn't go on with me any longer, but each time he listened, offered any advice he might have, and, in the end, told me to solve my problems, that he'd go along with me as long as possible."

Despite widely divergent styles, Billy Sullivan and Pete Rozelle shared a background that gave them a natural affinity for each other. Like the commissioner, the president of the New England Patriots had made his way up in life through public relations. Born in 1915 and one of five children, "Old Billy" grew up in a part of Lowell "where, as the Irish would say, you were rich if you had fruit on the table when nobody was sick." Sullivan enrolled in Boston College with the aid of a scholarship and a part-time job, and made a point of praying in the chapel every morning. "Frankly," he later explained, "I wasn't one of the great scholars of history. I figured I needed Divine help." When he graduated, Billy was selected to deliver the Class Day address. The speech took him six weeks to write. It was a verse epic that included the names of all 284 graduates, which he memorized and delivered without referring to notes.

In 1938, Boston College hired him to be their first public relations director. The job was Billy's idea. He pointed out to the dean at B.C. that Harvard had a whole department to project the university's image. It was Billy's luck that Frank Leahy, future legendary football coach and athletic director, arrived at B.C. shortly thereafter. Leahy transformed the school into a collegiate football power, and one of Sullivan's chief responsibilities was flacking that team. Leahy took Sullivan along to Notre Dame as special assistant to the director of athletics in 1940.

Billy Sullivan moved into professional sports in 1945, when the Boston Braves made him the first full-time publicity director in professional baseball. Sullivan eventually left baseball to join his old mentor, Frank Leahy, in a venture called All-Star Sports, Inc., which eventually folded. He went to work for Boston's Metropolitan Oil Company in 1955, and by 1958 had been named the firm's president. By then, Billy Sullivan's eyes had already turned to professional football. His first step was to approach the NFL's commissioner, Bert Bell.

"I spoke to Bell about getting a team into Boston," Sullivan recalled, "and he told me to come back when I had a serious plan. So I had an architect draw up plans for a stadium. It was the first stadium with a roof and those executive boxes. . . . We got an option on some land in Norwood and the [baseball] Red Sox agreed to share the stadium with us. But they said they didn't want any of this to get out until the details were finalized. They didn't want to upset the community. Now a lot of money for this was coming from some beer people in western Massachusetts. One of the fellows was Bissell from Hampton Brewing . . . and he wanted to take the architect's model of the stadium home to show some friends. Well, he paid for it, so we couldn't say no, but we asked him to be very careful about the press and publicity. Then came April 1, 1958. I remember the date because that's the date I became president of Metropolitan. It's also the day I was driving to work and on the radio I heard a report about our stadium and plans. . . . Well, the Red Sox were annoyed and walked away from the plan and soon after, Bell died. So I decided to make a try for an AFL team."

On Sunday, November 19, 1959, Billy Sullivan got his first phone call from Lamar Hunt. A week later, he was at his first AFL meeting. "Men like Hunt, son of a millionaire and a millionaire in his own right, and Barron Hilton, whose father started the Hilton hotels," Sullivan marveled. "I wondered what I was doing there."

The Patriots were football's weak financial sister from day one. To help pay for the effort, Sullivan brought in what became a group of nine other investors. Billy would become their president. The franchise started life with no home field and played its first "home" game in Birmingham, Alabama. It lost money steadily. Jumping from stadium to stadium around Boston with year-to-year leases, the Patriots were rumored to be considering a move on a number of occasions prior to the merger. Sullivan twice led unsuccessful drives among the voting shareholders to stem the tide of red ink by selling a majority interest in the club to out-of-state buyers. Sullivan's interest in selling evaporated when the AFL-NFL merger "made the Patriots financially viable."

It did not, however, insure they would stay in Boston. Despite the exemption Sullivan had garnered for his team's "ownership situation," he could not escape the requirement that all teams in the League have a home field with a minimum seating capacity of fifty-five thousand. The Patriots were given until the end of the merger's four-year transition period to bring themselves into compliance.

By 1969, Billy had exhausted Boston's supply of ready-made stadiums. They'd tried Boston University Field, Fenway Park, and Sullivan's alma mater, B.C. Harvard Stadium, their last stop, required they put down a new playing surface but would only allow them to use one locker room. That was given to the visiting team; the Patriots themselves dressed for games in a nearby Ramada Inn and met under the stands at halftime.

The city was unwilling to construct a new stadium, and things looked grim for football in Boston. The 1970 NFL annual meeting was scheduled for March and, by then, Sullivan pointed out, Boston had to produce or else. There were relocation offers from Tampa, Memphis, Birmingham, Seattle, Toronto, and Montreal. "We don't want to leave," Sullivan told *The Boston Globe*, "but we have to come up with an answer by the time of our next League meeting." And Billy had run out of ideas.

Over the next month, a plan to combine the resources of the city and the state for a new stadium surfaced but, despite being pushed by Massachusetts Governor Francis Sargent, whose brother owned a large chunk of Patriot voting stock, the attempt came up empty. Rozelle "said he was very pleased by the governor's response," Sullivan remembered, "but would be more pleased if the stadium had been voted into law. I asked the commissioner about the possibility of getting an extension, but I couldn't get an answer one way or another. He just told me that the owners from the other teams in pro football will have to make that judgment. If we get to the owners' meeting in Hawaii without an answer, all I can do is fight for more time. I'll just have to sit down, individually, with every owner and see if they can give us a break.''

When the 1970 annual meeting convened, Sullivan had to spend all his considerable energies fending off ''the necessity of a decision on the location of the franchise.'' He had two things going for him in that attempt. The first was the emergence of yet another stadium possibility in the days just before the meeting convened. The village of Foxboro, about halfway between Boston and Providence, Rhode Island, had come up with a proposal. E. M. Loew, owner of the racetrack, was prepared to donate land for a site if someone else came up with the money to build. Just where that money would come from was not at all clear, but it was a possibility and Billy Sullivan made sure everybody knew about it.

Billy Sullivan's second advantage was the continued tolerance of Pete Rozelle. At Billy's request, the commissioner appointed a committee to study the Patriots' plight. The three men recommended that ''the Patriots continue to explore every possible method of keeping the franchise in Boston or at least the New England area.'' While saying a solution must be ''prompt,'' the report set no specific deadline. Billy Sullivan emerged from the NFL's final session, the *Globe* noted, ''wearing his first smile in days.''

While Sullivan was in Hawaii, the Patriots had already begun to explore the possibilities in Foxboro. The pivotal role in that process was played by stock-owner Dan Marr. The critical question was how cheaply a stadium could be constructed. The Marr family business was erecting structural steel, and Dan had an idea. By sinking two-thirds of the structure in the earth, enormous savings could be reaped. Marr hired consulting engineers, put together a rough set of specifications, and solicited informal bids. The result, he informed Sullivan, was a stadium that could be built for $6 million—relative chickenfeed in the stadium business.

On April 5, 1970, Billy Sullivan called a press conference and announced that the Patriots were moving to Foxboro. Later, they would change their name from ''Boston'' to ''New England.'' To finance their new home, an independent real estate investment trust (REIT) was being formed for public subscription. On September 18, Sullivan announced the stadium would be built. ''The eleven-year struggle of the Patriots to find a home,'' *The Boston Globe* noted, had ''come to a happy ending.'' When

"Old Billy" officially announced as much to the next meeting of the NFL, the owners stood and cheered.

The groundbreaking for Foxboro's Schaeffer Stadium was held on September 23, 1970. The Foxboro High School Band played "Let the Sun Shine In." Commissioner Pete Rozelle, "tanned and lean and smooth as maple sugar," was visibly relieved. The credit, he said, belonged to Billy Sullivan. "Billy isn't a millionaire sportsman like some of our owners," Rozelle elaborated, "but nobody in the NFL has devoted as much time, effort, and money to his ball club as Billy and his family . . . yet he's one of the few people who always thinks of the League first, who pays more than lip service to the good of the game. The New England fans are very, very fortunate to have an owner who cares so much."

28
Saving Football for New England—and Fighting for Your Life

Around Boston, Schaeffer Stadium was considered something of a miracle and Billy Sullivan was the miracle maker. That reputation only grew when construction was completed on time and under budget. Billy Sullivan, now "the man who saved football for New England," cut a considerable civic figure. Still president of Metropolitan as well as president of the Patriots, he and his wife, Mary, had had six children, a house in Wellesley and a summer place in Cotuit. Sullivan attended Mass every morning and his biggest passion in life was letter-writing. He often wrote more than eighty before leaving for work each day and was renowned for spending more on his personal postage than anyone in Boston except Cardinal Cushing.

In the iconography of the NFL, Billy Sullivan embodied the "rewards of persistence." Schaeffer Stadium was a monument to Old Billy's now legendary doggedness. That persistence was, in turn, one of the primary reasons his fellow owners believed him when he promised to comply with ownership policy if given enough time. Having watched Old Billy finally bag a stadium after eleven years, his NFL friends were prepared to believe he was up to keeping any promise he might make. "I've watched this man butting his head against a wall, trying to make things go on a shoestring budget," Lamar Hunt pointed out. "I admire him so much for his stick-to-itiveness and the way he's fought, scrapped, and clawed. . . . Personally I find it very heartwarming to see the success he's having. . . . I think he's done a wonderful job."

Inside the Patriot franchise itself, however, opinions of their President were decidedly more mixed. From 1966 to 1972, the team had won only 27 games while losing 54 and tying 3. Among Sullivan's partners, there was now a growing feeling that the franchise needed a new approach. They were "up to here" with his endless speeches about someday making the Super Bowl. Despite his status as a local legend, Sullivan was vulnerable in his own backyard and that vulnerability was a function of precisely the ownership policy violations he had been promising since 1967 to correct. As the *Boston Herald* put it, the Patriots' ownership was "split more ways than a $3 pizza."

Billy Sullivan would later call taking partners into the Patriots "a mistake" and claim that he could have borrowed enough money to make a go of the Patriots single-handedly. Nonetheless, to do so would have meant risking everything he owned and "risk" was probably an understatement. The AFL in 1959 was a shaky investment all over the map, but nowhere more so than Boston. In their first season, the Patriots sold five thousand season tickets, eighteen hundred of them to Billy Sullivan. The franchise lost $1 million during its first four years in business.

In those days, having partners was very useful, though Billy claimed to have approached them all not as investors, but as "friends who had helped me during my life." One hundred thousand voting shares in Patriots, Inc., were issued and, as Billy Sullivan remembered it, he "very foolishly" let all his friends have the same piece of the action as himself.

Sullivan's next group of partners entered the franchise en masse a few months after the first nine, when the franchise sold 120,000 nonvoting shares to their football watching public at five dollars a share.

By 1973, the board of directors made up of Patriots, Inc.'s, voting shareholders was an entirely different arrangement from the group of "friends" envisioned by Sullivan in 1960. Billy himself personally owned 23.7 percent and controlled the votes of the additional 12.5 percent owned by Billy's cousin. The remainder of the voting stock broke down into three significant blocks. The largest, thirty-four percent, was owned by two New York investors, David McConnell and Robert Wetenhall. Billy would later describe their relationship as "unfriendly, at best." The second block of voting stock outside Sullivan's control was the fourteen percent belonging to Bob Marr and Dan Marr Jr. Bob, the younger of the two, was the verbal point man. While not particularly close to McConnell and Wetenhall, the Marrs shared the New Yorkers' opposition to Billy. Voting together, the two factions were usually joined by two other minor interests for a total of forty-nine percent. "What you have to remember," Bob Marr pointed out, is that the Patriots' franchise, despite being identified in the public mind with Billy alone, "always has been a coalition" and "Billy has never been a unanimous choice for the job."

The swing vote that had kept Sullivan in the Patriots' presidency was a fourteen percent block of Patriots stock owned by George Sargent's widow, Hessie. Like her late husband, she was an old friend of Billy's and his wife, Mary. While habitually loyal to Billy, she was under increasing pressure to switch sides, primarily from her son, Lee. In the early days, Lee had been the Patriots' ball boy and by the time Schaeffer Stadium opened, was "more involved" in the Patriots' workings than his mother was. He did not share her attachment to Sullivan's presidency. "Bill had it for a long time," Lee pointed out. "Now maybe it's time for someone else's chance."

By the time the board of directors of Patriots, Inc., met in January 1973, shareholder support for New England's "man who saved football" was, as *The Boston Globe* put it, "shakier than a bathtub of Jell-O." Once the discussion started, it was apparent that Billy Sullivan's days were numbered.

"The whole franchise was adrift," Bob Marr explained. "The team was not doing well. Boston was down on the team and the sale of season tickets was down. We had to have some changes made." Though Marr's opinion wasn't new, Hessie Sargent was now prepared to go along with it.

Her old friend Billy Sullivan, however, was not about to leave without a fight. When informed he was going to be replaced, Marr remembered, Sullivan "came all apart." Sullivan pleaded to the board. If they would vote him just one more year as president, he promised that he would resign his position when it was done. Billy's emotional plea was aimed at Hessie Sargent in particular and landed on fertile ground. The two had been good friends for too long for her to do less than accede. The board made Sullivan's reelection unanimous on the condition he resign in January 1974.

The board's decision was "secret" but word of Old Billy's downfall soon reached Greater Boston as a rumor and then as an outright announcement by Sullivan himself. "Disenchanted seems like the proper word," he offered in description of his feelings. "I expect to remain with the club in some capacity. I'll just be shedding a lot of responsibilities."

This was not, however, a promise Billy Sullivan meant to keep, and the closer his scheduled resignation got, the more obvious that became. Despite his initial stoicism, Sullivan spent a good part of his last year on the job trying to buy control of the franchise so he wouldn't have to leave. His cousin agreed to sell her 12.5 percent. Then Billy turned to Hessie Sargent again. If she would sell him her fourteen percent, his problems would be solved. Hessie said she would talk it over with her son, Lee, and when McConnell and Wetenhall learned of Sullivan's move, they cried foul. The New Yorkers claimed that Old Billy had promised them first refusal anytime the Sullivan family bought or sold any Patriots' stock. The issue was referred to Pete Rozelle for resolution.

In the meantime, the Patriots' board meeting scheduled for January 1974 was postponed and Billy Sullivan was instead observed at Super Bowl VIII "bubbling over with enthusiasm and confidence . . . not acting like a man about to step down from anything." Shortly thereafter, Rozelle ruled that McConnell and Wetenhall had no right of first refusal but that Sullivan was obliged to offer them the same price he offered Hessie. It was a hollow victory for Sullivan. In fact, whatever Rozelle might rule, there was no one who was willing to sell. Lee Sargent was adamantly opposed and his mother agreed with him. "My mother and I have been kind of dependent on each other," Lee explained. "We worked together and we've been quite sure of our position for a year now." The meeting at which that position would be exercised was now scheduled for March 21.

On February 24, Billy Sullivan arrived in Bal Harbour. He represented his by now frantic buy-out strategy to his fellow members as an attempt to bring the Patriots into compliance with the fifty-one percent provision in the commissioner's ownership policy, but admitted he was "backed up against my own goal line." They wished him the best, but most figured this was Old Billy's last appearance in the National Football League.

29

Joe Robbie—How to Start With No Money and Lots of Partners and End Up With Lots of Money and No Partners

No one in the NFL would miss Billy Sullivan more than Joe Robbie, owner of the Miami Dolphins. Robbie and Sullivan had been close friends since Miami entered the AFL. At the time, Robbie had replaced Sullivan on the bottom rung of the League's financial ladder. The two were something of an odd couple. The Lebanese Robbie, characterized by *Sports Illustrated* as "tough as a wharf rat and charming as a rent collector," had none of Old Billy's Irish lovableness. He was, with the exception of Sullivan, something of a loner and not terribly popular. "If someone killed Joe Robbie," one NFL executive observed, "the list of suspects would be the Miami phone book."

One of the few things Billy Sullivan and Joe Robbie had in common was finances. *Sports Illustrated* described Robbie as "the poorest man to obtain a sports franchise in the last twenty years." He was also, by reputation, the cheapest. An attorney with eleven children, he had never made more than $27,000 in a single year before joining the AFL in 1965. "He runs a $2 million business like a fruitstand," one owner observed. His employees described him as someone who counted paper clips and "hardly ever signs checks promptly, if at all." Hook-nosed and squat, with thick-framed glasses, Robbie had none of the glamour usually associated with the NFL, nor any of the flash traditionally associated with Miami. "He looks like a business agent for a labor union," one sportswriter observed, "wears electric-green anklets, and his grip on a cocktail glass is that of a longshoreman holding a schooner of beer." Joe Robbie was quick to point out that he didn't get into the football business to be liked.

"Once," Joe Robbie offered, "people sympathized with the guy who could climb up the ladder, the Horatio Alger thing, you know. But I think in this affluent society, where lots of people have lots of money, they resent a working stiff making it . . . particularly in the glamorous area of professional sports. . . . I know how to fight. I come from a town called Hard Times."

More precisely, he came from Sisseton, South Dakota, where his father had emigrated from Lebanon in 1900. By age fourteen, Joe was working part-time as the sports editor of the *Sisseton Journal Press*. He then worked his way through college and finished with a law degree. While in college, he was student body president, and at law school, a debate champion. "I loved to talk," he remembered. "I learned that it could be a weapon too."

During the War, Robbie served in the navy and returned home with a bronze star. During the next six years, he practiced law, was elected to the legislature, served as state Democratic party chairman, and ran unsuccessfully for governor.

Robbie had significant political connections. He was a close friend of Hubert Humphrey and he served as campaign manager in the then senator's failed 1960 presidential campaign. He kept a photo of himself and John Kennedy on his office wall and never missed a Democratic National Convention. Joe Robbie's political connections had a lot to do with his joining the NFL.

The particular connection that proved invaluable was his friendship with Joe Foss, AFL commissioner. Foss was a much decorated World War II aerial ace who had come home and made a career in South Dakota politics. There he crossed paths with Robbie, another young veteran doing the same thing. In 1965, Robbie was hired by a client to approach his friend Commissioner Foss about an AFL expansion franchise in Philadelphia. Foss informed Robbie that the AFL was indeed going to add a franchise, but not in Philadelphia. The league wanted no more intra-city combat with the NFL. "If you want a franchise," Foss advised, "make it Miami." Robbie's client wanted nothing to do with Miami, but Robbie, uninhibited by his $27,000-a-year income, decided to pursue the franchise himself.

Despite Foss's advice and backing, Miami was by no means the favorite location for expansion among AFL members. It was a hard town in which to sell a ticket and Robbie, residing two thousand miles away, would have an additional outsider's disadvantage. Lamar Hunt thought that a resort area would have little civic enthusiasm for a football franchise to tap. Robbie pointed out that professional football exhibition games there had drawn well and that Miami's attitude about a professional football franchise had changed. In fact, the deal Robbie eventually cut with Miami would long be considered the best lease in the league.

In 1965, however, Miami was running a poor third in the AFL's expansion discussions. The first choice was Atlanta, but suddenly, the NFL put a franchise there, effectively closing the market. The next choice was New Orleans, but during the AFL 1965 All-Star game several black players had been subjected to racial harassment, and New Orleans became a potential public relations nightmare. In August 1965, Miami was voted in as the upstart league's first and only expansion franchise, which was awarded to Joe Robbie, a total unknown to both Miami and the world of sports. The price tag was $7.5 million.

If convincing the AFL to risk a team in a city heretofore considered a football graveyard was a significant accomplishment, Joe Robbie's gifts became truly obvious as he went about solving the problem of buying the franchise without any money of his own. Robbie found the answer in the form of a limited partnership.

The limited partnership is, in effect, a two-story legal structure. On the first floor are the general partner or partners, who are personally liable for the partnership's debts and have exclusive decision-making power. The second floor is occupied by the limited partners, who own a piece of the venture but are simply investors with no personal liability. The form allowed huge depreciation benefits while sheltering significant amounts of income. Limited partnership status also insulated the investor from anything more than paper losses. "I am where I am now," Robbie would later say, "for one reason. That's because nobody wants to put their own money up. They want something for nothing. . . . That's why I have the club. I took the risk." His twenty-year contract as managing general partner allowed Joe Robbie to run the team as his own. His personal investment was $100,000.

In the first of three Dolphin partnerships Joe Robbie would form, he was the only individual general partner. The other general partner was a corporate entity headed by Danny Thomas, himself a fellow Lebanese and a very visible and wealthy figure. He proved instrumental in soothing any worries about Robbie's threadbare finances and in attracting limited partners.

The franchise spent as little money as possible. Despite living in Minneapolis, Robbie signed every check the Miami team wrote. "We never had any money," the business manager remembered. "I couldn't even write a check for a pencil sharpener. . . . I was in charge of business operations but there was no money to run the business." Six months after Robbie joined the league, Al Davis became commissioner, and confirmed the franchise's shaky finances. "Danny Thomas was supposed to be the money man. . . .[but] we found out [Danny Thomas Sports, Ltd.] was a shell corporation with $25,000 [in the bank]. I was greatly concerned with who was going to end up paying. . . . We had a big problem with Miami."

That "problem" eased somewhat when Danny Thomas was bought out by Robbie and Willard Keland, a wealthy Wisconsin developer. The price was not a matter of public record but, judging from Thomas's public response, it was attractive. "Did I lose money?" he chuckled. "You got to be kidding. Did you ever hear of a Lebanese losing money? I don't lose money. I only make money." Thomas told the press, "Robbie is a great guy in my book, rough and tough. Joe put the club together. I trust Robbie implicitly."

Joe Robbie's new general partner, Willard Keland, came to a strikingly different conclusion a year later. "When we bought out Thomas," Keland claimed, "Joe didn't come up with the money to buy his half, so I figured I was in control. But it didn't work out that way." Keland learned as much when he attempted to fire Robbie. Their dispute soon ended up in Pete Rozelle's lap. When Rozelle upheld Robbie's contract, Keland sold out. "I bear Joe no ill will," Keland said afterward. "I learned a lesson from him. If you're going to run with sharp operators, you've got to be smart. He came up with a group from Miami to buy me out, and I guess he's got them doing the same thing for him, supplying the money so he can run the club."

By 1968, Robbie had moved his wife and children to Miami. South Florida, he pointed out, was now his home. All the new partners were Miami residents. "This is what I've wanted for four years," Robbie proclaimed. It also marked the point at which Robbie finally gained what *The Miami Herald* called "undisputed operational control of the Dolphins."

Like Leonard Tose, Joe Robbie left a lot of ex-friends in his wake. By 1970, he had already fired four business managers and a number of secretaries. "Nobody thinks much of him," one of his ex-employees told *Sports Illustrated*. "For a big man he's very small." But by 1974, his franchise was worth more than twice what it had originally cost. Robbie himself was a recognizable figure along the Orange Bowl sidelines, as *Sports Illustrated* described him, "[sprinting] up and down the yard stripes, pounding players on the back, yelling as if he were in the charge at Manassas and banishing people from the area who have suddenly incurred his disfavor." He had also won himself something of a reputation inside the NFL. When asked about the move he was then making on Wayne Valley inside the Raider franchise, Al Davis explained that he was taking the "Joe Robbie approach."

At Bal Harbour in 1974, Robbie's circumstances stood in stark contrast to those of his friend Billy Sullivan. While old Billy was perceived as a defeated man, Joe Robbie arrived in triumph. Despite all the jokes about his Arab-trader approach, the team he started from scratch and built using willpower in place of cash had just won two consecutive Super Bowls. It was also the first and only team ever to go the length of a season undefeated.

Yet, among his fellow owners, Joe Robbie's achievement only transformed what had been contempt into a more respectful resentment. "Robbie's a hard guy to like," one of them explained. "You've got to pretend you're talking to someone else."

30
Robbie—Fighting Rosenbloom *and* Rozelle

No one in the NFL disliked Joe Robbie more than Carroll Rosenbloom. Their relationship had been perpetually off since 1970, when Robbie had made the uncharacteristic decision to spend some money—at C.R.'s expense.

While Joe Robbie may have been cheap, he was a shrewd businessman and understood that you had to spend money to make it. Robbie was prepared to spend borrowed money because the Dolphins had won only three games the previous season, attendance was still spotty, and it was obvious that only winning teams would generate the gate he felt he needed. In the spring of 1970, Joe Robbie made his move. What Robbie "bought" was head coach Don Shula.

In 1969, Shula had three years left on a contract with Carroll

Rosenbloom's Baltimore Colts. He had coached the first NFL team to lose a Super Bowl, and when the Colts had followed that with an 8-5-1 season, his relationship with C.R. had soured. Rosenbloom took steps to reduce the coach's authority inside the Colts and made little secret of the fact he blamed Shula for the franchise's lack of ultimate victory. Even from as far away as Miami, Shula looked ripe for a change of job.

NFL rules forbade "tampering" with anyone else's coach without first getting his employer's permission, and no one had yet talked to Rosenbloom. A *Miami Herald* sportswriter called to see if Shula would be interested "in coming down to Miami as the head coach and also becoming involved in ownership." Shula called Robbie about it to see whether he was serious about ownership. Joe Robbie said he was. Shula then said he would inform the Colts.

At the time, Carroll Rosenbloom was vacationing in Bangkok and his son Steve was minding the business. Steve gave Shula official permission to talk to Robbie. By the time Shula and C.R. finally talked, Shula had decided Robbie's offer was too good to refuse. "In the beginning," according to Shula, Rosenbloom "was very kind and understanding." Then, "he turned very curt and very businesslike and said he wanted to call the commissioner," which he did only after Robbie had announced Shula's signing. By then the Baltimore press had jumped all over Carroll for letting Shula get away and he responded by denouncing Robbie to the commissioner and the public at large for "tampering."

While Rozelle found it "hard to believe" that Steve Rosenbloom hadn't secured his father's permission before letting Shula proceed, "the rule said you had to talk to the operating owner," so he awarded the Dolphins' first choice in the next player draft to the Colts. Joe Robbie thought it was too much. Carroll Rosenbloom thought it was too little and made what Rozelle called "a lot of public noise about it." Joe Robbie attempted to make peace and placed a call to C.R.

"Carroll?" Robbie began, "this is Joe Robbie."

"I don't want to talk to you about anything," Rosenbloom snapped, then hung up. Later he publicly announced he would never talk to Robbie or Shula again.

It is doubtful Joe Robbie lost much sleep over C.R.'s attitude. After three years of Shula, the Dolphins were selling out the Orange Bowl and well on their way to making Joe Robbie rich. He was also used to having people mad at him, whatever their reasons. "Joe Robbie is an enigmatic man," *Sports Illustrated* pointed out, "a case study of the type of guy who would pick a fight with Bo Derek on their wedding night." Even Don Shula was not immune.

At the Dolphins' 1974 team banquet celebrating their second straight Super Bowl, Shula was late and Robbie found his coach outside the banquet hall, waiting for his wife. Robbie was furious. "It was very evident," Shula told *Sports Illustrated,* "that he had been drinking." The apparently well-lubricated Robbie opened up by yelling at Shula to get the hell into the room. Shula responded in kind. "Yell at me again," he told Robbie, "and I'll knock you on your ass."

Though Shula continued to work for Robbie, he reportedly referred to his boss in private as "that asshole." It was a description of Joe Robbie already in wide circulation around the League. Asshole or not, Robbie was a devoted family man in all his endeavors, including football.

From the beginning, Robbie's Dolphins were a family affair. Robbie invested his wife's life savings when he entered the football business and "she participated in virtually every aspect of the Miami Dolphins. . . . She is in on all the debts. . . . It's all our family money. It isn't mine and it isn't hers. It's ours." That "ours" included eleven younger Robbies.

The Robbies were by reputation a close family, but not without their tragedies. His daughter Kathleen, a student at the University of Mexico in Mexico City, drowned in the ocean off Acapulco in 1971. His oldest son, David, a graduate of Notre Dame and the University of California School of Medicine, jumped to his death off the Golden Gate Bridge in 1975. By the early 1970s, his next oldest son, Mike, was working as director of ticket sales and his other four sons, Robbie was proud to point out, "have the same kind of interest in sports."

Robbie's collision course with Pete Rozelle's ownership policy was set in 1972, shortly after that policy was first formalized. At the time, Miami had a North American Soccer League franchise called the Gatos, whose ownership recently had gone bust. Harper Sibley, one of Robbie's new limited partners, was hosting a party to try to collect a group of people to buy in and save soccer for Miami. As Joe remembered it, the Robbies got involved when "Harper Sibley, toward the end of the meeting, pointed to Elizabeth and said, 'We ought to have a woman in this. How about you, Elizabeth?' " Elizabeth said yes and subscribed for a limited partner's "rooting interest." Joe Robbie joked he was "happy Elizabeth is in soccer," because now she could "quit running the football team." Thus the NASL franchise was rescued. Renamed the Miami Toros, it would lose some $900,000 over the next three years.

In 1973, Elizabeth dramatically increased her liability for those losses when she agreed to replace one of the general partners who was dropping out. When Rozelle learned of Mrs. Robbie's increased NASL role, he agreed that it was at least technically outside the purview of the League's ownership policy resolution. But he also targeted the arrangement as a potential "conflict of interest" that ought to be formally prohibited whenever the subject again heated up. For his part, Robbie found Rozelle's ownership policy arguments specious. Among other things, attorney Joe Robbie noted, the constitutional amendment Pete Rozelle wanted was an open invitation for a lawsuit under the Sherman Act.

31
The Battle to Control the Redskins— Edward Bennett Williams

The only other attorney on the NFL's membership rolls, Edward Bennett Williams of the Washington Redskins, shared Robbie's assessment. Coming from Williams, however, the opinion carried infinitely more weight.

Edward Bennett Williams was already renowned as perhaps the premier courtroom performer in the nation. Among his more famous and notorious clients were Teamsters President Jimmy Hoffa, Congressman Adam Clayton Powell, *The Washington Post,* the Democratic party, Senator Joseph McCarthy, bookmaker Frank Costello, and CIA Director Richard Helms. By 1974, Williams's law practice yielded him some $1 million a year. A conservative Catholic Democrat, his name was often raised in connection with cabinet level posts but none of the offers was good enough to lure him out of private practice. An invitation to Williams's box at R.F.K. Stadium "was among the most sought after badges of prestige in Washington" and his guests included "a procession of senators, cabinet members, and even a President of the United States."

Williams did little of the day-to-day running of Washington's NFL franchise. "I delegated that," he explained. "My whole philosophy in running the company was to get the very best people that I could, turn the operation . . . over to them, and do nothing to interfere . . . except to look at the end results and make a judgment at the end of the year." His fellow football owners loved to listen to Williams talk, although, as Lamar Hunt noted, "Mr. Williams has a way of expressing himself where I'm not sure whether you know what you hear after you've heard it."

Williams was perhaps the only owner for whom the NFL's power and celebrity were actually less than those afforded in the rest of his life. He was there because he liked to win and made a point of seeking out opportunities to do so. "There are three occupations that involve what I call 'contest living,' " he explained, "sports, courtroom law, and politics." Williams was involved in all three and "in each one you may be absolutely brilliant on a given day, but you still may lose. It's the most agonizing way to live, but it's also the most exhilarating." It was the kind of life Ed Williams had always wanted, and getting what he wanted was a Williams trademark.

Born in 1920 in Hartford, Connecticut, Edward Bennett Williams anticipated big things for himself from the beginning. His father never made much money but was considered a brilliant man who had high expectations for his only child. As a teenager, Williams already wanted to be a lawyer and used to mount a chair and imitate Franklin Roosevelt. Williams went on to a full scholarship at Holy Cross and graduated first in his class and summa cum laude. Next came Georgetown Law School in Washington, D.C. His stint at Georgetown was quickly interrupted by World War II and an enlistment in the Army Air Corps. A year later, the plane he was flying crashed and Lieutenant Williams suffered a severe concussion and a back injury that would plague him all his life. Discharged for medical reasons, Williams returned to Georgetown where one of his professors described him as "the brightest student he had ever encountered."

Hogan and Hartson, one of Washington's most prestigious law firms, interviewed Williams shortly before his graduation from Georgetown in 1944. "I chatted with Ed," the head of the firm's trial department recalled, "and I was so impressed . . . that even though he had a couple of weeks yet left to finish in his school and had not yet taken the bar . . . I made the determination that I wasn't going to let the guy get out of the building except that I had a commitment from him." After two years at Hogan and Hartson, Williams married Dorothy Guider, granddaughter of one of the firm's senior partners, and decided to get out of the law firm.

On his own, Williams had become a visible legal figure by the early 1950s, when he shepherded clients in front of the House UnAmerican Activities Committee. That began three decades of assisting a long list of highly visible and generally controversial clients. Along the way, Edward Bennett Williams attracted a certain controversy himself. At issue was his willingness to say whatever might bolster his client's case. "There was something upsetting about the performance of this lawyer who stands near the top of his profession and commands such respect," a *Chicago Tribune* editorial complained.

However controversial, Williams's legal and oratorical mastery earned him a handsome living. By 1982, the attorney's net worth was reported to be "at least $50 million." Included in that were several office buildings in downtown Washington, a hotel, an estate, a summer home in Martha's Vineyard, a commanding interest in the law firm of Williams and Connelly, and 14.3 percent of the Washington Redskins' holding company, Pro Football, Inc.

Williams's investment in Pro Football, Inc., had begun as a five percent interest, in 1962. Williams described the purchase as "the most highly speculative investment you could possibly make." At the time, the Redskins' principal shareholder was still George Preston Marshall, who owned fifty-two percent. Twenty-five percent was owned by Canadian millionaire Jack Kent Cooke. The remaining eighteen percent was owned by two Washington attorneys. George Preston Marshall was, as the *Washington Monthly* described him, "an erratic and unpredictable man . . . who had practically disowned his two children when his wife divorced him years before," but he had "a soft spot in his heart for Williams. Williams was like the perfect son to Marshall, the type of son he had always wanted." By December 1963, Marshall was suffering from cerebral arteriosclerosis, emphysema, and heart trouble. In 1965, Williams assumed the franchise's presidency. That summer, Williams, described by his biographer as a "frustrated jock," showed up at the Redskins' training camp, "wearing shorts, a Redskin T-shirt, and athletic shoes. He proceeded to go through a workout with his players, running laps, doing calisthenics, and impressing squad members by demonstrating that at forty-five he could catch long passes and withstand the rigors of an entire workout." When his team opened the season by losing five straight games, Williams blistered the players with a two-hour speech behind closed locker room doors and they promptly won three in a row.

By then, Edward Bennett Williams's role in the estate of the now incompetent George Marshall had already become the subject of what would be described by *Washington Monthly* as one of Washington's "ugliest" running courtroom battles. The challenge came from Marshall's two children who, under the terms of the will of the senile majority owner of the Redskins, were to be left no more than ten thousand dollars a year apiece. Marshall himself was now completely incapacitated, without the ability to speak or even to gesture in a meaningful way. When Williams had been Redskin president for little more than a year, Marshall's children escalated their objections. They had learned their father's will left the bulk of his estate, including his controlling interest in the Redskins, to a foundation for underprivileged children and, in 1966, set about trying to get him to sign a new will. At one point, Marshall's son went so far as to break into his father's home late at night in order to discuss the subject. Williams was furious and went to court and enjoined the children from "interfering with their father's estate . . . especially . . . from attempting to have him execute legal documents," but the Marshall children and their attorneys showed up at their father's house on July 2, 1966, with a new will for him to sign, that included an express direction that the will be signed by someone else on his behalf. His son and two of the attorneys did so. The new will bequeathed everything to the children.

Williams demanded the children be cited for contempt of court and ordered to surrender this new document immediately. Marshall's son refused and charged, "[Williams is] stealing a football team for himself." After five weeks in prison, Marshall Jr. finally agreed to give up the will. The terms of George Preston Marshall's two wills became items of active legal dispute in 1969, when the founder of the Redskins died. After further public name-calling, the case was eventually settled in January 1972. Each of Marshall's children was awarded $750,000 plus $10,000 a year and, in return, the 1966 document was declared invalid. Of the outstanding shares Edward Bennett Williams emerged from it all, still Redskins president. He managed to increase his share to over fourteen percent without spending any of his own money. By conservative estimate, this "highly speculative" 1962 investment of $75,000 was now worth $2.4 million.

When Edward Bennett Williams reported on the status of the Redskin ownership at Bal Harbour, however, the last 260 share buyout resulting from Marshall's death had yet to be finalized. Since it would, in effect, create a new majority owner of the franchise, Rozelle had ruled that it required a formal endorsement, even though no new parties were entering the League. That endorsement, in turn, was subject to the conditions of the 1972 ownership policy resolution.

As a result, Edward Bennett Williams's Pro Football, Inc., would eventually become the first and only NFL ownership to comply with the policy of which Williams himself was the most vocal opponent.

32
Cooke in the Backseat

At issue specifically were the holdings of Jack Kent Cooke, Pro Football, Inc.'s prospective majority owner. Cooke's interests in professional basketball and hockey were clear transgressions of the commissioner's post-1972 cross-ownership prohibition and as far as Rozelle was concerned, to let Cooke move into a controlling ownership position without accounting for that violation was out of the question. Cooke left direct dealings with the League to his partner, Edward Bennett Williams.

Williams disputed the need for a vote at all. He remembered. "I didn't think this kind of transfer had to be approved because it was an intramural transfer. My understanding of the purpose of transfers of ownership being approved [by the rest of the League] was to keep undesirable persons out of the game." Williams went along with the rule nonetheless. "We did it," Williams explained, "just so there wouldn't be any dispute. . . . We weren't looking for a quarrel with the commissioner's office." Over a barrel, the nation's foremost trial lawyer recognized the situation would have to be finessed.

Apart from his cross-ownership violations, Jack Kent Cooke, then sixty-two, was an ideal candidate for an NFL franchise. Not surprisingly, Jack Kent Cooke's favorite books featured Horatio Alger. Born in 1912 in Hamilton, Ontario, to which his father had emigrated from Australia, Cooke's family were "awfully well-to-do" throughout his childhood. The Cookes' wealth evaporated in the opening rounds of the Great Depression. Jack Kent immediately dropped out of high school and began earning a living as leader of a band called Oley Cooke and his Orchestra. He also worked as a runner on the Toronto stock exchange and sold encyclopedias door to door. Next he went to work for Colgate-Palmolive and "sold more soap than anyone in the history of the company."

What Jack Kent Cooke later called "the great break of my life" came when he was hired to manage radio station CJCS in Stratford, Ontario, for $25 a week in 1937. Within two years he had become partner and within four more years, a millionaire, owning radio stations and magazines. Cooke soon added more companies, including Canada's largest manufacturer of plastics. He purchased his first sports franchise in 1951, taking over Toronto's struggling minor league baseball team. By 1952, he had made it a success. Cooke was also a championship yachtsman, a voracious reader, and the composer of more than a hundred copyrighted songs.

In 1960, Jack Kent Cooke moved to California, eventually settling in Bel-Air, next to Beverly Hills. His neighbors there included Tony Curtis, Jerry Lewis, and Greer Garson. "A hearty laugh takes the edge off his pomposity," the *San Francisco Chronicle* observed, "and he is frequently interesting if you don't mind all the quotes from Shakespeare and Bismarck. He delights in correcting other people's grammar. . . . His sentences more often than not demand exclamation points." Cooke became an American citizen almost immediately upon emigrating by virtue of special legislation that was shepherded through Congress by a friendly representative from Pennsylvania who cited Cooke's "fervent pro-Americanism" as reason enough. Cooke's first new enterprises as an American citizen were an investment firm and a cable television company.

In 1961, Jack Kent Cooke bought into the football business. He purchased 250 shares in Pro Football, Inc., from broadcaster Harry Wismer, who had become one of the eight founding owners of the AFL and needed cash. Wismer was also tired of fighting with George Preston Marshall. According to *The Washingtonian* magazine, Wismer's problems with Marshall had begun when he "discovered that instead of paying profits to shareholders, Marshall was spending the team's earnings on himself. Some of the money went to maintain a stable of women in other cities so that when the Redskins played a road game, Marshall could count on finding a friendly face. Marshall also sold his home in Georgetown to the Redskins, but he continued to live in it, paying nominal 'rent,' well below the market rate. . . . He [also] used Redskin employees as his personal servants.'' Wismer sued unsuccessfully for a greater share of the profits and then decided to get out.

Ironically, the first prospective purchaser for Wismer's shares was Edward Bennett Williams. In February 1961, the attorney and Wismer had agreed on a sale price of $250,000, but Williams needed Marshall's approval to consummate the purchase. In 1961, Marshall was the only owner in football who refused to hire black players, and Williams had ''strong moral and practical'' objections. Williams told Marshall he would not ''come into the company if he did not break the racial barrier, because I thought it was an absolutely disastrous policy.'' Marshall was furious. According to Williams, he ''. . . told me that under no circumstances would he change and I was not welcome in the ball club.'' A year later, Marshall would hire his first black and sell Williams his initial five percent, but at the time, Williams's deal with Wismer had already collapsed.

Jack Kent Cooke learned about the availability of Wismer's stock by accident, during a trip to New York City, when he shared a cab with a friend who knew of the collapse of Williams's deal. That evening, Cooke and another friend had dinner at Manhattan's ''21'' Club and the friend mentioned he had once worked for Marshall. Before the meal was finished, the friend had called Marshall from their table and secured Marshall's permission for Cooke to buy in. Wismer then agreed to sell for $350,000 and Jack Kent Cooke had his original twenty-five percent. By the time Pro Football, Inc., had arranged the final buyout of the dead Marshall's shares at the franchise's expense, Cooke's investment comprised more than seventy percent of the outstanding stock and was worth at least $12 million.

Cooke's basketball and hockey holdings dated from 1965, four years after his entry into football. First, he bought the National Basketball Association Los Angeles Lakers. A year later, he'd bought a National Hockey League expansion franchise and named it the Kings. Cooke spent $16 million building his own arena, in which the teams could play, The Fabulous Forum, in Inglewood. Dismissed as ''Cooke's folly'' when first announced, the Forum made money from the day it opened and eventually drove the rival L.A. Sports Arena to the edge of bankruptcy.

A key influence on the strategy Edward Bennett Williams chose in order to secure NFL approval of Cooke's Redskins buyout was Cooke himself, who was battling a string of other difficulties and didn't have the time to bash about with Pete Rozelle. Cooke's run of bad luck had begun in 1973, when he suffered a heart attack. To recover, he retired to his ranch in the Sierra Nevada mountains to write songs, only to have that retirement end when his cable television business collapsed.

Cooke owned sixteen percent nonmanaging interest in Tele-PrompTer, Inc., the nation's largest cable television firm. The summer of 1973 ended with news that the Securities and Exchange Commission had suspended trading in the company's stock, and by November 1973, Cooke had moved in to take personal control of the company and try to salvage his investment. When Pete Rozelle demanded a League vote on the final buyout of Marshall's Redskin shares three months later, Jack Kent Cooke was up to his ears in trimming dead wood out of TelePrompTer Corp., and asked Williams to settle it all however he could.

Edward Bennett Williams's plan was strategic retreat. While he agreed with Joe Robbie that the commissioner's ownership policy was an invitation to a lawsuit, Williams did not intend to file it himself. He wanted a compromise and took the best terms he could get. Williams's compromise entailed two concessions. The first was the establishment by Cooke of a "voting trust" whereby the operational power of his Redskin shares was vested in Williams, his trustee. The second concession amounted to the firmest and most definite promise to divest yet offered by any opponent of the commissioner's cross-ownership prohibition. "Mr. Cooke authorized me to say that he would divest his conflicting interests," Williams remembered, "by the time of the next [annual] meeting." According to Rozelle, "on the basis of Mr. Williams's commitment, there was little or no discussion and the member clubs voted approval of this transaction."

Though it amounted to Williams eating a little crow and was accounted a Rozelle victory, the compromise was not necessarily a defeat for Edward Bennett Williams. The last Marshall buyout had been confirmed and his control over the franchise was secure. Whatever ground he'd given up on the issue of ownership policy would be regained in spades the next time the issue heated up.

33

Threatening the Empire—The World Football League Surfaces

In 1974 the NFL still presented a single face to the world and that face, of course, was Pete Rozelle's. League Think was in its ascendancy and the clamor for the NFL's product gave the exclusive twenty-six-man club enormous leverage over how America saw itself. However else a city might try to boost itself, the only sure way to get listed in capital letters on the national map was to have a home team in America's Game. Six years of phenomenal growth had passed since the NFL had added a new location and there was now an impatient assortment of cities outside the League hoping to be let in. "Having created an opiate for the people," *Sports Illustrated* noted, the NFL "can no longer deny it to those who can support the habit." That the membership would be enlarged was by now an accepted NFL fact, but where, by whom, and under what terms were all still hot issues.

Like ownership policy, expansion had long been a League issue. To Rozelle, the inclusion of new locations was at the cutting edge of the League's public relations and marketing, both his home turf. It was also the principal currency of the League's political influence, which, under the terms of League Think, was exclusively Rozelle's to spend. The last time he had done so was in the scramble to secure antitrust exemption for the merger with the AFL in 1966. Then, Rozelle had assured Congress that the exemption and the cessation of interleague warfare, would "guarantee" that football would spread. To prove his point, he promised two new franchises by 1968: The New Orleans Saints and the Cincinnati Bengals. Rozelle had also promised to "study the possibility" of even more expansion after that. By late 1972, however, no such study had been done, and when pressured for a comment on the possibility, he said only, "I believe there will be expansion in this decade." The comment did little to assuage the anxiety of the impatient cities, in which Pete Rozelle was fast acquiring a reputation for arrogance.

In 1972, citizen groups from Memphis, Phoenix, Seattle, and Tampa met with him about redeeming his promises of future growth. They were all at the commissioner's office at the appointed time; the commissioner, however, was not. They were greeted by one of Rozelle's assistants, who informed them, "The commissioner is out of the office today." The assistant listened to the group's presentations, then responded by admonishing them for having released news of its meeting to the press.

The pressure soon became both more official and more effective. As Rozelle remembered it, "Congressmen and senators began hearing from affluent people in their city or state and then the NFL got pressure from politicians for the first time." The commissioner learned about the virtues of Memphis as an NFL site from Senator Baker of Tennessee. At another meeting, Senator Scoop Jackson of Washington gave the commissioner an earful about Seattle. Both no doubt reminded Pete Rozelle that Congress expected his earlier promises to be kept. Rozelle in turn reminded them it was the owners' decision, and added that some of them would be a hard sell. The conversations nonetheless had a visible effect.

When the League met in 1973, Rozelle was convinced that the time had come to expand. He simply announced that football could now accommodate two more locations and "it was time to investigate expansion." As the discussion went around the room, there was both "strong, strong interest" and "some resistance." The resistance centered on the fact that admitting new members took money out of the current members' pockets. Though any new ownership would have to purchase its franchise from the League, the League would have to split its television revenues more ways. The prospect caused several owners to hesitate. Rozelle "had to sell them on the concept this would benefit the whole League, that we would become stronger as a whole." Congress, he noted, was applying pressure and at the moment was considering some forty-four different pieces of legislation that affected the football business in one way or another. Before adjournment, the "member clubs" had instructed the commissioner to appoint an expansion committee.

The committee Rozelle appointed was not a group likely to throw any surprises the commissioner's way. Dan Rooney was named chairman. "I wanted people on the committee who could make good business judgments," Rozelle explained, "but could also evaluate the various connotations." Dan Rooney was also, like Tex Schramm, another committee member, one of the commissioner's close personal friends. The procedure worked out by Rozelle and the committee was two-tiered: first, select a city and set a price; then choose specific individuals to whom to sell the new franchises. In all, some twenty-five cities expressed an interest, and Rooney's committee investigated each. By the Bal Harbour meeting, the time had come to narrow the list and start talking about price.

Enlarging a monopoly was a process fraught with potential dilemmas. While expansion might mean risking overexposure, unsatisfied demand created a vacuum, insuring instability in the market and risking external competition. When Rooney's group started work, the threat of new competition had already added pressure to the issue and served to push the expansion committee ahead with all due speed. The new factor was the World Football League, started in October 1973. It was the first challenge to the NFL's monopoly since the merger. "The NFL has grown arrogant and complacent," Gary Davidson, the new league's founder, charged. "The doors are open to a rival. The war is on."

Pete Rozelle would later describe the WFL as a minimal factor in the NFL's decision to expand, and expressed great skepticism about the new league's capacity even to wage war, much less win it. Davidson, however, came on strong. "We are far better off than the AFL was when it was founded," he claimed. The WFL would play its first season in fall 1974 with twelve teams, including franchises in Anaheim, Jacksonville, Portland, Honolulu, Birmingham, Memphis, Charlotte, Detroit, and Philadelphia. According to the WFL master plan, the initial twelve would form the league's American Division. Within five years, a second division would be added in Tokyo, Madrid, London, Munich, Paris, Dusseldorf, Rome, Mexico City, and Stockholm. Initially all games would be scheduled on Wednesdays, ceding the weekend to the NFL, and played using a football with phosphorescent stripes.

Pete Rozelle's skepticism about the World Football League reflected his own sense that while football appeared to be a simple business, it was not nearly as simple as it seemed. It also reflected his sense that Davidson was in it for a quick profit and didn't have the resources to pull it off.

By 1974, Gary Davidson was a familiar face in the sports business. He had already started two new leagues, the American Basketball and World Hockey Associations. In each, he had subscribed all the new franchises, saving one for himself, and established the league with a public relations coup, usually a raid on the existing league for celebrated players. Then Davidson sold his own franchise on the inflated bull market and headed for his next venture.

Of greatest longterm significance to League Think was the signal the mere existence of the WFL sent in the NFL's direction. Professional football franchises were a commodity for which there was far more demand than supply and the wider the differential became, the more that demand would generate forces at variance with the interests and structure of the NFL's monopoly. More than a few cities were already desperate for a place in America's Game, prepared to do whatever it took to secure a franchise, with or without the League's blessing. Put to the uses of Carroll Rosenbloom, Al Davis, and the players of the Superstadium Game, that runaway seller's market would eventually propel the NFL into what Pete Rozelle called "anarchy" and make his worst nightmares come true.

34
Lining Up to Get Into the NFL

The demographic minefield that would eventually blow the ground out from under League Think was discussed in a December 1973 report, *Socioeconomic Information on Candidate Areas for NFL Franchises*. The document, prepared by the Stanford Research Institute, amounted to a detailed map of the football market *outside* the NFL's 1973 boundaries. In retrospect, it would read like a guidebook to coming battle zones.

At NFL direction, SRI made a preliminary investigation of twenty-four possible locations and then went into fourteen of those in detail. Of the cities investigated, ten seemed promising. The two weakest candidates for expansion were Honolulu, Hawaii, and Birmingham, Alabama. Each of the remaining locations had a relatively strong case for membership.

Seattle, Washington, was the capital of the American northwest, one thousand miles from the closest franchise, and encompassed a metropolitan population of almost two million, who already supported professional basketball and hockey franchises. Indianapolis, Indiana, encompassed 1.2 million people but another 2.7 million were within a one-hundred-mile drive and more interstate highways converged in Indianapolis than in any other section of the United States. Phoenix, with a population of 1.1 million in 1973, was growing fast. It's National Basketball Association franchise ranked fifth in the league's attendance, and the local college football team filled its stadium every Saturday.

Tampa's population was roughly equal to that of Phoenix and Tampa had supported "the largest number of [NFL] preseason games played at any neutral site during the last six years." Attendance at those averaged almost forty thousand. Memphis, Tennessee, was rated higher than only Birmingham and Honolulu among the final ten.

The remaining three municipal regions on SRI's top ten were of a somewhat different species than the other seven. While all three represented untapped potential markets, all were within a seventy-five-mile radius of an existing franchise. Yet, their demographics were the most compelling of all:

Nassau and Suffolk Counties on Long Island were already part of a Greater New York market that included more than eleven million residents, currently serviced by the Giants and the Jets. Considered apart from nearby Brooklyn and Queens, Nassau and Suffolk Counties were by themselves the ninth largest metropolitan area in the United States, with a population of 2.5 million. The area ranked first in per capita spendable income. Greater Chicago was a metropolitan area of more than seven million, serviced by one franchise, the Bears. The untapped potential market there was enormous. The area was the nation's largest producer of capital goods, and in the last ten years its "disposable household income after taxes" had increased "more than any other major area of the United States." The Anaheim metropolitan area in Orange County was the eighteenth largest in the country with a population of more than 1.5 million. As a county, it ranked seventh in the nation in retail sales and twelfth in the number of households earning twenty-five thousand dollars or more. The only local supply of professional sports was the California Angels professional baseball team based in Anaheim. To consume football, Anaheim had to drive into West L.A. and watch the Rams.

Stanford Research Institute's conclusions were simple. "According to all the economic and demographic criteria studied, the New York [Nassau and Suffolk], Chicago, and Los Angeles [Anaheim] areas rank substantially above all the candidate areas, even when data are divided by two or three to account for a shared market."

The demographics detailed by SRI presented the football monopoly with two fundamental dilemmas, both of enormous longterm consequence. The first was implicit in the size of the market SRI located. Even after adding two more franchises, some twenty-two percent of the NFL's potentially profitable franchise outlets would remain fallow and the NFL would continue to be significantly smaller than its market. On the plus side, that available reserve of locations created a strong upward pressure on the value of existing franchises and gave NFL members enormous leverage in the Superstadium Game. The negatives were that the pressure that had driven the NFL finally to expand by two in 1974 would remain largely unsatisfied. The potential consequences of that frustrated demand were not, however, a subject on which the expansion committee spent much time. Both Rozelle and Rooney considered expansion a "case by case" situation and made no attempt in 1974 to devise a long-range plan. The principal question as they saw it was to choose from among the current options in a way that "strengthened the League and made it more truly national."

The second of the NFL's dilemmas was crystallized in SRI's somewhat unexpected conclusion that the NFL's best option was to put more franchises into its current three largest markets. But despite their independent size, Nassau, Greater Chicago, and Anaheim were all still "suburbs" according to the terms of the NFL's monopoly, and hence not significant enough for membership. In the long run, this stance would insure that the largest untapped markets for live football were not only frustrated at lack of inclusion in the NFL but even further frustrated by the lack of consideration at all. Within four years, that frustration would set off a chain of events that eventually ended with the crushing defeat of League Think at the hands of Al Davis.

There were two reasons for Rozelle's 1974 attitude. The first was television. In the question of "suburbs," the League's broadcast and live gate markets were somewhat at odds. To protect the live gate, the League had always put restrictions on televising games within a seventy-five-mile radius of a franchise's home game. If the home team didn't sell all its live tickets, its game could not be televised, nor could any other games be broadcast into its market. If the home team did sell out, its game could be televised and at least one other as well. Since three games were normally televised into the markets without home teams, simply having a franchise in any market reduced its potential. Having two or more teams in the largest markets of all reduced their TV potential even further. Rozelle considered the television reduction already experienced in New York and San Francisco a "problem" and was not about to add more "problems" to it.

The second reason was built into the NFL constitution and made the possibility of expansion into markets already within a franchise's home turf virtually nil. The location of a franchise "within the home territory of any other club shall only be effective if approved by unanimous vote." In 1974, the need to protect each owner's home territory from encroachment was a truism that no one bothered to discuss. Thus, the possibility of more franchises in the New York, Chicago, and Los Angeles video markets was summarily dismissed. The purpose of expansion was to extend the League's monopoly, not reduce it.

"SRI did a good job," Rooney explained, "but they didn't consider all the factors."

35

Charting a Course Through the "Demographic Minefield"— Dan Rooney

Pete Rozelle considered Dan Rooney, president of his father's Pittsburgh Steelers, the "ideal" owner to stage-manage expansion. Young, bright, and articulate, he talked about football ownership as an almost religious obligation. "Our responsibility is the good of the game," Rooney argued. "Owners have to protect the game. We are trustees and, unless we're careful, that trusteeship role may get lost in the name of doing business." Trained as an accountant, Rooney was a devoted backer of League Think. Short and handsome, with dark looks and prematurely graying hair, Rooney was considered level-headed and modest. "In this business," Rozelle noted, "ego can be a narcotic. Dan is a rare exception. You just don't run into very many sports figures who have it under control the way he does." Rooney was also the leading spokesman for the Old Guard, the bedrock upon which League Think and the Rozelle era had been built. The faction's boundaries included almost all the ownerships whose presence in the League predated Rozelle, a block of some six votes in 1974. It was a powerful faction not just for its numbers, but for its influence as the keeper of the League's fifty-four years of tradition.

The Old Guard's sacred icon was the Green Bay Packers. Green Bay, Wisconsin, joined the infant League in 1921 and chose the name Packers after the original owner's Acme Packing Company. Green Bay's population was approaching 100,000—off the bottom of the chart as far as standard metropolitan statistical areas went. That Green Bay had managed to survive as part of the NFL was a source of great pride to Pete Rozelle. It was also central to the iconography of League Think. Left to Green Bay's native economic base, Rozelle was quick to point out, the Packers would have died in the modern age. The town had no media market to speak of, but thanks to Rozelle's 1961 television-sharing policy, that didn't matter. "Where else could a place like Green Bay play the likes of New York and Los Angeles?" Rozelle asked. "It says a lot for our League that they are still, and will always be part of it."

The Old Guard's two living saints were George Halas of the Chicago Bears and Dan Rooney's father, Art. The reverence now accorded them embodied the League's ritualized yearning for a simpler age. "It doesn't seem too long ago," Art Rooney pointed out, "when we could settle every pro football problem in a quick discussion around a table. The guys who ran the League then were Bert Bell, Tim Mara, George Marshall, George Halas, and myself. We ran it pretty well too. Nowadays, though, the owners don't arrive at a League meeting by themselves as we once did. Each is accompanied by a squad of lawyers, accountants, tax experts, and more advisers than I even can name. When we were struggling to survive, pro football was a fun thing. The bigger we get, the less fun there is in it." Of the Old Guard's living saints, Halas was held in awe, but Rooney, "with his broad Irish face, his frosty white hair, a cigar propped between his lips, and a laugh bubbling up at the least provocation" was, according to Don Kowet's *The Rich Who Own Sports,* "the most beloved figure in all of professional football."

The Rooneys had first come to Pittsburgh from Pennsylvania's rural coal country when Art's father moved there to found Rooney's Saloon, soon the favorite watering hole of the city's Irish sportsmen and politicians. Raised a devout Catholic, young Art was

also one of the city's better amateur baseball players and boxers.
"I could have gone to the 1920 Olympics," Art remembered,
"but I turned pro." Rooney soon retired from the ring and went
into politics. Throughout the 1920s and 1930s, he was the chief
ward heeler for James J. Coyne, Pittsburgh's Republican king-
pin. One of his specialties was raising campaign funds by staging
semi-pro football games. The games were spirited but informal,
with Rooney coaching one or both of the competing teams.

Art Rooney bought into the NFL in 1933. The Pittsburgh
franchise cost him $2500. At first, the team was called the
Pirates and its offices were off the lobby of the Fort Pitt Hotel.
In those days, one historian of the period noted, "political
cronies and gamblers and priests would shuffle in and out, any
hour of the day." The Fort Pitt was, by all accounts, a modest
beginning. "Once upon a time, I suppose, the Fort Pitt had been
a high class hotel," Rooney recounted, "but I can remember
guys rushing in, pulling down their flies, and me having to tell
them that they had come to the wrong place—the men's room
was next door." Art Rooney kept his franchise alive with win-
nings at the track. His most famous exploit was a two-day
stretch, one at the Empire City track and another at Saratoga,
where he turned two twenty-dollar tickets into an eventual $250,000
payout. Since Pittsburgh's NFL franchise lost money for its first
twelve years, Rooney's prowess at the track was essential to its
eventual success.

Art Rooney still remembered the NFL's old days well and
made no bones that they'd often been a mess. "At one time," he
pointed out, "the League had an executive committee of three,
rotated among the owners, to screen proposed legislation before
each League meeting. One year, Charlie Bidwill [of the then
Chicago Cardinals] and George Marshall [of the Redskins] and I
were on the committee, and we met in Chicago, just before the
League meeting. As usual, Marshall had about a hundred proposals to make to the League. Charlie and I agreed with every
one of them and we got finished in less than an hour. Marshall
said it was a great thing that the League finally had a progressive
executive committee. Charlie and I just wanted to get out to the
racetrack. We did, but the next day we met again with Marshall
and just as calmly voted against every one of the things he had
proposed the day before. And that was the end of that executive
committee."

Rooney was an unalloyed booster of Rozelle. "Pete Rozelle has
had more to do with the growth of this League than anyone else.

He was on top of things from the first meeting he ever had. He started well and grew with the job. We were very, very fortunate to have had him. Rozelle made the NFL the strongest of major league sports. He's very honest and very fair. He's been tough when he had to be and compassionate when he had to be. His judgment is just about perfect. I hope Pete stays a long time. It would be very, very difficult to replace him.''

The significance of Rooney's endorsement only grew as Art's sainthood burgeoned. By 1974, when Rooney was seventy-one years old, that status was unquestioned. All of Rooney's wealth was mingled with that of his five sons in a company named Ruyanaidh, a Gaelic word pronounced "Rooney." It was the umbrella for some ten different corporations, most of them sporting enterprises: Penn Racing Association, Green Mountain Park racetrack in Vermont, Liberty Bell track in Philadelphia, Yonkers Raceway in New York and the Palm Beach, Florida, Kennel Club. Art's oldest son, Dan, was, of course, president of the Pittsburgh Steelers.

Dan had been born the same year as the Steelers and was raised in his father's strict Irish Catholicism. Dan was an outstanding athlete himself. As a high school senior, he quarterbacked the football team to the city championships. In 1955, after graduating college with a degree in accounting, he went to work in the family football business. Over the next ten years, Dan worked in every phase of the Steelers' management. "Dan never thought there was any job too menial,'' one of his brothers remembered. "Now, with the possible exception of coaching the team, there's not a single facet of this business he doesn't know inside and out.'' After Dan had been running the team for almost ten years, his father handed over the title of president.

Dan Rooney's approach to football, like the rest of his life, was notoriously clean-cut and straight arrow. One owner referred to him as "Rozelle's head Boy Scout.'' He had married his grade school sweetheart and had nine children. They lived in "a typical Pittsburgh suburb.'' His luxuries were skiing in Colorado and a single engine Beechcraft airplane. His wife Patricia's biggest complaint was that he made himself "so available to the team and the League alike.'' Physically, Dan Rooney still looked "like a fifties college student'' except for the patches of gray growing in at his temples. "This is not a plaything,'' Rooney said of his franchise. "It demands and deserves everything I can give it. It's my sole livelihood. It may not have been run like a business before my time, but it is now.''

While some of the reverence afforded his father overlapped onto Dan, he had also built a significant influence inside the League on his own. When asked to name the League's three best "football men," other owners invariably listed Rooney's name with those of Tex Schramm and Al Davis. A second factor in Rooney's influence was his relationship with Rozelle. Close in age, the two men had become good friends when Rozelle was still general manager of the Rams. Like his father, Dan Rooney was a strong Rozelle supporter. "Pete's integrity and intelligence carry him," Dan observed. "I've seen him under situations where it's very tough and I've seen him have as much integrity as anyone I've ever met."

Dan Rooney's report to the Bal Harbour meeting on behalf of the Expansion Committee marked the beginning of the formal process of expanding the League. As such, it also marked the end of the period in which expansion was defined by Rozelle's informal sense of what was called for, subject only to the approval of Rooney and three others. Now the League as a whole was involved and, soon, formal votes would be taken concerning location and price.

Of the two questions, location proved the least controversial. The Expansion Committee had reduced SRI's top ten to five locations for further study: Seattle, Phoenix, Tampa, Memphis, and Honolulu. Honolulu's inclusion was basically a public relations gesture and not a serious possibility, so the list was in fact reduced to four. The hardest part for Dan Rooney had been dropping Indianapolis. "We had no choice," he observed. Indianapolis had no suitable stadium. Rooney said the committee would be ready to report on the five finalists at a meeting devoted to expansion the following April.

The committee's report ran into a lot more rough air on the question of price. Their recommendation was $12 million in a wide spread of payments at interest below prime. Setting the price that low was a particular concern of Rozelle's. The tricky part of expansion, he argued, was making sure the new franchise took. It was counterproductive to weigh it down with too large a debt before it even began operations. The League, he reminded everyone, had thrived by nurturing its weakest links. Dan Rooney agreed with the commissioner, as did Tex Schramm, and both argued strenuously for the lower price.

Even so, it was soon apparent the argument wasn't going to wash. "Jesus Christ," Leonard Tose sputtered, "I owe more than that to the bank." Others were clearly uncomfortable with the recommendation as well. Football was a business in which each franchise sale redefined the value of all the rest. In this instance, the committee's recommendation meant that the League itself was officially setting a value of $12 million—$4 million less than Tose had paid for the Eagles and $8 million less than the Rams had been valued at in Carroll Rosenbloom's 1972 swap. A number of men in the room had outstanding loans or tax returns that valued their franchises at prices significantly higher than the one at which the commissioner was prepared to sell. Following Rozelle's lead meant costing themselves money.

No vote on the question of price was taken at Bal Harbour. Finally, "the membership voted unanimously to meet in the League office on Tuesday, April 23 . . . for the sole purpose of discussing the many aspects of expansion."

The stage was now completely set for the civil war to come.

36
On Top of the World . . . But Not For Long

On the afternoon of February 27, 1974, the National Football League annual meeting gathered in executive session once more before leaving Bal Harbour. The agenda offered no hint of the fate awaiting League Think. If anything, there was only more seeming proof to the contrary. Two such items stood out.

The first was the report of the NFL's finance committee. The committee had finished negotiations on Commissioner Pete Rozelle's employment contract and recommended it be "amended and extended for ten years from January 1974." The League unanimously confirmed the committee's recommendation. The extension insured at least another decade in the Rozelle era. The amendments set Rozelle's new salary level at or around $500,000 a year and coupled it to a package of retirement benefits Rozelle described as "generous." Also included was the explicit modification of the commissioner's expense account to cover the travel expenses of the new Mrs. Rozelle. To sweeten the package further, the League agreed to provide a separate $300,000 loan at

seven percent interest to help the Rozelles redo their new home
in Westchester.

The second apparent proof of Rozelle's firm grasp on the
NFL's reins was a constitutional amendment that added the
explicit "authority to arbitrate" to the commissioner's existing
powers of "full, complete, and final jurisdiction" over internal
football business disputes. Though the measure was considered a
piece of bureaucratic housekeeping that brought forth no discussion, its passage by rote reflected the extent to which Rozelle's
dominance was assumed in February 1974. No one seemed to
think it could ever be otherwise.

The only hint of the future came up at the commissioner's
final press conference on February 28, when Rozelle had to
reassure the press that Robert Irsay's Colts would not leave
Baltimore, even though it was now obvious that the new stadium
Irsay thought Carroll Rosenbloom had promised was not going to
materialize. "It will be a burden on Mr. Irsay financially,"
Roselle announced to the reporters, "but the team will stay in
Baltimore."

Aside from that, League Think's horizon seemed remarkably
clear. No one recognized any signs that the League everyone
called "Rozelle's" would not remain so in perpetuity. The
"greatest commissioner in football history" left Bal Harbour
tan, in love, and making more money than he had ever made in
his life. To all concerned, he seemed destined to sit comfortably
in the catbird's seat for years to come.

Things would never look quite that good for Pete Rozelle
again.

PART TWO

THE
PLOT
THICKENS

1
Garvey's Game Without Rules

Though internal disorder was the catastrophe lurking in League Think's future, that disorder was still largely concealed by the warfare raging outside the NFL's borders. Two such external threats dominated Pete Rozelle's attention when he returned from Bal Harbour in 1974. The more worrisome of them was the NFL Players Association led by young Ed Garvey.

Sports unions presented one of the oddest relationships in American labor. They were the only unions in the U.S. that did not negotiate members' salaries, which were negotiated by each club and each player or player's agent. The NFLPA restricted its activities largely to retirement benefits, working conditions, and the establishment of standardized pay for exhibition games, a minor part of football economics. The union's 1974 grudge dated from the "failed" negotiations on their last contract in 1970.

Pete Rozelle's posture in 1970 had been to cast himself as arbitrator, the "impartial" representative of the entire game. However, the players refused to accept his mediation through most of the negotiations. At the time, the union was represented by John Mackey, its president, and Alan Miller, then executive director. Ed Garvey entered the picture when it came time to sign the agreement offered by the owners. Mackey sought out Garvey's law firm for a second opinion, Garvey told him to refuse to sign, and was brought onto the team as a consultant.

The union's attitude was typified by an exchange between Carroll Rosenbloom and Mackey, one of C.R.'s employees. As the possibility of a strike during the 1970 preseason loomed, Rosenbloom intervened personally. While vacationing in Florida, C.R. called Mackey to point out a strike was hopeless. "We don't need football," Rosenbloom argued, "but you do."

Mackey responded that the owners needed football in a much worse way than the players did. "If you didn't have tickets to give away," he told his boss, "you wouldn't have any friends."

C.R. hung up.

By August 1970, players went on strike and were boycotting

preseason training camps. Then Pete Rozelle intervened; he locked the two sides in a room together and forced them to find agreement. The meeting lasted twenty-two straight hours. According to Garvey, however, "the story of Rozelle's intervention was bullshit. . . . In order to get the owners to the bargaining table at all, we had to let Rozelle chair the sessions."

The meeting convened on August 2 and the sessions got "grueling" when the air-conditioning broke down, but Rozelle kept his coat and tie on throughout. Whenever the group split into its respective halves, Rozelle left with the management team. "If you're so goddamn neutral," Mackey groused at him, "why do you always leave with them?" The next time a similar occasion arose, Rozelle stayed in the room with the players until Mackey invited him to get out.

"I thought you said you wanted me to stay," the commissioner explained.

When an agreement was finally reached, "There wasn't any winner," Mackey reported. Garvey was succinct. "The owners," he remembered, "gave us nothing."

According to one of the NFL's attorneys, "negotiators of the 1970 agreement shook hands, settled their differences, called off the player strike, and left to the lawyers the task of putting their understandings on paper. Mr. Garvey thereafter spent almost a year raising new issues and reopening old ones before the agreement could finally be executed." By then, of course, Ed Garvey was the NFL Players Association's new executive director.

His predecessor, Alan Miller, was asked to resign in January 1971 "on the grounds that he didn't seem to have the union's cause sufficiently at heart." Miller's exit, according to *Sports Illustrated,* "may have been brought about by a Mata Hari. During summer 1970 Miller had been introduced to an aspiring young actress by someone close to Cowboy owner Clint Murchison. A romance blossomed. Miller, who was divorced, flipped on the girl to the point where he told friends he was contemplating another marriage. But when the negotiations were finally concluded, the girl was suddenly too busy to see him." The suspicions surrounding Miller and his girlfriend were typical of the attitude the 1970 negotiations had nurtured in the union. "In any negotiation people start getting paranoid and suspicious," Garvey pointed out, "but here an atmosphere of distrust had been created to the point that people began to think that their rooms were being bugged and that they were being spied upon."

When news of the union's suspicions became public, Rozelle

was quick to smooth the public waters and deny the stories. Privately, Rozelle called Mackey to complain about the insinuation. "How could you think we tapped your phones?" he asked. Rozelle also reportedly offered to take a lie detector test, which Mackey thought was a good idea. But according to Garvey, nothing more came of the polygraph offer.

As the NFLPA's new executive director, Ed Garvey was characterized by Pete Rozelle as "a prototypical early sixties radical, a militant ideologue who is unable to see any good, any justice, in any action of management. He is unable to see in any shades of gray, no in-betweens. He has no ability to get close to the center of an issue."

Ed Garvey himself could not have cared less what Rozelle thought. He felt the 1970 negotiations had failed for lack of unity and was quite prepared to vilify the owners in order to fill the void. They were, he would later point out, an easy group to make look like bad guys. "The idea of dealing with athletes as equals is obnoxious to them," Garvey pointed out. "These guys are union busters in the classic sense."

Filing *Mackey v. NFL* in 1972 was the first step in Garvey's strategy and its defiant tone helped turn the situation around. For the rest of the energy he hoped to infuse into the union, he relied on his own considerable political skills. A Robert Kennedy Democrat, Garvey had considered running for Congress in Wisconsin before accepting the job at the Minneapolis law firm that led him to the NFLPA. The challenge of the task he set for himself was considerable. The union not only negotiated a unique version of labor contract, it was structurally unique as well. The average career of its members was a little over four and a half years, meaning a twenty-three percent annual turnover in the union's composition. Since contracts were negotiated every four years, only some ten percent had a statistical likelihood of having been around during the previous bargaining sessions. "There's no institutional memory," Garvey pointed out. "You have to reorganize the union every year."

That particular characteristic of the NFLPA allowed Garvey himself to provide the continuity and made stamping his identity on the union a relatively rapid process. Said one player representative on the union's six-man executive committee: "The executive committee was more or less who Garvey wanted. He liked to have guys who [sic] he could mold. Ed was real skillful at controlling meetings." By 1974, Ed Garvey had made himself the single most critical ingredient in the NFL's labor supply.

In preparation for 1974 contract negotiations, Garvey made personal visits to each of the teams, trying to whip up enthusiasm. That process culminated in an NFLPA convention where the words "strike" and "solidarity" seemed to be on everybody's lips. At the union's final plenary session, new president Bill Curry asked the crowd if they were "willing to stay out until Freedom?" All in favor were to stand. Everyone stood and clapped. "We went into negotiations with a great sense of unity," Garvey remembered. "We were confident we could get what we wanted."

The NFL Management Council brought their own grudges to the encounter, the most immediate of which dated from the filing of *Mackey v. NFL*. The second layer of NFL grudges dated from the 1970 negotiations, when the NFLPA had been officially certified as the bargaining agent for football. At the time, the NFL had conceded to this rather than force an election that would have postponed bargaining for months. By 1974, some NFL members wanted to roll that decision back. Owner Joe Robbie was the most vehement proponent of that position: "I felt at the time that the labor laws were never enacted for the purpose of granting independent contractors, called football players, the right to collective bargaining and no less an authority than [AFL-CIO president] George Meany expressed the same opinion." Ed Garvey considered the Miami owner's labor views "neanderthal."

The two conflicting agendas collided when negotiations began in March 1974. Ed Garvey read a two-page prepared statement:

> It has been four years since we looked across the bargaining table at one another. We have not forgotten the way you conducted yourself during the 1970 negotiations. . . . Your attitude for the past four years has been to disregard the union, to avoid compromise at any cost . . . and to continue to suppress the rights of individual players. . . . You are guilty of indifference to societal changes which have occurred since the early '60s. You have perpetuated an unjust system of control over athletes headed by those who have demonstrated disdain for the constitutional rights of athletes.

That statement was followed by a list of some fifty-eight demands. Chief among them were "elimination of the Rozelle Rule" and the creation of total "free agency," "a union shop provision for all players from the beginning of their employment," "elimination of the commissioner's authority to discipline players," and a host of "freedom issues." Among the latter were the right of veteran players to veto any trade, the banning of "all psychological and personality testing," and a provision stating that "no player representative or elected officer of the NFLPA shall be cut or traded without his consent."

Wellington Mara was appalled. "These demands," he responded, "reflect only one thesis—that the experience of generations is worthless, that a structure that has evolved through the years should be torn down and replaced by nothing. . . . We estimate [your monetary demands] would cost the clubs $100,000,000 more this year. We do not say that our system is the only system. . . . [or] necessarily the best system for maintaining the high popularity of professional football. What we do say is that it is a system that has worked. . . . With all the conviction at my command, I urge you to reexamine your values."

The union's proposals were, the management council argued, "a demolition of the structure which has taken the NFL more than fifty years to build, with no organization proposed to take its place. . . . We draw the line at a system with no rules, and we cannot be asked to bid against ourselves in altering a structure with which we have no major complaint."

It appeared that hostilities on the labor front would be longterm at best.

2
The WFL Raid

The other front monopolizing Pete Rozelle's attention in spring 1974 was the World Football League. Right after the NFL annual meeting adjourned, Gary Davidson mounted the long-awaited player raid that was his league-building trademark. His target: the legendarily cheap Joe Robbie.

Actually, Tom Keating, the agent representing three of Robbie's star employees—Larry Csonka, Jim Kiick, and Paul Warfield—had been approached in February. The WFL wanted to know how much money it would take for Keating's three clients to sign with them. The agent came up with $2.7 million. "You're kidding," was the response. At the time, Joe Robbie was paying each of the stars between $60,000 and $70,000 a year.

It was widely known that the WFL had no one who brought the financial stature Lamar Hunt had given the infant American Football League, but John Bassett, heir to a fortune based in Toronto, was as close as they got. Bassett's original intention was to field a Toronto team called the Northmen. The Canadian government objected to the importation of American football, however, and he quickly moved the franchise to Memphis and named it the Southmen. Wherever his team was, Bassett's finances stood out by WFL standards. Most of the other owners were, in Bassett's words, "a lot of people who wanted to play with other people's money."

The principal financial reason the football business was an attractive investment to men of Bassett's means could be found in the Internal Revenue Service tax codes. "When a team is successful," *Fortune* noted, "its returns are in a class with those found in the sort of real estate deal that generates cash flow, tax benefits, and longterm appreciation . . . a very cost-effective means for enjoying public stature. Professional sports teams qualify for so many tax advantages as to render their . . . 'book' profit or loss figures meaningless." There was just one small problem, as John Bassett and the rest of the WFL soon found out. The tax magic worked only if the team generated revenues. While an owner was trying to establish a revenue base, the losses were real, not paper. Over the next year, that drain averaged $1 million per club and, given the new league's underfunded character, Bassett pointed out, it would be tough "finding people with enough money to keep things going." Bassett had more to do with setting the scale of those losses than anyone else in the WFL, when he raided the NFL in the spring of 1974.

First, Bassett called Keating and said he wanted to talk about Csonka, Kiick, and Warfield. "I've heard about the figure you came up with," he told the Dolphins' agent. "Are you serious?" Keating said he was and Bassett said he wanted to do business. Keating then checked out Bassett's finances. Impressed, he arranged for his clients to come to the Toronto negotiating sessions in the Prime Minister's Suite in Toronto's Sutton Place Hotel. The night before, Bassett, his general manager, and his attorney went out for drinks and dinner with Keating and his clients. For Keating, it was a critical opportunity to size up the opposition. "Psychology plays a tremendous part in negotiations like this," he later explained. "With some owners you've got to be low key—talk softly, go fishing with them. With others, you might have to pound the table and have a few drinks. The secret is to get the other guy as close to the corner as you can without pushing him against the wall." On the basis of dinner conversation, he decided to use the soft approach on Bassett.

Negotiations included Bassett's three-man team and Keating. (Keating's clients had been sent to a clothing store to pick out some custom-made suits courtesy of one of Bassett's minority partners.) Keating presented three separate salary demands totaling $3.884 million and including a million-dollar signing bonus. Csonka was demanding $1.4 million over three years, Kiick $700,000, and Warfield $900,000. Csonka was asking almost eight times what he currently earned from Joe Robbie, not counting a signing bonus. Keating also presented Bassett with a long list of alterations his clients wanted in the standard NFL player contract and a short list of desired "extras," such as a "a fully equipped luxury automobile" every year and a three-bedroom luxury apartment. Keating's palms were sweating when he handed the memos over.

After a morning spent fruitlessly hashing around terms, Keating offered that "it doesn't look like this is going to work out" and stopped the negotiations. At that point, Bassett left to confer with his attorney and Keating had "the sick feeling that it was about to slip away." But Bassett worried he would lose any chance at the three Dolphins if he quibbled. He also said the signings "would make the club and the league." When he rejoined Keating, Bassett shuffled the papers the agent had given him. "Ed," he said, "you've got a deal." Keating said he'd have to talk it over with his clients.

The ball was in Joe Robbie's court. Keating was "afraid the Canadians might rescind or lower their offer if we waited too long," so he called Don Shula, Robbie's coach and general manager, and asked to talk to Robbie himself by the next day. Keating's clients had few illusions that their current boss would match Bassett's offer. "I can't conceive of Joe Robbie giving us a Mustang," Kiick pointed out, "much less a Cadillac." Robbie refused to negotiate long distance and refused to fly to Toronto to talk.

Shortly after Joe Robbie hung up, Larry Csonka, Jim Kiick, and Paul Warfield signed with John Bassett's World Football League Northmen/Southmen/Grizzlies. *Time* called it "the deal that astonished sports." Al Davis offered that the new league was taking up where the AFL left off—with one difference. "It took us [six years] to figure out how the weaker league could bring the stronger league to its knees," Davis said.

Pete Rozelle, however, remained unimpressed. While admitting the WFL had "raised the price of doing business," there was no evidence the new league could honor the contracts it signed. In the meantime, Joe Robbie had lost the heart of his Super Bowl team and was furious. He considered the whole process "blackmail" and complained loudly about having to buy his team all over again.

3
Sullivan's Last Stand

Robbie got a lot of sympathy for his complaint from his friend Billy Sullivan, but, by then, almost all the air was out of Old Billy's NFL balloon. Since the Bal Harbour meeting, Billy had been fighting his last stand. "Instead of a smooth transition," Bob Marr remembered, "he made it an emotional trauma for everyone. He did everything he could to hang on."

The object of Sullivan's strategy was still the shares belonging to Hessie Sargent. Marr pointed out that she "was under terrible pressure by Billy, his wife, Mary, the whole family. Billy was crying on her doorstep every night." In depicting the situation, Billy described it as a palace coup "spearheaded by David McConnell and Robert Wetenhall," the Patriots board members to whom he referred derisively as "the New Yorkers." To Billy, they were just interested in money. There were also hints dropped that the New Yorkers meant to move the franchise once they were in the driver's seat. Bob Marr described the insinuation as "bullshit."

The day before the Patriots' annual board of directors meeting, in March, Sullivan's personal attorney asked for a temporary restraining order postponing the gathering in order to give Billy more time to purchase stock. His attorney claimed that the Sargent Trust and Hessie Sargent were prepared to sell to Billy but "their stock would be voted against him if the meeting were held today." Billy claimed he would need as much as sixty days but the best he could do was postpone his fate for a little more than two weeks.

Though Sullivan's strategy succeeded only as a momentary holding action, it marked the advent of another character who would prove to be the dominant force in the franchise's future: Billy's son Chuck. Thirty-one years old, Chuck was an associate at a Wall Street law firm. When first contacted by his father about what was going on, Chuck immediately involved himself in a behind the scenes role in preparing the Suffolk Superior Court request for time. From then on, his involvement became virtually total. Chuck had little of Old Billy's native charm. Moon-faced and balding, his eyes were squinty and his body was short and somewhat pear-shaped. Where Billy was verbose to the extreme, Chuck chose his words carefully. "There wasn't a hint of glitter surrounding him," *Fortune* observed. "His only apparent gleam emanated from his well-polished shoes." He was quite adept at the nuances of finance law, an expertise that would prove of no small use to his father. However, Chuck Sullivan was an unlikely candidate for the role of football business heavyweight. "He had no idea whether a football was pumped up or stuffed," one acquaintance noted. "He didn't know squat about the game, not at all." That ignorance was inconsequential to the business Chuck Sullivan would eventually do.

In the immediate moment, however, it was too late to do much at all. Try as he might, Billy Sullivan had been unable to bring Hessie Sargent around, and on April 9, 1974, the board of directors meeting he had been fighting to avoid finally took place. Billy would later remember that day as one of the low points of his life. As expected, he no longer had the votes to keep the presidency. "He took it very bitterly," Bob Marr recalled. "There were no tantrums or tirades but he expressed bitterness to some of the board who he thought owed him their votes." It was all to no avail. The new president of the New England Patriots was Bob Marr, the new vice-president, Lee Sargent, Hessie's son. Following the meeting, the new Patriots' management held a press conference.

Marr attempted to smooth the transition, so he spoke more kindly about his predecessor than he in fact felt, then continued, "Much has been made of the current change in management. We have read a great deal about power struggles and bitter feuds. This is not so." Lee Sargent also made light of any conflict. "We had disagreements at meetings," the new vice-president admitted, "but the disagreements have been nothing like they have been reported in the media. They were greatly exaggerated.'' Sargent went so far as to claim Old Billy'd had no desire to serve another term.

The fiction was easily penetrated. If that were indeed so, *The Boston Globe* asked, "why wasn't Sullivan at the press conference to wish his successor good luck?'' The reason was that Billy Sullivan had no such generous feelings toward his successors. "I'm not a sorehead,'' he told the *Boston Herald*, "but I am shocked at the way this was done.'' He was most upset by the board's failure to name him to even an honorary post. "I understood I'd be given the opportunity to serve as chairman,'' Sullivan went on, "but it was not offered to me at the meeting. I felt I could have done the club a real service by representing it at League meetings. Now that we're doing well, I get thrown out. But I hung in there before and I'll hang in there now. The Patriots have been my real life's work. I had been given every indication I'd be allowed to buy enough stock to own fifty-one percent of the club and had raised the money to do so. Then everything turned around and I was voted out. I don't want to say anything in anger that might hurt the ball club, but my absence from the press conference should speak volumes about how I feel.''

When Old Billy got home, his cousin Walter was waiting in the driveway. "What are you doing here?'' Billy asked. Walter said he was worried about him. "If what happened to you today had happened to me,'' he explained, "I would have jumped off the nearest bridge.''

"You don't know your cousin,'' Billy Sullivan chuckled grimly. "I guarantee you as sure as I'm standing here today that in another year I'll be back in the driver's seat. Then,'' Billy promised, "the next Patriots board of directors will have people named Sullivan on it and no one else.''

4
The NFL Expands

When the NFL convened in April 1974 for a special executive session on expansion, the first order of business was the introduction of Bob Marr. While Marr was frankly thrilled to be there, the feelings of most of the other men in the room were at best mixed. Ralph Wilson of the Buffalo Bills took the floor and spoke about "the fine record of past service that Bill Sullivan had given." A long discussion of the WFL followed and the subject of expansion itself did not come up until the League reconvened after lunch.

Dan Rooney opened the afternoon session by reporting on the four serious finalists. The key issue was stadium availability, and Seattle's situation rated at the top of the list. King County, Washington, in which Seattle was located, was already building a new domed facility called the Kingdome, a multipurpose indoor stadium which would seat 64,984 football fans. The facility would be finished by the 1975 football season and, according to the Stanford Research Institute, "will be made available to an NFL team franchised in Seattle at reasonable rental rates."

Tampa Stadium was an outdoor, football-only facility with a current capacity of 46,486, and, should the NFL commit to locate there, this number could expand to as many as 70,000 seats. The Tampa Sports Authority had passed resolutions establishing rental rates of $150,000 a season or ten percent of the gross, whichever was greater, for any Tampa NFL franchise.

Memphis's situation was similar to that in Tampa. The Memphis City Council had recently passed a resolution approving expansion of the 1965 stadium from its current capacity of 50,164 to 72,164 seats, contingent on the NFL designating Memphis as an expansion site. "If accomplished," SRI pointed out, the enlargement "would make the Memphis Memorial Stadium one of the largest in the League." The city of Memphis was also "highly desirous of obtaining a professional team tenant for the stadium. Although a recent feasibility study of stadium expansion indicated that rental rates for a professional team would be on the order of eleven to twelve percent of gross ticket receipts, private conversations have indicated that a somewhat lower rate would be charged an NFL tenant."

Phoenix's stadium availability was the most questionable of the lot. "Phoenix," SRI reported, "has no stadium at present but is in the process of planning . . ." Present plans called for a nonprofit stadium corporation to implement construction of a 55,000 seat stadium. Should the project not be completed in time for the 1976 season, Sun Devil Stadium on the Arizona State University campus was a possible interim site.

Among the four finalists, Seattle was the most obvious choice. Rozelle was its most influential booster and the case he made was strong. "I respected Seattle as a good sports community. I was high on it as an expansion site, in part because there wasn't a great deal of entertainment competition there." Additionally, Seattle would give the league geographic coverage in the only region of the country with no football franchise at all. However obvious the choice of Seattle might have seemed, it was not an easy one to make in April 1974. The principal hangup was in getting Kingdome officials to translate the "reasonable terms" they had earlier promised into actual "reasonable" numbers. The *Seattle Times* was reporting that King County officials were demanding twenty percent of gross admissions, five percent higher than any other NFL lease.

The second favorite was Tampa. The League liked Florida, a state where many of them regularly vacationed, and Tampa had a particularly strong backer in Carroll Rosenbloom. C.R. had wanted to move the Colts there when they were still his. The Tampa Sports Authority had also been on record for three years offering a ten percent lease, which qualified easily as "reasonable," particularly since they would also undertake expansion of the stadium at their own expense. The final factor boosting Tampa was that Joe Robbie, owner of the only current Florida franchise, did not make a fuss about keeping the state for himself. Most of his tickets were sold immediately around Miami, so Tampa represented no lost markets. According to Rozelle, "Joe Robbie had surface misgivings about another Florida franchise but didn't make an issue of it. He probably saw it from the standpoint of a potential intrastate rivalry that would generate a big preseason game every year."

Phoenix and Memphis were the clear also-rans, though still attractive. Phoenix's problem was its absence of a reliable stadium. Memphis's problem was the WFL. By then, John Bassett had beat the NFL to Memphis Memorial Stadium. In addition, Pete Rozelle remembered, "the World Football League sent us a wire saying that if we went into any of their cities . . . they would construe it as an attempt to run them out of business and they would sue us." Gary Davidson's threat of a lawsuit ruined what was otherwise a strong Memphis case.

On the issue of location, the League recognized that the only real dilemma left was how best to pressure the Kingdome into getting "reasonable." The rest of the issues discussed, however, were not nearly so easy to resolve. How, for example, would the expansion franchises be stocked with players? To field a team, the two new entries would have to select from a pool made available by the existing franchises. Just how that ought to be done proved complex and controversial and the subject produced a long discussion and no resolution.

The issue of price, however, could not be postponed and things got very loud when it came up. Leonard Tose was demanding $20 million. He was by no means alone. Others still stuck obstreperously to Rozelle and Rooney's original recommendation of $12 million. Rozelle was prepared to accept a $16-million compromise and pushed for it. Young Bob Marr, was immediately impressed with the commissioner's technique. "He worked beautifully behind the scenes," Marr marveled. "He had his mouthpieces push his ideas but it was obvious who they were coming from." By late afternoon, discussion was pretty much used up, but rather than try to put something on paper immediately, Rozelle first had Tex Schramm report about some playing rule changes proposed by the competition committee. The effect was to sap the meeting's energy even further. Then, on the verge of adjournment, Rozelle called for a vote.

The resolution on the floor, moved and seconded, was,

RESOLVED, that the National Football League grant an expansion franchise to the City of Tampa to begin play in the 1976 season and that the NFL expand by at least one more city before the end of 1974. The price for the franchise is to be sixteen million dollars . . . The Expansion Committee is authorized to research potential ownership for the Tampa franchise and to make recommendations to the full membership. . . .

It passed by a 25 to 1 vote.

The news was received with great glee in Tampa. In Seattle, it provoked impotent rage. "The owners went for the big buck," the *Seattle Post-Intelligencer* complained, and went on to rant about NFL greed and arrogance, as well as to suggest that Seattle take its business to the WFL. Officially, Seattle remained sanguine and confident. "I would interpret this as meaning," a King County official observed, "that the League wishes to refine the terms on the stadium lease. There is no question that Seattle remains the most attractive possible franchise and . . . barring a totally unreasonable decision, professional football will be here in 1976."

When the NFL's Executive Session reconvened in June, that prediction finally came true. Again, however, it took all day and shortly before adjournment, a resolution was finally passed:

> RESOLVED, that Seattle be admitted to the National Football League as the 28th franchise under the same terms and conditions under which Tampa was admitted last April and it be reaffirmed that unanimous consent be required of the membership to change the required payment of $16 million no later than the spring of 1976.

The minutes made no record of what new stadium concessions Seattle had offered, but whatever they were, they seemed sufficient. The resolution passed with twenty yes votes, five nos, and one pass.

The commissioner announced Seattle's selection. "It's the sixteenth largest market in the country," he pointed out, "and falls into the NFL schedule for the largest cities in the country." Recognizing the disappointment he knew the also-rans felt, Rozelle went out of his way to indicate that the NFL was not through expanding. "I wouldn't expect another city to be added this week," he continued, "but the expansion committee will explore additional expansion. . . . Any city would be a candidate. . . . Future expansion is a totally open deck. Going from twenty-eight to thirty clubs is probably the next logical step."

While the commissioner's hints about throwing open the NFL doors no doubt gave immediate heart to Memphis, Phoenix, Anaheim, Honolulu, Nassau County, Birmingham, Orlando, and Charlotte, in the long run they would only add to Rozelle's reputation for arrogance. The expansion consecrated on April 24 and June 4, 1974, would be the last in NFL history. The door was now shut for good and, as a consequence, the volatility of the seller's market would increase geometrically over the remainder of the decade.

5
Ownerships Old and New

Next, Rozelle and Rooney's committee had to select owners for Tampa and Seattle. They began by crafting a set of standards for choosing from among the many requests for consideration. They came up with four key factors. The first was "financial responsibility." Rozelle wanted assurance that the two new members would have the cash to carry most of the franchise by themselves. Thus, the expansion committee eliminated "those that indicated that they wanted to put a group together." New NFL members had to play with their own money. Hustlers of the Joe Robbie mold need not apply.

The second factor was, Rozelle explained, ". . . living in or in the general geographic area of the franchise itself. . . ." The third concern was "the character" of applicants, and to investigate this, the NFL security department was dispatched to compile a workup on all serious contenders. The fourth standard was willingness to adhere to the League's ownership policy. A number of the men interested in ownership might have financial interests in other sports and the commissioner wanted that eventuality accounted for up front. All potential owners engaged in such "conflicts of interest" would be required to promise they would divest their other interests upon entrance.

Although 1974 was shaping up as the worst year for American business in almost two decades and the League's standards additionally circumscribed a great deal of the potential ownership pool, a number of interested parties nonetheless emerged.

On the Tampa list, the most familiar face was Tom McCloskey, who had purchased the Philadelphia soccer franchise from Lamar Hunt. McCloskey had extensive financial interests in the

Tampa area. Another familiar face vying for Tampa was Hugh Culverhouse, the Jacksonville, Florida, attorney who had been competing with Carroll Rosenbloom for the Rams in 1972. Though he lived on Florida's northeast coast, Culverhouse was prepared to expand his business into west central Florida and live in Tampa a good portion of the year. Others included Austin Knowlton, a Cincinnati businessman, Harry Mangurian, a millionaire in partnership with professional golfer Jack Nicklaus, and Edward DeBartolo Sr., a Youngstown, Ohio, based shopping center developer with "extensive shopping center interests in Florida."

The list for Seattle, like everything to do with the League's second choice, would develop more slowly and not nearly as smoothly as Rozelle had hoped. The only genuinely homegrown candidate was a partnership built around Seattle's Nordstrom family. Lloyd Nordstrom, board chairman of Nordstrom, Inc., a clothing store chain in the northwest, was the central figure and planned to bring in his brother, three nephews, his daughter, and son-in-law as well as a number of other partners. Other candidates were a group headed by Minneapolis millionaire Wayne Field that included former NFL and University of Washington football great Hugh McElhenny and already called itself the "Seattle Kings." Sam Shulman was a Los Angeles resident but kept a condo in Seattle and was prepared to give up his basketball interest if the NFL would let him in. Larry Weinberg, part owner of the Portland Trailblazers, also wanted in badly enough to get out of basketball and according to Rozelle claimed to "have been more or less in the Seattle area for a couple of years." Los Angeles resident Clarence Martin, once a minority owner in the Rams, closed out the list. Martin had grown up in Washington and his father had once been governor of the state.

The expansion committee planned to interview each of these finalists before coming to a final recommendation to take to the membership. Those interviews were delayed by the League's continued preoccupation with the impasse on the labor front and would not take place until late September.

In June, the only ownership decision immediately confronting Rozelle was Billy Sullivan's final desperate attempt to avoid the inevitable. It was perhaps among the sadder incidents in Pete Rozelle's career. Bob Marr would later call it "ludicrous." Billy had appealed to the commissioner for a ruling on Marr's recent election. Sullivan claimed that the Sargents had violated a previous agreement with him to vote their stock for his candidacy. The agreement, Billy argued, should have precluded them voting for Marr. Invoking the NFL constitution, Sullivan asked Rozelle to exercise his power to resolve ownership disputes, reverse the decision of the Patriots board of directors, and reinstall him as president. The request led to a hearing in June.

Though the Patriots had a corporate counsel who might have accompanied Marr to that meeting, the man serving in that role was a Sullivan intimate and, with the approval of the Patriots board, Marr hired outside representation. Billy's case was not hard to puncture. The Sargents said their agreement applied only to the potential sale of their stock, not to any vote on the board of directors, and their stock was not for sale. In addition, Sullivan's name had never been officially placed in nomination at the April board meeting, therefore any agreement to vote for Sullivan made no difference since doing so was formally impossible. "Sullivan felt he could lobby the owners to put pressure on Rozelle," Marr commented, "but Rozelle played it pretty even. He wasn't obviously partial. He went through it all at Billy's request and was probably embarrassed at being put in that position." When Rozelle ruled for Marr and the Patriots board of directors, it was the first and only time he would ever rule against the Sullivans. Nevertheless, Billy Sullivan was now officially out of power. Whether that would be a permanent condition, however, remained to be seen.

Billy's son Chuck was already planning his father's comeback. The campaign to get Hessie Sargent to sell continued unabated. According to Bob Marr, it included calls from Billy's wife worrying that Billy was going to have a heart attack unless all this got "straightened out." His dismissal had been, Billy himself noted, "a terrible, terrible shock." Chuck Sullivan had confidence his father could bring Hessie around, but even then the situation would be far from simple. The further complexities flowed from an interlocking network of buy-out agreements that connected all the Patriots factions and ultimately meant that Billy's return to power could cost him more than $6 million.

Had that power meant outright ownership of the club, Sullivan could have easily collateralized a loan for that sum with the assets of the franchise itself. In the case of the Patriots, that was impossible because of the outstanding stock held by some 2,600 different individuals. Their continued presence meant Billy Sullivan would have to buy his way back to power using his own resources. As of June 1974, his net worth was some $4 million and his annual income with which to service any new debt was $96,900.

Chuck Sullivan's dilemma was finding a bank that would loan Billy at least $2 million more than he was worth. First, of course, he would have to convince them that his father could pay it back. Neither task would prove at all simple.

6
Strike Breaking

On July 1, labor impasse became open strike and the ensuing fracas at least momentarily obscured the rest of the issues facing the League. While the NFLPA had presented fifty-eight demands in March and added thirty-three more in May, the Rozelle Rule was at the top of both sides' lists. Pete Rozelle and the management council maintained the League could not survive without it and Ed Garvey and the players union were unflinching in their demand it be dropped entirely.

"Players demand freedom," former NFLPA President John Mackey wrote in *The New York Times*. "They demand the rights of citizenship. They demand the Constitutional protections afforded all other citizens of this country. . . . I am appalled that in the United States of America people can still make economic arguments to justify the taking away of a man's freedom. . . . Some say that freedom for athletes will destroy the NFL. I say nonsense. . . . But I also say this: If freedom will destroy the NFL, then the NFL should be destroyed."

One NFL attorney answered, "The players' demand for 'no system' would constitute anarchy." Part of the reason for the League's resentment of the union's attack on the Rozelle Rule was the "unfairness" of Garvey's larger strategy. While on the one hand claiming in *Mackey v. NFL* to need the intercession of the court under the Sherman Act in order to correct a condition the union would be otherwise powerless to change, Garvey was at the same time making the condition an active issue of negotiation backed by a labor boycott. The League didn't feel he should be allowed to do both, but Garvey did both anyway.

The young union leader wanted to get the Rozelle Rule however he could. According to Garvey, the rule had existed as a "gentlemen's agreement not to sign free agents" prior to 1963. Then Carroll Rosenbloom violated the agreement in his thirst for championships in Baltimore and signed one R. C. Owens, the NFL's first and only uncompensated free agent. In the aftermath, the League "quietly adopted a new provision, which we now know as the Rozelle Rule, [calling] for compensation for any player who signs with another team." The effect of the arrangement allowed "club owners to control both on-field and off-field conduct of their employees in their industry, to hold wages down. [It also allowed] a team to restrict the right of free expression and deprive the individual of the right to employment of his choice." Garvey wanted to break with this legacy of subjugation once and for all.

Garvey's attitude was evident from the beginning of negotiations. He had as many players as possible sit in on negotiations and, according to one League negotiator, he played to them as a gallery. "The players liked to watch him," the negotiator noted. "They liked to see big management getting jerked around."

Negotiations broke off, and on July 1, the union announced that none of the League's veterans would report to training camps two days hence. "I am confident we can hold out until a new collective bargaining agreement is signed," Ed Garvey told *The New York Times*.

The strike's first public skirmish centered around the opening of the San Diego Chargers' training camp on July 3. That day rookies were scheduled to report. They were not members of the NFLPA, but the union was nonetheless calling on them to join their boycott. That morning, Ed Garvey led a fifty-man picket line in San Diego, each man wearing a T-shirt emblazoned with a clenched fist and the slogan NO FREEDOM, NO FOOTBALL. Chargers owner Gene Klein was waiting for them at the entrance and cut a street corner deal with Garvey. If the pickets wouldn't enter the training camp grounds or block traffic, the police who had been called would depart. Klein said Garvey agreed but the very next day led pickets into the training camp. According to Klein, when confronted with his breach of faith, Garvey responded by saying, "This is July Fourth, Freedom Day, and the deal doesn't count." By then, Klein had long since sworn to field a team "if I have to use bartenders."

Wellington Mara had reached the same conclusion in New York. The strike had a deep personal impact on him. "I never really believed it would happen," he remembered. "The relationship between an owner and a player should be a lot different than the usual employer/employee relationship. Their demands were so outrageous I could only respond with disbelief and indignation." Mara called all the Giants' rookies to a meeting and addressed them in somber tones. "I hope we can play this season with veterans and rookies," he announced, "but if we can't, we'll play it with rookies. . . . We must operate."

The National Labor Relations Act required granting the NFLPA controlled access to those in training camp, a condition to which both Klein and Mara acceded. Mara, however, insisted his representatives sit in on the NFLPA's recruiting session. "That's my football team," Mara snapped in explanation. "You wouldn't walk out of your store and leave the cash register untended." *The New York Times* described Mara's stance as "the strongest and most definitive" of any owner in the League.

Most football owners simply intensified their vilification of Garvey. Though his position would change, Carroll Rosenbloom was in the front row of 1974's anti-Garvey chorus. On July 16, he accused Garvey of "using" the players. "This fellow," C.R. claimed, "has told them, 'Look, you should go to a camp where coaches won't be able to say anything but yes, sir, and no, sir. You won't have to practice unless you want to practice. There will be no rules. You can bring your wives or girlfriends to camp.' That's pretty cute. The players themselves will tell you that would destroy the game." By the time C.R. issued his statement, seventy-seven union members had crossed the picket lines and gone back to work.

On July 18, the two sides met and again rejected each other's demands. By July 21, the League reported 108 union defections and by July 29, the figure had grown to 248, almost twenty percent of the NFLPA's total membership. When the two sides returned to the table, the exhibition schedule had begun, using mostly all rookie teams. The union claimed ticket sales for the first week of exhibitions were down $1.8 million from the year before. But despite the continued air of public defiance, after thirty-six days on strike, the union's resolve was crumbling and Garvey knew it. The League was applying pressure and finding weak spots all along the solid front Garvey thought he had built. On August 7, the NFL had 360 union members now in camp.

The heaviest pressure of all was against the twenty-six player representatives upon whom the whole union superstructure rested. Ken Reeves, Atlanta's player rep, was walking a picket line when Falcon owner Rankin Smith drove up in a car with the

eam's coach and told Reeves to take his picket sign to New
Orleans because he'd been traded. Within a year, a total of
twenty union officers and player reps had been cut or traded. Of
the seven men on the union's negotiating committee, only two
would still have jobs a year after they set up their first picket
line. Wellington Mara set the tone: by September 15, 1974,
"almost every Giant who stayed out during the player strike"
would be "gone."

On August 10, the management council sensed the strike's
imminent collapse and threatened to walk out and not return until
the "freedom issues" had been completely dropped. "They
smelled blood," Garvey remembered. He offered to take the
freedom demands off the table and let them wait on the trial in
Mackey v. NFL. The League said no, it wanted *Mackey v. NFL*
dropped as well. When Garvey refused, the Management Council walked out of negotiations to let the union appreciate the
weakness of its position. "The strike collapsed and we lost,"
Garvey later admitted. "It was time for Plan B."

Plan B was to return to work without a contract and "continue
the fight in the courts." His player reps were divided on the
issue. Some were upset, Garvey explained, "because they knew
just by going back in they were going to be cut. The other school
of thought was 'live to fight another day.' " At this point,
according to Garvey, "the only thing management had agreed to
was to no longer force players to shave their mustaches." There
was, Garvey offered, no option to Plan B except outright surrender. When Garvey announced Plan B, he caught many observers
and the League itself by surprise. While he described the return
to work as a "fourteen-day cooling-off period," those fourteen
days evolved into semi-permanent irresolution as both sides geared
up to fight *Mackey v. NFL* in Federal Court.

According to Garvey, "management went crazy" at having
been denied a definitive victory. "They were vindictive and we
had cost them millions of dollars and nothing was settled. They
had their camps full of scabs and didn't want to let players back
in but they had no choice. They were an inch away from
destroying us, then we jumped out of the ring."

Ed Garvey's first meeting with the union membership after
Plan B commenced was with the Falcons in Atlanta. He was
nervous about it, but one of the Falcons offered him some cogent
advice. "Just be honest with them," the player suggested. "Players
understand winning and losing, they don't understand ties."
Garvey followed the advice. "We didn't stick together," he told

the meeting, "so we lost." Now the NFLPA would "raise dues to fight it in court." Garvey considered the approach successful "Right now it's like we're behind twenty to zero," he offered "Do we quit or do we still try to win?" While Ed Garvey made it clear he meant to win, he conceded that "it's clear by the attitude here and elsewhere that we will try to avoid another strike." He hoped the Sherman Act would give him the leverage his union was unable to muster on its own.

While the NFL and its commissioner found Plan B enormously frustrating, they had no choice. All they could do was to hire lawyers—and wait.

7
League Laughs—Inside and Out

While the NFL was still tied up with Ed Garvey, the WFL had opened for business. The new league started its season in the third week of July and its opening numbers must have sent some tremors through the strikebound NFL. Attendance for that week's WFL schedule was an announced 258,624, an average of better than 43,000 a game. In Philadelphia, the Bell, thought to be the league's weakest franchise, drew 55,000 to its game with the Portland Storm. The Jacksonville, Florida, Sharks drew 59,112 against the New York Stars. WFL Commissioner Gary Davidson pronounced himself "awestruck" by his league's immediate success.

That patina of vitality lasted for less than a month before collapsing into scandal. While Garvey was launching Plan B against the NFL, *Sports Illustrated* revealed that of the 120,253 who allegedly attended the WFL Philadelphia Bell's first two games, 100,000 had been admitted free. To cope with the scandal, Gary Davidson suspended the Bell's vice-president for forty-eight hours. By then, the NFL was back to work and the WFL had picked up the nickname "World Freebie League." When the NFL regular season opened in September, the WFL's credibility was losing altitude each week.

By October, its shaky financial substructure had been exposed. The Detroit Wheels started the month by filing for bankruptcy. During September, the franchise had run out of adhesive tape and couldn't afford to get its uniforms back from the laundry. "They were just thirty-two jerks who thought they'd be millionaires overnight," one Wheel player described the franchise's owners. The owner of the Jacksonville Sharks had been unable to make his payroll for four weeks. At one point, he borrowed $27,000 from his head coach and then fired the coach the next week. The Houston Texans fled Houston for Shreveport, Louisiana. On their last day in Houston, the team bus driver refused to drive the players to practice unless he was paid his sixty-one-dollar bus rental fee in advance. The owner of Anaheim's Southern California Sun was indicted on three counts of "making false statements to obtain loans." Only Birmingham, averaging a legitimate forty-three thousand a game, and Memphis, fueled by John Bassett's money, were in good shape. "Any new league is going to have problems," Bassett pointed out. The WFL's October pratfall no doubt inspired chuckles and sighs of relief around the NFL, which was not without its own embarrassments that fall. The year 1974 was, after all, when Robert Irsay came into his own in Baltimore.

The differences in style between Irsay and his predecessor at the Colts, Carroll Rosenbloom, had been obvious to Baltimore immediately. Tall and stylish, Rosenbloom was a Maryland patrician, accustomed to great wealth, and capable of generating enormous, if occasionally devious, charm. Squat and bull-necked, Irsay was crude, blunt, and boisterous, and incapable of subtlety, let alone refinement. In 1974, he was still commuting to Colt games from Chicago in one of the three Learjets he claimed to own. During football season, he was in Baltimore for no more than six days a month but bridled at being described as an absentee owner. "That's more than Carroll had been around," he pointed out.

In 1974, the specter of Carroll Rosenbloom still haunted Robert Irsay in several significant ways. First, he was particularly galled to discover in fall 1972 that Rosenbloom had loaned $650,000 of the franchise's money to Colt players so that they could buy businesses for themselves. "I'm no financial consultant, like Carroll Rosenbloom," Irsay told the *Chicago Tribune,* "but I'm a good man. I'm not going to demand payment before the season is over, but . . . I'm not in the loan business—I'm in the football business. . . . We're going back to the good old days," he vowed. "I'll keep the players fired up or I'll fire them, either way."

Carroll Rosenbloom's shadow also fell on Robert Irsay in Baltimore's Memorial Stadium, the Colts' home field. Essentially a baseball stadium converted to stage football games, it was old, small, rickety, and getting only more so. Irsay believed C.R. had promised him a new stadium was in the works, and he viewed the long string of hassles he had over his home field as an albatross Rosenbloom had personally hung around his neck. In the fall of 1974, those hassles took the form of a series of unsuccessful negotiations with the city of Baltimore and the state of Maryland over a proposal for a new downtown stadium complex. The Colts owner complained, "If they're not going to put up a new stadium, I would insist they start a complete renovation." He would get neither.

Thirdly, the memory of Carroll Rosenbloom dogged Robert Irsay in the inevitable comparisons of the franchise's performance on the field. C.R. had left Baltimore with a Super Bowl trophy and, under his ownership, the Colts had acquired the reputation of a League powerhouse. C.R.'s Colts sold out Memorial Stadium every Sunday. Irsay's Colts quickly reversed the trend. Under Irsay, the Colts started badly and were getting worse. During Irsay's first season they won 5 games and lost 9; his second, 4 and 10; his third, 2 and 12.

From the beginning, Baltimore's press corps was worried that Irsay, like his predecessor, harbored notions of moving the Colts. "You're gun-shy about moving," Irsay lectured them in 1973. "We have absolutely no idea of moving the franchise. . . . Tell the people to keep the faith, that the Colts will be back as soon as possible." Irsay also prided himself in knowing a thing or two about football. "I was just a little squirt when I was trying to play college football," the Colts owner told *The* [Baltimore] *Sun,* "but that's not the part I'm proudest of. I was also carrying twenty-three semester hours in an engineering course and washing dishes besides. That wasn't easy. . . . We've shown before that we can reach goals. I did it in the Marine Corps and in college and in business and we can do it now."

At the time, Irsay was still claiming to have been a Marine lieutenant who fought at Guadalcanal, Tarawa, and New Britain. He also claimed to have graduated from the University of Illinois. One story about Irsay's career in the air-conditioning business recounted the time he walked into a union negotiation conspicuously armed with a .45 caliber pistol. Asked if he would use the weapon, he answered, "Who knows?" The Chicago millionaire took pride in being a man who would not back off. "We're here and in this to stay," he pledged. "The Baltimore

Colts are going to be winners. The Baltimore Colts are going to the Super Bowl. You have my word of honor.''

In many ways, Robert Irsay *was* a more natural match for the city than C.R. Baltimore prided itself in being a blue collar town and Rosenbloom was a lot closer to the gold neck chain set. In December 1973, Irsay scored a local PR coup when he attended a party of ordinary Colts fans after a game. According to the organizer of the event, Irsay's ''humility'' had made him the ''hit'' of the evening. ''There were two hundred people here and he talked to all of them.'' Irsay addressed everyone as ''Tiger.'' The boisterous owner even got in a beer-drinking contest with one of his players and downed three quick bottles. Before leaving for Chicago, Irsay quietly picked up everyone's tab. ''He was just like a blue collar worker who made it big,'' the organizer raved. ''He seemed wonderful, strictly a shirt-sleeves kind of guy.'' There was, however, growing evidence that Robert Irsay might be less wonderful. ''He's a liar,'' Bert Jones, one of his players, complained to *The* [Baltimore] *Sun*, ''a cheat, crude, with no manners, and he drinks too much.''

Drink quickly became a permanent part of the Irsay legend, and by 1974, the local press was already speculating that he ''appeared intoxicated on Sunday afternoons.'' One agent who negotiated a player contract with him remembered Irsay arriving at negotiations already flushed and then consuming ''six or eight vodkas'' during the next two hours. Irsay's wife, Harriet, denied drinking played an important part in her husband's personality. ''He acts the same if he's had a drink or he hasn't,'' she explained. ''He just hates to lose, and when he does, he gets mad.''

No one could deny the intensity he brought to football games. On a typical fall Sunday, he would rise at 7 A.M., then his Lear would fly him and five or six friends to Baltimore. ''During the game,'' *The Sun* observed, ''he swears, cheers, criticizes, and exults.'' By the third quarter, Irsay would make his way through the stands down to the Colts sideline. He was often greeted with catcalls from fans seated along his path. ''Stick with us,'' he'd yell back. ''We're trying.''

Like the members of the NFL, Baltimore had expected Irsay to be little more than the creature of his general manager, Joe Thomas. Irsay himself made a point of reinforcing the assumption. ''I've tried to stay out of the limelight,'' he explained in May 1974. ''A lot of owners have tried to run the team by being present all the time. I have chosen to do it through Joe Thomas.

I've always felt that if you have two captains making the decisions, you'll have trouble with the crew.''

However, there was also growing evidence that Thomas was not nearly as in control as he seemed. In 1972, after just four months as an owner, Irsay personally fired the team's head coach. "I've watched this team on the field," the owner pointed out, "and I think a high school team could beat them." In 1973, Irsay stormed into the Colts' locker room after yet another loss and cussed out the team's starting quarterback. "First, everybody thought he was joking," one of the players who observed the scene remembered. "We were all laughing, then all of a sudden things got serious. . . . It frightened me." Thomas managed to defuse the situation and quickly pulled his boss to another part of the room. "Anything Irsay said was in jest," the general manager offered in an attempt to smooth things over.

The incident that finally convinced Baltimore that Irsay was more than Joe Thomas could handle occurred on September 29, 1974, when the Colts lost 30–10 to Leonard Tose's Philadelphia Eagles. The [Baltimore] Sun reported that Irsay was behaving like "a raving, swearing, intoxicated man" at the stadium that day, all of which Irsay later denied. By the second half, he was down on the sideline, barely able to contain himself. Finally he stormed up to his head coach, and, with a string of expletives, ordered the man to take the quarterback out of the game. Using his own group of expletives, the coach refused. Irsay stalked away and held his tongue for the rest of the game. Then the Colts owner headed for the locker room in a rage.

Gathering the players around him, he announced that he was firing the head coach, the fourth head coach in two years. Just ten days before, Joe Thomas had publicly guaranteed the coach's job for at least the rest of the year. "Joe Thomas is now the coach," he informed the players. "This fucking ball club will go on that field to win even if I have to play myself." The last man to learn of all the changes was Joe Thomas. When he did, he was "visibly shaken and soaked with perspiration." Thomas arrived in the locker room just as Irsay was leaving, "red-faced, with jowls sputtering prophecies, threats, and expletives." The two men passed in the hall. "You're the coach," Irsay growled at his general manager, "as of right now."

When Pete Rozelle's office was questioned about Irsay's behavior, it could only point out that the Colts were, after all, Irsay's franchise. "The League is not in a position to decide how an owner operates his team," a spokesman for the commissioner patiently explained.

8
Power Plays: Selecting New Owners

The NFL was no doubt looking for people as unlike Robert Irsay as possible for the League's two new franchises. The League was scheduled to decide on its two new members at the October meeting. Each city presented an opposite dilemma.

The problem in Seattle was scarcity of appropriate applicants. That shortage was exacerbated further when the "Seattle Kings" group headed by Wayne Field dropped out of the running. Of all the applicants, the Kings had been in the hunt longest. The reasons they gave were financial. The factors cited for adding to the group's financial worries, above and beyond the $16 million pricetag, were the continuing strike by the NFLPA and a recent IRS challenge to the heretofore monumental tax writeoffs granted sports franchises. In retiring from the contest, Field recommended the League select Seattle Professional Football, the group clustered around the Nordstrom family and represented by Herman Sarkowsky.

The Sarkowsky group was the only genuinely homegrown Seattle applicant, but nonetheless suffered from ownership policy problems. For starters, the group offered no single fifty-one percent owner. The closest thing to such a clear majority were the holdings of the whole Nordstrom family, more than a half-dozen separate individuals. Sarkowsky owned only ten percent but, to help assuage the commissioner's worries, was scheduled to be named the franchise's managing general partner, in much the same manner as Al Davis's arrangement in Oakland and Joe Robbie's in Miami.

But cross-ownership presented an even larger problem for the Sarkowsky group. At the time of the applicant interviews, Herman Sarkowsky still owned forty percent of the National Basketball Association Portland Trailblazers. In addition, he owned a small piece of the Seattle North American Soccer League club, as did several members of the Nordstrom family. One of the first issues raised in Sarkowsky's interview was divestiture. According to Rozelle, Sarkowsky responded that "he would divest himself of the basketball team to conform with our policy and said he would . . . sell a rather sizable chunk of [basketball] stock . . . that would place him in a very minority position and then when business or taxwise it made sense for him, he would complete the divesting." Despite those assurances, the problems attached to the League's Seattle vacancy insured it would sit unfilled much longer than Tampa.

In Tampa, the NFL faced a relative surplus of "viability." Two candidates there ranked almost equally high, though neither was technically "hometown." The first was Tom McCloskey, the Philadelphia contractor and soccer owner. According to Rozelle, McCloskey "still had the bulk of [his] construction business in the Tampa area" and "was a voting resident of Florida, although he resided in Philadelphia." What made Tom McCloskey particularly attractive was his "extended identification with sports." His soccer franchise had won the NASL championship during its first season. Rozelle was familiar with him from the 1969 bidding over the Philadelphia Eagles in Jerry Wolman's bankruptcy case. Prior to finishing second to Leonard Tose, McCloskey had been given a clean bill of health in a League investigation.

This would likely be Tom McCloskey's last shot at a franchise and he was eager to do his best at the expansion committee interviews. He also knew that his soccer team would not be looked on with great favor, champions or not. For advice, he consulted Leonard Tose, who told him to divest himself. To Tose's great satisfaction, McCloskey followed his advice. Unlike Seattle's Herman Sarkowsky, Tom McCloskey was not about to dicker over the terms of divestiture. Rozelle remembered, "He readily agreed to sell his soccer investments promptly . . . in any manner that the NFL asked him to do." Rozelle himself could not have asked for a more correct response.

McCloskey's principal rival for the Tampa franchise was Hugh Culverhouse, the Florida attorney. Culverhouse's specialty was tax law, and he was also a director of Barnett Banks of Florida, Inc., the Barnett-Wilson Corp. that operated food services in Tampa International Airport, the George Washington Life Insurance Company, Mode, Inc., condominium developers, the Port Everglades Steel Corp., the Miami International Merchandise Mart, and San Juan, Puerto Rico's, Ivanhoe Insurance agency. In Jacksonville, he cut a considerable civic figure. His only previous involvement in sports had been as a collegiate boxer at the University of Alabama, where he fought on the same team as Governor George Wallace.

Hugh Culverhouse was fond of quoting Louis Pasteur to the effect that "chance favors the prepared mind." It was certainly the lesson of Culverhouse's own rise to wealth. Reared in Birmingham, Alabama, during the Depression, Culverhouse, age fifty-five at the time of his Tampa application, had started life in the white collar middle class. In 1947, he graduated from the University of Alabama Law School, then in 1949, he joined the Internal Revenue Service. Culverhouse's last posting with the IRS was as an assistant regional counsel covering Atlanta and Jacksonville. It was the first time he had lived in Florida and his primary job there was investigating organized crime figures. By 1956 he had become attached enough to Florida to turn down a transfer to Dallas and go into private practice. At that time, he was making less than $20,000 a year.

Culverhouse's wealth was a function of "the wise investment of increasingly sizable legal fees" accrued in his private practice. By 1974 he was worth somewhere between $30 and $40 million. Much of that accumulation was in real estate. Everyone who dealt with Hugh Culverhouse considered him a shrewd businessman with a knack for knowing how to make money. "Hugh takes a piece of everything that crosses his desk," one associate noted, "and more stuff crosses his desk than anyone I ever heard of."

Culverhouse's application for membership was no surprise, since he had attempted to buy the Los Angeles Rams two years before. Like Tom McCloskey with the Eagles, he had already come within inches of joining the League. Unlike McCloskey, he had not accepted his shortfall without protest. That made Culverhouse somewhat more controversial than his rival.

Culverhouse had learned of the Los Angeles franchise's availability in 1972 from one of his golfing partners. His partner knew that the Reeves estate had an offer, but if it fell through, would be looking for new bidders. Over that weekend, Culverhouse and an associate worked up what they thought the numbers of such a business might look like and got excited. The following week, the offer ahead of him in line fell through and he flew to Los Angeles to talk to the Rams' general manager, Bill Barnes. Barnes noted that Culverhouse had done his homework better than anyone who had yet expressed an interest. When Culverhouse then detailed his estimates of what the Rams' balance sheets must look like, Barnes admitted the Floridian was "very close." After Culverhouse reported on the financial worth of himself and his groups, Barnes said the asking price was $20 million.

Culverhouse returned with $17 million and, according to him, it was accepted. On June 6, Culverhouse met with Barnes and the attorneys for the Reeves estate, to sign the sale agreement and pay the $100,000 earnest money to seal the bargain. According to one source close to the deal, while Culverhouse was waiting in the attorneys' outer office, Carroll Rosenbloom was inside finalizing his own last-minute deal for Robert Irsay to buy the Rams for $19 million and trade them to Rosenbloom for the Colts plus $4 million in cash. When the lawyers and Barnes finally met with Culverhouse, they refused to accept his earnest money and said they had decided that the franchise was "best kept within the football family" and were consequently selling the franchise to Rosenbloom.

A month later, Hugh Culverhouse filed suit in New York federal court under the Sherman Act, naming Rosenbloom, Barnes, the Los Angeles Rams, the executors of Reeves's estate, Robert Irsay, the Baltimore Colts, the National Football League, and Pete Rozelle as defendants. He claimed Rosenbloom and the others had acted "to further monopolize the monopoly power acquired by them in the business of professional football in the territory of Los Angeles and its environs."

Not surprisingly, the suit never reached trial. Hugh Culverhouse was a lawyer who made far more money staying out of court than getting in. C.R. and Culverhouse met somewhere in Florida. The two quickly reached "a meeting of minds." The specific terms were not part of the public record. According to Rozelle, "Culverhouse wanted and got assurances that litigation would not be held against him in the future awarding of expansion franchises." Whatever the deal, it did not seem to make much difference when the League met in executive session on October 30, 1974. Dan Rooney reported about candidates for ownership. In the case of Seattle, the committee recommended waiting a bit longer until all the options had been further explored and "problems" nailed down. In the case of Tampa, they recommended Tom McCloskey. Rosenbloom, Steve remembered, was "upset" and "a little unnerved" at the announcement. Nonetheless, "without dissent," the League passed the following resolution shortly before adjourning:

RESOLVED, that the [Tampa] franchise . . . in the National Football League . . . be granted to Thomas B. McCloskey upon his acceptance in writing of the following terms: McCloskey is to pay . . . [16 million dollars . . .] McCloskey is to agree to divest himself of his interest in the Philadelphia Atoms of the North American Soccer League. . . . Written acceptance of these terms and conditions is to be accompanied by a minimum One Hundred Thousand Dollars in earnest money.

After the meeting, Rozelle announced McCloskey's selection to the press. Seattle's ownership, the commissioner explained, would be chosen "within a month."

Seattle greeted the League's inaction with a certain nervousness. On October 31, Herman Sarkowsky exchanged several phone calls with the League office. "We were led to believe our decision would come much sooner [than a month]," Sarkowsky griped. But in fact, the first action the expansion committee took was to offer the franchise to Hugh Culverhouse. Fortunately for Sarkowsky's group, Culverhouse declined. "No thank you," he said, "but I will wait and see where there is future expansion."

Culverhouse's wait turned out to be exceedingly short. Tom McCloskey's tenure was the briefest in NFL history. During his first few weeks in Tampa his performance was unimpressive. "Tom McCloskey seemed an okay guy," the *St. Petersburg Times* observed, "but the Tampa team appeared to be only one of a thousand interests with this construction wheel from Philly." Before Tampa had much chance to be bothered, however, McCloskey suddenly vanished from the scene. At the end of November, he informed the League that he would not be making his December payment. Rozelle would later describe the dropout as "a strange thing." One owner explained that McCloskey was in a divorce proceeding, and when his wife learned of the purchase, immediately demanded half the purchase price as her share. Another owner speculated, "I assume some pressure was brought to bear, but I don't know what happened behind the scenes." An inside League source maintained that McCloskey had been a less than serious candidate thrown in place momentarily to conceal the deal Rosenbloom and Rozelle had cut with Culverhouse back in 1972. One thing was certain: Hugh Culverhouse was now in the NFL to stay. On December 5, Culverhouse's selection to replace McCloskey in Tampa was announced along with the selection of Herman Sarkowsky's group in Seattle.

Culverhouse would become increasingly central in League business. Short and obese, with a nose widened by his days as a boxer, his courtly southern manner and slow drawl concealed what one owner called "a cool slick mind that knows how to

operate." The NFL was now among the business crossing over
Hugh Culverhouse's desk and, within a decade, he would amass
enough power and influence to rank with the likes of Tex
Schramm and Art Modell.

9
Odd Bedfellows in Cleveland

By the time Hugh Culverhouse's first check cleared the NFL's
bank, Art Modell was finishing up his first year as his own
landlord. His Cleveland Stadium Corp. reported a net 1974
income of $13,789, but its longterm financing was decidedly
shakier than it seemed.

That shakiness began in February 1974 when Modell received
a letter notifying him that his friend Shelly Guren's U.S. Realty
Company was withdrawing its commitment to form a real estate
investment trust to finance Stadium Corp. and was withdrawing
from its $8 million commitment to interim financing as well.
U.S. Realty was involved in what Robert Gries Jr. described as
"a major real estate scandal," the biggest such in Cleveland's
history. Lawsuits emanating from it would last another nine
years. Clearly, participation in Stadium Corp. was now financially impossible. The banks turned to Modell to assume Stadium Corp.'s financing personally and to do so, Modell pledged
all his Browns stock and the land he had bought in Strongsville
as collateral. He considered it a temporary arrangement and
started looking for new partners to share his loans.

Modell's search focused on Robert Gries Jr., his partner in the
Cleveland Browns. Though invisible to the football business's
public, Gries had an abiding interest in the Browns and a significant civic standing in Cleveland. Both factors made him seem a
natural for Cleveland Stadium Corp. His father had taken the
family into the football business in 1936 when he purchased a
piece of the Cleveland Rams. Robert Gries Jr. considered the
Grieses the fourth oldest family in the NFL, after the Halases,
Rooneys, and Maras. Robert Gries Sr. remained an owner until
1943, when the franchise was purchased by Dan Reeves. In
1946, Reeves moved the Rams to Los Angeles and that same

year the Browns were founded in the old All-American Conference. Robert Gries Sr. was among the Browns' original owners and his presence in the new ownership had been a precondition of the sale to Modell in 1963. "To my father," Robert Gries Jr. remembered, "football was a civic kind of enterprise."

Gries Jr. had been educated at an eastern prep school and then graduated from Yale in 1951. After working for the family business until 1963, he started Gries Investment Company, his own venture capital business. Despite what he called the business's "very high risk" nature, Gries did well at it. Thin and handsome, Gries ran marathons for relaxation and served on the boards of fifty civic enterprises, from hospitals to universities. When his father died in 1966, Robert took the helm of Gries Sports Enterprises, the family's football holding company.

Ironically, it was Gries who initiated contact with Modell over Cleveland Stadium Corp.'s longterm financing. Gries thought Guren's withdrawal presented a potentially lucrative "corporate opportunity" for the Browns. There were, Gries pointed out, great advantages to the football franchise in controlling its stadium. Since he considered the Browns' twenty-five-year lease "the bulwark of what made this whole Stadium Corp. idea viable," why should the two operations be separate? Why not have the Browns buy in?

Art Modell's response was both negative and, according to Gries, "adamant." The baseball Indians, Stadium Corp.'s other tenant, "would never allow it," and on top of that the city "prefers a separate entity" as well. Gries argued that at least the Browns ought to consider it. The Browns, Modell countered, had neither the money nor the credit worthiness for this type of project. They could not afford to get involved in a $10 million obligation. When the franchise had an outstanding debt of $8 million. He had "worked out an extremely favorable lease for the Browns," Modell pointed out, and "under no circumstances" would he consider bringing the Browns into Stadium Corp.

Art Modell's attitude irritated Robert Gries Jr., and he seriously considered taking Modell to court for allegedly violating his obligations to Cleveland Browns, Inc., but instead, he finally suggested that perhaps they should "explore an equitable participation in Cleveland Stadium Corp." Unable to make Modell budge on selling to the Browns, Gries was willing to discuss having himself and Gries Sports Enterprises buy into Stadium Corp. That, of course, was what Art Modell had wanted to hear all along. He wanted Gries to come in for forty-five percent of

Stadium Corp. and involve his family in guaranteeing Stadium Corp.'s bank loans. As part of the package, Modell was to be given an "employment agreement providing for reasonable compensation." In addition, Cleveland Stadium Corp. would purchase Modell's 192 acres in Strongsville for $2.1 million, almost three times what he had paid for the property three years earlier.

On this last point, Gries took a "vigorous position" and held his ground. He was, he told Modell, interested in the Browns and not the land development business in Strongsville. Modell protested that he had bought the land "to protect the Browns," but he finally backed off and dropped the Strongsville land from his proposal.

Though slowly, he and Gries continued refining the possible terms of Stadium Corp.'s reorganization through much of 1975. The Cleveland patrician and the New York hustler made an oddly matched couple for the very few who knew they were partners.

10
1975 Woes: Labor and Competition

Pete Rozelle led off the 1975 NFL annual meeting with his customary report. "1974 had included the third largest attendance in league history . . . [and] a Super Bowl game that attracted the largest number of viewing homes for any type of program in the history of television." The two principal problem areas Rozelle identified were the NFLPA and the WFL. The required response: increased devotion to League Think. The NFL could continue to be successful, "if the power, intelligence, and poise the League commands [is] used wisely and without divisive pettiness and purely emotional reactions."

On the WFL front, all the news was good. In spring 1975, seventy-five percent of its players were still owed back salary. Collective losses among the twelve franchises totaled $3.2 million and only five of the original ownerships were still around. *The New York Times Magazine* had dubbed the first WFL championship game "Super Flop I." It had pitted the Florida Blazers against the Birmingham Americans. The Blazer players had not been paid for ten weeks and their coach personally had to supply toilet paper for the locker room. The Americans, who won the game, had their game jerseys confiscated by creditors while they were celebrating. WFL Commissioner Gary Davidson, who had once claimed "there is absolutely no way this league can fail," was now retired from the football business.

Davidson's replacement was Chris Hemmeter, who planned to salvage the WFL by pursuing a drastic reorganization. According to his plan, all teams would have to adopt a standard internal economics: 42 percent of gate and television revenues to the salaries of players and coaches, 10 percent to stadium rental, 10.5 percent to league assessments, and 37.5 percent to fixed costs such as offices and travel. During the 1975 off season, each owner was required to pay league debts, make a down payment on delinquent player salaries, and provide working capital. Seven of the eleven WFL ownership groups now included at least one banker. Hemmeter struggled mightily to rebuild the WFL's credibility, insisting, despite his monumental problems, "This is the league of the future."

The statement was a subject of NFL laughter. The WFL's revival plan was dependent on the players accepting a percentage of the gross, an unprecedented step, and even if they did accept Hemmeter's forty-two percent figure, the longterm contracts that had been given NFL stars to lure them away were still in force and had to be paid regardless. Typically, the contracts of former Joe Robbie employees Csonka, Kiick, and Warfield with owner John Bassett that had set off the player raids were for "personal services." That meant, one player observed, "even if there's no football team, those guys got to walk around and do whatever the dude say do. But that's cool if they get paid."

Chuckle as they might, the NFL's own labor relations were almost as problematical. There had been some hope in 1974 that the NFLPA Plan B wouldn't work. With no contract in place, Ed Garvey had to collect union dues himself. Eventually, the union offered belt buckles to teams whose dues were paid up. Garvey himself went "in debt up to my keester" and the NFLPA reported $600,000 in losses. Nonetheless, Plan B had held into 1975 and the deadlock continued. The League insisted that any contract include acceptance of the Rozelle Rule and Garvey held his ground, saying the Rozelle Rule should be left up to courts and *Mackey v. NFL*.

The Mackey case was central to Garvey's strategy. "You had to break the Rozelle Rule to have an effective union," he argued. The argument that carried the most weight inside the union was financial. The average NFL salary had remained at $25,000 a year since 1968. Free agency was the most obvious way to break out. Garvey argued that once they won *Mackey v. NFL*, it would "force them to negotiate with us to get it back instead of us begging for scraps. . . . We had to win," Garvey remembered. "If we lost *Mackey,* we were out."

Mackey v. NFL began trial in February 1975, in Minneapolis. Both sides had agreed to have the case decided by a judge rather than by a jury. "We had two attorneys," Garvey recalled, "one of whom was me. The NFL had eight or nine. On the opening day, one of their lawyers said, 'This case is all about young men who've grown rich and famous beyond their dreams who have come to malign the system that made them rich and famous. . . .' We heard that rich owners would devour the weak by purchasing all the talent, build a superteam, and thus destroy the very entity he seeks to dominate. . . . We heard that elimination of the Rozelle Rule would kill the NFL as we know it today. We heard . . . that poor Green Bay and Minnesota would soon lose their franchises in a free market. In modern times there has never been a free market for professional athletes, so clearly any such speculation is exactly that; nevertheless, it is used to justify all the controls used to deny players their freedom of choice.''

All told, *Mackey v. NFL* consumed fifty-five days in court, generating more than twelve thousand pages of testimony. At its current rate, the attorneys noted, the trial would not finish until July and a decision might not be issued until 1976. Any appeals might well consume at least another year after that. In the meantime, the League could only wait.

11
Al Davis: Some Charges Are Made

Among the "legal, political, and public relations problems" Pete Rozelle predicted for the NFL in March 1975, no single person would be more responsible than Al Davis, the Oakland Raiders' managing general partner. Immediately after the 1975 annual meeting, Davis was preoccupied with securing his control over the franchise once and for all. The last stumbling block in that process was Wayne Valley, the man who had hired him in the first place. In May 1975, two years after it was filed, *Valley v. Davis* came to trial in California Superior Court. It was the second most watched courtroom drama in the NFL that spring.

Valley v. Davis opened with Wayne Valley on the stand. He admitted that Davis had made an obscure reference to the new contract some six weeks after Valley's other general partner, Ed McGah, had signed the document sight unseen in June 1972. The next Valley had heard on the subject was in October 1972, when Buffalo Bills owner Ralph Wilson mentioned to Valley that Davis had claimed McGah had given him a new contract. "I don't believe it," Valley responded. "I would know about it." Valley actually saw the document when his auditor found it among the franchise's business records. When he confronted Davis about it in February 1973, Valley claimed Davis had responded, "Wayne, I could write a twenty-five-year contract myself and you couldn't do anything about it." That Valley considered Davis unscrupulous at best was obvious.

The shadows surrounding the persona of Al Davis darkened dramatically on June 1, after *Valley v. Davis* had been running for less than two weeks and before Davis himself had taken the stand. That morning's [Oakland] *Tribune* featured a front-page story about Davis's real estate partnership with one Allen Glick. At the time, Glick, controlled four Las Vegas casinos and was described by federal investigators as "a straw party controlled by the organized crime syndicate." When checking Glick out, *The Tribune*'s reporter had run across the name "Allen R. Davis" as an investor in some of Glick's California real estate holdings.

183

The reporter was puzzled. "What is he doing in business with Allen Glick?" he asked.

The correct answer, was "making money," something for which Allen Glick seemed to have a knack. Five years earlier, Glick had been an obscure San Diego lawyer and real estate developer. Now, *Business Week* labeled him "a contender to Howard Hughes" for the title "King of the Las Vegas strip." Glick's meteoric rise began with a financial vehicle called Saratoga Development Corp. After serving as assistant to Saratoga's president for two years, Glick claimed to have been "more or less given" a forty-five percent interest in the San Diego based company, though he was less than clear about the circumstances. In 1972, he connected with Al Davis through a San Diego attorney who had once played for the Chargers in the AFL. At the time, Saratoga Development Corp. "were very successful developers with a very impressive clientele," an attorney remembered. "They were doing real estate deals with private capital [and] they had a number of professional athletes working for them. . . . I thought Al Davis would be a prospect and so I brought them together."

"I listened to one or two propositions," Davis later recalled. "They involved a minimal amount of investment. Some complexes in La Jolla. I am not sure. I think it was a million or two million dollars. And I liked the deal. . . . I sent an attorney down to see the property, and, et cetera, like that. [Then] I formed a limited partnership with several owners in the National Football League. We invested in the deal." The limited partnership Davis formed was Red Dog Investors and its participants included Carroll Rosenbloom, Buffalo Bills owner Ralph Wilson, and Don Shula, Joe Robbie's coach and minority partner. The rewards were apparently high. "That deal became a very profitable situation for us," Davis admitted, "so we formed another partnership. This time, I don't know, we invested somewhere between a million and two million dollars." This second limited partnership was called Blue Chip Investors. Davis also formed his own partnership with Glick, called GWD Associates.

In 1973, Saratoga Development Corp. became a springboard to Las Vegas. Glick's first purchase there was the Hacienda Hotel and Casino. His share of the deal was $2.3 million, which was loaned to him by Saratoga Development. Shortly thereafter, he also bought the Stardust and Freemont Hotel-Casinos with financing supplied by a Teamsters' pension fund to the tune of

$62,750,000. In one stroke, Glick, age thirty-one, with "exactly four and one half years' experience in the business world," had become the second largest borrower in the history of the Teamsters' pension fund and he was by no means yet done. By 1975, he built the Las Vegas Airport Marina Casino, again using Teamster pension fund money. The fund itself already had a reputation for borrowers "who had been jailed by federal authorities for crimes ranging from fraud to kickbacks." When asked by *Business Week* why the fund was so supportive of him in particular, Glick cited his "management ability" and "timing."

By 1974, however, Allen Glick was, *The* [Oakland] *Tribune* revealed, under investigation by the Justice Department's Organized Crime Strike Force, the Nevada Gaming Control Board, the Labor Department, the Securities and Exchange Commission, and the Internal Revenue Service. Davis quickly withdrew of all the football money he had brought into Saratoga Development through Red Dog and Blue Chip. "Allen became linked with . . . a supposedly federal inquiry into his ties with Central States Fund and the Mafia," Al Davis remembered. "At that time, I . . . got every owner and every coach and everyone out of their investments with all their money back."

"Everyone," of course, but Davis himself. He saw "nothing wrong" with Glick's Las Vegas connections. Instead of backing off, he loaned Saratoga Development some $250,000 to help liquidate Red Dog, Blue Chip, and their own GWD. Davis also began a new investment with Glick around the same time called Eastmont Mall Associates, headquartered in Oakland, which was the tip of the iceberg first stumbled over by *The Tribune* in spring 1975. Opened in 1966, Eastmont Mall was originally financed with a $25 million loan from the Teamsters' pension fund. Its previous owner had been arrested in a federal gambling raid in 1970 and died in 1973. Glick took over Eastmont in 1974 after agreeing to assume the payments on the pension fund's loan. Glick offered Davis twenty-five percent of the limited partnership of Eastmont Mall Associates. Davis remembered that he was "a limited partner with no management affair in the business. They thought by bringing me in in Oakland, it would somehow or other bring image or stature to the shopping center. . . . It was the most expensive shopping center built in the United States."

It also generated very profitable tax losses. At one point, the facility's manager would claim Glick and Davis fired him for making the shopping center "too successful." Over the next ten years, though Eastmont made no money itself, Al Davis's $5000 investment would save him an estimated $1 million in taxes. Saratoga Development filed for bankruptcy in May 1975. One of Glick's original partners in Saratoga would die in prison from a heart attack. Another, who was working as a "consultant" to Eastmont Mall in 1975, would be found dead in her living room, shot five times in the head and neck, just six months later.

Neither Davis nor Glick was "available for comment" on *The Tribune*'s June 1 story. In the meantime, the revelations fueled a flurry of headlines along the wire services—"Financier Denies Tie With Crime" and "Davis—A Link to the Mob?" Pete Rozelle also refused any public comment on Davis's connection with Glick. The most *The Tribune* could get was a comment from a "spokesman" for the commissioner that the Davis-Glick partnership "looks like a small investment."

On June 5, Ed Garvey demanded an investigation. "Every time there is the slightest suggestion of a player being involved with 'unsavory characters,' " the union head pointed out, "there's a hue and cry." Garvey focused his attack on Rozelle, telling the New York *Daily News,* "He's always been a puppet of the owners. . . . It's obvious you can't expect anything but a double standard from the commissioner." While Garvey's acid comments no doubt stung Rozelle, he maintained his public silence. Privately, however, he dispatched "one of the League security guys" to interview Davis shortly after *The Tribune* story came out. The investigator, according to Davis, "found that all it was was a business deal." Later, Davis claimed, he and the investigator would laugh "about the fact that the League . . . was using the Allen Glick association to try and hurt me publicly." In the meantime, Rozelle explained, "the League didn't feel it could do anything. We asked Al to get out but, in effect, he refused. It was never really a League matter."

Al Davis also continued to refuse all public comment. Privately, according to *The Tribune*'s George Ross, "He just passed the word out that I had engineered the whole thing to embarrass him" in the middle of his suit with Wayne Valley. If that was indeed the intent, it had none of the desired effect. When Davis took the stand, he showed no signs of intimidation. He had, he maintained, informed Valley in person of his new contract before he and McGah had signed it and over the telephone afterward. There was, he claimed, nothing out of the ordinary about the new powers it granted him and that he had always operated the Raiders with "a free hand." McGah, he pointed out, thought the arrangement was a good deal.

To reinforce that notion, the defense called Leonard Tose of the Philadelphia Eagles. Tose claimed he had tried to hire Davis in 1971 and 1972, immediately before the new contract was signed, and was "so anxious" to do so that he offered him ten to fifteen percent of the club. "Al," Tose recalled saying, "you can write your own ticket." Davis admitted he had been "intrigued" by Tose's offer and had also entertained similar proposals from the Houston Oilers and Los Angeles Rams. He also repeated that Valley knew about the new contract ahead of time.

On June 18, the judge heard final arguments and then took the case under advisement. His decision was delivered two months later. The outcome appeared a tie: Davis's new contract was upheld, but the expanded powers it included were thrown out. "A Solomon-like decision," Wayne Valley offered, "he cut the baby in half." The real winner, however, was Al Davis. "Al kicked his ass," a Davis associate bragged, "and Valley couldn't take it anymore." Preoccupied with other business and unwilling to stay in the Raiders with a man he no longer trusted, Valley would sell all his holdings in the franchise by January 1976, leaving Al Davis with absolute control. "A lot of people were sorry to see Wayne Valley go," Lamar Hunt remembered.

When Davis arrived at the NFL's June 1975 meeting, he acted as though Valley were already gone. Never short on confidence, he seemed unfazed by having been linked to the mob and called a liar by his partner in open court. If anything, the experience only seemed to have made him bolder. "Al Davis always wanted to be commissioner," Gene Klein pointed out. One of the proofs later offered to support that statement would be Davis's behavior when the NFL discussed the WFL.

During the preceding spring while the new league was reorganizing, Davis and Carroll Rosenbloom had met with the WFL's John Bassett, who, according to Rozelle, "was hustling the idea of a merger." Neither Davis nor Rosenbloom would ever report to the rest of the League about their discussions, but in June, Davis tried to seize the initiative on the issue. Walking to the blackboard, Al Davis chalked the figure $12 million per franchise and then multiplied it by ten. That, Davis told the group, was how much money they could make by merging themselves with the infant league and putting their war to an end. It was, he claimed, "a great way to make a lot of money."

Gene Klein immediately laughed out loud. Rozelle pointed out that there would be Sherman Act dilemmas, just like the last time. Tex Schramm observed that Davis "must have thought he was talking to the World Football League." Leonard Tose thought it was the "dumbest idea Al Davis ever had." Art Modell called it "really Disneyland." According to one of the NFL attorneys in the room, the predominant response was "snickering."

12
Old Billy on the Rebound

Al Davis made no formal report to the NFL's 1975 meeting about the status of Oakland's ownership. The only such ownership reports were by Edward Bennett Williams, about the Washington Redskins, and Bob Marr, about the New England Patriots.

Williams addressed his now one-year-old promise that Jack Kent Cooke would divest his cross-ownership "conflict of interest." Cooke had not, according to Williams, "been able to perform, and the commissioner had been assured that he tried." The problem was the market; Cooke couldn't sell for what he thought his holdings were worth. He would, of course, continue "to try," but exactly what that meant was "clouded at this point." Some owners' vented their continued frustration on the issue of compliance with ownership policy, it led to no resolution.

Marr's report followed, and many in the room counted the news as exceedingly welcome. Hessie Sargent had finally given in out of "loyalty to her departed husband." George Sargent had been the very first outsider involved by Billy in the Patriot ownership, a fact the Sullivans had not let Hessie forget during the fourteen months since she had voted for Billy's removal. With the Sargent shares his, Sullivan would now control a clear majority. The membership was first notified officially of the proposed transfer by a letter in which Rozelle "recommended that the transfer be approved." An immediate vote was taken by telex.

Old Billy lobbied hard in advance of the vote. Exile was not a comfortable situation for him. He told anyone interested that he was keeping busy writing a biography of Cardinal Cushing, but it was obvious that football was where he wanted to be. The day votes were wired in, he showed up at the offices of the New

York Jets and visited his friend Phil Iselin, Jets president. Billy asked Iselin to phone Rozelle's office and find out the results. Iselin gladly did so. "I want to be the first to verbally augment my telex vote," the Jets president told the assistant he spoke to.

"You're too late," the assistant responded. "People have been calling all day. Mr. Sullivan has the votes." Officially the count was twenty-seven yes, one no. The no vote had been Bob Marr's.

By itself, however, the vote was not enough to return Billy Sullivan to the NFL. Two significant roadblocks remained. The first of those was financial. Rozelle had ruled earlier that whoever bought control in the fight would also have to offer to buy out the others. Since McConnell and Wetenhall had an agreement whereby they could force the sale of the Marrs' interest as well, the Marrs also would have to be paid. That kind of money was thought to be enough to stop Billy in his tracks. The New Yorkers had not, however, counted on Chuck Sullivan. Chuck understood financing from his Wall Street law practice and knew where and how to get it. Buying out the voting shares was only phase one of his strategy.

In order to finance phase one, the Sullivans had to go even further and, in a second phase, buy up all the nonvoting shares, whether their owners wanted to sell or not. In so doing, the franchise itself could be pledged as collateral and the whole package could be financed. The LaSalle National Bank of Chicago was prepared to take the majority of the offering but only if the Sullivans offered as additional security the entire assets of the New England Patriots: "the franchise granted by the National Football League, all of its contracts with its players and coaches, all proceeds and revenues from television and radio contracts . . . and its rights as lessee to Schaeffer Stadium, Foxboro, Massachusetts, or any other location where it plays its regular season home games." For those assets to be pledged, the franchise had to be Sullivan's personal property. Making it so would amount to phase two. Thus, even with financing in place, it was still, as Bob Marr made clear in his League report, by no means a certainty.

The second remaining roadblock was legal. The Sargent shares were held by the George L. Sargent Trust and their sale would require both the approval of both its trustees and the probate court. The trustees were no problem. The difficulties were in Probate Court, where McConnell and Wetenhall had decided to make their last stand. "If the court tells the trustees that it would be in the best interest of the Sargent heirs to sell to Sullivan at this time," *The Boston Globe* explained, "then Sullivan would gain enough stock to put him back in command."

The New Yorkers were asking the court to enjoin such a sale. Though the Sargent Trust was bound by written agreement to sell only to Billy, if the trustees waited until December 1977, when that agreement ran out, McConnell and Wetenhall were prepared to purchase the shares at a much higher price than Sullivan had offered. The trust's beneficiaries would be better served, they argued, by taking the second offer. Chuck Sullivan responded in court that the New Yorkers' offer was "frivolous." McConnell and Wetenhall's then produced a certified check for $1,000,000 as a nonrefundable deposit. The New Yorkers' case was significantly strengthened when Lee Sargent, Hessie's son and one of the trust's two beneficiaries, joined in asking that the Sullivan sale be blocked.

Marr was nonetheless unwilling to admit defeat on June 25. "This is just another move in a game that has been going on for years," he pointed out for the benefit of those already prepared to celebrate Old Billy's resurrection. "No one, I mean no one, knows how this is all going to turn out. Whatever happens is going to take a long, long time."

13
Rosenbloom versus the Rozelle Rule

Whatever happened in New England, the League's dominant concern throughout that summer continued to be *Mackey v. NFL* and defense of the Rozelle Rule from Ed Garvey's Plan B. The courtroom confrontation with the NFLPA continued until July 19. Among the horde of witnesses called to bolster the NFL's position were two former players association presidents and the union's former legal counsel. Also, the League managed to maintain its own solid front. Even C.R. fell into line. He testified that the Rozelle Rule was "essential" to maintain football's "competitive balance."

Shortly thereafter, however, Rosenbloom went his own way again and set off more than a year of open conflict with Pete Rozelle. Later, the League remembered their series of collisions as a "war." At the time it began, both men had absorbed many changes in their personal lives and, at least outside of football, seemed content.

For Rozelle, those changes revolved around his marriage to Carrie. Gone was the apartment on Sutton Place and the evenings spent catching a movie with Bill McPhail or a few laughs with Art Modell. Gone also were his days as a single parent. In their place was the new red brick Tudor house in Westchester and a suddenly bustling family life: his daughter from his first marriage and Carrie's four children from her first marriage lived with them. The suburban life-style suited Pete. There was a swimming pool out the back door and tennis courts on which to battle the bulge at the waist of his once skinny frame. The Tudor was the first house he had ever owned, and he soon came to prefer quiet evenings there to socializing in the city. He described himself as "very comfortable" financially.

Asked to describe the most difficult thing he'd done as commissioner, Rozelle answered "the merger with the AFL." Asked to describe his job vis-à-vis the owners, he chose the words "counseling" and "educating." The worst thing about his job was "the loss of privacy." And he claimed to have adjusted to spending an ever-growing portion of his work time in court. "Litigation has become a way of life for me," he explained. "It's an unpleasant way of life, but I'm inured to it now. We get sued all the time. The first time, I was uptight. . . . Now I just ask my attorneys when I have to give my next deposition." There was, however, much worse to come.

For Carroll Rosenbloom, the adjustment to southern California had been easy. "He has become," the *Los Angeles Times* pointed out, "a dedicated Californian . . . with a carefully chosen California life-style." Most of his friends were in the entertainment business and C.R. and his wife spent a lot of time playing tennis with them. By this point in his life, while not revered like the saints of the Old Guard, Carroll was still considered something of a dean in the football business and he enjoyed the stature.

While in New York for the June League meetings, Rosenbloom was the guest of honor at a dinner of the Pro Football Writers Association, where he was awarded the Arthur Daley Memorial Award for long and meritorious service. In accepting the award, "Rosenbloom repeated what he has been saying for some time—lashing out at the owners, blaming himself and the others for 'stupidity' in outrageously squandering so much money, and for building up inflated operational budgets." C.R.'s greatest vituperation was reserved for the litigation process in which the

League seemed mired. He said that lawyers were costing each of the NFL's members at least $200,000 a year. "We never get out of court," he complained. "One day lawyers and accountants may own every franchise in the League."

Back in California, Rosenbloom's life was divided between his estate in Bel-Air and the house at Trancas Beach, his favorite. He began his days there at 7:00 A.M. with breakfast and business calls, but by 8:00, he was on the beach with his dogs. He repeated the routine in the evening and usually managed to get in several sets of tennis in between. He prided himself in looking much younger than his almost seven decades. Most everyone who met C.R. considered him handsome. When the Rams were in training camp, a helicopter ferried him there every morning, where he mingled among players and coaches, addressing each by name. During afternoon rush hour, he helicoptered back to Trancas Beach.

One of the great solaces in Rosenbloom's southern California life was living next to the Pacific Ocean. "When night comes," Rosenbloom explained, "I love to go to bed with a good book and listen to the waves." Even when staying in Bel-Air, he slept with the stereo playing one of "those records that have nothing but the sound of the ocean washing up on the beach. . . . I've been a beachcomber all my life. The ocean does for me what the desert does for others. They like the stillness. I never tire of listening to the ocean or looking at it." Four years later, those words would have a haunting quality.

While Rosenbloom's relationship with Rozelle had been relatively quiet since C.R. had moved west, the Rams owner's resentment had by no means diminished. He was also considerably vexed about how the League was doing business. His son Steve remembered, "The League had hired an in-house attorney and Rozelle had turned him into his personal employee. When Carroll complained, the guy took the position he was the commissioner's attorney, not the owners'. . . . That upset my father. He was also upset that he couldn't get financial information out of the League office . . . and he wanted to know how the money was being spent. He was a business guy. He didn't go for being brushed off. It got to the point where he was going to have the League audited. Carroll needed a good fight and felt Rozelle and the League office were getting too arrogant. He was one of the few who would stand up to them. Most of the rest of the owners were jellyfish. Carroll had scared the League shitless a number of times." In July 1975, yet another of those times was approaching rapidly.

Carroll Rosenbloom's greatest frustration in life remained his failure to win a Super Bowl with the Rams. Carroll was convinced he was only one additional player away from the championship and he already knew who the player was: Ron Jessie, wide receiver for William Clay Ford's Detroit Lions. Jessie's contract with the Lions had expired with the 1974 season and he was technically a free agent, covered by the sanctions of the Rozelle Rule that C.R. had just finished defending. However, Rosenbloom signed Jessie before the trial's closing arguments.

Despite his reputation for smoothing rough edges, Rozelle was not averse to what he called "putting my foot down." Known for not picking fights, he had a surprising record of taking them when offered. In this instance, the penalty he announced was arguably the most severe in the history of the Rozelle Rule. On the four previous occasions Rozelle had invoked his rule since it was formally established in 1963, none of the awards had involved veteran performers. Looking over his shoulder at the Minneapolis federal court then considering a decision in *Mackey v. NFL*, Rozelle apparently felt the timing of C.R.'s move deserved a precedent-setting penalty. On July 25 the commissioner announced that his award to the Lions was one Cullen Bryant, a promising Ram fullback and two-year veteran. Depending on Bryant's contribution to the Lions during the next season, Rozelle also held out the possibility of giving the Lions some unspecified Ram draft choices as well. "Rozelle Rule Hits Rams," the *Los Angeles Times* headlined.

Rosenbloom was anything but pleased with the decision. He was convinced Bryant was on the verge of stardom and the commissioner's ruling left him still one player short in his obsessive quest. Cullen Bryant filed suit, attempting to invoke the Sherman Act to void Rozelle's award, and it was, as one L.A. sports columnist remembered it, "no secret that Carroll had set up Bryant's fight." Rozelle reached the same conclusion. It was a stab in the League's collective back and worse still, in its opening round, the suit looked decidedly threatening.

At an initial hearing in District Court, the judge delivered what was described as a "stinging rebuke to the NFL" and temporarily enjoined any enforcement of Rozelle's award. "I think the Rozelle Rule . . . violates Section I of the Sherman Anti-trust Act," the judge declared. Another preliminary hearing was set for August 12. However, Rozelle was not about to let *Bryant v. NFL* get that far. He was in a potentially lethal legal crossfire and had no choice but to cut his losses and regroup. On

August 2, the commissioner voided his previous award to the Lions and replaced it with the Rams' first and second round choices in the next player draft. Rozelle offered no comment on his change of mind.

The same could not be said of the Lions. The franchise's head coach, Rick Forzano, aimed straight at Carroll Rosenbloom. He told the *Los Angeles Times,* that Rosenbloom was the "most selfish owner in professional football. . . . I believe Rosenbloom wants to win so badly he would really go as far as this—to cheat another team. He is hurting professional football . . . [and] he could destroy the strong foundation of the game's support."

C.R. gave the criticism short shrift. "If you call 'selfish' attempting to bring the best possible team together for our fans," he replied, "well, yes, I am selfish. The Rams have acted according to the regulations and the spirit of the regulations of the National Football League. All this is a matter of record and nothing further needs to be said."

Ignoring Rosenbloom's admonition, the Lions responded the next day. This time the complaint came from William Clay Ford, their owner, in a public letter to C.R. Ford's presence in the fight was extraordinary: the automobile heir played virtually no active role in NFL affairs. His letter was one of two cameo appearances in the decade. "It is my opinion," he wrote Rosenbloom, "that you and your organization have done more to harm professional football than anyone in the history of the NFL. Several weeks ago you testified in Minneapolis that the so-called Rozelle Rule was necessary to maintain 'competitive balance' in the League, but this was apparently hypocrisy. . . . You have made a mockery of the compensation rule. . . . I hope all sports and football in particular have not been too badly damaged."

C.R.'s answer was again short and testy. He was waiting for Rozelle to enforce the section of the NFL constitution that prohibited owners from making public criticism of each other. His wait, however, was fruitless. Rozelle simply let the issue drop.

Rosenbloom was furious, convinced that if he was in Ford's position, Rozelle would have levied a fine. Now, not content with having bloodied Rozelle and forced him to back off on the Rozelle Rule, Rosenbloom wanted, as one NFL owner put it, "to get" Pete Rozelle any way he could. His first step was to hire a private detective to collect whatever dirt on Rozelle he could find before the next League meeting.

14
The WFL Collapses

When the 1975 season began, the League still awaited a decision in *Mackey v. NFL* and stalemate continued on the labor front. In the League's other external war, however, victory was in sight. The reorganized WFL had begun its second season and even its most prestigious owner, Memphis's John Bassett, could offer little optimism about their chances. "It's like a brand new car," he told *Sports Illustrated*. "Once you've wrecked it, no matter how well it's fixed up, it's never the same." By October, impending collapse was apparent everywhere:

First went the Chicago Wind, expelled in September for failing financially when the franchise's two principal investors withdrew. Asked to identify those investors, one of the Wind's vice-presidents replied, "George and Rich from California. I don't know their last names, but one's an Arab and the other's a Greek."

When the Southern California Sun played the Philadelphia Bell in Philadelphia, the scene was stark. "When we came out to warm up," a Sun wide receiver remembered, "I looked around and there wasn't one person in the stands. Not one. . . . I think we ended up with 3,100." The Bell had arrived at the stadium in an old school bus that was losing its back door. At first the stadium guard thought it was a busful of migrant workers and wouldn't let it in. When the bus finally clunked inside, the back door broke open and several players fell out. "To save money," the Bell's quarterback remembered, "we always seemed to arrive at a hotel at one in the morning and then played the game, leaving as soon as we showered. Once . . . we got on a bus in Philadelphia and it broke down and we had to get out, carry our bags, and hitchhike."

When a storm knocked out power to the Honolulu Hawaiians' locker room, the players assumed it was an economy measure and the coach ordered the team bus to shine its lights through the locker room window. The Charlotte Hornets' practice field had no goal posts or yard markers and it's locker room had only four showers. Eventually they were evicted for nonpayment of rent. During a game between the Hawaiians and the Sun, a fight broke out on the field and both benches emptied. When the referee threatened to fine anyone who didn't stop immediately, a player yelled, "Fined from what?" and everyone started laughing so hard the fight died.

By October the death of the WFL was imminent. John Bassett's attorneys met with Pete Rozelle and his assistants to formally notify the NFL that the WFL was "in danger of financial collapse." Bassett's Memphis franchise and the group running Birmingham would "obtain title to all of the WFL's good players" and both Bassett and Birmingham intended to apply for membership as "ongoing entities" in the NFL. Rozelle only noted that anyone who wanted to was free to apply at any time. On October 22, the WFL's end was official. Commissioner Chris Hemmeter wrote to Pete Rozelle, praising the NFL and sadly admitting there was little possibility a second league could survive. Fittingly, the Hawaiian Hemmeter signed the letter, "Aloha."

The WFL's capitulation was complete and final. When Hemmeter's announcement was made, the Southern California Sun's phone bank, ringing regularly the moment before, immediately went dead—disconnected. The San Antonio Wings' public relations man cleaned out his desk and headed for his company car, provided gratis by a local Chevrolet dealer. Before he reached the parking lot, the car had been repossessed.

It must have been a satisfying moment for Rozelle. This was his first victory over a rival league and was at least some counter to Al Davis's sneering claim to have whipped him the last time out. It was also some balm for his recent thumping at the hands of Rosenbloom. But most important, the NFL's monopoly over the business of football was once again without exception. On that front at least, his much-cherished "stability" was intact and League Think triumphant.

15
Old Billy Comes Back

That fall, the commissioner added another entry in his "stability" ledger as well, this one concerning ownership policy. By the end of October, the New England Patriots were about to redeem Billy Sullivan's nine-year-old promise to comply with the fifty-one percent rule.

At the Probate Court hearings, Chuck had reinforced his father's case by invoking the Sullivans' credentials with the NFL. Billy's friend Joe Robbie made a strong witness to that effect, arguing that it would be a mistake for the Sargent Trust to wait and hope for a better deal from the New Yorkers. He maintained that the "other NFL owners would never approve McConnell and Wetenhall as majority owners." Billy Sullivan was a "League leader" and McConnell and Wetenhall were an unknown. The NFL preferred Sullivan "to continue to be the voice of the Patriots." The judge took the case under advisement and scheduled another hearing to announce a decision in early October.

Old Billy's breakthrough came before the judge could act. "McConnell and Wetenhall got cold feet," said Bob Marr, and accepted a last minute offer to sell out. That meant all the club's voting stock would become Billy's and the probate court action would no longer be contested. According to Marr, "McConnell and Wetenhall were afraid that if the court decision went against them, then their stock would lose a lot of value when Billy took control." To complete the settlement, Sullivan borrowed $5.3 million from two banks and bought the stock of the Sargent Trust, the Marrs, and McConnell. Wetenhall was paid with a $1.7-million note to be paid off by 1982. The only other outstanding voting stock was owned by Billy's cousin Mary, and she assigned its votes to Billy by irrevocable proxy.

As part of the paperwork for Billy Sullivan's loan, Pete Rozelle dispatched a letter to the bank, establishing the terms under which it would dispose of the franchise should Sullivan default. It was a standard League procedure whenever NFL holdings were pledged as collateral and in Billy Sullivan's case it seemed

particularly appropriate. The total financial obligation he assumed in the buyout was more than twice what he was worth.
Billy's "financial situation was marginal at the time," Rozelle
remembered, "but this was an individual who had helped found
the AFL in 1959, and I knew that the member clubs were
intending to support him all the way."

"It's been a long hard struggle," Billy crowed when his
victory over the New Yorkers became public knowledge. "I've
put so much into the Patriots and I just didn't want to give up.
This was just a very happy moment for me. I just had a feeling
of tremendous relief that all of this trouble was behind me."
Though the comeback added a whole new chapter to Billy's
legend, it was his son, Chuck, who gained the most stature from
the transaction. "Chuck Sullivan worked out the myriad financial and legal moves for the family end-around play." *The
Boston Globe* pointed out. "He discovered clauses in the agreements to sell stock. He devised ways to apply pressure. He found
sources of money. He won." Unlike his father, however, Chuck
was well aware the Sullivan's troubles were by no means yet
behind them, and quickly turned his attention to phase two.
Without it, everything could still fall apart.

In the meantime, Billy's first step was to name a new board of
directors, Four of whom were named Sullivan. Their first act
would be to elect Billy president.

For his part, Bob Marr was sad to leave. He was convinced
that if the New Yorkers had waited for the probate court to
decide, everything would have gone the other way. Whatever
Marr thought was now, however, of no import. "Billy's back!"
the *Globe* exclaimed. "You wonder how Pope Rozelle has run
the religion without him. . . . Billy gave us a million laughs, a
million tears, a million smiles, a million scowls. . . . He may be
delightful and/or destructive, but he won't be dull."

According to Rozelle, "a lot of people were happy to have
Billy back," himself among them.

16
Rosenbloom Leaps for the Jugular

The NFL meetings in November 1975 belonged not to the Sullivans, but rather to Carroll Rosenbloom. Still seething, C.R. arrived in New York prepared to go after Rozelle in no uncertain terms.

One of C.R.'s frustrations was his private eye's lack of success. Pete Rozelle was an exceedingly difficult person upon whom to find dirt. The commissioner didn't run around with women and, though he drank, it was rarely to excess. He had nothing to do with gambling outside some navy poker games during World War II. He was scrupulous about his personal behavior. With or without a scandal, however, Rosenbloom had come to New York to attack.

His anger just simmered through the first two days while the members set up the mechanics of stocking the two new franchises with players. The November 6 executive session spent the first hour or so considering the technicalities of player contract signings. Then Carroll Rosenbloom addressed the meeting. His address lasted for well over an hour. C.R. had been up late the night before working on it and referred to notes on a yellow legal pad. "He had stood up several times before and had something to say," his son Steve remembered. "He got more and more upset that Rozelle's arrogance was not being challenged. Carroll expected business answers to business questions and all he got was the runaround. I knew he was upset. He talked softly and got people's attention. He controlled his anger and said a number of things."

"He gave Rozelle a beating," Leonard Tose remembered. "He was unmerciful. He said Rozelle was a crook. . . . It was so degrading, it was repulsive to me. Everybody was listening to it, though. I don't recall anyone leaving the room."

Bob Marr, sitting in on his final executive session, called C.R.'s diatribe "mostly emotional, not much substance. I got the impression," he noted, "that it had happened before and would happen again."

"Carroll blasted Pete with a slashing attack," Art Modell remembered. "He threatened the League and everybody. I thought it was a totally unjustified attack, but I was impressed with the way Pete handled it, with enormous patience and fortitude."

"I just tried to be cool," Rozelle explained.

Rosenbloom's anger seemed to feed on itself as he went along. Toward the end, he made no reference to his legal pad and just rocked back on his heels and railed. A decade and a half of grievances gave him plenty of ammunition. Finally he ended his tirade with a promise: "I will never attend another meeting," he stormed, pointing his finger at the commissioner, "as long as that man is in the chair." Then he headed for the door, stopping once for a final threat. "I'll get even," Rosenbloom snarled. "If I can't get you in here, I'll get you out there." His arm waved vaguely in reference to the outside world and then he turned and was gone.

A dead silence followed, until Rozelle finally broke it. "Anyone who would like to talk to me privately about the charges you just heard," the commissioner offered in his calmest voice, "feel free. But for now, let's continue the meeting."

The next item was the formal approval of Sullivan's stock transfer and it was quickly passed by unanimous vote. Then Wellington Mara suggested a recess for lunch; he "wanted to break the spell." After lunch, Mara arrived with what he hoped was an appropriate cartoon. The drawing depicted a cowboy, having been tossed over a cliff by his horse, holding on to a flimsy bush over the lip of the precipice. Above him, another cowboy was assessing the situation. "Hang on, old boy!" he shouted. Mara gave the cartoon to George Halas who then presented it to Rozelle for having endured the previous item of business. "Everyone laughed," Mara remembered. "It broke the ice."

The laughter was decidedly nervous nonetheless.

17
Union Victory

The "spell" generated by Carroll Rosenbloom's anger was finally broken by what Wellington Mara called "catastrophe" on the League's labor front. The decision on *Mackey v. NFL* came in on December 29 and it could not have been worse.

"The Rozelle Rule constitutes a *per se* violation of the antitrust laws," the court ruled. It also constituted "a concerted refusal to deal and a group boycott on the part of the defendants. The Rozelle Rule," the court continued, "is illegal under the Sherman Act. It is also an unreasonable restraint of trade at common law." Even the rule of reason was an inadequate defense. "The Rozelle Rule is invalid under the Rule of Reason standard. . . . The Rozelle Rule is unreasonably broad in its application . . . [and] is further unreasonable in that there are no procedural safeguards with respect to its employment. There is no hearing or opportunity to be heard. . . . The Rozelle Rule is unreasonable in that it is unlimited in duration. It is a perpetual restriction on a player. . . . He is at no time truly free to negotiate for his services with any club. . . . The Court finds that the existence of the Rozelle Rule and the other restrictive devices on players have not had any material effect on competitive balance in the National Football League. . . . Elimination of the Rozelle Rule would have no significant immediate disruptive effect on professional football.. . . . Elimination of the Rozelle Rule will not spell the end of the National Football League or even cause a decrease in the number of franchises in the National Football League."

The court then proceeded to cut off the League's only line of retreat. Even if the NFL were to negotiate an agreement about the Rozelle Rule with Garvey and the NFLPA, it would still be illegal.

Ed Garvey learned of the decision from a reporter who called for a reaction. "Congratulations," the reporter began, "you won the Mackey case."

"Oh my God," Garvey gasped.

The union's response was to throw a big party for the small band of people who "had put it on the line" and made the victory possible. When the union leaders had voted to file the case, it was assumed that whoever had his name on the suit would lose his football career. Mackey, then union president, had wanted his name on it nonetheless. An emotional discussion had followed in which, one by one, the others added their names to make it *Mackey et al.* All the players named in the suit were black except one, who dropped out. Garvey himself had mortgaged his house to raise money. Now the men who had risked everything seemed to have won everything. Plan B had carried the day.

The NFL intended to appeal the decision. In January 1976, the League convened for two days to discuss what to do next. The sense of crisis was palpable. Rozelle called it "the most turbulent period since I have been commissioner and very likely in the history of the League. . . . [The Mackey case] attacked the very structure . . . [and] . . . validity of the game." On the first day, the group agreed to appeal "to the Supreme Court if necessary."

In the next session, the subject was expansion beyond the Tampa and Seattle franchises. The Birmingham and Memphis remnants of the World Football League made presentations, officially asking to be let in. After a discussion among the members, no decision was made on the applications, and the League broke for the evening.

The next day, the lengthy discussion concerned "the uncertain future of professional sports in general and professional football in particular, especially in light of the recent Minneapolis court decision." New member Hugh Culverhouse of the Tampa Buccaneers, was insistent on "the need for an early clarification, in court if necessary," of the union's declared position that the League's plans for stocking its two new expansion franchises "raised antitrust issues." All the more than three hours of discussion yielded was a "general recognition of a need to study the future direction of professional football." To that end, the League formed its first "planning committee" with Rozelle as chairman and Tex Schramm, Art Modell, Paul Brown, Lamar Hunt, and Al Davis as members. The League then adjourned until its 1976 annual meeting in March.

The 1976 planning committee was, in Rozelle's words, "very much a spur of the moment thing that grew out of the Mackey decision. . . . It was felt that a think tank team . . . might be able to develop some contingency plans." According to Lamar

Hunt, the planning committee "only had one or at the most two meetings [before] the committee more or less just died." Rozelle credited that death to Al Davis. At first, the commissioner thought it might be just the right committee for Davis, who Rozelle remembered, "worked better solo. . . . Al Davis couldn't fit in a structured thing, thinking just League." Rozelle hoped the idea-mongering involved in the planning committee would tap Davis's genius without putting the League in any jeopardy. Davis was already known for his "original ideas" about the labor issues that had prodded the committee into existence.

The planning committee's one and only meeting was held just before the annual meeting in San Diego. Al Davis established his presence early. Davis was not one of those owners intimidated by free agency. If anything, he expected it would give him an even greater advantage over the rest of the League. In Palm Springs, he proposed that the League "make everybody a free agent." Davis also had definite feelings about the role of the planning committee itself. It was, he thought, an excellent way to handle the League's business and suggested that it ought to operate as an executive committee.

Though his peers knew he was power hungry, Al Davis was by no means a shunned figure. He and Tex Schramm got along well and that helped ease his dealings with Rozelle. One evening, after the day's committee dealings were over, Davis, Schramm, and Rozelle sat out on the patio watching the sunset. The view of the mountains in the distance, looming over the desert floor, was inspiring. Davis mentioned that he had always been fascinated by Mt. Kilimanjaro. He had read a lot of Hemingway, he said, and the mountain had always intrigued him. When I win the Super Bowl, he told Schramm and Rozelle, no football for a couple of months and I'm going to climb Mt. Kilimanjaro.

"Gee, Al," Schramm quipped, "you think it will still be there then?"

Al Davis's greatest frustration was still the absence of a single Super Bowl victory, but he took the joke at his expense without flinching.

In those days, there was still humor attached to the League's view of Al Davis. He was still thought of as "a character" who had "his own way of doing things." There was some lingering resentment of what he'd "done" to Wayne Valley, but Davis's fellow owners had become accustomed to his silver and black clothes and his habit of speaking in obscure half-sentences so the listener could not be sure of his intentions. The rest of the NFL knew Al Davis always had a hidden agenda, but just what it was still didn't seem to matter much. Nonetheless, the fear he had inspired ten years earlier when leading the AFL into battle was still tangible. As much was apparent in the fate of the planning committee.

The committee's last two hours of existence came at the end of the 1976 annual meeting. "The entire session," according to the minutes, "was devoted to the discussion of a possible planning council." The idea was Davis's and in his speech on the subject, the half-sentences were few and the message clear. Davis's speech, according to one of the men who heard it, "was about how the planning committee should be made into a full-scale junta and run the whole League. He clearly saw this as an opportunity for a power grab. . . . When he stood up at San Diego and spelled out what he thought the powers of the planning committee ought to be, everybody just looked at him and that was the end of the planning committee. Everybody said we don't need this committee anymore and that ended that."

18
The Ownership Policy Fight Continues

The most familiar issue at the San Diego meeting was ownership policy and, again, it was raised at the insistence of the commissioner, who wanted to eliminate all such "causes for litigation." In the three years since the last major discussion on the NFL's ongoing ownership policy resolution, prohibiting cross-ownership and pledging League members to their "best efforts" to divest, things had been allowed to lapse. Due to an "oversight," the ownership policy resolution had not been reaffirmed upon expiration in 1975. The commissioner had not noticed the oversight until the following year.

The issue, however, had not become any less touchy in the meantime. The discussion was loud, occasionally hot, and included the by now ritualized acrimonious blast at Lamar Hunt from Leonard Tose. "My position has always been the same," Tose pointed out. "Get the hell out [of other sports]." As usual,

Tose confronted Hunt personally. "I said," Tose remembered, " 'Give us a price for your soccer team . . . maybe some of us can get together and buy your interest out, or give us a price on your football team, if you want to get rid of that, so that you can make a choice.' His reply was, 'I will think it over,' but . . . there was never ever a corresponding follow-up on it." Joe Robbie remembered, "[Lamar Hunt] had invested a lot of money in developing that soccer franchise and wanted to recover it if he were to sell out." As Rozelle remembered it, "many of the owners' tolerance was starting to ebb" and the discussion was "basically directed to Mr. Hunt and the fact that he was promoting a [soccer] league." Those promotional efforts by Hunt still "generated a great deal of ill will and some rather sharp discussion."

"Almost every time the subject came up," Hunt remembered in testimony later, "there would be a variety of suggestions, some in writing, some verbal, as to amending it, how it would work, how it could be modified , , , how it could be, handled in the future, whether it should be done away with, whether it should be continued, but I don't have specific recollection of individual meetings. . . . It was brought up frequently." But the ownership policy's most implacable critic remained Edward Bennett Williams, though while the March 15 discussion raged around him, the nation's foremost trial lawyer was quiet, scribbling an occasional note to himself on a pad of paper.

Williams's first note was comical. "*How do you make a small fortune in sports?*" he questioned. "*Start out with a large fortune,*" he answered.

"That was just a piece of whimsy," Williams later explained, "that I wrote to myself . . . during the discussion. I didn't intend it as a serious profound observation . . . just whimsy. I was, I guess, just ruminating while I was upset during the . . . meeting. I was just writing to myself."

"*Sports have a community of interest,*" Williams next wrote to himself. "*Should have one commissioner's office. Speak with one voice to Congress.*" "I don't believe that sports are in competition with each other," the Redskins president pointed out. "I think [if] there is success in one sport, in one town, [then there will be] great success in another sport. I believe very deeply that it is good for a city with a football team to have a baseball team; good for a city with a baseball team to have a football team. I think it is good for a city with a hockey team to have a basketball team. I think it is good to have a soccer team. I think it is good to have people get into the habit of taking their children and their families to sports events. It is part of the culture of the city. . . .

"*Don't circumscribe prospective purchasers*," he scribbled next. "*Passage deflates value of interest. Distress sale.*"

"The people who are interested in sports and who are prospective investors in sports constitute a rather small reservoir of entrepreneurs on the American economic scene," Williams argued. "There is a strong tendency on the part of someone who is an investor in one sport to maybe invest in another sport and . . . if you passed a rule which proscribed this, you would be circumscribing the prospective purchasers. . . . If [a constitutional ownership policy prohibition] were passed and people were required to make a selection as to what they were going to divest, obviously they would be making a coerced or mandated sale and we all know from just the basic rules of economics that a mandated sale produces less in the way of revenue than a voluntary sale.

Williams's last note to himself reaffirmed his complete opposition to all facets of the commissioner's policy: "*Must have corporate ownership, must have multiple ownership. No other sport has such restrictions.*"

"I have not just been opposed to the ownership policy of the National Football League insofar as it relates to cross-ownership," the attorney reaffirmed, "but also those policies that inhibit a corporation from buying franchises. I've also been opposed to those rules which historically have required a person to own at least fifty-one percent of the franchise. I have been for fragmenting and liberalizing ownership policies. I have said this, but without much response from my colleagues in the League. The ownership policies of the National Football League by my lights are wrong. I believe they are counterproductive to the best interests of the National Football League and to their owners, to players, ultimately to the fans. . . . I think it should be permissible for a hundred people to own a National Football League franchise and each have one percent, or fifteen, and each have seven or eight percent, and I also think you should be able to have ownership in more than one sport. . . . I don't think that there is anything accomplished by keeping people out of investing in the National Football League, making it more difficult to get in."

Finally, Williams attempted to derail any talk of making this a constitutional amendment and to delay any consideration of the issue as long as possible. "I said," Williams remembered, "have we really reflected on the legality of this? Have we really gotten an opinion on it? . . . I would like to have a view of some reputable counsel with respect to whether there were legal problems in this matter. . . . They agreed to get a legal opinion on it, so I was persuasive, I thought, at the time. At least they would explore whether it was lawful or not."

Williams had calculated the impact of his request well; the tactic irritated the commissioner's office. "It was just Ed rattling his chain," Jay Moyer, the League's in-house legal counsel observed. "We sent a legal opinion over to him and never heard another word." Williams claimed never to have seen such an opinion. According to Joe Robbie, "that legal opinion was not forthcoming until after the 1978 [annual] meeting. . . ." In any case, the request itself was enough to momentarily derail the ownership policy express until the next League meeting in June. At San Diego, the League did, however, commit itself to "adhere to the terms of the [previous ownership policy] resolution even though it expired in 1975."

When the proposal came off the table in June, it would be stripped of all references to amending the constitution and amount to the same ongoing resolution, first passed in 1973, only this time passed in perpetuity and "subject only to change by 21 votes or amendment by 21 votes." The vote was unanimous. "The resolution ultimately evolved because it was obvious that a constitutional amendment was not going to pass," Joe Robbie pointed out in explanation of the vote's reported unanimity. "We were simply compromising by reducing this to nothing more than a policy. . . ."

In 1976, even Pete Rozelle claimed to favor that approach. "At this time," he later testified, "we did have violations of this [policy] and I didn't feel that it made sense to put something in the constitution which was being violated, and it was better to keep it in resolution form until Mr. Hunt, Mr. Robbie, and Mr. Cooke were in compliance."

19
Shrinking Possibilities for Expansion

The second issue of longterm consequence raised at the 1976 annual meeting was, once again, expansion. It was a question that simply refused to go away. Encouraged by the League's irresolution on the issue, both Memphis and Birmingham contingents arrived at the meeting in force—potential owners, civic boosters, and potential fans. Worried that it would be years before the League would expand again, both cities had, in Tex Schramm's words, "come on strong." Both were proud of their relative success in the WFL, but Rozelle was doubtful about growing again so quickly. Tampa and Seattle had yet to be assimilated, and *Mackey v. NFL* was still on appeal. The commissioner's reluctance doomed Memphis and Birmingham to the less than big leagues for the foreseeable future. Before proceeding to other business, the League passed the following resolution:

> RESOLVED, after a thorough review of the major problems presently confronting the NFL, that the member clubs do not believe they can formally commit to specific expansion arrangements at this time. The clubs do, however, reaffirm their desire to bring total League membership to thirty teams as soon as possible after resolution of current problems and assimilation of the new Tampa Bay and Seattle teams. At that time, Memphis and Birmingham, which have most actively sought admission in recent months, will be among the cities receiving strongest consideration for NFL franchises.

The vote was twenty-five to three, with Ralph Wilson, Robert Irsay, and Al Davis voting no. The door to the NFL had slammed shut once again.

Reactions varied, but perhaps the most bitter was John Bassett, who eventually filed a lawsuit under the Sherman Act, *Mid-South Grizzlies v. NFL*. In it, Bassett et al. would accuse the NFL of conspiring to boycott them by refusing Memphis an NFL franchise. The suit would be one of the few Sherman Act suits the League managed to win over the next eight years. Perhaps Indianapolis had the most optimistic response to the NFL's expansion resolution. NFL boosters in Indiana began a long scramble to prepare for the unspecified future date when the League would expand again. Indianapolis's 1974 bid had been thwarted by the lack of a big league stadium, and in 1976 a small group of local business leaders began what would become a very long campaign to erect a domed stadium complex in the heart of downtown. It was a high-risk venture, but within a year, the city of Indianapolis would take an option on a seventeen-acre site. It was a start.

Phoenix, however, was the first to stake out the strategy of the future. Their logic was simple: The only real option for Arizona was the possibility of an existing franchise abandoning its current hometown and moving there. It was that option Phoenix chose to pursue. In March 1976, a private group of NFL boosters from Phoenix approached Robert Irsay about pulling his Colts out of Baltimore. For Irsay, the approach offered an opportunity to push his effort in the Superstadium Game. His complaints about Baltimore's Memorial Stadium were by now a NFL truism and he meant to use Phoenix as leverage. At the moment, he told *The Baltimore] Sun*, he had the Arizona offer on the back burner. "I'm going to be in Baltimore for three months, raising enough hell to get some of the things the stadium needs. I might even go door-to-door explaining our situation. There are things we would like to have done to make the stadium a better place. . . . I will give it ninety days, then I will take another look."

Few took Irsay's threat to move seriously. "Sources close to the NFL's New York headquarters" told *The Sun* that Irsay's chances of doing so were "nil." Under Section 4.3 of the NFL constitution, such a move into new territory would require the approval of three quarters of the membership. "The Pete Rozelle regime prides itself . . . that there has never been a franchise shift during Pete's term as commissioner," one unnamed owner pointed out. "Baseball [has] moved franchises all over the place. We don't. Irsay would need the votes of twenty-one owners to get approval to move out of Baltimore. I'd say he has no shot."

The owner's description of the situation was slightly inaccurate. The last shift in location by an NFL franchise, while set in motion by Bert Bell, had in fact been consummated in 1960, during Rozelle's commissionership. The move took the Cardinals out of Chicago and into St. Louis. At the time, it had been considered the solution to a longstanding NFL problem—how to share what was then the nation's second largest market with George Halas's Bears. The pressure that put the move over the top came from CBS. Chicago was then the League's only shared market and, since TV sets in cities where a home game was taking place were then completely blacked out from football programming, it meant that the nation's number two market was largely inaccessible. Shortly after Pete Rozelle began his commissionership, a deal for moving the Cardinals to St. Louis was finally worked out. Since then, however, everyone in the NFL had stayed put.

In 1976, Robert Irsay professed not to understand why his Colts should not be allowed the privilege of moving. Typically, he raised the issue at the San Diego meeting, but after hours. Late one evening, Pete Rozelle received a phone call in his hotel suite. Robert Irsay, one of his assistants reported from the lobby, was at this moment holding forth in the nearby bar. His precise state was undetermined, but he had reached the loud stage. He was talking about "storming the beaches" and "threatening at that moment, even before the bar closed, to transfer the Colts to Phoenix." To hell with the commissioner and Section 4.3 or whatever it was.

"Rozelle," the [Baltimore] *News-American* noted, "prevented any such late night or early morning move" and, for the moment, managed to shut Irsay up. Like most things about Robert Irsay, however, that silence would prove fleeting.

20
Rosenbloom Calls the Dogs on Rozelle

San Diego saw yet another battle in the war between Carroll Rosenbloom and Pete Rozelle. Despite the boycott of League meetings he had announced the previous November, C.R. came to San Diego. Rosenbloom's presence did not, however, represent a change of mind. Carroll had, once again, come to fight.

Nor had his feud with Rozelle cooled in the meantime. Indeed, Rosenbloom's list of grievances had only grown. On

Christmas Eve in 1975, Rozelle made it clear C.R.'s threats had not intimidated him when he announced the year's final round of fines. Rosenbloom, Al Davis, and Ralph Wilson were each assessed $5000 for having criticized game officials. Davis made no comment, Wilson made little, but Rosenbloom was icily sarcastic. "Since an agreement exists between the owners and NFL Commissioner Pete Rozelle that fines will not be discussed publicly," C.R. announced, "I am not in a position to elaborate. I helped make the rules and I try to abide by them. In 1971, I was notified by Rozelle on a fine in the Don Shula matter. Abiding by League rules, I refused to discuss the matter publicly. However, Rozelle saw fit to discuss the fine at the next Super Bowl game, when he had a maximum media audience. Therefore, I refer you to Rozelle for any further information. I feel certain if he does not care to elaborate further at this time he will, in all probability, be happy to do so at the upcoming Super Bowl."

That Super Bowl would be yet another for which Rosenbloom's Rams fell one game short, upping C.R.'s frustration yet another notch. After besting the St. Louis Cardinals at the L.A. Coliseum, 35–23, the Rams hosted Tex Schramm's Dallas Cowboys for the right to play in the Super Bowl against the Pittsburgh Steelers and lost 37–7. It was the Cardinals game that put C.R. on the NFL's San Diego agenda.

The confrontation had begun in the week prior to the game, when the Cardinals had requested use of the Coliseum for a pregame workout. C.R., looking for whatever advantage he could get, said that was impossible due to the terms of the Rams' lease with its landlord. The Cardinals complained to the commissioner's office, and the League's treasurer checked it out on their file copy of the Rams' lease. In the process, the treasurer discovered some discrepancies in the way C.R. had handled the question of rent for postseason playoff games. The gate from playoff games was, once expenses were deducted, forwarded to the League office for equal distribution to all member clubs. Over the previous years, whenever such a game was held in LA, Rosenbloom had deducted ten percent for rent before sending the receipts along. The treasurer's examination of the Rams' lease revealed that the franchise had not actually paid anything in rent during the playoffs and C.R. had been billing for expenses he never incurred. "He was stealing money from his partners," Gene Klein observed, "pure and simple."

In early 1976, Rozelle confronted C.R. about the discrepan-

cies. Rosenbloom, according to Rozelle, was "very upset."
Trying to avoid any charge of having picked on C.R. because of
the November incident, Rozelle referred the question to the
League's finance committee, which reported at the Executive
Session at San Diego. The finance committee backed up Rozelle
and demanded Rosenbloom pay the money back.

C.R. was, according to Rozelle, "very upset for the next few
years." After the meeting, Carroll burned the last of his bridges
to Rozelle's camp. Rosenbloom's relationship with Art Modell
was already in an "off" stage, and Tex Schramm quickly joined
him. According to Steve Rosenbloom, his father's San Diego
falling out with Schramm "had to do with a vote at a meeting.
He and Schramm had been friends, but he felt that Tex had lied
to him. Carroll felt betrayed and when Tex tried to explain his
way out of it, it got worse. He didn't talk to Schramm for two
years." It was obvious to everyone in the League that the
Rosenbloom-Rozelle war was far from over. That spring, according to several NFL sources, Carroll finally redeemed his
November promise to "get" Rozelle, "out there" if "in here"
wouldn't work.

What gave rise to their suspicion was a visit to the NFL
offices by two investigators from the Internal Revenue Service.
They wanted to see Pete Rozelle and the League's treasurer and
it was not a casual visit. The IRS agents read the two men their
Miranda rights against self-incrimination and informed them they
were under criminal investigation.

The object of the IRS's inquiry was the $300,000 loan at
seven percent which the League had given Rozelle in 1974 for
the purchase of his house. The IRS wondered whether the "loan"
under such favorable terms was simply a way of hiding either a
"gift" or "income," upon which Rozelle had failed to pay tax.
Certainly the house transaction was one the League had gone to
great lengths to hide. Since Rozelle and the finance committee
worried that Ed Garvey would make a big deal out of the
expenditure in collective bargaining, the title to the Westchester
property had been held for the last two years in the name of one
of the League's attorneys. The IRS subpoenaed League records
and interviewed all the members of the finance committee. After
two years, the investigation was dropped without explanation.

There can be little doubt that Rozelle's own suspicions focused fairly quickly on C.R. It wasn't lost on the commissioner
that the man who had brought gambling charges against
Rosenbloom in 1963 had subsequently faced a similar IRS inves-

tigation. Years later, when Carroll's wife, Georgia, bragged that she had the name of a New York lawyer who could get anybody she wanted investigated by Internal Revenue, Rozelle no doubt had his suspicions even further confirmed.

None of that was, of course, evidence. Rosenbloom himself had refused to talk when the IRS agents attempted to interview him. Even so, a number of owners shared Rozelle's suspicions. "Somebody motivated it," Art Modell pointed out, "and it was concurrent with Pete's troubles with Carroll. Someone planted the notion of wrongdoing in the NFL office and it had to have come from inside. I, for one, am sure it started with Rosenbloom. Carroll played for keeps."

On the subject of the rent dispute that touched it all off, Modell, like Gene Klein, considered it a matter of Rosenbloom "stealing from his partners, pure and simple."

21
Cleveland Gets Its Stadium—and More

"Stealing from his partners" was a charge that would eventually be thrown Art Modell's way as well. By spring 1976, the situation from which the charge would emerge was now firmly in place. After more than two years up in the air, Cleveland Stadium Corp.'s longterm financing was at last set and Robert Gries was, once again, Modell's minority partner. Gries's investment did not, however, take quite the form Modell had originally envisioned.

Negotiations between the two men had never ceased being difficult. The final and most telling sticking point was over the issue of how, if Gries were to buy in for a proportion similar to his share in the Browns, the debts of Stadium Corp. would be secured. Modell's deal with the city of Cleveland required the corporation to spend at least $10 million in improvements over its first ten years as landlord of Cleveland Stadium and that money would, of course, be borrowed. Gries's idea was that each entity would guarantee its own portion of the debt. "I don't think the banks will go for it," Modell responded. He wanted Gries to guarantee the entire amount. The two men discussed a number of "different formulas," but the negotiations were still at an impasse in November 1975, when Robert Gries Jr. had to leave the country on business. In December, Gries, in Indonesia, received a telegram from his brother-in-law. His attorney and his brother-in-law reported that negotiations had reached the point where it was proposed that Gries take a simple ten percent of Stadium Corp.'s stock without guaranteeing the bank loans. In addition, Gries, as part of the agreement, would be given "a put"—the right "to get out at a set price" whenever he so chose. Gries's negotiators said it was either take that or proceed with suing Modell for double-dealing and betraying his fiduciary responsibility to the Browns. There were no other options left. Robert Gries, aware he couldn't negotiate from Thailand and couldn't yet return to the United States, simply said "go ahead, wrap it up."

As "wrapped up," ten percent of Cleveland Stadium Corp.'s stock was taken by the combination of Robert Gries Jr., Gries Sports Enterprises, and Richard Cole. Gries later described the interest as a way "to keep a foot in the door and an eye on Modell." Another ten percent went to what Modell described as "employees, lawyers, and others." The remaining eighty percent was Art Modell's. The $10 million would be borrowed at a point over prime, for which Modell pledged "all the leases, assignments on the leases, assignments on all sources of revenue, and my own personal signature and that of my wife" as collateral.

As part of the final agreement, Cleveland Stadium Corp. buttressed Modell's personal finances by purchasing his land out in Strongsville for $4 million, almost five times what he had paid for it three years earlier. Gries still considered the price outrageous and might well have backed out of the deal over it, but at the last moment Modell wrote out a further agreement that the fate of the land in Strongsville would have no effect on "the put price" given the Gries interests. "With that," Gries pointed out, "I really didn't care what he did with the land."

As with the Browns, in 1976 only a handful of people even knew Modell had partners. To greater Cleveland, Art Modell was now Cleveland Stadium as well as the Cleveland Browns. Of the two, he claimed to be having the most fun "building something here in the stadium. I'm very proud of what I've done. It's a physical thing I can see and develop. I've had more fun with this thing, despite the gamble, than I've had, perhaps, with my ball club. In retrospect, it's the greatest thing that has happened to me in my professional life, because I do see a renaissance taking place in downtown Cleveland. . . . I'm an activist owner and this is a way I have a slight edge over my competitors.''

Stadium expenditures took two forms—structural improvements and what Modell termed "potential income producers." The problem was striking a balance between the two. It turned out to be a curious balance. The lion's share of the budget went to "income producers" such as a scoreboard that would yield as much as $1 million in a year in advertising revenues. It would be the second largest scoreboard in North America, with some twenty-three thousand lamps. Most of the income producing renovation expenditures went to construct Cleveland's version of the luxury box, called loges. During Cleveland Stadium Corp.'s first two years, Modell constructed 108. They were all decorated at the direction of Pat Modell, Art's wife, and she was there herself on the last night before the baseball season opened, down on her hands and knees putting the final touches on the carpeting. The boxes would generate as much as $2.4 million a year for Stadium Corp.—welcome news, no doubt, to Art Modell's bankers. Perhaps just as important to Modell himself, they also cemented his reputation for having "saved" the stadium and, thereby, helped save Cleveland's downtown. Art Modell loved to hear that kind of talk about himself and took it to heart.

No one in Cleveland talked about Art Modell being an outsider anymore. The former part-time Brooklyn pool shark had transformed into a figure high on civic Cleveland's masthead. His short and increasingly chunky figure was immediately recognized when Cleveland's upper echelons gathered to bolster their hometown. Modell's address was as good as could be found in that part of Ohio, and his personal life was inconspicuous and built around his family. His wife, Pat, was by all accounts devoted to him. "I would rather have someone compliment me on my looks than say I'm bright," she explained to The [Cleveland] Plain Dealer, "I think my life is to enhance a man's."

Art and Pat were a very visible couple in Cleveland's cultural activities. Modell's special passion was the city's symphony. One of his first philanthropic outbursts was to stage a fund-raising concert by the symphony in Cleveland Stadium. In white tie and tails, the orchestra was to assemble on the fifty-yard line and upwards of forty thousand were expected to attend. The event collapsed when a sixty-mile-an-hour rain squall blew off Lake Erie while the crowd was still filing in. As the audience fled for cover, Modell remained at the railing of the upper deck, out in the weather and refusing to move. Next to him stood Pat, her hand placed on her husband's arm. "Nice try, darling," she soothed him. "Nice try." She kept repeating, "Keep cool, darling, keep cool." His greatest disappointment was that the orchestra had refused to take the field in the face of the storm. Though Modell afterward wondered out loud "whether I'll ever do anything for the orchestra again," his stature as a bulwark of the arts in Cleveland was only enhanced.

In 1976, Modell would spearhead yet another civic rescue, enhancing his reputation even further. When the Sheraton Cleveland Hotel, an enterprise whose success was considered "essential for the stability of downtown," went bankrupt, the bankruptcy judge turned to Modell. Modell put together eight civic-minded investors to contribute $1 million apiece to establish an equity in the hotel, then borrowed an additional $10 million with which to remodel from "all the city's banks." According to Robert Gries, Modell "had hopes of a great profit." Whatever Modell's motives, even Gries admitted the hotel rescue was "a very fine gesture." *The Plain Dealer* saw fit to thank Modell in its lead editorial. "He used his business expertise and contacts to draft the help of a group of businesses that ensures a new wave of interest by the total community in the future of the once grand Sheraton Cleveland. . . . Modell was the man to do it," *The Plain Dealer* raved.

Among the enterprises anteing up $1 million to save the old Sheraton Cleveland was Cleveland Stadium Corp.—now, much to Robert Gries's discomfort, in the hotel business as well as land development and stadium management.

22
Billy Sullivan's Comeback: Phase Two

Billy Sullivan was another NFL member about whom "cheating his partners" would be claimed by some of those partners. In the spring of 1976, his son, Chuck, was well into phase two of the family's takeover of the New England Patriots and it would prove exceedingly controversial. The target this time was the 139,000 shares of outstanding nonvoting stock.

On January 16, 1976, Chuck met with his father's bankers to discuss how they were going to accomplish the complete ownership they had promised by the coming fall. Sullivan began by disclosing that the Patriots' off-field financial success had vastly exceeded their on-field playing record.

Chuck then proposed a reorganization that would be accomplished by establishing a new Patriots corporation, with which the old Patriots corporation would merge. As a condition of that merger, all holders of old Patriots stock would be forced to sell their interests to the new corporation—owned, of course, exclusively by Sullivans. Chuck anticipated completing the reorganization by July, so he could free up cash in order to start paying back the bank.

Cash was a question about which both banks continued to be nervous. Before the meeting adjourned, LaSalle National Bank's vice-president "very strongly stated to Chuck Sullivan . . . that the banks expected the first interest payment to be made when due, irrespective to the status of the reorganization. Chuck Sullivan did not seem to be particularly disturbed or surprised, and indicated that although he did not feel that they could borrow money from the Patriots, that other sources of family funds could be tapped to take care of this obligation."

Of the two financial institutions, LaSalle was the less nervous. "As you know," one of its vice-presidents wrote Rhode Island Hospital Trust in February, "LaSalle is the main bank for the Miami Dolphins and the St. Louis Cardinals, as well as the Patriots. Our lending experience in this field dates back to 1968, when we made a loan to Joe Robbie so that he could purchase control of the Dolphins. In 1973, we made a similar loan to Bill Bidwill of the St. Louis Cardinals. . . . When we recently met Pete Rozelle at the Boys' Club Dinner in Chicago honoring George Halas, Mr. Rozelle's first reaction was to thank us for our participation with the teams in the League. . . . We will be traveling to New York sometime in the near future for dinner with Mr. Rozelle to better solidify our position with the League office and get acquainted. . . ."

As well as being quite obviously taken with the idea of becoming the NFL's banker, LaSalle was also quite convinced of the value of the franchise. "I am confident," the LaSalle V.P. continued, "that a minimum price of $12,000,000 to $14,000,000 could easily be obtained [should the Patriots have to be foreclosed and sold]. The recent new franchises given to Seattle and Tampa were at a price of $16,000,000. Rhode Island Hospital

Trust's vice-president was more conscious of the dilemmas posed by their Patriots loan. "One of the continuing risks of this loan," he noted, "is the [possible] cessation of the continued willingness of rich men to pay prices for NFL teams which are in no way justified by the earnings of those teams." Even more disturbing to Hospital Trust was the fact that the merger plan being developed by Chuck Sullivan would require the approval of at least two thirds of the affected nonvoting shareholders. The requirement came as news to the Rhode Island Hospital Trust's vice-president, who, at the time of the loan approval . . . [understood] that no vote was required."

Chuck Sullivan was also worried about the two thirds vote. The Sullivans' strategy in response to that obstacle was to get the law changed. First, they approached Barney Frank, a liberal Democrat recently elected to the Massachusetts House of Representatives. At the time, Frank was dating Billy's daughter, Kathleen. "We went together for about a year and a half," Frank remembered. "I was at a lot of the family get-togethers. The old man used to like to talk to me about business. He said I was antibusiness."

On Christmas Eve, 1975, however, Billy offered Frank an opportunity to redeem his record. "We were sitting around talking," the representative later claimed, "when Billy came over and said he had a way I could help business in Massachusetts. He told me there was a law on the books that was bad for the businessmen of the state. He said it would really help if someone could change it. This was the law regarding mergers and what kind of vote it took to put through a merger. I really didn't know anything about it. Chuck came over and joined the conversation. He showed me a piece of paper, and out in the margin was a check mark beside the words 'two thirds.' I told them I would look into it."

The Sullivans proposed reducing the merger provision to 50.1 percent approval, a bare majority. Frank passed the proposal along to Representative David Schwartz of Haverhill. "I didn't want to file the bill," Frank explained, "because I thought it would be a conflict of interest, going with Kathleen at the same time. Dave knew something about this law and said it wouldn't be bad, that about twenty states had it at fifty percent. . . . [When I learned] what was going on that summer when the bill was about to pass, I felt used."

"I did it for Barney," Schwartz later remembered. "Besides, I liked the bill. I thought it would be a good one. It did go through very fast. It's not often you see something go through with unanimous approval of both the House and Senate." By August, House 5153 would be on Governor Michael Dukakis's desk, awaiting signature.

"I think it very possible that the bill may become effective in time for the Patriots' merger," Rhode Island Hospital Trust's attorney wrote his opposite number at LaSalle. "I have also been told by two or three completely independent sources that Billy Sullivan is behind all this. One could not hope," the attorney warned, "that this would be excluded as evidence in any lawsuit that might be brought."

When later asked under oath what he had to do with getting House 5153 passed, Billy Sullivan would answer, "Nothing."

23
Gene Klein: A Challenge to the Franchise

The National Football League owner with the most pressing partner problems at the time of the 1976 annual meeting in San Diego was Gene Klein, baron of the city's Chargers. By then, Klein was in his third year of just running his football team and trying to "enjoy life."

When in San Diego, Gene Klein stayed in his Spanish-style house overlooking the ocean. He kept three Rolls-Royces in the driveway, a sedan, and two $47,000 Corniches. For relaxation, he told the *Los Angeles Times,* he liked to "put the top down and take off through the desert or along the ocean." When Klein first bought his San Diego mansion, he envisioned living there with his second wife, Nancy, but that relationship soon fizzled and in less than a year he was back on his own.

By the time of the NFL meeting, Klein had married his third wife, Joyce, more than twenty years his junior. "Usually we're together about eighteen hours a day," the new Mrs. Klein explained, "And that's because we really like each other." Joyce also evinced a great taste for her husband's football franchise. "It's so much fun sitting in our box with our friends and watching the games. I've been going crazy because of all the excitement."

Despite their attachment to the Chargers, the Kleins' principal residence continued to be their mansion in Beverly Hills. There, Gene indulged his passion for collecting modern art: Henry Moore, Modigliani, Chagall, Ernst, Picasso, and Degas, among others, in rooms described as "overflowing with paintings and sculpture that read like an exciting modern art lecture."

However many pieces of art he accumulated, Gene Klein's favorite possession remained his football team. It, in turn, continued to perform miserably. In 1974, the Chargers won 5 and lost 9 and in 1975, they fell to 2–12. While still bitter about the drug scandal that had led to Rozelle's 1974 fine, Klein's only continuing grudge from the incident was against Dr. Arnold Mandell. In 1976, Klein charged that two years earlier, Mandell had illegally supplied amphetamines to Charger players and was personally involved in the manufacture of drugs. Mandell, however, was eventually "cleared" by the California Board of Medical Quality Assurance and returned to anonymity as the co-chairman of the University of California at San Diego's Psychiatry Department.

Gene Klein's partner problems began in February at a meeting of the Chargers' entire ownership group. Klein himself owned only sixty-one percent of the franchise. The rest was in the hands of a group of ten limited partners. The most significant of those was Barron Hilton, the hotel heir and "playboy" who had founded the franchise. When Hilton sold the club's majority to Klein in 1966, he had retained a twenty-percent interest, later enlarged to thirty percent. Among the remainder of the partners, the most visible was John Z. DeLorean, then still the whiz kid of the automotive world. According to Klein, it was DeLorean who engineered the ambush that greeted him on February 18. "DeLorean wanted to sell me his interest and was trying to jack up the price. He didn't like the way the club was going and persuaded the others."

At the time, the most visible figure in the attempted coup was Hilton. According to his attorney, "Mr. Hilton stated that in his opinion, the team while under the direction of Mr. Klein had acquired a bad image in San Diego as well as with the entire League and that a change in management was needed. Mr. Klein responded that he was not going to resign as general partner . . .

and that he intended to continue to manage the club. When Mr. Hilton suggested that the limited partners had the power to remove Mr. Klein as general partner, Mr. Klein retorted that if so removed, he would appoint a new general partner who would give him a management contract at a big salary to manage the club." The impasse was created by the Chargers' ownership agreement which required two thirds of the limited partners to remove the general partner, but allowed the appointment of a new general partner by a simple majority vote of all the club's stock.

"They were unhappy that we were losing games," Gene Klein remembered, "and thought I should make some changes. I said, 'Fellows, no. . . . In my opinion, we're going to be all right in two or three years. This is a five-year program, and we just have to suffer.' Then they started the lawsuit."

The lawsuit was filed three days before the NFL's annual meeting convened nearby. The plaintiffs, Barron Hilton, John DeLorean, and five others, sought the removal of Klein as president and CEO of the franchise. "Due to the poor business and management techniques employed by Klein," Hilton told the court, "my partnership has suffered in both financial terms and otherwise. . . ."

Gene Klein was furious. "This is obviously a grandstand play before the League meetings," he exploded to the *San Diego Union*. "Those people tried to force me to buy them out and this is an effort to force me to pay the price they want me to pay. . . . Most people know Barron [Hilton] doesn't have an over-abundance of brains. The smartest thing he ever did was pick his father."

Among the charges leveled at Klein was "extravagant" use of the partnership's funds: the leasing of yet another Rolls-Royce, spending more than $1000 on his wife's birthday party, and billing the club for a "twenty-two-day junket to Europe, purportedly to look for a place kicker." Both sides charged each other with wanting to move the team out of San Diego.

It was not the first time such a move by Klein had been speculated about. In 1974, rumors had floated around Seattle that he was going to abandon the Chargers and apply for the expansion franchise there. In 1975, he was approached by Memphis's John Bassett about selling the team to Tennessee. "He said the club was not for sale," Bassett remembered. In March 1976, however, Klein claimed it was his partners who wanted to move. "They're not interested in the team or the city," he told the *San*

Diego Union, "they just want to make money. But I repeat what I have said for nine years. I intend to keep the team in San Diego."

A week after the rest of the NFL left town, the superior court made its first ruling in the suit. The news was headlined "Klein Wins the First Round." In that ruling, the judge agreed with Klein's contention that according to the NFL constitution, Commissioner Pete Rozelle had the authority to resolve the dispute. Gene Klein was jubilant at the decision. "The court has spoken," he crowed. "I'm a guy who likes to live by the rules. The commissioner has sole power. Whatever he decides will be right."

For more than a year, Rozelle would discuss the problem with Klein and his partners without issuing any ruling. Eventually, according to Rozelle, "they worked it out themselves." Sixteen months after Barron Hilton and John DeLorean opened their rebellion, the records in the *Hilton v. Klein* lawsuit were sealed. According to Klein, the settlement had been concluded when "Barron . . . said he was sorry he started it. He understood what I was doing and [said] let's drop all the animosity. I said, fine. I didn't start it. . . . Now we're very good friends."

24
Owners Versus Players

The League's overwhelming 1976 concern continued to be the war with the players association. On that front, the annual meeting had yielded the first hopeful signs in almost two years.

The hope was started by Dick Anderson, the new NFLPA president. When Anderson addressed the Executive Session, the new union president's attitude was conciliatory. "We can come up with an agreement," he asserted. Anderson took particular care to take the focus off Ed Garvey, an almost obsessive issue among the owners. "Look," Anderson pointed out, "Garvey is our executive director, he works for us. He is still with us, but our policies are set by the elected officers and a seven-man executive council, all players." The union wanted to discuss issues, not Garvey. "He made the point he was not a puppet of Ed Garvey," Dan Rooney remembered. "At the very least it showed that Anderson was willing to talk and that was progress."

Though Anderson's didn't know it, the NFL was also worried

that personalities were getting in the way of resolving the situation—particularly Wellington Mara's personality. The Giants owner defended himself. "If I believed that any members of our committee were an obstacle to settling problems, I would do everything I could to get a change."

Whatever his public position, it was apparent to his fellow owners that Mara was having trouble handling his role as chairman of the management council's executive committee. "I was close to an emotional breakdown a couple of times," Mara admitted. "It was the first time I had to face this kind of situation. There was enormous frustration. Things just got worse, not better. The things we believed in we were told were wrong. Our good faith was always questioned." Rozelle also recognized that a genuine opportunity was in danger of being lost. The commissioner found Anderson, a Joe Robbie employee, someone "I could talk to. He spoke quite rationally and reasonably and that was a welcome change from the kind of stridency we got daily from Garvey. . . ." Anderson was, Rozelle noted, "at odds with Garvey on a number of issues." As such, he presented an opening the League could not afford to pass up.

The League's first overt response to Anderson's speech was the appointment of Dan Rooney to take over the management council's negotiations. "They wanted a new face," Rooney explained. "I had a relationship with Garvey that was O.K. We understood each other. I'm not opposed to unions. Some people in the League called Garvey a Communist, but he was a good person, following what he thinks is the right way to go. . . . He'll tell you a lot of things that are just not so, but if he tells me something eye to eye, I believe him. You can't pay attention to the rhetoric."

The person Dan Rooney began dealing with, however, was not Garvey but Anderson. Rooney remembered, "I convinced Anderson that they wouldn't get an agreement if we just continued this way. I said Garvey wants to force total free agency down the League's throat but, given the recent Minneapolis court decision, we didn't need an agreement to get that. Why should we hand out benefits, what do we get out of it? We talked about what the League was willing to do in the way of pension, minimum salaries, and protection for players' rights. In return, the NFL wants preservation of its system of the draft and compensation for free agents. It would be chaos without it." At one point, the discussion focused on the development of a formula for Rozelle Rule compensation that would be acceptable to the union. "It was basically Anderson's idea," the commissioner remembered. "He thought it was a good way of compromising. We massaged it."

By the beginning of August, Anderson and Rooney had reached an agreement. In it, the gains of *Mackey v. NFL* were modified in exchange for a large increase in benefits. Neither the NFL nor the NFLPA was bound by the agreement Anderson and Rooney had reached, but both participants signed a letter "admitting our lack of authority but pledging we would both try to sell the arrangement to our two sides." Of the two, Anderson had the toughest selling job by far.

By this point, the union's membership had shrunk to sixty percent of its potential because of the lack of an automatic dues checkoff and "the association," according to *The New York Times,* "is torn between anti-Garvey and pro-Garvey forces," with Garvey having "the backing of the more militant of the members."

"Anderson stuck his neck out," one NFL executive remembered. "He thought he could get it done, but Garvey didn't like someone coming in the back door and undermining him." Their confrontation came when Anderson presented the agreement to the union's executive committee meeting in Chicago. Ed Garvey, however, would have nothing to do with the deal. Anderson's private initiative amounted to the first serious challenge to Garvey's leadership since the 1974 strike and Garvey moved quickly to dismantle it. "He accused Anderson of making under-the-table agreements," one union officer remembered. "Anderson's proposal was shot down quickly and it would have been voted down no matter what was in it. You can't cut deals without the knowledge of the executive committee. . . . There are always people pissed off at every contract and you have to have the perception of fairness, otherwise it won't work. You have to defend a contract for years, and twenty percent always think they got fucked. Garvey was right. It's no way to do business."

Once the union vote was held on August 31, the NFL grudgingly returned to the drawing board.

25
Davis Makes His Play in the Labor Impasse

The League's public resentment over the collapse of the Anderson-Rooney agreement naturally enough focused on Ed Garvey. Inside the confines of the NFL's executive sessions, however, Anderson and Rooney's failure also cast an air of suspicion over Al Davis.

Davis's ideas about labor were known to be at odds with most of the League's, making him an easy figure to resent. He had also been the only owner to break the NFL's solid front in responding to the *Mackey* decision. "We've got to be intelligent enough to modify, change, and rebuild our rules to deal with what the courts have ruled," he argued. "The judges are placing the rights of individuals above the interests of a group structure like ours so we have to do away with what's illegal."

NFL members also knew that Davis had also been working on his own plan to resolve the labor dispute. To many, it was yet another example of Al Davis "playing commissioner" at his own quest. Davis proposed compensating the signing of free agents with money instead of players and it was thought that he had communicated his plan directly to the union, bypassing the owners' negotiating team. By the summer of 1976, Al Davis was already forecasting "a change in the labor policy in our League" to grant "much more freedom for the players to move themselves from location to location." Rozelle maintained such an eventuality would destroy the football business. Later, Davis would say, "I think that wealth will be the prerequisite for greatness in the eighties."

That attitude made his fellow owners wonder just whose side Davis was on, and with some justification. "Al was a union supporter," one of his employees observed. Then the employee added a qualifier. "That is, of course, as long as he had a guy in the union in a position of power."

That "guy" in this instance was Gene Upshaw, Raiders player

representative, member of the NFLPA executive committee, and a rising star in the union's internal politics. Upshaw had played a major role in the devastation of Anderson's proposal. According to Davis, he and Upshaw "discussed the position [Upshaw] would take on every matter I think we have ever had between the players and the owners." In addition, since April 1975, Upshaw had been a "member" of Eastmont Mall Associates, Davis's shopping center partnership with casino king Allen Glick. Davis himself admitted it was "possible" that he had told one member of the now defunct planning committee that "he could get Gene Upshaw to do whatever he wanted." Not long after the Raiders' player rep had helped kill Anderson-Rooney, according to Rozelle, "word came through that Al had helped scuttle the deal through Upshaw."

According to Al Davis, the exact opposite had happened. "The League wanted to push through the Anderson-Rooney agreement," Davis remembered, "which was a stacked agreement. I didn't agree with it for a number of reasons, and they wanted me to urge Upshaw to push it through. And I wouldn't do it. . . . I have great influence on Gene. He is a friend of mine and I would never do anything to impugn his integrity, and when I was asked to do that, I wouldn't do it. . . . They wanted to get Ed Garvey out as a power [in the union] and wanted me to use Upshaw to do that. . . . I thought it was wrong, but most important of all, I never thought we would have an agreement without Ed Garvey and several owners, close friends of mine, chastized me on it. . . . We got into violent arguments over it."

Independent of the maneuvering around Anderson-Rooney, Al Davis remained an easy person for the rest of the NFL to dislike. "A combination genius and devil," his black suit, white shirt, and silver tie gave him a look *Sports Illustrated* dubbed "the appearance of a mobster in an old George Raft movie." *The* [Oakland] *Tribune* noted, "strangers sometimes express surprise when they find he has much charm."

"I don't know what they expect," Davis would observe, "maybe a fat, tough-talking guy with a big cigar in his mouth. I suppose they expect a flashy show-girl type on my arm. I guess it's a shock when they learn I've had the same wife for twenty years." Though Al Davis refused to appear on television or radio shows, his image was important to him and he made a habit of stroking the press corps. Every Christmas he distributed binoculars, TVs, stereos, and even cash to the Raiders' regular reporters. Davis called it nothing more than "a little appreciation for the guys who live with us," but in at least two instances, reporters were removed from the Davis beat by their editors for having compromised themselves by accepting his appreciation.

Central to the image Al Davis crafted for himself was victory in whatever form it was available. "My kick comes from trying to figure ways for us to win," Davis explained, "with the rules that everybody else makes. I'm no rule maker. Football is a game you play to win. Otherwise, like they say, why do we keep score? You play, you win, the money comes; and the recognition, if that's what you want."

Davis's hostility toward the commissioner was yet another factor that reinforced the "member clubs' " suspicions. "Davis is an implacable enemy of Pete Rozelle," *The Tribune* noted, "though he is more restrained in his criticism of the commissioner than Carroll Rosenbloom. . . . Of the two, Davis represents the more danger to the commissioner. The difference, it is said, is that Rosenbloom wants Rozelle's head; Davis is after his job."

Before the dust from Anderson-Rooney's rejection had settled, the rest of the League's owners had yet another incident upon which to hang their resentments of Al Davis.

On the opening day of the 1976 season, Al Davis's Raiders were pitted against Dan Rooney's Pittsburgh Steelers on national television. The two teams had a particularly vicious relationship of long standing. The play that set everything off occurred late in the first half. As described by *Sports Illustrated,* "Lynn Swann, the splendid wide receiver of the Steelers, ran a pattern down the right side of the field, then cut to the middle. He was covered by George Atkinson, a tough but hitherto unheralded defensive back for the Raiders. As the play unwound, [Steeler Quarterback] Terry Bradshaw was forced to scramble, eventually firing a pass to [Steeler running back] Franco Harris, who thundered downfield. As Harris caught the ball, fifteen yards away Atkinson rushed up behind the unsuspecting Swann and cracked him with a forearm at the base of the helmet. Swann dropped as if he were shot. He suffered a concussion and missed the next two games. No official saw Atkinson's blow, no penalty was levied."

The game's huge national television audience had witnessed everything, however, and saw it over and over again in slow motion replay as the game progressed. Even the hometown [Oakland] *Tribune* described Atkinson's blow as "dirty foot-

ball.'' Pittsburgh head coach Chuck Noll was incensed and made
it clear after the game that he considered Atkinson's play part of
a Raider strategy to maim the Steelers' best players. ''You have
a criminal element in all aspects of society,'' Noll charged
through clenched teeth. ''Apparently we have it in the NFL
too.'' Noll suggested that players like Atkinson should be ''kicked
out of the League.''

The burgeoning public relations disaster was dumped in Pete
Rozelle's lap. It was a week before he issued any judgment, and in
the meantime, the League office was ''swamped with calls and
letters about Atkinson's hit.'' On September 20, the commissioner's office announced it was fining Atkinson $1500 for what
Rozelle called as ''flagrant'' a foul as he had seen ''in sixteen
years in this office.'' He also fined Noll $1000 for his remarks,
under the NFL bylaw that forbade public criticism by a member
team of another.

Less than satisfied by the ruling, Dan Rooney fired a private
letter back to Rozelle charging ''direct premeditated, unemotional
efforts by the Oakland Raiders to seriously injure Lynn Swann.''
These efforts, Rooney charged, involved ''the Raiders coach
staff'' and, by implication, Al Davis. For his part, Davis's only
public stance was to blame the furor on the press. ''No one was
killed,'' he snapped when approached by a *Tribune* reporter.
''Why get excited? Yet you wrote as though the Pittsburgh game
was the My Lai massacre. You guys are the problem. You want
us to win. You want us to be tough. But when we're in a vicious
game with the Steelers, a team that is notorious for busting up
opponents, you seize on an incident involving one of our men
and you hammer away. Do you realize what would happen now
if we went back to Pittsburgh for one more game?''

Behind the scenes, however, Al Davis had a more aggressive
strategy in mind. ''Chuck Noll,'' he pointed out, ''had condemned certain individuals playing for the Oakland Raiders and
labeled them 'criminals' and I felt it was important that we get
rid of that label.''

George Atkinson, Davis's employee, did not take kindly to
being branded a ''criminal'' either. For him, the charge had a
particular kind of sting. In 1975, Atkinson had been brought to
trial in San Francisco on federal charges of embezzlement and
larceny for having allegedly convinced two female bank tellers to
steal some $3200 from two different Alameda County banks.
After one jury deadlocked for conviction, a second trial had

acquitted him on all counts. According to a teammate, "Al Davis was paying the bills" for Atkinson's defense.

Atkinson filed a $2 million slander suit against Steeler Coach Chuck Noll. "Pro football is on trial here," the attorney argued. "If a jury rules that Atkinson is not slandered by being called part of a 'criminal element' then the term 'criminal' has been judicially certified as a viable, proper, accurate definition of the game. After this, every time a player is injured . . . he could bring a criminal suit for assault. Hell, you could bring a class action suit against showing the 'criminal' violence of football on TV. Pro football could be X rated." The attorney's case would also focus "on the contention that there was a conspiracy on the part of the Rozelle-Rooney establishment to get the outcast upstart Oakland crowd led by Al Davis."

Rozelle, for one, was convinced that Al Davis was the one really suing and that the parties really being sued were the Pittsburgh Steelers, Dan Rooney, and the NFL itself. "Al Davis financed and ran the case," Rozelle charged. "Al didn't care how he did it. Hurting the League didn't bother him at all." It was the kind of behavior which Rozelle felt deserved a response.

Noll's defense would be financed by the Pittsburgh Steelers. Dan Rooney considered it an attempt to damage the Steelers on the playing field. "Davis was behind Atkinson," the Steelers' president complained. "In reality, it was Raiders v. Steelers, and that was the way it was fought." By the time the suit came to trial in June 1977, Davis's alleged pivotal role would be the official NFL position. "Mr. Atkinson was a nominal party in that lawsuit," one of its attorneys would claim. "The Raiders were the real party interest. . . . A lawyer for the Raiders actually conducted the examination of the principal witnesses . . . and the questions posed by [that lawyer] were the result of notes handed him by Mr. Davis sitting in the courtroom."

Al Davis would claim the opposite. "We didn't get into the case," he explained. "We sat there and watched it. . . . Chuck Noll called our players criminals. . . . It was a misrepresentation. It was unfair. . . . I resented it and the commissioner didn't do anything about it."

While *Atkinson v. Noll* was awaiting a place on the federal court trial docket in fall 1976, Dan Rooney warned the rest of the League. "It was the first suit by one NFL team against another NFL team," he pointed out. "It set a precedent and I pointed this out a number of times at League meetings." One fellow owner responded that rather than a precedent, this was really a "unique" case, much more tangled than one team against another.

"No it's not," Rooney snapped. "This is Raiders versus Steelers." Once the precedent of one team taking another to court was set, it would, he claimed, open the doors to potential disintegration of the League. Three years later, Rooney's prediction would become fact.

26
Carroll's Coliseum

Nevertheless, in the fall of 1976, the League's trepidations were still focused primarily on Carroll Rosenbloom. The IRS's visit to Rozelle had shocked a number of members and they were well aware that Rosenbloom's anger would not be easily extinguished. Since the San Diego annual meeting, however, C.R. had been relatively quiet.

For most of 1976, C.R. had his hands full with the second round in his Superstadium Game against the Los Angeles Memorial Coliseum Commission. His lease was due to expire at the end of the year and Rosenbloom had long since become totally disenchanted with his landlord. "The LAMCC was the worst kind of political body," his son Steve remembered. "It was divided into three parts and the president's position rotated each year. Every year we would tell the new president what we wanted and we'd get lip service but nothing else. Year after year it was the same thing."

In 1976, the president of the LAMCC, Pete Schabarum, and Rosenbloom had many discussions about the extension of the Rams' lease. C.R. presented two principal demands, but, according to Schabarum, "was not genuinely interested in a lease extension." The first demand was that the playing field be lowered, eliminating the running track that currently separated the audience from the game and making room for more seats. C.R.'s second demand was luxury boxes and, on this issue, negotiations made more headway. Rosenbloom wanted more than a hundred boxes strung along the rim of the Coliseum, "securing financing to bring into being [an] overall Coliseum, improvement program." As drawn up by architects, that program included lowering the field and squaring the oval shape at one end of the structure as well. On a "contingency" basis, the LAMCC agreed to provide design help, a bond counsel, a consultant, and "the initiation of a sales program offering those suites to the public." The contingency, according to Schabarum, was that a 1976 attempt to generate advance sales would be successful and that Rosenbloom would subsequently sign a longterm lease. Before football season, the Rams and the Coliseum announced the effort had begun.

The Coliseum, the sales brochure raved, "today stands on the threshold of a new era of achievement in stadium design and development. . . . Combining the rich tradition of the Coliseum's fifty-five-year history and a new concept of intimacy and game view improvement, a major renovation program will be completed [by the opening of the 1977 season], enabling the Coliseum to take its place among the nation's finest and most modern. . . . The addition of 138 luxurious, air-conditioned suites . . . will allow you and your guests to view the game in comfortable, relaxed surroundings. . . . Every seat in every suite is a winner! The sight lines between you and the playing field are superb. Every convenience awaits you and your friends, offering the ultimate in spectator luxury. . . . Add to this the advantage of parking spaces close to the Coliseum and private access to your suite!

"Because of the high interest already generated," the brochure claimed, "now is the time to arrange for your Coliseum suite."

In truth, the promotion was an early flop. Only a smattering of commitments came in. "L.A. may not have been ready for it," one LAMCC official noted. There was, as Rozelle later described it, "overwhelming disinterest." At that, C.R.'s deal with the LAMCC "unraveled" and he ended up accepting another three-year extension on the lease he already had. He was convinced the Coliseum would never be the kind of football palace he wanted and thought he deserved.

Not surprisingly, from fall 1976 on, Rosenbloom's concern about stadiums ranged all over the southern California landscape. To Al Davis, he mentioned he had considered Dodger Stadium in Chavez Ravine and the possibility of buying the baseball Dodgers in order to gain access to it. Rosenbloom also looked into building his own stadium in Inglewood or on a site near Hollywood racetrack. On "many occasions," Davis later testified,

C.R. also discussed the possibility of moving to Anaheim, right next door in Orange County.

Rosenbloom's superstadium preoccupation had not completely diminished his desire to lash out at Rozelle. The barrage he loosed in the commissioner's direction at the end of September was an elaboration on a theme C.R. had begun working the previous April, when the League's 1976 schedule was announced. At that time, the *Los Angeles Times* reported "a source with Rams connections" as saying that "every time the League could have gone one way or another, it went against the Rams." On September 30, C.R. seized the gauntlet again personally. The commissioner, he charged, had "deliberately" scheduled the Rams to play a 4:00 P.M. game in Miami the following Sunday at the start of Yom Kippur, the Jewish religious holiday. Carroll's wife, Georgia, would later describe the incident as his "Yom Kippur caper." It was one of the few times C.R., a titular Jew, raised the question of religion in his entire public life. Scheduling the game for Miami at that time was, Rosenbloom raged, "insensitive, arrogant, and stupid. But Rozelle has no sensitivity. Yom Kippur is the most important holiday to Jewish people. This is a thing that was done with malice aforethought. They said, 'Let's put the Jew in Miami for Yom Kippur and see how he likes it.' I just know Rozelle and his stooges were giggling about it on the day they released the schedule. . . . I make no claim to being a religious man, but I am Jewish and this is an insensitivity that has offended many people.

"The whole schedule of the Rams was based on punishing me," Rosenbloom continued. "It is a punishment and a warning to other teams that if they criticize Pete Rozelle, they will also be punished. . . . Every team that is a contender, we play away from home. . . . If Rozelle could have arranged to have us play at midnight in Nome, Alaska, he would have done it."

Rozelle responded on October 1. "We attempt to avoid scheduling conflicts with all religious holidays," he explained. "Unfortunately, it is not always possible to do so. This League was obligated to provide a national network telecast this Sunday beginning at four o'clock Eastern time. The Rams, by scheduling rotation, play the Dolphins in Miami, and this was the only attractive game available." Privately, Rozelle managed to chuckle over the attack. "One of the Jewish owners in the League called me," the commissioner noted. "He said, 'I'd hate to have been hanging by my toes since the last time Carroll went to temple.' "

Carroll's son Steve agreed with the gist of the joke. "My

father was no more Jewish than you are,'' he offered to one Protestant reporter. "He really didn't want a late afternoon game and it gave him an excuse to jump on Rozelle." In the fall of 1976, the commissioner and the League braced itself for the next attack, but what followed instead was an eerie calm. Rosenbloom put his Rozelle feud on hold and devoted himself to winning his Super Stadium Game once and for all.

27
Winning the Labor War

On October 18, 1976, the appeals court sitting in the case of *Mackey v. NFL* announced its ruling. "The National Football League's Rozelle Rule, which applies to every League player regardless of his status or ability, which is unlimited in duration, and enforcement of which is unaccompanied by procedural safeguards, as enforced, unreasonably restrains trade in violation of the Sherman Act." If, however, the Rozelle Rule were a condition specifically accepted in collective bargaining, such a labor contract would exempt the arrangement from Sherman Act jurisdiction. At first the response of everyone in the league was depression. "It was another loss," Wellington Mara remembered. Only Ted Kheel, one of the council's two leading labor attorneys, thought otherwise. "This is not just a victory," he crowed, "but a great victory."

"Everyone laughed at him and called him the captain of the *Titanic*," Mara remembered, "but I soon saw his point. Garvey analyzed the appeals court decision and saw that he should start consolidating his gains."

Kheel's opinion was soon that of the entire League. "The union position," Rozelle explained, "had been that antitrust laws were on one side of the equation, labor law on the other, and that the antitrust law overrode the labor laws. . . . The owners felt Garvey always wanted two bites out of the apple—whatever he could get or was entitled to under the labor laws he wanted, then he'd go to court and try and get it under antitrust laws. The *Mackey* appeals court came down saying the issues shouldn't be resolved in court, but instead in collective bargaining. Once the union realized its major legal premise had been pulled out from under it, he decided to bargain.''

Ed Garvey also felt the effects of more than two years without a payroll checkoff with which to collect NFLPA dues. ''Our membership was down to about three hundred,'' one union source later told *The New York Times*. ''You have no idea how close we were to going out of business.'' While Garvey considered the appeals court decision a ''victory,'' talks with the League resumed before Christmas. The talks commenced in a Washington, D.C., hotel suite decorated with red velvet wallpaper. Both sides were well aware of past failures in similar situations. ''If you absolutely do not trust them,'' Garvey explained to *Sports Illustrated,* ''and they do not trust you, then you can't get a settlement.'' The Management Council's chief negotiator, attorney Sargent Karch, arrived with what he hoped would be a new approach. ''Settling was just a matter of trust,'' Karch remembered. ''Everybody assumed we could not agree because of Garvey, so I started to think in terms of what was important to Garvey and the union.''

''We reasoned that the Rozelle Rule . . . was *not* all that important to Garvey,'' Karch explained. ''Getting rid of the Rozelle Rule would help the wealthy players at the expense of the poor ones. The way we began to view it, the Rozelle Rule [was] simply the way Garvey was getting his leverage and he was getting more leverage with every court decision. Then we concluded that three things were important to Garvey: 1) the strength of his union, 2) outside arbitration of player grievances . . . and 3) cash settlements of the lawsuits striking down the Rozelle Rule. . . . I decided to make a last try with Garvey and bring up these three issues.''

''For the first time,'' Garvey agreed, ''there was a discussion of things we wanted to talk about instead of just what they wanted to talk about. . . . They'd never bargained before.'' At the meeting's conclusion, Garvey expressed pleasure with their progress. ''Sarge,'' he said to Karch, ''I hope you're not kidding me.''

''When Ed said that,'' Karch remembered, ''it told me a lot. It was then that I knew a settlement was possible.''

More discussions followed in January and February in 1977. On February 9, however, everything seemed to come apart. That afternoon, ''angered by the owners' sudden refusal to discuss the major issues,'' Garvey walked out of bargaining sessions and returned to his nearby office. Dan Rooney arrived at

NFLPA headquarters shortly after Garvey and began talking to him, one-to-one. At dinnertime, the two men adjourned to a nearby steak house and were joined by Karch and two members of the union's negotiating team. "It was the first time we'd ever broken bread together," Garvey remembered. "We managed to talk over a good many things informally and by the time we paid our own checks, we'd gotten back on the track."

Shortly before midnight on February 16, 1977, the two sides agreed on a seventy-six-page contract, ending the longest labor war in football business history.

The union gained status as what Dan Rooney called "a full-fledged National Labor Relations Board union, an agency shop where you have to pay dues even if you don't join. It was significant to the union," Rooney noted, "and a major issue among the owners. There were some who fought it all the way and there was much argument. I told them, 'We will maintain the system, we will continue to operate. The union will play a bigger role and that is just the way it will be. It's a fact.' "

The union also won concessions on Rozelle's authority over player grievances, a $107-million package of benefits spread over the five-year life of the contract, and a number of the "freedom issues" with which the strike had begun. In addition, the NFL would pay $13.65 million over ten years to settle the damages arising from *Mackey v. NFL*. This money would be distributed among active and former players. In return, the Players Association accepted the Rozelle Rule, completely abandoning the free agency it had won little more than a year earlier, and making the NFL's system once again legal. It was the most controversial concession Ed Garvey could have made. One player's agent would later describe the move as "the biggest sellout by a union in sports history." Garvey, however, considered it worth it.

As did Pete Rozelle. Almost three years of continuous external warfare were over and, at last, it seemed as though the forces of "stability" were again on the rise.

28
Solidifying New England

At a New England Patriots stockholders meeting on December 8, 1976, the Sullivans eliminated the last publicly traded stock in the NFL and, Billy Sullivan redeemed his ten-year-old ownership policy promises in full. From Rozelle's point of view, "stability" in the franchise was now "assured."

Chuck Sullivan's phase two had not, however, been easy to pull off. The younger Sullivan would eventually be known throughout the NFL for his capacity "to get things done," especially where banks were involved, and that reputation was first earned in the last six months of 1976.

The Sullivans' problems began arising when H.B. 5133, reducing the state requirements for corporate mergers to 50.1 percent, reached the desk of Governor Michael Dukakis in August. Though they were both on the same political side, the relationship between Dukakis and the Sullivans was uncomfortable. In 1974, when Dukakis was the Democratic party's candidate, Billy had publicly snubbed him at a large party fund-raiser, embarrassing everybody there except perhaps himself. There was also increasing opposition to the measure, led by the Boston Bar Association and the Associated Industries of Massachusetts, both of whom had written Dukakis asking him to block H.B. 5133. "There was tremendous pressure on everyone up there to get this done for Billy Sullivan," one state politician told *The Boston Globe*. "Everyone was in line."

While Chuck Sullivan was confident his family could secure the governor's signature, timing remained a problem. The banks required Billy to pledge the entire Patriots franchise as additional collateral by October 1, 1976; the deadline for accomplishing his "freezeout" was rapidly approaching. In response to that urgency, the State Senate had added a provision to H.B. 5133 making it effective on September 18, 1976. The House, however, struck down that provision, meaning the bill would not become law until ninety days after the governor

236

signed it. Dukakis did so on August 29 but it would not be available to the Sullivans until November 26.

As a consequence, the Sullivans were at the mercy of their banks, where things were not going all that smoothly. Not only did it look as though the Sullivans would miss their deadline, but to finance phase two, the banks were to loan Billy another $1.4 million with which to make the bulk of the nonvoting share buyout, and the banks were getting more nervous about their money every week.

Prior to H.B. 5133 becoming law, the banks' principal worry stemmed from a Federal Securities and Exchange Act rule that, in the view of the Rhode Island Hospital Trust, called for the purchaser to "make full and complete disclosure of all facets of the proposed merger." The minority stockholders also had the right, even if the deal went through, to sue for the face value of their stock. It was this, Rhode Island Hospital Trust's senior vice-president emphasized, that "causes us the most concern."

Chuck Sullivan drafted the prospectus making the required disclosures to the stockholders in the course of the merger. The proposed price was fifteen dollars a share and among the "corporate purposes" allegedly served by eliminating the minority shareholders was compliance with NFL ownership policy prohibitions of publicly traded stock. The banks responded to this prospectus by reporting that, "it was felt that the business reasons for the merger as set forth in the preliminary copy of the proxy material were misleading as stated because they inferred that the NFL was requiring the Patriots to 'go private.' " In addition, since . . . "the [nonvoting] stock would have a value of fifty to sixty dollars a share, . . . the validity of a fifteen-dollar-per-share offering price is questionable." To Hospital Trust, the shortfall posed an enormous dilemma. "To make the necessary disclosures to the public holders of the [nonvoting] stock pertaining to the value of their stock," the memo gloomily concluded, "would probably kill Sullivan's proposed merger." With it would die the security on Hospital Trust's loan.

Chuck Sullivan was unfazed. "We did not try to hide anything. In our opinion, and that of our counsel, everything was put into the proxy statement that should have been there." Sullivan submitted his draft to the SEC and they returned to him a six-page list of recommended changes. Again unfazed, Chuck complied and, though the SEC would eventually investigate the buyout after the fact, nothing it found would be considered actionable.

Reaction among the actual holders of nonvoting shares was decidedly mixed. One stockholder concluded that the fifteen-dollar offering price meant the Sullivans were attempting to buy "a $16,000,000 franchise for the total price of $6,743,637." Another angry shareholder declared, "You can tell the Sullivans to go to hell; my stock is not for sale at any price."

By then, the legal worries of the national banks had been enlarged to include the impact of H.B. 5133. They had assumed a vote of sixty-seven percent would be required and "were relying heavily on that protection" in their commitment to the Sullivans' $1.4 million loan. Now, their loan was more legally exposed than ever. The exposure, they worried, would enlarge even further if Billy voted the 11,026 shares of public stock he either owned or controlled. In September, the banks modified their agreement so they would be held free of any possible litigation in the merger. In addition, the banks insisted Sullivan not vote the stock he controlled until after a majority of the publicly traded shares had already been reached.

Billy Sullivan complained bitterly. To the banks, he claimed the restrictions "would be extremely detrimental to the success of the transaction." Then, at the end of October, twenty-eight days after the original deadline had passed, phase two of Chuck Sullivan's plan for his father's comeback collapsed. LaSalle announced it "did not wish to continue further in the recapitalization financing." Chuck Sullivan, "took the news calmly." He asked if this meant LaSalle was demanding repayment of his father's outstanding loan. The executive vice-president responded that "he hadn't come to that point, but would be studying his bank's position" over the next few days. Chuck's only response was that he would find another bank.

Despite their actions, both LaSalle and Hospital Trust's vice-presidents wanted to give the Sullivans room to save their merger. "LaSalle and we will assess the situation," Hospital Trust's representative noted the following day, "hopefully to the satisfaction of the Sullivans. We both like them very much."

Good will or not, for Chuck Sullivan, the entire financial structure he had created was quivering. He now not only had to find a new $1.4 million to buy out the nonvoting shares, he also had to find someone to take over the debt left from buying out the voting shares a year earlier. By November, Chuck had convinced LaSalle and Hospital Trust to agree that, while "reserving the right to demand payment on the Note at any time, in order to enable the Patriots to proceed with alternative financing plans, the Banks confirm that they do not have any present intention of demanding payment.'' Sullivan was assuring LaSalle and Hospital Trust that First National Bank of Chicago was going to ''come in,'' but the details still had to be worked out. Finally, on December 8, Chuck Sullivan arrived at the New England Patriots' stockholders meeting with his father's financing intact. The meeting was presided over by Billy. Less than one hundred of the twenty-six hundred stockholders attended. A number spoke against the merger, a few spoke in favor. Then the counting of proxies began. Fittingly, it was Chuck Sullivan who announced the results. ''The shareholders,'' he intoned, had ''approved a plan of corporate restructuring.''

The public credit was all Chuck's. ''I don't care for the guy,'' one of his father's former partners allowed, ''but I do admire the way he pulled the whole thing off. This is his deal all the way.''

If Chuck himself gave credit, it was in private and likely included a large measure of gratitude to H.B. 5133. With Billy's almost 11,000 shares, the total majority approving the merger was 59 percent. Without them, it was 51.2 percent. Under the Massachusetts corporate statutes that had been in effect until only twelve days earlier, Billy Sullivan's comeback would have collapsed on his son's head, eight percent short of success.

The Massachusetts merger laws would be changed back to two thirds again in 1981 and at the time, the principal question would be why the reversal had taken so long. ''What happened with the bill for the Patriots,'' one Boston politician explained, ''was an embarrassment to a lot of people. Everyone knew what happened and they didn't want to be further embarrassed by changing it back the next year.''

The actual payout to effect the merger began before Christmas, using $1.4 million from the First National Bank of Chicago. Within three months, LaSalle, Rhode Island Hospital Trust, and the First of Chicago would all be paid off by a new loan from Industrial National Bank of Rhode Island. The Industrial of Rhode Island loan was at lower interest rates and, according to Chuck, ''we ended up with a better situation all around.'' By then, Chuck Sullivan's burgeoning reputation for finance had made him a rising NFL star in his own right.

29
Davis's Star Rises

If there was any omen of the NFL's future as 1976 turned to 1977, it was the presence of Al Davis and his Raiders in the January 9 Super Bowl XI. The next round of turmoil in the football business would make the previous three years seem tame and Al Davis would be one of those at the heart of the disorder.

For Davis, Super Bowl XI was a personal landmark. Since losing Super Bowl II, his team had not been back, though over that time the Raiders had accumulated the best record in the League. Fittingly, victory came at the end of the first season during which control of the Oakland franchise had been Davis's alone. Just as fittingly, the Raiders reached the Super Bowl by thrashing Dan Rooney's Pittsburgh Steelers, his current courtroom adversaries. But why it had taken him so long to reach the Super Bowl? As hoopla for the "Game of Games" mounted, *Newsweek* noted, "Al's boiling mix of ego, tunnel vision, and genius demands that he play down the Super Bowl just a bit."

"Isn't it great to be on top?" someone asked him.

"We've been on top for a long time," Davis snapped.

And what a "top" it was. Super Bowl Sunday was the culmination of a four-month period during which an estimated nine billion American manhours had been spent watching the NFL. It was also the biggest single day of the year for bookies and an estimated $260 million would be wagered one way or another. Over 100,000 people would attend the game in Pasadena's Rose Bowl and for the week preceding it, a Super Bowl ticket was the hottest item in the United States.

Those tickets were also an item of sharp contention inside the League. As of yet, the League had no set formula for distributing tickets to its newly minted classic, so tickets for each Super Bowl were allocated at the preceding year's annual meeting, a system Al Davis found "unique" and "unheard of." As approved unanimously, each team not playing in the game would be given 1,000 tickets apiece, each of the two participating teams would get 15,000, while 10,000 went to the League office, and 8,000 were offered for public sale. What Davis found "unique" was that the remaining 30,000 highly prized tickets were all allocated to the host franchise, the Los Angeles Rams. Just a day after charging him with "stealing from his partners," the League gave C.R. enough tickets to make it Carroll's Super Bowl, whether his team got there or not. Al Davis was especially irritated that the League office had "upped their ante for Super Bowl tickets" as well. Davis later testified, ". . . the people who were getting all the Super Bowl tickets were the host city and the commissioner's office, and the two competing teams who might need the most tickets were given an allocation just to satisfy them and keep them in place."

Then came the issue of price. The hottest tickets in the country had a face value of just twenty dollars. As a consequence, scalpers were peddling them for ten and twenty times as much, usually through travel agencies packaging tours that included a seat for the game. When some owners suggested upping the ticket's face value, Pete Rozelle considered it bad public relations and kept the price down. "As far back as 1974," Davis remembered, "different owners . . . asked why the commissioner has not raised ticket prices for the Super Bowl commensurate with the demand for those Super Bowl tickets. . . . I remember Lamar Hunt standing up and saying, 'We are selling a twenty-dollar ticket that should be fifty.' And I remember asking one owner in a League meeting, 'Why the hell doesn't he do it?' "

When his Raiders were headed for Pasadena, Super Bowl tickets became a source of direct contention between Davis and Rozelle. "At that time," Davis remembered, "I called the commissioner and I said, 'Listen. I have got a tremendous problem here. We have got a minimum amount of tickets. We have a demand that is unbelievable. The fans are in an uproar. I need some more Super Bowl tickets. . . . I don't know why you need as many as you got and certainly the Rams don't need as many as they got, and I would like an allocation of about another three to four thousand . . .' I told him that if I were playing in Miami, I would understand the amount we were getting. We were playing in Pasadena, which is a short plane trip . . . for our fans, and they wanted tickets. The press was on us tremendously." Rozelle, Davis recalled, said "he would see what he could do about it."

The commissioner told Davis he could arrange a "loan" of two hundred tickets from the Rams. "What about the League office?" Davis demanded.

Rozelle said all theirs were gone.

"I was upset," Davis remembered, "[but] I took the two hundred tickets."

Al Davis would later claim to have been even more upset when he found out just what C.R. was doing with his tickets. According to Davis, Rosenbloom "asked me what I was going to do with [the Raiders'] tickets, and I said we are going to give them to our fans, give them to the people we thought were necessary to give them to."

"What are you going to sell them for?" C.R. asked.

Davis replied, "Face value."

Rosenbloom objected that he was a fool to do so. "Look," the Rams owner offered, "I have a guy who knows how to handle this. He knows how to market these tickets. We could make a fortune."

"I said I wouldn't do it, and was committed to go ahead the way we were doing it, and I was quite shocked about it," Davis claimed. "I asked him who the guy was and he said it was a fellow by the name of Harold Guiver. . . . Carroll said Guiver owned a ticket agency." Davis also wondered what C.R. planned to do about Rozelle's response. "You're going to get in a lot of trouble," he pointed out.

Rosenbloom, in the derisive tone he used when mentioning the commissioner, asked if Davis was kidding. "Rozelle is in this up to his neck," C.R. claimed. "He knows what is going on. This is where he makes his big score."

Later Davis testified, Rosenbloom "talked to me about what he had done with the Super Bowl tickets that had been allocated to the host city . . . and told me they made a killing."

"For Christ's sake, Carroll," Davis responded, "you got a lot of guts."

"This time again," the Oakland owner remembered, Rosenbloom said in roundabout words that Rozelle "is in this up to his neck. . . . What is he going to do about it? He knows about the scalping. He knows about the travel agencies who are making a fortune. . . . He is well aware of it. We talked about it at League meetings. He has never done a thing about it."

"I was just shocked about it," Davis repeated. "I was then told that other owners are in the travel agency business . . . and that they are using their tickets for their travel agencies. He wanted to know if I would like to start a travel agency. . . . I told him, no, that I didn't want to get involved in it. I didn't want any part of it, and I was again led to believe that the commissioner . . . was using these tickets not only for his self-gain, but as a way of getting around people throughout the country.'' Despite his protestations, Davis discussed the travel agency idea with Carroll face-to-face, but nothing ever came of it.

Almost four years later, when the struggle between Al Davis and Pete Rozelle had reached the no-holds-barred stage and gone public, Davis revealed C.R.'s charges against Rozelle, and Rozelle denied every one.

At the time, Davis said nothing. In fact, he was most conspicuous by his invisibility. While Pete Rozelle was throwing a $100,000 party for some two thousand members of the press, Davis was off somewhere in a room that smelled of sweat socks, watching film and diagraming plays. "I have no roundness in my life,'' he admitted. "I've got to be all football, all sharp edges. If I want something else, I've got to find time at two in the morning.''

On the morning of Super Bowl Sunday, he was spotted loitering around the sidelines before anyone but the TV crews had entered the stadium.

"Where have you been?'' a reporter asked.

"Aw, you know me,'' Davis joked. "If I come around, I say something controversial, and the commissioner doesn't get the headlines.''

During the game, Davis was in his traditional seat in the press box, jaw clenched, wearing sunglasses, eyes glued to the field. With five minutes left to play, the Raiders led 32-7. At that point, *Newsweek* reported, "reporters and well-wishers began to swarm around Davis. They grabbed his hand and slapped his back, probed at him with microphones and even spilled coffee on the ledge in front of him. Aides scurried to clean and shield their dictator's territory. But Davis's gaze never left the field.''

"I don't want to lose track of the game,'' he snapped.

"Hey, Al, congratulations,'' someone shouted. "Your team's playing great. Really super.''

"What bullshit,'' Davis muttered, eyes still riveted to the game below.

When final whistle blew with the score 32-14, Al Davis hurried to the Rose Bowl locker room to celebrate with the team and accept the Super Bowl trophy from Pete Rozelle under the TV lights set up there.

Though it never dented his appearance, it must have been a nervous moment for Rozelle. On the other side of the lights,

Raiders, covered with turf stains and adhesive tape, were pouring champagne on each other and jumping up and down. Among them, George Atkinson, official plaintiff in *Atkinson v. Noll,* was delivering "a vividly worded diatribe" against the commissioner for everyone to hear. For his part, Davis had the look of a man standing right where he knew he would always be.

"I'm sorry it's not silver and black," the commissioner joked as he handed over the two-foot-tall pedestal topped with a silver football, "but it's close. Al, your victory was one of the most impressive in football history."

Taking the trophy, Davis was exultant. "This is magnificent," he crowed. "I said we'd get it someday and we have." After the obligatory thanking of everyone in the Raider organization, he then addressed the issue of Oakland's fans. "What concerns me," he said, "are the season ticket holders we had to leave home. I'm going to push for more tickets when a Super Bowl team comes from a city near the site. That we upset some of our loyal fans is the only negative part of this whole thing. I hope the fans will forgive us."

It was, of course, a dig at Pete Rozelle, but at that time, only Davis, Rosenbloom, and Rozelle knew it. Over the next six years, Rozelle would present two more such trophies to Al Davis. With each, the scene would only get more difficult and its portent more dark.

PART THREE

THE
POT
BOILS

1
No April Fool Davis

When the National Football League convened its 1977 annual meeting on March in Phoenix, the football business was on the verge of the most damaging sequence of internal struggles in its history, but again, no one seemed to notice. After three years of open warfare with the WFL, and with the players association, the League's own politics seemed little more than random skirmishing of a familiar type. The commissioner's public comments consumption still focused largely on the war just gone by. "There have been some negative feelings toward us that began during that turbulent period when new leagues were started," he pointed out to *Sport* magazine. "From that you've had player movement, you've had strikes, you've had a number of things that were turn-offs, but I think we pretty much nipped it in the bud."

In Phoenix, Rozelle's opening report was bulging with superlatives. Paid attendance for the previous season had "exceeded eleven million for the first time in history," and overall attendance "was 15,071,846, second only to the record year of 1973." The record breaking numbers for television were just as staggering. Super Bowl XI reached an estimated audience of 81.9 million. But the greatest accomplishment of the previous year in Rozelle's eyes was the agreement reached with the NFLPA, which the commissioner reported, "paves the way for intelligent planning and implementation of steps to solidify the franchises and the League."

One such step was the rewriting of Rozelle's contract as commissioner. The process had begun the previous December, when the owners had created a three-man committee chaired by Leonard Tose, "to negotiate a new long-term contract" with Rozelle. On January 16, the members approved a new ten-year contract for Rozelle by a vote of twenty-seven to one. Though the financial terms were not released to the public, it was described by one owner as "another handsome increase." To no one's surprise, the one vote against this "strong reaffirmation" of Rozelle's authority had been cast by Al Davis.

The relationship between Davis and the commissioner was, by now, volatile at best. The antagonism was not lost on the rest of the League, but most still tended to look past Davis toward Rosenbloom when fearing trouble. Al Davis's free-lancing continued to be measured on a scale of personal eccentricity rather than political threat, despite Dan Rooney's repeated warnings to the contrary. Rozelle was convinced he had to deal with Davis's transgressions in no uncertain terms and he arrived in Phoenix prepared to begin putting the Raiders' managing general partner in his place.

First, Rozelle took steps to cover his own flank. A proposal to standardize the formula for dividing up Super Bowl tickets was among the "steps to solidify the League" the commissioner had heralded in his opening address. The proposal allocated one percent to each of the League's twenty-six nonparticipants, ten percent to the League office, twenty-four percent to the host city, and twenty percent to each of the participants. The measure passed twenty-one to seven.

Three days later, Rozelle laid the groundwork for his move on Davis, though the step seemed innocuous at the time. According to the minutes, "the member clubs approved by unanimous vote [that] . . . the commissioner will in consultation with the conference presidents appoint standing committees of the League and would make replacements on an irregular rotation basis." Apparently, the import of the policy was lost, even on the wily Davis. The expression of policy formally confirmed the commissioner's power to "irregularly rotate" owners. When it was passed, Rozelle was already preparing to use that power in a dramatic fashion. His target was Al Davis's seat on the powerful Competition Committee.

The Competition Committee, chaired by Tex Schramm, was charged with "recommending all changes in rules in the area of on the field competition." Its purview also included scheduling, roster sizes, and the trading and waiving of players—a majority of the actual mechanics of the football business. Schramm was most impressed with Davis's contribution there, and the two had formed a close working relationship. "Tex and Al had a good time working on rules together," Rozelle remembered, "but people on a committee should be thinking for the League, what's best for the League. Al had dropped out of NFL Charities, was suing another club using George Atkinson as a straw man, and played a role in the failure of the Anderson-Rooney agreement." In Rozelle's eyes, Davis was using his role on the committee to "give validity to positions contrary to League policy." According to one NFL executive, Rozelle intended to put a stop to it.

Pete Rozelle had made his reputation by getting along, but in spring 1977, he was not looking to smooth things over with Al Davis. The Competition Committee was the one thing Al Davis wanted that Pete Rozelle could deny him. Such was the intensity of Rozelle's intentions that he did not bother to consult Schramm in advance. In all other instances of the removal of owners from committees, Pete had always talked it over with Tex. But this time, when the Cowboys president learned of the move, he would publicly describe it as a "disservice" to his committee and to the League. "He took me off the Competition Committee," Al Davis remembered. "Never faced me man to man and told me. Just did it, and then leaked it to the press so that . . . it would be a big story, make him strong."

In March 1977, Al Davis already assumed the commissioner's ill will, but made no moves to reduce it. His first Super Bowl victory had not mellowed him. "You keep fighting," he pointed out. He still watched miles of game footage and still saw things his coaches had missed. Even when out to dinner, he often ended up diagraming plays on the tablecloth. Al refused to patronize restaurants in which there was no phone to bring to his table; he even bought an interest in a restaurant near the Raiders' practice field to insure he would always have a place nearby where he could both eat and talk on the phone. To relax, he lifted weights, drank ice water, and attended sporting events. "The dictator hasn't lost his drive," *The* [Oakland] *Tribune* noted.

Inside the Raider organization, Davis now called all the shots. He still had Ed McGah for a general partner and a dozen or so limited partners as well, but that only meant that he had to pay lip service to an annual meeting. His principal lieutenant was Al LoCasale, a stumpy man who had been with Davis at the San Diego Chargers when Davis was still an assistant coach. "LoCasale was a strong manager," a Davis acquaintance observed. "He took a lot of the day-to-day weight off Al's shoulders without being a threat. LoCasale was a smart man who made himself a very strong colonel to Davis's general. He became Al's voice to the public when Al himself didn't feel like talking. As Al rose in stature, he used LoCasale more and more. LoCasale made himself conversant with Davis's views and made himself a second voice. There was not, however, any doubt about who was in charge."

Davis's organizational model was apparently Germanic. "He

was a great admirer of Hitler and the Nazis," Davis's former partner Wayne Valley remembered. Given that he was Jewish, Davis's admiration was all the more remarkable. "I didn't hate Hitler," Davis explained. "I was captivated by him. I knew he had to be stopped. He took on the whole world." Al Davis's religion was, like the rest of him, personal and free-lance. "Al was barely conversant in Judaism," one Davis intimate remembered. "It was a personal thing that was largely a reaction to his father's death while he was still in San Diego, before the Raiders . . . the only day you can be sure Al will make it to a synagogue is the anniversary of his father's death." Whatever the particulars of Al Davis's theology, it made him neither self-conscious nor timid. "Al was a slick son of a bitch," one of his friends pointed out. "When he wanted to do something, he found a way to do it. I sure wouldn't want to get in a fight with him. He just doesn't back off."

That Al Davis had no intentions of smoothing Rozelle's feathers was apparent on April 1, when the annual meeting discussed "the various commitments made to NFL Charities by various clubs." Davis made it clear he intended to continue "requesting receipt of royalties" from NFL Properties "rather than contributing to Charities." When later asked to explain Davis's continued refusal, Rozelle offered, "Because I suggested it." On that April Fool's Day, few members were yet prepared to give Davis's attitude the significance it deserved.

2
San Francisco for Sale

The item on the 1977 annual meeting's agenda that drew the most attention was the admission of a new member. The San Francisco 49er franchise was being sold to one Edward DeBartolo Jr., and formal League approval was sought to finalize the transaction. The sale had been gestating for more than a year and a half, and a number of familiar characters had been involved in the process.

First was Wayne Valley, Al Davis's ex-partner. Lou Spadia, 49ers president, had notified the commissioner in the summer of

1975 that the Morabito sisters were looking to sell their ninety percent interest. When Rozelle asked Valley if he would be interested in buying the 49ers, Valley's immediate response was "yes." By Christmas, it seemed Valley and Spadia had cut a deal. The price was $11.3 million cash. Valley, however, still had his doubts whether the sale would go through. The owners' minority partner, Franklin Meuli, had the right to block any sale by exercising his own rights of first refusal. Meuli, Valley pointed out, was a friend of Al Davis and Davis would not stand by while his ex-partner set up shop right across the bay.

Valley's prediction was on the mark. According to *Sports Illustrated*, Davis "convinced" Franklin Meuli "to exercise his first refusal right" and stalled the sale for almost a year while Meuli attempted to gather enough partners to make a formal offer. In April 1976, Rozelle tried to get Meuli and Valley together in the hope that the two of them might combine to buy the San Francisco franchise, but the attempt was ill-fated. A meeting was arranged but shortly after it began, according to Valley, Meuli stood up without explanation and left.

The episode was the last in Wayne Valley's football career. Rather than pursue the 49er opportunity, he decided to get out for good. "The fun had gone out of it and I didn't buy," he remembered. "The game had changed."

At this point, Al Davis explained, "Valley was knocked out of the purchase" and for the rest of 1976 Franklin Meuli held center stage. Meuli was a former advertising executive with little relative wealth and it was no secret by fall 1976 that Meuli was having difficulties raising capital. As his December 1 deadline approached, Meuli even made overtures to Valley again, but Valley would have none of it. Things were not going smoothly between Meuli and the NFL office either. Meuli's professional basketball team was a source of "significant concern." Rozelle pointed out that the League's continuing ownership policy resolution prohibited cross-ownership by new members. If Meuli wanted in, the commissioner observed, he would have to get out of basketball as well. On December 1, 1976, Meuli failed to make a solid offer and disappeared from the picture.

While Al Davis was glad Meuli had derailed Wayne Valley, he was no doubt also pleased at the collapse of Meuli's position. Davis's continuing problem with the 49er sale was the price. "It was bigger than a Brink's deal," he pointed out. "The heist was on." By the end of 1976, the price of football franchises had become an unsettling issue throughout the NFL and, though most of the League still preferred Wayne Valley, Davis had done them all a service by blocking the $11.3 million offer. After close to two decades of continually rising franchise values, something of a price panic had now set in, instigated by a new tax law. Under the revised IRS code, only a maximum of fifty percent of any sports franchise's purchase price could be ascribed to the value of its player contracts and thus depreciated over a four-year period—the tax law's definition of a player's useful working life. "The new bill will reduce franchise values substantially," one tax accountant predicted. Had the $11.3 million sale gone through, that prediction would have been substantially proven and, on paper, everyone in the League would have been worth $4 million less. Instead, Davis now moved to confound the prediction entirely.

Shortly after the Super Bowl in January 1977, the attorney for the Morabito sisters approached Davis and asked for his assistance in finding a buyer. Davis proved ideal for the task. "Davis is a man who loves to move behind the scenes," one Davis associate told the *San Francisco Chronicle*, "set things up, work out details—the more complex the better. This deal was a natural for him."

A familiar face soon entered—Joe Thomas, the man who'd brought Robert Irsay to Baltimore. In January, two of Irsay's attorneys had informed Thomas that if he didn't resign, he would be fired. Since Thomas still had a year to go on his contract, he refused and was fired. Back on the streets but undaunted, Thomas set out to find himself another owner. In February, Thomas called Edward DeBartolo Sr. and asked if the Ohio construction magnate might be interested in buying the San Francisco franchise. DeBartolo told Thomas he would buy the San Francisco franchise only on the condition that Thomas would run it. Thomas signed a general manager's contract before negotiations for the purchase of the franchise had even begun. Thomas then approached Al Davis, asking his assistance. At the time, Davis claimed to have been on the verge of approaching DeBartolo himself.

Edward DeBartolo Sr. was already something of a familiar commodity in NFL circles, at least by reputation. When he had been considered for Tampa's expansion team, he had impressed the League with his "financial clout." Called "the richest man in Ohio," (*Forbes* would later estimate his net worth at "well over $500 million") DeBartolo had made almost all of it himself. Born in 1910 in Youngstown's Italian "hollow,"

DeBartolo had lost his natural father, who had died of a heart attack three months before his birth. Taking the name of his stepfather, an immigrant paving contractor who neither read nor wrote, DeBartolo worked his way through Notre Dame and graduated with a degree in engineering. After the war, he founded the Edward DeBartolo Corp., then a fledgling construction company.

By 1977, the DeBartolo Corp. was considered the largest developer in the United States, pioneer of both the shopping center and the enclosed shopping mall. Some seventy different companies in all parts of the country were under its overall umbrella, including thirty-four shopping complexes, a free trade port, four Holiday Inns, hundreds of acres of land, some gas wells, and three Florida banks. Edward DeBartolo ran it all from his Youngstown headquarters, working twelve to fifteen hours a day. Soft-spoken, short, thin, and well-dressed, he had never taken a vacation in the history of his corporation. What time off he did take, he spent at home with his family. It was common for him to spend five hundred hours a year flying to his various projects. For short trips, he used a three-passenger Super Helio Courier, for longer trips, he took his Learjet. He employed three pilots full-time.

DeBartolo's previous participation in sports had been largely through his corporation. DeBartolo Corp. had purchased, renovated, and revived Thistledown racetrack outside Cleveland, Balmoral racetrack outside of Chicago, and Louisiana Downs near Shreveport. It also owned the Pittsburgh Civic Arena. "Mr. D's" only personal holding was ownership of the Pittsburgh Penguins in the National Hockey League. Now sixty-seven years old, he did not intend to hold the 49ers franchise in his name. It was to be owned by his only son, Edward DeBartolo Jr., known as "Eddie." Thirty years old, Eddie was, along with his father, mother, and sister, one of the directors of the privately owned corporation. He would become the youngest owner in the NFL.

Short and chubby, Eddie wore his dark hair thick and over his ears and could be seen driving around Youngstown in a corporation Cadillac. He had married his sweetheart, and his best friend was still a foundry worker with whom he'd hung out since he was a sophomore. Eddie wanted to be an athlete, but at five foot seven and 160 pounds, that was a frustrated yearning. "I didn't treat him like an altar boy," Mr. D pointed out. "He wasn't sheltered. I wanted him to face the world. He's a plain sort of person, like I am." He was also, according to the *San Francisco*

Examiner, "a carbon copy of his father in avoiding people on the telephone, forgetting promises, and ducking those whose hopes he has raised through overzealous enthusiasm." Unlike his father, he took an occasional afternoon off for golf, and short vacations in the Caribbean and Las Vegas. The relationship between Eddie and Mr. D was, by all accounts, loving, and Eddie still kissed Mr. D whenever his father returned from one of his innumerable trips.

It was not, however, easy being Mr. D's heir apparent. Eddie would later describe the self-imposed pressure of his position as "brutal. It almost broke up my marriage before I realized I can't fill those big shoes. . . . My father has helped me overcome that pressure by letting me handle things my own way, to be my own man." Part of that process was buying the San Francisco 49ers. In the course of the actual purchase, however, it was Mr. D who carried the ball, so much so that both San Francisco papers would mistakenly identify him as "the new owner" when news of the sale broke. Joe Thomas, as promised, would be the new general manager, though he would last little more than two years before being fired.

The critical middleman between the DeBartolos and their football franchise was Al Davis. "I kind of brought them all together," Davis later explained. "Mr. DeBartolo had enough faith in me to ask me to sit down in negotiations and I sat in. . . . I think the transaction took approximately a month and I would say I spent ten to fifteen days on it." The price for eighty percent of the franchise was some $18.2 million, placing the total value in the neighborhood of $21 million. For his services, Al Davis was paid a "consultant's fee."

The last step in the process was securing League approval of Eddie's bid for membership. Pete Rozelle would later claim that NFL Security spent "an extraordinary amount of time" investigating the DeBartolos and "found nothing that would preclude them from ownership in the League." The "extraordinary" time taken with Eddie's application was likely a reflection of what Mr. D would later call the "innuendo" that already surrounded the DeBartolos. They were Italians, in the construction industry as a family business, and one of the first questions asked by the *San Francisco Examiner* was whether DeBartolo Corp. was connected with the Mafia. Mr. D found the question offensive. "If we were connected with the mob, why would some of the biggest companies in the world—like U.S. Steel and Mellon Bank—be in joint venture with me? I got where I am by working my can off every day of my life. Check our records. We never borrowed a single cent from a Teamsters union or a pension fund. And like everybody else, I had rough times in my career. I could have turned to certain characters in this town. I'm not saying I don't know them. But I solved my own problems."

Rozelle's most significant concern about the DeBartolos was with regard to ownership policy. Eddie's NFL franchise and Mr. D's hockey ownership, though not technically a violation of the current continuing ownership policy resolution, intimated cross-ownership and potential conflict of interest. The commissioner's uneasiness was apparently easily satisfied. Eddie explained that Mr. D kept the franchise afloat as a "civic duty" to Pittsburgh and added that his father "did want to get out of it when he could reasonably do so."

While the annual meeting considered Eddie's membership in Executive Session, Eddie himself waited nearby in the hotel. According to one of the owners present, "Rozelle pushed it through," though there was little controversy about Eddie himself. "He was a young rich kid," another owner offered, "he seemed basically decent." Eddie's membership passed by unanimous vote. Shortly thereafter, he entered the room and took Spadia's seat.

The controversy that had prolonged the discussion was about Al Davis's role. Far from thanking Davis for the money his intervention had saved them, a number of League members were "furious" at him for taking a finder's fee as part of the transaction. Art Modell described it as "rather unusual," "appalling," and "outrageous," questioning the "ethics" of the arrangement since the League's constitution forbade any owner to have a financial interest in any franchise other than his own. On that point, Rozelle came to Davis's support. "The financial arrangement with Al Davis was fully explained," he offered. "There's nothing in the constitution against it."

Davis again did nothing to smooth feelings. "Al didn't give a shit what we thought about it," one NFL member observed. "If anything, he figured he was worth a lot more than he'd been paid." Davis told his fellow owners that his fee had been $100,000 and was defiant about having taken it. "I'm no different than Hugh Culverhouse," he argued. "He's a lawyer and he's doing the tax work on this deal. I'm sure he ain't doing it for nothing. . . . I found the DeBartolos. I handled every phase of the sale, including the payoff formula, so I wasn't really a finder as much as I was a consultant." Leonard Tose was

Davis's most vocal defender. "It's a little unusual," he admitted to the *Los Angeles Times*, "but Al Davis is an unusual guy. I'm not opposed to the idea. Al obviously rendered a service and was paid for it." Tose's arguments made little headway against the resentment Davis had already provoked. Al Davis thumbed his nose at the sentiment.

A reporter later asked Davis about the controversy over his "$100,000 finder's fee." The usual finder's fee, the journalist pointed out, was ten percent. In the case of the 49ers, that amounted to something like $1.8 million, not $100,000.

"I didn't receive anything like that," Al chuckled, "but it was," he admitted, "a lot more than $100,000."

That the statement put the lie to what he'd told the Executive Session four days earlier did not seem to bother Davis. Several of his critics would later describe the attitude as "no big surprise."

"That's just like Davis," one of them complained. "After himself, there's not much else Al cares about." The same critic would later say the same thing about Eddie DeBartolo, despite having voted to admit him to the League.

3
Hess's Jets

Eddie DeBartolo wasn't the only new member admitted to the NFL during the spring 1977 executive session; he was just the only one requiring a vote. The other new member, Leon Hess, required no formal approval under League rules.

Hess had been a partner in the New York Jets since 1964, when he and four other men bought them out of receivership. The franchise was called the Titans then and had been the first casualty of the AFL-NFL war. The purchasing group had been put together by Sonny Werblin, who, like Hess, held almost twenty-five percent. Werblin served as Jets president until 1968, when the other partners forced him out of office and bought his share for some nine times what he'd paid four years earlier. The next partner to run the team was Don Lillis, who died two months after being named president. The next new president, Phil Iselin, dropped dead from heart failure in his Jets office on December

28, 1976. Hess, shortly to be a fifty percent owner by virtue of buying out Iselin's widow, "reluctantly" accepted the Jets presidency in February 1977.

Leon Hess could certainly afford a team. *Forbes* placed his "minimum net worth" at $320 million. Like Eddie DeBartolo's father, he'd started with next to nothing. His father had emigrated from Lithuania in 1904. Leon, the youngest of Mores Hess's three sons, was born in 1914. The elder Hess was a meat dealer until 1925, when he bought an old oil wagon and began delivering fuel around New Jersey. By 1933, Mores's fuel company had filed for bankruptcy and been forced to reorganize. The new Hess Oil Company retained Mores as its titular head, but was run by Leon, then eighteen years old and fresh out of high school. Within five years, Leon had made Hess Oil into a major bidder on U.S. government fuel contracts in New Jersey. Leon himself had already acquired a reputation for his toughness and ability to run his family business on a shoestring. While most oil bids were submitted typewritten, Hess still scrawled his with a pen. During World War II, Leon enlisted in the army and spent the duration procuring and transporting fuel in Europe to supply George Patton's armored troops. He was discharged as a major and awarded a Bronze Star for his efforts. "It taught him about planning," one of his friends said of Leon's military career. "He became very orderly in his way of going about any problem."

Back at Hess Oil, Leon planned to build a major integrated oil company, just like Standard, Shell, and the rest. To begin, he took Hess Oil into supplying residual fuel for power generation and soon made it the biggest such oil supplier in New Jersey. He also began importing oil, and by 1957 was handling thirty-eight thousand barrels a day. By then, Hess was also into refining. In 1960, he moved into retail gasoline sales. He started with twenty-eight stations. By 1969, he had more than five hundred, each pumping five times as much as the industry norm. A "fanatic about cleanliness," Hess regularly inspected all the company's facilities and, one of his employees told *Fortune*, "raised hell if everything isn't just right." In 1970, he merged Hess Oil with the Amerada Corp., one of the largest independent producers of crude oil in the world. The new corporation, Amerada Hess, was controlled by Leon, and with its advent, his grand design had been realized.

By then, his business stature was uncontested. "He built a local delivery service into a major integrated oil company," *Fortune* applauded, "in his lifetime, starting with nothing."

Though possessed of "supreme self-confidence," Hess, balding and owlish in plastic-rimmed glasses, had surprisingly little ego. Until his father's death in 1965, Leon gave the old man a higher title in the corporation than his own and let him sign all Hess Oil's checks.

Leon also had "an almost pathological aversion to publicity. He is not a recluse on the order of Howard Hughes, but . . . when attending public functions, as he sometimes must, Hess will practically wither at the sight of a camera."

"Part of his shyness," *Fortune* went on to explain, "comes from the fact that he is a strong-minded, volatile man, apt to say things he shouldn't, sometimes in off-color language. Part of it stems from the fact that he is very rich, and has been bothered by cranks and parasites. Hess also explains that his parents, humble Jewish immigrants from Eastern Europe, beseeched him at an early age 'not to toot my own horn' and to 'let my actions speak for me.' "

Hess's passion for invisibility was a trait unusual to NFL members. He had bought into the Jets originally only as a favor to Werblin, but over his first seven years as Jets president, Hess would nonetheless increase his share of the team to one hundred percent—all the while continuing to shun the celebrity trappings that came with owning a piece of America's Game. Once, when spotted by a reporter watching a Jets practice session, he asked that the man not write that the Jets owner had been present. "I'm supposed to be working," Hess pointed out. Not until 1982 did Hess personally attended a League meeting as Jets president. When he did, he would quickly acquire a reputation as "one of Rozelle's stalwarts," pushing the League's fight with Al Davis because "Rozelle's honor was at stake."

Leon Hess clearly meant business from the first day he took personal control of the Jets. Running corporate enterprises had few mysteries left for Hess, and after twelve years in this one, he had already formed strong opinions about the Jets' problems. His strongest was about its home field, Shea Stadium, and its lease with the city of New York. A month after Phil Iselin's funeral, the new Jets president set out to better his franchise's position. Hess's problem in 1977 was not with the physical structure of Shea, but with the Jets' lease and Shea's other tenant, the baseball Mets. Shea Stadium had been originally built in 1964 to house a baseball expansion franchise acquired in the civic panic that set in after the Giants and Dodgers left for California in 1958. The deal the city had given that franchise, the Mets, was often described as a "sweetheart" arrangement. Among other things, the lease agreement gave the Mets "the right to restrict the use of the natural grass field from February 20 through the end of baseball season" in October. The Mets, exercised that right without variance. That meant the Jets had to play all their preseason and their first five regular season games away from home. By the time of their first home game, the turf field at Shea was well on its way to mud and the approach of winter had turned the horseshoe-shaped stadium into a haven for perverse freezing winds.

The 1977 struggle over that arrangement was three-sided, with the city of New York sandwiched between Hess and the Mets' owner, Donald Grant. Hess's lease then had seven years to run and Grant's had option clauses allowing him to extend its terms well past the year 2000. Grant was willing to let the Jets play one preseason and two regular season games while baseball was still on, but, according to *The New York Times*, insisted that those games be postponed if a "baseball game had to be played after a football contest in rainy weather." Such postponement of scheduled games was unacceptable to the Jets and the NFL. To at least mitigate the disadvantages of winter games, the Jets offered an interest-free $4 million loan to the city of New York to install artificial turf, but that was rejected by Grant out of hand.

On February 4, two days after officially becoming Jets president, Hess moved to break the stalemate. That day, officials of the Jets met with New York's Mayor Abraham Beame and Beame, as usual, pointed out that his hands were tied. On February 7, Hess wrote Beame a letter. "We do not want to leave New York," the Jets owner maintained, but Grant's offer remained unacceptable. "It is impossible to permit [anyone] other than officials of the National Football League to postpone a game." Without "satisfactory solutions to the problem," the Jets "must explore any and all options, including the use of another stadium. . . ." Love of New York notwithstanding, Hess continued, the Jets had been "forced" into discussions with New Jersey's Meadowlands because the current situation, in effect, compelled them to negotiate with "another tenant" instead of their landlord.

The struggle went public on February 10, when New Jersey Governor Brendan Byrne announced that he hoped his state would soon have a second professional football team. The next morning's *New York Times* bannered the story "Football Jets

Negotiating Jersey Move" and cited sources close to the Jets as claiming the two parties were "very, very close to a verbal agreement" that would start with the 1977 season. "We would love to have another professional football team," Sonny Werblin observed. "The Giants are not exclusive. It's up to the Jets. We can certainly accommodate them."

Leon Hess made no comment on the story but Abraham Beame and Donald Grant were not nearly so reserved. "The Jets are absolutely inflexible," Grant complained. "This whole situation is easy to resolve. I have offered Mr. Hess a compromise. . . . I'm very surprised they're talking about going. I think they're trying to put pressure on the city to get us to change our lease." Grant was, of course, stating the obvious. Hess had tossed a political grenade in Abraham Beame's lap. He knew exactly what he was doing. Recluse or not, Leon Hess was also astute in the mechanics of politics. In election years, he spread his money around. In 1968, he donated some $100,000 to Hubert Humphrey's presidential campaign. In 1972, Hess and his corporation donated $250,000 to Richard Nixon. In 1976, Hess voluntarily admitted having paid "substantial" bribes to "a foreign government official." The statement, like all of Hess's, was issued through a corporate spokesman. No such statement was issued in response to Donald Grant's. Instead, Leon Hess waited to see which way the mayor would move. Having already made his way through several decades of the political rough-and-tumble surrounding the oil business, the Jets president had no qualms about playing hardball with Abraham Beame.

Beame knew he was sandwiched. New York City had already lost the football Giants, the North American Soccer League Cosmos, and a good portion of its harness-racing crowds to New Jersey. In addition, the city was convulsed in the worst financial crisis in its history and facing bankruptcy. Losing the Jets would add humiliation to defeat and insolvency. Even if he weren't responsible, Beame knew he would take the blame. His immediate response was noncommittal. "We're extremely concerned," he offered on February 11. "New York shouldn't be without a football team."

By February 14, the mayor had settled on a strategy. "We are determined to use every weapon at our command to insure that the Jets remain in New York and play at Shea Stadium," he announced. "I am particularly incensed at the interference of the New Jersey Sports Authority," the mayor continued. "It is ironic that the same man who signed the original Jets lease is now heading that authority and is trying to induce the Jets to leave the city and the fans who have supported them for years." Beame said the city was exploring the law to see if it had grounds for legal action against New Jersey for "inducing a breach of agreement."

On February 15, Beame, Grant, and Hess met for an hour and a half. Afterwards, the mayor's spokesman announced that "positions remained unchanged." Grant proclaimed that "the Mets' offer is still on the table." Hess said nothing and was nowhere to be seen. The following day, Hess called Beame to say the NFL would not accept any postponements, and to make a counteroffer that was announced to the press immediately there-after. "The Jets told the mayor that they would be willing to give up the exhibition game in Shea," the spokesman explained. "However, they made it clear that they would not compromise on the two regular season games. The Jets made their offer contingent on the mayor's understanding that it was only the first step—for this year only—in reaching absolute equality with the Mets by 1978 in scheduling games at Shea Stadium." Hess's counteroffer was relayed to Grant by Beame. According to Grant, the mayor was "annoyed" that Hess had made the offer public. Grant himself called it "a backwards step."

By February 18, a deal had been cut. The Mets would accept one exhibition and two regular season games during August and September with no postponement. The artifice crafted to let Grant swallow his hard line was the agreement that the mayor himself would hold the Mets' former postponement rights and the mayor in turn agreed to waive them. "This proposal," Beame pointed out, "was made with the understanding that the Jets would agree to play in Shea Stadium for the duration of their lease and will make no further demands for additional playing dates during the baseball season. I'm very pleased about it. I presume since this is what the Jets and Mr. Hess asked for, they're going to adhere to the conversations we had." The mayor trumpeted the agreement as a victory over the New Jersey Sports Authority.

It was the reclusive Hess who got the best press from the affair. "Leon Hess," the *Times* proclaimed, "the New Jets' Muscle." The nation's newspaper of record said, "The oil baron displayed an attribute that had been missing since Sonny Werblin departed—strength." Though the description of Leon Hess may well have been accurate, the assumption that the battle at Shea was over was not. By the first week of March, Beame's deal had fallen through. Grant initiated the collapse by claiming that the mayor could not cede his right to make postponements to save the grass field from damage. Grant's reversal led to a week of frantic negotiations to no avail. Then, on March 16, Leon Hess played his trump card.

For the upcoming season, the Jets would play their first two home games in the New Jersey Meadowlands and then the rest of their schedule back in Shea after baseball season ended. "We will not completely remove ourselves at this time," Hess's statement read. The Jets would compensate New York with $100,000 for the two missed home dates and should they eventually move altogether, would buy out the remaining years on their lease. "We are choosing not to abandon New York City. That would be an easy course for our minds, but not for our hearts. The ownership of the Jets will not do anything further to further demoralize a city in crisis."

Beame responded by announcing that the city of New York was going to sue the Jets, the Mets, the NFL, and the New Jersey Sports Authority. The Jets would be forced to play all their home games at Shea, the Mets would be forced to rewrite their sweetheart lease, the NFL would be enjoined from scheduling Jets games anywhere but Shea, and the New Jersey Sports Authority would be enjoined from inducing the Jets to break their lease. "It's a sad day for major league sports that we must resort to the courts to force parties to fulfill their obligations to the city," Abraham Beame pointed out, "but I am determined to see that those obligations are met." New York's suit was the first episode of the Superstadium Game to reach the judicial system. There would be more, and this first one was by far the shortest.

On May 11, the court ruled that the Jets could not play home games anywhere but at Shea Stadium. Justice Harold Baer also "strongly urged" the Mets to accommodate the Jets' September home games. The Jets immediately appealed. On May 26, the case was settled out of court. The terms for dropping the action were hammered out at the Mets' expense. Baer's plan required Grant to give the Jets two September dates immediately and, starting the following year, guarantee them two October dates as well. The Jets would also be allowed to play one game this year in New Jersey but none for the rest of their lease with Shea. "If you don't agree to this," the justice lectured Grant's lawyers, "you're going to be sorry." The justice eventually relayed his threat to Grant directly on the telephone and, according to one of the attorneys present, "Grant finally caved in."

This time the deal stuck and *City of New York v. New York Jets Football Club, Inc. et al* was history. Having won what he set out to get, Leon Hess resigned himself to another seven years at Shea and did his best to resume being invisible.

4
Robbie, Winter, Irsay, and C.R. Play

Others were playing the Superstadium Game in 1977, as well. The seller's market for football remained volatile even after expansion into Seattle and Tampa, providing a key strategy for owners who wished to play.

In Miami, Joe Robbie had commenced a decade-long fight with the city over the Orange Bowl. The stadium, a huge 1930s bowl inside the city limits, still had wooden benches and most of its game-day parking area consisted of front lawns rented in the surrounding neighborhood. As far as Robbie was concerned, all of it cost him money. The seating capacity of nearly eighty thousand meant Dolphin tickets were easy to get and the stadium's facilities made the tickets less desirable than they ought to be. The lack of parking lots meant the Dolphins were one of the few NFL franchises without significant parking income. When his lease came up for renewal in 1976, Robbie had demanded that something be done.

Before his lease negotiations with the city of Miami began, Robbie announced the Dolphins were developing plans for a modern football facility. He claimed such a facility could be built for $30 million, a figure Miami officials scoffed at. It was, the *Miami News* offered, "just a dream," and indeed, the idea had gone nowhere by 1977. But by then, Robbie had signed a new ten-year lease which gave him the option to leave for another stadium on three years notice. Its rental terms were still among the best in the NFL.

The city of Miami also sought to soothe their principal tenant's feelings by proposing a 1977 bond issue to finance some $15 million in improvements. It was a failed gesture almost as soon as it was made. "I don't think anyone being nice to Joe Robbie gets anywhere," Miami Mayor Maurice Ferre observed.

Robbie was quick to oppose the refurbishing measure. By July 1977, the Dolphins had sold only thirty-six thousand season tickets and their owner was more adamant than ever about what a white elephant the Orange Bowl was. He had made it clear that it wasn't fit to hold another Super Bowl in and he didn't blame Dolphin fans for not wanting to come to it. "I can't support this bond issue. I could support it if there were an alternative proposal to build a new stadium. . . . I definitely think Broward County will build a stadium and I think Miamians would be much happier with a superstructure with all the modern conveniences, even if they have to drive a little farther to get to it. . . . I can't tell the fans that if they vote for this, I'm staying here. I'd be misleading them."

The lease Joe Robbie had signed was in fact just a truce to buy time while he waited for his "dream" to ripen.

In Minnesota, the dilemma facing Vikings majority owner Max Winter was the same, but the setting and circumstances were different. The Vikings' home field, Memorial Stadium in suburban Bloomington, was the smallest in the NFL, with only 48,500 seats; even less than the League's official minimum. An open bowl configuration, the field was frozen solid for much of the last half of the Vikings season and games occasionally featured wind chill factors of two degrees Fahrenheit. Max Winter had been complaining about the stadium for more than a decade. His options were either to get a new stadium built or move to another city, and Max had a lot of roots in Minnesota.

Going on seventy-three years old in 1977, Max Winter had come to Minneapolis at age ten from Austria. Max's earliest memory of America was eating a banana for the first time in his life when the boat docked in New York. Now worth $30 million, "Max," the *Minneapolis Tribune* noted, "has perfected the art of the hustle to a fine degree." His first success was selling women's hair-care products, despite knowing next to nothing about hair care. In the 1930s he made a name for himself promoting local boxing matches. From there, he went into restaurants, real estate, and vending machines. From 1947 to 1957 he was co-owner and general manager of the Minneapolis Lakers professional basketball franchise, Minnesota's first big league team. After Max sold out, the Lakers had left town for L.A. A friend of Art Rooney and George Halas, Winter had first begun approaching the NFL about a Minneapolis football franchise in 1955.

Though Max did not want to leave town, he was more than fed up with the stadium in Bloomington. For years, progress on a new stadium had been bogged down in the political cross-currents surrounding the issue of where such a publicly funded stadium would be located. When nothing had happened by 1973, Winter made his first noises about moving the franchise. When the issue finally reached the State Legislature in 1975, the Vikings scheduled an exhibition game in Phoenix, Arizona. In February 1976, a proposal for a $47 million stadium in downtown Minneapolis was formally submitted to the legislature but was almost immediately hamstrung by the pro-Bloomington forces. Shortly thereafter, Winter opened discussions with New York about the possibility of moving east to play in Yankee Stadium. They paid a visit to Memphis to discuss possibilities there. The Vikings also continued to refuse to sign anything more than a one-year lease on the stadium they had.

In May 1977, the Minnesota House of Representatives voted to establish the Metropolitan Sports Facilities Commission, which was empowered to select a site for a new stadium and then issue bonds for construction. By July, the commission had narrowed the field down to three locations; a year later, the field was narrowed to two. Meanwhile, Max Winter was ready to play his hometown off against whoever was available.

In Baltimore, Robert Irsay's discussions with the city on the stadium subject had never gone anywhere. Though the lack of a modern football facility was a continued source of frustration to Irsay, he was at the moment basking in the highlight of his career in the NFL. The previous season, his Colts had won eleven and lost three, the best record an Irsay team would ever produce. In spring 1977, Irsay considered himself on the verge of a dynasty that would, he forecast, put the memory of Carroll Rosenbloom's Colts behind him once and for all.

Winning seemed to have softened Baltimore's attitude about Irsay as well. The local papers had little bad to say about Irsay's success. But even at his high point, Irsay felt no great allegiance to the city of Baltimore. In spring 1977, he made an appointment with Paul Oakes, chairman of the stadium task force in Indianapolis. At the time, Indianapolis was still trying to figure out what kind of stadium to build, where to build it, and how to pay for it. None of those questions was close to being answered, but Oakes had arranged the meeting anyway. "I had heard he was unhappy with Baltimore," Oakes recounted to *The Indianapolis Star*.

Oakes showed up at Irsay's office with a delegation that included Indianapolis's mayor. They told the Colts owner that the city was currently discussing constructing a sixty-thousand-seat stadium downtown. "If you break ground," Irsay told the group, "I'll move the Colts there."

Indianapolis's representatives left Skokie ebullient. Another meeting with Irsay was scheduled, but by then the group realized it was way ahead of itself and discussions were dropped at the city's initiative. Nonetheless, Baltimore's Robert Irsay was obviously ready to listen to all relocation offers and, just as obviously, loved being asked.

In Los Angeles, Carroll Rosenbloom seemed to have ended his Superstadium Game by signing a lease the year before, but that was an illusion. C.R. was determined to find someplace besides the Coliseum to play and would do so shortly. When he finally succeeded, all hell would break loose.

5

Tose: A Brush with Bankruptcy

Though all episodes of the Superstadium Game were accompanied by a litany of alleged financial woes, only one NFL owner, Leonard Tose of the Philadelphia Eagles, was in serious money trouble in spring 1977, and Tose's difficulties were decidedly his own fault. "Tose was just spending money and selling his assets to cover his expenditures," Sidney Forstater, his personal financial adviser, later testified. "For some time, we were able to meet expenditures only by making substantial loans. When the loans became due, it was necessary to sell valuable assets to meet the payments. Mr. Tose said he wasn't going to run out of money. He kept saying he'd be dead before the money ran out."

When making that prediction, Leonard Tose seriously underestimated his own skill at losing money.

Tose's assets, excluding the Eagles, had been worth some $12.5 million in 1969, the year he entered the NFL. By the end of 1976, those same assets were worth $2.5 million and sinking. Tose Trucking, his principal nonfootball worth, had lost $2.5

million since 1973. On paper, Tose's only income during the same period was the combined salaries he drew from his trucking company and football team, some $110,000, roughly equal to the annual costs of his personal helicopter. Thus, Tose charged off as much of his life-style as possible to the Eagles franchise, and, despite ranking near the top of the NFL in attendance, the franchise lost almost $1.3 million in 1976.

Tose's profligacy had also added to the growing list of people who wished they'd never had anything to do with him. By now it included Herb Barness, a man Tose had once described as his "best friend." Barness owned a twenty-nine percent share of the Eagles and had backed Tose in 1971 when three other investors had filed suit. By 1976, he was threatening suit himself and demanding full access to the club's financial records. Early in 1977, Barness informed First Pennsylvania Bank, holder of the Eagles' note, that he was considering legal moves to put the football franchise into receivership. By March, Barness and Tose were discussing what Barness's share might cost. Barness was prepared to take $2.5 million. Tose asked if he'd take $2 million cash instead.

"Len," Barness answered, "put it on the table and see what I do." Herb Barness doubted Leonard Tose could actually lay his hands on that kind of money. In that respect, he was by no means alone.

The most logical place for Tose to find such a sum was First Pennsylvania Bank. Tose had reduced his borrowings there from $10.3 million to $5.3 million and, according to Tose, paid First Penn some $6.2 million in interest over the seven years since the bank had loaned him enough to join the NFL. By December 1976, however, the Comptroller of Currency had adjudged its loan to Leonard Tose "substandard" and the $5.3 million borrowing with the Philadelphia Eagles as collateral had been assigned to First Penn's problem loan division. Earlier, First Penn had forced Tose to sign an agreement restricting his salary and expenses, but it had proved a futile gesture. In 1976, Tose exceeded his personal Eagles budget by $200,000 and in the first three months of 1977, he had already drawn and spent more than his entire annual salary. He had also already overspent his annual Eagles expense account by $25,000.

In March 1977, the supervisor of Tose's loan recommended that the loan be called. He noted that calling the loan would probably force Tose to put the team on the market. Herb Barness owned first refusal rights should Tose sell, and the supervisor's memo suggested that Pete Rozelle be approached through Barness once Tose's loan had been called. However, First Penn was not yet ready to take such a radical step. The bank's president, John Bunting, vetoed the proposed foreclosure because football teams were "not easily resold." Instead, Bunting summoned Tose to a meeting at bank headquarters on March 25, shortly before the Eagles owner left for the League's annual meeting in Phoenix. Tose arrived with his attorney. Bunting began by lecturing Tose about the Eagles' financial condition and complaining about Tose's life-style. Tose listened with little interest. "First Pennsylvania wanted us to buy cheaper tape to tape our athletes," he fumed. "They checked lunch boxes. They found there were two pieces of fruit in them and they wanted only one. . . . Bunting said he doesn't like my life-style. He doesn't like my style because he doesn't have any style and I guess if you don't have any style, you don't like anybody's style."

Despite Tose's failings, Bunting continued, First Penn had decided to "try to save the club." Bunting then offered to help Tose buy out Barness once and for all. "We had to get Barness out of there," First Penn's president explained, "because the tension [between Barness and Tose] was creating a cancer," jeopardizing the club, and raising the threat of a protracted public lawsuit. Any loan to purchase Barness's twenty-nine percent, First Penn's president pointed out, would be conditional upon Tose permitting First Penn to appoint an Eagles financial officer with the power to control expenditures. But the only concrete result in March was agreement to a future succession of meetings to discuss the club's financial ills.

The first meeting was held after Tose's return from Phoenix. They discussed a First Penn plan to cut some of the almost $2 million the Eagles annually spent on administrative expenses. In addition to holding Tose strictly to his agreed upon salary and expenses, it recommended firing or retiring some five front-office employees, including Tose's personal secretary. Tose resisted agreeing to specifics, but promised to adhere to the goals of the plan. Things got testier when Bunting informed Tose and his attorney that the bank had discussed the possibility of buyout with Herb Barness. Tose's attorney responded that he was "shocked" at Bunting's behavior because Barness might then jack up the price. Everything just sat up in the air all spring and by summer, the Eagles' finances had not improved and the bank made its insistence on financial restraint even louder. First Penn also framed the message in words they were sure Leonard Tose could understand. The man who delivered them was First Penn vice-president John Pemberton. "I've got to treat you like a jackass," Pemberton snarled at Tose. "I've got to mount you and put my spurs in you." Much to the bank's irritation, the effect of Pemberton's rhetoric on Leonard Tose was virtually nil.

First Pennsylvania Bank would have even been more irritated had they known what other financial dealings Tose had been up to that spring. He was very quietly looking elsewhere for a loan of $200,000 to repay the Eagles for his 1976 overdrafts. He had a number of short-term personal loans from friends that had to be repaid as well. Tose was introduced to one Bruce Rappoport, owner of the Swiss-based Grove Corp., a shipping firm. At the time Rappoport was a controversial financial figure, linked to what *The Philadelphia Inquirer* called "allegations that Rappoport had grossly inflated contracts to build oil tankers for Indonesia." That spring, he agreed to loan Tose $1 million. Without informing First Pennsylvania Bank of the transaction, Tose posted his holdings in the Eagles, already completely pledged to First Penn, as Rappoport's collateral. Now, the Eagles were not only in "financial chaos" but, as Tose's attorney later admitted, "doublehocked" as well.

The situation was further complicated in June, when another former football partner of Leonard Tose jumped into the legal ring. The partner, John D. Firestone, had sold his 5.1 percent to Tose, his former friend, in November 1976. Part of the transaction was a $375,000 promissory note upon which Firestone claimed Tose had defaulted. During the first week of June, Firestone filed suit, charging that during 1976 the Eagles had lost money in large part because of "extravagant and wasteful" spending by Tose on "activities wholly unconnected with and unrelated to the business or interests of the club," all of which was a violation of the limited partnership agreement. Among the "wholly unconnected" activities cited in Firestone's complaint were trips to Acapulco, Beverly Hills, and New Orleans by Tose and a trip to Las Vegas by "a female acquaintance of the defendant and her mother," all billed in whole or in part to the Philadelphia Eagles. The club was also billed for the "female acquaintance's" visits to Bonwit Teller, Henri Bendel, and Giorgio's on Rodeo Drive. To send Leonard Tose to watch the Super Bowl that year had cost the football franchise $10,000, including $3300 in limo rentals, $3000 in hotel bills, and a $2000 tab at one restaurant alone. Tose had also charged the Eagles for $9100 of his helicopter expenses and $2000 so his

daughter, Susan, in Miami could buy sixteen season tickets to
see the Miami Dolphins. Firestone cited Tose's $200,000 over-
draft on his salary as well.

By virtue of *Firestone v. Tose*, First Penn's collateral was now
not only "in financial chaos" and "doublehocked." It was, at
least momentarily, "legally encumbered." It was not at all what
John Bunting had hoped for back in March.

On July 28, First Pennsylvania's president peremptorily summoned Leonard Tose and his attorney to bank headquarters. "I
perceived Mr. Bunting sitting behind his desk as being pompous,
hostile, and arrogant," Tose remembered, "and I said to myself,
'I wonder what this meeting is all about?' He told me to sit down
like [I was] a schoolboy." Tose's attorney described Bunting as
"icy calm."The news he had to deliver was blunt. The bank
wanted Tose to replace himself as chief financial officer with
Sidney Forstater immediately, and give Forstater full financial
control. If Tose refused, First Penn would call in his loan and
begin bouncing the franchise's checks.

Tose asked for two weeks in which to find a new bank, but
Bunting refused. "He said, 'I'm calling in your loan,' " Tose
later testified, "Five and a half million or something like that,
and I was to have it paid by the next morning. I was sort of
shocked." Tose claimed, "He threatened me. He said, 'I'll
make sure you don't get any financing from any bank in Philadelphia.' I was stunned and he went on, showing his power, and
said that he would see that I didn't get any financing anywhere in
the country." Bunting would later testify only to advising Tose
he was "an undesirable bank client."

When Tose's arguments failed, his lawyer stepped in. During
previous discussions, he argued, First Penn had promised a
ninety-day period in which Tose could find alternative financing
should the bank ever decide to call its loan. The lawyer demanded the ninety days, telling Bunting that Tose could find
new financing because the franchise was valuable. Just a month
earlier, he pointed out, Herb Barness had offered Tose $21.5
million for it. "You should have taken it," Bunting replied.

For the moment, Tose had no choice but to do everything the
banker had ordered. On July 29, Sidney Forstater became chief
financial officer of the Philadelphia Eagles. It was, *The Philadelphia Inquirer* noted, "the equivalent of a second string lineman
replacing a charismatic superstar." Forstater and Tose had been
on the outs for several months; Forstater later described Tose's
approach to money as "a philosophy of life that I didn't sub-

scribe to.'' On August 1, a bank delegation arrived at the Eagles' training camp to read the coaches a formal letter detailing Forstater's new powers. "Mr. Tose told me to go along with whatever they have to say," Head Coach Dick Vermeil remembered, "to make no fuss. But then I asked why financial details of the Eagles operation . . . were leaked to the newspapers. Mr. John Pemberton jumped up and said if we didn't cooperate, he'd 'blow this blankety-blank team out of the water.' '' Within hours, Forstater had begun laying off front-office employees and implementing plans to slash expenses to the bone. "They were going to destroy the team," Tose whined.

But there was little Tose could do about it. He had to find new financing and that was proving as difficult as Bunting had predicted. "He tried to borrow from every bank in the city," one Eagles source observed. "And in the state for that matter. Nobody would touch him." The more he was turned down, the more desperate Leonard Tose became. Though he still owned the team, he had been required to pay cash up front for tickets to the Eagles' first preseason game. "It was a very difficult period for me," Tose admitted. "I was terribly humiliated and despondent. I couldn't sleep."

The move by First Penn also created severe dilemmas for the NFL as a whole. For Rozelle in particular it was déjà vu of the worst sort. He had been solving "the Philadelphia problem" since he became commissioner and the Eagles' financial collapse in 1977 was a decided embarrassment. Worse, it was also a challenge to ownership policy itself. The Eagles were, in effect, now operated by a corporation, First Pennsylvania Bank, an arrangement Rozelle himself had forecast as the beginning of the end for the NFL. Rozelle was also less than enamored by Sidney Forstater's approach to the football business. Within Forstater's first week, Rozelle had intervened in at least one contract dispute and forced Forstater to spend money he didn't want to. Through most of that same week, Forstater was bragging that "Leonard Tose is dead."

Forstater, however, had not calculated on the NFL raising Leonard Tose from the grave. Tose asked Rozelle to "Help me." It was, Tose noted, the first time in his memory he had ever used the phrase. The NFL response was immediate. Art Rooney, Bill Bidwill, Wellington Mara, and Art Modell all called the Philadelphia owner to see if they could help find a bank. The most important call came from William Clay Ford, owner of the Detroit Lions. Ford was a director of Manufacturers National

Bank in Detroit and suggested Tose try there. On August 9, Manufacturers National, despite its reputation as a conservative institution, loaned Leonard Tose $5.3 million with which to pay off First Penn. The money was described as a bridge loan, due the following February and designed to buy Tose the time to find longterm financing. Also included in the loan was $1 million to pay off Bruce Rappoport and eliminate the franchise's doublehock. Asked how he felt when the money actually changed hands, John Bunting responded, "As if Santa Claus had just arrived."

In debt or not, Leonard Tose was back in control and relishing the fact. His first step was to fire Sidney Forstater. "Sidney had illusions of grandeur," Tose explained. "I think he was promised big things from First Pennsylvania and probably from Barness. I could [sic] care less now." The next morning, Tose called a press conference and went after John Bunting and First Penn. Bunting was, Tose offered to *The* [Philadelphia] *Bulletin,* "a son of a bitch" and the bank had been part of a "plot from within to get me." The paper described Leonard Tose's return "one of the greatest comebacks in recent Philadelphia sports history" and Tose himself credited "Rozelle and his fellow NFL owners who rallied around him when he was down."

The task of explaining why the NFL had chosen to do so fell to Art Modell. "You must understand that there is a great camaraderie among the owners," Modell offered the day Tose's return was announced. "When one of us is in trouble, the others come to his aid. This camaraderie, that's what makes the NFL such a beautiful thing to be part of. While there is no love lost on Sunday [when games are played], it's all for one and one for all the rest of the time. We have strong feelings for Len Tose. We want to see him succeed." They should have known better. Far from being accomplished, the financial rescue of Leonard Tose had in fact only just begun.

6
Dirty Football's Day in Court

Only one NFL owner stood noticeably outside the boundaries of the "one for all, all for one" ethos articulated by Art Modell in the summer of 1977. He was, of course, Al Davis. By the time the League had rescued Leonard Tose from First Pennsylvania Bank, *Atkinson v. Noll* had been to trial, confirming Davis in his outcast role. "Al didn't care how he did it," Rozelle claimed. "Hurting the League didn't bother him at all. He just wanted to win that case."

The slander suit turned into what *Sports Illustrated* called "a nasty spitting contest that seemed, at times, to be aimed mainly at proving in court whether the Steelers or the Raiders were the dirtiest team in football." As such, it was a public relations disaster. Davis was not, however, the only owner pushing the confrontation. Dan Rooney and the Steelers were equally adamant. Rooney's insurance company urged him to settle the suit with a $50,000 payment to Atkinson, but Rooney steadily refused. "The wrong people were being sued," Rooney explained. If we settled, every player would be suing every time he was criticized. We felt we had to go to court to save the game."

Court opened on July 11 in San Francisco. Coach Noll's attorney argued that Atkinson's hit on Lynn Swann was an "illegal act," violating two clear NFL rules, and provided the context for the Pittsburgh coach's description of Atkinson as among the League's "criminal element." Atkinson's attorney responded that football was "a game of violent physical contact, rough and tough and injury-producing." Indeed, even the NFL's legal hits were enough to cause permanent physical damage. "It is," Atkinson's attorney pointed out, "legal combat which television shows to sixty to eighty million Americans," every weekend, September to January.

Atkinson's case made excellent use of the footage collected from NFL Films. On the stand, Noll was deluged with video examples of Steelers doing mayhem and ultimately admitted that at least four of his own players belonged on any list of the

League's "criminal element." The commissioner's office was disgusted with the approach and made no bones about it. "The whole thrust of the defense was 'you think this is bad,' " one NFL attorney complained, " 'see how dirty these other bastards play.' That such talk hurt the League is obvious." Rozelle himself was particularly disgusted with Davis. "Al sat near the jury box," Rozelle remembered, "and every time they would show [film clips of] another play, he'd wince and make noises for the jury's benefit."

Atkinson also contended that the League's action against him was the product of what his attorney called "a conspiracy on the part of the Rozelle-Rooney establishment to get the outcast upstart Oakland crowd led by Al Davis." Atkinson's attorney even wrote Davis: "Rozelle and Rooney want to dismantle your team. . . . Every official works for Rozelle and every discretionary play from now on could go against you." Rozelle had little doubt Davis was the argument's architect. "It was," he remembered, "the first example of Al Davis's line."

When Al Davis took the stand, he was dressed in a white shirt, silver tie, and "dead-black" suit—what Noll's attorney snidely called his "sincere" outfit. For Davis, the issue was defending his player and ridding his team of Noll's "label." "Anytime anybody steps on the football playing field," he testified, "there is an element of risk. Every player assumes that. It's part of his contract." George Atkinson's blow to Lynn Swann had been part of that assumed risk and Noll's description of him as "criminal" had diminished his value. "Right now Mr. Atkinson is in limbo," he continued. ". . . his trade value has lessened. He has an erroneous label that I think has to be reversed." Trying to single Atkinson out was also hypocritical. "In every game that I have ever observed," Davis pointed out, "we have the paradox—the hypocritical thing—that there are some things that are legal that are more violent than things that are illegal. Our problem is to confront this."

Pete Rozelle took the stand the next day. He could have substituted a deposition for personal testimony, but nonetheless decided to appear. The reason, according to *Sports Illustrated*, was that he "had decided that his and the League's reputations were at stake." He looked tan and fit in a business suit and evinced no doubt that his fine of Atkinson had been appropriate. "I am fully convinced that there is no place in professional football for the kind of fouls committed by George Atkinson," Rozelle offered. "Such conduct is clearly outside the rules and calculated either to disable opposing players or to intimidate them into less effective performance." He did not, however, admit to the existence of a "criminal element." He described Atkinson as "an outstanding defensive back" and speculated that Noll's comments might well have enhanced Atkinson's value because they made him more recognizable and hence a candidate for work in commercials. Atkinson's attorney called Rozell "a professional witness."

Rozelle's cross-examination epitomized the tone of Atkinson's case. Having already described the League's offices as a "castle on Park Avenue," Atkinson's attorney started his questioning by looking over Rozelle's tan and asking if he'd just returned from the Greek isles. The answer was "no." The questioning concentrated on Rozelle's relationship with Rooney and the Steelers. Rozelle denied that he and Rooney were friends (only "close acquaintances"), and denied he had done anything "unusual or unfair" in handling Atkinson's disciplinary action. Rozelle admitted, however, that he had spoken with Rooney perhaps fourteen or eighteen times in the nine months preceding the trial and that he hadn't talked with Al Davis once on the phone in the same period. "I get the impression the Oakland organization isn't interested in having much contact with the League office," he responded somewhat wryly.

In the final arguments, Noll's attorney went after Atkinson, pointing out that he had been previously charged with embezzlement, carrying a concealed weapon, and threatening to castrate a man. "Since injury to reputation is the gist of slander," he pointed out, "a bad reputation must be considered." Noll's attorney also sought to lift the onus of violence off the League and onto its audience. He noted that the Oakland crowd had cheered when George Atkinson hit Lynn Swann and called it "a sad commentary on the motives of our generation. It's sadistic," he continued, "this secret love of violence, the spectacle of liking to see others hurt, happiness at pain, enthralled by the love of blood. That's the America of George Atkinson." And, by inference at least, Al Davis.

Atkinson's attorney, whose fees were reportedly paid by Davis, went after the NFL, calling the League "second only to the U.S. government in terms of power, scope, and potential." Atkinson's mistake had been being "a rag-tag kid brawling with the establishment." He was a "pawn" between Davis and Rozelle, "because he wore a Raider helmet" and "there were differences" between the commissioner and Davis dating back to 1966 and the AFL war. "Glib Rozelle," the attorney warned, "came out here to give aid to his friend, Dan Rooney. He is very smooth and very clever, but he came in and brainwashed the truth."

The jury returned a verdict four hours later: no slander, no malice, no damages for Atkinson. "Raider Star A Loser," *The* [Oakland] *Tribune* proclaimed. Al Davis made no comment.

Though hard-won, the victory was also hard for the victors to savor. "This has been the most depressing thing I've ever done," Dan Rooney observed. Rozelle had difficulty celebrating as well. Win or not, he pointed out, "the ugliness of it had stained everything and everyone involved and may well continue to smear the NFL for a long time to come." The damage was done. It would not, however, go unpunished. Rozelle would see to that in October, the next time the League met.

In the meantime, *Atkinson v. Noll* was a victory, and it was not without impact inside the NFL. The case set an important emotional precedent, if not a legal one. Davis had been taken on in court at his instigation and he had been beaten. Rozelle had been an impressive witness and Davis much less so. Most important, Rooney's decision to "go to court to save the game" had been vindicated. The jury's verdict gave Rozelle, Rooney, and the rest of the League confidence in doing the same thing for the same reasons and with the same expectations of success when next faced with a legal challenge from Al Davis. *Atkinson v. Noll* had escalated the antagonism toward Davis to a new level of intensity. Almost everyone in the League enjoyed seeing Davis beaten.

Gene Klein was a case in point. Once indifferent, even friendly to Davis, he was now well on his way to an extreme anti-Davis position. His bad feelings had been nurtured by the presence of Klein's Chargers in the Raiders' division and Davis's history of thumping them regularly. Klein knew Davis would go to any lengths to gain an advantage and considered him someone who wanted one rule for himself and another one for everybody else. *Atkinson v. Noll* made Klein feel his resentment was justified. That resentment was even further intensified by an incident during a preseason game, several weeks after Atkinson's suit failed.

Klein's team went to the exhibition in Oakland in something of a state of flux. His star quarterback, Dan Fouts, was holding out for a new contract. Because of that star's absence, the Raiders had promoted the game by hyping San Diego's second string quarterback, James Harris, one of the first blacks ever to play that position in the NFL. Given that Oakland was more than half black, it was a natural promotion. Klein's coach, however, pulled the second string quarterback after four plays and used a white third stringer the rest of the game. Davis was furious, feeling Klein had spoiled his promotion and failed to let the Raiders play against top-flight competition, thus diminishing the value of the exhibition. As a consequence, he refused to send Klein his share of the gate receipts, and only did so when Rozelle's office intervened and forced him to.

"He's an asshole," Gene Klein charged, "and he wants to run the whole League. Rozelle had no choice about dealing with him. If you don't put a guy like Davis in his place, pretty soon you got no League left."

7
The $5 Million Deal

Pete Rozelle delivered Al Davis's comeuppance in October at a League meeting in New York. Typically, Rozelle's final assault on Davis's Competition Committee seat came late in the afternoon, when everyone was tired and sentiments were running very much the commissioner's way. Rozelle delivered his blow without fanfare. It was the next to last item on the agenda and amounted to no more than the distribution of a list of new committee assignments. The list, according to the minutes, included "some changes and additions." Some ten League and five Management Council committees with a total of sixty seats were included and Al Davis's name was nowhere to be seen. The minutes noted no discussion of the document, and Davis himself was not in attendance. Apparently anticipating Rozelle's move, he had dispatched his assistant, LoCasale, in his place.

The big committee list winner was Hugh Culverhouse, owner of the new Tampa Bay Buccaneers. In the midst of only his second season of fielding a football team, Culverhouse was nonetheless named to both the three-member Congressional Relations Committee and the four-member Finance Committee, two of the more important postings. The idea of using the Tampa owner that way had originally come from Carroll Rosenbloom, in his anti-Rozelle tirade two years earlier. "Carroll complained about how people with skills were not being used on committees," Rozelle remembered, "and pointed to Hugh Culverhouse as an example. I thought it was a good idea. Culverhouse is just a real sharp guy who gives of his time." Culverhouse was also a relatively unthreatening presence. "He's the sweetest southern gentleman you could hope to meet," one owner observed.

In the NFL's lexicon, Culverhouse was a "business guy," not a "football guy." In October 1977, his Buccaneers had a lifetime record of no wins, twenty-one losses. He also played the role of owner with a decided absence of flash. Already fat when he joined the League, he had added twenty-five pounds since. On game days, he and his wife often wore matching outfits in the Buccaneers' colors and at NFL meetings he was known for wearing gaudy sport coats that clashed with his slacks. He attended all his team's games. In Denver the previous year, he had been late getting back to the buses after the game and reached the stadium parking lot just as the last one drove off. Tampa's owner chased after his bus as best he was able, throwing rocks at its back window in an attempt to get it to stop, but it didn't and he was forced to hitch a ride with Denver's team doctor. When Culverhouse finally caught up with his team, he delivered what several staffers described as "the worst chewing-out he ever gave us." Henceforth, the last Buccaneer bus was on standing instructions not to leave unless the owner was on it.

Hugh Culverhouse was not a particularly easy boss to please. He had entered the football business thinking he could rely on "pros to do the job for him" but then, according to his accountant, "found that he and his office had to do more in the daily operations of the team than he had ever suspected." Close to a dozen members of the front office were let go in Culverhouse's first two years in business. During the same period, he acquired a reputation as a "tightwad" among his employees, complaining about items as small as the cost of the paper in the office copying machine. He also did "a personal economic analysis of the future of pro football," and in the end, rather than rely on "pros," Culverhouse became one himself.

It was precisely that expertise Rozelle sought to tap by putting Culverhouse on the finance committee. Culverhouse in turn made good use of his position. Seven years later, one NFL owner would call him "more the vice-commissioner than Tex Schramm." Culverhouse's rise would coincide with his usefulness. "He did everybody's taxes for them," one NFL observer pointed out, "and he became the commissioner's adviser on finances." He was also the right man with the right expertise at the right time. The cash flow of the football business was about to escalate sharply, making Culverhouse even more useful.

Rozelle had announced that escalated cash flow as the first item on the meeting's agenda. He had spent the previous six months hammering out a new four-year agreement with the networks. The actual numbers involved had been the owners' favorite subject of speculation since the negotiations began. "The clubs of the League would be calling me as the television negotiations were under way," Rozelle explained, "and they called the other TV committee members as well. Like a kid at Christmas: 'What do you think it's going to be?' "

Most assumed the contract would be larger than the $2.2 million a year they were each currently receiving. "I heard three million dollars from a number of sources," Billy Sullivan remembered, "and I think some of the more optimistic predictions were running three and a half. But it was strictly speculation because the commissioner . . . at no time indicated what the figures would be, because, frankly, there are critics of the commissioner and some of the people that wanted to hurt him were throwing huge numbers out so if he didn't reach that, they would say he'd done a poor job. . . . One of the owners in the League who was constantly trying to depreciate [sic] the commissioner's position was talking numbers out of sight." Sullivan identified the "out of sight numbers" as "over four million." Sullivan didn't identify "one owner," but Al Davis was the most likely candidate. Davis would later claim to have expected a sharp escalation rather than the incremental growth assumed by the rest of the League.

Davis was certainly correct. The new television deals Rozelle announced would pay each club an average of $5.2 million a year, an increase of 133 percent. In return, the League would go to a sixteen-game schedule, add a "wild card" to the playoff system, and stage at least an additional four prime time games. *The New York Times* later described the new arrangement as "the biggest deal in television history" and noted that "never before in an industry in which program life is short have such rich long-term commitments been made." It was also a historic moment in the NFL. For the first time ever, the average team's income from the League's shared television revenues would now exceed its income from its own live gate.

Almost everyone greeted the numbers with awe. Most were also quick to give Rozelle the credit. The acclaim was predictable and provided Al Davis with another good reason for missing the meeting. He could not have wanted any part of the commissioner's moment of triumph, especially since it coincided with his own comeuppance at Rozelle's hands. Davis made his presence felt, however, in a manner calculated to piss the commissioner off.

After the League's treasurer presented "a summary of the annual club cash flow projections" over the life of the TV contract, the Television Committee presented six proposed amendments to the constitution, designed to simplify the commissioner's job of scheduling games under the new arrangements with the networks. Four of the six were special guarantees given the New York Giants, New York Jets, San Francisco 49ers, and Oakland Raiders at the time of the merger agreement ten years earlier. They required the commissioner to get the permission of those teams in order to schedule their home games any day but Sunday or schedule competing home games on the same day in the same market. The terms had been included in the merger agreement to ease the friction of sharing the same market and had been informally ignored almost since their inception. Their elimination was considered necessary to provide Rozelle "more latitude in the development of the playing schedule." It would require a unanimous vote.

The Raiders, represented by Al LoCasale, voted no on all four amendments and all four failed by votes of twenty-seven to one. When asked for an explanation, the minutes reported, "Mr. LoCasale said Oakland was voting no because of insufficient time to examine and study the effect of the proposed amendments." Rozelle maintained his veneer of politeness and "asked that he be notified as soon as possible if Oakland were to decide to change its vote." To no one's great surprise, no such notification was ever forthcoming.

8
Rosenbloom's Roving Rams

While Al Davis no doubt shared some of his darker thoughts about Pete Rozelle with his closest friend in the League, Carroll Rosenbloom, Rosenbloom's own relationship with the commissioner was headed in the opposite direction. C.R., having already raised hell in no uncertain terms, was now content to make peace. The reasons for his turnaround were several.

The first was a certain amount of persuasion applied by other owners, like Hugh Culverhouse, C.R.'s tax advisor and one of the executors of his latest will. Culverhouse was also an apostle of getting along with the commissioner. Perhaps the most effective persuasion came from Leon Hess, owner of the Jets, who urged Carroll to lighten up on Rozelle. "Carroll liked Hess," his son remembered. "They were both the same age and both successful businessmen. When Carroll talked to me about the visit, he said Hess hit the right chords. Also I think my father was beginning to get enough satisfaction from the commissioner's office and wasn't nearly so irritated."

A second reason was Carroll's sense of his own mortality and his worry about his legacy. "I've had a lot of fights with guys in the League," he mentioned to his son Steve. "I think I should patch things up so you don't have a problem when I'm gone." Carroll remade his relationships with Tex Schramm and Art Modell, as well as the commissioner himself, by early 1978.

The third and perhaps overriding reason was that Rosenbloom had other fish to fry and it would be a lot easier if Rozelle were on his side rather than against him.

More than anything else, C.R. wanted out of the L.A. Coliseum. "When I came out here in 1972," he said "I tried to work with the Coliseum people to get the stadium improved. First, I wanted to spend my own money. I offered to buy the Coliseum . . . I didn't know at the time that they couldn't be free of it because they have to support that other thing, the Sports Arena. I've tried every way in the world to get something done . . . and the Coliseum is [still] not that safe and enjoyable."

If anything, C.R.'s description of his home field was charitable. The *Los Angeles Times* called the L.A. Coliseum "an aging monolithic structure in south-central Los Angeles assaulted on three sides by what socio-economists would call urban blight." Due to several well-publicized muggings in the stadium parking lot, the Rams now employed "a special security force of husky young men in T-shirts and windbreakers" who were "purposefully conspicuous in great numbers" on game days. Even so, the Rams' average attendance had slipped from seventy-six thousand a game in 1974 to fifty-three thousand in 1977, despite fielding winning teams. When the Rams sent a questionnaire to their ticket holders asking how Rams games could be improved, ninety-nine percent of the respondents complained about the Coliseum.

Rosenbloom still had the dilemma of where to go, and by October 1977, he had decided on Anaheim. Twenty-eight miles outside Los Angeles's city limits, it was well within the seventy-five-mile radius allotted each NFL franchise for its home turf and, in League eyes, a move to Anaheim would be no different from the Cowboys moving to Irving, the Giants moving to Jersey, or the Patriots moving to Foxboro. Carroll had spotted its possibilities in 1972. He considered Big A stadium, then housing only a baseball team, as "spotlessly clean" and "an enjoyable safe place to go." He had even begun preliminary negotiations with the city's stadium manager. "Our proposal to the Rams at that time called for the city to provide the land for Rosenbloom or others to build a stadium he would control," the manager recalled, "a basic football stadium next to the Big A or across the street."

In the fall of 1977, C.R. secretly dispatched an assistant to make contact with Anaheim, while he also began discussions with the LAMCC. His lease in Los Angeles ran through 1979, but he wanted to know what the LAMCC was willing to do now to keep him. Before, Al Davis noted, "Carroll got advantages from the Los Angeles Coliseum when he threatened to leave the Coliseum. This time, he used the Coliseum—that he might stay there—as a lever and he got the advantages from Anaheim." Anaheim was pleased to be in the bidding. The city had been searching for a football franchise since 1966, but at present had no hope of obtaining a new NFL franchise. So when Rosenbloom came knocking a second time, Anaheim offered him everything it thought he might want.

Most of what it had was land—ninety-five acres immediately

adjacent to Big A. Anaheim had wanted to develop the parcel for a long time and used the inquiry from Rosenbloom to put the idea in motion. The city suggested a two-tiered arrangement: Big A Stadium would be expanded to seat seventy to eighty thousand, including luxury boxes, and then leased to the Rams on better terms than the franchise currently had in L.A. In return, Rosenbloom would also sign a longterm lease with option to buy on the adjoining ninety-five-acre parking lot. There, he would put up a hotel or office complex or whatever development both he and the city could agree on. Anaheim figured the rent receipts and the taxes generated by the ninety-five-acre development would cover the costs of redoing Big A and put Anaheim in the big leagues to boot.

Rosenbloom was intrigued by the offer, but by no means sold. "Carroll's concern was to get a new stadium," his son Steve pointed out. "But Anaheim also wanted to do something with the parking lot. They'd tried before and failed. . . . They're Disneyland people. They talked about building a monorail from the stadium to Disneyland and crazy shit like that. Carroll didn't like real estate and was leery of it all. As a businessman, he thought it was a big risk." A developer other than Carroll Rosenbloom would have to be found by the city for the deal to go forward.

Using the possibility of the Rams as fresh bait, Anaheim now went shopping for developers and it found Cabot, Cabot & Forbes, a Boston-based company with projects all over the United States. Said James Kenyon, a senior vice-president, "We reorganized and we really were looking for a bellwether, high prestige, quality development to do in the western United States. We felt that the draw of the Rams, the modernization of the stadium, the identity, the developer's dream of controlling a large parcel of land so you can properly master-plan it was terrifically egotistically interesting to CC&F." He remembered, that Anaheim "wanted a national developer, somebody with some image." For its part, CC&F wanted a joint venture and the partner it wanted was Carroll Rosenbloom. "It was obvious to us," the vice-president explained, "for two reasons: one is that Mr. Rosenbloom was reputed to have a very large net worth, a financially successful guy. Number two, the Rams are the tenant that put the biggest stress on the [proposed] usage. It was logical for us to tie the two of them together."

A month after getting acquainted, CC&F sent Jerry Blakely, its chairman of the board, out to Anaheim to pursue the discussion further. C.R. was receptive enough to the possibility that the chairman arranged to meet with him again soon to get more specific.

In the meantime, the developers did more of their homework, so they could make a presentation to Rosenbloom back in Los Angeles. It included "an analysis of the last twenty-seven stadiums built in America, about the parking ratio, the sight lines, all of the various buzz words when it comes to stadiums." They offered C.R. pictures and brochures about previous CC&F developments. The discussion was aided by the rapport between Rosenbloom and Blakely. Their sons had attended the same eastern prep school and they both served on the school's board together. Blakely "told Carroll that we would not move forward with the deal unless he was a partner, for obvious reasons. We needed a partner and we felt that the combination of a tenant who potentially is going to average sixty-five thousand people in the stadium was important because you had to work collectively." For his part, C.R. remained enthusiastic but noncommittal. "Carroll was awfully hard to pin down," CC&F's senior vice-president noted, "an excellent businessman."

By the time 1977 had become 1978, however, CC&F felt it had to have some kind of commitment before it could go forward. There were still other developers in the picture who had been approached as Anaheim shopped around, and CC&F wanted some guarantee of exclusivity.

Rosenbloom complied, and in January signed a letter of intent with CC&F. The letter bound him to CC&F as his exclusive partner should he move forward "to develop the stadium and develop the peripheral land." The letter specifically stated his intent to form Anaheim Stadium Associates, fifty percent of which would be owned by a Rosenbloom holding company, and fifty percent of which would be owned by a wholly owned subsidiary of CC&F. Together, they would see what kind of terms they could extract from the city of Anaheim. Now C.R.'s Superstadium Game was in high gear.

News broke in Los Angeles a week later when the *Los Angeles Times* ran a story headlined "Rams Appear Closer to Anaheim Stadium." From the L.A. Coliseum's perspective, the news could not have been worse. The LAMCC had been continuing conversations with the Rams, but was waiting to find out if its bid for the 1984 Olympics would be accepted before committing itself to any improvements. The *Times* story made that strategy dysfunctional. With the Rams "closer to leaving Los Angeles than at any time since they came west in 1946," something would have to be done soon. Steve Rosenbloom pointed out that "If the Coliseum could offer us the same things that Anaheim can offer, we'd stay at the Coliseum." If the Rams left, the nation's second largest city would be without a football team and the Los Angeles Coliseum and Sports Arena would have to be bailed out of potential bankruptcy. "If we don't get the message this time," the L.A. Coliseum general manager observed to the *Times,* "we're pretty stupid."

While the LAMCC struggled to get a counteroffer together, a group calling itself "The Committee to Relocate the Rams to Orange County" bought a full page ad in the *Times* for "An Open Letter to the Los Angeles Rams." The committee included representatives of business, industry, and local government, including the mayors of Orange County's twenty-six cities. Their letter described Anaheim as "a modern, attractive place" to watch a game and called on Rosenbloom to move the franchise there "for the betterment of professional football."

The vice-president of the L.A. Coliseum called the ad "a declaration of war." At the time, the statement seemed like hyperbole. Six years later, it would sound like understatement.

9
Keeping Tose on His Toes

By the time Anaheim made its declaration of war, Carroll Rosenbloom was back on speaking terms with Pete Rozelle.

C.R. broke the ice by reporting to the commissioner on developments with the L.A. Coliseum. "He telephoned on several occasions," Rozelle recalled, "and he told me that the Los Angeles Memorial Coliseum Committee would do nothing to improve the stadium. . . . His phone conversations with me developed a pattern of growing disenchantment and then he mentioned the possibilities he felt existed at Anaheim. . . . It was not an extensive discussion. . . . He just said he felt it would be an attractive deal."

At the time, Rozelle said nothing that might jeopardize his

newfound communication with C.R. The commissioner did not treat Rosenbloom's mention of Anaheim as a cloud of war on the League's horizon. Nor did he express concern over just what effects a vacancy in the nation's second city might have on the NFL. Rosenbloom's Superstadium Game was considered his business, not the League's, and was simply tracked from a distance by the commissioner's office. At the time, it was one of the less pressing developments demanding Rozelle's attention.

Perhaps the most pressing was, once again, Leonard Tose in Philadelphia. The bridge loan supplied by William Clay Ford's Detroit bank in August was coming due in February 1978, and finding a replacement proved no small task. Both Tose and Rozelle turned to Chuck Sullivan, Billy Sullivan's oldest son. Chuck's rescue of his father had established his reputation as the best man in the NFL at dealing with banks. At the moment, Chuck Sullivan was also the League's rising star. Executive vice-president of the Patriots, he handled all the franchise's finances. He was also in the process of becoming personal attorney for Carrie Rozelle's family. In June 1977, he was voted chairman of the Management Council, replacing Wellington Mara, despite the complete absence of any experience in labor negotiating. Chuck had also been the first person in memory to push himself for the job.

Though he was already reaping the benefits of its success, Chuck Sullivan's brilliant quarterbacking of his father's comeback was not yet complete. Two outstanding items remained unsettled: several suits filed by the nonvoting shareholders, none of which was close to trial, and the Patriots' taxes. The new tax depreciation laws were putting an unanticipated strain on the Sullivans' cash flow. To help ease the strain, Billy approached the IRS for an adjustment. Sullivan's argument was that since he had already begun the process of taking over sole ownership in 1975, months before the tax change, he ought to be treated under the old law, even though the takeover had been finally consummated after the new law's deadline. When no adjustment was forthcoming, Billy sought an act of Congress to allow him the benefits of the old depreciation system. The legislation was first introduced by Massachusetts Senator Edward Brooke in 1976 but failed in the House. In 1978, Brooke planned to reintroduce it, this time as a rider on another, unrelated bill. "I'm just asking to be treated like every other sports team," Old Billy explained. Billy's new tax bill was just in the talking stages when Chuck took on the task of finding Leonard Tose a bank loan and, since politics was his father's bailiwick, the effort in Washington required little of Chuck's time.

Chuck Sullivan's involvement with Leonard Tose's finances would later be characterized as an extension of his management council duties, but "He did it for the money," Tose later explained. Sullivan's fee was no doubt considerable, but it was also well-earned. Finding a bank willing to have Leonard Tose for a client was a genuine challenge to Chuck's skills. What Sullivan was looking for was actually two loans: $7 million to repay Manufacturers Trust in Detroit; and $2.5 million to deal with Tose's "personal debts." By January 1978, a dozen New York and Pennsylvania financial institutions had turned the loan down. Even the League's stated willingness to guarantee Tose's borrowings with the Eagles' $5 million a year in television revenues had produced no immediate takers.

There were two significant roadblocks to Leonard Tose's refinancing. The first was his twenty-nine percent partner, Herb Barness, now suing Tose over club finances. "That's why the banks won't lend money to Tose," a "banking source" told the *Philadelphia Daily News*. "They're afraid of the lawsuits Tose may get from his partners. The partners are upset that he's agreeing to too many long-term commitments. He makes agreements with coaches, players, and water boys. There's no question he's up against the wall. Loans are scarce now and he's lost credibility. The League will have to step in for him." Unbeknownst to the *Daily News*'s source, of course, the League already had.

In January 1978, Chuck Sullivan met with Herb Barness, whose "main issue," according to Sullivan, was "personal salary. He wants Leonard to settle for a $35,000 salary when the other owners take home about $175,000 apiece. We told him we thought his demands were unfair." However, in February, a Philadelphia Court enjoined Tose from taking more than $60,000 in annual salary. It also required him to submit an itemized expense account to the court within ten days of the end of each month. The accounting had to be certified by the Eagles' accountants, with a copy sent to Herb Barness. Ironically, Tose's reversal in court was at least partially reassuring to those banks still thinking of loaning him money.

Tose's second major refinancing roadblock was his own reputation as anything but frugal. "The banks aren't worried about the Eagles' ability to pay back money," one Philadelphia banker observed. "They're worried about the personal tab Tose has run up." Tose's previous lenders did nothing to ease their worries. After New York's Citibank had been approached, one of its assistant vice-presidents then phoned John Bunting, First Penn's president, asking for his assessment. "He said Tose was 'a big spender,' " the banker recalled, "a 'high liver with debts all over the country and I wouldn't touch him with a 170-foot pole.' "

As Tose's February 9 deadline rapidly approached, speculation began about whether any bank would touch the Eagles' owner. Chuck Sullivan surfaced to calm the waters. "Leonard's credit rating with the NFL is Triple A," he contended. "The Eagles are one of the best managed teams in the NFL. Because of the new TV contract, a loan to the Eagles is as strong as a loan to IBM." Sullivan said refinancing would not be a problem. "You know," he pointed out, "banks have been making loans to teams since 1922, and no bank has lost as much as a dime on an NFL team."

According to Eagles general manager Jimmy Murray, Manufacturers National was applying no pressure for immediate repayment. "We have an excellent relationship with the Detroit bank," he claimed. "I don't know how we'll resolve the issue. . . . Leonard's the only one who knows what he's going to do, but he's not talking." And Tose was waiting for Sullivan to do what he was being paid for. Chuck was negotiating with Manufacturers National about possibly rolling the bridge loan over. As their deadline approached, Sullivan wanted to buy a little time. He finally succeeded. On February 9, instead of repaying the full $7 million Tose owed in Detroit, a $350,000 interest payment was made. The money, according to the *Philadelphia Daily News*, came from a $1.5 million "personal loan" Tose had secured from an unknown source. Herb Barness expressed amazement that anyone would make a personal loan to Leonard Tose.

Chuck Sullivan expressed a certain amount of relief. "His personal finances have all been straightened out," Chuck said of Tose. "We paid the interest today and, in view of the fact that several banks have expressed interest in refinancing . . . everything is in great shape." There was still long-term financing to be arranged, but to the press, Chuck was sanguine about that too.

In the meantime, Leonard Tose had the full backing of the NFL. The League had bailed him out before, Sullivan pointed out, "and we'll do it again if we have to. We bought Leonard

Tose, not anybody else. He's the man the NFL wants to control the Eagles. We will stick by him. Leonard Tose is a very important part of the NFL owners' team. . . . Speaking for the rest of the NFL owners, I can say that we will make sure Leonard Tose keeps control of the Eagles until breath leaves his body."

10
Robbie Rubs Rozelle the Wrong Way

Pete Rozelle was also concerned about Joe Robbie in early 1978, but for very different reasons.

Robbie liked to play the rogue elephant on labor issues. These labor proclivities combined with his contempt for the commissioner's ownership policy and became, in Rozelle's eyes, yet another threat to the integrity of League Think. A collision between Robbie and the commissioner became inevitable.

Joe Robbie's stirrings on the labor front dated from spring 1977, when the ink on the League's new five-year collective bargaining agreement was hardly dry. The incident that set things off occurred on May 4 in Miami. That evening Miami police arrested two of Robbie's football players, Randy Crowder and Don Reese, and charged them with attempting to sell a pound of cocaine to an undercover cop. Robbie suspended the two, pending the outcome of their trial, scheduled for the middle of the next football season. Reese and Crowder filed a grievance under the new contract, claiming that Robbie's action amounted to prejudging their case and that all action should await the proof of their guilt or innocence. Under the terms of the League's labor agreement, their grievance was heard by the Player-Club Relations Committee, composed of two union representatives, Len Hauss and Gene Upshaw, and two owners, Dan Rooney and Wellington Mara.

The decision the hearing reached displeased Robbie even more than the hearing itself did. On Friday, July 29, the PCRC announced its ruling, final and binding to all parties under the terms of the 1977 contract. Robbie's Dolphins would have until the following Monday to either trade, waive, or reinstate the two players. Players association Executive Director Ed Garvey called it "an excellent settlement for all concerned."

Joe Robbie was furious. "It will take virtually a case of mistaken identity before I want Reese and Crowder back on the Miami Dolphins," he stormed. "It's completely unfair to give us a deadline like that. It's obvious nobody's going to trade for them under those circumstances. I am not taking issue with the collective bargaining agreement, but . . . the action of the PCRC establishes a dangerous precedent and could rise to haunt the NFL in the future in protecting the integrity of professional football. What will happen if two players are arrested for fixing a football game? . . . What happens in a case involving murder or manslaughter? Must the player be paid in jail or out on bail while he awaits trial?"

Robbie immediately took his complaint to Rozelle. He wanted the commissioner to suspend Reese and Crowder for life. Rozelle, however, had already decided to stay his hand "until the judicial process played itself out" and could offer Robbie no satisfaction. Robbie also asked for an extension of the deadline and was refused. On August 1, his Miami franchise grudgingly complied with the PCRC and placed the two players on irrevocable waivers. They were now, Joe Robbie noted, "free agents."

The next day, Joe Robbie announced that he intended to sue the NFL and the NFLPA in an attempt to have the PCRC ruling reversed. Such a suit was, of course, the last thing the NFL needed. Having struggled for three years to get a contract, it would have been a disaster to now have it sabotaged by one of the League's own members. Fortunately, Robbie's threat of suit became moot when Reese and Crowder pleaded guilty on August 10 and were sentenced to a year in prison. Their suspension for that period was now automatic and Robbie backed off from using the courts to make his point. Nonetheless, Rozelle remained leery about the possibility of Robbie rattling Ed Garvey's cage on a free-lance basis. Garvey, the commissioner was quick to point out, was hard enough to deal with as it was.

The commissioner had hoped the new contract, making the NFLPA more secure and prosperous than ever would yield labor peace for a while. Certainly the union was no longer struggling for survival. The settlement had increased the union's net assets from minus $233,000 to plus $608,000 in one year. Ed Garvey's annual salary had been raised from $56,000 in 1976 to $114,000 by the end of 1977. Prosperity did not, however, make Ed Garvey easier to get along with. "Garvey took every chance he could to attack, attack, attack," one Rozelle assistant complained. "In enforcing the contract, there were a lot of very technical objections. A lot of stuff that was just pure bullshit. We tried to be patient. We listened to him, sifted it out, responded to him, and tried to ignore it all, but it was hard."

By the end of 1977, however, Garvey was not giving the NFL his full attention. He was looking around for other areas to organize. "Ed envisioned himself being a big man in the AFL-CIO," Bob Moore, one of the NFLPA vice-presidents, remembered. "He envisioned a Federation of Professional Athletes that would include all sports, with Garvey as its head. . . . The biggest problem it faced was that the union leaders in baseball, basketball, and hockey all hated Garvey, so that part never got off the ground. In the meantime, he went after the unorganized sports." Garvey tried to organize motorcycle racing, rodeo riding, and soccer. Soccer was the most concerted of those campaigns and was well under way by the beginning of 1978. His target was the North American Soccer League and his new union was named the NASL Players Association. To fund the effort, according to Moore, Garvey's NFLPA loaned his NASLPA some $500,000.

When Ed Garvey took on the NASL, the would-be sports labor czar soon crossed swords with Joe Robbie again, much to Pete Rozelle's consternation. Robbie's wife, Elizabeth, owned the league's Ft. Lauderdale Strikers, formerly the Miami Toros. When Mrs. Robbie took over the franchise in 1976, she inherited an indebtedness of more than $900,000 and, in so doing, insured a family commitment to making the NASL succeed.

When questioned by Rozelle or his fellow NFL owners about the soccer franchise, Robbie described it as a separate enterprise, of which Elizabeth was the "sole proprietor." In operation, however, the two franchises blended much more closely together. "My wife and I don't have separate wealth," Robbie explained. "As a matter of fact, we don't have joint wealth really. The profits that we make in the Miami Dolphins are available to us for whatever other purposes, including the Strikers. . . . It's all the same jackpot. . . . I get a copy of every business letter that is sent from the Ft. Lauderdale Strikers and my wife gets one from the Miami Dolphins and I read that file to keep currently abreast of what's going on." In addition, one son was about to become general manager of the Dolphins, and another was assistant general manager of the Strikers.

The other NFL owners were irritated not so much by the

assistance he gave his wife's club as by the assistance he afforded to the NASL as a league. In 1976, he had served as an
advisory member to the NASL's planning committee and participated in three or four league policy "brainstorming sessions."
He had also furnished the soccer owners with information "concerning the profits per team that an NFL club receives from NFL
Properties" and "how much profit each club obtains from NFL
Films." All of it was information other NFL owners considered
confidential. "We compared notes about how best to operate a
professional franchise," the Dolphin owner explained.

Even more irritating in the beginning of 1978 from the NFL's
point of view was Robbie's service on the NASL's recently
created labor relations committee, again as "advisory member."
The committee had been formed, according to Robbie, "for the
purpose of dealing with the attempt of Edward Garvey . . . to
obtain certification of a union to represent the NASL players."
He considered his efforts at those NASL meetings an attempt "to
stiffen their backbone and make them stand up and fight Mr.
Garvey and the union more so than the NFL did over the years.

"I've told the NASL to avoid our pitfalls," he went on to
explain. "I did not feel that all twenty-four teams in soccer, for
example, should have to deal as one with the players union. I felt
that the individual club was the appropriate bargaining unit and I
wanted that tested. . . . I was intensely interested personally in
what was going on between the NASL and Mr. Garvey and his
union."

By the end of 1977, Garvey was already complaining about
Robbie's NASL involvement. "We now face an interesting recognition question in soccer," the architect of the Federation of
Professional Athletes testified. "NASL owners say they believe
unionization of the NASL is 'inevitable' and that they don't
mind a union in soccer. The problem is that they do not want *this*
union in soccer and so we are now before the National Labor
Relations Board seeking an election."

Chuck Sullivan, chairman of the NFL's Management Council,
considered the exposure "very adverse," especially since it
came during a period when the NFL was trying "to have some
semblance of a harmonious relationship with the players union."
Leonard Tose, vice-chairman of the Management Council and by
far the loudest NFL critic of cross-ownership, was predictably
more vociferous about the dangers such behavior posed. According to Tose, Robbie was giving Garvey extra leverage, which
was, of course, one of the express goals of Garvey's Federation

of Professional Athletes scheme. Pete Rozelle was even less sanguine about Robbie's adventurism. The commissioner pointed out that "from what we've heard of the Robbie situation, it would appear that it is Mr. Robbie who is on the soccer committees, not Mrs. Robbie, and it is Mr. Robbie attending meetings, not Mrs. Robbie. I would say that . . . there is a conflict . . . with the spirit and intent of ownership policy."

It was not, however, a violation of the letter of the continuing ownership policy resolution then in effect and Rozelle was powerless to do more than observe it. The "Robbie situation" was yet another irritant in the commissioner's open wound over the cross-ownership issue. None of the unspecified promises of divestiture had been lived up to, none of the conflicts of interest eliminated. Rozelle was now sure they wouldn't be until they were meticulously banned and that ban entered in the League's constitution. It had been five years since he had last tried for that solution, but he had not forgotten it. Joe Robbie provided only the most recent of the reasons Rozelle thought it ought to be done.

On the agenda for the 1978 annual meeting in March, a "discussion of dual ownership or investment in other major team sports by NFL owners or their immediate families" was scheduled for Executive Session. From Rozelle's perspective, the time had come to force the issue to its conclusion.

11
Crossing Swords Over Cross-Ownership

The 1978 annual meeting lasted a week, but most of those in attendance remembered most clearly the Executive Session discussion of cross-ownership on the morning of March 16. "This is the point where the tolerance had ebbed," Rozelle explained. "There was an escalation of feeling on the part of some members . . . that something should be done about the conflicts [of interest] and the lack of success of those individuals [owning other sports interests] in resolving the conflicts as they had pledged to do."

As traditional, Leonard Tose opened the issue with a blast at Lamar Hunt, set off by Hunt's ongoing media hype of the NASL. Tose was infuriated by an article that appeared in *American Way* magazine, the in-flight publication of American Airlines. He carried the magazine in his fist and brandished it like a cudgel when he addressed the rest of the League. Tose recounted, "What particularly disturbed me . . . was the fact that Mr. Hunt was quoted as saying soccer is going to replace football."

Hunt was not pleased by Tose's remarks. "There were . . . at least six clubs that had people with ownership interests in other sports," he complained, "and whenever this conversation would come up in the meeting . . . invariably I would be the only one that would be asked to respond. . . . I would look around the room, and [the other cross-ownership violators] wouldn't say a word and wouldn't participate in conversation and yet all of the conversation was pointed at me and asking me questions." Hunt considered Tose's attacks "very disruptive toward the harmony of the League."

Lamar Hunt also thought he'd done nothing wrong. From his point of view, he had made his "best efforts" to divest and had kept the commissioner's office informed of those efforts by letter. The last such letter had been sent a year earlier. He had, he informed Rozelle, made his basketball interest in the Chicago Bulls available, but it was "without real prospective buyers." In the case of his soccer franchise, the Dallas Tornado, Hunt had encountered two interlocking "difficulties." He had hoped to put together a group of one hundred one-percent owners to replace himself and "assure the stability of the team." Unfortunately, the Tornado was at the moment in a very public dispute with Southern Methodist University over the use of their soccer stadium. "With an ongoing dispute in the newspapers," he explained, he "didn't feel it was practical to even broach the subject" of his plan.

In the meantime, of course, Hunt had continued trying to make the NASL a success. Like Joe Robbie, he served as an ex-officio member of the soccer league's planning committee, whose goal was to make a long range plan for NASL success. Among the items discussed were soccer's future television policy and how the NASL might "alter the way it marketed its TV rights if and when the NFL shifts to pay TV." Hunt later admitted that he "might possibly" have provided the soccer owners with information about the NFL, but he claimed it was only things that were "essentially public knowledge." He also provided the NASL commissioner with a list of "people who were interested in an NFL team in their cities'' but again insisted that none of it was a conflict of interest.

At the 1978 annual meeting, Lamar Hunt's response carried less weight than ever and Tose was by no means the only person prepared to say so. Wellington Mara offered that Lamar should divest either his soccer or his football and do it soon. When Max Winter spoke up, he sounded like a Leonard Tose clone. The two men were ''good friends'' and talked about soccer regularly. Winter told the other owners that the NASL's Minneapolis franchise, the Minnesota Kicks, ''are hurting the Vikings, our sports dollar, and that they are drawing and we are losing ground as far as media exposure and fan participation.'' Even the Sullivans, close to both Hunt and Robbie, saw fit to complain. Since they were considered a ''family team,'' like the Rosenblooms and Rooneys, the Sullivans were allowed two representatives in Executive Session and both Billy and Chuck were there. ''We,'' Chuck explained, ''have had the opportunity within the last ten years to purchase the Boston Red Sox [baseball franchise], the Boston Celtics [basketball franchise] . . . the Boston Bruins [hockey franchise] . . . the Boston Tea Men [NASL franchise]. . . . In each event we turned these opportunities down because it was our feeling that our family had become identified with the NFL and identification with . . . other enterprises would take away from our primary objective of promoting the NFL. . . . If Lamar Hunt were to devote more time to the promotion of the Kansas City Chiefs and less time to the promotion of other sports interests, I think the NFL would significantly benefit.

''My family made a commitment that we would bring ourselves into compliance with the rules,'' Chuck continued. ''It cost us ten million dollars to do that. We expected Mr. Hunt, who had made the same commitment, would do the same thing and bring himself into compliance.'' Instead, Chuck went on to note, just as Tose had, that Hunt kept promising to divest but never did so.

Hugh Culverhouse made a point similar to Chuck Sullivan's. He had turned down the opportunity to purchase a Tampa NASL franchise. Culverhouse also spread the onus beyond Lamar Hunt. He pointed out the possibility that Edward DeBartolo Sr., father of the NFL owner, was a likely buyer of the NASL franchise that Culverhouse had refused. He also noted that the Nordstrom family, central to Seattle's NFL ownership, owned a piece of a soccer team as well. So did Joe Robbie, Culverhouse pointed out.

Joe Robbie was not at the meeting to defend himself. None-the less, the ''Robbie situation'' was, as Rozelle remembered it, "the pivotal family relation issue that was discussed." The majority felt that a situation such as Robbie's ought to be prohibited and that the ownership policy's cross-ownership prohibitions should include "immediate family . . . husband or wife and sons and daughters of owners." In the course of that discussion of Robbie, the names of Eddie DeBartolo and his father, Mr. D, came up again as a sidebar on the question of "what ground rules we should have for family conflicts of interest." Eddie himself had left the meeting before the discussion of cross-ownership had begun. The most articulate opponent of Rozelle's ownership policy ideas, Edward Bennett Williams of the Washington Redskins, was absent as well. His substitute pointed out that the Redskins "will conform" to the ownership policy resolution then in effect, but that Jack Kent Cooke, the majority owner, had not yet divested his basketball and hockey interests. The problem was, for the moment, out of Cooke's hands. His wife was suing for divorce and until that case was settled, Cooke was under court order not to sell any of his assets.

Of all the excuses for failure to divest, Cooke's was the one with which Rozelle was most sympathetic. Rozelle's wife, Carrie, was Cooke's former daughter-in-law and considered Cooke's wife one of her best friends. It was, Rozelle knew, a sensitive situation. "I didn't want the divorce," Cooke explained. "She did." The dissolution was, the Redskins majority owner admitted, "a very unhappy" turn of events.

With Williams and Robbie absent and Hunt maintaining his usual silence on cross-ownership, the most discordant note to Rozelle's ears was sounded by Al Davis. Davis's complaint was aimed principally at Rozelle's lieutenant, Art Modell. Davis claimed the Cleveland owner was up to his neck in cross-ownership conflicts of interest himself and that Rozelle's tolerance of those violations at the same time as he decried others' was a double standard and hypocrisy of the first order.

Certainly Modell's case was an example of the gray areas surrounding the definition of "conflict of interest." First, though he was never involved in ownership per se, Modell had, for several years, sought to get an NASL expansion franchise situated in Cleveland. He hoped to find another tenant for his stadium. Modell had tested the Cleveland soccer waters by staging a number of soccer games in the mid-1970s. He had several meetings with the NASL's commissioner to discuss "the needs of the soccer league." Modell insisted that "I made it clear from the beginning [that] the extent of my interest was occupancy for the stadium, but if I can help assemble a group for ownership of a soccer franchise, I will." Nothing ever came of Modell's offer and by 1978, his soccer interest had dissipated.

It was not soccer, however, but baseball that was the principal subject of Davis's objections. Modell was also on the board of directors of the Cleveland Indians baseball franchise, though he had no outright ownership interest. Again, according to Modell, the reason was his stewardship of Cleveland Stadium Corp. By the end of the 1977 baseball season, the Indians, one of Cleveland Stadium's two principal tenants, were "on the verge of bankruptcy" and Modell was admittedly "terrified of losing baseball to New Orleans or some other city and leaving eighty-one playing dates [for Cleveland Stadium] vacant" and forcing the stadium—and Modell "very close" to bankruptcy. "It would have been a disaster," he pointed out. Privately, he later admitted, "Had it not been for the NFL's cross-ownership rule, I would have bought the Indians myself."

Instead, he sought to rescue the baseball franchise by finding a new owner. The owner he found was F. J. "Steve" O'Neill. At the time, O'Neill owned a small piece in the New York Yankees. "I asked him would he consider taking control of the Indians," Modell remembered, "to save it for Cleveland and, secondly, save it for the stadium." O'Neill agreed and Modell was named to the board of directors in the new baseball ownership. His presence, he claimed, "was designed to ease the transition from one ownership to another. . . . It was cosmetic. I did not function on any committees. I did not participate in any player . . . or broadcast negotiations."

Cleveland was appreciative of Art Modell's gesture, if Al Davis was not. Davis's point was that civic gesture or not, if Lamar Hunt's absentee ten percent ownership of the basketball Chicago Bulls was a conflict of interest, so was Art Modell's presence on the board of the Cleveland Indians, even without an ownership interest.

Pete Rozelle was quick to defend his friend and lieutenant. "[E]veryone at the time Mr. Modell became a member of the board of directors of the baseball team realized it was part of a business arrangement that Mr. Modell had made with the city of Cleveland to refurbish the stadium. . . . I only saw it as a conflict when it gave Mr. Davis an opportunity to bring it up in a meeting. I like to eliminate divisiveness among our people, if possible, and anything that can be used like that and prevent us from going forward with a single voice, I don't think is good."

In the interest of "going forward with a single voice," Art

Modell promised the meeting that "rather than get in a problem with Mr. Davis," he would not stand for reelection to the Indians' board when his current term ran out two years hence. It was an act he later described as "my decision to get the hell off." He explained, "It wasn't worth the embarrassment to the League. It wasn't worth the controversy."

When the dust cleared on the session, it was tallied a big victory for Rozelle. The "sense of the meeting" for which he had been waiting five years had arrived. Now, there "was a growing impatience with the inability of several of the clubs to divest their holdings" that was "getting progressively more heated," according to Rozelle. "The consensus was the only way to achieve what had been sought for a number of years was to vote specific sanctions" into the constitution. Ownership policy was at last to be given teeth. "The commissioner," the minutes recorded, "said the League office would develop for the June meeting alternatives to consider regarding penalties for noncompliance with League policy on this subject. In the meantime, he asked for strong best efforts to divest of such holdings before June."

Sensing only long-awaited breakthrough, it apparently didn't occur to Pete Rozelle that he might be opening a Pandora's box in League Think's closet.

12
Alluring Anaheim

Carroll Rosenbloom played no significant role in the cross-ownership debate, though his sympathies were apparent in his behavior.

The Rams' owner had flirted with the notion of owning other sports franchises, but never made a purchase. In 1976, he talked with Lamar Hunt about purchasing the NASL's L.A. franchise for one of C.R.'s sons. Rosenbloom, Hunt remembered, "felt there might be merit in having a combination situation where the Rams . . . and a soccer team . . . would play in the same stadium and might help get some stadium improvements that he was negotiating for." That idea, like the improvements themselves, went nowhere, but in 1977 Carroll had considered another cross-ownership, this time in indoor soccer. He tried to draw his friend Al Davis into it, but they finally backed away.

Obviously far less than a fan of the commissioner's ownership policy, Rosenbloom nonetheless kept his peace at the 1978 annual meeting. For him, the Superstadium Game was now everything. Anaheim Stadium Associates had begun hammering out the details of an agreement with the city of Anaheim; Los Angeles and the LAMCC had commenced their last ditch effort to keep his Rams; and Carroll had to convert pressure on his second front into leverage on his first. It was a critical stage and he avoided distractions.

The LAMCC's drive had begun with reorganization, specifically, the rotation of Bill Robertson, a Los Angeles labor leader, into the Coliseum commission's presidency. Over the next six years, he would become arguably the most important external civic figure in the history of the NFL.

Robertson was originally from Minneapolis. After high school, he pitched in professional baseball until what he called his "drinking problem" destroyed his career. That drinking problem lasted almost fifteen years; four of which were spent living in skid rows and being "a bum." When not on the skids, he worked as an auto worker, a marine electrician, and a packinghouse worker. He'd been a member of the United Auto Workers, the construction trades union, the packinghouse union, and even, for a brief period, the Newspaper Guild. In the mid-1940s he began working as a bartender and manager of bars and restaurants and joined the hotel and restaurant workers union. In 1950, he gave up alcohol altogether and was a "changed man."

In 1953, Robertson moved to L.A., started tending bar, and joined Local 694. He was then elected president of Local 694 and served in that post for ten years. In 1967, he joined the staff of the L.A. County AFL-CIO Labor Council. One of his first tasks was directing the ten-union strike at the *Los Angeles Herald Examiner*. He was soon the director and chief spokesman for more than six hundred thousand workers in Los Angeles County. Robertson oversaw the union programs for education and safety and the like and helped the four hundred locals with their negotiations, but his prime responsibilities were political. As such, he was a key player in California's Democratic party.

Robertson was appointed to the LAMCC in October 1977 by California's governor, Jerry Brown. Originally, Brown had wanted to appoint his labor ally to the board of the state college system, but Robertson, a sports fan, asked for the Coliseum commission instead. The state appointed three of the commissioners, the county of Los Angeles supplied three, and the city of Los Angeles supplied three. Two months after Robertson joined the state's contingent, the presidency of the LAMCC made its annual rotation among the three components. It was now the state's turn and Robertson became president.

Bill Robertson and Carroll Rosenbloom first laid eyes on each other in February 1978. The two met in C.R.'s office at Rams headquarters. "I told him," Robertson would later testify, "that we were determined to do everything possible . . . to keep him as a tenant." Rosenbloom, he remembered privately, was "decent enough," but "crafty" and tried his best to "stroke" the Coliseum commission president. Robertson had brought a proposal with him which included construction of a new double-decked air-conditioned press box, replete with its own kitchen, and a new private owner's box. The LAMCC also proposed to build a new "state of the art" scoreboard, larger dressing rooms, larger lavatories, new escalators, and a new "communications center." Rosenbloom told Robertson he "appreciated" the proposal. "He said he would look it over thoroughly and he would be back to us." When Robertson asked about the status of Rosenbloom's dealings with Anaheim, Rosenbloom answered that "he was looking around."

The proposal fell short on at least a couple of significant points. Rosenbloom wanted the running track eliminated so the playing field could be lowered and the track area filled with seats. Robertson couldn't promise that because L.A. still hoped to host the 1984 Olympics. C.R. also wanted a closer practice facility than the current one in Long Beach. Robertson described the practice site as "a reasonable request" that he was powerless to meet. "It just wouldn't sail politically," the LAMCC president explained.

But not satisfying C.R. also posed political dangers. The man most threatened by a Rams move was Tom Bradley, L.A.'s mayor and southern California's foremost Democratic politician. The first black man ever to be elected mayor, Bradley was looking forward to an unprecedented third term and had fought a long battle with the City Council to get the Olympics bid made. Should the city lose that bid and lose the Rams as well, Bradley might face becoming the mayor who lost professional football for Los Angeles.

The mayor and Bill Robertson were close political allies and Robertson did not make light of the difficulties of trying to keep C.R. He thought Rosenbloom already had a deal with Anaheim waiting in the wings. "The Anaheim stadium people are bubbling," Jim Hardy, the L.A. Coliseum's general manager, noted. "They think it's a *fait accompli*." Nonetheless, Robertson continued playing out his end of the negotiations. In March, he arranged a meeting with Rosenbloom, himself, Bradley, Hardy, and City Councilman Gil Lindsay in C.R.'s office. Robertson wanted to reassure Rosenbloom that L.A. wanted him badly.

Rosenbloom recited his historical grievances with the LAMCC. He felt his requests had been legitimate and he was treated cavalierly. In response, according to Robertson, "the mayor and City Councilman Lindsay made a very strong appeal to Carroll Rosenbloom that they as public officials would do all in their power to see that the program that we submitted would come through. . . . Carroll, as [was] his nature, treated us very cordially; but he still said he was looking around, talking. We knew he was talking to Anaheim. . . . So it was clear that there was a real danger of him leaving Los Angeles."

Robertson asked what would happen should Rosenbloom leave. "In the event that you decide to go to Anaheim," the LAMCC president pointed out, "we are going to pursue an effort to get an NFL team to replace you. What are your feelings about it? Would you object to it?"

"No," C.R. answered, "I would not."

By the end of the month, the *Times* headlined a story, "Coliseum Will Try for a New Team If the Rams Leave." Rozelle's office pointed out that "the unanimous consent of League owners would be required to move either an expansion team or existing franchise into Los Angeles." That meant Carroll Rosenbloom had veto rights. And C.R. was not answering public questions about the issue. "If that time ever comes," he explained, "that would be the time to discuss it."

When Rosenbloom made that remark, he and Anaheim Stadium Associates were in the process of drawing up a proposal to the city of Anaheim and Anaheim Stadium, Inc. They proposed to build an "approximately twenty-seven-thousand-seat addition" to Big A Stadium, as well as "press box, private box, and locker facilities of a character to make the Stadium suitable for use by the Los Angeles Rams." Anaheim Stadium, Inc., Big A's official controlling entity, would issue bonds and lend the money raised to Anaheim Stadium Associates, who would retain title to the improvements and lease them back to the city. The city of Anaheim would in turn lease the stadium to the Los Angeles Rams for thirty years, and Anaheim Stadium Associates would lease the city's adjoining ninety-five acres with an option to buy the parcel at $40,000 an acre. That property would eventually be developed according to a master plan over which the city would have approval.

With that proposal, serious bargaining with Anaheim began. It was a process Anaheim's city manager described as "clarifying various points in the proposal and securing modifications where necessary." Perhaps the greatest clarifications were required on the lease and option prices on the ninety-five acres. The city of Anaheim thought the acreage was worth four times more than Rosenbloom and CC&F had offered.

CC&F assumed Anaheim would settle for $8,000 a year rent and an $80,000-an-acre option price. On the ninety-five acres covered by that arrangement, CC&F envisioned that Anaheim Stadium Associates would erect mid-rise office buildings, low-rise office buildings, a five-hundred room hotel complex, four theme restaurants, two "commercial projects," and parking garages to replace completely the parking stalls previously housed on the acreage. CC&F projected a positive cash flow of some $2.5 million a year from the development to Anaheim Stadium Associates.

"Rams to Move to Anaheim Stadium in '80," the Times predicted on April 28. C.R. would only say that he had made a lease offer to Anaheim but would meet again with the LAMCC before "we arrive at any decision. We owe them that courtesy," he explained. In the meantime, Rosenbloom was said to be looking at homes around Orange County's Newport Beach. By June, however, when Carroll and his son Steve left for League meetings in New York, no such announcement had been made.

During the spring, Rosenbloom had phoned Rozelle "a limited number" of times to keep him informed. Mostly he complained about the LAMCC's inability to give him what he wanted. There was only passing reference to "some real estate investment." Rozelle's "impression was that it was an office building or hotel or something of that sort." Rosenbloom provided no financial details. "It was not," the commissioner explained, "an extensive discussion."

Rosenbloom was more "extensive" with his friend Al Davis. The two talked "almost daily" throughout Rosenbloom's negotiations with Anaheim. They discussed the possibility of Davis moving his Raiders into the vacated L.A. Coliseum. Often, Davis's remarks took the form of "teasing that I may come down there with our little ol' team and we would have a hell of a competitive market and really go at each other and things like that. Sometimes he would think I am serious and sometimes he wouldn't." When C.R. thought Davis was serious, according to Davis, "he would always talk to me about not moving, why I shouldn't move. Certainly he didn't think it was right that I move to Los Angeles and invade his territory." Davis once told Rosenbloom he was "going to come to L.A." during a "social occasion" when C.R.'s wife, Georgia, was present. Later, Carroll told Georgia that Davis was being "facetious." Georgia disagreed. She thought Al Davis was "serious."

13
Tose's Italian Quarterback

To Rozelle's eye in spring 1978, however, things still seemed to be stable. Leonard Tose had finally resolved his finances. After almost a year of turmoil and uncertainty, Chuck Sullivan had at last found him a longterm loan.

Sullivan revealed the loan on April 19. The principal borrowing was for $8 million from New York's Citibank, the second largest bank in the world. The two other participants in its syndicate were Central Penn National of Philadelphia and Midlantic Bank of West Orange, New Jersey. Chuck Sullivan described the loan's structure as a "longterm deal." *The Philadelphia Inquirer* described it as "unique." Divided into two parts, $5 million was to be paid back within four years; the remaining $3 million was of "indefinite term." Sullivan explained: "It's actually working capital and a credit. It could go on forever and ever." In addition to the $8 million loaned the Eagles, another $2 million was loaned to Tose as a separate personal loan.

Chuck Sullivan was proud of the deal he had wrought. Leonard Tose, he declared, "is now free and clear. The key is the television revenue. The actual TV money secures the loan, which is the same for eight other NFL clubs."

However, Sullivan was not yet through. To further stabilize the Eagles, he immediately began negotiations to buy out Tose's minority partners and end the threat of legal encumbrance once and for all. The principal immediate target was Herb Barness, owner of twenty-nine percent, then came Wally Leventhal, the remaining six-percent partner. Both were reported to be in the mood to sell when they learned of Tose's loan. Barness ultimately sold his share to Tose for $3 million. Within a year, Leventhal sold for $1 million and the Eagles were all Tose's.

The night the Citibank loan was finally secured, Tose took all those who helped him to dinner at Brussels, a fashionable New York restaurant. From his point of view, he had a lot to celebrate. Even his enemies admitted Tose had scored a considerable coup just in surviving the previous year. Tose seemed to derive his greatest pleasure from the comeuppance his new financing gave to First Penn and its chairman, John Bunting. That humiliation was still fresh for Tose. "Mr. Bunting said to me, 'I'll make damn sure you won't get any loan from another bank,' " Tose railed, "and he also said, 'I'll bury you.' . . . He did a helluva job. There wasn't a bank in Philadelphia that would even give us an interview or look at our records." Bunting, Tose maintained to the Associated Press, had been the lynchpin in a "conspiracy" to run him out of football. They meant to deny him credit and make it impossible to keep the Eagles, but, Tose bragged, "that will never happen. I have too many friends in the National Football League and in the banking community."

The most useful of Tose's NFL friends was, of course, Chuck Sullivan, his hired gun. However, Leonard Tose remained a difficult man to advise, and he proved it with Chuck less than a month after their celebration dinner. At issue between Tose and Sullivan was the revenge Tose wanted to seek from First Penn and John Bunting. Tose believed their "conspiracy" was a violation of the Sherman [Anti-trust] Act and he wanted to sue everybody involved. Sullivan wanted nothing to do with Tose's strategy and said so. "I think litigation really is self-defeating," he explained.

Leonard Tose hired a lawyer who agreed with him and the result was *Leonard Tose v. First Pennsylvania Bank et al.,* filed on May 5, 1978. Tose's counsel was Joseph Alioto, former mayor of San Francisco and one of the country's foremost antitrust litigators. Though his work for Tose would prove a sideshow, Alioto would soon acquire Al Davis for a client as well and, at Davis's behest, establish himself as a regular feature in League Think's worst nightmares.

In May 1978, the dominant irony of Tose's hiring of Alioto was that while ignoring Chuck Sullivan's advice, the Eagles owner was nonetheless keeping his legal business within the greater Sullivan family. Alioto, one year younger than Chuck's father, Billy, had recently married Chuck's sister Kathleen, age thirty-two. Tose had settled on Alioto at the recommendation of several other NFL members. He was, they said, aggressive and relentless and, in previous years, had both cut the League up and defended it to the death. The cutting up had been in *Radovich v. NFL,* the 1958 suit that had first established the jurisdiction of the Sherman Act over the football business. The suit had germinated from an encounter between Alioto and Radovich when the latter was waiting tables in Los Angeles. When he told Alioto his story, the attorney drafted a brief for his case on a napkin, attacking the League's "blackballing" of his client as "a conspiracy to monopolize commerce in professional football."

Alioto's defense of the NFL had come in *Kapp v. NFL*, a 1974 suit claiming the standard NFL player contract was a violation of the Sherman Act and seeking $12 million in damages. On that occasion, Alioto trumpeted on behalf of the NFL, saying "these rules have generated the greatest mass entertainment . . . in universal history, in the history of the world. All that can be lost if we let the prima donnas of this game have their way, and if this thing turns out to be a lawyer's paradise instead of a spectator's delight." The jury went with Alioto, and awarded no damages.

In *Tose v. Penn*, Joe Alioto's first duties were to accompany his client at the May press conference announcing the suit. There, he characterized his client as a victim who had been forced to fight back.

Tose himself cut his usual natty figure at Alioto's side. Still the NFL's best-dressed member, *Philadelphia* magazine described him as favoring "crisply starched French cuffs, fastened by gold Eagles cuff links, well-cut and expensive suits, conservatively striped shirts rakishly set off by white collars and cuffs, and his trademark tie clip placed just a few inches higher than it should be." He lit his cigarettes with a jeweled lighter featuring an eagle and the number one. Tose characterized his action as a crusade for the average guy. "If this kind of thing can be perpetrated against the Eagles," he pointed out, "God help the poor people. God help my truck drivers. God help everybody." Being on the side of the little guy against the big bad banks, Tose went on to say, "Bunting's been to bat and he's struck out and now Leonard Tose is going to bat." He was claiming $12 million in damages and if he won, those damages would be automatically trebled to $36 million.

When Leonard Tose joined the rest of the League at the June meetings, he was already calling the attorney "my Italian quarterback" and waxing optimistic about his chances of hitting the jackpot at First Penn's expense. Many of those he talked to were fans of Alioto's and tended to agree with him. But by the time the suit reached trial in spring 1980, many of those same men were already wishing they'd never heard Joe Alioto's name.

14
Cross-Ownership Crossroads

The earliest date when League Think actually started coming apart was at the NFL Executive Session on June 7, 1978. At that time, the momentum began to shift and Pete Rozelle would go over to the defensive for the duration.

That executive session focused on ownership policy. Rozelle raised the issue himself. Armed with his "sense of the League" from the previous March meeting, Rozelle delivered a lengthy presentation, which he closed by again telling the story of Dick Boe, the owner of both the New York Islanders hockey franchise and the New York Nets basketball team who "took money from the successful hockey team to help keep the basketball team afloat and, in so doing, apparently created rather serious problems for both franchises. I pointed out . . . that this could happen in football and that sports are a risky business. . . ." After a break for lunch, the commissioner announced, "The topic would be discussed fully."

Rozelle began the afternoon session by opening the floor to what Joe Robbie described as "round-robin discussion" and "called on each club to express itself." Very quickly, "Leonard Tose delivered himself on the subject" again. Tose, Edward Bennett Williams remembered, "spoke with some feeling with respect to the policy and what he said was a commitment on the part of Mr. Hunt to use his best efforts to divest." As usual, Tose maintained Hunt's word was worthless and yelled at him to get out. Lamar Hunt listened with his usual detached look.

While Robbie and Williams, the two loudest critics of the commissioner's ownership policy, found both Tose and Hunt's behavior predictable, the rest of the discussion was much more unsettling. Most of the men who spoke wanted a deadline for divestiture set and wanted specific penalties for exceeding it as well. The discussion also took up where it had left off in March on the issue of prohibiting cross-ownership by immediate family.

Joe Robbie had missed the March meeting and was outraged by this new aspect. "There had never been mention of familial ownership at any prior meeting," he explained. "I got up and took strong exception to the National Football League attempting to tell my family what investments they could make in professional sports. I said that there was no way my five sons could all run the Miami Dolphins. That would be bedlam. . . . I told the NFL that we stood to lose substantial money to sell off the Ft. Lauderdale Strikers as a result of this family policy. . . . I think it's illegal," he emphasized. "I think it's contrary to public policy, especially as it relates to family. . . . I don't see any reason why a person can't have an investment in more than one major league team sport."

Robbie was, however, in a distinct minority. Banning cross-ownership, Tex Schramm remembered, "was a necessity and to have strength it needed to be in the constitution and it needed teeth." It also needed a deadline. Whatever the total length of time given, Art Modell remembers that Hugh Culverhouse added, "It should be a January cutoff date to allow a taxable year to commence and give people . . . a chance to attend to their own individual tax problems as they saw fit." There were also, Rozelle recalled, "a number of suggestions made regarding specific sanctions that would be involved after an agreed-upon point in time."

To Joe Robbie and Edward Bennett Williams, the notion of sanctions was perhaps the most unsettling aspect of all. Robbie noted that "the discussion got rather heated about the imposition of penalties. There was almost a bidding contest to how much they should be. . . ." At this point, Robbie pointed out, "Williams also took strong exception. He repeated that he had assured the NFL on many occasions that Jack Kent Cooke would exert his best efforts to resolve the problem with regard to dual ownership . . . 'in spite of the fact that I consider your policy to be illegal . . . but . . . when you start talking in terms of amending the constitution and bylaws and imposing penalties of the sizes that are being discussed here, then I think you would do better to put down in writing exactly what you have in mind and call a special meeting for that purpose.' " For Williams, the suggestion served the purpose of at least delaying the procedure. He also wanted to put more pressure on Rozelle's sense of the meeting and suggested a straw vote.

Williams proposed, "Why don't we [approach] the subject in stages? Let's ask, number one, how many are in favor of the general policy of cross-ownership, and then . . . how many people want to extend that policy . . . to members of the family, and then later break it down and see what the sanctions should be to enforce it, and finally, how much time should be given to someone who is in violation of the policy . . . to divest himself. . . . They accepted that suggestion and they voted on four different things."

Williams approached the vote with the same strategy he'd been keeping to since the issue first arose. "I voted no on the policy," he remembered, "and then said if you have it . . . it should apply to everyone, because I was anxious to defeat the policy and I thought it would have less chance to pass if it applied to everyone in the family, because that was ludicrous on its face, and then I came out for the minimum sanction and the maximum period to divest." On all those issues, he was in an enormous minority.

The question of amending the constitution was the first considered and, in Williams's view, the most critical. He and Joe Robbie cast the only two distinct no votes. Four owners passed, one was absent, and twenty voted yes. Though twenty-one votes would be needed actually to accept an amendment, a quick look at the group who had passed or been absent made it clear the commissioner could easily get the majority he needed. Two of the passes, Lamar Hunt and Al Davis, weren't likely to vote for him, and Seattle, a third pass, might respect its own soccer cross-ownerships enough to deny the additional yes, but the other two were the Sullivans and Max Winter. Even if the Sullivans didn't give Rozelle the vote he needed, Max Winter, who had been on the phone when the vote was taken, was second only to Leonard Tose in his rabid backing of anything that was against cross-ownership.

The votes on the subsequent three questions were, from Williams's standpoint, just as bad. The "consensus" on them was "extensive" coverage of "family relations," sanctions ranging from $10,000 to $50,000 a month, and complete divestiture of all interests in other major league team sports by January 31, 1980. The minutes recorded that "the League office was directed to draft a bylaw proposal reflecting the position expressed by a majority of the member clubs relative to ownership policy." The lawyers began drafting the amendment the next day.

After eleven years of patient struggle, Pete Rozelle was now on the verge of getting the constitutional amendment he had always wanted. Edward Bennett Williams, however, had the final word. The vote had changed none of his thinking. "I told them they would have certain litigation if they enacted this," Williams remembered, "I said the League is being led by lemmings into the sea."

15
The "Grand Duchess" Stands Empty

There was, of course, another storm brewing on the NFL's horizon that summer. This storm was in L.A. and, like the June cross-ownership struggle in New York, its significance went largely unappreciated in the immediate moment. What was going on in L.A. was still, Rozelle noted, "Carroll's business."

And C.R. was taking his time in conducting it. The only public stirring on the question of a Rams move that month was a well-publicized June 28 visit by C.R. to Anaheim's Big A Stadium. It was the third time in his life Rosenbloom had been there and the first time he'd met many of the Anaheim city officials. C.R. explained, ". . . we're getting to the point where they need to know and we have to make up our minds, certainly by the end of July."

Rosenbloom's visit to Orange County set the stage for his final face-to-face meeting with Bill Robertson. On July 9, Robertson offered a detailed verbal rundown of what the $9 million the LAMCC was committed to raise would buy for the Coliseum. Robertson also gave his word that the money would indeed be forthcoming. C.R. didn't doubt Robertson's promise. "I have faith in you," he told the LAMCC president, "and if you had been aboard a year earlier, all of this would not have happened." Robertson remained convinced he already had a deal in his hip pocket for Anaheim, but Rosenbloom continued to be noncommittal.

Robertson pushed the issue a little and asked the Rams owner to give some sense of what L.A.'s chances were. "Oh," C.R. mused, "I would say it's sixty-five to thirty-five I'm going to make the move to Anaheim." Robertson pointed out, "my charge is to either retain the Rams or to get another football team. I am going to pursue that with all the vigor at my disposal. Would you oppose such a move?"

"No," C.R. reaffirmed, "I wouldn't."

After that meeting, the remainder of their communications were by phone. The most heartening of those calls came a week later when C.R. called the LAMCC president at home and asked if he could have the verbal proposals L.A. had made over lunch in writing. Rosenbloom claimed he "wanted a chance to study them." Despite his sense that the die was already cast, Robertson quickly complied.

The letter Robertson sent to Rosenbloom on July 17, 1978, included a six-page schedule of where the Coliseum's $9 million would be spent. Robertson also sweetened L.A.'s offer. "The Coliseum commission desires to make substantial additional improvements" as well, he pointed out. "These improvements will be funded from a $12,000,000 to $15,000,000 allocation we expect to receive shortly after a contract is executed for the award of the 1984 Olympics to Los Angeles." In closing, Robertson tried to evoke Rosenbloom's loyalty to his adopted home:

> I would like to urge you to give the most serious consideration to the interests of the citizens of Los Angeles. I know that you must be deeply concerned with their welfare, just as I am. As president of the Coliseum commission, I am more than willing to do everything within my power to make it possible for our football fans to continue to enjoy the finest in professional football. . . . You know, of course, that Mayor Bradley is also fully dedicated to this goal. Under these circumstances, I am confident that, working together, we can overcome whatever difficulties have existed in the past and assure a long and successful future for the Rams in the Coliseum.

Bill Robertson's plea to Carroll Rosenbloom was, in truth, a waste of paper. The day after his meeting with C.R. and a week before his letter was written, an agreement had already been settled upon between Anaheim Stadium Associates and the city of Anaheim. Stadium Associates would build a twenty-seven-thousand-seat addition to Big A, for which CC&F would act as "construction supervisor." Stadium Associates would hold title to the bulk of the new addition, but Rosenbloom alone would own the stadium's "approximately one hundred" new luxury boxes. The stadium's adjoining ninety-five acre parcel would be rented by Stadium Associates for $8,000 an acre, with an option to purchase that was good for fifteen years.

By the time Robertson's letter reached Rosenbloom, the Rams owner had already notified Commissioner Rozelle of his intentions as well. "He just told me that if he could consummate a deal" with Anaheim, Rozelle remembered, "he wanted to move there and he was going to announce that." Later, Rozelle recalled, "I didn't debate it with him on the telephone. I just listened. I did, however, send him a personal letter on the subject."

Rozelle typed that letter personally and kept no copy. The typing was all in lower case, a style Rozelle described as "a throwback" to "my PR days. . . . I wanted Carroll to view it as somewhat of a personal letter and I hoped that he would give it some consideration," he explained. "I had some feelings for the L.A. Coliseum. That was the first place I saw football games when I was a youngster. . . . I felt it was more attractive for [Rosenbloom] and his wife to play in the Coliseum. A lot of their friends were in West Los Angeles and I thought they would like the Coliseum better than Anaheim."

There is no evidence that Rosenbloom reflected further on the move, as Rozelle had asked him to. On July 21, he had his last phone conversation with Robertson. The Rams owner still maintained that he was only "leaning" toward Anaheim even though a press conference with Anaheim city officials had been on C.R.'s schedule since at least July 10. He promised to call Robertson before announcing any decision one way or another. Bill Robertson never heard from him again.

On July 25 was the press conference at Big A Stadium. "It will be with feelings of deep regret that we leave the Coliseum," Rosenbloom explained. "But we shall look forward to having our playing site, our training facility, our coaches and management together. We believe that this, coupled with a closed, intimate stadium, where fans can be more a part of the game, will help us win." Despite the move, however, Rosenbloom planned to continue calling his team the Los Angeles Rams. "It's our name," he claimed, "and we'll continue to use it."

Rosenbloom also said he would not oppose another NFL team in the soon to be vacant L.A. Coliseum. Los Angeles bit its public tongue and said nothing. "We made no effort to stop the Rams," Robertson observed. "We believed that Carroll Rosenbloom, like any other businessman in this country under our capitalist, free enterprise system, had a right to move if he so desired."

Of course, Bill Robertson immediately set out to find another

franchise to take the Rams' place. The first two steps in his
strategy were accomplished within three weeks of Rosenbloom's
announcement. The first step was to tie his search into the
stature and office of Tom Bradley, L.A.'s mayor, by creating the
Mayor's Professional Football Search Committee. Bradley had
agreed to it after a lecture from one of his closest advisers. The
problem, he pointed out, was that the Coliseum had been incompetent over the years. Robertson was the best man for the job,
but he'd come on the scene too late to do anything, and his hand
had to be strengthened before anything more would get done.
Because of its tripartite composition and rotating officials, the
LAMCC was dysfunctional. "Tom," his adviser warned, "if we
just let those turkeys handle it, there's going to be no football
team and no Coliseum."

The stakes were high. C.R.'s departure for Anaheim would
leave the L.A. Coliseum with a $750,000 annual deficit, the first
time in its history it would ever have required public funding. If
public money didn't rescue it, "the Grand Duchess of Stadiums" and the LAMCC would be bankrupt. The search committee's chairman was Bill Robertson. "The mayor," Bradley's
adviser explained, "wanted to give Robertson independent leverage on the LAMCC."

Second, Bill Robertson wanted to find out just where the NFL
and Pete Rozelle stood. For this, L.A. called on Kenny Hahn,
member of both the LAMCC and the Mayor's Search Committee. Hahn, a longtime L.A. politician, had been an instrumental
figure in luring the baseball Dodgers west from Brooklyn twenty
years earlier. Hahn had first made contact with the commissioner's office the day before Rosenbloom officially announced his
departure, in a telegram requesting the commissioner's help in
securing a new team for the Coliseum. On July 25, he followed
up his wire with a phone call, asking to discuss L.A.'s future
with the commissioner in person. The issue was a possible
expansion franchise. They arranged to meet in early August.

"We had a very cordial discussion," Rozelle remembered. "I
told him, 'Kenny, we aren't prepared to expand. . . . It
would probably be five or six years before Tampa and Seattle
were . . . sufficiently established [to warrant further expansion].'
So he asked me about L.A. getting a franchise and I said, 'I have
always thought highly of L.A. [but] I don't have a vote. [But] I
would see that L.A. was given serious consideration.' . . . Mr.
Hahn [then] said to me, 'I have some people that I know might
be interested in ownership of an expansion franchise.' And I

said, 'Fine. I will see that they are given consideration for ownership should we come to Los Angeles.' It was very cordial."

Robertson and Hahn, however, considered Rozelle's response "very negative." The formal letter from the commissioner's office that followed was, from their standpoint, even worse. Rozelle began by suggesting that "some forthright comment on the L.A. situation is called for." He continued:

Decisions as to expansion of the National Football League are made by the member clubs collectively. . . . The National Football League has recently added two new teams. There are already four NFL teams operating within California, more than any other state. . . . Hurried expansion has never served the interests of any sports league. Experience in other professional sports has repeatedly and emphatically demonstrated this. There also exist within the United States other major population centers which do not have a professional football franchise and which have actively sought NFL franchises for many years. Thus, while the League's membership may decide to add additional franchises at some time in the future, and while the Rams themselves have publicly indicated that they will not oppose any form of future expansion which will serve the League's interests, I cannot predict early expansion action by the League. Nor can I provide any assurance as to the direction such expansion will take when and if it is decided upon.

Still further, as NFL commissioner, I cannot in good conscience encourage any existing NFL franchise to leave its present metropolitan market without professional football. While such decisions are not within my control, I take pride in the fact that no NFL club during the League's modern era has taken such an action. Other professional leagues have had a more spotty record in this respect, and have left a residue of ill will in the wake of uprooted franchises.

I fully appreciate the concern which you and the Coliseum authorities have with the prospect that the Coliseum may lose one of its present football tenants. But the Rams' proposed move to Anaheim should not, in my view, be considered a metropolitan area departure. While all stadium shifts within the NFL have differed on their particular facts, the Rams' proposed move is not wholly dissimilar to that of the Patriots' move to Foxboro, Massachusetts, the Cowboys' move to Irving, Texas, the Giants' move [to New Jersey], or the Lions' move to Pontiac, Michigan. . . .

In short, candor compels me to state that I do not believe there is any great prospect that the League will add additional franchises in the near future and I can provide no assurance that Los Angeles will be preferred over other potential franchise sites in any future expansion that may take place. I regret the need for replying to you in this fashion, but I believe it important that we understand each other as clearly as possible.

> Sincerely,
> Pete Rozelle,
> Commissioner

The letter infuriated Robertson. "It was arrogant and an insult," the president of the LAMCC fumed. "He just told Los Angeles to get in line with everybody else."

16
Impending Anarchy

If Pete Rozelle was somewhat deaf to Los Angeles's outrage, it was, at least in part, a function of the uproar his ownership policy initiative had provoked at the same time.

On June 28, the commissioner dispatched the draft amendment on ownership policy. The bylaw proposal was accompanied by a memorandum to the NFL's membership on the subject of "Ownership in Major Team Sports." While requesting "thoughts and suggestions on the draft," Rozelle used the bulk of the memo to remake his arguments against cross-ownership. Prohibition was necessary to avoid the dilution of the resources, energies, and loyalties of NFL owners, he again pointed out. It would prevent "conflicts of interest" and insure "appropriate confidentiality of marketing and other strategies."

"The NFL's success depends on fan interest and loyalty," he emphasized. "The League competes with other major team sports for that interest and loyalty as well as for gate receipts, TV revenues, advertising dollars, and media coverage. Connections with NFL personnel may well enhance these competing team sports, both in fact and in the public's perception, at the expense of the NFL."

The amendment itself would replace Article IX, Section 9.4 of the NFL constitution. Subsection A of the new 9.4 stated that "No person (1) owning a majority interest in a member club, or (2) directly or indirectly having substantial operational control or substantial influence over the operations of a member club, or (3) serving as an officer or director of a member club, or (4) any spouse or minor child of any such person may directly or indirectly acquire, retain, or possess any interest in another major team sport (including major league baseball, basketball, hockey, and soccer)."

Subsection B expanded A to "also apply to relatives of such persons (including siblings, parents, adult children, adult and minor grandchildren, nephews and nieces, and relatives by marriage) (1) if such person directly or indirectly provided or con-

tributed all or any part of the funds used to purchase or operate
the other sports league entity, or (2) if there exists between such
person and any such relative a significant community of interest
in the successful operation of the other sports league entity."
Subsection C gave the commissioner the power to "investigate
to the extent he deems necessary or appropriate any reported or
apparent violation."

Subsection D was the kicker. Members had until February 1,
1980, to divest themselves and afterward, any member "found
to have violated subsection (A) or (B) above will be subject to
fines of up to $25,000 per month for each of the first three
months of violations; up to $50,000 per month for each of the
next three months; and up to $75,000 per month thereafter."
Such extended violations could also be considered sufficient
grounds for revocation of the member's franchise. If the fine
levied was not paid within twenty days, the League office was
empowered to seize the fine as the club's television money
passed through its hands.

A special meeting to discuss and vote on the amendment was
scheduled for October. In the meantime, Rozelle asked for
reactions. The ensuing uproar came from three parties.

As usual, the most quiet was Lamar Hunt. "The whole tenor
of the proposal is considerably different [from previous policy],"
Hunt complained. "It asks for . . . a time limit that would, to say
the least, be punitive. . . . It would make it very, very difficult
to sell [my other interests] at a fair price." Though Hunt considered the policy neither "necessary nor reasonable," he said he
would be willing to cooperate.

Joe Robbie was much more blunt. "I am flatly, unalterably
opposed to it," he responded. Predictably, Robbie's outrage was
at the inclusion of relatives in the cross-ownership prohibition.
"That wipes my family out in every direction," he said. It also
galvanized his urge to stop the amendment however he could. "I
probably would have expressed myself in stronger terms earlier," he explained, if "I'd had before me then [the amendment]
subsequently sent me . . . . I suppose if a grandchild of mine at
some future time should marry somebody involved in professional sports, that person would have to divest or they would
have me paying the penalties. . . ." Robbie considered Rozelle's
draft absurd.

So, too, of course, did Edward Bennett Williams. "The resolution which has been operative through the years covers only
those persons who have a majority interest," he pointed out, and

"it has no sanctions. The proposal that came forth from the League office . . . is very, very broad and sweeping and purports to cover not only majority owners, but members of their families. . . . It imposes sanctions that go up to a million dollars a year. . . . No company in this League could stand it."

Sports was good business for all sports, Williams argued. He also called at least one other owner and repeated his warning of "certain litigation" if the League proceeded any further. The most likely plaintiff was the North American Soccer League. Indeed, by August 28, the NASL had voted to "retain counsel to seek a preliminary injunction against the NFL." In September, the NASL's attorneys made contact with Rozelle. "The draft amendment had got into their hands," the commissioner remembered, "and they came marching over here to our [Park Avenue] office. They sat us down for several hours and told us that they were going to sue us unless we voluntarily retracted the amendment. They weren't just going to sue if we passed it; they were going to sue if we put it on the agenda. They, in effect, said if you don't stop it right now, we will sue. We told them we weren't going to stop."

Meanwhile, the League's southern California front was erupting as well. L.A. was also about to make their intentions a legal issue; this was step three in Bill Robertson's strategy. It was obvious that the only solution to the LAMCC's dilemma was to convince another NFL owner to do to another stadium what Carroll Rosenbloom had just done to L.A.'s. The chief obstacle was Article IV, Section 4.3 of the NFL constitution, which required that "no member shall have any right to transfer its club or franchise to a different city outside its home territory except with the prior approval of the members of the League." Further, "any transfer of an existing franchise to a location within the home territory of any other club shall be effective only if approved by unanimous vote; any other transfer shall only be effective if approved by the affirmative vote of not less than three fourths."

In September, L.A. filed *LAMCC v. NFL*, contending that Section 4.3 was a violation of the Sherman Act. The suit was immediately put on hold by the federal district court because no one had actually yet been prevented from occupying "the Grand Duchess of Stadiums" through the enforcement of Section 4.3, but it served to put Robertson's leverage on the table for all his potential allies to see. It also got the NFL's attention. Discussion of the suit was added to the agenda for the League's special meeting in October.

At the time, the principal subject of the meeting was still the ownership policy amendment. Before the end of September, however, that agenda underwent a drastic alteration, provoked by *NASL v. NFL,* a suit charging that the League's proposed ownership policy amendment violated the Sherman Act. Since the NASL was able to quickly win a restraining order preventing the NFL from acting on the proposal, the discussion of it was now confined to discussion of the suit itself. The complaint listed twenty-one of the NASL's twenty-four franchises as plaintiffs and twenty-five of the NFL's twenty-eight as defendants. The unnamed parties were Seattle, where the Nordstroms owned most of football and some of soccer, Miami and Ft. Lauderdale, where Joe Robbie owned football and Elizabeth Robbie owned soccer, and Kansas City and Dallas, where Lamar Hunt owned all of both. All three would be required to foot the legal bills of both sides of the suit. During the NFL's discussions of *NASL v. NFL,* the three would be asked to leave the room so as not to compromise the League's legal strategies.

Edward Bennett Williams didn't need to tell his fellow owners that his prediction had indeed been accurate. Joe Robbie expressed no regrets. "It's one way of trying to resolve the issue," he observed. Lamar Hunt said only that *NASL v. NFL* put him in "an awkward position" in which he was "divorced from himself either way."

Leonard Tose, the loudest proponent of the contested amendment, was only more adamant about Hunt in response. "Hell," Tose fumed . . . [Hunt] is the guy who originated it. He is the perpetrator. Whatever the hell the word is, he is the guy."

For Pete Rozelle, *NASL v. NFL* was a blow to League Think's solar plexus. It was also a dangerous precedent. "I know of no previous instance," the commissioner later testified, "where an NFL owner has been on the minority side of an issue and subsequently played a role in having that decision challenged in court. . . . [It] tears right at the guts, at the foundation, of the harmony and unity that you attempt to build for the success of the League. . . . I can see this leading to anarchy."

17

The Meeting in Chicago, Day 1

The NFL special meeting in October would eventually become one of the most minutely examined gatherings in NFL history, but not for the anticipated reasons. The NFL was now enjoined by the federal court from voting on Rozelle's constitutional amendment on ownership policy and the discussion of *NASL v. NFL* was inconsequential. Instead, *LAMCC v. NFL* and the "Los Angeles problem" assumed the League's center stage.

Discussion of the issues raised by L.A. began on the first afternoon. Rozelle and the League office presented to the membership "bylaw proposal number two," a package of constitutional amendments principally designed to modify Section 4.3 to require only a three-quarter vote for all types of franchise moves. Since the provision to be replaced required a unanimous vote, a unanimous vote would be required to amend it. To the commissioner, the logic behind such a move was obvious. The LAMCC suit, he remembered, "prompted my thinking about the rule which, of course, I'd say had gone back into probably the founding of the League . . . I thought it was silly to try to defend in court something that didn't have an important business interest."

The discussion was opened with a report from the League's attorney, who pointed out that the current unanimous provisions of Section 4.3 left the League with "no defense" should *LAMCC v. NFL* ever be activated. Rozelle then bolstered the attorney's judgment with his own. He said that he could not guarantee that the LAMCC would drop its suit or that the changes would mean victory in court, but he felt "strongly" that three quarters would be "less offensive than the unanimous vote." In his judgment, the LAMCC wanted "to knock out territorial exclusivity," and the object was to make that principle defensible. The current Section 4.3, the commissioner argued, was indefensible and "no longer necessary." He then opened the subject up for round-robin discussion. "I don't recall opposition," he later testified. "I recall discussion and a couple of clubs requiring clarification as to what was being done."

319

Al Davis would remember it very differently. "There were many speeches made on this," the Raiders owner claimed during a pretrial deposition, "many objections, actually violent arguments between owners . . . .To get the [three-quarters vote] rule, the commissioner needed the unanimous consent of all the members of the League. . . . The commissioner . . . polled the owners approximately five times that day hoping to get the unanimous consent . . . and he couldn't get it."

Leading that opposition was Davis himself. "We had one purpose," he complained, "knock the rule [Section 4.3] down so the L.A. Coliseum would drop the lawsuit." On the subject of the proposed change to a three-quarters vote, he added, "There was no real thought as to whether it was a functional, workable rule relative to someone wanting to move. . . . It was such a dire necessity in their minds to negate that Coliseum lawsuit. They made it sound like it was the most important thing in our lives, and I didn't feel that way."

Instead, Al Davis felt no Section 4.3 whatsoever was a much better option than an amendment. Davis opined that any required vote about franchise movement would be struck down if taken to court. His own lease would expire at the end of the 1979 season, just like Carroll Rosenbloom's. "I told them I may want to move," Davis remembered. "I told them I don't think I need a vote to move."

Most of the other owners figured Davis's stance was another dose of his obstreperousness. "It was just the Al Davis approach," Steve Rosenbloom remembered. Wellington Mara, however, claimed to have seen it coming. "Al," he pointed out, "is a guy capable of bringing the roof down around his own head." While the discussion was raging, he and Carroll Rosenbloom had a short side conversation about what Davis was up to.

"I think what Al is after is the Los Angeles pay TV market," Mara told C.R., who expressed disbelief, but given that Rosenbloom and Davis had already had a number of conversations about precisely that possibility, C.R.'s response to Mara was less than credible.

For his part, Rozelle claimed he "had no idea the Raiders were thinking of moving to Los Angeles." Davis was incredulous at Rozelle's claim. "All I was concerned about was Los Angeles," he pointed out. "All the membership talked about for a day and a half was Los Angeles. And I don't think there should have been any question in anyone's mind as to what city I was talking about." He also personally mentioned the possibility of his franchise filling L.A.'s vacancy to Joe Robbie, Tex Schramm, Eddie DeBartolo, Chuck Sullivan, and Leonard Tose.

Certainly Los Angeles was, in one way or another, very much on the minds of the three other owners who joined Davis's opposition. Joe Robbie thought the proposed amendment would have no effect on L.A. at all. When the Rams would move to Anaheim at the end of the next year, he argued, L.A. was not going to allow itself to be left without a franchise, whatever the League's rule. The situation Rosenbloom had set off by moving to Anaheim was not like the Giants moving to New Jersey. "There is less difference between New Jersey and Manhattan than between Orange County and L.A.," he warned. "The county of Los Angeles will fight us in the courts, the Congress, and the state legislature." They would keep "the pressure on" until Los Angeles got another franchise, whether or not Section 4.3 was altered. The only solution was "either keep the Rams in L.A. or move another franchise" there. Robbie was the only owner to suggest keeping the Rams where they were.

Buffalo Bills owner Ralph Wilson also disapproved of the move. Like most other owners, he knew nothing of Rosenbloom's development deal with CC&F and Anaheim, but understood that the move would "financially benefit" the Rams. In general, Wilson thought no team should move "to get better financial arrangements" unless they were under "dire financial stress," which certainly Rosenbloom was not. He thought the Coliseum was "a fine stadium," that the Rams had a loyal following there, and that "moving to Anaheim in another county" was not "in the best interests of the League."

The opposition's final and loudest voice was Robert Irsay, who launched into a largely incomprehensible address punctuated with pieces of diatribe about Carroll Rosenbloom. "He couldn't make sense," one owner remembered. "Everybody looked at each other and thought he was crazy. We just let him rant and rave and tried to pay as little attention to it as possible." Apparently, Irsay "flatly opposed" changing from unanimous vote because he believed that some owners, like Rosenbloom, could get the necessary votes, but others, like Irsay himself, could not. "He did view himself as unpopular," Rozelle later testified. "Mr. Irsay is a high-strung, emotional individual and sometimes it is difficult to understand exactly what he is feeling or saying. . . . He is very florid and vociferous in his speeches. . . . For some reason he felt this might help Mr. Rosenbloom and he was against it for that reason. . . . He was talking without any real . . . consideration of it and he finally ended up and just said, 'I want to talk to my own attorneys.' "

Perhaps the loudest among the twenty-four votes supporting the bylaw was Gene Klein. He called it an essential step to put the question of franchise movement "in line with everything else we do." His own attorneys had informed him *LAMCC v. NFL* would be "easy to defend" once Rozelle's amendment had been passed. A longtime resident of Beverly Hills, Klein also knew Bill Robertson of the LAMCC, who had indicated in private that the change to three quarters would be sufficient to get the suit dropped.

"Mr. Klein represented to the ownership that he had met with Mr. Robertson," Al Davis later testified, "and that if we changed the vote, [the LAMCC] would drop the lawsuit. That was the theme all day. . . . Gene Klein said it three or four times during the meeting to try and get the ownership to adopt the lowering of the unanimous [vote]. . . ." Klein himself, under oath, could remember only that he "might have mentioned Robertson" and denied ever having said the LAMCC would drop their suit. In any case, Davis was unmoved by the argument. "Quite frankly," the Raiders owner later admitted under oath, "I had advance information that Mr. Klein would do this."

Throughout, Al Davis continued to hold his ground. "I felt the rule was entirely too restrictive," he pointed out, ". . . we don't need a rule; we need guidelines." Davis's call for guidelines set off the only direct intervention by his friend Carroll Rosenbloom. C.R. supported Rozelle's bylaw proposal for reasons of his own. "The change was closing the door after the cows are out," his son Steve explained, "but we didn't want to be accused of blocking any move into the Coliseum after we left." Rosenbloom's intervention was an attempt to find some sort of middle ground that might satisfy Davis. His idea was to craft a definition of home territory that included specifics of "population, geographical area, stadium suitability, economy, travel, demographics, and TV market coverage" rather than just a seventy-five-mile circle. Such an arrangement might very well give Davis the latitude he felt he needed. C.R. advanced his plan in individual discussions around the room. Rozelle recalled, "If it ever came up, it was rejected immediately because it didn't make sense. We never had a lengthy discussion or any sizable discussion on standards."

Among the other side conversations, there was at least one between Rozelle and Davis. "He and I talked . . . about Los

Angeles," Davis remembered. Rozelle said "He also knew how I felt. . . . He knew my lease was up, that I was in an untenable situation and I wasn't anxious to get this thing into new focus . . ."

Rozelle remembered that Davis "said some things that made me feel he might change his mind. He said, 'I don't want to block what you're doing. I don't want to stop you.' Then he would raise objections." Rozelle elaborated, "It is difficult to know what Al is saying. . . . It isn't fair to say he had said one thing at one time and one thing at another, but he was equivocating. . . . He seemed to want to stay flexible and to reserve all his options, whatever they might be."

Rozelle's sense of Davis as obscure about his intentions was corroborated by Robert Schulman, the Washington attorney sitting in for the absent Edward Bennett Williams. At one point, Schulman remembered, "the commissioner asked Al how he was going to vote. Al waffled . . . did not give him a definitive answer."

However obscure Al Davis may have been, Pete Rozelle could read the handwriting on the wall as the meeting approached adjournment. Al Davis, Joe Robbie, Ralph Wilson, and Robert Irsay still held "reservations." The chances of getting a unanimous formal vote on October 4 were obviously nil, so, Rozelle explained, "I let it go until the next day."

18
The Meeting in Chicago, Day 2

The October 5 session opened with more uproar. The clamor grew out of a phone call Ralph Wilson had placed to Bill Robertson in Los Angeles at 2:00 A.M. Wilson wanted to verify Gene Klein's claims of the previous day.

"Bill," Wilson asked, "did you at any time tell Gene Klein that if the NFL reduced the requirement [to three quarters] you would back away from the lawsuit?"

"Absolutely not," Robertson answered.

When the League reconvened, Wilson informed the other owners of the phone call. According to Al Davis, at this point,

''Mr. Rozelle and Mr. Carothers threw their hands in the air with exasperation and everyone yelled at Mr. Wilson, 'Why did you do that?' ''

Wilson remembered that among the most vocal objectors to his phone call was C.R., who, as Rozelle recalled it, pointed out that Wilson had no business talking to Bill Robertson about private League business. Wilson responded that he would talk to anybody he wanted about anything he felt like.

In the melee that followed, Al Davis pointed out that the principal argument in favor of bylaw proposal number two had just been shown up as an ''outright lie'' but his point was lost. Most of the ensuing discussion was just more speeches in favor, and the number of owners in favor had grown since the previous afternoon. The last straw vote on October 4 had been twenty-four in favor and four ''reservations.'' The first poll on October 5 came out twenty-seven yes and one pass. Davis was now alone.

Ralph Wilson had changed his position despite his phone call to Robertson out of his concern for ''stability'' and some ''uniformity of rules'' within the League. The amendment seemed ''in order'' because of the widespread use of the three-quarters vote in other League business. He maintained that going to three quarters was ''a logical compromise.'' Joe Robbie's reservations had apparently been satisfied overnight as well. Robbie himself was now absent and was being represented by his son, Mike. Mike voted yes with no explanation.

Robert Irsay's mind had also been changed—by none other than Steve Rosenbloom, who called his assignment ''tougher than Al Davis.'' The younger Rosenbloom had approached Irsay's general manager, a friend of his, and asked him to talk some sense to his boss. The next day Irsay was absent. His GM assumed his seat and voted yes, saying he was doing so with the full approval of his boss.

Even alone, however, Al Davis had the upper hand. His refusal to cast the twenty-eighth yes vote still had the commissioner stalemated. At this point, however, Davis later testified, ''someone stood up and made the statement, 'Mr. Davis, this is probably the most important decision we ever had to make. Why can't you give us your vote?' And I told them why. Because I may want to move in the future. . . . I said furthermore the presentation made by Gene Klein the day before, that the Los Angeles Coliseum would drop the lawsuit if we changed the vote . . . we now find is not true. I said, 'So that is another reason.''

Then Davis turned to Rozelle. "You can't pass this thing," he said. "I will not give my vote."

The principal topic then became whether or not the vote could be considered unanimous without Davis's yes. The question was specifically whether a vote of twenty-seven yeses and one pass constituted universal agreement. Davis alone argued it was not. When Rozelle finally called for a formal verbal ballot, "I could see what was coming," Davis claimed.

He turned to Chuck Sullivan and asked the lawyer to "give me some language to be sure I made the proper statement." Davis claimed Sullivan wrote it out for him on a piece of paper: *I reserve the right to move my team as I see fit if you are going to declare this unanimous when it isn't.* The piece of paper was later lost and, though he remembered talking with Davis immediately prior to the vote, Chuck Sullivan would later testify to having "no recollection" of ever writing anything.

When Davis voted, first he cast a "pass" and then, he remembered, "I said to the commissioner, 'If you are going to consider that unanimous, and it isn't, then I reserve the right to move the Oakland Raiders as I see fit.' "

Rozelle remembered Davis making his point much more "obliquely," saying only, "I pass and reserve my rights." Rozelle asked two more times what he meant by that and claimed Davis's only response was "half-sentences and mutters." The League attorney remembered listening to Davis and thinking, "I wonder what the hell he means by that?"

Davis himself thought he'd been perfectly clear. "I felt that if they were going to . . . violate my rights, . . . then I would reserve a right . . . to go my own way. And when they didn't respond to it, I felt that they accepted what I said . . . I thought they ratified my right to move."

Rozelle claimed to have interpreted Davis's stance as just the same old Davis approach. "I inferred that Al Davis was doing what he has done on a number of other occasions in League meetings," Rozelle explained. "Rather than voting yes or no on a motion, he will pass and be either oblique or noncommittal . . . that's the way Al likes to be. He had done it before. The last thing in my mind was that he was saying to the meeting that he was reserving his rights to move to Los Angeles."

Others in the room had their own perspectives: Leonard Tose agreed with Al Davis. "Al put them on notice," Tose remembered. "He was clear. He was very clear." Gene Klein agreed with Pete Rozelle. "Al Davis was a great double talker," he observed. "He was a mumbler. He never reserved any right to move." Jim Kensil, the Jets executive representing Leon Hess, later made a written report to his boss. "The proposed reduction passed by a vote of twenty-seven yes and one pass," he reported. "The pass vote was by Oakland [which] claimed it may wish to assert in the future that no votes at all are needed to move a team."

Robert Schulman, representing Edward Bennett Williams, was taking notes as the meeting progressed. He wrote, *Al Davis on record as not accepting any right to approval of a move. Al Davis reserves rights.* "When it came to Oakland," Schulman remembered, "Al made clear . . . that he was reserving his rights, whatever they might be, [but] nobody knew what the rights were. We were all vague."

Vague or not, whatever Al Davis was reserving seemed to be a commodity the rest of the League wanted as well. Gene Klein voted after Davis. "I don't think any team in this League should have more rights than any other team," Klein offered. "We'll vote for the amendment, but we want to reserve the same rights, whatever they may be, that Mr. Davis or anyone else has." Robert Schulman jumped on the bandwagon. "Whatever rights San Diego's reserved," he said, "I want to reserve as well."

At this point, Rozelle intervened. According to the minutes, he "noted that, upon adoption of the amendment, all NFL clubs would have equal transfer rights regardless of the proposed site of the transfer." Afterward, the vote got moving again. While it proceeded, Schulman jotted down, *Rozelle states flatly everyone has the right to upset new bylaw.*

The final vote was, as expected, 27–0–1. When it was complete, Rozelle conferred with legal counsel in "a low voice" for a moment, and then ruled that twenty-seven yeses and one pass "constituted a unanimous vote . . . in accord with prior [League] practice." Section 4.3 was now officially amended and bylaw proposal number two in the books.

All that remained was to officially approve the Rams' move to Anaheim and that took no more than ten minutes. "We felt there might be some reason in the future that we would want to approve a move from one city to another within a home territory, so Mr. Rosenbloom waited until after that amendment had been made and . . . we called for the first time for a three-quarters vote to move to another city within the same territory," Rozelle explained.

C.R. gave a brief report on the change but made no mention

of the real estate deal involved. "He only mentioned the gate at Anaheim and what the visiting team could be expected to receive," Rozelle remembered. "He said he anticipated sellout crowds and that the visiting team should get a bigger share."

During the ensuing vote, Al Davis apparently didn't know whether to vote yes or pass, so he left the room, as did Chuck Sullivan. The final count on the question of whether Rosenbloom ought to be allowed to leave L.A. was twenty-six yes, zero no, and two absent. It, too, was recorded in the minutes as "unanimous."

Then the League adjourned. That meeting on October 4 and 5, 1978, would haunt Pete Rozelle forever after.

"It's a strange thing," the commissioner later mused. "Of all the meetings over which I presided, I will never forget that meeting. We must have been awfully dumb not to realize what Al Davis had in mind."

19
The Grand Duchess
Hunts for a
Tenant

Bill Robertson of the LAMCC was not surprised by the League's official approval of Rosenbloom's move. Nor was he impressed by their modification of Section 4.3. He never considered dropping the Coliseum's suit in response. "I was committed to this," he remembered. "I knew it was the right thing. The Coliseum had to have an NFL team to stay solvent. It was the only choice we had." He spent that late summer and early fall looking for an NFL franchise that might want to move.

Robertson's quest had a lot of emotional support around L.A., the most vocal of which was coming from sports columnist Mel Durslag in the *Los Angeles Herald Examiner*. Durslag attacked Rosenbloom for leaving and the NFL for indifference. He credited Rosenbloom with "having consummated perhaps the fattest deal in the history of sports." The other NFL owners, according to Durslag, "are such fat felines today . . . that they can't picture any force big enough to hurt them." And he made no secret of his own partisanship. "The territorial battle of southern California is just beginning," he vowed as the 1978 football season opened. "Very lively days are ahead in this little niche of sunshine."

Mel Durslag and Bill Robertson saw eye-to-eye on what was going on. "Mel believed L.A. was getting screwed," Robertson remembered. "He thought the Anaheim deal was obscene. He became a crusader and was a catalyst." Robertson needed his "many connections with the NFL owners and such." If Robertson was going to find a tenant for the Coliseum, he needed face-to-face access to make his case, something Durslag could provide.

The closest of Durslag's NFL connections was with Ralph Wilson, owner of the Buffalo Bills. Durslag put Robertson in touch with Wilson before the Chicago meeting, and the two spoke five or six times during the last six months of 1978. According to Robertson, "Wilson said that he would love to be playing in Los Angeles . . . because of what he saw as the tremendous potential here because of our population. . . . He was also attracted by the climate." Nonetheless, he turned down Robertson's invitation to move.

"Wilson never misled me," Robertson remembered. "He made it very clear that he had a lease in Buffalo and was not looking to break it. He was a decent human being." Wilson offered Robertson advice, and little hope. While telling Robertson that he would vote yes should L.A. find a possible tenant, "Wilson also said that he felt it would be impossible for us to get the votes [needed for a franchise to move]."

Mel Durslag also connected Bill Robertson with Gene Klein. According to Klein, Durslag and Robertson "tried to convince me to move to L.A. I said 'under no circumstances.' " Robertson's version was quite different. "I asked him how he would feel about coming to Los Angeles, and his response was . . . 'I would be delighted to come to Los Angeles, but I can't. My attorneys have checked my lease [in San Diego]. There is no way to break it.' " According to Robertson, Gene Klein held out little hope of "getting any established team or an expansion team into Los Angeles," because "we would be unable in his judgment to get enough votes." In addition, Klein admonished Robertson over the Coliseum's lawsuit. "He didn't think it was wise of us to file an antitrust suit. He thought that would hurt our chances of getting a team [even more]." When Robertson and Klein next saw each other, Robertson remembered that Klein again gave him "the distinct impression that he would love to be in L.A. rather than San Diego." Klein also "still felt it would be extremely difficult to secure the required votes to get a ball club [for Los Angeles]. It was his feeling that the owners . . . and Pete Rozelle were opposed to it."

Despite the discouragement he and Durslag were getting, Robertson would claim "real sincere interest" from at least two owners by the beginning of 1979. The first of those was Max Winter of Minnesota. Winter still did not have the domed stadium he wanted and the issue was still hung up in the state legislature. When Durslag called Winter on the L.A. Coliseum's behalf, Winter said he was "interested" and Durslag connected him to Robertson. In the summer of 1978, Robertson asked if Winter "was interested in sitting down and exploring the possibility of the Minnesota Vikings coming to Los Angeles." Winter was receptive and they met in Minneapolis. Robertson admitted that he knew Winter would rather stay in Minnesota and that "the only reason to motivate a move would be the fact, if it became a fact, that he couldn't obtain a domed stadium in downtown Minneapolis." Nonetheless, Robertson proceeded to point out the advantages of a move to L.A.—among them "the media value" of the nation's number two TV market, the climate, and the population Winter's franchise would draw upon, some ten million or so.

Winter responded that there was "no question" he would rather stay in Minneapolis, but he "had become very frustrated in his efforts to get cooperation from various politicians" so the stadium he wanted could be built. "He was anxious to see what we could provide. . . . He said to me that if he had to move out of Minneapolis, he felt that Los Angeles would be the place to move if he could get over the obstacle . . . of getting the required votes to permit that move within the NFL." Winter "wasn't in any position to make any type of commitment," but he wanted to "continue discussion" while he waited to see what the state legislature would do.

Bill Robertson and Max Winter next met in January of 1979. Winter was in Los Angeles for an NFL special meeting. The agenda was filled with odds and ends. Fittingly, the most time-consuming of those was Max Winter's continuing stadium problems. The Minnesota legislature's latest stadium financing bill was something with which the entire League had to concern itself. They had included in the stadium package a provision requiring the NFL to commit itself to "assurances" that a franchise would remain in Minnesota for "as much as thirty years." It also contained a provision "conditioning the new stadium on local telecasting of [Viking] games . . . if ninety percent of the tickets were sold seventy-two hours prior to the game," rather than the NFL's own requirement of one hundred percent.

Robertson and Max Winter met "off the record" on the morning of January 28. Winter, according to Robertson, then "made it clear to us . . . that if he didn't get a domed stadium [in Minneapolis], he was going to look elsewhere. . . ." Winter was also, Robertson noted, "very cognizant" of Section 4.3 of the NFL constitution. Should he move the Vikings to L.A., Winter pointed out, "we will have a problem unless I can convince the commissioner and my fellow [NFL] members. However, I think that I'll have a good chance to be able to do that because they recognize my plight." Robertson remembered: "Pete Rozelle had assured him he would do all he could for him if he didn't get that desired domed stadium."

After a lot of legal discussion, the league owners authorized Rozelle "to execute a certain form of agreement relating to the continuing of a National Football League franchise in Minnesota." On the question of lifting the local TV blackout, however, the League reinforced its own one hundred percent standards. Afterward, Max Winter, pessimistic about how the Minnesota legislature would respond, "asked that alternative solutions to [his] stadium problems be reviewed in executive session at the [upcoming] annual meeting," in March.

In the meantime, Bill Robertson had little choice but to watch developments in Minnesota and wait to see which way Max Winter jumped. His only other "sincere" prospective tenant in the beginning of 1979 was Al Davis. Robertson had written "at least one letter" and placed "several phone calls" to the Raiders owner, but, prior to the special meeting on October 4 and 5, Davis "never responded . . ."

During that period, Davis did, however, make contact with Mel Durslag, supposedly, Davis explained, "to patch up a tremendous feud that had grown between Carroll Rosenbloom and Mel Durslag. I was fond of both of them. . . . [Durslag] had written a couple articles that were negative and Carroll took exception. . . . I was very friendly with Mr. Durslag and Mr. Rosenbloom and had to walk a tightrope between the two, but I did it." While Davis was unable to patch up things between

C.R. and Durslag, he and Durslag eventually got around to talking about the coming vacancy in Los Angeles. Davis remembered that ". . . he wanted to know if I would be interested in coming to Los Angeles. I told him no. . . . Mel knew this fellow Bill Robertson and wanted to put me together with Robertson [but] I refused. . . . I didn't want to get involved in that kind of publicity."

After the October meeting, Davis phoned Robertson directly. Davis told the LAMCC president that he was talking to him now only "because I have been assured by Mel Durslag and others that you are a responsible person and will respect my confidentiality. You must recognize I am in a sensitive position in Oakland."

"He didn't want to do anything to destroy the season ticket sales," Robertson explained, "or create a controversy. . . . I assured him that . . . everything we talked about would be off the record." After that, Robertson "indicated that we were extremely anxious to get a football team here and we would welcome the opportunity to discuss all facets of a possible move." The two men arranged to meet when Davis came south for the January League meeting.

Despite Al Davis's concern for confidentiality, his flirtation with L.A. was a matter of public speculation in Oakland even before he and Robertson ever laid eyes on each other. "The Rams are moving . . . to Anaheim after next [football] season," *The* [Oakland] *Tribune* noted on January 18, and "the Raiders' contract with the Oakland–Alameda County Coliseum runs out at the same time. That might be an unhappy coincidence [for Oakland]. Davis could be using the availability of the larger L.A. Coliseum to negotiate a favorable new lease and stadium expansion with the Oakland Coliseum. Or he really might be hungering for appreciation from the glittering star colony in the southland where he has many friends and where it's said the warmer weather suits him better."

Robertson himself remained puzzled about Davis's intentions after their informal meeting. For his part, the LAMCC president spoke about L.A.'s "desire to get a football team" and indicated his commission "would do anything reasonable that we could deliver to get Oakland to come here."

Davis responded that "he recognized Los Angeles for a number of reasons as being attractive to him. He likes the area on a personal basis and there was no question in his mind that the area could support his football team. . . . He said that a number of times."

Robertson also stressed that he was not about to try to match Anaheim. "I told Mr. Davis that we were not in a position to give in to any excessive demands by anyone," Robertson remembered. "I don't want to be critical of Anaheim, but . . . if we tried to put together a similar deal in Los Angeles . . . we would be run out of town on a rail. . . . I made it clear to him we didn't have a lot of money to deal with. We felt that this area could stand on its own in supporting a football team and that we didn't have to make an attractive economic package for them. He said he understood that, but there were some things he felt he needed." Among them were luxury boxes, a training site, and "some sort of office comparable to that which he has in Oakland."

Later, Robertson would describe Davis as having both "indicated interest" and acted "not particularly receptive."

After the meeting, Robertson readily admitted that he "never had a handle on how serious Al might be." Davis was, he noted, "very cagey" and that January, "I didn't feel a great deal of optimism."

20
The Mellowness of Victory

Among the other items covered at the January meeting was "a brief legal report" about *NASL v. NFL*. All the recent skirmishing over Section 4.3 had somewhat obscured its issues, but the suit was still a topic of great concern. The League's attorneys did not expect to be in court with the NASL for at least another year. After their report, Ralph Wilson raised the subject of cross-ownership, but Rozelle quashed it, announcing that it "would be discussed in executive session with legal representation present at the [March] annual meeting."

Perhaps the most noteworthy development on the ownership policy front was Leonard Tose's sudden lethargy on the subject. He was no longer in the mood to push the question. "Edward Bennett Williams predicted everything that was going to happen," he later explained. "There was no way to stop cross-ownership. We were kidding ourselves."

No doubt one source of that disillusionment was Tose's own exhaustion. The fierce financial warfare he'd been engaged in for the last two years had taken its toll in a number of ways. "His feelings of public humiliation linger," *The Philadelphia Inquirer* noted. "He feels removed, distant from city and fans. . . . He remains deeply suspicious, embittered by past events." If Tose had an obsession at this point in his life, it was with *Tose v. 1st Penn*, his revenge against the "conspiracy" that had tried to dethrone him. *Tose v. First Penn*, like *NASL v. NFL*, was still more than a year from trial. In the meantime, Tose observed, "the situation hasn't changed a hell of a lot. I probably have one friend."

That one friend was Jimmy Murray, his general manager. Jimmy, forty-one, was native Philadelphia Irish. Overweight and pleasant, he'd worked as a public relations man in minor league baseball and then signed on with the Eagles in 1969. In 1974, Tose named him general manager at $25,000 a year and by 1976, his salary was raised to $80,000 a year. He earned it right away. In the battles that July and August, he was Leonard Tose's chief lieutenant. "We were at war," Murray explained. "It was the worst part of my job at the Eagles." Murray created subterfuges and Murray championed Tose's cause when Tose retreated into public silence. When Tose finally bought out Herb Barness, the last of his partner "friends," he turned around and made Murray a one percent partner. The arrangement gave Tose a more favorable tax status than sole ownership, but it was also an expression of affection.

"He was my best friend," Tose pointed out. "We were in constant communication. If I can't trust Jimmy Murray, who can I trust?" He even wrote an addendum to his will giving the right to operate the Eagles to Murray after his death. "I picked him over my daughter," Tose continued, "not to own it but to run it. . . . I treated him like a son. I just turned everything over to him. I trusted him with anything in my life."

No doubt Murray inspired such trust because he understood his boss. "Because people see Len's limousine, his helicopter, his Beverly Hills suit, that's how he's judged," Jimmy explained. "He's a very private person really, and for that reason the public perception of him is superficial. He has a great deal of humility, actually. He's always telling me, 'Don't underestimate me,' and the curious thing is that so many people have underestimated him."

Jimmy Murray was by no stretch of the imagination a threat to Tose. Leonard's friend was also his employee and that inequality in status made him the perfect foil to Tose's high-rolling sense of himself.

As one former Eagle employee remembered, "One day the owners were all meeting in New York. Leonard decides to go. It just so happens that Rozelle has a lot of important things to go over. [Rozelle] puts everybody in a lecture room [in the NFL offices]. It looks like a classroom. It has three rows of student desks, the kind with the flip-down arm to take notes. Leonard takes one look at this setup and barks, 'What the fuck.' You know Leonard, he can't go through a sentence without f-sharp. So, he sits down and tries it out. Then he screams again, 'Jimmy, get the fuck over here. What the fuck is this? I can't sit in this. I can't sit here. Are you gonna take care of this? What the fuck? Get me a fuckin' chair.' Now Jimmy's main job is to keep Leonard happy, so Jimmy hustles out and goes looking for a chair on the streets of New York. After lunch, the meeting resumes and in comes Murray, sweating, dragging this huge executive swivel chair with him that he's just gone out and bought. Leonard sits down with a big smile. They clear the desks away and Leonard crosses his legs and leans back. Everybody in the place is roaring by this time. Leonard says, 'That's more the fuck like it.' I think they still have the chair in the NFL offices."

By 1979, the toll Len's troubles had taken on him was no laughing matter. That risk of heart attack was dogging Tose's heels. The previous November, a physician had recommended open heart surgery, so Tose had checked into Dr. Benton Cooley's Texas Heart Institute. The following morning, Dr. Cooley fitted Tose's heart with a plastic replacement valve. When the Eagles owner came out from under the anesthetic, the first face he saw was Jimmy Murray's. The general manager was kneeling by his boss's bed, praying.

"Leonard has a lot of courage," Murray told the press afterward. Murray also encouraged his boss to sell. As Tose admitted soon after the operation, "[Jimmmy Murray would] tell me, 'For your own sanity and health, why don't you sell?' I knew it was probably the right thing to do. . . . but I don't know what I'd do without the Eagles."

Tose's brush with mortality did not significantly affect his life-style. "I've always believed in living every day like it's your last," Tose noted. However, his rehabilitation program was uniquely his own. Shortly after the operation, Dr. Cooley invited Tose to lunch along with two other Philadelphians upon whom he'd recently performed the same surgery. The subject of how they were taking care of themselves came up early. Cooley's other two patients ordered Perrier and told Cooley they "run five miles a day, don't smoke, don't drink."

"What do you do?" the doctor then asked Leonard Tose.

Tose had ordered a scotch on the rocks. "I drink ten scotches some nights," he answered, "smoke three packs of cigarettes a day, and go with a lot of young broads."

Cooley turned to the waiter. "Give me whatever Mr. Tose is drinking," he said.

Tose's recovery had indeed been remarkable. There's a good possibility that his newfound passivity on the subject of ownership policy was emotional, rather than medical. In the football season during which he'd had his heart surgery, his team had found success at last. With it had come a certain mellowness; perhaps he no longer needed to cut up Lamar Hunt to feel good about himself. During 1978, the Eagles won nine and lost seven, and finished second in their division. Though they were immediately eliminated by Rankin Smith's Atlanta Falcons, making the playoffs brought Tose the appreciation of Philadelphia and he reveled in it. People who wouldn't talk to him when First Penn was on his back now called for tickets. People who didn't recognize him now did.

Leonard Tose basked in the spotlight. Dressed to the nines, he moved about Philadelphia night life escorting a "young broad" and lighting his cigarettes with his diamond-studded lighter. In deference to his doctor, he tried to get to bed by 10 P.M. If he did, he often woke up by 2 A.M. and smoked until he could get to sleep. He averaged about six hours sleep a night. On game days, he woke so nervous he couldn't eat. Suddenly, however, it all seemed worth it.

After one Eagle victory, Tose took his football coach out to dinner at Philadelphia's exclusive Vesper Club. "We walked in," Tose remembered, "and we got a standing ovation. I never saw anything like that in my life. The Vesper Club is not the kind of club you walk in and get a standing ovation. . . . I was really amazed. That was the first time I got a real feel for what the people think." At least for the moment, Leonard Tose was having too good a time to pick any fights.

21
The Super Stadium Game Heats Up

Leonard Tose chose to skip the discussion of cross-ownership held at the March 1979 annual meeting. According to the minutes, "the commissioner asked for an expression from the member clubs that the League intends to vigorously continue defense of the antitrust suit brought by the North American Soccer League. He said such an expression would have no bearing on the League's current dual ownership policies and that a vote in favor would not indicate a vote in favor of the proposed bylaw that had been drafted . . . that the League's dual ownership policies continue in effect pending the resolution of the soccer suit for [all] team sports other than soccer, and that violations would be considered conduct detrimental to the League."

Rozelle's ownership policy reminder was aimed principally at Edward Bennett Williams. His franchise's majority owner, Jack Kent Cooke, still owned teams in basketball and hockey. Previously the commissioner had gone out of his way to extend sympathy to Cooke, but Cooke and his wife had finally agreed on a divorce settlement. Once that was finalized, Cooke would no longer be bound by a court order not to sell his holdings. Earlier, Williams said that Cooke intended to sell his hockey and basketball interests as soon as he could. If he did, he would be the first owner to do so since the ownership policy resolution had taken effect eight years earlier.

However, Williams was long since on record that *NASL v. NFL* was a "bad suit." Once again, his opinion made little difference. The League passed a formal resolution to "continue to vigorously defend the antitrust lawsuit brought against them by the North American Soccer League." The formal vote was twenty-three yes, two no, three pass. Edward Bennett Williams and Joe Robbie were the two nos. Lamar Hunt, Herman Sarkowsky, and Eddie DeBartolo were the passes.

Apart from that resolution, the action at the annual meeting was largely dominated by the Superstadium Game. The most publicized episode involved Joe Robbie and the city of Miami. It arose while the League was hearing presentations from various cities and stadiums seeking future Super Bowls. Among those was Miami, boosting its Orange Bowl. Having already hosted a record five Super Bowls, Miami was confident of more games. Joe Robbie, however, was not at all pleased with his adopted hometown.

Robbie's antagonism toward the Orange Bowl was longstanding, but now he was in a particularly irritated state. In January 1978, the city of Miami had repealed a longstanding local prohibition of alcohol sales in the Orange Bowl. Robbie, the stadium's exclusive concessionaire, had long sought the change, but rather than automatically award the new arrangement to its exclusive concessionaire, Miami advertised for public bids for the first Orange Bowl beer concession in history. The city's move was guaranteed to piss Robbie off. Robbie immediately filed *Miami Dolphins, Ltd. v. City of Miami*, charging violation of contract. When the court ruled in Robbie's favor, the city proceeded to appeal and piss Robbie off even further.

Robbie's irritation had escalated another notch just a week before the 1979 annual meeting when, after a series of "secret negotiations," the city turned down Robbie's offer of a settlement that would have given him both the beer concession and a new scoreboard. When Miami made its Super Bowl presentation, *Miami Dolphins, Ltd. v. City of Miami* was still pending, Robbie still had no beer concession, the Orange Bowl still had a "bush league scoreboard"—and Joe Robbie meant to make Miami pay through the nose. He interrupted the program to deliver what Miami metropolitan area Mayor Steve Clark described as a "tirade." Pete Rozelle described the faceoff as "a blowup."

When the NFL vote on the Super Bowl sites for 1980, 1981, and 1982 were announced, Miami was awarded nothing. The Orange Bowl would never host a Super Bowl again and Joe Robbie made no secret of the fact that he thought it was Miami's own fault. "I've been loyal to the city," he claimed. Robbie also said that if Miami had any sense, it would build a modern stadium suitable for a Super Bowl. In that case, he'd do everything in his power to get the League to select it.

The 1979 meeting also witnessed another presentation from a stadium that would never host a Super Bowl again—the L.A. Coliseum. Even before the L.A. Coliseum's fate was sealed by *LAMCC v. NFL*, the NFL had registered its opinion: The 1979 Super Bowl had already been awarded to southern California, but the League had selected the Rose Bowl out in Pasadena rather than the "Grand Duchess." To make its point even clearer, the League awarded the 1982 Super Bowl to Pasadena as well.

The action came as no surprise to Bill Robertson. His real motive in coming to the meeting was to look for prospective longterm tenants. His list of "sincere" prospects had not grown at all. He had, however, begun a fresh list of prospects who were "less than sincere." Not surprisingly, Baltimore's Robert Irsay was the first one on it.

Irsay had been brought into the L.A. picture by Supervisor Kenny Hahn. When the League met in January, Robertson met with Robert Irsay. Irsay had recently reached a verbal agreement with Baltimore to extend his lease through 1981, but Carroll Rosenbloom's departure for Anaheim seemed to have set him off on another direction. Apparently the Colts owner meant to sue C.R. on the grounds that he had made a fabulous deal in Anaheim and therefore owed him more money from their 1972 swap. Irsay claimed that if he had said something about suing Rosenbloom, he was only "kidding." Irsay was also once again fed up with Baltimore. There were delays on the new Colts training facility, for which Irsay himself was footing the bill. Construction permits were still snarled in red tape. "Look," Irsay told *The* [Baltimore] *Sun* before the meeting arranged by Hahn, "I like Baltimore. I have said I never plan to leave, but. . . . This has been going on for over a year. . . . If they don't want me to build my facility, then maybe I should go someplace else."

At his meeting with Los Angeles, Irsay came on like gangbusters. "I must say that he gave an impressive performance," Robertson pointed out. Robertson, L.A.'s official football negotiator, offered the same $9 million package he'd developed for Carroll Rosenbloom. Robertson explained his approach "not to go overboard and don't make any promises that you don't have some reasonable assurances you can deliver on." Hahn, however, seemed to subscribe to some other theory. He proceeded to promise Irsay new freeway off ramps, additional parking, and a new training facility to be constructed in what was now a public rose garden—all without assurances L.A. would or could pay. Finally, Robertson intervened and shut Hahn up. The incident didn't spoil the meeting, however. Even Robertson felt Irsay was "sincere." The Colts owner told the meeting that he was "ninety-five percent sure" he would move to L.A. next season. They immediately arranged another meeting at which Irsay could make his feelings known to the full LAMCC. Sensing a triumph, Hahn even invited the press.

The politicians and press who assembled in the Coliseum commission's board room to meet Robert Irsay on January 29 waited and waited. Hahn tried to reach the Baltimore owner on the phone, but nothing came of it. Finally, everyone figured he wasn't coming. The LAMCC contingent straggled out with egg on their faces.

For his part, Irsay simply issued a statement before leaving town. "There was no reason to meet again," he said. "We have a commitment to play next season in Baltimore and they still have the Rams playing there in 1979. There will be no further talks until after the season." Earlier news reports of Irsay's January flirtation with L.A. had provoked Rozelle to put himself on record. "It's of great concern to me," the commissioner admitted. "Any time a team leaves an area there's a void and we don't like to see it. I don't think any existing team can justify moving into L.A. . . . I think one thing that has helped make our League great is the fact that we have had such stability. We haven't had franchises floating around." Bill Robertson pointed out that the commissioner's statement conveniently avoided the "void" Carroll Rosenbloom had left in Los Angeles when he "floated around" to Orange County.

For his part, Rosenbloom was still maintaining his public stance that he would refuse to block any move to L.A., but it was by now widely reported that he would expect to receive a generous financial compensation for agreeing to share the nation's second largest pop off at the LAMCC. "I was made all sorts of _____ises by the Coliseum commission too," he pointed out. "But, like me, Irsay will never get any of them. That group is good at promising things and never doing anything about it."

Irsay responded only to Rozelle. "Nobody can tell me I can't move my own property," he threatened. "A federal judge has said that no one could prevent a man from moving his franchise." The case to which Irsay referred did not exist, but he offered no further clarification.

Bill Robertson did not even bother to approach Irsay when the League met in March. He did, however, breakfast with Max Winter. Max's situation was basically unchanged. He was still having problems with the legislature and repeated that if he didn't get his domed stadium, he would move. He was also still optimistic the League would approve that eventuality. Winter's confidence was reinforced by the executive session meeting. The League heard a report from the Vikings about the continuing hassles over their proposed stadium. In the course of the state's debate, one Minnesota legislator had flung Rozelle's earlier response to Irsay into the argument, pointing out that Max Winter could not get permission to move and had no leverage. The legislator had wired Winter earlier that day and challenged the Vikings owner to get the League's permission to move.

Winter wanted the League to respond and, according to the minutes, Rozelle complied, saying that ". . . the member clubs would not lock any club into an untenable situation in perpetuity, and that financial condition was only one of the many pertinent considerations in membership evaluation of a proposed transfer." According to Rozelle, "what we wanted to say was that . . . if [a club] had a difficult situation, they could come to the League, and if they had a good enough case, the League could decide whether they were to move or not."

"The League takes pride in the stability of its franchises," the commissioner announced at a press conference following the executive session, "but we don't like our stability being thrown at us. It is untrue that teams never get permission to move. The Vikings are not seeking to move, but the sentiment seems quite strong that the League would not like to be frozen until they lose a million dollars. Metropolitan Stadium [in Bloomington, Minnesota] is below the League guidelines and has been for years. Today, the Vikings are O.K. financially but in sports, changes come dramatically."

When Bill Robertson ran into Winter, Winter repeated that the League "already gave a clear indication that he would permit a move." Robertson still found it difficult to share that confidence. He and Rozelle had their own "very brief" conversation during the meeting at a reception thrown for the League by one of the television networks. "I told him that we were certainly disappointed that the Rams made the move to Anaheim, [but that] we were determined to do all we could to get another football team." Rozelle responded that he didn't see "any viable likelihood of getting an established team" for Los Angeles. With that, the conversation was over.

Robertson recognized that the commissioner's position might very likely amount to the kiss of death for L.A. He also knew that there was only one owner prepared to buck the League if it came to that. "If I moved my team," Al Davis had told *The* [Baltimore] *Sun* in January, "it would be unilateral. I would not need a vote to make that move." Davis, however, remained something of a mystery to Robertson. His lease with Oakland would be up at the end of 1979 and he was dragging his feet in his negotiations there. On the other hand, Davis was still keeping his distance from Los Angeles.

22
"Come Autumn, and the Roar of the Crowd ..."

Had the circumstances remained the same as they were at the 1979 annual meeting, Bill Robertson might never have come any closer to finding a tenant. Rozelle's opposition was enough to make any owner think twice and, if that weren't enough, lurking behind the commissioner was Carroll Rosenbloom. Despite C.R.'s public utterances, few in the League felt they knew just what Carroll would do if someone actually tried to move into his territory. C.R. could prove a formidable foe. Enough, perhaps, to intimidate even Al Davis.

That threat vanished on April 2, 1979, and neither L.A. nor the League would ever be the same again.

C.R. had skipped the Honolulu meeting and sent his son Steve in his place. He had had some oral surgery done, then he and his wife took a winter vacation in Florida. C.R. mostly played tennis there, ran along the sand, and swam. He tracked his investments on the phone in the morning and went to sleep to the sound of the surf at night. On the morning of April 2, he called Steve in California. They discussed the recent annual meeting. "He sounded relaxed," Steve remembered. "He was enjoying himself." At about 11:00 A.M., Carroll called Rozelle in New York to "chat" about "League business." Rosenbloom noted that the day outside had turned blustery and he'd been driven indoors by it, at least for the moment. "He said he couldn't play any tennis," Rozelle remembered. "It was too windy."

It was not, however, windy enough to keep Rosenbloom out of the water. Despite heavy surf, Carroll apparently decided to get his early afternoon exercise in the Atlantic rather than in his

own swimming pool. It was a decision that would forever mys-
tify his son Steve. "Carroll was never a good swimmer," Steve
explained. "He had a natural fear of the water. He never went in
by himself. I used to swim with him. He knew how to react in
the water, but he wasn't the kind to just jump in, swim out, and
come back. He was just in the water to get wet. To do what he
did, he broke the habits of a lifetime. I'm just a son who knew
his father, but I'm not satisfied that what happened was ever
explained." The water Carroll ventured into was later described
by Golden Beach's chief of police as "extremely rough," the
undertow as "very, very strong."

The last person to see Carroll Rosenbloom alive was a
middle-aged French-Canadian tourist, standing on the beach.
Rosenbloom was at least 150 yards out to sea, screaming for
help. The Canadian charged into the water and fought his way
out to where C.R. was, but his heroism was to no avail.
Rosenbloom had been floating facedown for five minutes before
he reached him.

Someone called the Golden Beach police about 2 P.M. and the
chief and another officer rushed down to the water. "When we
got to the beach," the chief reported, "we saw two men in
heavy surf about 150 yards from the beach. One man was trying
to support the other. We took off our clothes and went into the
water, but by the time we got there, the other man was near
exhaustion. There was no apparent sign of life [in Rosenbloom]
when we got to him." Before Rosenbloom's body could be
brought ashore, the rescuers were dragged almost 150 yards
north along the face of the beach by the heavy seas.

Georgia Rosenbloom was notified shortly thereafter. Rozelle
notified the rest of the League. "Everyone was very shocked that
Carroll had died like that," Rozelle remembered. "No one could
understand the drowning because Carroll had lived there in
Golden Beach off and on for several years. They couldn't understand it." Still somewhat stunned, Rozelle spoke with the press
that afternoon. "Carroll Rosenbloom played a major role in the
growth and success of the National Football League," the commissioner observed, "both through the teams he produced and
through his active participation in the League's decision-making
processes. We had some differences over things in the League
that he felt affected his team adversely. I was very pleased that
in recent months it was considered past and gone and we had a
very close relationship."

Steve Rosenbloom learned of his father's death after returning to the Rams' offices from an errand. When he walked in, Steve's pregnant wife, Renee, was there crying. Renee had got the news earlier but had been unable to find him. Steve immediately prepared to fly to Florida for a private family funeral in accordance with Jewish ritual. First he met with members of the Rams' coaching and office staff. "There's no danger of any changes," Steve reassured them. "C.R. wanted the team to remain with the Rosenbloom family and he's taken great care to make certain it would."

As Steve flew east, Los Angeles was already eulogizing his fallen father. Even Mel Durslag in the *Herald Examiner* found kind things to say. "The life of Carroll Rosenbloom comprised adventure and character development that would never even be found in the contemporary works of Harold Robbins," Durslag wrote. "A fascinating man, quietly mysterious, he moved in an incredible sphere of excitement, couched in a duality that made him a different individual to different observers. To adversaries, he was ruthless. To those within his social orbit, he was witty and warm. . . . At times, rival owners, incensed by his transgressions, took solemn oaths they never again would speak to Carroll. Some swore revenge whatever the price. But it usually developed they returned to the nest, yielding to the horsepower of his unusual charm. . . . It isn't easy to picture football without Carroll."

Most assumed the franchise would now pass to Steve. But like many assumptions about Carroll, it was off the mark. In fact, Rosenbloom left behind no sole heir to his football team. Steve was charged with "managerial and operational" responsibility, but actual controlling ownership was left to his widow, Georgia, who inherited seventy percent of the club's stock. The remaining thirty percent was split equally among C.R.'s five children from his two marriages. "He wanted Georgia to have the income and status," Steve explained, "and he wanted me to run it."

Georgia, however, did not see herself in quite so passive a chief executive role. "I know what Carroll wanted," she pointed out to the *Los Angeles Times* several days after C.R.'s death. "Carroll knew he'd live through me. He still runs the Rams. I'm just an extension of Carroll Rosenbloom. I don't want to sound kooky, but I feel as close to him as ever. We were never apart, you know. We talked over everything. It was Carroll's wish that the Rams continue as a closely knit family operation and I look forward to working with Steve."

The two-headed organization C.R. left behind was on shaky

ground from its first day. Steve thought Georgia had been "good for my father," but was not otherwise close to his stepmother. At the family funeral, he was put off even further. "She was already into talking about the will," he claimed. Steve was even more upset by her behavior at the service itself. To start with, Georgia was more than an hour late and kept everyone else waiting. Her attitude, according to Steve, was "less than the grieving widow. . . . She could have pretended to care at least. She didn't even talk to Carroll's brothers."

The memorial ceremony Georgia staged back in L.A. positively turned Steve's stomach. "C.R. didn't want a service," his son complained. "He told me and Georgia that at the same time. . . . The thing she had was like a coming-out party. It was the sleaziest thing I've ever been to. There was dancing on the tennis court, for Christ's sake. It was no more like Carroll than the man in the moon. It was pathetic."

According to the *Los Angeles Times,* Georgia's memorial service ". . .was handled as a celebration of life rather than a mourning over a death. All the music was upbeat and the tone, as set by Mrs. Rosenbloom, was light and loving." The eulogies were given beneath a large green and white striped party tent. The guests—among them Pete Rozelle, Al Davis, Hugh Culverhouse, Billy Sullivan, Leonard Tose, Robert Irsay, Mayor Tom Bradley, Warren Beatty, Kirk Douglas, Cary Grant, Jimmy Stewart, Rod Steiger, and Henry Mancini—all waited under the tent almost an hour before Georgia finally made her appearance. She then kicked things off with a welcoming speech. "Carroll didn't want any tears," she said. "He didn't like sad songs or sad endings." Then she turned the program over to comedian Jonathan Winters. "He was a special man," Winters observed of the departed. "He wanted the Super Bowl more than I did." Winters was followed by ten other eulogists, including a rabbi, a priest, three football players, two actors, and two owners of football teams. The rabbi observed that Carroll would have liked this ceremony. Of the two football owners, Art Modell and Al Davis, Davis's remarks were by far the more memorable.

"Among the great people in my world," Al Davis observed, "Carroll Rosenbloom was the giant. It will never be over with me. Come autumn, and the roar of the crowd, I'll always think of him."

Afterward, the memorial service, according to the *Times,* became "a buffet party" on the Rosenbloom tennis court, complete with "string orchestra," "festive flower-laden tables," and "strolling musicians." Georgia Rosenbloom was a charming hostess. Steve Rosenbloom left early.

Steve's stepmother was now his boss and he set out to make the best of the arrangement. "In a sense we are acting as one and I'm sure we'll continue to have a great relationship" Steve claimed in May. "My father asked me to take over the operational end, but Georgia owns most of the store and she has a good head for this business. . . . Before any step is taken, she and I will have talked it over at length. The thought I'm being guided by is my father's—we have to stick together."

Georgia evinced the same spirit. "We're going ahead just as if Carroll were on vacation," she pointed out. "I do have the final say, but the best way to think of this is as a partnership between the children and me. . . . I am obviously not going to go into the office every day—neither did Carroll—it's also obvious that I'm not now capable of making technical football decisions. But I know what Carroll thought and did for the last twenty years, and why he did it, and I'll learn the technical things. Steve and I are conferring and we'll continue to confer on all the major things."

Behind the scenes, however, Steve found educating his stepmother in the football business an exasperating process. At one point, he went to her because one of their players was about to become a free agent. "Well," Georgia answered, "if he only has a free agent, why don't we pay to get a professional one for him." Steve shook his head and found it hard to believe this was happening to him.

Georgia and Steve Rosenbloom attended their first NFL meeting together on June 6. Georgia became the first woman in NFL history ever to represent a team in Executive Session. Some found her presence disconcerting. At one point in that day's discussion, Leonard Tose said "fuck" three times in two sentences, and then stopped in midstream, turned to Georgia, and apologized. Georgia laughed and allowed she had already heard some of those words before.

After several items of business, Georgia Rosenbloom officially introduced herself to the NFL with a speech. Still beautiful and shapely, she spoke in a gentle voice. While some of the men in the room were as shocked by Georgia's inheritance as they had been by Carroll's death, she was given a polite and friendly reception. After Georgia's speech, Hugh Culverhouse suggested that "the owners prepare and present a proclamation to the Rosenbloom family in gratitude to Carroll for his service to the League." The suggestion was adopted unanimously. The proclamation honored him for being "the architect of a team which posted the best record in the NFL during the period 1958–71," and the man who "directed that team to six consecutive NFC Western Division titles."

Though the tribute was at best a limp reminder of Carroll Rosenbloom, it didn't much matter. The impact on the League's future of C.R.'s drowning was the same whatever his survivors now chose to inscribe on a plaque. To the vacuum of a vacant Los Angeles Coliseum was now added the further vacuum of Rosenbloom's absence, and there was nothing anyone could do to bring him back. Nor was there anything Carroll Rosenbloom could now do to keep someone else from filling the spot he'd left open.

23
Leaning South

The most noticeable change Bill Robertson encountered after C.R.'s death was in the posture of Al Davis. Davis now wanted to talk specifics.

Davis and the Oakland Coliseum Commission had been talking intermittently since January, to no avail. The commision knew what it was in for. In previous years when options had come up for renewal, the process had been difficult. "For years," according to one of Davis's former friends, "Al had been engineering a position from which it would look like the Raiders were being abused. He was working on short-term leases and his negotiating always became obstructionist. He would make demands, sit down to talk reluctantly, and then finally sign a new lease after extracting what he wanted."

In 1979, Davis wanted luxury boxes. This major source of income was denied him at the moment. "Unfortunately," he noted, "the Oakland Coliseum has a very untenable situation as to building suites because of the structure of the stadium. . . . The most we could build . . . was sixty-four suites." Davis wanted the Coliseum to loan him the money necessary to build what boxes were possible. He also wanted a Raider Hall of Fame located nearby and improvements in the team's practice

facility. On top of that, he was irritated at sharing the stadium
with the Oakland A's baseball franchise.

When negotiations kicked off in January, Coliseum chairman Robert Nahas proposed using the baseball team to get what
Davis wanted. The A's were threatening to move, but to do so,
they would have to buy out their lease for, Nahas hoped, at least
$4.5 million. "Nahas eloquently told me that they would let the
baseball team go if I would sign a ten-year lease," Davis later
testified. "They would fill in the stadium with approximately ten
thousand more seats and do a few other gratuities for me. . . . I
told them then that I would like to think about that because I felt
I am not in favor of the baseball team moving."

Davis also thought Nahas's buy-out figure was too low. He
concluded $6 million was a minimum figure, but he never got a
chance to tell Nahas. "They told me they couldn't go ahead
with it," Davis claimed, because "the mayor put his foot down.
He was adamant that it wouldn't happen." The turnaround irritated Davis and he was also irritated that some of the substance
of his negotiations were being leaked to *The* [Oakland] *Tribune*.
If news of their conversations got into the papers, he warned,
"that's it"—the negotiations would be over for good.

In March, the commission learned that sixty-four luxury boxes
would cost around $4 million. Oakland promised to make the
additions, but to do so would require issuing new bonds, which
would in turn require a longterm lease. At that point, discussion
came to a halt. Al Davis categorically refused to discuss any
lease "anywhere" for more than seven years. "From here on,"
an inside source claimed, "Al started dragging things out, not
agreeing to sit down, doing everything through LoCasale rather
than personally. He was becoming more and more difficult."

Two weeks after Carroll Rosenbloom drowned, the deadline
for Davis to renew his lease came and went. The Coliseum
Commission considered this no more than a standard Davis
"negotiating ploy." Unbeknownst to Oakland, Davis had also
begun a parallel set of negotiations with L.A. Both would be
protracted.

The people in L.A. got a very different impression of Al
Davis from the one his current landlords had formed. "He's one
of the straightest, clearest people I ever met," one source noted.
"His pattern of speech wasn't precise, but he gets the message
across. When he was through with a point, you knew where he
stood. He was never shy or modest about his demands but he
was always guarded. . . . There was no double talk or breach of

commitment. If he said it, you could count on it. He was always gentlemanly. He also pushed for the last dime, very tough but completely honest. He always said he wanted to come to L.A., but that he had to deal with Oakland. He told us not to be nervous about it. He said he didn't think Oakland would come up with anything.''

The list Al Davis had for Los Angeles once again began with luxury boxes. ''There are a lot of people,'' Davis noted, ''who want to be able to go to a game and entertain and have the television and be able to drink and have their own quarters. Seems to be an in thing. Seems to be sweeping the country.'' Davis hoped L.A. could come up with the boxes—143 in total. He wanted to lease them for $35,000 per box per year for the first four years and then raise the price. He also wanted to lower the field, eliminate the running track, and reduce the total number of seats significantly. ''I thought it was more important to fill the stadium and lift the blackout so that we could be exposed to the entire Los Angeles area,'' he explained, ''than it was to sell out the [larger] stadium.''

From the beginning, Davis's motives for a move to L.A. were entirely financial. The box arrangement alone could gross $5 million a year. The sixty-four less attractive boxes Oakland offered would gross $1.6 million at best. Luxury boxes were not the only motivation he found for heading south. According to Robertson, ''he saw significant pay TV somewhere down the line. It is his theory that in four or five years, professional football will be really into pay TV and this being a very large market, this would be an attractive place to be.''

Robertson's motives for bargaining were financial as well, as the possibility of insolvency of the LAMCC grew larger. And by the middle of May, Al Davis was the only ''sincere'' prospect Bill Robertson had left.

The Minnesota state Senate, the Minnesota House, and the City Council had passed a new financing bill to fund Max Winter's domed stadium in downtown Minneapolis. Max Winter was now off Robertson's list entirely.

Winter's departure from the scene certainly brought fresh motivation to Robertson in his discussions with Davis, but, in truth, Robertson didn't actually have much else to offer Davis. The changes Davis wanted would obviously cost more than the $9 million package originally developed for the late C.R., and even that offer was now shaky. California had passed Proposition 13, an enormous local tax reduction, and Robertson knew that at the very least, every dollar would be a struggle. Robertson told Davis as much, but said he wouldn't promise anything that he wouldn't also commit himself to get.

One of the first understandings the two men reached was that "before any final resolution would be made . . . anything we agreed on had to be in writing." Robertson additionally pointed out that he couldn't sign anything without the approval of the LAMCC and "unless I was assured that this area . . . would indeed be available for the entry of an NFL club."

"I consistently pointed out to him my fear of him being unable to get League approval to move," Robertson remembered. "He responded two different ways at two different times. His first response was that if it came to the mechanics of getting the votes required, he was not at all confident of getting them, but he said, 'Regardless of that, if I want to move, I will just move.' "

"You say you will just get up and move," Robertson observed, "but what if the NFL refuses to schedule your games?"

"They can't do that," Davis insisted. "It won't bother me."

Though the threat that the League would not approve lurked in the background, it was insufficient to keep Davis and Robertson from trying to work out a deal. Neither of the two was an easy man to best at negotiating and their discussions were often a cycle of tests and responses. Typical was the issue of moving costs. "He expressed a concern," Robertson recalled, "that if he did make the move down here, that he should get some help on moving costs for key personnel. I responded by saying that we would try to work out anything that was reasonable and I didn't know what kind of money he was talking about. . . ." Davis did, however, detail some of the things he expected to be covered under that category. Among them was that "he would like very much to get a house in the Beverly Hills area . . ." As the list got even longer, Robertson had to interrupt. " I didn't see how we could do it," said Robertson. "And I put it to him almost point-blank, that if he was going to be insistent on this, that we had quite possibly reached an impasse."

"Well," Davis relented, "I don't want you to feel that way."

Nonetheless, Robertson remembered, "he still tried to persuade me to in some manner get some movement going to provide for some moving costs. He said, 'You can do it, you have a lot of ability, you have a lot of friends,' and all that. I told him again, 'Don't depend on it because I am not going to be out there. . . . I am not going to do it.' "

The negotiating process had gotten little further than this kind of jockeying when Al Davis flew to New York for the League meeting at which Georgia Rosenbloom, the new owner of the rights to professional football in greater Los Angeles, was introduced. Al already knew her better than most of the League. Carroll had once told Georgia that if he was dead and she needed help, Davis was the person she should talk to. Georgia Rosenbloom didn't worry Al Davis at all.

24
Farewell, Golden Forked Tongue

The Rams were not the only ownership change making news when the NFL met in June. The other big story was the Washington Redskins. In May, Jack Kent Cooke, eighty-six percent owner, announced that he was selling his L.A. hockey and basketball teams. It was the first and only divestiture in the history of the NFL's formal prohibition of cross-ownership and, as such, the high-water mark of Rozelle's ownership policy.

When the sale was announced, Cooke denied he'd been under any pressure from the League to sell. He meant to get out of California entirely. The sale included not only the hockey Kings and basketball Lakers, but also his Fabulous Forum entertainment complex and his thirteen-thousand-acre ranch in the Sierra Nevadas. The total price was $67.5 million. The buyer was Jerry Buss, a local real estate magnate, described by the *Los Angeles Times* as a fancier of "fast cars, fast women, and fast scores in business." He was asleep when Cooke phoned on the morning of May 29. "Oh-oh, he may call off the whole thing," Buss remembered thinking. "Instead, he was extremely congenial. He asked, 'Are you ready?' Even though I felt the deal was imminent, I was in a state of shock. You see, I've been hanging so long. The terms of the deal must have changed something like six times." It would be "a couple of months" before the sale would be finalized.

In the meantime, Cooke was glad to be leaving the Pacific Coast. His divorce had been a trying and bitter experience about which he did not like to speak. According to one of his friends, it had split his entire family down the middle. "I think he wants to start fresh in the East," one friend observed. "California, to put it simply, reminds him of his wife."

While Cooke's sale was being finalized, Edward Bennett Williams continued as the Redskins' president. Williams was not particularly pleased that Cooke had kept the promise he'd made five years earlier, but that submission did not measurably diminish Williams's sniping at ownership policy.

At the June 1979 League meeting, ownership policy discussions were still largely confined to mounting the defense of *NASL v. NFL,* and Williams ambushed that process. His move caught Rozelle unaware. Williams gave a report about an eight-year-old lawsuit over Washington's RFK Stadium. Then, according to Rozelle, he "attacked the League position on the soccer case. He strongly objected to us defending the case. I was really surprised. It was out of order, out of the blue. He made a very strong advocacy against defending the case." It was a bad suit, Williams warned once again. There would be "big damages" involved and it would end up "screwing the League" and everything the League had going for itself. It was "folly" to persist.

Rozelle was pissed off and had "harsh words" with Williams. "Look, Ed," he complained, "when you speak, you speak as an attorney as well as a club member. Now we're going to have to get the League attorneys over here to explain their views."

Rozelle thought he'd played it fair with Williams and felt he deserved better treatment. From his point of view, the defense of the NASL suit had been discussed and approved in March. This was just useless obstructionism. As promised, the commissioner summoned the NFL legal team to the executive session and managed to undo some of the damage from Williams's attack, but it took only a little of the edge off Rozelle's irritation.

The only solace was, of course, that Williams's days in the NFL definitely seemed to be numbered. It was commonly assumed that Jack Kent Cooke would now want the Redskins' driver's seat, and the possibility of the two men sharing that seat was commonly dismissed. "Merely envisioning those two overpowering men residing in the same office is too shuddering to describe," one Cooke friend noted. Though Cooke had not yet clarified his intentions, most signs pointed toward him taking over the actual running of the franchise and leaving Williams a fourteen percent partner along for the ride.

The most obvious sign of impending change was that Cooke was house-hunting around Washington, D.C. He purchased a

fifty-acre estate in the Virginia horse country, thirty miles from
the Redskins' headquarters. When finished, according to *The
Washingtonian*, it featured "paintings by the masters and lesser-
known moderns; thousands of books . . . antiques . . . rare rugs;
a wine cellar that Cooke is very proud of; a collection of snuff
boxes; and sculpture, including a bust of Cooke by his ex-wife."
The grounds included: "a large cottage that serves as an office
for several accountants, secretaries, and other employees of Jack
Kent Cooke, Inc.; a stable that houses five horses; a swimming
pool and a small lake stocked with bass; hidden gardens, in one
instance linked by a wrought-iron door fashioned by Louis XIV's
ironmonger; and topiary gardens filled with shrubs shaped into
peacocks, dolphins, and other creatures."

Also, the five-year voting trust under which Williams had run
Cooke's Redskins' interest had been quietly terminated the previous March.

While Cooke's advent in Washington would certainly get
Williams out of the commissioner's hair, Cooke was no less
formidable in his own way. Cooke's detractors, according to *The
Washingtonian*, called him a "pirate" and "highwayman."
While possessing great charm, one of his former employees
noted that he "constantly plays his employees off against
each other" and approached all business with a "tiger's smile."
Having already run hockey, basketball, soccer, and minor league
baseball franchises, as well as a baseball league, he didn't need
to be told how to operate his business. *Sports Illustrated* once
dubbed him "the Sol Hurok of sport." Cooke also "loathed"
organizations and attending meetings, considering both "a waste
of time." Nor was he particularly a fan of Rozelle's, due,
perhaps, to what Art Modell called "family bitterness," directed
toward Rozelle's wife, Carrie, his former daughter-in-law. "He
hates Carrie," one of Cooke's friends noted. "He can't stand
her." Cooke's antagonism toward Rozelle himself was still,
however, of the smoldering variety.

Williams's antagonism was more immediately active. He was
indeed destined to leave the inner circles of football shortly, and
the way he left—thumbing his nose—pissed off Rozelle even
further, effectively ending any remaining goodwill between the
two men. The issue, as usual, was ownership policy.

While Cooke was shopping his L.A. properties around, Williams had quietly entered the baseball market. In 1978, he had
been hired by former Treasury secretary William Simon to try
and purchase the Baltimore Orioles. When that deal fell through,

Williams pursued the idea himself and on August 3, 1979, while still the chief operating officer of the Washington Redskins, he announced his new ownership of the Baltimore Orioles.

When asked by *The Washington Post* if owning a baseball team wasn't in violation of NFL ownership policy, Williams scoffed. "There is no rule in the NFL on cross-ownership," he pointed out. "There is nothing in the constitution or bylaws on cross-ownership. Therefore, I am not breaching any rules."

However, Williams privately took steps to make sure he was "meticulously in compliance" with the continuing ownership policy resolution. Before the November consummation of his baseball deal, he and Cooke, the only holders of the Redskins' holding company, reorganized their corporation. The functions of the president, Williams, were transferred to the chairman of the board, Cooke, making Williams a minority partner, outside the purview of the resolution he had resolutely opposed. He was also, in effect, out of the football business.

None of that lessened Pete Rozelle's anger. In all those speeches Williams had given about saving the League from "folly," the commissioner pointed out, "Ed had spoken with a golden forked tongue." All the while, he had been planning to buy into baseball. "That irritated a lot of club members," Rozelle claimed. "He wasn't speaking for the NFL, he was just speaking for Ed Williams."

After Williams's baseball purchase was finalized, Rozelle would try to do something about it, but the attempt was futile. He formed a committee to investigate "a possible conflict" in Williams's "dual role as a club official" for both the Redskins and baseball's Baltimore Orioles. "I had a meeting with Ed Williams in his office," Chairman Gene Klein remembered. "We worked it out amiably." There was no use the NFL kidding itself. There was absolutely nothing they could do about Williams and both Klein and Williams knew it.

25
Georgia Takes the Reins

About the same time Edward Bennett Williams made his leap into baseball, C.R.'s two-headed legacy was heading for the rocks. Four months together told Georgia Rosenbloom and her stepson Steve that they were not suited for sharing power with each other.

Steve, now thirty-four, was assessed by the *Los Angeles Times* as a "beer-and-pizza guy." His first job with his father's Colts had been picking up dirty towels and socks. In college, he had kept a pig in his dorm which he took to basketball games on a leash. While executive vice-president of the Rams, he had a license to drive eighteen-wheelers, and occasionally took the wheel of the team bus. When still in Baltimore, he liked nothing better than to cruise Interstate 695, looking for stranded motorists. "You always see people in trouble," Steve pointed out. "I stop and help them out, maybe change a tire. You meet interesting people that way. They don't know who you are and people in trouble are always friendly. Maybe it's an escape for me."

Steve had resisted moving west with his father in 1972. For a year after the Rams-Colts swap, he stayed in Baltimore and ran a dog kennel. Carroll twisted his arm to persuade him to move to L.A. and resume the football relationship they'd had in Maryland. Steve started as his father's assistant and, according to Rams Vice-President Harold Guiver, "gradually assumed more responsibility and authority until he actually was running the team on a day-to-day basis." Steve always selected the cold cuts for the team plane and made the sandwiches himself. No one ever mistook him for the late C.R., who dressed impeccably. Steve preferred Levi's jeans and wore his prematurely gray hair tousled in several directions at once. Carroll was infatuated with the glitter of L.A., Steve couldn't have cared less.

"After home games," a Rosenberg employee observed, Steve goes to ". . . this little bar in Manhattan Beach, where some of his old Baltimore cronies hang out. They shoot the breeze and throw beer on each other if they feel like it. That's Steve. No phony airs. No pretenses. No flaunting his position. Treats everyone the same. Steve Rosenbloom is not a Bel-Air type of guy."

His stepmother, on the other hand, was very much a Bel-Air type of gal. "During her life with Carroll," one of Georgia's friends noted, "she pretty much had to toe the mark, and it was different. Now she loves the life she's leading. She's free to do what she wants." Georgia shopped on Rodeo Drive, hired a personal publicist, and kept seven or eight servants at her mansion in Bel-Air. The Super Bowl trophy her late husband had stolen from Robert Irsay remained in the study. Georgia liked to sleep late and stay up a good portion of the night. A devotee of astrology and numerology, she would claim to "rely" on Carroll for several years after his drowning. "I can't really say I've gotten over his death," she observed. "I don't cry anymore, but I can't sleep more than four hours a night. My brain keeps flashing back to that beach in Florida where he drowned."

To fill the vacuum in her life, Georgia threw dinner parties, always arriving late, even though the events were in her own home. When she made her entrance, according to the *Los Angeles Times*, it was by "sweeping into the room with kisses for all, a carryover from her show business days." She often had East Coast crab and lobster flown in. Afterwards, she serenaded her guests with a medley of show tunes. It was also "customary for every male present to dance with her on the portable dance floor set up for the occasion."

One of those males invited to dinner with increasing frequency was Dominic Frontiere, a forty-six-year-old Hollywood composer of such film scores as *Gumball Rally, Pipe Dreams,* and *Freebie and the Bean.* He had spent most of his career creating music for television series. An acquaintance of some three or four years, he became "a family friend" shortly after Carroll's drowning. Fewer than four months after Carroll's death, Dominic Frontiere had moved into the guest house at Georgia's Bel-Air estate. Frontiere would later explain that Georgia "began to receive threats and a great deal of criticism" as the result of owning the Rams and when she became frightened, he agreed to move in "for security purposes." He was described in the *Los Angeles Times* as Mrs. Rosenbloom's "personal lyricist." Steve Rosenbloom described him as "a sleaze bag," and as, simply, "The Frog."

When Dominic Frontiere was moving into Bel-Air, the bitterness of his own position had already begun to well up in Steve

Rosenbloom. "My problem was that overnight, one woman turned it all around, took a tradition, and flushed it down the toilet. I saw it coming. She moved faster than I thought she would but it unfolded exactly like I thought. . . . I began to hear things. I knew she didn't want C.R.'s son around. Georgia didn't want any of C.R.'s old people around. She wanted to get her own people in."

Steve and Georgia knocked sparks with increasing regularity. It often took him three or four days to get hold of her, but she nonetheless insisted on being consulted on everything. When Steve acted anyway, that infuriated Georgia. He also took to ignoring some of her requests for information, infuriating her further. On August 6, she attempted to stop Steve's behavior by circulating a memo that included some twenty-eight items of franchise business that everyone was now instructed to act on only with her full consultation and approval. Among the items listed were all contracts, anything to do with "budget," "assignment of parking spaces," all hiring or firing, any check "in excess of five thousand dollars," and anything to do with Anaheim.

It took Steve little more than a week to violate her memorandum, and when he did, she went for his jugular. On August 16, Georgia kicked Steve out of the organization. "Carroll always told me," she later explained, " 'if the little bastard ever gives you any trouble, get rid of him.' So I did."

Georgia's attorney did the firing and Georgia said nothing. Steve asked to be allowed to go out to the training camp and say good-bye to the players. By the time he got there, Georgia's office had canceled the team meeting Steve had intended to address. Most of the players stuck around anyway. There was talk of a protest strike, but Steve objected. "I just wanted to tell them good-bye," he remembered, "wish them good luck, and tell them they had the ability to go to the Super Bowl." Before long, Steve was out of football entirely.

Afterward, Georgia described firing Steve as "the hardest thing I've had to do in my life. Right now I'm so exhausted I can hardly think. We love each other, but we can't live together. It's like getting a divorce. If I hated Steve, this would be simpler. I want people to understand the why of this, so they don't think I'm some woman sitting up here with the power to chop someone's head off. I have to think of the business first and I can't be concerned what people think. But I do care. . . . I fear they'll think the worst, that I'm just the ugly stepmother."

Georgia recovered quickly. With Steve gone, she didn't

have to share the Rams stage with anyone. Soon she was dubbed "the Boss Mama of the Rams" by the sporting press. Her style was clearly her own. In her first few months on top, she attended some Rams games and visited training camp, but usually for no longer than twenty minutes. Thus far in 1979, the longest time she had spent there was posing for pictures on one end of the practice field while the team was going through its paces at the other end. Her poses involved attempting to kick a football off a kicking tee. To the players, only a bevy of photographers and a shapely blond woman were visible in the distance. "What's going on?" one player was asked.

"Some Hollywood broad," he answered, "doing publicity shots."

Georgia Rosenbloom was, for the moment, the football business's most meteoric figure. In the Rams' 1978 press guide, she had been identified only as Carroll's "beautiful wife." In 1979, her biography ran for 313 words, written by her personal publicist. It credited her with mastery of skiing and skating, and stardom in light opera. She was also, her bio noted, "a poet of note." Among Georgia's better efforts was "The Future Is Suddenly Now," which included the lines,

Well, I thought & thought and I said at long last
There's one thing for sure—I can't bring back the Past!
However, the Future that I dreamed of before
Is suddenly NOW—and we've settled a score
So today is all mine—I can clearly see. . . .

But all was not pleasant for Georgia, alone at the apex of the Rams. As Steve had predicted, she soon began a housecleaning. The entire corps of executives brought to L.A. by Carroll and Steve was eventually dismissed, one by one. She was soon complaining in private about all the bad publicity Steve was giving her. For advice, she phoned Pete Rozelle.

According to Georgia's later testimony, she had seen the commissioner only on social occasions until she became president of the Rams. Since C.R.'s death, she had phoned him several times, but seldom talked just "straight business talk."

"I didn't really advise her," Rozelle remembered. "We discussed things." The commissioner claimed to have told both Georgia and Steve to stop any public sniping at the other. "It wasn't helpful," he explained, "to the franchise or the League."

The next problem Georgia took to the commissioner arose at

the Rams opening game of the 1979 season against the Oakland
Raiders. It was also the kickoff for the Rams' final season in the
Grand Duchess of Stadiums. The game was preceded by a
memorial eulogy for the late C.R. delivered by Davis. Davis's
Raiders then proceeded to win, 24–17. At the time, Georgia was
still publicly committed to Carroll's position on anyone moving
to fill the coming vacancy in L.A., but her private sentiments
were significantly less approving. That much became clear at the
Raiders game. For the last month, the L.A. papers had been full
of speculation that Davis might move his team there. Georgia
had her staff clip any articles that appeared about either the Rams
or the Raiders.

During the course of that opening game, someone hung a
banner on the outside of the press box proclaiming WELCOME LOS
ANGELES RAIDERS. Georgia couldn't see the banner from her
owner's box, but when reports of it reached her, she was furious
and immediately demanded that it be taken down. She also
demanded to know who had put it up there in the first place. It
was eventually removed, but not before making the lead photo-
graph in the Monday morning newspapers all over southern
California.

Mrs. Rosenbloom called Rozelle shortly thereafter. "She was
very upset," he remembered. "She felt she was a part of the Los
Angeles community. She didn't want to go to Anaheim in the
first place. And she was very upset that she was not viewed as
the Los Angeles team." She was also worried specifically about
the Raiders moving onto her turf and the competition it might
bring. Rozelle tried to calm her down. He told her not to worry.

26
Tragedy Interrupts Davis for a
Moment

In the fall of 1979, the argument for not worrying about Al
Davis still seemed strong and Bill Robertson was the first to
admit it. "Pete Rozelle controls the League and he's adamantly
opposed to our getting a team in Los Angeles," he said. "The
NFL is run with a country club attitude. They're not interested in

the public, just the almighty buck." As for the intentions of
Davis himself, Robertson remained uncertain. "I don't know that
Al Davis is interested in moving," he admitted. "He's exploring
his options. We're still a long way from fruition."

In the meantime, the odds against Davis ever getting NFL
permission to make such a move only increased. "Our League
has built its success on continuity and stability," Art Modell
pointed out. "If Al Davis came in and said he had a problem,
he'd have an attentive audience. That doesn't mean he'll move.
I've got problems, too, do I move to Phoenix?"

In October 1979, only two NFL owners were prepared to
commit themselves to public support of a possible Davis move to
L.A. One was Georgia Rosenbloom. "I wouldn't oppose it,"
she claimed to *The* [Oakland] *Tribune.* "We have all the fans we
need in Orange County." According to Davis, her private conversations with him indicated the same position. "Georgia told
me she would not block a move," he claimed. "In fact, she said
she would okay the move." Al Davis's other yes vote was Eddie
DeBartolo, for whom Davis's departure would mean not having
to share the northern California market with anyone. "I would
be for a move," he offered. "I'd be crazy if I wasn't." That left
Davis nineteen votes short of approval, should he put the issue to
a vote.

The opposition he faced did not drive Al Davis back in
Oakland's direction, where negotiations were still stalemated. By
September, the Oakland Coliseum negotiators were sufficiently
frustrated to make a public announcement on the state of the
negotiations, a move of which they knew Davis would disapprove. The Coliseum claimed Davis's desired improvements would
cost between $15 and $20 million, while he refused to sign
any lease for a longer term than three years. "That's more than it
cost to build the stadium in the first place," one Oakland official
pointed out. It was an impossible figure unless the Raiders made
a longterm commitment sufficient to amortize the whole arrangement. Davis's landlord was willing to build the sixty-four luxury
boxes he wanted, but, once again, the two sides disagreed on
financing. Davis's proposal called for the Raiders to get all the
income rental while the Coliseum insisted that income be used to
pay off the cost of construction.

In the meantime, Oakland's counteroffer to Davis's demand
for a three-year lease was a commitment to spend $1 million
over those three years and nothing more. The Coliseum's board

was irritated at Davis's tactics and felt secure that Davis would never get League approval to leave.

In fact, Davis and Robertson had been hard at negotiations since June. "Al Davis was edgy," one of the attorneys involved noted. "He would be risking his entire franchise. On one level, I would have been surprised if he actually went through with it, but I always thought he wanted to. . . . The real problem was that L.A. was in no position to do anything. Bill was really bargaining without authority. The LAMCC was so badly structured, it was next to impossible to get anything done. . . . To get money, he had to go to the city, the county, and the state. The state was a problem because of the North versus South issue. The city and county were a problem because to get those yo-yos to do anything is always difficult. There was a real question whether the governmental entities would go through with any deal they made. It would all have to be done with mirrors and baling wire. The credit goes to Robertson. He did a fantastic job. He developed a good relationship with Davis and he was patient. He evaluated Davis properly. He talked to him regularly on the phone and maintained an even balance throughout. Lots of people would have blown this deal."

Like Oakland, Bill Robertson figured L.A. would need at least $15 million to land Davis. Davis was also insisting on no lease longer than five years; Robertson was holding out for ten. "We were a long way from home," he remembered. Nonetheless, Robertson began to take steps to try to solidify his financial position. In September, he wrote a letter to the other members of the search committee to alert them to "the crucial circumstances now complicating the search for a National Football League franchise to replace the Rams in the coming year. . . . If we cannot guarantee the private boxes will be on line for the 1980 season, the interested NFL franchises will be forced to exercise other options," he wrote. Robertson requested a $15 million loan so that "construction of private boxes could begin on a timely basis." After noting the Coliseum's possible bankruptcy if no new tenant were found, Robertson concluded that "If the loan is not forthcoming, the prospects for this area are bleak."

The letter opened discussion of the question, and Robertson and Davis kept talking. From his side, Davis kept prodding on the financial issues. "Come on," he was fond of saying, "I have to show my partners something. They keep asking why take the risk." L.A., Davis pointed out, had to be willing to risk something too.

The risk he was referring to was, of course, the possible response of the rest of the League. "The real risk," one of the attorneys noted, "was whether Davis would be able to move, not whether he wanted to. The beginnings of all the League opposition was going on."

Pete Rozelle was monitoring the situation from afar. "I know that Al Davis feels unhappy," he admitted that fall, "but I have not explored it with him." He and Davis had spoken "briefly and generally . . . he may have either told me or inferred [he was interested in L.A.], more than likely inferred because Mr. Davis infers more than he makes declarative sentences." And the commissioner's position had not changed. "I don't like to see movement. We haven't had a franchise change cities since the Cardinals moved from Chicago to St. Louis in 1960. I don't have a vote, but I can recommend." There was, of course, no doubt about what Rozelle's recommendation would be.

"To ever get any kind of deal with L.A. was almost impossible," a source close to the negotiations remembered. "Nobody but Al Davis would have put up with it. The deal was always changing because of the politicians Robertson had to appeal to. He also had no strong allies other than Robertson himself. No owners were on his side and he had no strong city support. L.A. was quivering the whole time. He had to be a little crazy to do it. There had already been times when I thought most normal people would have backed out. But Davis was stubborn and self-confident. He had such a strong ego. He didn't want to let himself be pushed around. He possessed an extraordinary unwillingness to be defeated."

Davis also had motives of his own. "At some point," one of his Oakland friends observed, "Al was impelled to things by the opposition they engendered. He wanted to be the master of his own destiny. But there was also the stature factors. He saw L.A. as one of the two great places in the United States, along with New York. He wanted to be a bigger frog in a bigger pond and there was nothing Oakland could do to satisfy that."

Whatever Davis's internal reasoning, Bill Robertson maintained his faith that Davis was actually serious about coming. Mel Durslag, however, remained unconvinced, fearing Davis was just using L.A. as "leverage" in his negotiations with Oakland. Both the Oakland Coliseum and Pete Rozelle tended to agree with Durslag.

But the whole process was suddenly put on hold by a near tragedy in Davis's personal life. According to his friends, the incident marked the one and only time Al Davis had even momentarily "abandoned his obsession for football power."

In mid-October, Davis's wife, Carol, suffered a massive heart attack and lapsed into a coma. From then until the end of November, her welfare became his one and only concern. He spent almost all his time in her Oakland hospital room. In the beginning, Carol's prognosis was anything but good. During the initial moments of her attack, she had been technically dead for five minutes, and if she finally managed to survive, her doctors worried, it would likely be as a "vegetable" forever after. "When she was lying there in a coma," one of Davis's friends remembered, "and there was nobody who could do anything for her, Al was calling up people, looking for anybody who could help, any doctor with an idea. He went to war."

Al Davis fought death tooth and nail. "We met when I was coaching at Adelphi," he remembered of his struggling wife. "I was a kid. She was a super kid, a man's girl, a little wild. She knew sports, she was smart, well versed in the things that were. She was my kind of woman." Instead of giving her up, Davis moved a cot into a tiny storage room next to Merritt's coronary care unit and spent twenty-four hours a day in the hospital, much of it sitting at Carol's bedside.

"Don't worry," he said to her over and over again. "Everything's going to be fine." She was comatose, but he knew she heard him.

Much of the rest of Davis's time was spent on the phone, consulting doctors around the world. "I'm not gonna let her lie there," he swore to one of his friends. "They tell me they can't do anything for her. I don't believe this. Somebody, somewhere in this world has an idea."

During his vigil, Davis made no contact with either Oakland or Pete Rozelle. He did, however, phone Robertson on several occasions. Robertson told Davis about the time his son had been in an auto accident on the Ventura freeway. The son had been in a coma for thirteen days, but came out of it and was now fine. "Al never gave up hope," Robertson remembered, and that hope eventually panned out. After weeks of coma, Carol Davis regained consciousness and proceeded to make what one surgeon called "one of the most dramatic recoveries I've ever seen."

Once she was out of danger, Al Davis would joke with her about the ordeal. "When we were married, I said the only thing that would take me away from football was life or death," he kidded, "but I didn't think you were going to put me to the test." They celebrated Thanksgiving together in her hospital room. When Carol finally checked out of the hospital, Al gave a new color television set to everyone who had helped her, doctors, nurses, and bedpan changers alike.

Come December, Al Davis would return to the football business, single-mindedly set on making up for lost time.

27
Irsay's Flirtatious Colts

Even before he withdrew to look after his wife, however, Al Davis had been at least momentarily displaced from center stage by Robert Irsay.

On June 11, Irsay reportedly announced to the press that he would be moving his franchise from Baltimore to southern California as soon as the Coliseum was vacated by the Rams. "In 1980 we will come to Los Angeles. I met with the mayor [Tom Bradley] and the governor [Jerry Brown]. I had a nice conversation with Governor Brown. We will move here next year."

Irsay claimed that his decision had been provoked by the indifference and discourtesy exhibited by Maryland's governor, Harry Hughes. "The governor doesn't want to talk," Irsay charged. "I canceled my vacation to meet with Governor Hughes on Monday the eighteenth. He called me yesterday and said he was not available until further notice. That's three dates canceled by the governor. I guess Maryland elected God, not a governor. Well, I've had it with Maryland, and the governor can go to hell. My goal is to move to L.A. There will be no more monkeying around."

As usual, Irsay's outburst proved off the wall. He had never met with Tom Bradley or Jerry Brown. Nor had he notified the LAMCC, who had heard nothing from him since he'd stood them up in January. For his part, Governor Hughes of Maryland had never had an appointment scheduled with Irsay on the eighteenth and had never called Irsay to cancel it. Nor had he ever canceled any previous meetings with Irsay.

"I haven't talked to anyone from the Coliseum," Irsay later admitted, "but it doesn't have to be here. I can go down the road to Phoenix if I have to." Not yet in southern California, he was already threatening to leave there for Arizona.

Predictably, Irsay's outburst had little impact. "Popgun Effect," The [Baltimore] Sun declared, "New Irsay Blast Fails to Impress Anyone." It did, however, prompt a series of conversations with Pete Rozelle which lasted, according to Rozelle, "off and on for a period of maybe a month or six weeks." The commissioner tried to be patient and to reason with Irsay. Rozelle pointed out that moving to L.A. would mean that the NFL's Eastern Division would have to fly all the way across the country to play him. That added travel would more than likely insure that the votes of those franchises would be cast against giving him permission to move. Rozelle remembered that he "encouraged him to meet with the Baltimore people—because that city has supported the League for many, many years—and press for improvements." Irsay listened to the commissioner, but ignored his advice. Instead, he started shopping around for a new home closer than L.A.

The first candidate he came up with was Jacksonville, Florida. In early August, Irsay admitted that he had received an "unsolicited offer" from the Florida city, which was "about the same" as the offer L.A. had allegedly made. "I am very serious," he added. "I'd say it's a good possibility of moving to Jacksonville, based on what I've been told the city can produce. Jacksonville is only one of several cities I'm looking at. I love Florida. In fact, I have a home in Bal Harbour." The probability of his remaining in Baltimore past the current football season was, according to Irsay, "one percent. The other ninety-nine percent is divided among Phoenix, Los Angeles, Jacksonville, Memphis, and Indianapolis."

Of the cities Irsay named, aside from Jacksonville, only Memphis actually had an active interest in getting the Colts. Memphis, however, had yet to communicate that interest to Irsay. In August, Jacksonville was first in line and meant to make the most of the opportunity. "I knew Jacksonville would someday be a big time sports town," its mayor, Jake Godbold, gushed to The [Baltimore] Sun, "but I never thought it was going to happen this fast. I'm prepared to do whatever it takes—as long as it's feasible and reasonable. I think we can meet their requests." To help the city prepare its offer for Irsay, Godbold had secured the services of Hugh Culverhouse, owner of the Tampa Bay Buccaneers and still a Jacksonville resident.

When Irsay actually showed up to look the town over, Jacksonville pulled out all the stops. When Irsay's private jet taxied to a stop at the Jacksonville airport, the city delegation waiting for him included Mayor Godbold, a number of civic dignitaries, and a bevy of curvaceous women wearing T-shirts embossed with I GOT COLT FEVER. Irsay was then ensconced in a silver and black Rolls-Royce and, led by a phalanx of police cars and followed by a fleet of Cadillacs, was driven downtown for a private lunch. The route he took boasted more than two hundred signs, some of billboard proportions, saying WELCOME BOB.

Irsay made it very clear that he wouldn't come cheap. He wanted Jacksonville to remodel its Gator Bowl stadium completely. He also wanted the city to guarantee the sale of sixty-five thousand season tickets over his first ten years, plus provide a forty-acre parcel for the Colts' training facility, grant him a percentage of parking and concession revenues, and assure him "a profitable radio network." All of this, he pointed out, would have to be forthcoming before the end of October, when the League was scheduled to meet in Dallas. Afterward, he described Jacksonville's reaction to his proposals as "positive."

Irsay was "positive" as well, especially after Jacksonville's sales pitch reached a crescendo that evening. The public expression of zeal in the Gator Bowl was unlike anything Irsay had ever seen in Baltimore. Some fifty thousand people were on hand, and another ten thousand were trapped in a traffic jam leading to the stadium. Irsay was landed at midfield in a helicopter. "We want the Colts," the crowd chanted, "we want the Colts." The welcoming ceremony featured sky divers, free food, marching bands, and a galloping horse dubbed the Jacksonville Colt. After watching somewhat dazzled by it all, Irsay took the microphone himself. "Anybody in his right mind has to be very pleased and enthused by the welcome I've had here," he pointed out. "I can't believe all these people came out to see me. This will be a very big part of my decision." When his speech was over, the stadium lights were extinguished and each person in the crowd lit a match "to illustrate [sic] a spark to get the Colts to Jacksonville."

The next day, Irsay lunched with Pete Rozelle and Chuck Sullivan. "He filled me in on what happened in Jacksonville," Rozelle remembered. "I got the impression, or feeling, that if something were done in Baltimore, he would be happy to stay there." After their lunch, Rozelle saw fit to take Irsay's side against Maryland—at least partially. "I think they should try harder," he commented to the press.

By then, Baltimore Mayor Donald Schaeffer had already attempted to contact Irsay. It was, the [Baltimore] *News-American* noted, "the first tangible effort by local officials to mend fences with the team owner since he threatened to move the team last spring." Irsay told Schaeffer that "many other cities have made an offer" and that he considered Governor Hughes to be his biggest problem in Baltimore. "It's up to us to show him we want him here," the mayor explained. "I happen to like him. He's a flamboyant individual and he was exuberant over how he was received in Jacksonville. When you have fifty thousand people cheer you, you have to feel good."

Schaeffer arranged a meeting on August 29. Robert Irsay, Mayor Schaeffer, and Governor Hughes had a thirty-minute discussion about improving Memorial Stadium which the governor later described as "very friendly." According to *The Sun*, "Mr. Irsay was on good behavior. He did not tell the governor where to go, nor did he accuse the Colt fans of nonsupport. He talked rationally and set forth his demands. . . . A tone of cooperation permeated the meeting and all sides agreed to have their intermediaries meet further to work out the details."

Afterward, Irsay told city business leaders that "time is of the essence." The NFL was going to meet again at the end of October, and by then, he had to decide whether or not to ask them to allow him to leave Baltimore. Maryland's governor and Baltimore's mayor were sympathetic to Irsay's hurry but, in truth, their hands were tied. The price tag for Irsay's improvements could run as high as $25 million. The state legislature was the only possible source for that kind of cash and the legislature had made it clear that any such appropriation would only be in response to longterm commitments from both the stadium's tenants, Irsay's Colts and the Baltimore Orioles baseball team, recently purchased by Edward Bennett Williams. Williams pointed out that the improvements offered nothing to the Orioles, and he was not about to sign any longterm lease on that basis. Until Williams's mind changed, Maryland could only try to mollify Irsay as best they could, while hoping the League held to Rozelle's attitude about "franchise stability." Irsay's response was already on the record. "I can go anywhere I want," he pointed out. "It's a free country."

By September 26, Irsay was back in Jacksonville. Again Irsay's jet was met at the airport and he was driven to a private four-hour lunch. The occasion was the official presentation of Jacksonville's written offer. The city was willing to guarantee sales of some forty-one thousand season tickets for ten years. It would also spend $14 million to remodel the Gator Bowl. Among the improvements would be 105 luxury boxes, a forty-thousand-square-foot training facility, enlargement to seventy-two thousand permanent seats, brand new press facilities, a ground-level restaurant, and construction of numerous "access roads and pedestrian walkways." Irsay characterized Jacksonville's presentation as "the first financial offer of any substance," but claimed there were more on the way. Along with Jacksonville, L.A. and Memphis were still in the running. "It is no longer a question of *if* I'm moving," he announced, "but a question of *where.*"

As usual, L.A. had no idea it was supposed to be working up an offer to Irsay. Meanwhile, Memphis was getting a lesson in the Irsay style of negotiation. When he met with civic leaders, he told them, "I give you my word we are moving out of Baltimore. At this moment, it's either Memphis or Jacksonville." When a Memphis delegation finally presented the city's official offer, ". . . we got a little more than twenty percent through it, at which point certain questions came up," the Mayor's representative remembered. "We started discussing the questions and the meeting deteriorated from there." Finally, Irsay excused himself to go to the bathroom. The waiting Memphis group heard Irsay close the bathroom door, then heard the toilet flush. Afterward they heard the hallway door slam shut. Irsay had walked out and disappeared without so much as a word.

The Mayor's representative later explained: "Our chances of getting the Colts looked bleak. But having dealt with Mr. Irsay [before], I know that he is a very complex individual, so I decided to call and check with him again. I really felt we were dead, but I have been trying to get a National Football League franchise for our city for the last five years and I wanted to check once more before I wrote off the final chapter in that quest. And I'm glad I did. Irsay said he was still interested in our proposal." The proposal guaranteed Irsay an annual stadium gross of $7.3 million for nine years, more than $1 million larger than Jacksonville's ten-year offer. It would also build him a training site and increase Memphis's Liberty Bowl stadium from fifty thousand to seventy-four thousand seats. *The* [Baltimore] *Sun* later described it as "the richest commitment ever made by a city to a sports team."

Offers in hand, Irsay intended to go to the NFL's meeting on October 31 and ask for a vote. Beforehand, however, Pete Rozelle began to maneuver a bit. He met with Baltimore's

Mayor Schaeffer and Governor Hughes to talk about what they would have to do to keep Irsay. Maryland then came up with $22 million in improvements to Memorial Stadium in exchange for a longterm Irsay lease. Hughes and Schaeffer discussed the offer with Irsay. Rozelle noted that he was "very encouraged." Hughes described himself as "satisfied," Schaeffer "did not express any disappointment," but Irsay still planned to ask the League to vote under Section 4.3.

By the time of the NFL meeting, that request was easily its hottest topic. Robert Irsay was spotted in the hotel lobby and immediately besieged by reporters. He tried to hide behind an abutment, then fled into the kitchen, where he was finally cornered in a utility closet. Irsay then told the reporters to "talk to my wife." She in turn told them he had proposals from Jacksonville, Memphis, and Baltimore, and that Irsay would "probably ask the other owners to vote on them." She characterized Baltimore's offer as "just talk," since the state legislature would not be meeting until the following January and could then "throw everything out." Memphis's offer was described by Harriet Irsay as "very good." At this point, Irsay himself intervened. "Harriet has a big mouth," he told the press. "She doesn't know what she's talking about." He and Harriet then disappeared into the elevator.

Escaping the press was easier than escaping Rozelle. That night, he and the commissioner had an extended meeting. Rozelle did not want a vote and made a strong case for the damage such a move would do to the League. Rozelle pointed out that Memphis's renovations would not be complete until 1981, so Irsay had nothing to lose by waiting to see what Maryland would do on his behalf. They met again before the League convened as a whole and the commissioner no doubt pointed out that Irsay had no more than six votes supporting him, some fifteen short of what he needed.

The commissioner soothed the League's most savage beast. "Irsay gave a very nice presentation," Gene Klein remembered with a certain astonishment. "He didn't ask for anything and acted totally inside the confines of the League rules." Irsay retracted his request for a vote under Section 4.3 and simply reviewed his discussions with Memphis, Jacksonville, and Baltimore. "He was almost eloquent," another owner gushed. "He made an excellent impression."

Irsay himself explained his turnaround as the best option of the moment. "Even if I had gone through with [it]," he pointed out, "the move probably could not have been made until 1981. As it now stands, I have left the door open to the cities I have talked to [and] . . . I want to thank Memphis and Jacksonville and the other cities, and I still have them in mind."

Irsay's "open door" did little to mollify the municipalities with whom he'd been dickering. The "bad news," according to the *Memphis Commercial Appeal*, was that "the Colts are staying in Baltimore." The "good news" was "so is Robert Irsay." "He told us two hundred times he might be coming here," one negotiator complained. "I absolutely don't trust him." Jacksonville now felt much the same way. "He'd cock his head to one side, give us that teddy bear smile, and tell us he was being sincere with us," Jake Godbold remembered. "His name is mud here." Even his "hometown" *News-American* described Irsay's last minute allegiance to Baltimore as no more than a "Sudden Change of Fickle Heart."

In any case, the NFL entered November with Robert Irsay once again safely stashed beneath its decks.

28
Getting Ready for War

With Irsay under control, Pete Rozelle's uneasiness soon shifted back to Al Davis. On November 20, Davis met with Jack Maltester, a member of the Oakland Coliseum's board recently assigned the task of reopening negotiations with the Raiders. The meeting was little more than an illustration of how fervently Al Davis did not want to be nailed down. Davis claimed Maltester elicited a set of complaints from Davis and then afterward sent Davis a letter, listing his various complaints as demands. Davis responded by adamantly refusing to admit to having any list of demands. He also characterized Maltester's letter as "something that shouldn't have been done." Maltester's worst violation was that the letter was "written as a public release," once again violating the secrecy insisted upon by the Raiders' boss.

According to Maltester, "I sat down with Al Davis and I put down notes of what he asked for. He wrote $8.5 million worth of stuff on the blackboard that I hadn't seen before. When I sent him a letter outlining what they were, what I felt we could do, he denied he'd ever proposed them.'' Maltester subsequently turned the task of negotiating over to a three-man committee, claiming he found further efforts with Davis impossible.

The obvious animosity was reflected on both sides. "The Raiders owe the people of this area something,'' Maltester complained to the press. Instead, all Davis did was say, "To hell with the Coliseum and the Coliseum board. . . . Don't they owe anything to these people? They're making money. If they said they were losing money, I'd be sympathetic. Really, what *do* they want? . . . They care nothing about the people. It's a greedy organization and I never thought I'd say that. It's a helluva thing for me to say. Most of the limited partners are friends of mine.''

Davis doubted "the ability and competence'' of the people Oakland sent to negotiate. "I don't even know who has the authority,'' he pointed out. Being at his wife's bedside also seemed to have provoked some hard thinking on Davis's part about just what it meant to stay in backwater Oakland rather than risking the southern California big time. After Carol was fully recovered, according to one NFL source, he hinted as much. "Would *you* want to bury *your* wife in Oakland?'' Davis asked.

Throughout his wife's ordeal, Al Davis had maintained contact with Bill Robertson in L.A. Davis had no contact at all with Pete Rozelle. At this stage, Rozelle noted, "I still didn't think the move idea was real. . . . I didn't think Al Davis would attempt to violate the constitution.'' In the last week of November, Rozelle attempted to contact Davis for the first time in six weeks. He contacted Al LoCasale at the Raiders and informed him that he and his wife were going to be in the Bay Area on November 29 and wanted to know if they could visit Mrs. Davis in the hospital.

On November 28, Al LoCasale called the Rozelles in their hotel room. LoCasale said "he wasn't certain whether [the Rozelles] would be able to see Mrs. Davis or not the next day.'' According to Rozelle, LoCasale also "may have said something to me . . . that I would be queried the next day [at the San Francisco Press Club] about [the Raiders] moving and he wanted me to be as soft as I can or, if possible, say yes, the Raiders can move.'' LoCasale wanted what he later described as "the Minnesota treatment,'' in honor of the press conference threat Rozelle had delivered in Hawaii on Max Winter's behalf. The Raiders, LoCasale reminded the commissioner, were in the midst of very sticky negotiations with Oakland.

The next morning, LoCasale called again. The commissioner remembered that "Mr. LoCasale told me that I would be able to get in touch with Mr. Davis by phone from the Press Club and he would know more about the situation regarding his wife." When Pete and Carrie reached the Press Club, LoCasale was already there. Again he requested "the Minnesota treatment," and Rozelle responded he would do his best.

As Davis's assistant had predicted, the possibility of a Raiders move was one of the first items raised during the commissioner's question and answer period. "I tried to take as soft a line as I could on Davis," Rozelle claimed. "I said that of course the League liked permanency to our franchises, but I hope they can work it out. I was more or less dancing on water there, trying to say I hope they stay here and I hope we can work something out."

Afterward, the commissioner talked with Davis in their first communication since his wife's coma. Most of the ten-minute talk was, quite naturally, about Mrs. Davis. She had just been moved to another hospital, so a visit was impossible. According to Rozelle, Davis eventually "told me he was having great difficulty in negotiating a lease with the Oakland Coliseum." He also said, "I don't think that you helped us out at all at that luncheon meeting."

"I felt I went as far as I possibly could in trying to help him," Rozelle remembered. "I said to Al, 'I helped you as much as I could. I did not have the right to say you could move your franchise. That's up to the member clubs.' I said that Al had not come to me. Al had not asked for a move. That's what I told the press. I said, 'I hope that he can conclude the negotiations with the Oakland Coliseum successfully.' So I said all the soft things to the full extent that I could at the time. . . . He wanted me to say more than I did and I told him that I thought that I had gone as far as I could on my own." Al Davis was unsatisfied, but, for the moment, dropped the subject. "I think I might want to sit down with you soon," he mentioned in closing, "and talk."

"Fine," Rozelle answered. "Just let me know when you are free."

Though it went unstated, both men now understood that the subject of this conversation would be Los Angeles.

In the meantime, speculation about Davis's dealings with L.A. only escalated. On December 17, the *Los Angeles Times* claimed that Bill Robertson had at last found a way to wriggle around L.A.'s financial crunch. L.A. had won its Olympics bid and now, according to Olympic Organizing Committee Chairman Peter Ueberroth, was prepared to use its advance revenues to underwrite the $15 million of improvements Davis wanted. "We have developed, with Bill Robertson," Ueberroth explained, "a plan that we feel would . . . get the facilities needed to attract a team."

The news was received with great uneasiness in Oakland. "There's no way we can get in a bidding match with the Los Angeles Coliseum," Jack Maltester groused. Oakland was increasingly relying on the assumption that the League wouldn't let Davis move. Otherwise, they had been outmaneuvered. "We don't feel like we're the bad guys," the Oakland Coliseum's general manager observed, "although there has been a strong attempt to make us look that way." Asked how the Coliseum and Davis were getting along, the GM admitted, "It hasn't been very good lately." Asked if the relationship had ever been any good, the GM said, "No comment."

The increased speculation brought some disquiet to L.A. as well. Shortly after the *Times* story, Georgia Rosenbloom again called Rozelle. "Have you seen the papers?" she asked. "The Raiders are in the headlines again. They're coming to town." Georgia was feeling "hurt" that Davis had not consulted her on his plans.

"Don't worry, Georgia," Rozelle advised. "It won't happen."

The commissioner later explained that he used "Don't worry" ". . . because that's the way I get off the phone with owners after lengthy calls. . . . I said, 'Don't worry. Al hasn't come to me. He hasn't said anything about wanting a vote, wanting to move to Los Angeles. . . . I think it's probably at this point just a negotiating ploy.' "

Bill Robertson had come to the opposite conclusion. In "the latter part of December," Robertson remembered, "my gut feeling was that Al Davis was seriously thinking of coming to Los Angeles." Once, Robertson had considered Davis simply "sincere"; now he upgraded Davis to "a hot prospect." The possibility of Olympic financing had a lot to do with Davis's attitude. "There were certain requirements that we needed to move to Los Angeles financially," he later explained, "and Bill Robertson was trying to put his package together so that the money would be there the day that I agreed to come. . . . In December, we met at the Olympic [Committee] office and every time we would finish the meeting, after we got done discussing details and money, Ueberroth would come up to me and say, 'I want you to know that the minute that you sign, the money will be there. You will have the money.' "

With that assurance, negotiations between Davis and L.A. accelerated. On Christmas Eve, Davis, Robertson, and a handful of attorneys and assistants spent the entire day closeted at the Beverly Wilshire, poring over details. Al Davis was insisting "that he will not move the Raiders to L.A. and sign a lease with the Coliseum unless the Coliseum guarantees to make a number of specified improvements." At the time, it was understood that "the Olympic Organizing Committee . . . has agreed that it will advance the Coliseum money . . . to help finance the costs. . . . The remainder of the financing will be through a bank loan [to the LAMCC]."

A week later the two sides got even more specific. The L.A. GM claimed that "An agreement was reached concerning a practice facility for the Raiders, including a clubhouse, training facilities, lockers, weight conditioning rooms, meeting rooms, offices for the Raiders' coaches and executives, two full-sized natural turf practice fields, a seventy-yard Astroturf field, all to be completely fenced in for privacy and security. The parties also agreed on insurance costs, the responsibility for day-of-game expenses, the disposition of income from the VIP executive suites, scheduling dates, and who would pay for moving costs. In addition, the parties reached an understanding . . . regarding the general amount of rent for the Coliseum, the length of time to be covered by the contract, and the splitting of concession income. The Coliseum expressed its willingness to grant Davis's request for a five-year contract, provided only that the term of the bank financing to pay for the improvements does not exceed five years."

Al Davis and Bill Robertson were closer to a deal than they had ever been, but two "ifs" remained. The first was if L.A. could really produce the money it was preparing to commit itself to spend. The second was if Davis could really get the League to let him move. Like the agreement itself, those dilemmas were still playing themselves out in private when 1980 began.

Oakland, of course, had no idea Al Davis and L.A. had gone as far as they had. By January 3, however, it was apparent something was up. The suburban *Hayward Daily Review* printed an exclusive interview with Davis. It marked the first time in the last year that Davis had broken his public silence on the issue of his Oakland lease and the gist of it all was decidedly negative in Oakland's direction. "They have not negotiated with us for ten years," Davis complained. "They still haven't done it. . . . There were a few concessions along the way . . . [but] the concessions were peanuts. We never got any of the things we deserved. . . . You know who built the Coliseum. They can talk about this guy or that guy, but you know. You know who's had a commitment to excellence. We may not have been as good as we'd like the last two years, but we've done our part. I don't think they've done their part, by any means. That's obvious, otherwise we would have solved the lease. . . . They'd have told us to go stick it except that something came up over the horizon that scared them a little bit." Davis also hinted that Oakland would soon pay for its folly. "I think this thing has gone much further than you assume," he warned somewhat obscurely. "It's like getting ready for a world war and you're still worried about Iran."

Oakland claimed the blast was just more Al Davis. "To me it sounds like just one of their maneuvers," Jack Maltester commented. "I think the chances are very much in our favor that the League will not let the Raiders move," he argued.

In the first week of 1980, however, Al Davis was moving on the League front as well. Over the weekend of January 5, Pete and Carrie Rozelle were in Tampa for the playoff game between the Tampa Bay Buccaneers and the Los Angeles Rams and had dinner with Georgia Rosenbloom and several others on the evening prior to the game. Rozelle raised the subject of Davis's designs on L.A., saying he now thought Davis was serious about moving there and didn't want Georgia to read about it in the papers. The change in Rozelle's estimate of the situation had grown out of a recent phone call from Davis, who now wanted "to sit down and talk." That the portent of such a talk was ominous went without saying.

29
Davis and Rozelle, Head to Head

Al Davis and Pete Rozelle met in Manhattan on January 7, 1980, alone, behind closed doors. "It was not an angry meeting," Rozelle remembered. "It wasn't explosive or vitriolic." None-theless, the commissioner would later wish there had been a witness in the room.

According to Rozelle, Davis began by explaining "the diffi-culties he was having in negotiating what he felt was a satisfac-tory lease with the Oakland Coliseum people. . . . and he said that he felt that they just were not negotiating in good faith and he said, 'I'm strongly thinking of moving to Los Angeles, to the Coliseum.' "

"Al," Rozelle responded, "if you decide you want to go to Los Angeles, let me know and I'll schedule a League meeting."

"I don't intend to submit this to the League for a vote," Davis announced. His position was the same as in Chicago, more than a year earlier.

"Well, Al," Rozelle shrugged, "it's my job to enforce the constitution, and that's going to present a conflict."

There would later be little dispute over the content of the exchange between the men, but much dispute about its tone and the respective postures of the participants. "It was one of the few times Al Davis had ever been humble in his life," one of Davis's L.A. associates claimed. He said he wanted to move to L.A. and needed Rozelle's help. Pete just said, 'You have to put it to a vote.' Al Davis knew who the vote was, he didn't stand a chance." Davis himself claimed that Rozelle "could not give any reason why I shouldn't move and even agreed that L.A. . . . could be the finest franchise in the National Football League."

Once Davis was gone, Rozelle discussed their conversation with his lawyers. "I told Mr. [Hamilton] Carothers what Mr. Davis had said to me," Rozelle explained. "That he was strongly leaning toward moving to Los Angeles and did not intend to ask for League approval." Carothers responded that it was "impor-tant to go on record promptly, having had that news from Mr. Davis. I think what Mr. Carothers intended to convey . . . to

Mr. Davis was that it was a rather serious decision that he was making and that he should be aware of the potential consequences." The result was a letter from Rozelle to Davis, drafted by Carothers and dated January 10, 1980:

Dear Al,

In our conversation last Monday you took the position that no vote by the NFL's member clubs is necessary for you to move the Raiders from Oakland to Los Angeles. Reflection on that conversation suggests that I should make clear what I believe the other clubs' reaction will be if you attempt to take such a step. . . . The requirement of member club approval of a franchise transfer . . . is in the interests of every member of the League [and] I do not know what the membership reaction will be to a proposal by the Oakland club for an immediate transfer of its home operations to Los Angeles. . . . But I think you would be extremely ill-advised to attempt to effect such a transfer without complying with the League's charter and submitting the proposal to the membership for its consideration. . . . When the Raiders entered the NFL, they entered as a franchise conducting their home operations in Oakland. They also agreed to accept the provisions of the NFL constitution and bylaws. The remaining NFL clubs will undoubtedly view the Raiders as contractually committed to remain in Oakland until the charter provisions are followed. . . .

I am, of course, aware of the antitrust litigation pending in Los Angeles [*LAMCC v. NFL*]. But if you are relying on that litigation as a basis for simply ignoring your contractual commitments to the other member clubs of the League, I think you are equally ill-advised. And if your reliance on that litigation is misplaced, which we think it clearly is, the costs, practical problems, and financial penalties inflicted on the Raiders franchise, including possible disciplinary action by the League and the imposition on the Raiders of the costs and expenses incurred by the League, will be quite severe. I therefore strongly urge you to take a responsible approach to the Raiders' interests and the interests of your fellow clubs by submitting your proposal for early consideration by the League's membership.

Sincerely,
Pete

Rozelle sent copies of the letter to all the member clubs and several called him to talk about it. They were, he later claimed, supportive of the stand he had taken.

Davis likely found the letter's threats invigorating. Getting hardnosed was something he enjoyed. Davis was obviously making ready to do battle, should it come to that. He retained the services of attorney Joseph Alioto—Billy Sullivan's son-in-law and Leonard Tose's counsel in *Tose v. 1st Pennsylvania Bank*. While not saying whether or not the Raiders were actually moving, Alioto had begun defending their right to do so before Rozelle's letter was even mailed. "We don't think anyone has jurisdiction," Alioto told *The* [Oakland] *Tribune*. "Carroll Rosenbloom moved. He didn't ask anybody. You can't justify that [move] as being in the same area. . . . If Rosenbloom did it without asking anybody, there's no reason to think Al would have to ask anyone." If the League tried to stop him, Alioto pointed out, it would be a severe violation of the Sherman Act.

Meanwhile, new developments were brewing in both L.A. and Oakland. In L.A., Bill Robertson continued to attempt to nail down financing. According to Robertson, "by early January, the prospects of the Raiders and the Coliseum committee reaching a mutually agreeable lease looked very probable." As those prospects increased, so did the pressure on Robertson. "Because of the urgency of arriving at an agreement with Al Davis," Robertson remembered, "we had to get some political action which would indicate support of a Raider move" and get it soon. Early in the month, Mayor Tom Bradley made it clear to Davis that Robertson had his full backing.

According to Robertson's new financial plan, $5 million would be supplied by an advance from the 1984 Olympics; another $5 million would be a loan from L.A. county, secured by projected income from advertisement sales on the new scoreboard and revenues from luxury boxes; and the final $7 million would be supplied by the city of Los Angeles. The arrangement made significant headway. The *Los Angeles Times* called it "a major step toward bringing the Oakland Raider football team to Los Angeles." L.A. Supervisor Kenny Hahn hinted that Davis might very well announce his move on the Friday before the Super Bowl.

Hahn, however, was off the mark considerably. One significant reason was that, in something of a late civic panic, Oakland had finally responded to L.A.'s challenge. The moving force was Oakland Mayor Lionel Wilson, who, like Tom Bradley in L.A., was the first black mayor in his city's history and the Raiders now loomed as the most significant challenge of his first term. The politician who stood to be blamed if Al Davis actually moved was the mayor. And he would be blamed for much more than just an empty stadium. As *The Tribune* noted, "Snatching the Raiders out of Oakland would rip the heart and guts out of the East Bay. . . . The Raiders are one subject that keeps the community mind on matters other than unemployment, high taxes, reduced services, and other despairs of present day life. . . . This isn't merely liking a team. It's almost love." The Raiders had put Oakland on the map; Oakland would have to scramble if it meant to stay there.

Wilson began his scramble on January 8 by calling for a meeting of all parties. Davis delivered his RSVP through Al LoCasale. "We're not going to a meeting with twenty-five people on one side and Al Davis on the other," Davis's assistant announced. "We're not interested in a meeting of political people who are ready to run to the nearest microphone the minute it's over." Wilson then canceled the larger meeting and arranged to meet with Davis alone on January 14.

On January 13, Davis went public for the second time, but it did little to clarify the situation. "The environment forces people to act," he philosophized to *The Tribune*. "I always believed I could beat it, I could make the environment work for me. But this time it's forcing me to act in a way I never thought I would. I don't want to blame anyone. I'll survive. No, I'll dominate, not survive." The next day he met with Lionel Wilson for the first time.

Oakland's mayor emerged optimistic from that January 14 meeting. Davis, he claimed, "wants to stay here. There was no mention of the terms of the Los Angeles situation. . . . I'm just satisfied that he is trying to find a way to stay here. The meeting was warm, very friendly. I think we've set the stage for further meetings." At the time, however, no such further meetings were scheduled. First Wilson had to put together a new and larger offer for Davis. He immediately convened his task force for precisely that purpose. It would take three days.

In the meantime, Davis flew to L.A. for the Super Bowl festivities. On January 17, he was at a private party with a number of other owners and Rozelle. The hottest topic of conversation was a column by Mel Durslag in that day's *Herald Examiner*: "Why the NFL Is out of Line Sermonizing to Al Davis." Starting with the theory that the greatest potential hazard on the NFL horizon was a challenge from Al Davis over the right to move south, Durslag wrote,

> Davis admits readily he could lose the vote in a politically inspired atmosphere in which the commissioner and

certain members have begun sermonizing on the evils of
deserting fans who have supported a club loyally. . . . In
blissful silence, if not with admiration, the commissioner
and the owners watched their late brother in Los Angeles
use his franchise to make the biggest heist in sports history
at Anaheim. . . . Did his colleagues concern themselves
with hometown loyalty in Los Angeles, which had supported
the Rams since 1946? . . . The owners have gone too far to
start sermonizing at this point. Having created the cut-throat
environment that they have, they can't sell anyone the notion
that their hearts bleed for the suffering fans of Oakland. If
they tell the fans of Los Angeles that their football needs are
being served in Anaheim, they also can tell the fans of Oakland
that their football needs are being served in San Francisco,
only a third the distance Los Angeles is from Anaheim.

Rozelle mentioned the column to Davis. "I don't remember the article directly," Davis explained. "Pete espoused
to me that a lot of them were upset about it and [said]
Georgia was one who was upset about it. . . . She had been
taken on quite heavily in the newspapers, and he mentioned that
to me [as well]." The two men did not mention Davis's negotiations with either Oakland or L.A.

Back in Oakland earlier on Thursday, Lionel Wilson had been
called out of meetings on several occasions to speak with Davis
on the phone. On Friday, January 18, Wilson had a new proposal to make. The big news of Friday, however, was on Davis's
L.A. front. The LAMCC dropped a new legal grenade in the
League's lap in Los Angeles Federal District Court. Stating that
the Oakland Raiders "are on the verge of transferring to Los
Angeles" it asked that *LAMCC v. NFL* be immediately revived
from legal dormancy. It also asked that the NFL be enjoined from
exercising Section 4.3 of its constitution and barred from taking
"punitive action against the Raiders." If such relief were not
granted, the LAMCC claimed, it would be "prevented from closing
a deal" with Davis. The move took the League by surprise but
didn't provide any definitive answer to its questions about Davis.
Since the Raiders were a defendant in *LAMCC v. NFL*, the NFL's
attorneys immediately contacted Davis's attorneys to ask if they
should continue to represent him in light of the LAMCC's most
recent action. Davis's attorneys, according to Rozelle, "called
back and said to continue to represent them until further notice."
Rozelle himself did not learn of the LAMCC's surprise move

until late on Friday afternoon. That evening was his annual party for the sporting press, a lavish affair for as many as three thousand guests. The new L.A. injunction was, according to Rozelle, "a major point of conversation [at] . . . that party." Rozelle remembered that at the time, the most common refrain "was 'What can we do to stop them if they are going to move without approval?' . . . I took the position of 'We should give Al an opportunity to come to the League and ask for a vote.' "

Though Davis skipped the party, Rozelle knew of his upcoming meeting with the group from Oakland. Lionel Wilson had called the commissioner and said the Oakland delegation would also like to talk to him while they were in L.A. Rozelle said he'd be glad to talk with them. However, "They said Davis had gotten wind that they were going to meet with me," Rozelle remembered, "and he had said he would not negotiate with them at all if they met with me." Oakland had "no choice" but to cancel their gathering with the commissioner.

Instead, they met with Al Davis. Wilson's offer totaled $8 million, including sixty-four luxury boxes, a $4 million unsecured loan, and a five-year lease. While it was not everything Davis wanted, it was a place to start. "They were well on their way to satisfying me," Davis remembered. "I was greatly encouraged. It was the first meaningful proposal I had ever had. [Now] I could make an intelligent decision where I couldn't rule them out. Up until the point they came to see me. . . . They weren't even close. . . . I gave them . . . the outline of an agreement as I thought it would be, and it was a list of all the things that were necessary for us to evaluate as to whether we stay in Oakland or not. . . . We then both went back to our respective locations."

Davis would later claim the meeting had made a significant impact. "I was pretty solid in the middle of January that I would move," he explained, but then "there was a change in developments that altered my thinking." Wilson apparently picked up on the shift in Davis's mindset. He said the discussion led him "to believe that Davis will remain in Oakland."

Others got the same message from Davis as well. He told Tex Schramm that Oakland had made an offer that he might have to take. Not long after Wilson had left, Davis saw Jim Kensil, who ran the Jets for Leon Hess, in the Beverly Wilshire bar. Davis had a glass of ice water and talked. "He led me to believe he was going to cut a deal with Oakland," Kensil remembered.

However, Davis had also used his time in L.A. to conduct a

more than six-hour meeting with Bill Robertson and the LAMCC's attorney. To the L.A. contingent he gave the opposite impression. "That day," Robertson remembered, "we knew Al Davis was serious about Los Angeles."

Al Davis left L.A. before the Super Bowl game. Since his own team wasn't in it, he decided to watch the game on television at home in Oakland with his wife. He gave his game tickets to Robertson. Before leaving town, he also called Rozelle's hotel room. According to Rozelle's later court testimony, Davis told him, " 'A lot of things are being said about the Raiders in the papers and otherwise the last two days that . . . aren't exactly true.' " Rozelle thought the statement reinforced his position "that we should give Davis every chance to come to the League for a vote." But, in truth, on Super Bowl Sunday 1980, no one in the League felt he knew just what Al Davis intended to do.

That, of course, was just the way Al Davis wanted it.

30
The Mob Makes a Play?

Perhaps the most anxious of those watching Al Davis at the Super Bowl XIV festivities was Georgia Rosenbloom. And her nervousness continued unabated. According to a source close to the Rams owner, she placed some thirty to forty phone calls to Rozelle—both at home and at work—during the first two months of 1980. Within a day of the commissioner's arrival for the Super Bowl festivities, Georgia had called him twice. The gist of her conversation was, according to her secretary's later testimony, "The Raiders are coming. Why do we have to put up with this? How can it be handled?" Once again, Rozelle told her not to worry, "it would be handled."

There were, however, a lot of other things besides Al Davis on Georgia's mind during Super Bowl week. She and Rozelle also discussed tickets to the game. Georgia had more of them than anybody else in the country—as one of the Super Bowl participants, the Rams were allotted 22.5 percent of the game's 102,000 seats. Since the Rams were the official host franchise as well, they were allotted another ten percent. That gave Georgia almost thirty-five thousand tickets with a face value of thirty dollars and a resale value of almost four times that much. In addition to being the single largest source of tickets, Georgia was also, according to *Time*, "the star" of the media hype that surrounded this year's NFL championship contest. Georgia nonetheless complained to Rozelle about her press coverage at regular intervals. She considered most things written about her "hatchet jobs."

However unfavorable, none of those stories questioned whether or not she ran the team. As Steve Rosenbloom had predicted, most of the holdovers from her late husband Carroll's organization were either gone or on their way out and Georgia was now charting her own course. One of the people she relied on for advice was her live-in personal lyricist, Dominic Frontiere. Another was Hugh Culverhouse, owner of the Tampa Bay Buccaneers and one of the executors of Carroll Rosenbloom's estate.

For the actual running of the team, Georgia relied on Don Klosterman, the most long-lived remnant of the C.R. days. Klosterman had grown up in and around Compton and Lynwood with Pete Rozelle, whom he'd known since he was eleven years old. According to Steve, Klosterman was "a survivor. He's like a cat landing on his feet. He doesn't really work, he's just a PR guy who does a lot of name-dropping." Steve had wanted to demote or fire Klosterman after C.R.'s death, but Georgia fired Steve instead. Klosterman was Steve's replacement. "The press has vilified Georgia," he argued. "And what did she do? She made C.R. happy for twenty years."

One of Klosterman's immediate duties after assuming the reins from Steve was liaison with his old friend the commissioner over questions of Davis and an L.A. move. The two had discussed the subject on five or six occasions, and Klosterman would later claim that he never objected on behalf of the Rams to a Raiders move but did express his feelings that Davis should come to the League for a vote. At the same time, Klosterman's public position was a little more nebulous. "There's the question of oversaturation of the market," he pointed out in September 1979. "We have four teams in California now. . . . There are other places—Phoenix, Indianapolis, Memphis, Charlotte, and Birmingham—worthy of consideration. Why not spread the wealth around?" Klosterman's private, unofficial position was apparently different as well. "The fucking Raiders aren't going to make it down here," he allegedly fumed, "no way."

Klosterman certainly assisted Georgia on the subject. She had only the barest grasp of the issues and strategies involved. Later she would claim she would have supported a Raider move if only Davis had been "nicer to me." When the LAMCC dropped its new legal bombshell on Friday of Super Bowl week, it registered only dimly on Mrs. Rosenbloom. Her lawyer told her that "something" had been filed in conjunction with *LAMCC v. NFL*, but she "did not understand what it meant."

Though it was the best role she'd ever played, Georgia was the first to offer that owning the Rams was no piece of cake. "Carroll always wanted the Rams to be fun for me," she claimed, "fun and profitable. That's why . . . he gave me the club. I should be having fun. I don't know why I'm not." One reason might have been the uncomfortable residue of the house-cleaning she'd begun by firing Steve six months earlier. It had generated bad press and public bitterness that was still continuing at the time of Super Bowl XIV. According to Rozelle, it gave rise to the most "bizarre" incident in the League's entire January sojourn in Los Angeles.

At the center of the incident was Harold Guiver, C.R.'s "vice-president of operations." Guiver and C.R. first got to know each other when Guiver began representing athletes and coaches in 1975. Later that year, Rosenbloom helped Guiver finance a shopping center project. In late 1976, C.R. touted Guiver to Al Davis as the man who could help them make a killing on the resale of Super Bowl tickets. C.R. began trying to recruit Guiver for the Rams around the same time as his discussion with Davis about scalping Super Bowl tickets, and by 1978, had succeeded. Mostly Guiver handled the negotiation of player contracts and similar chores. According to Don Klosterman, when Steve left and Klosterman became general manager, Guiver was "no longer needed."

Guiver had been a partisan of Steve and knew his days were numbered. By October 1979, the only question was whether he would resign or be fired. Guiver wanted to be fired, so the Rams would be forced to settle the employment contract C.R. had given him. Georgia wanted him to quit and said she would take care of him as Carroll would have. He ought to trust her, she argued, just like he would have trusted C.R. Guiver didn't, so they negotiated throughout the fall. C.R.'s previous deal with Guiver contained a number of aspects besides just salary. To lure Guiver to the franchise, Rosenbloom had forgiven a $140,000 note, given him a Mercedes, and promised him a minimum of 1,000 Super Bowl tickets at face value any time the Super Bowl was held in L.A. The biggest fight between Georgia Rosenbloom and Harold Guiver was over those tickets.

On October 24, according to Guiver's later testimony, he met with her in her Bel-Air bedroom suite. According to Georgia, he claimed that Steve had promised him 3,000 to 4,000 Super Bowl tickets and "to avoid embarrassment" he needed at least 1,000. Each claimed that the other "kept changing the terms" of the proposed settlement. According to Guiver, Georgia asked him how much Super Bowl tickets were worth. He said it was a matter of "speculation" but guessed $100 apiece, $70 more than their face value. When they reached a deal, Georgia claims Guiver suggested her attorney should draw up the agreement, and Guiver claimed he drafted and signed a letter of agreement that evening. The note he signed, which later became a trial exhibit, read:

The Rams will honor the commitment for 1,000 Super Bowl tickets made to me by Carroll Rosenbloom, and after the death of Carroll reaffirmed to me by Steve Rosenbloom. I agree to reimburse the Rams for the cost of the tickets and enclose my check for $30,000 to cover cost of same. These tickets will be used to fulfill the commitment I have made. The tickets will [be delivered] before Dec. 20, 1979.

Harold B. Guiver

Georgia informed her lawyer and told him that she wanted to get the League's permission to release 1,000 tickets to Guiver. To do so, she phoned Rozelle's office. Rozelle told her that Carroll's verbal promise of Super Bowl tickets was not in the contract itself but since Steve had confirmed it, he didn't see how she could get out of it. Given that Guiver "would be using them for public relations, clubs, and officials he had promised them to," Rozelle saw "no problem" from the League's standpoint. Soon thereafter, Guiver delivered a $30,000 check to her attorney.

By November, according to Guiver, Georgia had changed the terms; she was now insisting on $100 a ticket instead of face value, an extra $70,000. She wanted Guiver to disguise the payment by agreeing to pay $22,000 for his Mercedes, a "gift" from C.R. the papers for which were still held by the Rams, and $48,000 on his $140,000 note, which he claimed Carroll had already forgiven entirely. Guiver resented the demand, later describing it as an attempt to extort, but agreed to her terms. They also acknowledged "there is no ill will between us" and agreed that "each of us will keep this agreement entirely confidential between ourselves."

By the time Super Bowl XIV moved into L.A., however, Harold Guiver was upset with Georgia. "You have violated the confidentiality clause on probably more occasions than I know," Guiver claimed. "Someone very high in your organization said he knew I received 1,000 Super Bowl tickets in my settlement. A ticket broker told me the same thing and said he could supply locations. I denied any knowledge of this and the person in your organization said he could prove I was lying." Guiver was also offended at how he was being treated by the Rams. He was now, he pointed out, "persona non grata" and thought the treatment unfair. Guiver claimed that when he'd tried to get tickets for the big party celebrating the Rams' trip to the Super Bowl, Klosterman had not only vetoed his request, but did so in language that his secretary was embarrassed to repeat. When Guiver got tickets from another source, Georgia was surprised to see him. "What's he doing here?" she asked.

Mrs. Rosenbloom had her own worries about Guiver. He was associated with her stepson Steve and despite admonitions from Rozelle, Steve was known as the source of a lot of information to the press about what had gone on inside the Rams. What to do about Steve had been a subject of discussion among Georgia and her advisers throughout the fall. That January, she may well have been worried that Guiver, too, was funneling derogatory information to the newspapers, though he steadfastly denied it. "I have lived up to all the terms of the agreement, and the Rams have not!" he claimed.

The most severe of those Rams violations, according to Guiver, happened on the day of the commissioner's giant press bash. It began when someone identifying himself as "Jack Catain" called Guiver at home and said he would like to meet him "on unspecified business matters." A year and a half earlier, Jack M. Catain Jr. had been identified by *The New York Times* as "a key conduit in laundering at least $10 million in organized crime money." The *Times* also claimed "numerous financial and personal links between Mr. Catain and leading organized crime figures or their associates from all over the country. In addition, Mr. Catain has been involved with some of them in such activities as extortion and loan sharking." Although Guiver claimed that Catain was a stranger, he agreed to meet him at the Al Brooks Ticket Agency, the owner of which was one of Guiver's best friends.

When Guiver arrived for the private meeting, Catain had brought along another man whom he identified as "Cohen." Guiver described them both as "swarthy" looking. According to Guiver, Catain and Cohen told him that someone in the Rams had "set the visit in motion" but that they were not "sent by the Rams." They also told Guiver "he did not want to know who sent them." Their message was simple: Keep "his mouth shut" about the Rams. They also wanted Steve Rosenbloom to shut up as well. Guiver said he could speak only for himself, but that he had not said anything publicly against the Rams and promised he never would. Guiver later described Catain and Cohen in a trial deposition as being "gangsters" from the "Mafia" and claimed they had threatened his life before the meeting broke up. After Catain's visit, Guiver called Steve Rosenbloom, who Guiver described as "very upset."

Next, Guiver called Rozelle and arranged to meet at Rozelle's L.A. hotel, along with Rozelle's in-house counsel, Jay Moyer. Their conference lasted forty-five minutes. Guiver told Rozelle and Moyer about his visit from Catain and Cohen and now claimed he had "documentation that they were bad people." He wanted Rozelle to talk to everyone and clear it up. Specifically, he wanted the commissioner to arrange for him to meet with Klosterman so they could "get things straightened out." According to Guiver, Rozelle was "incredulous," but called Klosterman with Guiver in the room, asked if Klosterman knew Catain, and got a negative response. Then Rozelle explained to Klosterman what Guiver had been saying. "I said I would like Klosterman to meet with him," Rozelle remembered. "Klosterman said 'Sure.' Don said he hadn't had anything to do with it. He didn't particularly like Guiver but hadn't encouraged anyone to threaten him."

Soon afterwards, Guiver met again with Catain, this time at Guiver's instigation. Guiver again made it clear he had nothing bad to say about the Rams. "Frightened," Guiver then asked Jack Catain to accompany him to his meeting with Klosterman the next morning "and judge for himself."

To that meeting in Klosterman's apartment, Catain again brought along his friend Cohen. According to Guiver, Klosterman expressed surprise at Catain's presence. According to Klosterman, Catain was "uninvited" and Guiver told him he "was concerned people were talking about him in a degrading way." Klosterman claimed he said "let bygones be bygones" and that Catain started to say something but got no further. Klosterman interrupted Catain, said he was an uninvited guest and had nothing to say. Then Klosterman ended the meeting after it had gone on for no more than five minutes. He claimed to have been "very abusive" when speaking to Catain. According to Rozelle, Klosterman also claimed that Catain and Cohen had "threatened him."

In any case, Guiver, Catain, and Cohen left Klosterman's apartment almost immediately and neither Rozelle nor Klosterman heard any more from them. Just who had originally dispatched them to shut Guiver up was never clarified. There would later be newspaper reports that Catain had been a guest in Georgia's owner's box, but those were adamantly denied by Dominic Frontiere, now her constant companion. He claimed Georgia did not know Catain at all and that Frontiere himself had heard of Catain only "in connection with his charitable works." Georgia herself had learned of Guiver's charges on January 21 from

Rozelle. Rozelle had told her that Guiver was coming to see him the next day and was already maintaining that Klosterman had sent someone from the Rams to "tell Guiver to keep his mouth shut or something would happen to him." Georgia told the commissioner it was a "ridiculous" claim.

Nonetheless, when Harold Guiver was looking for someone to complain to about the affair after it was over, he wrote a letter to Mrs. Georgia Rosenbloom, dated January 28, 1980. "Georgia," Guiver objected, "the person or persons in your organization who instigated this ought to be *very* ashamed of themselves. That is a *dirty, foul* way to act and the tragic part of the whole matter is that the complaints about me are mere figments of someone's imagination. . . . Since I left, I have refused to talk to . . . anyone about Rams problems. . . . I have *no* desire to cause trouble to anyone in the Rams organization and I want to be left alone. . . . I am very hurt by what has happened."

Although Guiver claimed Rozelle had promised to "look into it," he heard no more. Klosterman talked to Rozelle and later sent him a formal memo about the incident, claiming he could not find out who had sent Catain. Klosterman also interviewed with the head of NFL Security. "It was absolutely bizarre," Rozelle remembered, "the entire situation." Nonetheless, the material Security accumulated went no further than a file in the League office.

By the time it had all been gathered, of course, Al Davis's Los Angeles front had broken open once again and Pete Rozelle had a lot more pressing questions to answer than where Jack Catain had come from.

31
Crossing the Rubicon

While Pete Rozelle was talking with Harold Guiver, Al Davis was back in Oakland negotiating. On January 22, he met with a representative of Mayor Lionel Wilson's task force, Cornell Maier, head of Kaiser Industries. After this talk, Davis remembered, "we started to have a meeting of the minds. . . . I was walking around thinking we had a chance to have a deal." That state of mind lasted through January. Davis had his attorneys meet with Kaiser Industries' attorneys to work on language and Davis himself made a tour of the Oakland Coliseum with its luxury box architect. On January 24, Davis announced that he now wanted Oakland to produce a formal offer from the Coliseum board. "The Los Angeles offer is more substantial," Davis noted, "but what Oakland has going for it is great tradition." Once Oakland's formal offer was in hand, Davis intended to decide where he was going by February 5.

None of these developments was lost on L.A. "This city is about to blow the Raider deal," Mel Durslag trumpeted in the *Herald Examiner*. "We've got a chance to get the Raiders. Al Davis is ready to move, believe me. But all he hears is promises, and promises aren't good enough for a smart businessman. Politicians are worried about some cost to the taxpayers but the only cost to the taxpayers here would be if the Raiders do not come to Los Angeles. A little city like Anaheim has the guts to assert itself and get the Rams while Los Angeles is left at the gate while politicians grandstand. Someone has to step forward now, pick up this issue, and run with it, but nobody has shown the guts to take the leadership. This city is losing the Raiders and deservedly so because elected public officials are sitting on their hands."

Durslag was angry at the L.A. County Board of Supervisors, whose $5 million loan was essential to pull off a Raider move. A number of their supervisors "complained that they had not been given adequate information about negotiations with the Raiders." One even called the expense of luxury boxes "inappropri-

ate for a publicly owned stadium.'' The strongest opposition
argument, however, was simply against going out on a limb. The
Coliseum, the *Los Angeles Times* observed, ''cannot consummate the deal with the Raiders unless they are certain the Raiders
will be allowed to move. Otherwise, they say, they could wind
up building the [luxury] boxes and be left without a team to pay
for them if the Raiders were denied permission.''

By the first week after Super Bowl XIV, the League's growing anger at Davis was a public fact. ''I object strenuously to
unilateral action,'' Art Modell told the *L.A. Times*. ''Either we have
a structure, a constitution and bylaws, or we don't. Davis has had
sellouts for thirteen years [in Oakland]. . . . It's wrong to litigate
to get a franchise shift.'' Modell was by no means alone. Herman Sarkowsky described Davis's approach as ''totally wrong''
and claimed ''most owners are like I am.''

''By early January 1980,'' Davis claimed three months later,
''the prospects of the Raiders and the LACC reaching an . . .
agreement looked very good. From that time . . . [till] the present, certain members of the NFL and . . . the Oakland [Coliseum]
commission, began a concerted campaign to intimidate and prevent the Raiders from transferring to Los Angeles. . . . From
that time forward, I received a variety of threats and warnings
from NFL Commissioner Pete Rozelle and from certain franchise
owners, such as Eugene Klein of the San Diego Chargers and
Mr. Sarkowsky of the Seattle Seahawks, that I had better not
take any steps to move to Los Angeles without *prior* NFL
approval. . . . NFL personnel stated publicly on a variety of
occasions that the Raiders could not obtain NFL approval of their
transfer and would have to remain in Oakland.''

The League's opposition was certainly a factor in L.A.'s
thinking. The odds against Davis winning an NFL vote were
already sufficient to make signing a binding lease before he
moved a political impossibility.

The League's opposition was also a significant factor back in
Oakland. There, it helped fuel a fatal counterattack, opened by
Jack Maltester, against Wilson and Maier's approach to negotiations. Maltester, president of the Oakland Coliseum board, claimed
the mayor and Maier had offered Davis a ''secret'' deal which
would give so much away that the Coliseum would run in the
red.

The Raiders responded to Maltester through Al LoCasale.
''Jack Maltester has not been a party to negotiations for a
number of weeks,'' LoCasale pointed out. ''. . . and I don't

want to give credence to what he says." Maltester's outburst was, however, only the opening round.

On February 1, the Oakland Coliseum board finalized its offer at a meeting in which Wilson and Maier were repudiated as negotiators. The offer was apparently at odds with the one to which Davis and Wilson had already agreed; for one thing, the lease changed from five years to ten. On that same afternoon, Wilson and Maier visited Davis and Davis remembered, "[they] told me they were no longer the negotiating committee, that the offer would have to be withdrawn. They were sorry."

Sorry or not, Davis's response was immediate and decisive.

"No one in good conscience can question the lousy way we've been treated," Al LoCasale told *The Tribune* on February 2. "We've discovered that the credibility and integrity of the people the Raiders have been dealing with has not changed. It's been this way for twelve years—arrogance, procrastination, deceit, and misrepresentation." A coliseum official pointed out in response that the Raiders had not even yet seen the Coliseum's offer but that apparently didn't matter. On February 3, the Raiders' PR director announced, "Negotiations are dead. I doubt we would even look at any new offer. Nothing will bring us back to the negotiating table with Oakland."

On February 4, when Oakland's attorney attempted to deliver the Coliseum's formal written offer of some twenty pages, Al LoCasale refused to accept the twenty pages and told the attorney to take them away with him. Instead, the attorney left the document on the counter and turned to go. At that point, according to Al Davis, LoCasale grabbed the document and "came over the counter," demanding that the attorney take it back. When LoCasale chased him into the parking lot and he still wouldn't take it back, LoCasale flung the lease offer on the asphalt and left it there. Davis later read the document, but only as a matter of curiosity. His attention was focused on maneuvering with the League.

Immediately after his visit from Wilson and Maier, Davis had called Rozelle and informed him that "Wilson and Maier had come to his office and said the offer they made was no longer available." According to the commissioner, Davis "then asked for a straw vote [over the phone] of the membership to find out where he stood" on the possibility of an L.A. move.

Rozelle refused. "I told him that if I were to take a straw vote," Rozelle explained, "there were a number of questions the members would want to know [sic] before they even gave a straw poll opinion. . . . I told him I couldn't call twenty-seven clubs on the telephone and tell them what was being considered . . . when I didn't have all the facts. I felt the best way was for him to ask for a League meeting.''

Concerned that any such meeting would end up being used to hold a formal vote which he did not want, Davis requested none. Asked to characterize the way Rozelle treated him at this time, Davis allowed ''at times he is pretty good and other times he is just as vindictive as can be.'' As evidence of this vindictiveness, Davis cited ''his public pronouncements, long before I ever considered moving, that I shouldn't move, that I should stay in Oakland; his . . . not telling the other owners as to what I was doing. . . . Instead, [he] polarized them.'' Bill Robertson in L.A. shared Davis's assessment. ''The League would have let Max Winter move,'' Robertson claimed. ''This was a personality thing, Pete versus Al. Al was not a rubber stamp kinda guy and Rozelle saw him as a threat.''

Rozelle steadfastly denied any such motivation. ''It's easier for Al to say it's a fight between him and Rozelle than to say it's a fight between him and twenty-seven other owners who disagreed with him,'' the commissioner explained. ''I enjoyed being with Al. The only difference I had with Al was on the League rules. You get a lack of unity, this disintegration, when one person can get away with violating the prime rule of the League. It also sets the stage for others to follow.''

Rozelle and Davis settled into an uneasy peace for several weeks after their February 2 phone call. Both were waiting to see how the court would rule on L.A.'s request for a restraining order on Section 4.3. Hearings on the request began on February 4 and lasted until February 21.

Meantime, Davis continued his negotiations with Robertson. Since a firm lease was impossible, the two had decided to draw up a memorandum of agreement that would frame the deal on paper. During Davis's final flirtation with Oakland, the total L.A. commitment had grown to $18.5 million: $14.5 million for improvements, and $4 million for relocation expenses. The agreement called for a seven-year lease, with an additional five three-year options to be exercised at the Raiders' discretion. The Raiders also would be ''compensated for the expenses involved'' if the League blocked their move.

Legally, the memorandum of agreement was little more than a nonbinding agreement to agree. The matter was subject to the agreement of the board of supervisors, to the approval of the

Coliseum board, and to county approval. While it was unlikely Al Davis really accepted the notion that any political approval would be a "formality," the situation had intensified enough that he was now willing to accept such assurance from Robertson and Halin. For most of February, the question was not whether Davis would sign L.A.'s memorandum of agreement, but only when.

Pete Rozelle awaited Davis's move in New York, and continued to take phone calls from Georgia Rosenbloom. The conversations were about all the votes Al Davis didn't have to support his move. A vote would be held, Rozelle assured Mrs. Rosenbloom, whether Davis requested it or not.

On February 21, L.A. Federal District Court granted the LAMCC's injunction against Section 4.3. The League then immediately obtained a stay of the order from the federal circuit court. Section 4.3 remained in force. On February 22, Oakland weighed in with its own action in California Superior Court, claiming the right to condemn the Oakland Raiders football franchise under the same eminent domain law with which it condemned land for freeways and housing projects. It also sought and got a temporary restraining order preventing the Raiders from moving without a court hearing.

By February 26, about to risk everything, Al Davis paused for a moment. Rozelle was already on record threatening the possible loss of his franchise should he fail, and even his support in L.A. was already shaky. "No one else would have gone forward at that point," one source close to Davis pointed out, "but Al Davis is built different than the rest of the League. In truth, he didn't have anything he could count on except Bill Robertson." For Davis, that was apparently enough. "I'm going all the way if you are," he told Robertson.

On Saturday, March 1, 1980, Al Davis announced his move, in the office of L.A. Mayor Tom Bradley. The press corps was there to watch the ceremony. Davis told them he had no intention of asking the League for a vote. He planned to move whether the League liked the idea or not.

The most decisive battle in NFL history was about to commence. "Al Davis has crossed the Rubicon," Bill Robertson crowed. "Al Davis has made a commitment. He can't go back to Oakland now."

PART FOUR

OPEN
WARFARE

1

Apocalypse Now

Pete Rozelle and Al Davis fought their first open skirmish in Dallas at a special meeting of the NFL's executive session on March 3, 1980.

Though the annual meeting was scheduled for just a week later in Palm Springs, Rozelle was convinced that this business could not wait. The special meeting had been called in response to the temporary restraining order granted the LAMCC in federal court. Then Davis had signed his memorandum of agreement with L.A.

Davis himself had few doubts about what he was in for or how he would handle it. "We know it's going to be tough," he admitted on March 1. "There are going to be a lot of obstacles in the way, but I consider obstacles normal and treat them that way."

Davis left his attorney behind in San Francisco when he flew to Dallas. "Al asked me if I would go to the Dallas meeting with him," Joseph Alioto explained, "but I said no because we are not seeking litigation." Nonetheless, Davis was prepared. "We just want the same approval Rosenbloom got under similar circumstances," Alioto noted. "Rosenbloom signed his agreement with Anaheim, then had a press conference. Four months later, the NFL approved the move. Saturday, Al signed an agreement with Los Angeles and held a press conference. Monday he will seek approval. The NFL is now in the position where if they continue their actions of interfering with that contract, they would be in line for a damage suit by the Los Angeles Coliseum involving millions of dollars. I think the NFL would be well advised to sit down and straighten things out right now because if they take any foolish actions, it could only become worse for them."

Pete Rozelle saw the issues as "apocalypse now." "The greater issue is anarchy," he noted. "The next step a team could take contrary to League rule could be to enter into a pay TV contract . . . or they could sell their team to General Motors or Caesars Palace."

When the Dallas special meeting convened, the twenty-eight owners had already been given the materials previously distributed at the Raiders' March 1 press conference and copies of subsequent press accounts. Rozelle's first order of business was to procure an explanation from Davis himself. Did Mr. Davis wish to make a report?

Mr. Davis was not then prepared to do so, but would consider doing so "after the lunch break." Then, the commissioner noted, the morning would be used "to review the situation . . . so that [the League] could be advised of the legal developments and what options they had."

Quite specifically that meant a report on *LAMCC v. NFL*, a suit to which Rozelle now considered Davis, for all intents and purposes, a party. He was treated as such at Dallas. The minutes reported that Rozelle suggested, on advice of counsel, "that the Oakland representative excuse himself while privileged legal matters were discussed. Mr. Davis then left the meeting." For the rest of the morning the League and its attorneys discussed their options. At 12:45 P.M., they broke for lunch.

When they reconvened, Davis was once again present and ready to report. The minutes described Davis's speech as "a general recitation of his recollection of the Raiders' negotiating history in Oakland and with the Los Angeles Coliseum Commission, which culminated in the Raiders taking an adversary position in the pending litigation and signing a memorandum of agreement with the Los Angeles Coliseum Commission." According to the *Los Angeles Times*, Davis "said he told the owners he was 'committed to Los Angeles.' He said he had 'a traumatic feeling about leaving the fans in Oakland' but found himself in an 'untenable position' in negotiations with the Oakland Coliseum. . . . Davis said he thought many owners 'were receptive and wanted to hear me,' but added that it was nothing more than an impression."

In the following question and answer period, the first inquiries were from Rozelle. "Do you intend to move to Los Angeles?" Rozelle asked.

"Yes, of course," Davis answered.

Rozelle's second question was, "Do you intend to come to the League for a vote?"

"No," was Davis's second answer.

"I felt that brought it to a head," Rozelle said.

When the other owners' questions for Davis were finished, Rozelle initiated the League's response. "The commissioner

commented that under the circumstances more complete information should be made available to the membership regarding all
aspects of the proposed transfer, in the event a vote should
subsequently be requested by the Raiders *or otherwise.*" He
appointed a fact-finding committee to investigate the situation
and report to the annual meeting one week hence. Al Davis was
angry. "The committee he created was unprecedented. . . . To the
best of my knowledge, at no time prior to the transfer by the
Raiders did the NFL ever bother to create a fact-finding committee to pass upon the desirability of the transfer of any NFL team.
Moreover," he continued, "and over my objections, it stacked
that five-man committee with certain persons who were publicly
avowed opponents of the Raiders' transfer."

"It was a tough committee to pick," Rozelle admitted. "It
was hard to try and find someone with stature, time, and who
wasn't already on record as antagonistic to Davis." The group
he came up with consisted of Art Modell, Herman Sarkowsky,
George Halas, Wellington Mara, and Bill Bidwill. Sarkowsky
was named chairman. Of the five-man committee, only Mara
and Bidwill were not yet on public record opposing Davis's
move.

Rozelle assigned Art Modell the task of "ascertain[ing] the
views of the three television networks." Because of his presence
in New York, Wellington Mara would join him. To Sarkowsky,
Halas, and Bidwill went the job of meeting with the L.A.
Coliseum representatives to "hear their side of it," with Oakland's representatives to "learn what they were prepared to do,"
and with the Raiders to "obtain any information the Raiders
wished to convey." As the commissioner explained, "I told the
committee that it was not to make a recommendation but merely
to report on what they had learned."

"I felt it was an unfair committee," Davis remembered. "I
told Rozelle so right there in front of the committee. . . . In
roundabout terms, I alluded [to the fact that] it was a stacked
committee."

Art Modell took umbrage at Davis's inference. "I assume you
are referring to me," he interrupted. Modell's assumption was
reasonable. By his own admission, Modell already had "strong
convictions." He felt such "casual moving would hurt the League's
image." He also felt Davis was reneging on his contract with the
League calling for him to play his games in Oakland and that the
League had "a strong moral obligation" to Oakland for its
previous support. Most important, Modell noted, he had yet to

hear of "a single benefit to the NFL as a whole" from what
Davis wanted to do. Modell was convinced any committee of
five NFL members would reach the same conclusion.

"If Mr. Davis objects to me," Modell offered, "I will be
happy to get off the committee." Al Davis did not fall into the
trap. He understood full well that the more he involved himself
in the committee's composition, the more credibility he would be
giving its conclusions.

According to Rozelle, Davis gave "an unintelligible half-
sentence answer" to Modell's offer to resign. "I believe he
said something to the effect of, 'Oh, that's all right . . . or 'It's
all bad anyway' or something."

According to Davis, Rozelle was the first to respond to the
Cleveland owner's offer. "No," the commissioner said to Modell,
"you stay on."

Then Davis spoke up. "Look," he said to Rozelle, "you
picked your committee. You go ahead." After that, there was
nothing left to discuss.

2
Art Modell Enters the Fray

That Al Davis's first combat with Rozelle involved Art Modell
as well came as no surprise. Davis knew that any attack on the
commissioner would be parried by Rozelle's lieutenants, and
since Tex Schramm was somewhat neutralized by his relationship with Davis, Modell, who would increasingly become identified as Rozelle's alter ego, bore the brunt. Butting heads with Al
Davis was a welcome task for Modell, whose description of his
relationship with Davis as "fair" was an overstatement of major
proportions. Davis's contempt for Modell's pack-running was
obvious and Modell's contempt for Davis's free-lancing was
equally clear. Modell also resented Davis's insistence on going
after his friend Rozelle rather than the League as a whole.
"Davis tried to make it all a personal issue with Pete," Modell
explained, "and Pete's just not that way." Modell also defended
League Think because of his own reverence for the League as
an exclusive club. "Before Davis," he pointed out, "the constitution was our court and we washed our linen in private."

By the time of the Dallas meeting, Modell had reached the pinnacle of his standing in Cleveland. He had already been mentioned as a possible Republican party candidate for lieutenant governor of Ohio and, within the year, his name would come up as a possible candidate for governor. As well as owning a majority of the Browns and eighty percent of Cleveland Stadium Corp., he now had significant corporate and real estate holdings. He also had invested heavily in oil and gas leases, and owned WJW Radio with two partners. Whenever Modell's name was linked to political rumors, his success as a businessman was always cited.

Despite that public acclaim, there was, by 1980, a certain amount of illusion to Art Modell's apparent financial success. His radio station had lost money for three consecutive years and his Whitney Land Company had gotten nowhere with its Strongsville development. American Metal Forming seemed healthy but, in truth, was just two years away from a collapse that would cost Modell at least $400,000. When the Premier Electric Company went belly-up in 1979, it cost Modell $1 million. By March 1980, Modell's net worth apart from his holdings in the football business had already dropped substantially and showed little sign of changing course.

Modell's most worrisome investment that spring was Cleveland Stadium Corp. In 1979, it had reported a $180,000 post-depreciation loss, down from a $330,000 profit the year before. Two more losing years would follow. "It's literally a nonprofit organization," Modell claimed in 1980. According to the corporation's treasurer, Stadium Corp. had been able to make the principal payment on its loan only once in the previous six years. One reason, *The Cleveland Press* noted, was that "the forty-seven-year-old stadium, built on constantly settling landfill, has required far more maintenance than originally projected." The previous winter, part of the stadium's roof had blown off and before that, the pipes froze and burst, the main concourse sank, and the remodeling work already done had uncovered even more rusted-out support beams. All of that cost Modell much more than he'd planned. Another reason for Stadium Corp's financial shakiness was the failure of the baseball Indians, its second tenant, to draw enough paying customers.

By far the biggest reason for Modell's 1980 worries was interest rates. He had borrowed significantly to finance the stadium improvements and Stadium Corp.'s acquisition of his Strongsville land, and that borrowing now haunted him. He initially "borrowed at one point over prime. It was fine when it was 6.5 percent prime, but now I'm paying twenty-one percent on $8 million . . . and it's strangling us." In addition, Modell was also servicing almost $7 million of personal borrowings from banks and "other lenders."

The value of his controlling share in the NFL Browns insured that Modell's assets still significantly outdistanced his liabilities, but he was nonetheless cash poor. To help relieve the pinch, Modell regularly drew interest-free cash advances from the Browns, above and beyond his $60,000-a-year salary. At the end of the year, he would deduct the annual bonus voted him by the Browns board from the amount he had advanced himself and "settle accounts." To do so in 1980 had required borrowing $1 million. By then, Modell was actively considering ways to get out from under the burden of Stadium Corp.'s interest payments. His first attempt was at a breakfast meeting with Cleveland's new mayor, George Voinovich.

"George," Modell offered, "if the city has the wherewithal to reimburse me all my costs, you can have the lease back for $1 and I'll stay here with the Browns." Voinovich declined.

By the time the League met in Dallas, Modell was considering selling Stadium Corp. "I wasn't feeling too good," he claimed, "and I was concerned about my estate."

But despite his financial pressures and concerns for his health, Art Modell handled his fact-finding committee duties with dispatch during the week before the annual meeting. He and Wellington Mara met first with ABC, the League's Monday night prime time broadcaster. ABC was "reluctant to become involved in the NFL's problem" but did allow that they would "not be happy" if Monday night football ended up blacked out in L.A. as a consequence of Davis's move. CBS's attitude was much the same as ABC's only they were "even more reluctant to engage in any dialogue" over Al Davis's plans for L.A. NBC made "no recommendation" one way or the other.

On the West Coast, Herman Sarkowsky handled the logistics. For health reasons, George Halas sent his general manager, Jim Finks, to represent him. Davis sent Al LoCasale, to talk to them and then the committee met with Oakland and L.A. "We went through a charade," L.A.'s attorney remembered. "There was no warmth but no unpleasantness either. Everyone was being polite, going through the motions. It was absurd, an obvious farce. It was just done so they could make a report and say Davis shouldn't move." Bill Robertson felt the same way. "It was a

Playhouse 90 that Pete put together," the LAMCC negotiator claimed. "It was like dealing with someone who has all the cards and their marching orders. We wasted a couple of hours and were stupid enough to pick up the check."

By the time L.A. and the fact-finding committee met, it was obvious to all concerned that the League had no intention of waiting for the committee's report. Neither, of course, did Al Davis. Instead, Rozelle had launched a new attack as soon as the Dallas meeting was over and Davis had responded in kind. The attack was *Philadelphia Eagles et al v. Oakland Raiders Ltd.*, a suit filed on March 4 by NFL attorneys in Oakland's superior court, charging Davis with breach of contract and asking that he be restrained from moving his franchise. Eventually, it would also ask that Davis's franchise be removed from his control and placed in receivership. "We wanted to stop their action," Rozelle explained, "and we took every step we could think of to achieve that." All twenty-seven franchises were party to the action though just why Leonard Tose was picked to lead the list was never fully explained. A likely explanation was that Tose, like Davis, was represented by Joseph Alioto and the overlap might well force Alioto to rule himself out over a conflict of interest. "We were all kind of surprised it was the Philadelphia Eagles who instituted the lawsuit," Davis remembered, "because the Philadelphia Eagles have always espoused that I should have the right to move. . . . The Eagles themselves didn't know that their name was put on the top of it." According to Davis, the step had been taken by Chuck Sullivan and one of the League's attorneys.

According to Pete Rozelle, *Philadelphia Eagles v. Oakland Raiders Ltd.* was a step a number of League members had been pushing since before Dallas. Roselle claimed that "I said . . . I think it's important to give Al Davis every opportunity to ask for a vote." Even so, Rozelle had prepared for other contingencies. He had already retained an attorney in Oakland on behalf of the League. And during the privileged legal discussion in Dallas, Rozelle did not mention a specific suit, but asked for and was given "clear authorization to do whatever I see fit to stop the Raiders from doing this and violating the constitution." When Davis refused to request a vote, Rozelle immediately filed a state court action on breach of contract. The papers for doing so had already been drawn up.

"It was a directly related attempt to move the lawsuit out the theater it belonged in," Al Davis objected. "It another attempt to bring more attorneys int pressure on me financially. . . . There was no breach of contract. . . . There was no reason for the receivership."

On March 6, while receivership motions were still being prepared, the judge in the case granted a temporary restraining order barring the Raiders from actually setting up shop in L. A. At that point, according to Davis, two NFL private detectives had been staking out Raider headquarters, watching "every move that the organization made," for several days.

But Al Davis was still one step ahead. Before the temporary restraining order was issued, Davis dispatched a telegram to Pete Rozelle saying he had already moved.

This communication is to notify you respectfully that the Raiders have legally and formally moved to Los Angeles. Our contract with the Los Angeles Coliseum is in precisely the same posture as the Rams at the time they held their widely covered press conference in July 1978, announcing their move to Anaheim. Moreover, the statements at our press conference were in substance similar to theirs. In fact, our move is in the same posture as all other recent moves. The Rams and the others were not charged with fomenting anarchy . . . nor should we be so charged in following their example. Our love and dedication to professional football . . . will continue to endure. The facts are that the Oakland politicians have effectively closed out negotiations by repudiating their own negotiators and their commitments as well as resorting to tactics favoring sham litigation. But in any event, it is imprudent in the highest degree in all of these circumstances to deny the historic Los Angeles Coliseum a right to life after the League itself ratified the Rams' move from Los Angeles County to the different world of Orange County.

I trust that you will view our actions in the same spirit that you viewed the others.

> Sincerely,
> Al Davis

meda County sheriff's deputies arrived at the Raider ffices on March 6 to enforce the restraining order, to impound were the telephones. All the rest ss was loaded in vans that had long since [Oakland] *Tribune* reporter found Davis d abandoned building that evening, looking "bleary-eyed, his tousled hair flopped over his forehead, and he sported several days' growth of beard on his chin."

"I feel a lot of nostalgia about it," Davis offered in a soft voice. "I've lived here for eighteen years. I love Oakland and the fans, I really do. I feel passive about it. I just think that you take a certain direction in life and you make things happen and you hope it all works out for the best. You anticipate the roadblocks and see various ways around them and you make it happen."

3
Hardball All the Way

The 1980 annual meeting was held at a resort in Palm Springs. Pete and Carrie Rozelle had a bungalow very close to that given Al Davis, who observed Art Modell, Gene Klein, Don Klosterman, Wellington Mara, Bill Bidwill, and Chuck Sullivan all go in to consult with the commissioner. Most of those Sunday meetings, according to Rozelle, were brief.

The longest was with Herman Sarkowsky, chairman of the fact-finding committee, who, Rozelle remembered, "told me that . . . he felt there probably was some fault on both sides [of the Oakland-Davis negotiations]." Sarkowsky also reported that the television networks "did not want to get very involved."

Perhaps the most telling of the commissioner's consultations, was his talk with Chuck Sullivan. Rozelle told Billy's son that he was through waiting for Davis to ask for a vote. Whether Davis wanted it or not, Rozelle "intended to see that a vote was taken." According to the commissioner, Chuck Sullivan was in accord with his intention, and offered to make the motion whenever Rozelle wanted the vote.

Pete Rozelle opened the annual meeting the following morning. The first item of business was the commissioner's annual report and, as usual, it was full of superlatives. Regular season live gate had passed thirteen million for the first time in history. Super Bowl XIV in L.A. had drawn an audience of more th one hundred million, making it the most-watched spo in the history of television.

During much of the morning session, small groups of owners caucused on the side in preparation for the afternoon's executive session at which Al Davis was to be discussed. Davis himself spent a good portion of the morning on his veranda, holding court with selected reporters. He claimed his team had sold more than thirty thousand season tickets during its first five days in L.A. and rented seventy of its projected ninety-nine luxury boxes. "I'm not for anarchy," Davis offered in his own defense. "I love the NFL. But I'll be damned if I'm going to let those Oakland people hold me hostage."

Back at the general session, according to *Sports Illustrated*, the commissioner "already looks tired and it's only Monday." Eventually, Rozelle left the meeting room for a cigarette, was cornered by reporters, and used the opportunity to fire his opening salvo. "Al says he's not for anarchy and I'm sure he wants a stable League," the commissioner pointed out. "He just wants anarchy for himself. I don't know why he didn't seek League support when he was having trouble over his lease with the politicians in Oakland. . . . I don't know why he didn't let the other owners know what was happening. When Bob Irsay had a problem in Baltimore, I had a meeting with the governor and the mayor. . . . Same thing in Minnesota last year. The Vikings are going to play in a new domed stadium in 1982. There are ways of working these things out and if you can't, then you go to the other owners. . . . But Al chose to do things his own way. I guess the carrot was just too big down there in L.A."

At the League's executive session, the first item of business was a legal report on the Davis move. Davis was immediately asked to leave and was readmitted two hours later. Next came the report by the fact-finding committee. According to Rozelle, "the television report was inconclusive because the networks said . . . we don't want to tell you how to run your business. In effect they said, 'You take your chances.' " Wellington Mara went slightly further. He, Rozelle remembered, "said that one or more of the networks . . . expressed concern about this entire situation if the League was not going to have control over where its franchises were located. They expressed concern for the . . . Davis remembered it, Mara held up a copy of the . . . and said the networks' concern was for the . . . book, this constitution and bylaws."

. . . Davis claimed.

. . . "reviewed meetings and conversations . . . in Oakland and Los Angeles." To

accompany his presentation, he had large display graphs of
Oakland's offer but none of L.A.'s. Davis remembered that
Sarkowsky ". . . told what they [L.A.] were going to offer and it
was a very fine deal and it was a very lucrative deal, and he
brought in the fact that they kind of threatened [that] if [the
League] didn't go along, [the League] would be sued. Then
[Sarkowsky] went into the meeting with the Oakland people.
And it was very subjective. It was not all the facts that were
given to them.''

In response, Al Davis stood and cut loose, addressing the
fact-finding committee. ''I told them that the thing was totally
subjective,'' Davis claimed, ''that I didn't like it and it wasn't
fair. . . . I told them . . . in no uncertain terms, that they are not
men. . . . I told Modell that. . . . I didn't think he acted with any
courage or truth. Sarkowsky, I told to his face . . . I didn't think
he did an honest job. Mara, I never said a word [to] about it. I
understand Wellington. . . .''

''I thought it was an unfair report,'' he continued, so ''I
explained to them about my negotiations with . . . Cornell Maier
and Mayor Wilson and how they were repudiated and . . . went
into the reason why I thought I ought to be allowed to move to
Los Angeles.'' At this point, ''some gentleman from Buffalo, an
attorney, Halpern, stood up and said, 'Mr. Davis, are you going
to abide by this constitution and bylaws? Are you going to ask
for a vote?' And I said I didn't think a vote was necessary. He
[again] said, 'Are you going to ask for a vote?' I said, 'I tell you
what I will do, as we so often do in this membership. Commissioner Rozelle, you poll the members. A straw vote. And see
what the vote will be. . . .' I said I am not going to ask for a
vote if I can't get a polled vote.''

Rozelle's lawyer recommended against any straw vote—a conclusion Rozelle himself had already reached. ''The Rubicon had
been crossed,'' he explained. . . .'' As Rozelle saw it, Davis
was asking for a privilege he had already forfeited. Rozelle also
claimed that he made no recommendation on the move himself,
but ''just chaired the meeting. . . .''

According to Rozelle, virtually everyone who spoke offered
arguments against Davis's move. One of reasons given, the
commissioner remembered, ''Was the theory of self-governance.
They felt that having a team move without a vote . . . was a very
unhealthy precedent for the League. . . . Two, the business
uncertainties, because the matter had not been carefully explored. . . . Also . . . the League had the right to derive the

benefits of an expansion franchise . . . in Los Angeles. I think an expansion franchise in Los Angeles would be worth more than the other cities in the League. . . . That money should be shared by the twenty-eight partners and they felt that they would be precluded if Oakland took it.'' On top of that, ''a number of them were concerned about what they felt was the erosion of goodwill for the League to have a team that had sellouts at the gate . . . leave it because it could do better elsewhere.''

Perhaps the most emotional of the speeches was delivered by George Halas, dean of the Old Guard. ''He brought up stories from the 1920s and 1930s,'' Rozelle recalled, ''to illustrate some early problems the League had on violations and how they were handled. . . . He was very concerned about the preservation of the solidarity of the League as represented by, in his mind, observance of the constitution. He was very upset that a team would attempt to move from its location without asking for a vote and then just saying, as the Raiders did on March 6, that they had already moved. And he said that he could foresee deep problems for the League in the future if that sort of conduct were to be condoned.''

When Halas was done, Chuck Sullivan took the floor and called for a vote. Rozelle would later admit that he knew Sullivan was going to make such a motion but denied having personally asked him to do so—one of the League's attorneys did.

Davis claimed the move took him by surprise. ''Is this a legal motion?'' he asked. ''I never heard of someone else being able to ask for a vote,'' he explained. For his part, Rozelle confirmed its legality.

Before any votes could be cast, however, Leonard Tose attempted to intervene. He had an idea to discuss, but that would require a ''privileged conversation.'' At that point, Davis remembered, Rozelle ''asked me to leave, and he said, 'Will you come back when I am done?' and I said, 'I will think about it.'. . . and . . . I left the room. . . . I thought the whole meeting was orchestrated. . . . I was called after I left and told I could come back and I said, 'No, I don't want to come back.' ''

With Davis out of the room, Tose spoke about the need to compromise and find a peaceful settlement. He proposed that Davis be allowed to move but fined $1 million for doing so. After brief consideration, Rozelle remembered, ''the consensus was that they did not feel that would be a satisfactory solution.'' Some even doubted Tose's motives. ''At the time,'' Gene Klein remembered, ''Davis was close to Tose. Tose was just being his stooge." Whatever his motives, the vote was only briefly delayed. Davis chose to stay on his veranda. He considered the outcome a foregone conclusion and claimed the owners "were inflamed by someone before the vote."

The actual polling included a number of explanatory speeches. Don Klosterman, representing Georgia Rosenbloom, abstained "upon advice of counsel," as did Eddie DeBartolo. Leonard Tose abstained because he still thought his plan was the best. Paul Brown of the Cincinnati Bengals abstained without explanation. The only "yes" vote was cast by Joe Robbie's son Mike, for the Miami Dolphins. After the vote was tallied, however, Mike changed his family's vote and abstained. The final vote was 0 yes, 22 no, 5 abstentions, and one absent. When the executive session adjourned, it was apparent to all concerned that the NFL had now crossed a Rubicon of its own.

Afterward, Al Davis doubted the League's capacity to make the fight to which they'd committed themselves. "We'll see what happens when this thing gets down to punitive damages," Davis sneered. "You'll see how many guys will back down rather than fight." Dan Rooney gave the League's answer. "I think he'll find that we're committed to go all the way on this thing," the Pittsburgh owner predicted. "Our constitution, our whole League, is at stake."

The coming conflict was now impossible to avoid. "It's a case of NFL capitalism vs. NFL cannibalism," one franchise executive observed. "The League will remain firm and not back down. Davis will remain firm and not back down."

"What does this mean?" the executive was asked.

"Hardball," he answered, "all the way."

4
Getting Personal

The NFL had a lot of throw weight at its disposal in this "hardball" game. Al Davis felt the impact as soon as the vote appeared in the papers. In L.A., the League's official disapproval collapsed the fragile coalition on the board of supervisors that Bill Robertson had spent months building.

Even before that vote, however, the L.A. County Board of Supervisors had become something of a political quagmire for Al Davis and his memorandum of agreement. The board had yet to approve a $5 million loan to the LAMCC *in fact,* rather than *in principle* as it had in January. Securing that approval proved an embittering experience. "Everybody gave their assurances to Davis," one L.A. participant noted, "but nothing happened with any of them. Once we started dealing with the supervisors, we found we couldn't count on them. . . . The board ended up being used as a forum from which to launch attacks on Davis."

The first of those "attacks" had been launched by Supervisor Baxter Ward even before Davis signed his memorandum of agreement. Ward had been the lone dissenting vote against approving the loan in principle, arguing that it wasn't a proper use of public funds. "In mid-January," he informed the board, "I became aware of rumors circulating that there was at least one business relationship between Al Davis, . . . and Alan [sic] Glick, who is said to be the subject of various federal investigations." Ward then suggested that the LAMCC "should ask Mr. Davis for a forthright statement regarding the allegations."

When Davis was invited to a board of supervisors meeting to discuss Glick and other subjects, Al LoCasale declined for him over the phone. According to L.A. County's chief administrative officer, "Mr. LoCasale also indicated that Mr. Davis wants to inform the board of his business relationship with Mr. Al Glick, namely: that Mr. Davis is a limited partner and investor in an Oakland shopping center, of which Mr. Glick is the general partner. Mr. LoCasale indicates that that is the extent of their association and that the association is winding down. Mr. LoCasale stated that any implications of wrongdoing would be totally irresponsible.''

Baxter Ward found the explanation insufficient and offered a resolution. "Clearly," his motion read, "it should be within keeping with public policy to inquire into the relationship between a key figure in the current Coliseum transaction and a person who is reputed to be 'the Chicago mob's main front man in Nevada and California.' . . . THEREFORE, as a matter of civic responsibility, I MOVE that the board of supervisors request the district attorney to inquire into the allegations and prepare a public report as to their truth or falsity.'' The motion to inquire was passed.

Davis considered Ward's attack a form of character assassination. "It's the same old stuff," he later commented. "A long description of Allen's notoriety and no real link between us. I'm a limited partner at twenty-five percent. The thing isn't worth much. It's losing money. It's a hell of a tax shelter. As soon as the tax ramifications are worked out, I'll divest. Look, it's a well-to-do shopping center in a black neighborhood near the [Oakland] Coliseum. It was built by the Teamsters. Allen got a good deal on it—that was before the notoriety. Some of our former players work there and help run it.'' Davis also refused to cooperate with Ward's investigation.

Despite his persistence, Ward would likely have remained isolated if the only issue were whether or not Davis had a relationship with a Las Vegas gangster. When Davis refused to cooperate with the district attorney, the board let the investigation die.

Of much greater concern was the League's vote on March 10 and Rozelle's announcement that the NFL would refuse to schedule any Raiders games in L.A. Robertson noted on March 11, "I talked to some politicians, and they were extremely skittish as a result of that.'' And their skittishness could not have come at a worse time. That same day, they were scheduled to have a second and final reading of the proposal to loan $5 million to the Coliseum. On March 12, the first payment of moving expenses to Davis under the terms of the memorandum of agreement was due. When the meeting convened, however, it was obvious to Robertson that his base had eroded significantly. His attempts to reverse the slippage had little success.

The two votes they were losing belonged to Supervisors Yvonne Braithwaite Burke and Ed Edelman. "Despite my strong belief that Los Angeles County would benefit by the proposed arrangement," Burke explained, "I have had to seriously reassess my position in light of recent actions taken by the NFL. I have learned . . . [that] the NFL has taken the position that it will refuse to schedule or play any games against the Raiders in Los Angeles. Obviously, if the Raiders are not able to play their home games in Los Angeles, many of the benefits which I believe justify the county's commitment of $5 million would not materialize.

Edelman's objections were similar. "Suppose the Raiders don't get here?" he asked. "What happens to that $5 million?" Edelman introduced a resolution "forbidding any advance of county money until the Los Angeles Olympic Organizing Committee first puts up the $5 million it pledged as part of the package to lure the Raiders to Los Angeles."

Stephen Reinhardt argued strenuously against Edelman. "I can tell you the effect of your refusing to act today," the attorney warned, ". . . we are in a war of nerves with robber barons who are sitting there trying (to see if, that by) flexing their muscle, they can show strength and that we won't." The League had "thrown down the gauntlet" and was trying "to intimidate the county."

"Nobody is going to intimidate the county," Edelman shouted. "I'm for the loan. I'm for bringing the Raiders here, but I don't want to sit here two years from now and feel that we've paid $5 million and we have no Raiders, no football team, and we can't get the money back."

"We're really getting out there on a limb," Burke agreed.

The best Reinhardt and Robertson were able to do was to postpone the vote for a week. Despite all the promises, Davis's money would not be delivered on schedule. "We're disappointed with the delay," Bill Robertson admitted, "but we've had many delays." Once again, Robertson was whistling in the dark. Before the week's delay was up, the League had hit Davis with another salvo.

This time the blow was struck on the Oakland front in *Philadelphia Eagles v. Oakland Raiders Ltd.* It was a graphic illustration that the NFL and Pete Rozelle were playing for keeps. On March 17, they formally filed their request that Davis be removed from control of his football franchise and replaced by a receiver of the NFL's choice. It was an act unprecedented in NFL history. The reason for it, according to Rozelle, "was that no action was being taken to sell tickets in Oakland" for the upcoming season, despite the fact the League was already scheduling games there.

One was a preseason game with Billy Sullivan's Patriots. The receivership motion was provoked by Sullivan, Rozelle remembered. "We either at that point had to try to get a receiver or file a motion saying that Al Davis should go to jail, which we did not want to do." While making no response to the receivership request, the court did continue the temporary restraining order Davis had escaped from on March 6.

The same day receivership papers were filed, Rozelle also authorized the League's attorney to write a letter to the LAMCC, the mayor, and the board of supervisors "telling them of the Oakland restraining order in the hope they would bring things to a grinding halt." The commissioner also had a letter sent to fourteen major banks enclosing a copy of the Oakland order. "We wanted them to be on notice what our position was." Rozelle explained that the ultimate purpose was "to stop any loans [to finance the Raider move] that might be in process or at least give those banks serious cause to think about it."

On March 18, the L.A. supervisors postponed their loan vote once again. "There are still a lot of loose ends in this thing," Ed Edelman explained. Those loose ends would remain untied for a long time. Soon after this second postponement, Robertson and Reinhardt went back to the drawing board in their search for financing. "We gave up on the board of supervisors," Reinhardt remembered. "We just dropped the original deal. As soon as the Raiders got here, they started raising questions. It was supposed to have been approved quickly. We finally withdrew the proposal after about three weeks of trying. Nothing the county had promised was ever delivered on."

On March 25, the Oakland court hearing *Philadelphia Eagles v. Oakland Raiders Ltd.* enjoined the Raiders from soliciting "ticket sales for games anywhere other than Oakland" or taking "any final action to move the franchise." As a legal maneuver this was the Eagles suit's high-water mark: Davis's Raiders would have no choice but to play their home games in Oakland. Their offices and training facilities, however, remained in L.A. and the team would commute four hundred miles north on game days. Pinned down, Al Davis would not abandon ground he had already seized.

Davis also fired back. On March 25, he, too, went into court, filing a $160 million damage suit under the Sherman Act and joining that suit to *LAMCC v. NFL*. To escape the potential conflict-of-interest trap set by the League for his attorney Joseph Alioto, the Raiders' action left only one franchise unnamed—the

Philadelphia Eagles, Alioto's other NFL client. Davis's suit also raised the stakes. Not content just to challenge the League as an anonymous entity, he also named specific individuals as having conspired to violate his economic rights, forcing them to defend themselves as well. The three he named were Pete Rozelle, Gene Klein, and Georgia Rosenbloom. Now the case could be personal. Its new official title was *LAMCC and Oakland Raiders Ltd. v. National Football League, Alvin Pete Rozelle, Eugene V. Klein, and Georgia Rosenbloom.*

"It became a personal issue," Tex Schramm remembered, "because Al Davis . . . framed it that way. . . . It didn't surprise me that Al did it like that. It was obviously a tool he felt he could use to distract attention and it was Al's nature to fight by whatever means are available."

5
Ownership Policy Goes to Court

In the public furor that followed, Davis was often mistakenly credited with being the first owner ever to sue his fellows, but that description ignored the precedent already set by Lamar Hunt and Joe Robbie in *NASL v. NFL*. Virtually from the beginning, the suit over ownership policy, once the most pressing issue on the NFL agenda, had been overshadowed by Davis and L.A. In April 1980, *NASL v. NFL* came to trial in New York City and almost no one outside the League noticed. Even for the NFL, it was considered something of a dry run for the battle to come.

The NASL case had two significant thrusts. The first was that the NFL's proposed ban on cross-ownership was starkly anticompetitive in intent. The NASL argued that the NFL's proposed ownership policy amendment was an "unreasonable" attempt by a combination of owners to reduce competition among major sports leagues and hence a violation of the Sherman Act. The NASL's second argument was that it and the NFL also competed in a "limited submarket" for "sports ownership capital and skill." There were, according to soccer's logic, only so many people either capable of or interested in owning sports franchises of any sort and the NFL's current membership comprised a "significant part" of that potential pool. For the League to deny the NASL access to that group was another contravention of the Sherman Act.

The NFL's attorneys responded to those arguments with two thrusts of their own. First, they maintained that there was no identifiable submarket in sports ownership capital; a member of the NFL was no more capable of purchasing and running a soccer franchise than any other wealthy or resourceful person.

Far more important was "the single entity defense." The Sherman Act specifically exempts the internal operations of "single economic entities" from all its provisions. The NFL claimed to be such an entity. Its proof was League Think itself; the League shared income and maximized the economic viability of the members' mutual enterprise. As such, its desire to prohibit the membership from buying into other sports leagues was legally no different from McDonald's requiring all its franchisers to serve Big Macs on sesame seed buns. What the NASL was seeking protection from was simply a more efficient, better organized, and stronger competitor, not an unfair combination. To find otherwise, the League argued, would restrict competition rather than enhance it.

When those arguments were tried in April 1980, the rifts running along the NFL's inner surfaces officially entered the public domain. The first NFL owner called by the NASL plaintiffs was Lamar Hunt. By then, of course, Lamar had already acquired a certain personal familiarity with the courtroom process. He had spent a good portion of 1977 and 1978 litigating with other Hunts after the death of his father, in November 1974. As Lamar and the rest of H.L.'s first family had feared, the bulk of H.L.'s bequest had gone to his second family, by his second wife, Ruth. The first family was "still suspicious that someone other than their father had helped write the will" and "seriously considered a challenge." Then tempers cooled, and the family decided to avoid a public feud."

Instead, a "third family" entered the fray in the person of Frania Tye, the woman H.L. had kept, and her four children whom H.L. had sired before taking up with Ruth. Frania claimed they had actually married. In November 1975, she and her children filed suit, asking for an equitable share of the moneys left the second family after H.L.'s death as well as the moneys provided the first family in their earlier trusts. To fight the charges, the first and second families made an uneasy alliance. The two sides finally agreed to settle by awarding Frania Tye and her children $7.5 million.

Back in court two years later, this time as part of the NASL's case, Lamar was defensive about being labeled an opponent of the NFL. "I am not testifying *for* or *against*. The things I'm saying are factual, I hope. [At least] I think they are." Among the "facts" Hunt helped establish was the importance of owner-ship for the success of a sports league. "Probably the most important reason" for the old AFL's success at starting from scratch, Hunt stated, "was in having a solid ownership group. . . . Sound ownership is very important to a sports team operation and I believe success in one [sport] leads to success in another."

Lamar defended his own previous votes in favor of ownership policy resolutions as a simple unwillingness "to be disruptive to the general tenor of the League." He also defended having furnished the names of potential owners accumulated by the NFL to the NASL. "They were people that . . . would come and attend cocktail parties at League meetings and bring eight or ten people from their city. . . . They might have a setup showing the stadium plans in their city. . . . It was in many cases a . . . Chamber of Commerce type operation."

Perhaps the most embarrassing part of Hunt's testimony came when he was cross-examined about the "best efforts to divest" he had promised the League over and over again. At the same time that he was making those promises in 1978, he had also received three separate leaguewide communications from the NASL commissioner asking to be notified if anyone in the soccer league wanted to dispose of his franchise. In none of the cases had Hunt responded. Hunt called his failure to respond "good business."

On April 7, the NASL called Edward Bennett Williams. Wil-liams, chief executive officer of the Washington Redskins when the events in question had occurred, now was the owner of the Baltimore Orioles baseball franchise as well as still a minority owner of the football team. The Redskins were a named defen-dant and Williams was served a subpoena to testify. To no one's surprise, the nation's foremost trial counsel proved a su-perb witness.

"I think that an investment in professional sports is such a highly speculative investment that there are very few people who are willing to take the gamble that it entails," he testified. "When you invest your money in real estate or in stocks and bonds of a solid company, there is a certain solidity. I had it very much impressed on me one time [when] the Redskins went to Cleveland one Sunday to play football and a disgruntled ex-player had brought a suit . . . on a workman's compensation claim and there was [an] attachment before judgment . . . and the sheriff came out and attached our equipment and there it sat in the middle of the room. There were shoulder pads and jerseys and towels and balls and helmets and it was a graphic demonstration to me. Those were all the assets we really owned in the world, tangible in nature. . . . All of the rest of the things we have are contractual in nature: leases, player contracts. And that, that kind of thing . . . drives away all but a very few prospective investors.''

Williams was quick to disassociate himself from the League's policy. "It's the commissioner's rule," he bristled. "It's the real Rozelle Rule. That is why we had it thrust upon us every year. . . . I had deep concerns when I saw [the constitutional amendment] that was circulated [in June 1978] and I spoke out very strongly. . . . I told them they would have certain litigation if they enacted this.'' Williams defended the Redskins' eventual compliance with the policy as simply a necessary step to keep the peace, but never an endorsement. When confronted with a copy of the League minutes from May 1972 that recorded a unanimous twenty-six-member vote for ownership policy, Williams dismissed the document's accuracy. When confronted with the minutes of June 1976, claiming the League had reached "general agreement on a moral commitment for strict observance" of the ownership policy resolution, Williams dismissed that as well. "I don't recall any such discussion ever taking place," he claimed. "There was a resolution. It got passed, so we abided by it.''

Williams's most obvious contempt was reserved for Rozelle's argument that the policy was essential to maintain the secrecy of internal League business. "My experience in twenty years at these [NFL] meetings is that there were no secrets,'' he maintained. "Within three or four hours, whatever took place at a meeting would be in the public domain. . . . We are not the CIA.''

When the NASL eventually rested its case, they dismissed Williams's Redskins as a defendant in recognition of his longstanding opposition to the policy they were suing to block. As Rozelle remembered it, "the Redskins went solo.''

The last NFL owner called by the NASL was Joe Robbie. Robbie admitted that he had welcomed the soccer league's suit as a way to clear this question up, once and for all. He also evinced sympathy for those football owners who resented the

NASL's competition. "I can understand their feeling about the competition with soccer in their communities," Robbie noted, "and if I felt strongly about that, I guess I would certainly want my family to be in soccer in Miami so somebody wouldn't be competing against us." Nonetheless, he argued, "The best way to sell tickets is to win."

Joe Robbie characterized his own relationship to the soccer business as a natural outgrowth of his family approach. "My wife is also interested in sports," he claimed, "and was extremely helpful to me in the early years of the Miami Dolphins. . . . I told [the NFL] that Elizabeth had the choice of folding a franchise in front of all the fans of the Miami Dolphins . . . or of continuing it. . . . I told them that we stood to lose substantial money to sell off the [NASL] Ft. Lauderdale Strikers as a result of the [NFL's] family policy."

"Have you ever told Commissioner Rozelle or anyone else that you intended to ask your wife to sell her [soccer] interest?" Robbie was asked.

"No," Robbie grinned, "I am waiting for her to come home and tell me I have to sell the football team because she is in soccer." The NFL's policy had, he noted, "been more honored by ignoring it than enforcing it. . . . I never saw any 'best efforts' to dispose of anything until Jack Kent Cooke sold his entire empire in Los Angeles."

The Dolphins' owner also buttressed the NASL's contention that there were a lot fewer potential sports owners than it often seemed. In his experience, Robbie said, "I generally found that if the conversation got serious, then the prospective purchaser wanted to go out and syndicate the interest that he was going to acquire so he could come in free. I don't put a lot of stock in lawyers calling saying they have clients who are interested in buying a pro franchise."

In its defense, the NFL called Bill Bidwill, Leonard Tose, Charles Sullivan, Art Modell, and, of course, Commissioner Pete Rozelle. Rozelle was the League's most substantial witness and stayed on the stand for the better part of four days. . . . The ownership policy, he testified, was an expression of "the philosophy that . . . you are only as strong as your weakest link. . . . One of the key things that a sports league needs is unity of purpose. It needs harmony. . . . But when you have to eliminate some of your colleagues in a meeting in order to have private discussions . . . it's a very unpleasant, unsettling situation." Whatever Williams might say, the commissioner emphasized, ownership policy was not his. "If this were just my policy," he complained, "I see no way this suit would have come about. . . . The decision to defend this policy . . . could not have been made by myself unilaterally.

Rozelle continued, "It is seldom that we have twenty-eight people agreeing, all voting yes on something, even on adjournment, but up until now, they have accepted the voting procedure and abided by it and moved ahead as one." Al Davis, currently the most glaring example of the League's lack of oneness, was not at issue in this trial, but his name came up anyway. The first time was in Rozelle's cross-examination.

"Is the reason you have not enforced the [cross-ownership] ban against Mr. Sarkowsky," Rozelle was asked, "because Mr. Sarkowsky is part of a 'small coterie of close associates' whom you favor, as alleged in the complaint in the Oakland Raiders case by Mr. Davis?"

"No," Rozelle answered.

Later, Rozelle made reference to Davis himself while bemoaning the dangerous precedent *NASL v. NFL* had set for the League's internal workings. "I know of no [previous] instance where an NFL owner has been on the minority side of an issue and subsequently played a role in having that decision challenged in court," Rozelle claimed. "The problem in California stems to some extent from what happened in this litigation. . . . The California litigation was triggered by someone saying, 'Well, if others are going to be selective in their observance of matters put to a vote by the NFL, then I am going to be selective.' . . . I can see this leading to anarchy."

The commissioner was followed by Bill Bidwill and Leonard Tose, both of whom provided little of import, one way or the other. On April 23, Chuck Sullivan was called to the stand and proceeded to paint the Patriots as a franchise that had gone out of its way to obey ownership policy, starting with its stadium problems in the early 1970s. Progressing to the battle to reinstate Old Billy, Chuck testified, "My family made a commitment that we would bring ourselves into compliance with the rules. It cost us $10 million to do that."

The last NFL owner to take the stand was Art Modell, who claimed Williams was ". . . wrong about sports feeding on each other's success. It doesn't happen that way. . . . We compete for the consumer dollars, we compete for space in the newspapers, we compete for the first item on the news show . . . and perhaps most importantly . . . we compete for the emotions of the people. I consider professional sports to be a continuing love affair with the public at large and the one that grabs the heart the earliest and holds on to it will maintain that hold for some time.''

Modell also pointed out that, as of the previous March, he had ceased serving on the board of the baseball Indians. ''I decided when the problem was raised by Al Davis at a League meeting,'' Modell explained, ''that this may indeed be a violation of our cross-ownership rule. I said, why beg the problem? I will not stand for reelection and I did not.''

Like Rozelle, Art Modell ended his testimony with a warning about the precedent this case had already set. ''The very fact that we are in this courtroom right now is a cause of concern to me,'' he argued. ''I believe that there is a pattern taking place in the National Football League which I find most disturbing of all . . . we have a self-governing system, and we have abided by it. I think it's a scary prospect to have an owner who may not get his vote, get his way, and looks to twenty-two teams, with others abstaining, takes them to court and tries to upset the voting of the League. It's happening in California right now . . . in the case of Al Davis.''

Everyone had to wait until November before the judge's decision was announced, but to the NFL, it was worth the wait. The court sustained the single entity defense and agreed with the NFL that there was no significant submarket in football owners. The League's elation would last until January 1982, when a federal appeals court reversed the lower level, found for the NASL, and banned any ownership policy amendments forever.

In 1980, however, *NASL v. NFL* was a significant confidence-builder for the League's legal strategists. Their single-entity arguments seemed to have worked. They would see no reason not to use them again when it came time to go to the mat with Davis.

6
Tose's Legal Bellyflop

In June 1980, there was another legal warmup of sorts when *Tose v. First Pennsylvania Bank* was finally heard in federal court. Because Leonard Tose's lawyer was Joseph Alioto, it was something of a trial run for Davis's side of the aisle. Now, the legal gunslingers had the chance to size up the quickness of Alioto's draw. Since he'd first entered the NFL's legal life in the 1950s, the League had yet to see Joe Alioto lose. That was, of course, the reason Leonard Tose had hired him in the first place.

Tose entered the courtroom that June in the best shape of his football life. He was current on his payments and his financing was stable. Even more important, his team continued to win football games. In 1979, the Eagles had won eleven, lost five, and advanced to the second round of the playoffs. One result was an $800,000 profit but Tose maintained that he was unconcerned about making money. "I don't dwell on figures," he pointed out. "It's not my goal to be the richest guy in the cemetery. I still believe you go first class or you stay at home. What the hell. I really believe that. And I don't stay at home."

His steady companion continued to be Caroline Callum, a former stewardess half his age. As he explained their courtship to *The Philadelphia Bulletin*, Tose had met her on a flight four years before. "You've got a beautiful ass," he offered. They had been together ever since. "I don't like her," Tose maintained, "I love her. I'm not happy being alone. I'm not for going out with one hundred different girls. I'm still old-fashioned."

Leonard Tose claimed to have significantly reduced his gambling. "I haven't played gin rummy for big money for years," he explained, "not since that thing with Andrea.* I used to play for big stakes, more than a buck a point. But no more. Same way with golf. I'd play $1000 Nassau, but in recent years I'd play $10 Nassau or a buck a hole. And the last two years, I've hardly played at all."

---

*Tose's earlier divorce trial, when his former wife testified as to his gambling habits.

Tose had not, however, lost his taste for luxury. He was still in the habit of giving $100 bottles of champagne to people he saw in restaurants celebrating birthdays or other occasions. The catered meals he provided the press corps on game days were described by *The* [Philadelphia] *Bulletin* as "lavish." He commuted to practices in his helicopter. "My life-style is that I go first class all the time," Tose explained. "I do everything for my comfort. . . . I don't think we're extravagant. Being first class means doing the right thing. We're not pissing away money."

Winning football games had escalated Tose's standing in the League's inner circles. "When I first came into the League," he claimed, "I couldn't even talk at the meetings. I now think I've gone from one of the least respected guys in the League to one of the leading guys getting respect." One role in which Tose asserted himself was the Management Council executive committee. "I speak out now," Tose noted. "I've had more experience with unions than anybody else."

Leonard Tose's confidence in his League clout had been apparent on the stand in *NASL v. NFL*, where he'd asserted his independence from Rozelle. "Mr. Rozelle is a good commissioner," he'd testified, "but . . . I do not work for Mr. Rozelle. When he's right and makes a suggestion, I consider it. If I don't like it, he above all people knows exactly where I stand and I guarantee you that most of the time we disagree."

That testimony was a dry run for Tose, who was the plaintiff's central witness in *Tose v. First Penn*, starting in June. The case Joe Alioto made in Tose's name leaned heavily on the Sherman Act. The defendants were First Pennsylvania Bank, John Bunting—now its former chairman, John Pemberton—still its vice-chairman, Provident National Bank, Girard Bank, Chase Manhattan Bank, Philadelphia National Bank, and Sidney Forstater—Tose's former financial adviser. Together, Alioto argued, they had "entered into conspiracies to unreasonably restrain trade." Their alleged purposes "were: 1) to form a 'banking boycott' which would deny plaintiffs access to the credit market in the Philadelphia area, and 2) to fix the prime interest rate so that all defendant banks would charge 'a uniform noncompetitive prime rate.' " In addition, the plaintiffs alleged that the ultimate object of all this had been to drive Leonard Tose out of the football business once and for all.

When Leonard Tose, sartorially splendid in a custom-made gray western suit, took the stand on his own behalf, he began by describing how he had worked sixteen-hour days in the 1960s "to transform his father's debt-ridden trucking company into a million-dollar operation." Then, his voice quavering with emotion, he told how John Bunting had called in his loan. "I was stunned," Tose testified. "I guess he felt his power growing because he said, 'I'll even do better than that. I'll make sure you don't get financing at any bank in the country.' " Tose recalled how John Pemberton had insulted him. "He told me, 'I've got to treat you like a jackass. I've got to mount you and put my spurs in you' . . . but the good Lord gave me the strength not to respond to that." He had managed to save his life in football, Tose claimed, only with a "desperate" last minute "bid for help" to William Clay Ford in Detroit. "I was totally humiliated," Tose shuddered. "I was despondent. I was a physical wreck. I couldn't sleep. I felt inside me that I should sell the team and not embarrass the players."

To no one's surprise, cross-examination bore in on Leonard Tose's life style. At one point, the bank's attorney interrogated Tose about a series of American Express charges billed to the Eagles by Caroline Callum. One was for $1238 at Giorgio's on Rodeo Drive in Beverly Hills. "I think it's a shop," Tose explained. Then the defendants' attorney wanted to know about $189 billed in St. Tropez, France. Tose said he couldn't remember it.

"Maybe she was there and you didn't know about it," the attorney suggested.

"You don't mean that," Tose snarled.

"Sure I mean that."

The judge interrupted. "Stick with the law case," he admonished.

"Wasn't one of the things Mr. Pemberton wanted you to do was lift Caroline's credit card?" the attorney continued.

"We did," Tose answered.

Then the defense questioned a $9100 bill in helicopter expenses. "That's the only bill [for helicopter expenses] that was ever rendered to the Eagles," Tose explained, "and if the true figures were ever billed to the Eagles, it would be much more."

The defense counsel, *The Philadelphia Inquirer* noted, "attempted to depict Leonard Tose as a man who went deeply in debt to support a flamboyant life-style that included a chauffeured Rolls-Royce and a private helicopter." First Penn's attorney also pointed out that he had once doublehocked the franchise.

"It was like a second mortgage," Tose maintained.

"Did you tell the bank [about it]?"

"No," Tose answered, "I did not."

In 1976, Tose paid some $42,000 in interest on his personal loans, the defense attorney noted. "Do you remember what was causing you to borrow all those monies?"

"To live in the style that I am accustomed to."

"And what is that style?"

"Graciously," Tose answered.

First Penn's attorney wanted to know what that meant. "That includes me being comfortable, sir."

"And is that still true?"

"Still true," Leonard Tose answered with a certain visible pride.

On re-direct examination, Joseph Alioto tried to undo some of the damage done by the defense. "Has any bank ever suffered the loss of a dime in dealing with you?" he asked.

"No, sir," Tose replied.

"And how many stockholders of First Pennsylvania Bank have suffered the loss of money because of Mr. Bunting?"

"All of them," Leonard Tose answered.

In the end, Joe Alioto's effort fell short. The judge ruled there was insufficient evidence to send the issue to a jury. After spending some $500,000 on making his case, the best Leonard Tose got was a legal bellyflop. From the League's viewpoint, the only significant contribution of *Tose v. First Penn* was the comfort of knowing that Joe Alioto was by no means unbeatable.

7
The Scalping Scandal

During the year before *LAMCC v. NFL* went to trial, the League's focus was on the struggle over public reputation that pitted Al Davis against Pete Rozelle, Gene Klein, and Georgia Rosenbloom, the three individuals Davis had charged with conspiracy. Each side tried to paint the other as black and sinister as possible, hoping to make the other backpedal and spend its energies defending its good name rather than its legal flanks.

In Gene Klein's case, the process had begun years before. In October 1979, *The* [Oakland] *Tribune* identified Klein as someone "who becomes irritated even at the suggestion of the Oakland Raiders moving to Los Angeles." In February 1980, Klein predicted that he "wouldn't be surprised if taxpayers' suits arise if the Oakland Raiders are permitted to move to Los Angeles." Bill Robertson responded immediately. Klein, he pointed out, had "personally told me during 1978 he would love to move the Chargers to Los Angeles" but "there was no way to break the San Diego lease." Robertson also charged that in the early 1970s, Klein had seriously investigated moving his franchise to Seattle. Klein's public contention that the L.A. Coliseum could have kept the Rams if they had only agreed to Carroll Rosenbloom's original demands was a statement that made Robertson "want to vomit." Ever since "he was involved in the San Diego drug scandal and got off easy with that $20,000 fine," Robertson argued, Klein had been nothing but "a puppy dog for the League office."

Rozelle stuck up for Klein the next day. "To say Klein is anybody's lackey is ludicrous. Gene is and always has been his own man." Gene Klein also stuck up for himself. "It's pretty obvious that the Ayatollah Robertson is trying to divert attention from the ridiculous actions of the Coliseum commission," he maintained. "It's ridiculous. They've lost one hundred percent of their tenants. They're really inept. . . . Robertson is Al Davis's lackey and he obviously is saying the things Davis wants him to say."

According to Robertson, the proof of his contentions about Klein came on March 3. While the League was meeting in Dallas, an attorney from L.A. filed a taxpayer suit asking that the LAMCC, L.A. County Board of Supervisors, and city of Los Angeles be prohibited from signing any loan agreements for the purpose of fulfilling their deal with Al Davis. The suit arose, Davis pointed out, just as Klein had said it would less than a month earlier. "You just don't have your average citizen walking into Wyman, Bautzer and saying, 'I want you to sue the Coliseum commission for me,' " LAMCC attorney Stephen Reinhardt observed. The law firm's late founder had been a Democratic National Committeeman and a close friend of Gene Klein's, who remained one of the firm's clients.

Klein steadfastly denied any involvement, which Davis found less than credible. He considered Klein's enmity one of the more obvious facts of the case. As much was apparent the last day of the 1980 annual meeting at Palm Springs. Accompanied by Joe Alioto, Davis met with League attorneys to be questioned under oath.

"Do you believe that the management of the San Diego Chargers has a personal animosity toward you?" an NFL attorney asked.

Alioto immediately interrupted. "You have got to be kidding," he laughed. "Even you can testify to that one."

Much of the public mudslinging during 1980 was rooted in the deposition process. Under oath, but out of the presence of a judge, the questions could be wide-ranging and provocative. The most embarrassing information offered or solicited in that process also had a way of leaking to the press afterward.

In the course of Davis's three deposition sessions, the League's principal interest was exploring Davis's relationship with the "Mafia front man" Allen Glick. Joe Alioto called for a break when the subject was first raised, and huddled with the NFL's attorneys. He warned them not to continue. If they did, he pointed out, two could play the same game. The NFL attorneys ignored his warning.

"Many of the people in the National Football League . . . were associated with Mr. Glick at one time," Davis explained. "Any representation that there was something other than just a simple business deal was purely irresponsible and misrepresented. . . . In early 1971, one of the players who played for the San Diego Chargers and one of the players who played for the Los Angeles Rams, namely Lance Alworth and John Hadl, came to me and told me they were working for a gentleman by the name of Dennis Wittman and a gentleman by the name of Allen Glick. They were in the real estate business and they had some very good real estate properties that I might be interested in, and they wanted to know if I would come down and meet with these people."

Was Wittman, Georgia Rosenbloom's lawyer asked, "the chap that died playing basketball in jail?"

"Yes."

Alioto interrupted at this point. "Anybody playing basketball at fifty years old deserves to die," he snapped.

"Ask Mrs. Rosenbloom about Dennis Wittman," Davis added. "He did a lot of work for Carroll."

In any case, most of Davis's contact had been with Glick himself and even that was minimal. "He was a war hero, decorated with honor," Davis continued. "And he was a very bright land developer and tax attorney . . . this is what the young people who came to me who I had coached, recruited, learned to live with, love, and assured me that these people were outstanding young people in the business world. . . . I don't know Mr. Glick very well. . . . I think I have seen Mr. Glick two or three times in the last four years.''

"Did you become aware that in addition to the fact that Mr. Glick owned casinos in Las Vegas in which gambling activities existed," Georgia's attorney asked, "that it was publicly reported that he had associations with organized crime?''

"Yes.''

"When did you become aware of that?''

"Oh,'' Davis answered, "I would say somewhere around 1977, '78. . . . I even welcomed the commissioner's investigation of my business dealings with Mr. Glick. . . . I was concerned to the point that I was doing everything I thought was right to eventually disassociate myself with [sic] Mr. Glick in a proper business manner, see to it that all our clients and constituents . . . were dealt with fairly, and certainly uphold everything that we believe in in the National Football League.''

After several hours, the League knew little more than what it had read in the papers. Glick was deposed as well, but spent most of the time taking the Fifth Amendment and provided no fresh weapons to use against Davis.

Davis himself was quick to strike back, as Alioto had promised. The subject he chose was ticket scalping. That an owner would claim anyone in the League was involved in it was an embarrassment itself, but Davis even claimed it was done with Rozelle's knowledge and tacit consent. First he told about C.R.'s approach in 1976, looking for tickets to scalp, and repeated what he swore were Rosenbloom's conclusions about Rozelle's relationship to such behavior. And that that approach had not been a one-time-only endeavor. In December 1977, Davis swore, Rosenbloom approached him again.

"I was again asked if I got into the Super Bowl would I like to use my tickets in a different manner than I had in the past and be thinking of charging above face value for the tickets and making a killing,'' Davis explained. "I again said no, I wouldn't do it, but how the hell are you going to do it this year if you are not in the Super Bowl. . . . He [C.R.] told me that . . . the New Orleans owner had gone along with the plan to use their host city tickets in a way of selling them above face value and using travel agencies, et cetera. . . . In February or March of 1978, there was a public announcement that John Mecom [owner of the New Orleans Saints] had arrived in Los Angeles to discuss a potential coach with Carroll Rosenbloom. . . . I learned at the time he was there not only to discuss a potential coach but how to handle the Super Bowl tickets because those two teams were going to be the host city teams for a number of years to come. . . . I was shocked. I was told that everyone in the League is doing it and everyone is doing it. I said doesn't he [Rozelle] know about it? I was totally shocked. Again, I am told he [Rozelle] is aware of it.''

Davis continued: Rozelle was also enmeshed in the world of travel agencies and Super Bowl tickets himself. In 1979, Davis claimed under oath, ''a fellow by the name of Ross from an Ask Mr. Foster travel agency which I later found out was owned by [Los Angeles Olympics Organizing Committee President] Peter Ueberroth [and which] the commissioner has been pushing for years . . . contacted me and said that they had the full approval of the commissioner of the National Football League, that he had investigated their tour package, thought it would be advisable that the League use this tour agency as their official agency and they wanted to meet with me in Hawaii [at the 1979 annual meeting]. I would not meet with the individual in Hawaii. I know that several clubs did. . . . Ross from Ask Mr. Foster [also] has told people in Los Angeles that he gets his Super Bowl tickets from Pete Rozelle.''

''When you look at the history of . . . the Super Bowl scandal . . .'' Davis concluded, ''and the statements made to me by different people in the League relative to the commissioner's actions with Super Bowl tickets and his tremendous interest in the Super Bowl, [this examination] leads me to believe that he certainly didn't want me in Los Angeles as the host team in a city that seems destined to have the Super Bowl in Pasadena at least five of the next ten years.'' Davis also intimated that another reason Rozelle did not want him in L.A. was that he was reserving that franchise for himself whenever he retired from the commissionership.

The NFL bristled at Davis's claims. ''You knew how dirty this was all going to be when they started all this bullshit about the Super Bowl tickets,'' an NFL attorney remembered. ''I never thought Davis would stoop that low,'' Gene Klein claimed. ''On a scale of one to ten, he has a character of zero.''

Even so, Rozelle had to respond when Davis's insinuations seeped into the press. Rozelle considered his reputation his principal asset and could not sit still while it was sullied. ''I can't understand all the statements Davis makes over and over,'' he was still complaining several years later, ''but there's no proof. I'm not interested in an L.A. franchise. . . . My wife doesn't want to live in Los Angeles. That's the last thing I want to do.''

Rozelle considered the ticket scalping insinuations preposterous. ''I was absolutely unaware [of] what Carroll was doing,'' he claimed. ''Davis offered no shred of evidence to the contrary. . . . As for the Ueberroth story, Davis heard it from Durslag, and Durslag heard it at a cocktail party. Ueberroth said he gets his tickets from Rozelle. Ueberroth had a travel agency and Don Ross worked for him. I've known Ross for thirty years. . . . So I would sell Ross between six to ten tickets. Most of those went to Ueberroth. . . . There was no substance whatsoever to what Davis was saying.''

Nonetheless, Davis's charges had accomplished his initial objective. Rozelle was now defending his reputation. Furthermore, Davis had found a critical chink in Rozelle's armor. Innocent or not, the commissioner's sense of himself made him vulnerable simply to the fact of an attack. ''It was the first time Pete's personal integrity had ever been challenged,'' one old friend observed. ''Having his integrity attacked really hurt Pete in a personal way and, as a consequence, I guess he sort of lost his cool over the Davis thing. It took a big toll on him.''

Rozelle began the fight at a disadvantage. It would only get worse. Sensing the commissioner's soft spot, Davis applied pressure to it relentlessly.

8
''Georgia Can't Swim''

Georgia Rosenbloom, was by no means exempt from the assault. She, of course, had public relations problems to begin with. Her ire at the L.A. press corps remained intense. She felt victimized by her coverage and after the Pasadena Super Bowl, refused to speak to reporters for eighteen months. She touched on her attitude in a poem called ''Cynics and Critics'':

A cynic is a critic that has lost his optimism.
His brain is filled with knives and barbs and petty pessimisms.

The muck and the mire that he sees as his news can hurt or
destroy, divide and confuse.
While hiding behind the freedom of the press, he gloats
with great glee at someone's distress.
We must try to reunite and resist the temptation, to build
and enhance this fool's reputation.

Georgia later enlarged upon that theme in a speech in L.A.,
telling the story of her recurring dream. In it, her staff convinces
her to have lunch with the press, so Georgia has them all over to
her house in Bel-Air for a meal by the swimming pool. During
the gathering, Georgia puts on her swimming suit and then steps
over to the pool. The water is solid. "I walk across," Georgia
recounted, "and nobody says anything. Then I walk back and
nobody says anything. Everyone leaves. Then the next morning's headlines are 'Georgia Can't Swim.' "

For Georgia, the public catfight she was about to enter with
Davis was, first and foremost, the end of a relationship. When
Carroll was alive, she and Davis had been friends. It was a
"social" relationship, Davis remembered, but "she used to,
once in a while, sing something [to me] over the telephone or
something like that."

Now Carroll was dead and nowhere was that more obvious
than the Rams front office. Georgia's housecleaning was close to
complete. Virtually the last vestige of Rosenbloom in L.A. was
Georgia's name and in July 1980, that changed as well when
Georgia took Dominic Frontiere for her seventh husband. Henceforth she was Georgia Frontiere.

Upon returning from their honeymoon, the Frontieres oversaw
the grand opening of the Rams' new Anaheim home field. None
of the real estate options for the adjoining ninety-five-acre parking lot had yet been exercised, but the Rams had new offices,
new practice facilities, and, of course, new luxury boxes. Georgia's suite left few doubts who the owner was. The size of three
normal luxury boxes, it was a split level with a private entrance,
a forty-five-foot viewing window, and seats for fifty. The two
levels were connected by a spiral staircase. Upstairs there was a
Jacuzzi, downstairs, a bar and buffet. The entire suite was
decorated in shades of lime, mint, and jade, Georgia's favorite
colors.

In September, the newlyweds also entered the entertainment
production business together, forming Empress Productions with
Dominic Frontiere as CEO. Currently in production, they an-

nounced, was a musical about the life of baseball legend Babe
Ruth scored by Dominic Frontiere. It was "intended as the first
of a sports musical trilogy," the *Los Angeles Times* reported.
Dominic was also reported to be one of the more important
advisers Georgia huddled with in trying to run the Rams. "He
attends meetings and he offers advice," the Rams new club
attorney, Terry Christensen, an old friend of Dominic's, observed. "And the first and last thing he says to me is, 'What am
I doing in those meetings? What do I know about football?'. . . .
However, I don't see him making any decisions in Georgia's
domain and I don't see her backing away from those responsibilities. She's head of the organization and runs the team. Any
press speculation to the contrary is simply wrong."

One source of such speculation was her stepson Steve
Rosenbloom. In August, he had been invited to the opening of
the almost new Anaheim Stadium, but the invitation had been
revoked after Georgia insisted that if Steve was there, she would
not be. "What has happened to that organization is a shame,"
Steve later told the *Los Angeles Times*. "It makes me sad. And
the problem isn't only that she can't make a decision, it's that
she has everyone else scared of making one too. There's a
hundred people at her ear, but she doesn't listen to anyone, even
those people that know what they're talking about. I'm also
hearing more and more that she can't make a decision without
Dominic helping her. I mean what's he know? He's an accordi-
onist."

Perhaps even more important than Dominic among Georgia's
inner circle was Hugh Culverhouse, the man who had married
them. He assisted her in dissolving the trust in which the Rams
had been left to C.R.'s children as well as to her, so that Georgia
could buy the children out and become sole owner. Within a
year, the *Los Angeles Herald Examiner* would note that,
. . . "Georgia Frontiere doesn't dare make a major move without consulting him." Steve Rosenbloom would call Culverhouse's
role "a curious conflict of interest." Steve explained that "The
other owners were a little uncomfortable about it. Here a guy, in
effect, has two teams all of a sudden."

The commissioner, however, expressed no reservations about
the arrangement. "He was executor of Carroll's estate and that
went on for several years," Rozelle noted. "He and Georgia
exchanged financial information about club operations. He was
just more conversant than she was with the specifics of running a
club. There was no conflict of interest as far as I was concerned.

Culverhouse was very sensitive to such a conflict. He wanted to settle the estate and get out of that role as soon as possible.''

In October 1980, ''one high-ranking Rams official'' told the *Times* that ''Georgia thinks Hugh Culverhouse is the smartest man on the face of the earth. Maybe so, but he's also very cheap.'' The effects were evident on a road trip to St. Louis that month, when the Rams were housed in ''a rundown old hotel whose best days were in the 1940s and '50s'' that was twenty dollars a head cheaper than the other options. ''Next week we'll probably stay at the Y,'' one player observed.

The franchise itself, however, was run with a style noticeably Georgia's. ''Mrs. Frontiere has had limited contact with the players,'' the *Los Angles Times* noted, ''and refused to meet with those with contract problems. She did tell one player she wanted to provide free singing and dancing lessons for those interested in show business careers after football.'' The approach was highlighted by a somewhat unique executive technique. ''Reporting to Bel-Air,'' one Rams employee explained, ''you are ushered into the study, where you usually are kept waiting one to two hours. One time, I was seated in the study waiting when she telephoned me from her room. Our whole meeting was conducted on the phone. Why, I asked myself, did I have to drive all the way from Anaheim for this?''

At best, Georgia's football efforts produced a mild levity among her NFL peers. Once, when she made her first personal venture into the player market, acquiring a quarterback from Baltimore, the deal was widely trumpeted as having been personally arranged between Georgia and Robert Irsay. That in turn became a joke in wide League circulation. ''The announcement was impossible,'' the joke went. ''Georgia doesn't get out of bed before noon and by then, Irsay is too drunk to talk.''

Another owner offered a more common reaction. ''She's a crazy cunt,'' he fumed. ''Her head rattles when she shakes it yes or no.''

Georgia was, however, one of the four most visible figures in the NFL fight over the L.A. Coliseum. The worst of the mudslinging began in August 1980, when Mel Irwin approached L.A. County Supervisor Kenny Hahn. Irwin and his wife, Dottie, had been employed by Georgia and the Rams between June 1979 and July 1980, when they were let go as part of a cost-cutting effort. Irwin told the supervisor that ''the newspapers did not have the full story,'' that he thought L.A. should have a team, and he thought he could help. Hahn called Bill Robertson.

"Mr. Irwin," Robertson remembered, "told me that . . . he owed no allegiance to Georgia and had some information that might be beneficial to us. He said that the [Frontiere] residence was taped and all phone conversations in the place were bugged. . . ." Irwin mentioned that Georgia had assigned him to listen in on "very confidential conversations" between herself and Rozelle, but "he wouldn't reveal them to me. He wanted to pursue it with responsible people. . . . I asked him if he would talk to attorneys and he said yes, so that's where I left it. . . . [then] I suggested to Al [Davis] that maybe his lawyers might want to talk to him."

Said Davis, "I was squeamish about talking to Mel Irwin. Quite frankly, I thought he was a plant. . . . [Mel Durslag] felt [Irwin] was an O.K. guy, what he knew of him."

When Irwin had a private meeting with the Raiders owner, Davis asked him about the conversations between Georgia Frontiere and Pete Rozelle that he'd mentioned to Robertson. Irwin recounted Georgia's panic at the possibility of a Raiders move to L.A. and how Georgia'd had him listen in. He had listened to some six to ten such calls over the previous year. Before Davis's move, Rozelle had always reassured her that Davis could not muster the votes to do it and that she shouldn't worry.

Two weeks later, Irwin flew back to Oakland for a second meeting and this time, Joe Alioto was also there. Alioto agreed that the information would be of some value and asked if Irwin would consent to a deposition. Irwin agreed and the resulting document was a somewhat startling window into Mrs. Frontiere's otherwise private operations. Irwin had begun his employment as director of community relations for the Rams, writing press releases and working mostly out of the house in Bel-Air. His wife, Dottie, was Georgia's personal secretary. After Dottie suffered a heart attack, Mel took over her duties. According to Irwin, Georgia was obsessed with getting everything on tape. Whenever Irwin drove her to the Rams offices or training camp, on the way she listened to tapes of phone and other private conversations often recorded, he related, without the knowledge of other participants. The house in Bel-Air included equipment to record both phone calls and gatherings in her meeting room secretly, and there was even a member of the staff designated to keep the equipment functioning properly.

"How come you are taping those phone calls?" Irwin once asked the resident soundman. According to Irwin, the soundman replied he had orders from "the boss." Georgia was also re-

ferred to as "Mrs." Irwin claimed that "Mrs." had confirmed
the soundman's assignment to him personally and instructed
Irwin not to "butt in." When she wanted to record conversations
outside her house, Mrs. Frontiere carried a transmitter in her
purse that broadcast to a tape recorder in the trunk of her car.
Irwin swore under oath that she had taped Steve Rosenbloom on
several occasions before firing him. While cleaning up her bedroom once he found two or three cassettes which Georgia had
labeled "Rozelle." Once when Georgia was meeting with Harold Guiver during their dispute over Super Bowl tickets, the
taping system broke down, and Irwin had to take Guiver out to
see the tennis courts while the machine was surreptitiously re-
paired. Guiver pointed out that he had seen the courts a number
of times already, having played tennis there with Carroll. Obviously, he noted, someone wanted him out of the house for while.
"What's the matter?" Guiver asked. "Tape machine busted?"
Irwin admitted it was.

But it was Harold Guiver himself who provided the most
scandalous contribution to the battle of depositions. Guiver,
officially terminated at the Rams earlier in the year, wanted to go
public about, among other things, Georgia's "ticket scalping,"
his visit from Jack Catain, and threats that had been made
against him at the direction of some unknown benefactor of the
Rams. As Davis recalled, "I think it was [Mel Durslag] who told
me that the intrigue of this thing is so great and the whole thing
is so big [it] rivals those two fellows Woodward and Bernstein
[who exposed the Watergate scandal]."

Harold Guiver was deposed on October 14. "I told him we
were going to discuss generally his relations with the Rams,"
Davis said. ". . . and I did tell him . . . that we were going to
discuss the Super Bowl tickets." Joe Alioto also promised that
"out of respect to Carroll," they would not ask him questions
about Super Bowls prior to the 1980 one for which Georgia had
allegedly charged him one hundred dollars a ticket.

Davis and Guiver met face-to-face on the day of Guiver's
deposition. By that time, Guiver had already met with the League's
lawyers. "What I told him," Davis testified, "was that I know
Pete [Rozelle] is involved in this, and I know you are going to
have to try and protect him. He told me that [the NFL attorney]
had come to see him and what [Guiver] was interested in was
getting at Georgia, nothing else. And I said to him . . . I am
interested to find out if Rozelle is involved in the ticket scandal.
I know he is, you know he is, and the question is, can he be

implicated. [Guiver] said he couldn't do it. . . . He said that [the NFL attorney] was interested in protecting the commissioner and the League [and] didn't care much about anything else." Guiver then entered the deposition hearing and told the story of Georgia and his one thousand tickets to Super Bowl XIV.

When Davis was next deposed in November, he pointed to Guiver's testimony as proof that Georgia was marking up tickets for resale and offered it as a motive for her conspiring to prevent a Raiders move. The commissioner, Davis reiterated, "is locked in on this . . . and I think the Harold Guiver situation certainly shows that he has been well aware of it."

The news of Georgia's Super Bowl ticket machinations broke on December 10 in Mel Durslag's paper, the *Los Angeles Herald Examiner*. Her attorneys immediately announced that they would seek to exclude the allegations from the upcoming trial of *LAMCC v. NFL* because they were "sensational, inflammatory, and fundamentally irrelevant." Once again, Rozelle felt he had no choice but to respond. "Rozelle: Scalping Allegation Is a Hatchet Job," the *Los Angeles Times* headlined on December 11. "It is apparent the *Herald* has access to information from a party to the litigation," Rozelle noted, "which chose to use the *Herald* to misrepresent the litigation in the L.A. area."

Pete Rozelle dismissed the move as a tactical ploy by Davis. "Davis knows that the League as a whole does not like distasteful publicity," he later told the wire services. "It's a form of intimidation. He figures that the League will get so tired they'll say, 'Al, you go to Los Angeles without a court case.' " That, Rozelle pointed out, was not about to happen.

9
Sticking It to the Commissioner

By the beginning of 1981, *LAMCC v. NFL* was as much blood feud as lawsuit. Each party saw it as an ultimate test of just what the League was, each claimed the other was bullying him, and both sides vowed to never allow themselves to be pushed around.

That mindset was apparent during the January American Conference playoffs. At stake was a spot in Super Bowl XV in New Orleans. The three principal contenders were Art Modell's Cleveland Browns, Gene Klein's San Diego Chargers, and Al Davis's Raiders. Of the three, Davis's team was the decided underdog. The Raiders had only barely qualified for the last playoff wild-card spot but, according to *Sports Illustrated*, "were a typical Oakland playoff team—mean and ugly and hungry."

The first face-off was Raiders v. Browns in Cleveland. The game was played on an icy field and into the teeth of a freezing wind. With fifteen seconds left, the Raiders were leading fourteen to twelve, but the Browns were within range of a three-point field goal. Instead of electing to try for the three points, the Browns attempted at a seven-point touchdown, throwing a wobbly pass toward the corner of the end zone. The Raiders intercepted the pass and the game was over.

Mel Durslag wrote about the Raiders' victory in the *Herald Examiner* the following day. Durslag wrote that "the Raiders should begin the championship round by asking for a change of venue, arguing that they can't get acceptable officiating within the confines of the fifty states." He went on to make a case against the way the officials had called the game. He concluded, "Certainly no proof exists the officials were groping for a way to beat the Raiders, but to be on the safe side, Oakland should ask for a change of venue [for the game in San Diego with Klein's Chargers], and, failing, should request an officiating crew from Canada."

Gene Klein's response to the column was immediate and unmitigated fury. "The afternoon newspaper in Los Angeles is an Oakland Raider mouthpiece," Klein fumed to the press.

"One of its columnists writes huge lies and makes incredible accusations. This is a devious plot to undermine the officials and intimidate the officials. . . . I ask you, gentlemen of the press, if that's fair, equitable, honest reporting or is the writer in somebody's pocket?"

Klein refused to mention Davis by name, but went after him anyway. "You know where it came from," he told the press. All of this was a "ridiculous smokescreen," fueled by "a group of people who are practicing the big lie, the same thing that Hitler's people practiced, and Mr. Goebbels. You keep telling the big lie over and over again and pretty soon, people start to believe it. . . . Nobody can play God. No owner has the right to say, 'I like rule one, two, three, four, five, but I don't like rule six, so I won't obey it. I'll do what I want.' . . . When I was in business, we had a saying, 'Losers litigate.' All this smokescreen, all this nonsense about scalping Super Bowl tickets has nothing to do with the merits of the case. . . . I live by the rules and that's the way most of the owners think it should be. . . . As Commissioner Rozelle told me several years ago, the only thing we have to fear is ourselves."

Mel Durslag issued an immediate response to Klein. "Mr. Klein," Durslag observed, "is a deliciously scurrilous individual who takes the position that if you are not on his side, you must be crooked. There is no reason for any logical person in Los Angeles to be on the side of the National Football League in the current argument. The National Football League is not above reproach, nor is Mr. Klein. All are fully capable, if not inclined, to punch to the pelvic region, describing people as being in the enemy's pocket, merely because they reject the political conspiracy that is keeping football out of Los Angeles. Klein voted for the Rams' move to Anaheim, openly embarrassed by the land heist involved in the deal. He told me personally it was embarrassing. He would tolerate such a caper and then turn around and call me a Coliseum and Raider house man for trying to encourage a replacement for that team. Klein should be ashamed of himself."

On January 11, Davis's Raiders handled Klein's Chargers thirty-four to twenty-seven. Afterward, Gene Upshaw, Raider captain and union rep, awarded the game ball to their owner. "This game ball goes to the one man in the organization who has taken more from the fans, the media, and the League than anyone in sports," Upshaw announced. "If anyone deserves a game ball, Al Davis does." Upshaw also made it clear that the team endorsed the larger struggle in which its owner was involved. "One thing that gave me great pleasure was coming down here and sticking it to Gene Klein," he told the press. "The only thing that's left is to win the Super Bowl, to stick it to our commissioner. I'm waiting for him to come into our locker room and present the trophy to us and find out what it's like to be booed."

That Super Bowl was scheduled for January 25 in the Louisiana Superdome. The Raiders faced Leonard Tose's Eagles and the matchup, Eagles v. Raiders, read the same as the Oakland court case in which the League had unsuccessfully sought to have the Raiders placed in receivership.

For Tose, the Super Bowl was the culmination of what once had seemed an impossible dream. But much of what this Super Bowl meant to Tose himself was buried in the avalanche of pregame hype anticipating the possibility that Pete Rozelle might be forced to award the NFL's greatest prize to his archenemy and legal foe, Al Davis. In response to a question about whether he'd rather give the trophy to Leonard Tose, the commissioner said, "It makes no difference to me. I totally divorce from my mind problems I and the other twenty-seven owners have with the Raiders when the game begins."

Those problems, however, were the major subject of Super Bowl discussion. If the League lost *LAMCC v. NFL,* he told the reporters, it would have "a very damaging effect" on his power as commissioner, but he would decide then whether or not to resign as a consequence. The commissioner claimed he felt defamed by the ticket scalping accusations. "It hurts me because I care about my integrity," he explained. "I have never scalped a ticket and I don't believe there's any evidence that I ever did." According to Rozelle, it was all part of Davis's strategy. "Al's attorney, Joseph Alioto, likes to find a villain in the case," the commissioner offered, "and I—as the authoritarian commissioner— was an easy figure. My differences with Al resulted from business matters. It's nothing personal. . . . I've always considered Al like a charming rogue," Rozelle admitted, "but in my business judgment, he's gone to outlaw."

Once again, Al Davis said nothing and, once again, Gene Upshaw, leader of the Raiders players, spoke freely. "I may not give Rozelle a chance to present the trophy," Upshaw said. "I may snatch it away from him. Rozelle sees me as the right arm of Al Davis and, if he can slap that arm, he will. . . . Maybe I'm blowing this out of proportion. Maybe he doesn't care. Maybe he's at a tennis club or on his yacht. Maybe he's worried who's

going to get his Super Bowl party tickets, the ones for the party
he has with his three thousand closest friends and none of the
players. . . . He is a PR guy cloned as a commissioner. With
that in mind, he doesn't want to do anything to disrupt anything."

The Super Bowl game itself was a thumping from beginning
to end. "We're not a bunch of choirboys and Boy Scouts,"
Upshaw observed of his Raider mates. "They say we're the
halfway house of the NFL. Well, we live up to the image."
While more than 100 million Americans watched, Davis's Raiders were, he later pointed out, "relentless." At halftime in the
Eagles locker room, their coach observed, "There was just an
eerie feeling, an eerie quiet feeling. There was a faraway look in
a lot of people's eyes. All of a sudden, there was a feeling of
shock, a feeling that we had lost it." The final score was
twenty-seven to ten. Among the very last people to leave the
victors' locker room afterward were Gene Upshaw and his boss,
Al Davis

An hour earlier, the moment they'd both been waiting for had
come. With 100 million Americans watching, Commissioner
Pete Rozelle put on his best smile and gave Al Davis his second
Super Bowl trophy. Davis took it. "Thanks very much," he
mumbled. "Thanks very much, Commissioner."

Despite Upshaw's prediction, there was no booing from the
Raiders players. Instead, most of them raised the cameras they'd
brought just for this occasion and snapped away, recording
forever the day they stuck it to the commissioner.

10
Modell's Maneuverings

Art Modell, like much of the League, worried that the public
skirmishing that pitted his friend Pete Rozelle against Al Davis
was an uneven match, weighted to Davis and hence unfair.
Davis was free to do what he wished. Rozelle, still married to
Caesar's wife, had to keep his demeanor dignified throughout.
Davis could be inaccessible, Rozelle could not. Davis looked out
for Davis; Rozelle had to look out for League Think. Davis
could snipe and bludgeon. Rozelle was bound by both his per-

sonality and job description to downplay and soothe. Davis had only to fight. Rozelle also had to clean up the battlefield during intermissions. Everything hinged on the trial of *LAMCC v. NFL*, scheduled for May.

Art Modell continued to defend the commissioner, but he also had problems to look after that spring. The problems were financial and they were mounting. Modell needed $2.2 million to service the interest on his personal debt over the next fifteen months, and Modell was cash poor. Modell described himself as "anxious to consolidate the assets and reduce debt where possible."

Cleveland Stadium Corp. was his most significant financial albatross. It was carrying over $6.1 million in debts. Cleveland Stadium Corp. reported a $232,000 profit for 1980 tax purposes but would have to pay more than $1 million in interest charges before the year was over. Modell was already worried that it would not be able to pay its debts before the stadium lease with Cleveland ran out in the 1990s.

Part of the reason was the continuing deterioration of the stadium. Despite Stadium Corp.'s expenditure of some $8.5 million to fix it, a new generation of problems seemed to be growing out of the fix itself. Typical was the playing field. The stadium had been improved in 1967 with new baseball dugouts and immediately adjacent box seats, but both had been built too low. Players in the dugout could see only the heads of those on the field and fans in the field boxes could barely see over the people in front of them. As a remedy, they lowered the field—and opened a Pandora's box.

Cleveland Stadium was built on landfill, and when Stadium Corp. scraped off nine inches of topsoil and another three inches of underlying cinders, there was as little as two inches of silty sand separating the surface and the landfill in some spots. A new drainage system had to be installed, but that didn't alter the field's spongy character. After particularly heavy rains it was treacherously unstable and prone to collapse in sink holes. Later that year, after a torrential downpour on the eve of a game, the groundskeeper was inspecting the sideline area when the dirt beneath him gave way and he fell six feet into the landfill. "I would not do it again if I was asked to," Modell commented with a certain disgust about his stadium. "I wouldn't touch it with a ten-foot pole. I would be happy to get out as landlord."

Worse, Cleveland Stadium Corp. was also carrying the burden of its nonstadium investments, particularly the land in Strongsville it had bought from Modell himself six years earlier. "When he

sold that parcel to Stadium Corp.," Modell's minority partner
Robert Gries remembered, "Modell had studies done, including
the possibilities of shopping centers, industrial parks, and hotel
chains. . . . But nothing happened. . . . There was a housing
boom in Strongsville between 1977 and 1979, so he went into
residential housing instead . . . and sold it off to two developers.
. . . The boom in Strongsville ended in the middle of 1979 with
the rise in interest rates, however, and never revived. The build-
ers Modell had sold the developed piece to went broke, and half
the houses they built didn't sell. It was a complete disaster."

Robert Gries, however, "had no idea [Modell] was in financial trouble." That "trouble" was the subject of a series of
communications between Art Modell and Central National Bank
of Cleveland during March. His interest payment on a $1.7
million loan was due that month and Modell's principal financial
adviser, made contact with Cleveland National, seeking a ninety-
day extension which was granted. On the subject of the larger
financial picture, Modell had the beginnings of a plan for financial consolidation. His idea was to merge Cleveland Stadium
Corp., of which he owned eighty percent, with the Browns, of
which he owned fifty-three percent. There were two ways to
accomplish that. The current Browns ownership could purchase
Stadium Corp. outright, or Modell could buy out all his minority
partners so he owned one hundred percent of both enterprises.
That would allow him to use the one to pay for the other and
consolidate both with the rest of his personal assets. The disadvantage to the latter plan, Modell admitted, was that "I would
have needed additional borrowing." The disadvantage to the
former, was that he didn't think the minority partners would
approve it.

On April 7, Modell's people and the bank continued the
discussion. One of the principal topics was a new loan of some
$7.5 million. The money would be used to buy out the Gries
family and the other Browns partners. Art Modell described the
proposal as "part of the consolidation of my assets and estate
planning."

Not long after the meeting, Goldman Sachs, the New York
financial house, estimated that the one hundred percent option
would cost at least $9.5 million—$2 million more than originally
thought—and Modell dropped the idea for good. On April 24, it
appeared that the dominant possibility was that the Browns
would buy Stadium Corp. at an anticipated price of somewhere
between $5.5 and $7 million. The man whose share of Stadium

Corp. would, in effect, increase more than fourfold in such a transaction, the patrician investor Robert Gries, had as yet no idea such a purchase was even being contemplated. It would be months more before he learned about it.

Meanwhile, Modell continued to use his public status as an elder statesman in the NFL to defend Rozelle and League Think. "Right now, it is a complex legal issue," Modell explained in phrases worthy of the commissioner himself. "I consider myself a National Football League man. I believe in the constitution and bylaws. You can't be selective in the rules you want to obey. . . . Oakland has been a great franchise and has sold out its games for thirteen years. Los Angeles is a large enough market to be considered in the future for an expansion team. . . . If it's made to sound as if I have a vendetta against Al Davis, I can only reply that such talk is fallacious. . . . Our biggest problems are internal. Sometimes we have nothing to fear but ourselves. I think we are going through a turbulent period. We ourselves, meaning ownership, need to keep the sport healthy. I hope we achieve a measure of stability."

11
Keeping the Colts at Home

Ironically enough, the only signs of rising stability in the NFL in spring 1981 came from Baltimore. Like all situations involving Robert Irsay, however, it had been reached only after a long succession of twists.

By now, Irsay's penchant for bizarre behavior was the stuff of NFL legend. According to accounts in the press, immediately after one Colts loss in which the team's kicker had missed four field goal tries, Irsay announced he was giving the man a ten-thousand-dollar raise "for trying." Shortly thereafter, the kicker was fired. After another Colt loss in Seattle, Irsay attacked the game's officiating, claimed the Seattle ownership had locked him into a luxury box during the game and would not let him leave, and threatened to sue the NFL for $5 million. "To hell with Rozelle," Irsay fumed, "let's see what a federal court has to say." No such suit was ever filed. During yet another Colt losing streak, Irsay began calling the team's plays from the press box, with no success whatsoever. When criticized for doing so, he pointed out that Al Davis did the same thing. "Irsay has never contributed anything to the League since he's been in it," one owner told *Playboy* magazine. "We would be better off without him." After the quote was printed, Irsay announced he was suing the magazine for $10 million. Again, no such suit was ever filed.

Unstable as he was, at least Robert Irsay was now confining his activities to Baltimore rather than shopping for a new home for the Colts. At the end of February 1980, Baltimore Mayor Schaeffer and Maryland Governor Hughes, met with Irsay to tell him they needed his agreement to sign a fifteen-year lease to assure the $23 million stadium renovation bond issue in the state legislature. Noting that the same demand was not being made of Edward Bennett Williams, owner of the stadium's other tenant—baseball's Baltimore Orioles—Irsay refused and demanded parity with Williams. Irsay also told *The* [Baltimore] *Sun* he made a counteroffer. If the bond issue was raised to $35 million, Irsay offered, "give me the whole $35 million bond issue and I would buy the stadium."

Later that same day, Irsay told *The Sun* he had never said anything about buying the stadium. "I don't want to buy the stadium," he claimed. "They asked for my personal guarantee on the [$23 million bond package]. Evidently they feel the stadium bill is in trouble. I told them I couldn't guarantee that kind of money." A spokesman for Governor Hughes described the meeting as "tentative" and the situation as "tenuous."

Irsay's refusal to sign a longterm lease without a matching commitment from Williams had thrown Hughes and Schaeffer back into a dilemma. Williams would have nothing to do with such a longterm lease. Far from committed to Baltimore, Williams was known to be privately considering building a new baseball park halfway between Washington and Baltimore. Publicly, Williams maintained that he would keep the Orioles in Baltimore as long as the town "supports" the team, but refused to define what he meant by the term. According to *The Washington Post*, "because of the conflicting nature of Irsay's and Williams's demands and also because of their apparent dislike of one another, Baltimore city officials have grown pessimistic about their ability to keep both teams."

On April 4, 1980, the state legislature ignored the dilemma and passed a $23 million bond issue to build luxury boxes, new locker rooms, and thirteen thousand new seats in Memorial Stadium. In order for the bonds to be issued, Irsay's Colts had to sign a fifteen-year lease. On April 9, Irsay told *The Sun* both that he was personally responsible for the bill's passage and that he would refuse to sign the lease it demanded. "I'm not going to sign anything he [Williams] doesn't sign." Williams only evinced disgust. "I didn't ask anything from the state or city," he said. "I didn't want anything. I supported them in their efforts to please Mr. Irsay. But I find his reaction to what the state and city have tried to do for him so outrageous that I can't comment."

On April 10, Robert Irsay reversed course again. "It's not fair for me to be required to sign a longterm lease if the Orioles do not have a similar arrangement, but it is not a condition. I never said I would sign a fifteen-year lease, but the fact remains that this will wash itself out. We haven't talked any further on the lease, but I see no problems." The "further" talk would consume the rest of 1980 without going anywhere.

In the meantime, Irsay continued to run his team as he saw fit and make sporadic visits to his "hometown" of Baltimore. On May 23, he attended the city's annual Saints and Sinners Roast to benefit the police Boys Club. The subject of the roast was Irsay himself. One of Irsay's players told the story of how his boss had come to the locker room looking to congratulate his star black running back and congratulated a white second stringer by mistake. The toastmaster noted that he would "hate to see Baltimore without a baseball franchise because it would mean we would be without a major league team." Another of Irsay's players joked about how his boss "goes out early for a liquid lunch." Even Irsay's wife, Harriet, got into the act. "He can't afford to divorce me," she noted. "He's not a cheap guy. Players get paid so much we just don't have any more money." Irsay took the jokes in good spirit and donated $1000 to the pot before flying back to his home in Skokie, Illinois.

Despite Irsay's intermittent acts of public goodwill, the popularity of his franchise continued to plummet as the 1980 football season progressed. The Colts won seven and lost nine, and the people of Baltimore avoided Memorial Stadium as though the Colts had the plague. In a stadium seating 60,000, Irsay's attendance averaged barely 41,000. On the final day of the season, they drew 16,941, the smallest crowd in the history of the franchise. The franchise was losing money. Even Rozelle now had to admit that Irsay "would have a stronger case for moving than he would have had in the past."

Instead, however, Irsay headed off on a new tack. On January 16, he mailed a personal appeal to Colts season ticket holders. "We are the Baltimore Colts," Irsay wrote. We want to play here, and we want to give you the kind of team you can be proud of again. This is our commitment. I'm a competitive person. I want to win. I've said some things maybe I shouldn't have. If I have offended the fans here, I apologize." Rozelle went out of his way to praise this fresh approach. "I'm very pleased with his letter to the fans," the commissioner pointed out. "I think it was a good thing and strongly indicates Mr. Irsay's position in regard to Baltimore."

To further indicate his seriousness about staying put, Robert Irsay purchased a condominium near the Colts' new training facility for a home away from home. On February 10, Irsay met with Mayor Schaeffer again and afterwards, Irsay told a reporter from *The Sun,* "Keep on your toes, there are going to be big things happening in a couple of weeks." At the time, there were rumors Irsay might be about to sell his franchise, but he scotched those emphatically. "The Colts aren't for sale," he explained. "About twenty people want to buy the franchise. I got a call from Steve Rosenbloom about selling the club and I told him, 'You would be the last person I would sell the team to.' "

In fact, the "big news" wasn't all that big. Four months later Irsay signed a two-year lease that would keep him in Memorial Stadium through 1983. The terms—one percent rent on the first $1 million, two percent on the second $1 million, three percent of the third $1 million, and ten percent of anything above $3.5 million—were the best in the NFL. Irsay called it the first step to a longterm lease that would be signed sometime in the coming year. In his ebullience of the moment, he even called Memorial Stadium "one of the best built stadiums in the country."

"The Colts are here to stay," Robert Irsay announced. By the time of the announcement, of course, the trial of *LAMCC v. NFL* was under way, and few in the League were paying much attention to anything else.

12
The Compromise Gambit

Perhaps the most critical pretrial legal skirmish in *LAMCC v. NFL* was the fight over where the trial ought to be held. The League wanted out of L.A., Davis and the L.A. Coliseum were opposed, and they won. According to Joe Robbie, the loss of the venue motion was a critical turning point. "Once we lost the change of venue," he later commented, "we should have settled the case. Your options narrow as courts hand down decisions. . . . The obvious resolution is a franchise for both Oakland and Los Angeles. It could have been settled but both sides bowed their necks."

Inside the NFL in spring 1981, Robbie's opinion was a distinct minority. There was more sentiment among the League for expelling Davis than for finding a way to cut a deal. Settlement possibilities were discussed at the League's annual meeting in March, but, according to one NFL source, "nothing proposed ever had any real prospect of flying." Other NFL members were willing to give L.A. an expansion franchise in 1984, but knew that Davis and the Coliseum had "a blood pact" to stick together and refuse such a blandishment. "There was no alternative in the League's mind to fighting Davis," Tex Schramm observed. "It couldn't be kept out of court." Rozelle's in-house lawyer agreed. "Settlement," he noted, "was never a realistic possibility at any time I can recall."

Nonetheless, the trial judge, Harry Pregerson, pushed for a settlement. On January 13, he summoned both sides to San Francisco for a settlement conference. Aside from attorneys, the NFL was represented by Pete Rozelle, Wellington Mara, and Billy Sullivan. Sullivan and Mara were included, Rozelle noted, "because I wanted Pregerson to understand that it wasn't just Rozelle versus Davis." On the other side were Al Davis, Bill Robertson, and their attorneys. Pregerson was pushing the idea of keeping the Raiders in Oakland but creating an expansion franchise in L.A. that would be awarded to Davis.

"Why are we talking about giving Davis an expansion team in

Los Angeles?'' Joseph Cotchett, Georgia Frontiere's attorney, asked. ''He won't come down here on those terms.''

''Why do you say that?'' Pregerson asked.

''Judge,'' Cotchett answered, ''I'll prove it to you.'' He turned to Joe Alioto, Davis's lawyer. ''Joe, I'll sell you the Rams right now. Would Davis like to buy the Rams?''

''No,'' Alioto responded, ''you're right. Al wouldn't do it. He'll only come down here with the Raiders.''

Nonetheless, Pregerson insisted the discussion of possible compromises continue. His suggested splitting the Raiders in half, with one piece going to L.A. and the other staying in Oakland under new ownership. Pregerson's efforts went nowhere. ''I thought the meeting today was not particularly productive,'' Bill Robertson commented afterward to the *Los Angeles Times*. ''I'm not too optimistic, but we all agreed we'd try to come up with creative ideas and get back to the judge.''

Robertson and Rozelle next saw each other at Super Bowl XV in New Orleans, a week and a half later. In their brief conversation, according to Robertson, the commissioner offered L.A. an expansion franchise if they would drop the suit. ''It's too late,'' Robertson answered.

Pregerson continued to push his formula for compromise throughout the spring. The closest it came to success was in a series of private meetings between Bill Robertson and Lew Wasserman, head of Universal Studios and an old friend of Rozelle's. Robertson and Wasserman were on friendly terms and Wasserman had also been a charter member of the mayor's pro football search committee. ''We started talking about the situation,'' Robertson remembered, ''and someone suggested Wasserman talk to Rozelle. Later I met with Wasserman and I told him up front that I thought something might be done. The best thing was for he and I [sic] to meet with Al Davis. . . . Wasserman was torn by his friendship with Rozelle. . . . He wanted the Coliseum to have a football team and tried to function as a mediator. He was sincere in his efforts.''

Sometime in late March, Wasserman and Robertson met with Davis. ''We were trying to work out some formula for splitting the Raiders,'' Robertson claimed. ''Al was courteous without indicating he was receptive.'' Wasserman's effort died not long after Mel Durslag wrote in his column that ''prospects for a settlement of the most volatile legal case ever to visit sports are beginning to brighten.''

''Wasserman got mad because Davis didn't call him back after their meeting," one source claimed. "Davis didn't really trust Wasserman and they both had huge egos." According to Robertson, "word came that Rozelle was not receptive and nothing ever came of it."

Either way, by May 1, the possibility of the case being settled was dead. On May 13, jury selection commenced. League Think's decisive battle was under way. The trial was expected to last four months, feature more than one hundred witnesses, and cost at least $5 million in attorneys' fees before any possible appeals would be completed. Privately, attorneys from both sides described the outcome as "up for grabs."

13
"Boy, Those Lawyers Can Kill You"

Though the case was composed of complex series of interlocking pieces, the issue that divided the two sides was simple at its core. The LAMCC contended that the NFL's Section 4.3 concerning franchise movement was "illegal in that it restricted the individual teams from moving and . . . anticompetitive in that it did not allow stadiums to compete for NFL teams." Davis's Raiders joined in that contention and also claimed that Davis "was not bound by the rule since he had an oral contract that he could move without a vote," given to him at the League meeting in October 1978. In addition to NFL's having acted in "bad faith" as a whole, Davis contended, Georgia Frontiere, Gene Klein, and Pete Rozelle "conspired individually to keep the Raiders out of Los Angeles."

In response, the League argued that there had been no conspiracy and that Section 4.3 was "valid, not anticompetitive, and a reasonable rule for leagues to have for the betterment of fan loyalty and stability." Most important of all, the League maintained, the NFL was "a single economic entity with a unitary product and [therefore] could not conspire together to commit an antitrust violation."

Pete Rozelle and Carrie moved to a hotel in Beverly Hills for the duration. Most days they sat together in the first row of the courtroom. On the very few occasions when Pete wasn't there, he was at the NFL's L.A. office, trying to conduct the ongoing League business. He looked tanned and composed in the courtroom, but the experience was enormously wearing. Usually a sound sleeper, he now woke often in the middle of the night and paced back and forth, thinking.

Rozelle was the first of the NFL's inner circle to be called to testify. He had been preparing for the performance for weeks and his attorneys acknowledged his would be the most difficult task of the entire trial. "He had a burden that I'm not aware of any other witness in any other trial having to carry," a League lawyer observed. "Pete had to answer hostile questions about literally anything and everything that had happened in this League for the previous twenty years." He would be on the stand for more than a week. In sum, the *Los Angeles Times* noted, "Rozelle's polished performance . . . was about what had been expected. His reputation as an exceptional witness had preceded him. While he lived up to it, he did not surpass it. . . . [Rozelle] was an urbane, cautious, well-spoken, persuasive advocate of the League position."

Rozelle evidenced irritation only at the very end of the first day, when Joe Alioto was questioning him about his telephone conversations with Mrs. Georgia Frontiere in the fall of 1979. Using material gleaned from Mel Irwin's deposition, Alioto wanted to know if Georgia hadn't said she wanted the Raiders stopped because she couldn't stand "the competition." His voice rising, Rozelle said he didn't think he'd ever heard Mrs. Frontiere use the word "competition." "That's a buzzword used for the purposes of this case," the commissioner snapped. "I don't think that word is in her vocabulary."

Alioto then hammered at Georgia's reactions to the "Welcome L.A. Raiders" banner hung in the Coliseum that September.

"She didn't know what it all meant," Rozelle answered. "I just knew she was under pressure, thrust into the limelight for the first time in her life." She was "angry and upset," but calls from owners in that state were part of his routine as commissioner. "One of my roles is to play psychiatrist," he explained.

"In your role as psychiatrist," Alioto wanted to know, did Rozelle realize her real problem was "she had a vehement objection to the notion of the Raiders moving? . . . Did you say, 'Don't worry'?"

Rozelle said that phrase was a routine part of dealing with owners. "It's my fastest way of getting off the phone at night," he explained.

On Friday, May 22, Rozelle and Alioto butted heads over Davis's alleged oral contract made at the 1978 League meeting. According to Rozelle, Davis had "absolutely not" been given assurances he could move during the vote on Section 4.3. He had merely said, "I reserve my rights." Just what those rights were, the commissioner testified, "was never clarified for me."

When court resumed on Tuesday, May 26, Alioto got Rozelle to admit that there were other violations of the constitution besides Davis's and some of them had gone unpunished. Next, Maxwell Blecher, the LAMCC's counsel, slashed away at the notion of the NFL as a single entity. While Rozelle pointed to the NFL's internal sharing as proof, Blecher kept hammering at the fact that there were significant differences in income between the member clubs. When court was over for the day, Al Davis took up the same theme with reporters on the steps outside. He claimed that the Rams had $2 million more annual ticket income than the Raiders and, counting their luxury box rentals, had made somewhere between $3.5 and $7 million more than he had the previous year.

On Thursday, May 28, Gene Klein took the stand. "Testimony Proves Klein Is Class Act," his hometown *San Diego Union* headlined, and went on to praise his performance for its self-possession, wit, and eloquence. Complimented by reporters on the job he was doing, Klein chuckled, "Boy, these lawyers can kill you." The remark would soon qualify as the most ironic of the entire trial.

Gene Klein seemed very drained during his final fifteen minutes on the stand. He began sweating profusely and answering hesitantly. "I was going to tell the judge I wasn't feeling well," he remembered, "and then the questions were over." When dismissed, Klein rose and walked straight out of the courtroom. "He didn't stop or say anything," Rozelle recalled. "I remember thinking it was strange, he can't have anything that important to do. I thought he would stay for at least the rest of the session and my testimony."

"I barely made it across the courtroom," Gene Klein explained. He had pains in his left arm and shoulder and violent feelings of nausea. "I don't think I can make it," he said at one point. A security guard called the paramedics and Klein waited for them, his head slumped on his hands, his shirt drenched with sweat. Ten minutes later Gene Klein was wheeled out to an ambulance and rushed to the hospital. He had suffered a massive heart attack. By evening he was listed in "satisfactory condi-

tion" in intensive care, but over the next week, his condition
was made "almost desperate" by a mysterious infection. When
the infection was finally in hand, he would be transferred to
Cedars of Lebanon Hospital, where his recuperation lasted another four months. "It was as tough a period as I ever had," he
remembered. "I had trouble even walking across a room."

Pete Rozelle learned of what had happened from Judge Harry
Pregerson. The commissioner had just resumed the stand when
Pregerson caught Rozelle's eye and Rozelle leaned toward him
to hear better. "Mr. Klein has had a heart attack," the judge
whispered. After trial was done for the day, Rozelle went out to
Klein's hospital but no one was allowed to visit with him. "I'm
shocked," Rozelle told reporters. "It's hard to believe. He was
so vibrant on the witness stand." Henceforth, however, Gene
Klein would be no factor whatsoever in *LAMCC v. NFL*.

On Friday, May 29, Rozelle spent his last day on the stand. It
was arguably his worst. He looked tired and, at times, uncomfortable. Perhaps the most uncomfortable moments surrounded
the letter he had written Al Davis in January 1980, warning him
of the potential consequences should he move without League
permission. The first line of the letter included the statement
"you took the position that no vote by the NFL member clubs is
necessary." The word "necessary" interested Joe Alioto. Heretofore, Rozelle had maintained that he knew nothing of Davis's
belief that he had been given an oral contract allowing him to
move on his own until after Davis had filed suit. "Necessary,"
however, implied that Davis had explained why he wasn't going
to ask for a vote. "What he told me," the commissioner insisted,
"was, 'If I decide to go, I do not intend to go to the League for a
vote.'" There was no discussion at all about what was "necessary" and its use in the letter was a "false" account of what had
transpired. The letter had been drafted "quickly" by the League's
attorney, Rozelle explained, and he had signed it "because I
wanted to get it out to him."

Al Davis watched Rozelle squirm from the middle of the
courtroom's first row. He would be in court, watching, every
day the trial was in session. While most observers gave Rozelle's
testimony relatively high marks, Davis was contemptuous.
"He's good at a press conference when he's got control of the
situation," Davis noted, "but when he was on the witness
stand, I wasn't impressed with the way he handled himself
under pressure. . . . He was caught being incorrect on several

cross checks or said on numerous occasions that he didn't remember."

Al Davis's turn would come soon. During the recesses out in the hallway, Davis told several reporters he was "nervous" about testifying. Most of them found that hard to believe.

14
The Primary Thing—To Win

Al Davis was preceded on the stand by Georgia Frontiere. She took the stand on June 8 and finished her testimony on the morning of June 9. She was wearing a periwinkle blue suit and her blond hair fell onto her back. On her way to the witness chair she gave Al Davis a long "how-dare-you" stare. There had been a lot of wondering just how Georgia would do, matched against Joe Alioto, but she acquitted herself well. "Her background as an entertainer showed," the *Los Angeles Times* observed. "She was a poised witness. She didn't devastate anybody, but she didn't walk into any manholes either."

When Alioto intimated she had been a show girl, Georgia took it in stride. "I was an aspiring opera singer," she answered in a frosty voice, "but I learned I couldn't make a living singing opera, so I went to singing more popular songs."

When Alioto noted that she had fired some twenty-seven Ram employees since taking over the L.A. franchise, she looked convincingly sad. "I don't keep count," she noted. "I never liked firing anyone." Georgia admitted that she had not been well prepared for some of the business and legal aspects of running a football team.

Al Davis and her late husband had been close. "He loved him," she said of Carroll's feelings for Davis. Prodded by Alioto, she also testified that Carroll had told her that after his death, "if you ever need any help and someone you can really trust, it will be Al." She had not consulted Davis because "I felt he was rejecting me. Maybe he couldn't see a woman as being equal, as an owner of a football team." On the day of the banner incident in 1979, Davis had been "withdrawn, cool, not the usual exuberant, affectionate Al." As a consequence, she had called Rozelle afterward. She had indeed been upset. "I didn't think that was a nice thing to do for Carroll's memory," Georgia testified about the banner and her subsequent call to the commissioner. "I hated to bother him, but I felt that I needed moral support . . . He reassured me everything was fine. . . . I was hurt and angry that someone wanted to hurt me. . . . They were calling us a lame duck team and I didn't even know what that meant." She had not told Rozelle that she couldn't stand the "competition."

Asked if the commissioner's surmise that the word "competition" was not in her vocabulary was true, Georgia hedged somewhat. "Well," she answered, "up until recently, I thought the only competition would be if a girl came along and tried to take my husband."

Since Judge Pregerson had ruled all the material provided by Harold Guiver was inadmissible as evidence, Georgia had to answer no questions about it, but she did have to respond to the deposition of Mel Irwin. "I have [recording] equipment," she admitted, "not to record telephone conversations, but to get information off the telephone."

"You've lost me," Alioto pointed out.

"I didn't tape phone conversations unless it was something I had to remember," Georgia explained.

And what about the two tapes marked "Rozelle" that Irwin had seen? Georgia thought one of them might have been from one of his press conferences and the other was "one with his favorite songs on it."

During much of her testimony, Georgia stared straight at Davis. After it was over, she was relieved. "It's a bit like an operation," Mrs. Frontiere told a reporter. "You don't know what they're going to remove."

The most controversial aspect to Georgia's testimony emerged after she had left the stand. Two of the jurors thought something untoward might have been going on when Georgia was testifying. According to the *Times* account, "a woman juror noticed on Tuesday [June 9] that Mrs. Frontiere was pausing and looking into the spectator section before answering questions. The juror followed Mrs. Frontiere's line of sight . . . and saw Frontiere moving his head, sometimes up and down and sometimes sideways. . . . The woman juror was reported to have nudged a male juror and called his attention to Dominic Frontiere's head movements."

Dominic Frontiere denied the allegations. He said he had noticed that his wife "was not completing all her sentences in her last hour on the stand Monday.'' He said he'd told her about it that evening and noticed improvement when she resumed her testimony Tuesday morning. Inadvertently, he said, he may have nodded approvingly.

Georgia was outraged. ''It's utterly ridiculous,'' she insisted. ''It's preposterous. No one has to tell me what to say.'' Pregerson apparently agreed with her. He finally ''. . . concluded that nothing improper took place''

Al Davis was on the stand from June 9 through June 18. First, he confirmed what Georgia had said about his relationship with her late husband. ''I was very fond of him,'' Davis offered. ''He was a close personal friend of mine.'' As he testified about Carroll, Georgia left the courtroom ''distraught.'' Her attorney later said that ''she was in tears and spent thirty minutes in a witness room outside the courtroom regaining her composure.''

The Al Davis visible to the jury in *LAMCC v. NFL* was, at least on the surface, a different man from the one the League was familiar with. Gone was the black suit, white shirt, and silver tie; gone was the amulet from oddsmaker Jimmy the Greek. Gone too the black and silver workout suit emblazoned with Raiders symbols. In their place were tasteful suits of blue and gray, light blue shirts, and quiet blue ties. His only jewelry was a single Super Bowl ring. His voice dropped often into southern tones as he testified and he always addressed Joe Alioto as ''sir'' and ''Mr. Alioto.''

The approach, according to the hometown *Times*, worked every bit as well as Rozelle's had. ''Davis,'' the paper reported, ''sometimes known affectionately and otherwise as 'the Genius,' was more blunt and less grammatical, but just as sharp and forceful. Rozelle was thought by some to have been too evasive too often. Davis, on the other hand, was said by NFL loyalists to have such sweeping recall that he could remember things that hadn't even happened. Rozelle, a seasoned witness, looked more at ease on the stand than Davis. But Davis did not look nervous, just intense. He was never close to cracking up.'' One NFL's attorney called Davis the ''most ringwise'' witness he had ever encountered. The *San Francisco Chronicle* offered a theory for his success. ''Davis could be a convincing witness,'' it commented, ''because . . . he believes what he's saying. This is classic behavior: Al Davis against the world. Much of his behavior over the years has been predicated on his belief that everyone else is out to get him. He has always believed others capable of the kind of action he would take. . . . Based on that kind of reasoning, it is only a short jump to the conviction that his fellow owners are united against him.''

On June 10, Davis testified about the oral contract he had received from the League in October 1978. Of the Chicago meeting's final day, after the other owners had attacked him for holding out, he testified, ''I said, 'If you fellows want to do what you want to do . . . I'll change my vote to abstain for the right to move without approval.' '' At that point, he continued, ''someone from the other side of the room shouted, 'That's it! ' '' Before the actual vote had been taken, he had a ''private meeting'' with Rozelle in which ''I told him I might want to move down the road and I mentioned Los Angeles.''

On June 11, Davis claimed that the Rams had made at least $4 million more than the Raiders in 1980. ''I just want parity, or close to parity, with top teams,'' he claimed. By way of an example, Davis offered international politics. ''If Russia has so many nuclear weapons, I want America to have at least a near equal number.''

With about an hour of court time left before the weekend, Joe Alioto handed his star witness over to the NFL for cross-examination. The first to go after him was Patrick Lynch, lead attorney in the League's case. Earlier in the trial, Lynch had referred to Davis's oral contract claim as ''trumped up,'' and Davis had responded that Lynch's statement was a ''falsehood.''

''I apologize for saying you trumped it up,'' Lynch offered in a quiet voice. The attorney paused a beat before continuing. When he did, his jaw was set and his voice raised to a shout. ''When did you trump it up?'' Lynch demanded.

Joe Alioto was on his feet in a flash, bellowing that Lynch ought to be cited for misconduct. Then, according to one courtroom observer, Alioto ''snarled some contemptuous words at Lynch out of the side of his mouth.'' Before trial broke for the weekend, the tone for Al Davis's next week had been set.

That week, the NFL's lawyers went at Davis in shifts. ''Didn't it strike you as puzzling,'' Lynch asked, that the commissioner's letter on January 10, 1980, made no reference to any oral contract? Davis answered that the only thing that ''struck'' him was ''that the letter was written by a lawyer, and it was written to protect Pete.''

Davis stood his ground about the October 1978 meeting. ''I've found a lot of people here under oath made statements related to that October meeting,'' he pointed out, ''and I dispute their integrity.'' The truth of the matter was, Davis insisted, that the NFL's own attorneys had called Section 4.3 illegal.

Davis's most effective tormentor was Joseph Cotchett, Georgia Frontiere's attorney. Cotchett noted that Davis had testified that the future possibility of pay TV had played no role in his decision to move but that his testimony was contradicted by Bill Robertson's, who claimed Davis had mentioned it among his reasons for wanting to come south. "Who is telling the truth?" Cotchett thundered. "Is it Mr. Robertson under oath, or is it you under oath?" Joe Alioto was on his feet immediately and forced Cotchett to withdraw the question and ask instead if Robertson was "mistaken."

"It is conceivable in the discussion the words 'pay TV' could have come up," Davis admitted, "but it was never discussed." Robertson's testimony expressed only "his feeling. It wasn't my state of mind."

Noting Davis said, like a southerner, "ah" instead of "I," Cotchett asked, "Is that accent an affectation of yours?" Davis said it dated from the 1950s, when he was a coach in South Carolina.

Cotchett also wanted to know what was "the primary thing" in Davis's life.

"To win," he answered without hesitation, "outside of life, health, and death—to win."

As the day was waning, Cotchett scrambled to score his last points. He began quizzing Davis about an interview he had given *Inside Sports* magazine. Davis was quoted as saying, "I didn't hate Hitler. He captivated me. I knew he had to be stopped. He tried to take on the whole world." Cotchett introduced the quote via overhead projector, so it was blown up on a giant screen.

Joe Alioto later called the move "a cheap shot" and "a stab in the back," and Judge Pregerson then ordered the jury to ignore all references to that Hitler quote.

Davis had given an impressive performance. "He's even better than I expected," one observer remarked to the *Los Angeles Times*. Judge Pregerson was reportedly among those most impressed. A federal court source said he later described Davis as the best witness he had ever seen.

"I sort of hate to see you leave," Pregerson noted as Davis stepped down.

"I'll see you around," Davis answered.

The courtroom audience laughed, but for many, it was more nervous gesture than spontaneous mirth.

15
"Will It Ever End?"

Though Al Davis, Pete Rozelle, Georgia Frontiere, and Gene Klein were the focus of the trial, a number of other NFL members also participated. Some came to testify and others just visited for a while, sitting in the courtroom, and left. Leonard Tose was one of the latter. He arrived with a well-developed cynicism about the legal process. "Lawyers are all full of shit," he observed. "The only thing they agree on is how much to charge."

Nothing Tose saw in Judge Harry Pregerson's court changed his attitude. The experience also further soured him on Pete Rozelle. "It didn't take me long to decide we couldn't win," Tose remembered, "so I met with Al Davis. Davis was reluctant to come, but I got him to agree to meet with Rozelle. Then I called Rozelle and suggested he meet with Davis and me. Davis would have settled, he was willing to go back to Oakland. He would have settled for money and stadium improvements there. He was reasonable and prepared to cut a deal. Rozelle called me back the next morning. He said he wasn't interested. Our problem was that nobody had balls enough to take Rozelle on. He made the decision to pursue the lawsuit. Davis would cut a deal, but Rozelle wouldn't even consider it."

Unlike Tose, other League members came to the trial to offer Rozelle moral support. Some testified, but their contributions were at best a mixed blessing. "There is a perception," the *Los Angeles Times* noted, "that the testimony of NFL witnesses has, at times, been more helpful to the other side than to their own."

Tex Schramm's was a good example. Though the NFL portrayed Davis as dealing in bad faith with Oakland negotiators from beginning to end, Schramm supported Davis's version. When the offer from Lionel Wilson and Cornell Maier had been made, Schramm testified, Davis had told him "he felt it was something he was going to have to accept." Herman Sarkowsky, chairman of the NFL's fact-finding committee on Davis's proposed move, also admitted that his impression was that Davis had bargained hard with Oakland, but not dishonestly.

457

Chuck Sullivan's testimony was abortive as well. He claimed that at the March 3, 1980, League meeting, Davis had stated that both Davis and Sullivan's brother-in-law Alioto were "concerned" at Sullivan's opposition to Davis's move. Then Davis had threatened him. "If you don't lay back," Chuck Sullivan claimed Davis said, "we're going to have to go after you." Al Davis later laughed that one off. "I've never thought of Mr. Sullivan as someone I'd go after," he noted. "I don't give him that much credibility. Mr. Sullivan is very young, he's immature."

Perhaps the most conspicuous blunder was made by Rozelle's friend, Art Modell. Modell had spent at least two months in L.A. often sitting next to Rozelle in the front row. "It's an important case to the future of football," he explained. "Either we have a set of rules or we don't. If the jury says these rules are illegal, then we have to start all over."

Modell's slip-up came under the pressure of Alioto's badgering. Throughout his appearance, the Cleveland owner had been adamant in refuting Davis's claim to an oral contract and Alioto swarmed all over his version of the events in the Chicago League meeting in October 1978.

During the roll call vote in Chicago, hadn't Davis said, "I reserve my rights to move"?

No, Modell insisted, he had said only, "I reserve my rights."

Alioto asked the same question over again and got the same answer. Undeterred, Alioto asked yet again and at last struck paydirt. "Mr. Alioto," Modell answered, "you can keep me here all summer long. I am not going to change my testimony. All he said was, 'I reserve my rights to move.' "

A stir moved through the courtroom, and Alioto asked for the court reporter to read back the transcript. Modell had indeed said, "I reserve my rights *to move*."

The audience laughed.

"I misspoke myself," Modell explained in chagrin. "All he said was 'I reserve my rights.' "

The six weeks that followed Al Davis's departure from the stand were torpid. "NFL vs. Raiders," the *Times* bemoaned, "Will It Ever End?" Most of the testimony concerned the precise shape of the football business, with one side claiming a single entity and the others attacking that notion.

Once during that period, unbeknownst to the bored onlookers, the whole affair came within inches of being declared a mistrial. The incident commenced when the NFL team began having questions about one particular juror. The judge had ordered, as part of jury selection, that the jury would be made up of a certain proportion from L.A. County. The juror in question had a residence in L.A. but reportedly spent most of his time at his girlfriend's house outside county limits. Looking for possible mistrial grounds, an NFL functionary had, said one source, asked a part-time security guard to call the juror at his girlfriend's, proving he was not a true resident of L.A. County. Instead, however, the security guard informed the Raiders and the whole mess ended up in judge's chambers. The discovery gave Joe Alioto the opportunity to move for a mistrial due to jury tampering then and there, but he declined to push it. Convinced he was winning his case, Alioto did not want to stop and start over.

The trial's final six weeks were exceedingly dry except for two legal rulings handed down by Pregerson, both critical in shaping the final outcome. The first came on June 26, after the plaintiffs, Davis and the LAMCC, had rested their case and the NFL had responded with a motion to drop all charges. The judge ruled that the trial of the NFL would continue, but the trial of the individual defendants, would not. "Reasonable jurors would not find that the three named individuals conspired," Pregerson ruled. When the ruling was finished, the *San Francisco Chronicle* noted, "Al Davis stalked out of the courthouse and declined to comment to reporters."

Pete Rozelle, on the other hand, was jubilant. "I feel like $160 million," he gushed. "Now Carrie can have another baby." Regaining his composure somewhat, he gave a more sober assessment. "The case has been cluttered with personal issues," Rozelle explained, "but the judge has done a fine job of carving them out. . . . and we can get down to the actual case."

Georgia Frontiere broke into tears when the ruling was made. "I'm most happy for Pete Rozelle and Gene Klein," she told reporters out in the hall. "They did not deserve to be here and neither did I. I learned a lot about the justice system. There's justice after all. I believe in justice and I'm thankful I live in America."

Even increasingly feisty Gene Klein made a statement over the phone. "Al Davis is a master of throwing crap against the wall and seeing what sticks," the recuperating Klein told the *San Diego Union*. "There was not a shred of evidence against myself, Pete Rozelle, or Georgia Frontiere. It was all part of the game Davis plays of putting extraneous things in orbit so he can take the focus away from the real issue. . . . Al Davis is really a bully . . . but he wasn't dealing with the new kid on the block."

Though it often seemed to be going nowhere, there was a drift to the trial's progress, and by July 20, the *Los Angeles Times* was reporting "that the wind has shifted and that the NFL is now sailing more or less into the teeth of it." That conjecture was confirmed on July 24, when Judge Pregerson made his second major ruling. In it, the *Times* noted, Pregerson "demolished the League's first line of defense."

"The undisputed facts preclude treating the NFL as a single entity for the purposes of this lawsuit," the judge ruled. "On its face, the NFL certainly appears to be an association of separate business entities rather than one single enterprise. . . . No two clubs have a common owner. The clubs share a large part . . . of their revenues [but] do not share profits or losses. They are managed independently. . . ." The jury was thus barred from considering the single entity question, but the jury still had to decide whether the NFL response to Davis was a restraint of trade and unreasonable. Nonetheless, the League case had been severely injured.

"The single entity defense was the primary defense argument," one of the League's lawyers complained. "We had pitched our case narrowly on that basis. Through the whole term of the litigation, Pregerson had refused to rule on that point, saying it was a jury question. Then, days before the end of the trial, he says he'd been thinking about it and decided it wasn't a jury question and ruled against us. It was very damaging to the NFL case. After the trial, the foreperson on the jury said, 'That was a pretty good defense and if the judge hadn't taken it away from us, we might well have found you were a single entity.' "

On July 29, *LAMCC v. NFL* was finally given to the jury to decide. Then on August 11, the impasse was broken and the trial, now eighty-four days old, began a rapid collapse.

The catalyst was juror Thomas Gelker, a sixty-six-year-old retired plastics manufacturer from Anaheim. On August 11, a reporter informed Judge Pregerson that he had learned that Gelker's cousin had once owned a team in the defunct World Football League. Since, as the *San Francisco Chronicle* pointed out, "all ten jurors were selected on a primary criterion of having virtually no knowledge or interest in professional football and no relations or friends involved in the NFL," the revelation raised a legal storm. Joe Alioto and Max Blecher argued that the information had been concealed by Gelker himself and that he should be dismissed from the jury. Pregerson took their motion under advisement and then interviewed each of the jurors individually.

Thomas Gelker claimed he hadn't seen his cousin in ten years, since before the cousin ever got into football. According to "a source" of the *Los Angeles Times*, "three jurors told the judge that Gelker displayed extensive knowledge of football though he had represented himself during jury selection as uninformed about the sport. . . . Gelker identified NFL Commissioner Pete Rozelle in a pretrial questionnaire as a 'baseball official' but later gave his fellow jurors a 'lecture' on how Rozelle's office distributes Super Bowl tickets." The jury foreperson, Carole Slaten of Big Bear, claimed that "Tom Gelker was biased against Al Davis." In the poll Pregerson took as he interviewed jurors, the split was eight for the plaintiffs, two for the defense, and Gelker was one of the two holdouts. Few jurors had any optimism at all that a unanimous verdict was possible. Late in the evening of August 13, Judge Pregerson declared a mistrial. The most decisive battle in the history of the NFL had ended in no decision and would have to be replayed.

The following day, Davis charged that juror Gelker had been "planted" by the NFL. "I anticipated this type of thing," he noted, "that the NFL would do everything it could to win. It's the law of the jungle." Davis was gratified that his "credibility" had been sustained by the vote of eight to two. He also intended to continue the case. Asked if that wouldn't hurt the League, Davis was defiant. "I am the NFL," he boasted. "I am the establishment. I believe in it. I'm not trying to make anyone squirm—but if I did, I think it would have been fun. . . . There's a couple of owners who try to act tough, but I don't think they're tough."

One owner to whom Davis probably referred was Art Modell. Modell, back in Cleveland when the verdict came in, was more ebullient about it. "Naturally," he pointed out, "I would have preferred a clear-cut victory, but. . . . It represents a victory in that it vindicates Pete's credibility, integrity, and honor, as well as the credibility, integrity, and honor of the other twenty-seven owners in the League. . . . Now we'll take our chances in a retrial."

Rozelle did not act vindicated. "I'm disappointed we didn't win it," he commented. "That's what we came here for."

After Davis's press conference, Rozelle was as agitated as any of the reporters had ever seen him, so much so that he attacked the press themselves, violating a cardinal rule of public relations. The articles that had run about Thomas Gelker set him off. "The message is," Rozelle complained, "if you're on a jury involving the city of Los Angeles and the Los Angeles Coliseum, you better be supportive . . . or you're just going to be castigated by the media.'' Rozelle went on to note that the "tone" with which the reporters had approached Davis at his press conference was "friendly and supportive," while Rozelle himself had been fielding questions that were markedly unfriendly. "I've had friends in the media I've known for thirty-five or forty years who are cutting the hell out of me," the commissioner complained. He felt the retrial should be held "any place" but L.A. Support for Davis "permeates the entire area" and a fair trial was impossible. "You people want a football team here," Rozelle whined.

Shortly thereafter, Pete Rozelle and his wife headed back to New York and Al Davis flew to Wisconsin, where his team was about to play an exhibition game. Of the two, Rozelle looked decidedly the worse for wear.

16
Garvey Gives The League No Peace

Bedraggled or not, there was no respite for Pete Rozelle. *LAMCC v. NFL* would not convene again until April 1982, and, in the meantime, there were other threats that also demanded his attention that fall. Fittingly, the most significant of those, like the problem of Al Davis, was yet another subject about which he could do little but worry. Once again, the National Football League Players Association was stirring.

The 1981 football season that commenced shortly after the L.A. mistrial would be the last one conducted under the 1977 contract. Ed Garvey was giving the coming expiration of the contract his full attention. Garvey's notion of a federation of professional athletes had long since collapsed in red ink, but the losses the NFLPA had incurred from Garvey's adventure nonetheless played a significant role in the 1981 situation. When the union accepted an agreement in 1977, the idea had been to use a portion of the damage settlement to accumulate a strike fund for the day when the contract was over. Next time, Garvey had pledged, they would go into their battle against management well armed. Unfortunately, the cash hadn't accumulated. Quite the contrary.

The union executive committee had first been informed of the dilemma during Super Bowl Week in January 1979. Bob Moore, one of the union's vice-presidents and its assistant director, was also one of Garvey's closest personal friends. He remembered, "Garvey came in looking white. 'What's wrong,' I asked. He then tells the executive committee that we're $1 million in the hole. Garvey had spent everything, including the $750,000 [from the Mackey settlement]. We asked Garvey, 'Where'd it go?' Garvey didn't know where it went. . . . I can't explain where the $750,000 went to this day."

As the union prepared for new contract talks in 1982, they knew they would have no strike fund to see them through. This added to the pressure on Ed Garvey when the union began designing its approach to negotiations during 1979 and 1980. He was already under pressure for having traded away all the rights to free agency won by the Mackey case and his critics claimed the players had nothing to show for it. Their average pay was still the lowest of the nation's three leading professional sports, largely because football was still the only one without any form of free agency to bid prices up. It was widely believed that Garvey would not continue to hold on to his job if he did not deliver in 1982.

Ed Garvey's response to that dilemma was a bold one. Rather than turn back in the direction of free agency, he pushed for taking the issue to its logical conclusion by seizing a piece of the business itself. Instead of demanding free agency, the union would demand that fifty-five percent of all NFL clubs' gross income be allocated to player salaries, distributed by the union according to a formula taking into account position and seniority. The union's figured players' salaries currently amounted to only thirty percent of the gross. Operating expenses accounted for thirty-four percent and owners' profits, thirty-six percent. In effect, Ed Garvey was suggesting that the union abandon its traditional position of negotiating only minimum levels and benefits and demand the right to negotiate salaries for all its members. Coupled with a percentage of the gross, Garvey argued, such an arrangement would be worth much more than free agency ever was.

Garvey's percentage of the gross demand spelled the disintegration of his friendship with Bob Moore. "At one point I thought he was my closest friend in the world," Moore later remembered with some bitterness. "Now, I can't stand him. He was in it for the visibility and ego. He would never answer his phone calls personally unless it affected his personal standing. He'd never talk to the average guy. He was a great speaker with a great sense of humor, but he was trying to be a senator."

Their falling out was not over the idea of demanding a piece of the action. Moore considered the idea a good one but it had become apparent to him that "the players didn't like it. Every guy believes he's the next superstar," Moore explained. "By the end of 1980, I became aware that percentage of the gross was a losing cause. I told Garvey, 'We don't know where we stand and we're going to have to go to war on this with the owners.' Garvey said no, the idea had vast support." Moore and Garvey also disagreed on what should be the union leadership's approach. Moore proposed that they present a series of options but, he remembered, "Ed didn't like doing it that way. His approach was that percentage of the gross was the best and we had to sell it to the players."

"He was like a fucking used car salesman," Moore complained. "The way Garvey sold percentage of the gross to teams was he would go to the chalkboard and do 'the numbers.'. . . The way he figured it everybody would make three times as much as they were making then. After that, Garvey would ask the players, 'What do you think?' Everyone agreed with him. He was amassing an overwhelming majority."

"Then things had come to a head," Moore explained. "There were four or five guys on the executive committee who wanted Garvey's ass, who felt we couldn't go on strike with him, and I called them. I told them this was our last chance to dump Garvey before it was too late." The four men Moore called were Gary Fencik of Chicago, Dewey Selman of Tampa Bay, Keith Fahnhorst of San Francisco, and Len Hauss, the union's outgoing president.

The dissidents met the night before a player reps' meeting and discussed who else might be on their side. Later that evening, according to Moore, "Garvey got word of what we were up to. We made some serious mistakes. We thought we'd just go in with our core group and fight it out, but he pretty much cut us off at the pass." Fahnhorst agreed. "Garvey blew us out of the water," he remembered. "We didn't seriously understand how powerful Garvey was." The next morning, before the meeting began, Ed Garvey approached Bob Moore.

"They're after us," Garvey warned his friend.

"I'm one of them," his friend answered.

According to Moore, Garvey offered to resign but then refused to do so when the meeting began. "The fight was on," Moore remembered. Moore started it by resigning his post as assistant director, arguing that he couldn't keep the post and try to oust the director. Then he launched his argument for dumping Garvey, emphasizing what he called the poor management of the union, Garvey's lack of respect in the eyes of players, and that the union could not get a good contract with him at the helm. The opposition to Moore was led by Gene Upshaw, incoming union president. According to Moore, there were three principal arguments for keeping Garvey but "no one said Garvey was the right man for the job." The first argument was that Garvey had announced the whole staff of some forty employees would resign if he were ousted. The second argument was that it was "too late" to fire Garvey. Negotiations would soon begin and there was no time to regroup. The third argument was that the attack on Garvey was "racially motivated," based on resentment of Garvey's multi-racial policies. "Garvey presented it as a black/white thing," Moore claimed, "and Upshaw got the blacks together behind it."

The result was a walk-over. "What we wanted wasn't even voted on," Fahnhorst remembered. "We ended up with a vote on whether or not to extend Garvey's contract, not terminate it." The vote to extend passed eighteen to seven, an overwhelming Garvey triumph.

When Ed Garvey and Bob Moore met outside the meeting, Garvey was very friendly and told Moore he wasn't going to accept his resignation. Moore resigned anyway and returned to California to finish law school.

Six weeks later, the percentage of the gross was entrenched as the union's position. By then, of course, management's position was fairly well set as well. Most of the work had been done by the management council's new director, Jack Donlan. Donlan had been hired in July 1980 and had a reputation as a "union buster." "Donlan was a hit man," Ed Garvey later complained, "not a negotiator. He was brought in to bust the union."

According to Garvey, the first time he and Jack Donlan met was in the summer of 1980. To get acquainted, he visited Garvey in the NFLPA's Washington, D.C., offices. "The first words out of his mouth," Garvey remembered, "were that they were canceling a joint labor/management career counseling program because they didn't think it made sense. I said, 'Fine, get the hell out of here. You're just here for show anyway.' It's

Rozelle, Schramm, and Modell who decide everything. I was so ticked off.''

Donlan has a different version of the encounter. ''I hadn't heard of Garvey before I looked at the management council job,'' Donlan remembered. ''I was struck that Garvey was already talking about a 1982 strike in August 1978. I thought that was strange. Unions use a strike threat to get something, usually at the last stage. They don't talk about it early. After three weeks on the job, I called Garvey and went to D.C. to meet him. He says to me that the biggest problem we have is we're supposed to have two arbitrators for injury grievances and we only have one because labor and management couldn't agree on a second. So when I got back to New York, I looked at the union's list of acceptable arbitrators and picked one. Then I called Garvey with his name. Garvey went off the wall. He says, 'Where do you get off choosing a neutral?' ''

During the first eight months of 1981, Donlan and the management council executive committee put together a negotiating position. ''We talked among ourselves about opening negotiations early, during the 1981 season, but Garvey's attitude vetoed that. Garvey was bound to put the worst face on everything we did, so we didn't want to negotiate during the season. It would just detract. By then, the owners were convinced Garvey wanted a strike.''

Al Davis disagreed. ''I don't think there will be a breakdown in labor negotiations if we handle it intelligently,'' Davis observed.

Pete Rozelle preserved his self-proclaimed ''neutrality,'' but worried nonetheless. After all the disastrous publicity being generated by *LAMCC v. NFL*, the last thing the League needed was a labor war. Art Modell was more vocal. ''There's always a possibility of a strike next fall,'' he told reporters in September 1981. Percentage of the gross was an ''unworkable'' proposition, he said.

In private, Donlan passed the same message to Garvey. ''Look, Ed,'' he said, ''the owners are not going to let you in their knickers. There's no way. It's just not going to happen.'' Ed Garvey ignored his advice completely.

17
Modell's Millions

Of all the NFL owners, Art Modell had the most immediate and personal reasons for fearing a labor war. Professional baseball had gone through a player strike in the summer of 1981 and, as the landlord of a baseball team whose rent was a percentage of gate receipts, he understood the grim financial reality of a strike. Cleveland Stadium Corp.'s revenues had dipped significantly during the baseball strike, while, at the same time, the interest rates rose from seventeen to more than twenty-one percent. As he put it, "the whole ballgame changed" that summer and Modell began scrambling to prop up Stadium Corp. and find someone to sell it to.

The most obvious buyer continued to be Modell's football franchise, the Cleveland Browns. On June 3, James Bailey, Modell's financial adviser, met with an officer of Cleveland's Union Commerce Bank, which held a good portion of Modell's debt. These notes were customarily rolled over when their due dates came. The bank considered Modell a "longtime customer" who had "never missed any interest payment on any loan" and the bank "wanted Modell's business." One plan they discussed was for the Browns to buy Stadium Corp., generating immediate cash for Modell to pay off his personal debts. Modell himself would later testify he didn't "seriously consider" that option until the late summer or early fall.

Preparations for some sort of sale, however, had begun the previous spring, when Modell called Joseph Thomas, the managing partner at McDonald and Company. In preparing their financial report, McDonald and Company had basically three assets to evaluate. The first and principal asset was Stadium Corp.'s lease with the city of Cleveland allowing it to treat the stadium as its own until 1998. The second was the parcel of vacant undeveloped land in Strongsville. The third was Stadium Corp.'s two-ninths interest in the hotel on Public Square. Two decades down the line, Stadium Corp.'s two ninths would be worth $4 million.

On August 12, 1981, while *LAMCC v. NFL* was teetering on

the doorstep of mistrial, McDonald and Company dispatched its initial report. It valued Stadium Corp. at between $5.2 and $5.9 million after deducting its outstanding debts. Modell asked for an "updating" on Stadium Corp.'s value if sold to the Browns rather than another buyer. "I do not accept your values," Modell told Joseph Thomas. "I think they are inadequate, but . . . I will live by your recommendation." Nonetheless, Thomas was soon working on a revision of its Stadium Corp. report.

Meantime, Modell took two significant steps to pave the way for a sale. First, he met with his minority partner, Robert Gries, in September to discuss the Browns, of which Gries controlled some forty-three percent. Modell mentioned that there was an "interest by an outside party" in Gries's football holdings. Though Modell did not identify him, the "outside party" was his oilman friend, Marvin Davis. Gries once again responded that he had no intention of selling. Most of their time was spent discussing the diversification of Cleveland Browns Football Company, Inc. Modell wanted to start a newspaper, the *Browns News Illustrated*, and had plans to put the Browns in the travel agency business, "to service our fans that go on road trips." In that context, he also mentioned the possibility of the Browns purchasing Stadium Corp. Gries apparently made little in the way of response.

Modell's second step was to pursue stabilizing Stadium Corp.'s finances. One employee recommended that an independent concessionaire might buy or lease rights from Stadium Corp. Modell gave the go-ahead and by October 9, discussions were under way with three different possible concessionaires.

By October 9, McDonald and Company had come back with better news, indicating that Stadium Corp. would be worth $1 million more to the Browns than any other buyer because of the peculiar advantages that arrangement would afford. In addition, McDonald had redone its figures and boosted Stadium Corp.'s worth by yet another $1 million for all buyers. Robert Gries, a venture capitalist himself, would later describe the accounting process they had used as "one of the strangest ways of trying to justify a million dollars I have ever seen in my life." As of yet, however, Gries knew nothing of what Modell was planning.

Modell was more forthcoming with Union Commerce Bank when they met in October. The good news, Modell announced, was that his oil and gas interests were being bought by his friend Marvin Davis for some $4.9 million. Modell was also enthusiastic about progress on the concession sale, which he hoped would pay at least a good portion of the corporation's $6 million debt, with $1.5 million left over to pay for the repairs still due to be made under the terms of his Cleveland lease. As for the sale of Stadium Corp. to the Browns, Modell contemplated realizing such a sale by March 1982 and indicated that he expected to net approximately $5 million from it, enough to "extinguish" his debts at Union Commerce and, combined with the sale of his oil holdings, extinguish his borrowings at Central National and National City as well. He and Union Commerce discussed the financial package that would be necessary for the Browns to make the purchase. Finally they discussed the fact that Modell might need a temporary loan in the immediate future to cover his personal obligations.

On November 11, Cleveland Stadium Corp. announced that a tentative agreement had been reached with Servomation, Inc., a national concessionaire. Under the terms of the agreement, Servomation would lend Stadium Corp. $6 million at nine percent over eight years on a schedule of accelerating payments. In addition, Servomation would put $1.5 million into capital improvements to satisfy Cleveland, all of them to the stadium's concession facilities. According to Modell, it wasn't until Servomation had entered the picture that he had become convinced that Stadium Corp. was the right purchase for the Browns.

Modell informed Robert Gries of that conclusion on November 24. Modell asked Gries to come down to the Browns office and bring his brother-in-law, Robert Cole. Cole was in the process of being divorced by Gries's sister, but the relationship was "still very amicable" and, for the moment, Cole was still a director of Gries Sports Enterprises. Modell informed Gries and Cole that he wanted the Browns to purchase Cleveland Stadium Corp. and expected to present such a proposal to the board by early 1982. Verbally, Modell pointed out, McDonald and Company had indicated that the increase to the original evaluation report would now be $1.5 million. The Browns, the Browns president contended, were the "logical" buyer. As president of Stadium Corp., he was prepared to make the corporation "available" for $6 million. That offer was followed by what Gries remembered as "a big build-up as to why he thought this should be done."

Gries took the McDonald and Company reports and said he would like time to look them over. "I couldn't comment much," he remembered. "This was the first I'd learned that reports had even been made." Noticing the August date on the initial document, Gries asked why he hadn't been shown the report before, since he was a stockholder in both the Browns and Stadium Corp. Modell answered that he hadn't decided on the move until now. The addition of Servomation had finally made it the right course for the Browns to take. When the meeting ended, Gries said he would look the reports over and get back in touch.

It had apparently been a good meeting from Modell's perspective; his financial adviser met with Central National Bank and stated that he "felt confident the merger [of the Browns and Stadium Corp.] would succeed."

Once Gries read the McDonald and Company reports, he shared none of Modell's confidence. "When I first read the October report," Gries remembered, "I laughed out loud. It seemed obviously just a way to get the value up to $6 million. Its reasoning was a little atrocious. When I looked at the report, I saw the land in Strongsville valued at $3.8 million. So I called a developer I knew and had a meeting. He knew the land in question. I said, 'What's it worth?' He said, 'Take a half a million dollars if anyone offers.' I also had an appraisal done of the hotel notes. They were overvalued by more than half a million. At that point, I knew I had problems." By Gries's own estimate, the whole operation was worth no more than $2 million net.

Gries's objections seemed to have little impact on Art Modell's plans. On December 23, he met again with Union Commerce Bank to discuss the possible consolidation of Modell's personal debts. Art Modell also needed a new loan of $1.5 million "to cover year-end funding of miscellaneous investments, internal advances, interest, and other requirements." The "internal advances" referred to the money he had been fronting himself from the Browns and paying back at the end of the year, a practice about which Gries as yet knew nothing. The total "consolidation" Modell asked for was $10 million. The term would be less than a year.

Asked how he intended to pay $10 million so quickly, Modell answered that part of the money would come from the sale of his oil and gas interests for $4.9 million in March 1982. The rest he intended to generate from the sale of Cleveland Stadium Corp. around the same time.

18

Uneasy Settlement Talk

Meantime, Art Modell also managed to participate in the major drama surrounding *LAMCC v. NFL* as it waited to be retried. The new trial also would be held in L.A., where the last jury had voted eight to two for Davis. The next trial would also be subject to the legal rulings made by Pregerson, making "single entity," the NFL's defense of choice, inadmissible from the beginning. One way out of the trap was to split L.A. away from Al Davis before the next trial started. Modell was a central player in the League's exploration of that option.

Modell's efforts began with L.A. Mayor Tom Bradley in September of 1981. By then, Bradley was in the first stages of his campaign to become the state's first black governor, trying to rally support outside the L.A. basin. On September 25, his campaign took him to San Leandro, next door to Oakland, to address a banquet. It was suspected he might encounter significant resentment from the crowd because of his city's enticement of the Raiders, and Bradley came prepared to mollify. "I'm not here to pirate away a team from any city," he told the labor leaders. Bradley claimed he did not want to see a second trial of *LAMCC v. NFL* and that he intended to approach Pete Rozelle to see "if there isn't some way to reach a settlement of the lawsuit." For his kicker, Bradley announced that he planned to ask Rozelle to "get an expansion team down in Los Angeles and leave your Raiders alone." The crowd cheered. L.A. reporters ran for the telephones.

The *Times* trumpeted Bradley's dramatic reversal: "Won't Try to Get Raiders, Bradley Says." Oakland's Lionel Wilson had nothing but praise for the announcement. "Now that Tom's got the message and he really understands that the Raiders have got to stay here," Wilson applauded, "I'm going to give him all I have in terms of making him the next governor of California." The LAMCC's current president, Mike Frankovich, confirmed that Bradley had already discussed the plan with him. Immediately after Bradley's speech, Bradley and Wilson announced they would call the commissioner to ask him to "get going on negotiations."

Tom Bradley's move caught the Raiders' other L.A. allies totally by surprise. "The speech was a mistake," one source close to Bradley explained. "He got carried away . . . the people traveling with Bradley were shocked." When the story of what Bradley had said ran in the Sunday morning *Times,* attorney Stephen Reinhardt immediately called Bradley and asked if that was what he'd really said. The mayor admitted it was, but it wasn't what he'd really meant. He'd meant that Oakland deserved a team, but not the Raiders. Reinhardt said he had to straighten the confusion out the next day or risk the Raiders' move falling apart.

That Reinhardt had successfully plugged the gap was apparent during the heralded conference call linking Bradley, Wilson, and Rozelle. Afterward, Bradley announced that he and Rozelle had agreed on "the possibility of beginning negotiations that will settle this issue." Bradley had imposed only two conditions. The first was that Al Davis had to be part of the ownership of any expansion team in L.A. The second was that the team be stocked by the League with players who would make it immediately "competitive with any team in the League." These conditions amounted to yet another reversal of position, said Wilson. "I did not know he was going to attach the conditions that he did." The conditions "tended to belie any reasonable chance of settlement," largely, the Oakland mayor noted, because of the insistence upon the inclusion of Davis. The NFL had already made it clear that Davis controlling any franchise in L.A. was "unacceptable."

Nonetheless, the negotiations Bradley had promised were actually begun. Each side sent representatives. L.A.'s were Robertson, Mike Frankovich, and Stan Sanders, another LAMCC member. The NFL's were Art Modell and Tex Schramm. "It was all to be very quiet," one source close to the negotiations pointed out. "I was surprised Rozelle had appointed Schramm and Modell. I didn't expect someone with authority." In essence, the discussion went nowhere. "Their demands were excessive," Art Modell explained. "They wanted a cash settlement and an expansion team." According to Robertson, the League's problem was Al Davis. "[Rozelle] wouldn't let Al Davis in Los Angeles under any circumstances," he claimed.

However, the issue was not put to rest. It was now obvious that Davis's control of his L.A. front was deteriorating rapidly.

"A lot of L.A. support was ready to sell Al Davis out," Robertson remembered. Robertson's friend and confidant, Mel Durslag, went further. "Rozelle was working very coolly," Durslag noted, "and had split the Coliseum commission. He had one faction convinced to drop Davis for an L.A. expansion franchise. Robertson was frantic. He'd lost a lot of votes on the commission. For a while Robertson had only three or four votes out of nine." According to Robertson, that erosion came because "the Coliseum commission was uptight about the financial situation involved in continuing the trial. Their attitude was: if a deal was possible, let's do it. I thought it wasn't possible."

Robertson was clearly no longer in control of things. "At one time," Robertson remembered, "I was the Coliseum's sole negotiator. I got a lot of heat. . . . My opposition . . . insisted we needed broader representation, so I added Stan Sanders and Mike Frankovich and made a negotiating committee." Robertson would later describe his creation as "a Frankenstein." To the NFL it seemed like a possible opportunity and they concentrated their efforts on Frankovich, working through Art Modell, who had known Frankovich for a long time.

Not long after the Bradley talks dissolved, Frankovich called Robertson with some "new information from the NFL" that made him think a deal could be worked out. Would Robertson be willing to meet with Rozelle? Robertson said he would, if they could meet in L.A.

The next Robertson heard of the proposal was several days later when he was in Oakland. Between two appointments, Robertson called his L.A. office and learned that Frankovich and Sanders had agreed to meet with Rozelle the next day in Dallas. "I was furious," Robertson remembered. At dinner, he told Al Davis what Frankovich had done.

Davis's reaction was instantaneous. "You gotta go," he exclaimed. Davis was worried the two others would cut a deal if left to their own devices. Davis used the restaurant phone to arrange for a car to take Robertson to San Francisco International in time for a plane to L.A. that allowed him to fly to Dallas with his fellow negotiators.

"We have to have an understanding among ourselves," Robertson told them on the plane. "We all have to agree to any proposal made and that there would be no deal unless it satisfies Al Davis." According to Robertson, both Frankovich and Sanders agreed with him. One of them said that the deal they should ask for would be an expansion franchise for Davis in L.A. and

$8 million. "Don't put it on the table," Robertson admonished. "Let's see what they put on the table first. Don't say anything about it." Again, Robertson claimed, the other negotiators agreed.

At the meeting, Robertson opened for L.A. "We need an understanding on one point right away," he announced. "Otherwise there's no point in talking. Whatever we're able to work out here has to be acceptable to Al Davis."

According to Robertson, Rozelle immediately "balked" and shortly thereafter, Robertson was undercut by his fellow L.A. negotiators. They suggested putting Robertson's demand aside for the moment and working on other things. They could come back to the issue of Davis. While Robertson looked on with irritation, one of the other L.A. negotiators then said they wanted a deal for an expansion franchise and $6 million. "He'd even reduced the figure he'd agreed not to talk about," Robertson noted with irritation. "I stopped things and called a caucus. 'What nonsense is this?' I asked." Robertson described the rest of the session as "a dog and pony show" that even "Rozelle knew was a nothing thing. It was just a bullshit session. . . . Rozelle thought that the Coliseum was weakening and caving in." Robertson also claimed that he was able to convince Frankovich and Sanders to that effect and that they reported to the LAMCC afterward that there was no chance of a settlement. "Al Davis was the stumbling block," he explained.

According to other sources, however, the talk in Dallas went further than Robertson thought. One source claimed Frankovich and Sanders "came back prepared to take an expansion franchise for L.A. It fell apart because Rozelle changed his mind about offering one. . . . A deal had been tentatively set up. There had been no promises yet by anybody, but Rozelle knew they were ripe and backed off."

Another source claims that, in fact, Robertson had "lost control. Frankovich and Sanders would have done anything," he explained. "They were like puppies with Rozelle. A deal had been discussed that they expected to be made. It wasn't acceptable to Davis but everyone thought it was going to be made anyway. It gave the League most everything it had wanted. L.A. would have gotten an expansion franchise and it wouldn't include Davis. The L.A. Coliseum would get $2 to $3 million and an expansion franchise within two years." The source claims the deal was actually "voted down unanimously" during confidential discussions of *LAMCC v. NFL* at the League's 1982 annual meeting. "The League was ready to accept it," he says, "but then they decided they had to fight. Someone scotched the deal.''

Joe Alioto, Davis's attorney, endorsed this version. ''The plan was to give the L.A. Coliseum an expansion franchise,'' he explained, ''and have the Coliseum settle the case out of court. It would leave the Raiders out to spit in the wind. There are a lot of angles to this thing. You have to recognize that Georgia Frontiere is represented by the law firm of Hugh Culverhouse and . . . Culverhouse took an active role in killing this thing because Georgia doesn't want another team out there. That's obvious to everybody. It's what the fight was about to begin with.'' According to statements made by Alioto to *The* [Cleveland] *Plain Dealer*, the new expansion franchise would have been awarded to Art Modell, who would have then sold the Browns and moved west. Modell denied any such intentions.

Whichever version was the more accurate, the conclusion was the same. No settlement was reached. ''By this time,'' one participant explained, ''things had gotten too personal for that.''

19
Cool-in-a-Crisis Chuck

The pattern of animosity generated by *LAMCC v. NFL* had long since become wide, deep, and readily apparent throughout the League. In the case of the Sullivans in Boston, it had even driven a wedge within the family. The schism centered on Billy Sullivan's son-in-law, Joe Alioto. As Al Davis's hired gun, Alioto was a particularly resented figure in Billy's circle. Alioto admitted that he and Billy never talked about the case and that it was never brought up at family gatherings. ''We're on opposite sides, no doubt about it,'' Alioto joked. ''I tell people it's the generation gap—Billy's a year older than I am.''

For his part, Billy Sullivan found it hard to laugh. ''When Kathleen and Joe and I sit down,'' he explained, ''we never discuss it. . . . He's a wonderful man, but he's on the other side. We can't talk. The three of us and Joe's son, Joe Jr., had lunch [once] and Joe Jr. started talking to his father about the case. I told Kathleen, 'I think I should leave.' . . . So I went and sat in a corner by myself. Kathleen came over with tears in her eyes. She said, 'Can't we even sit together?' And I had to tell her no, we couldn't.''

Despite the rift inspired within the family, not to mention the disruption it brought to the League in general, the Sullivan empire nonetheless expanded while *LAMCC v. NFL* was going on. Again, the growth was due principally to the energies of Chuck and his target was Schaeffer Stadium in Foxboro, where the franchise played its games.

Originally considered a miracle that Old Billy had somehow managed to produce at the last minute out of thin air, Schaeffer Stadium was controlled by Stadium Realty Trust, which Billy had constructed in 1971 to procure the necessary financing to build in Foxboro. To float the trust, Billy had bought more of its stock than any other individual and the Patriots more than any other organization. By 1981, however, this had become a ''problem.'' After several years it became apparent that Stadium Realty Trust wasn't getting other events at the stadium to help income, and the income from the Patriots alone was insufficient for sound maintenance, so the Patriots subsidized the stadium to keep it from falling apart. ''Because it wasn't a public facility,'' Billy remembered, ''we had the second highest rent in the League [and] we had the largest police payroll in the League. . . . When we still saw no efforts by Stadium Realty Trust to get other events to defray some of those costs, we decided to try to buy it.''

Once again, Billy pointed out, the takeover was ''a family affair,'' quarterbacked by Chuck, and revealed on April Fool's Day, 1981. ''The problem,'' Chuck explained to the *Boston Herald*, ''is that we've had an erosion of our season ticket holders from fifty-five thousand to forty thousand. . . . [Our fans'] general reaction was that they are high on the team and the game, but not on the facilities . . . the stadium is ten years old and needs a major overhaul. In part, Chuck was speaking generously of Stadium Realty Trust at this point because he had just made them an offer: $12 a share for stock then selling at $7. The stock would be purchased by Stadium Management Corp., a vehicle wholly owned by Sullivans. Down the line, the Sullivans intended to refinance and, in Billy's words, ''make it one of the best facilities in the NFL.'' By June, the board had rejected Chuck's offer as ''inadequate.''

The setback barely caused the Sullivans to pause. By July, a dissident slate of trustees had been nominated to replace the current board and a proxy fight had begun. The Sullivans' proxy statement informed shareholders that the current board had to be replaced "to provide a more hospitable home for the Patriots at Schaeffer Stadium and to eliminate the increasing distrust and disputes which have in recent years plagued the relationship between the Patriots and the management of the trust." The current trustees responded that the Sullivan offer "was not fair, adequate, or reasonable." *The Boston Globe* described the fight between the two positions as "nasty, even vengeful." By the middle of July, Chuck thought he had more than enough to get the two thirds necessary. Balloting was scheduled for July 28.

Before the vote could be held, however, a new bidder jumped in: Nelson Skalbania, who owned some $50 million worth of sports teams around Canada. He offered Stadium Realty Trust $16 a share and the Canadian had never even seen Schaeffer Stadium. Nonetheless, the sitting trustees postponed the scheduled vote to consider Skalbania's offer. Chuck Sullivan reacted angrily to the move. "Calling it an offer," he fumed, "is a misnomer. It is more an expression of interest."

Whatever it was, Chuck acted quickly to remove it and on August 4, the Canadian "reluctantly" withdrew his offer because of "business aspects" and some "nonbusiness problems." The men the Sullivans were seeking to depose thought they knew where those problems had come from. They "believed opposition by the Sullivans played an important role in Skalbania's decision." Even so, the trustees' days were now numbered. The day Skalbania withdrew, Chuck already claimed to have proxies in hand for more than 203,000 of the trust's 382,000 outstanding shares.

On August 13, a formal shareholders meeting was convened and on August 14, the proxy count would be announced. Billy Sullivan spoke for the dissident slate. "I appear here today . . . as a substantial stockholder in the Stadium and as owner of the prime and, I think, only tenant in the facility. . . . This is not the ordinary garden variety form of stockholder proxy fight . . . our guys versus their guys. [The current trustees] are friends of mine since well before the stadium was built. Indeed, in some cases, answered my invitation to serve as trustees. This is not the Sullivan family versus the trustees." Confident of victory, Billy thanked his opponents for their "dedicated services" and the shareholders in general. However they voted, Old Billy noted with a twinkle, "they participated in a very great part of demo-

cratic society, the proxy fight.'' The next day, the Sullivans'
slate won.

One hurdle remained: a formal vote by the same shareholders
to approve the trust's liquidation and sale to Chuck Sullivan's
holding company. Once again the Sullivans prevailed. ''I'm just
delighted with the vote,'' Chuck beamed afterward. Football and
Sullivan were now synonymous throughout New England. Once
the owners of less than forty percent of a football franchise with
no stadium, they now owned the football team and the stadium
as well.

While enlarging the family empire, Chuck Sullivan also continued to play a major role in League affairs. Between the trials
of *LAMCC v. NFL,* most of Chuck's NFL energies went into his
job as chairman of the management council executive committee, which was attempting to ready the League for potential labor
war. While the union was headed for the confrontation with no
strike fund to speak of, Chuck was busy arranging a $150
million unsecured line of credit for an owners' strike fund that
would be in place not long after negotiations began.

The management council's opening session with the NFLPA
was held on February 16, 1982. The council was represented by
five negotiators, none of them owners. The union was represented by Garvey and some thirty others, most of them players.
Gene Upshaw, now NFLPA president, noted the absence of
owners and described the management group as ''virtually a
subcommittee.'' Ed Garvey was ''disappointed.'' Nonetheless,
they proceeded to present their demands. ''They had a twelve-
page document,'' Jack Donlan remembered, ''and they all took
turns reading it aloud. It was like a high school pageant.''
According to one source in the room, the most embarrassing
moments came when two of the players couldn't pronounce the
words Garvey had written for them.

The part the management council had been waiting to hear,
dealing with percentage of the gross, came last. It was a disappointment and a frustration because Garvey's document stopped
short of actually saying what percentage the union wanted. Instead, it demanded to see the owners' books so it could determine for itself what percentage it intended to ask for.

The counterproposal from the management council was described by Gene Upshaw as ''an insult to our members.'' It
refused access to management's books, demanded new player
dress codes, and refused to improve the pension plan. By the end
of the opening session, people were shouting at each other. On

February 18, the two sides met again for ten hours, once again ended up shouting, and suspended negotiations. Ed Garvey described that meeting as "the worst experience I've been through in my twelve years of dealing with the NFL." Chuck Sullivan made no comment.

20
The NFL Goes to Washington

Pete Rozelle, of course, took no direct role on the League's labor front, explaining that he was "the commissioner of all of football," not the representative of one interest over another. At the time, he also had his hands full with other League business.

Two items preoccupied Rozelle between trials. One was the negotiation of a new television agreement with the networks, a contract he intended to announce at the 1982 annual meeting in March. The other preoccupation was breaking out of his *LAMCC v. NFL* encirclement. Once Rozelle had developed a strategy on that front, he pursued it single-mindedly.

The plan was remarkably daring for a man with Rozelle's cautious reputation. Rather than seek a piecemeal victory, he went for the whole ball of wax—eliminating the League's Sherman Act vulnerability once and for all. To do that, he shuttled back and forth between New York and Washington, D.C., campaigning for a "sports bill" that would exempt the NFL from many of its current antitrust dilemmas. It had been more than a decade since he had last petitioned Congress for a limited exemption and almost two decades since he had sought anything as broad as what he now had in mind. If not exactly home turf, Capitol Hill at least afforded more possibilities than were available in front of a judge in L.A. The congressional strategy had great allure: If he was successful, he would beat Davis and save League Think once and for all.

The commissioner's campaign started with congressional hearings in December. Beforehand, he worked privately, meeting with congressmen and senators to discuss the issues. In politics, the operative principle is quid pro quo, and the League made its case accordingly. What it had to offer was expansion, and Rozelle was not averse to pointing that out in private or in public. "A lot of cities have talked to us about expansion," the commissioner explained, "and we're ready to expand. But the situation is this. We can't expand without fear of litigation. We've said that as soon as the sports bill has passed, which gives us the same rights as multidivisional corporations, we'll expand. . . . As the sports bill is passed, we'll appoint an expansion committee to give us two more teams for a total of thirty."

With the concept of expansion in his back pocket, Rozelle met in November with Senate Republican Leader Howard Baker of Tennessee. Baker, according to the *Memphis Commercial Appeal,* had "been spearheading Memphis's attempts to get into the exclusive NFL club for a couple of years." He was more than happy to discuss expansion with the commissioner. Though their meeting of minds was not complete, Baker and the commissioner made some headway. According to one of the people present, the meeting ended "in a posture of Rozelle saying there'll be expansion when they get their antitrust exemption and Baker saying there'll be antitrust exemption when Memphis gets a team." Nonetheless, Senator Baker emerged optimistic enough to tell his constituents that Memphis "has the best chance of any city in the country" to be included in NFL expansion. "Rozelle didn't promise anything," he pointed out, "but he just left me with a good, strong, positive feeling."

On December 10, Pete Rozelle formally launched his campaign with a tour de force in front of the House Judiciary Committee's subcommittee on monopolies and commercial law. The subject was "the effects of antitrust laws and policy on professional sports leagues," a field, the commissioner pointed out, "that remains utterly confused and unsettled after three decades of constant litigation." There was, however, a solution. "In my view," the commissioner read from his prepared text, "the time has come for Congress to directly address this subject with legislation."

"If some of my statements today are strong," Rozelle continued, "it is because the case for legislative clarification is overwhelming. Put simply, professional sports leagues are at a point where—because of the novel business form of sports leagues—every league action, every league business judgment, and every league decision can be characterized as an 'antitrust' issue. . . . I am not a lawyer, but I have probably spent more time in litigation matters than many members of the bar. . . . In my judgment, it is clear that the antitrust laws, as now applied to sports leagues, do more to frustrate the very consumer and public interests that they were designed to promote than to serve them."

The commissioner presented, in essence, the same single entity defense that had been disallowed in the last L.A. matchup with Al Davis. "The relationship among the clubs within the League is unique," he emphasized. "It is found nowhere else on the American business scene. On the playing field, the teams are clearly competitors. But in producing and marketing the NFL product, the clubs are co-producers and co-sellers, not competitors. They are partners acting together in a common enterprise. . . . The antitrust straw is thus about to break the camel's back unless antitrust doctrine comes to recognize the true novelty of the sports league economic relationship. . . . If sports leagues cannot act as unified business operations, . . . then responsible league sports can be added to the endangered species list."

The reason, Rozelle noted, was that "the antitrust courts are in the process of rendering leagues powerless to act. They are putting leagues in a catch-22 situation—where the individual clubs are regarded as separate, independent entrepreneurs, outside the plane of League decision making, while all of the rest of the League's members remain obligated to conduct all of their operations on whatever conditions are established by the individual club or sought by some outside party. The inability of the League to make and enforce operating principles equally binding on all members threatens many serious consequences for professional football and the public."

Rozelle suggested several such consequences. "For one thing," he continued, "it risks foreclosing future expansion of the NFL. . . . [If] the League's choice of location and decision to create a new partner can be challenged as a 'conspiracy' with antitrust consequences, then there is simply no practical way to continue to enlarge the League. . . . [I]t is unlikely that the NFL's pattern of stable team-community relationships will continue if antitrust concepts are used to make leagues powerless to influence or control team location decisions. . . . There is not even the assurance that the NFL's established patterns of revenue sharing will survive."

The most irritating aspect, Rozelle testified, was that "leagues are regularly damned in antitrust if they do, and damned in antitrust if they don't." He offered four examples. The first was in 1960, when the NFL was first sued for placing its broadcasts on more than one network and then, when it moved to unify on just one network, sued for that as well. Second, the World Football League had threatened suit if the NFL expanded into Memphis and then, the following year, the League had been sued for declining to expand there. The third example was *LAMCC v. NFL,* where the League had been sued for failing to permit a transfer. If they had permitted it, Oakland was preparing a suit against doing so. The fourth example was *NASL v. NFL,* which Rozelle claimed was in compliance with antitrust law "prohibiting interlocking directorships" but nonetheless subject to litigation for precisely that prohibition.

Rozelle discussed the confusion inherent in legal thinking on this subject. The federal court in Philadelphia, he pointed out, had ruled that the NFL is "a unique type of business" and its clubs "must not compete too well with each other in a business way." The federal court in Minneapolis, on the other hand, ruled the NFL is "like any other business" and "open unfettered competition must take place among its clubs." The federal court in New York deemed the NFL a single economic entity and the federal court in L.A. had most recently declared them "business competitors" and not a single economic entity.

That court in L.A. was, of course, the subject of some of Rozelle's most intense attention. "Now," the commissioner lamented, "the NFL is involved in exhausting litigation over whether the League's executive committee could evaluate the Oakland Raiders' proposed move to Los Angeles—and, ultimately, prevent an NFL club from abandoning its home territory when the League's membership believed the club had no sufficient reason for walking out. The recurring antitrust confusions and contradictions are illustrated in this litigation. Before the Raiders tried to abandon Oakland, antitrust law as to League decisions regarding location of franchises seemed clear. . . . In 1976, the Department of Justice told the House Select Committee on Sports . . . that team transfer issues probably did not even present an antitrust issue.

"Yet," Rozelle went on, "when the Los Angeles Coliseum challenged the NFL's decision not to endorse the Raiders' effort to abandon Oakland, prior antitrust learning went out the window: the local Los Angeles area federal court found not only an antitrust issue but an antitrust violation. . . . After three months of trial, the jury could not reach a verdict, and unless the courts sharply change their view, we must try the case again in Los Angeles. . . . Under ever-changing antitrust concepts, the League is now tied down like Gulliver in its efforts to keep the Raiders in the Oakland community."

As he wound up his testimony, the commissioner's plea for help was adamant. "Let me be unequivocal," he asked of the congressmen. "I do not regard all sports league antitrust issues as requiring a legislative solution. . . . The greatest danger lies in the use of the antitrust laws to attack the internal structure of a sports league and to permit even league members to second-guess every league operating principle. . . . [S]ports leagues simply need to be recognized as the common economic enterprise that they are. This would accord the leagues antitrust treatment equivalent to that already received by other single enterprises. . . . Today the only way a sports league could avoid antitrust involvement and treble damage exposure is to cease operations altogether and simply turn the whole thing loose. . . . [W]e have already arrived at the stage where wrongly transplanted antitrust concepts are going to make the leagues powerless to prevent such results."

The League's next step was to start shaping the solution and, in early 1982, League lawyers began drafting possible legislation. According to a NFLPA lobbyist, the first draft was "an extraordinarily broad exemption" that covered almost every possible situation. Meanwhile, Rozelle was assembling a team to push the legislation that would eventually include nine different Washington PR and legal firms, all working the Hill every day.

However, opposition quickly developed around two aspects of their proposed sports bill. The first was from the union, even though Rozelle had called on the congressmen to turn their "focus" to antitrust law "outside of the labor-management area." By the end of January, the NFLPA had begun a steadily rising drumbeat of negativity about the proposal. "If this law had been passed in 1970," its newsletter pointed out, "the NFLPA would have lost the Mackey case . . . and no one could have challenged the draft. The NFL could then concentrate on breaking the NFLPA and all players' rights would be gone." Garvey's attitude eventually meant that the AFL-CIO would lobby against the measure as well.

The second focus of opposition was to a particular provision that the League insisted on, a provision making its exemption retroactive to include court cases then under litigation. According to the League's chief counsel, such retroactivity was guaranteed to be controversial. "If we got it," he admitted, "we'd probably face lawsuits over it. There are precedents both ways. . . . When it's still in the courts and not yet final, Congress can do what it wants. Once it's final, it can't do a thing about it."

The issue created two types of problems for the League. The first was one of timing. During the same session that the League's sports bill began testing congressional waters there was also, a League attorney remembered, "a big debate going on about applying antitrust legislation retroactivity to exonerate a bunch of companies in the paper industry who had been convicted of price fixing. They had a big bill up there and there was a lot of opposition to that. . . . People who would privately say we support you would also say, but I can't do it openly because I'm opposing the paper industry bill and I'll be contradicting myself. . . ."

The second problem with the League's position was that it increased both the number and intensity of the opposition. Retro-activity was the League's new last line of defense in *LAMCC v. NFL* and immediately recognizable as such. It gave L.A. and Al Davis no choice but to add their considerable weight to Garvey's. With this provision, Joe Alioto thundered, the NFL was "giving even arrogance a bad name." It was "the worst kind of special interest legislation" that the League hoped "to sneak through" and overturn "well-reasoned court decisions." The political deals involved would amount to "a sale of votes for football franchises. Don't ever underestimate the power of the NFL," he warned, "particularly when they're out there dangling franchises that are worth $250 million."

Pete Rozelle's in-house counsel responded. "Alioto's allegations," he noted, ". . . are completely unsupported by the facts. . . . There is not, and has never been, any attempt to sneak through legislation. . . . The legislation we seek . . . would be public interest legislation. . . . I would view Alioto's comments as another in a long series of efforts to poison the well against the National Football League."

Nonetheless, the problems retroactivity posed for Rozelle's breakout strategy would only escalate. "Rozelle insisted on retroactivity," Steve Rosenbloom later remembered. "The exemption would have had a chance without retroactivity. The only real reason for it was that he and Al Davis hated each other so much. If Rozelle had let retroactivity go, he would have closed the door. Instead, he got caught up in the battle with Davis. It was an arrogant approach and Rozelle demonstrated an inability to cut his losses. His attitude was 'pro football is second to God, maybe first.' It didn't work."

21
Artful Manipulations

While his friend Pete Rozelle spent most of January 1982 on Capitol Hill, Art Modell was in Cleveland trying to put his financial game plan over the top.

Modell sent a letter to Union Commerce Bank on January 6, enclosing a statement of his net worth. If none of his assets was sold by April 1, his personal debt would have risen to $11.5 million. At the same time, he had less than $1 million in assets he could convert readily into cash. This was despite drawing a quarter million dollars a year average in salary and bonuses from the Browns over the last four to five years. Interest was the big factor, costing him $1.5 million a year that he was just rolling over into his debt.

Modell hoped to escape from that vicious cycle by selling his gas and oil holdings for $4.9 million. Still, his interest burden would be in excess of $1 million a year. Aside from more borrowing to cover himself, Modell's only other option was the sale of Cleveland Stadium Corp. The Browns, Modell told his banker, would acquire Stadium Corp. for $6 million. Of that price, $4.8 million would go straight to Modell, reducing his debt to a manageable $1.8 million. Modell's letter projected that transaction would close by February 1.

Modell expected opposition from Robert Gries and unless handled carefully, Gries could still torpedo the deal. Modell had anticipated those difficulties and moved to isolate Gries from the rest of the Browns' board, who would have to approve the purchase. The board had seven members, two of whom were appointed by Gries. Gries's other appointee besides himself was his brother-in-law Richard Cole. The financial difficulties Gries had helped Cole cope with the previous fall had continued to plague him and were exacerbated by his impending divorce from Gries's sister. In late December 1981, unbeknownst to Gries, Cole visited Modell and told him that he wanted to sell his interest in the Browns and noted that the franchise itself had right of first refusal. Modell responded that he would arrive at a value for Cole's interest and he would recommend the repurchase to the Browns board. If the board didn't want to buy the shares, Modell guaranteed he would purchase them himself. Relieved to have found a buyer and apparently intent on ingratiating himself with his new benefactor, Cole also provided Modell with information about Gries's intentions. His brother-in-law was opposed to the Stadium Corp. purchase, Cole explained, and he intended to sue Modell and the Browns if they proceeded with it.

By January 13, 1982, Modell and Cole had signed a letter of intent. The deal it framed was conspicuous for its generosity toward Cole: The Browns would pay Cole $661,000 for his 4.3 percent of stock. Cole would remain a director of the Browns for the next five years, and would also continue to receive the salary and Blue Cross coverage of a Browns vice-president until August 1987. On top of all that, the Browns would also purchase Cole's Stadium Corp. holdings for $192,000 and if they had failed to do so by March 1, Modell would purchase the Stadium Corp. interest himself.

That same day, Modell received yet another report from McDonald and Company, reflecting the value the new Servomation loan had added to Stadium Corp., and forwarded it to Gries. Modell also retained a law firm, having the "strong feeling" there might be litigation. Shortly after the new McDonald and Company report, Gries got to set up a meeting for January 19. It was in that discussion, Gries remembered, that "it all hit the fan."

"This was wrong from beginning to end," Gries claimed, "and I told him that." Gries was "very, very upset because no one represented the Browns in this transaction. Who was fighting to get the best possible price on behalf of the Browns?" His answer was no one. "If we are going to spend $6 million," he told Modell, "I guarantee you we won't be simply having one report and saying O.K." Modell responded that McDonald and Company was a good firm and their report was a good report.

McDonald and Company was a "good firm," Gries agreed, but said "this report is not a credible report." Its $3.8 million estimate on the worth of the Strongsville parcel was "outlandish." Gries had procured his own evaluation of Strongsville since he and Modell had met the previous Thanksgiving. His evaluator had used two different methods to assess Strongsville's worth. One came up with $400,000, the other with $700,000. That part of Stadium Corp., in Gries's estimate, was overpriced by at least $3.1 million.

Cleveland Stadium Corp.'s other nonlease asset, its notes from the sale of the hotel on Public Square, was, according to Gries, overpriced as well. "Unless the Browns have surplus money," Gries later argued, "they should not be getting into things that have nothing to do with football. I can't, in my wildest imagination, conceive of why the Cleveland Browns . . . would invest millions of dollars in something that is nothing but a twenty-three-year note payout." McDonald and Company had said the hotel note was worth $2.1 million; Gries's consultant said the value was no more than $1.3 million. "We can solve this disagreement right away," Gries challenged Modell. "We don't have to argue about its value. Ask McDonald and Company to go out and sell it right now."

Gries also objected to McDonald and Company's conclusion that Stadium Corp. was worth $1 million more to the Browns than anyone else. "This makes no sense," Gries argued.

"Control of the stadium by the Browns is really the important thing," Modell argued. He then launched into what Robert Gries described as a "very strong and impassioned, emotional speech about why the Browns must control their own destiny." The real issue, according to Modell, was to avoid the problems that had plagued other franchises who did not control their stadiums. The Rooney family's Pittsburgh Steelers were in that position and, according to Modell, "couldn't even raise ticket prices because the city wouldn't let them."

"What has that got to do with here?" Gries interrupted.

"Suppose someone else owned the stadium?" Modell asked back.

Gries pointed out that in any case they were not going to control Browns ticket prices. "Even if you could sell that right to somebody, you won't," he noted.

"Suppose I sell the stadium to somebody and they let the thing fall apart?" Modell pressed. "Then what will the Browns do?"

The Browns had a valid lease, Gries replied. "You told me it was a very favorable lease. I am sure it provides protection against a landlord if they let things run down. I am not convinced we have to buy protection because there is nothing appearing that we have to protect against."

Quite the contrary, Gries argued, from the standpoint of protecting the Browns, the purchase itself posed the most immediate danger. "I strongly objected to increasing the Browns' debt," Gries explained. The transaction "made no sense whatsoever for the Browns at this point in time." Labor negotiations were about to begin, Gries pointed out, and the NFLPA was already talking strike. In the face of that, "you just don't go out and take the Browns and load them up with this huge amount of debt."

After listening to Gries's objections, Modell remained unmoved. He was going to present the transaction to the Browns board, he informed his minority partner, and he hoped Gries would reconsider his opposition. Robert Gries remembered that that meeting ended "acrimoniously."

The following week, Modell asked Gries if he could come to another meeting on January 26. "I was anxious to avoid litigation at all costs," Modell remembered. He began by telling Gries that his complaints were "all wrong" and that he did not agree. "The McDonald and Company report is a good report," Modell affirmed, "and I will stand on it. We are going ahead. But, to give you comfort, I am going to give you a guarantee that the Gries family isn't going to come out any worse with this deal than if we didn't make the deal."

Gries called it an "interesting concept" and asked how it would work.

"I haven't worked out the details," Modell admitted. Maybe Gries could "figure something out" with Modell's financial advisers.

"I'll give it a shot," Gries promised.

Modell thought Gries was pleased and described him as "cordial" when the meeting ended.

The next six weeks Modell spent in southern California. There he vacationed, met with the rest of the League's television committee, and participated in some of the League's settlement flirtation with the LAMCC. It was during this stay that Joe Alioto became convinced Modell meant to move to L.A. permanently. "Beverly Hills is a glamorous place," Davis's lawyer pointed out. "Art likes to be around glamorous people and his wife, Pat, is a former actress and is thinking about going into some film production. Art is on the board of directors of Twentieth Century Fox. Life out here with all the glamorous people is heady stuff, real heady stuff. And when you finish making all the money you want and have everything else, you start looking for something else."

"All I will tell you about Joe Alioto," Modell responded, "is that he never lets facts interfere with a good story."

Alioto, of course, had no idea just how far Art Modell really was from having made "all the money you want." Debt was still socked in around him on all sides and, in Cleveland, his negotiators were making little headway with Robert Gries.

Gries proposed dropping the Strongsville land from the transaction altogether and if the hotel was to be included, should be sold off in "a reasonable time." If Modell's more optimistic projections actually happened, then he could get more money. Those ideas were rejected by Modell's men, who instead concentrated on finding terms for Modell's proposed guarantee. Their idea was, according to Gries, the "most unfair guarantee I've ever seen, ever. . . . Even if I got my money back, it amounts to an interest free loan of seventeen years."

"That is not a guarantee for us," Gries exploded. "That's a guarantee for Modell."

Modell's negotiators called him in L.A. and told him Gries found none of their guarantees acceptable. "What [Gries] wanted was guaranteed profit return," Modell explained, "contrasted with my offer of a guarantee against losses and if profits were to develop, so much the better."

Modell and Gries didn't square off again face-to-face until the third week of March, shortly after Modell returned from California intent on finishing off the Stadium Corp. transaction once and for all. That finishing off occurred at a meeting of the board of directors of the Cleveland Browns. When Gries arrived with his attorney, the six other directors were already there, having met privately ahead of time. Among the six were Modell, his wife, Richard Cole, and James Bailey. All of them had received a long letter from Gries several days earlier, stating his continuing objections to buying Stadium Corp. The first point Gries raised at the meeting was his right to have legal counsel present. Modell considered the request "unusual" and left the room for a phone consultation with his own attorney.

"O.K.," Modell told Gries's lawyer when he returned, "you can stay, but don't talk." The Browns president and majority owner then opened the issue of purchasing Stadium Corp., and turned the floor over to Gries, who, according to Modell, "expounded at length."

Much of it was the same thing he had already told Modell in January. Gries also presented the reports he had received contradicting the one drawn up by McDonald and Company, citing some fifteen experts he had consulted. As usual, his greatest complaint was about including Strongsville in the purchase. Gries had commissioned yet another appraisal of the property and this one said it was worth $335,000—$3.5 million less than the Browns were about to pay. At the mention of Gries's new report, Modell and his financial adviser, James Bailey, looked at each other and chuckled. Modell then admitted that there was "a problem" with the McDonald and Company evaluation of the Strongsville parcel. Bailey had procured another real estate appraisal that lowered the value to $2.5 million. To make up for that potential shortfall and give more "comfort" to Gries, Modell announced that he was going to forgive the $1 million note he still held from Stadium Corp. That note had been part of the original purchase of the Strongsville parcel and Modell's offer did not impress Gries in the least. "The note was only payable off the profits of the land," he pointed out, "which hadn't been realized to date, might never be realized, and if realized, it would be long in the future and hence, of far less value than $1 million."

Modell also presented a twenty-page document spelling out the guarantee he was willing to furnish his minority partners. Gries's attorney then asked if the meeting could recess long enough to let him study the document. Modell refused. "It's absolutely unnecessary," he told the attorney. "There's no reason for it. We're going on with the meeting." Later, Modell was more forthcoming about his motivation. "I honestly thought he was going to file suit the moment he got out of that room," he explained.

Much of the remainder of the meeting was spent questioning Gries. The exchanges became particularly sharp between Gries and Modell's wife, Pat. At one point, she demanded that Gries tell the rest of them the names of all these experts he had consulted. Gries refused "to give a laundry list of every person I had talked to." That wasn't good enough for Pat Modell. "Well, we did," she complained. "We gave you ours. Why don't you make them available?"

"I'll make them available in court," Gries snapped.

Gries was convinced that Stadium Corp. was worth no more than $2 million, a third of its price tag, "even if you accept management's figures, which is a big if." By now, however, it was more than apparent that the rest of the board wasn't much interested in what he thought. Before an actual vote was held, he requested a short recess so he could consult his attorney.

When the board meeting reconvened, Modell remembered, Gries "made a statement that all his remarks were extemporaneous and he reserves his rights." Next came the vote. To maintain appearances, both Modell and his wife abstained. The tally was nonetheless four votes in favor of the purchase and only Robert Gries against.

Once the board had given its approval, Central National Bank, carrying seventy-five percent of the loan with which the Browns would pay Stadium Corp., would transfer $4.8 million to Art Modell's personal account. Modell would then transfer $4 million of that to Union Commerce Bank, settling his debts there. At 5:00 P.M., not long after the board meeting, Union Commerce's legal department informed the vice-president that there "might be an attempt to file a temporary restraining order to block the transaction on the following morning," but both Modell and his money man, James Bailey, urged speed in completing the exchange. Robert Gries filed suit shortly after the courts opened at 10:00 the next morning, but was too late to block a dime.

His business done, Art Modell left for Phoenix, where the 1982 annual meeting was scheduled for March 21.

22
Temporary TV Euphoria

The 1982 National Football League annual meeting was full of both good news and bad news. The good news was delivered in executive session on the morning of March 22 when the League's television committee reported on the outcome of its negotiations with the networks.

Tactically, this television pact was of prime importance to Pete Rozelle, more so perhaps than any he had ever negotiated. The commissioner had been entrapped in trench warfare since shortly after the last TV agreement was announced in 1978 and, as yet, had few, if any, victories to show for an enormous expenditure of effort on several fronts. Rozelle did not have to be told that if that pattern continued, his position would eventually be ravaged by attrition. A big win now would bolster his backers and provide fresh financial incentive to keep the League's solid front intact. It was also Rozelle's first opportunity in almost two years to break away from legal quibbling and reaffirm just how valuable he and League Think actually were.

As usual, he had entered the negotiations well armed. The 1981 season had been the NFL's best year ever for combined television ratings. Both ABC and CBS had logged all-time highs during the regular season. Super Bowl XVI had been the most watched live production ever. More than 110,000,000 Americans saw Eddie DeBartolo's 49ers win its first Super Bowl over Paul Brown's Cincinnati Bengals and 14,000,000 more listened on the radio. The NFL's average live gate for the season topped 60,000 for the first time in history.

Normally, final statistics for the last year of a television contract had little effect on negotiations because negotiations were usually finished by the time such numbers were available. This year, however, *LAMCC v. NFL* had delayed everything and the TV committee did not begin its final preparations for bargaining until after Super Bowl XVI. Then Rozelle, Art Modell, and Gene Klein huddled for a week and when the trio had come up with the figures they wanted, they sent Rozelle back to New York to tell the networks. Their demands were rumored to be "enormous" by all previous standards.

"For the first time, in the 1982 negotiations the TV committee had more involvement than ever before," Rozelle remembered. Modell and Klein joined Rozelle in some network meetings, and at another time, a CBS executive flew to L.A. and negotiated with Klein alone, the first time since 1960 that any network representative had ever negotiated football programming outside of Rozelle's presence.

All the networks were stunned when told what the League wanted. "We had been expecting a one hundred percent increase," one television executive explained, "but he hit us with 150 percent from the start and that was a surprise." Nonetheless, Rozelle at first found the going relatively easy. Taking the networks one at a time, he started with ABC and relatively quickly got them to agree to pay $680 million over five years. Next came NBC, who demanded a share of ABC's prime time slot but soon "knuckled under" and agreed to $640 million. CBS, however, put its foot down when Rozelle asked $770 million. "CBS didn't want to pay," Klein remembered, "so we went at it head to head." The CBS executive told Rozelle that CBS would drop the NFL entirely if their price didn't come down. "They stood eyeball to eyeball for a while," a source close to the negotiations remembered. "Then Pete blinked." CBS signed for $720 million on the day before the annual meeting.

The package presented on March 22 was still beyond almost everyone's fondest imaginings. The three networks had agreed to pay the League a total of $2 billion over five years. Split twenty-eight ways, that was $14 million per club per season, almost three times their current $5.2 million. "There were lots of smiles," the commissioner remembered. "They were very happy." For good reason. At the time, the average total annual expenses of an NFL club was in the neighborhood of $11 million. That meant the average club was guaranteed a profit before it even began counting the live gate. "Once again," *Sports Illustrated* declared, "the wiliest sports commissioner of them all had gone to the network treasuries and come back loaded with untold riches." When it came time to vote on the package, Rozelle remembered, "it was the quickest yes vote we've gotten from the Raiders in a long time."

Just how happy the owners were with Rozelle became apparent immediately after the TV committee's report was finished. "At noon," according to the minutes, "the commissioner and League office employees were asked to leave the room." Gene Klein then took the floor to make a motion:

RESOLVED, that a committee of owners be chosen and authorized to negotiate and execute a contract for the further employment of Pete Rozelle as NFL commissioner.

The motion was passed by a vote of twenty-seven to one, with, once again, only Al Davis dissenting. "The membership then nominated and approved a three-member committee." The members were Hugh Culverhouse, Gene Klein, and Leon Hess. The three said they would accept the assignment on "the proviso we can finalize the deal without coming to the membership for a vote." Such authority was given, twenty-seven to one. The committee was now free to give Rozelle whatever it felt was appropriate. It would be two years before most of the owners even learned what was in the contract.

"We corrected some terrible financial injustices to Pete," Gene Klein remembered. "If he was a standard CEO, he would have had stock options so that the success of the enterprise would have made him a lot of money. Pete can't do that, so we tried to make up for it. Only Al Davis objected."

While Pete Rozelle no doubt felt a certain vindication in the glory surrounding the new television deal and his employers were certifiably richer than ever, none of that changed the fact that the rest of the news facing the 1982 annual meeting was bad. Three issues in particular dominated the League's worries.

The first was, of course, *LAMCC v. NFL*. To the great frustration of the NFL's attorneys, none of their new change of venue motions had proved successful and less than a week after the meeting adjourned, trial would resume in L.A. Already there was talk about winning this one on appeal. Bolstered by the prospects of a television bonanza, however, the League was in a fighting mood, and the executive session minus Al Davis voted unanimously "to give no further consideration to settlement."

The second concern was Ed Garvey and the NFLPA. At that point, labor negotiations were looking like a replay of 1977, only worse. Even the League's optimists were counting on Garvey's position collapsing rather than modifying. Art Modell thought that the worst that could happen was "a show of unity" by the union during next season's training camps. A number of other owners, however, were already convinced there would be a full-fledged strike because that's what Garvey wanted.

Lastly, for the first time since 1975, the League was about to face the prospect of external competition. Within two months, a new football business calling itself the United States Football League would announce its existence. Both rumors and accurate information about the USFL had been in circulation for the last year. Perhaps the first NFL owner to learn about the plans for a new league was Al Davis. Davis had been approached by one of the league's initial organizers shortly after the 1980 annual meeting. The approach was in response to a statement Davis had made to the press shortly after walking out of executive session while the rest of the League voted on his move to L.A.

"I've just been thinking about . . . starting a new football League," Davis had told a reporter. The idea would be to field eight teams to stage eight games a month. The broadcast rights would be sold to cable and pay television outlets, which, Davis figured, would net the league $48 million, $6 million per team. "I'm not planning this or anything," Davis had pointed out. "I'm just thinking about it. You know, just talking . . ."

Shortly thereafter, Al Davis received a phone call from George Allen, former coach and general manager of the Washington Redskins. Now out of the NFL, Allen was enthusiastic about Davis's comments. "George called me," Davis remembered, "and said, 'Why don't we do it?' And I would talk to him about it . . . he would ask me questions about budgets and things like that, which I would help him [with] . . . and [I] advised him what I thought he would have to do to make a new league work. . . . I told him how much money he would have to get from the networks per team to succeed." When his fellow NFL members eventually learned of Davis's cooperation, it would become yet another reason to resent him.

In March 1982, however, it was not clear just how much of a challenge the USFL was going to pose. Rather than go head to head, the new league intended to play games in the spring and summer. It would not compete directly for audience, which was good news, but it might well compete for players, which decidedly was not. That March, it was the USFL's organizers' stated position not to try to buy away NFL talent but to build a league on the leftovers, almost like an NFL farm team. "As far as competing for players," Modell noted, "they have limited payroll budgets . . . so that should not be a problem." The pessimists noted that there had never been two football leagues without a bidding war between them and that the USFL was recruiting owners with money to spend. The pessimists were right. Just as the NFL seemed to have found the goose that laid the golden egg, the cost of doing business was about to go through the roof.

Euphoria from their television contract apparently blinded a number of League members to the actual direness of their situation, but, on paper, it looked like Rozelle's worst nightmare. For the next year, the League would have to fight a trade war, a labor war, and a civil war all at the same time. Rich or not, League Think was in deep trouble.

23
The New Raiders

The most immediately pressing of those potential disasters was *LAMCC v. NFL*. In March 1982, most of the League wanted to whip Al Davis. One owner even had a parrot trained to squawk "Fuck you, Al Davis" stationed near the check-in counter when Davis arrived at the annual meeting.

Davis's detractors claimed the issue was much larger than Davis himself. "You can't have a rule and then abide with it when you agree and say the hell with it when you don't," Art Modell argued. "This is a far more important thing than merely if the Oakland Raiders move or not."

Davis himself remained largely silent between trials, but there was little doubt he found the rest of the League's arguments specious. "It's stupid," he told *Sport* magazine. "It's ridiculous. It's the same lament and cry from Rozelle and the other owners in the NFL for the last ten or fifteen years. When Congress lifted the TV blackout, Rozelle told Congress it would destroy the home gate. On the contrary, it's grown. Every time one of our illegal rules is struck from our constitution, it's meant 'doom' for the League. But in reality . . . the NFL has become a better League. . . . It's the old fear package, something that's typical of Rozelle."

According to Davis, Rozelle was the reason for it all. "He had a nickname for a while, Sneaky Pete," Davis told *Sport*. ". . . He knows that. And that's the way he operates. . . . Rozelle is the most powerful man in professional sports and he does not want to give up his power base. This [trial] is a challenge to it. He tried to destroy my negotiations in Oakland. He's sent me letters threatening disciplinary action that would, in essence, take my team away from me. He's sent letters to banks in Los Angeles, telling them not to loan me any money. All of those things are personal, there's no question about it. . . . The League has what we call its police force. It's a thing that started out as a security force to protect the League from gambling influences and things like that. Instead, it has become a personal gestapo for the commissioner . . . . God, the investigations that we've gone through. I know one owner in particular, I don't want to mention his name, who was called in within the past two years and told to get in line or else. And he has gotten in line. . . . My life has been gone over with a fine-tooth comb."

Davis still claimed that Rozelle's motive was in part a lust for L.A. for himself. "I really don't think that I would have had any problems if I wanted to move my team to Phoenix. I strongly believe that he wanted the territory for himself. . . . Pete lived there, his family lived there. He wants equity. He doesn't want to be an employee, to have his salary docked. He's gotten older and he's reached a stage where he wants to play tennis, be a big socialite." According to Davis, Rozelle's own needs had even affected the new TV contract. "I think we might have made a mistake in signing a five-year contract, I really do. . . . [W]e should have signed a shorter contract. . . . He wanted that $2 billion figure. It gives him a chance to look for a new contract for himself. It also gives him a power base with the networks that he wants very badly when he has to influence

Congress or the country on certain issues. The League probably has the most massive media control of any entity in America other than the President." Rozelle, of course, continued to maintain his decorum and ignore Davis's sniping.

By March 30, the day the *LAMCC v. NFL* retrial's opening arguments began, the difficulty of the commissioner's role was also becoming apparent. The battle was now etched under Rozelle's eyes in shadows and puffy ridges. There was more sag to his cheeks and there was already a sense of something battered about him. The year 1982 would be his third straight one without a vacation, and there was yet another to go after that.

Though the retrial process would not be as physically grueling as what had happened the previous year, it would prove just as wearing or even more so. The new trial was essentially a severely foreshortened version of the first. Since personal charges against Rozelle, Klein, and Frontiere had been previously dismissed, there was no need on their parts to either prove or disprove a personal conspiracy. The same, of course, was true for the NFL's single entity defense. Even the jury was smaller; six women with no discernible knowledge of football. The one constant was that Al Davis and Pete Rozelle remained the star attractions.

The main issue was framed by the LAMCC's Maxwell Blecher in his opening statement. "The real subject matter is monopoly and monopoly power," the attorney argued. "All the Oakland Raiders and the Coliseum commission have done is to request an equal opportunity to compete on the merits in the marketplace. . . . We say the NFL does not own Los Angeles. They cannot make the decision who will play in our ballpark. . . . The NFL is fighting about money and property rights. We're here fighting about freedom."

Rozelle's testimony lasted four days and had few variances with what he'd sworn to in 1981. Those few discrepancies, however, were picked at mercilessly. During his first day on the stand, he sought to modify his earlier testimony that the L.A. Rams had benefited more than any other party from the League's refusal to allow Davis to move south. Upon reflection, he pointed out, he had noted that the Rams games in Anaheim had been sold out and the absence of any other unsold home team tickets in the L.A. media market meant the Rams home games could be televised. "The biggest winners," he now observed, "were the followers of professional football in southern California."

Naturally enough, Blecher wanted to know why the commissioner had omitted such calculations the previous year. "I guess I have a lot to think about," Rozelle explained.

The change that damaged the NFL most emerged on Rozelle's last day on the stand. Heretofore, he had resolutely refused to admit that the League had any pecuniary motive of its own for refusing Davis. Before going on the stand that morning, however, the League's attorneys instructed him to add one, their reasoning was that the admission might be useful in the appeal process. But Rozelle's new testimony was like a crowbar in Joe Alioto's hands.

"The League has a right to derive benefits of an expansion franchise in Los Angeles," the commissioner pointed out. He also noted that such a franchise would be worth "considerably more" than one in Oakland or any number of other cities. "It's a corporate right of all twenty-eight clubs . . . to share the benefits." That right, Rozelle admitted, allowed the rest of the League to say that Davis "must stay where a franchise is worth less money."

Did this NFL rule, Alioto probed, mean that eight owners could say "we want a franchise for ourselves and we'll divvy up the money" and then "vote their pocketbook against Mr. Davis?"

"Yes," Rozelle admitted, "but Mr. Davis would share equally."

So if Section 4.3 of the NFL constitution, granting them that right, were invalidated, Alioto continued, "it would be competitive to your right to put a franchise in and divvy up the money?"

If Section 4.3 were invalidated, Rozelle retorted, "we couldn't put a franchise anywhere."

Try as Rozelle might to put his statement in context, the next morning's headlines were ominous for the League. "Testimony by Rozelle May Hurt NFL," the *Los Angeles Times* noted. "He Tells of League's Financial Motive in Blocking Raider Move."

When Al Davis took the stand, the closest the defense came to catching him in a contradiction came on April 21. At issue was Davis's testimony that the L.A. Coliseum, was "superior" to Oakland's newer stadium.

So you have never been critical of the L.A. Coliseum as a place to watch football? one of the NFL attorneys asked.

"Never," Davis answered.

The attorney then produced the clipping of a 1973 interview Davis had given to the *Los Angeles Times* in which he said the exact opposite. "The [L.A.] Coliseum is tough on football games," he had told the *Times*. "Los Angeles fans sit so far away they don't feel involved," he said. "It's like looking at a parade from a helicopter. . . . Football as a spectator sport was meant to be played in an intimate, closed-up stadium. When the spectators are on top of the players, the game is never dull. Every play is exciting when you're in the thick of the action, when you feel involved. . . . [And] see and hear the violent and artistic things that make football what it is. . . . If a Rams fan could attend a game sometime in Oakland, he'd understand what I mean."

Davis's immediate response was to deny the quote entirely. Under pressure he admitted he had probably talked to the reporter, but continued to deny the quote itself. Though described as "stunned" by the clipping when the attorney produced it, Davis could not be shaken any further and that was as close as the NFL came to breaking him the second time around.

On May 7, when the case went to the jury, the wait was short. The jury in the first trial had hung after more than twelve days in deliberation. This new jury took just six hours. It had two counts to decide. The first was whether Section 4.3 violated the Sherman Act. The second was whether the League had also breached its contractual duty of good faith and fair dealing with Davis. The jury found for Davis and the LAMCC on both counts.

When the court clerk read the verdicts aloud, the *Times* reported, "Al Davis was sitting in his usual front row seat and beamed." Pete Rozelle immediately issued a press release saying the League intended to appeal the verdict and fight all the way to the Supreme Court.

Joe Alioto called the verdict "a smashing victory over a very worthy and very resourceful opponent," but his boss, Al Davis, objected to the use of "victory."

"It's just an injustice that has been rectified," Davis claimed. "I'm not emotionally elated. I wish I could say it's a victory, but I can't look at it that way. . . . I thought we were going to win all along." Warming to the subject, Davis did note who the loser was. "I think we showed Mr. Rozelle that he can't treat people like that," he added. "He can't push people around like that."

The League's optimists thought the verdict would not affect its immediate behavior, and Art Modell went so far as to predict there was "no chance" the Raiders would play in L.A. for the upcoming 1982 season. "The game isn't over," he pointed out.

In response, Joe Alioto explained the risk the NFL would be taking if it didn't allow Davis to move while the appeal was being made. *LAMCC v. NFL* would be reconvening soon to hear testimony on what damages should be awarded the plaintiffs.

"It's going to compound damages," Alioto observed, "which are running about $8 million a year." Since antitrust damages were, as a matter of federal law, automatically trebled, the actual price would be $24 million a year. Given those numbers, the lawyer added, "You can understand why a lot of those people are getting nervous."

Within a month of the verdict, the League included the new L.A. Raiders in its 1982 schedule. A little more than two years after he set out to make the move, Al Davis was at last free to do so. For the moment, at least, Los Angeles was his.

24
Deflation in Washington

Pete Rozelle returned quickly to New York and fell back on his breakout strategy. On May 21, Congressmen Fortney Stark and Don Edwards of California and Henry Hyde of Illinois introduced the Major League Sports Community Protection Act of 1982, prohibiting "a franchise from using antitrust laws to attack a sports league" and requiring "teams to receive league approval before moving to another city." On July 12, a similar version of the act was introduced in the Senate.

The Senate bill was the focus of the most legislative attention. It was submitted with the stated purpose of allowing Congress "to clarify the application of antitrust laws to professional team sports leagues [and] to protect the public interest in maintaining the stability of professional team sports." It specifically exempted votes on franchise relocation and "rules for the division of League or member club revenues" from the Sherman Act. If Rozelle could convince Congress to pass the retroactive act before the *LAMCC v. NFL* appeals ran out, the day would be saved.

To effect that rescue, Rozelle called out the League's lobbying blitz. In addition to the nine firms it retained for that purpose, a number of the League's owners participated directly as well, visiting senators and making political contributions. By August, Senate Democratic party leader Robert Byrd of West Virginia had received the maximum legal campaign contribution of $1000 from Georgia Frontiere, Hugh Culverhouse, Joe Robbie, Gene Klein, Bud Adams, Rankin Smith, and Leonard Tose. "Now the League is stepping up the fight in the only other arena left to them," Joe Alioto complained. "Rozelle and his people are trying to make an end run around the courts. . . . They're dangling franchises in front of states with influential congressmen, . . . and they're hiring some of the most expensive lobbyists in Washington."

"The NFL is trying to bribe its way through Congress," Al Davis said.

Leonard Tose would later claim that Davis needn't have been so worried. Despite the League's enormous mobilization, Tose remembered, "there was no organization. It was amateur night. I went down and saw a couple senators and, frankly, they had more important things to do than help the NFL. I talked to one senator I know well and he told me, 'You guys are just playing with yourselves. You're not going to get anything.' "

Tose's information did nothing to dent the commissioner's effort. When the Senate Judiciary Committee held hearings on the act, Rozelle was again the League's lead witness. His argument was much the same as he had offered to the House the previous December, only now *LAMCC v. NFL* was at the top of his list of complaints. If that decision were allowed to stand, he pointed out, "it would be anarchy. . . . We sit down at a League meeting, and under the decision in Los Angeles . . . everything we do—I include picking where we are going to have a League meeting—could be a conspiracy."

Rozelle's principal opponents at those hearings were Ed Garvey of the NFLPA, Bill Robertson of the L.A. Coliseum, and Al Davis.

Garvey testified immediately after Rozelle on August 16. Six days earlier, the union's membership had voted strike authorization, although no date for the strike had been set. "I guess it is fair to say," Garvey told the senators, "that we would not envy a senator from the states that are considering expansion. . . . There is enormous pressure on them to try to accommodate the NFL so that the NFL will indeed expand. But in a real sense, I think what the NFL is saying to the Congress is what each team says to its city: 'Unless you do certain things, we will move or we will do something else.' . . . To just trust the monopoly I think is folly." Even League Think's revenue sharing was not out of bounds for Garvey. "We suggested . . ." Garvey continued, "that it was time to take a long hard look at revenue sharing because it has hurt the player market pool and we do not see that it has helped competition. More importantly, it has given the NFL enormous power to make sure that other leagues could not form, and it allows them to decide when and where to expand.''

Ed Garvey also did not buy the League's claims that S. 2784 would not affect its labor/management relations. "We also hear,'' Garvey continued, ''. . . that they are very concerned to make sure that this bill does not in any way impact adversely on the players. Anyone who looks at the antitrust laws and the history of sports litigation could not reach that conclusion. . . . If the Congress declares [the NFL] to be a joint venture, then by . . . force of law, they will be able to successfully argue their way out of Section 1 of the Sherman Act. . . . They have tried it every time they have had a case come before the court. . . . The courts have said, 'Follow the rule of reason: come up with something less restrictive: negotiate with the union, and you have no problems.' And, indeed, that is what happened. Yet, if this bill passes, they know perfectly well then they have an incentive not to reach agreement with the union, but to continue what they have been trying to do for years, and that is not to have a union at all.''

Bill Robertson testified shortly after Garvey. "NFL Commissioner Rozelle has maintained that the NFL is the proper determinant of what constitutes public interest as it applies to professional football,'' Robertson complained. ''. . . such an assertion is incredible. . . . If they [the NFL] are chronic [antitrust] violators—and indeed I submit they are—it is only because of their arrogant and willful insistence that they should be above the law. . . . Given a choice between letting the free market decide versus twenty-eight NFL aristocrats, we believe the public interest is best served by a free market economy . . .''

Al Davis testified on September 20 only because "forced'' to do so by Joe Alioto. He began nervously: "I appreciate . . . very much [the opportunity] to talk about my opposition to [S.2784] . . . I am very much opposed to it. . . . I have spent seven months in the courtroom out in Los Angeles and had a trial by jury, . . . in which the case of the Raiders was won. . . . We won in every court decision, so far, between the National Football League and the Raiders.''

"This bill,'' Davis continued, "would now give the National Football League, the owners, the opportunity to go back to unanimity, unanimous vote before somebody could move or eight people could decide they didn't want somebody, based on any reason whatsoever. Pete Rozelle admitted, under oath, that the reason they did not want me to move to Los Angeles was that the Los Angeles franchise was worth a lot more money than the Oakland franchise and that by my moving to Los Angeles, I would get a valuable piece of property that other owners thought they should have and they should divvy up amongst themselves. . . . I do not think it is fair. I do not think it is necessary. I think that the National Football League is twenty-eight individual owners who are individual competitors and I would go a little further and say vicious competitors. . . . We do have common rules. We have common scheduling, but we do not share profits and losses. We do not share them at all. And to make us a single entity is totally unfair because that is what we are not.''

Davis contested the idea that he was trying to live outside the rules. "I do abide by the rules," he insisted, "especially if they are legal rules, but if you remember this, when we won the trial in Los Angeles, the Raiders, at the beginning, did not contest Section 4.3. What I contested was that even if the rule was legal, they acted in bad faith . . . and we won that unanimously. . . . They put every type of harassment in front of me, and I have abided by the rules all the way and I think the court bears that out. . . . I really do not think these sports bills are necessary for the good of the National Football League and the good of the American public. I think that these sports bills take away the right of cities to protect themselves. They give us a hammer and a wedge to do whatever we want.''

"Are you telling this committee," one senator persisted, "that if these pieces of legislation were amended to include standards and guidelines that that would be acceptable to Al Davis . . . ?''

". . . I have won in court," Davis responded ". . . but I am willing to do anything that is reasonable. . . . I do not want a continuing confrontation with the commissioner. In fact, I am willing to let him win in some way, if that is what he needs, a victory. I am willing to let him win.''

Pete Rozelle found Davis's claims to "reasonableness" laughable. Even he, however, had to admit that by the time Davis testified, the League's bill was facing significant problems, mostly on the League's labor front. On the morning Davis testified, Ed Garvey announced the NFLPA was on strike and the three-week-old football season came to a grinding halt. "As soon as the strike was first announced," Rozelle remembered, "some people who had been supportive of the legislation said to hell with it." No one on Capitol Hill wanted to intervene in a labor dispute.

The news could not have been worse. While Pete Rozelle had been concentrating on Davis, League Think had been taken from the flank by the NFLPA. The League had no choice but to drop its business in Congress and square off with Ed Garvey for the fight of its life.

25
Garvey Gets a Cold

The 1982 strike marked the first time that an NFL regular season game had ever been canceled by a labor dispute. Though the League's relations with the union had always been conflict-ridden, the events of 1982 were a quantum leap beyond simple animosity and irritation. This time, the fight cost the League large amounts of money and threatened its very status as America's Game. Coming as it did, when League Think was reeling from civil war and the League had been exhibiting its dirty laundry in federal court for two years, the strike culminated in a public relations disaster of enormous proportions. It was also the climactic episode of the NFL's decade-long relationship with the Ed Garvey.

From the owners' viewpoint, it was Garvey's strike all the way. "Garvey is a horse's ass," Leonard Tose railed. "He promised the young people in the union the moon and they thought he could deliver. He never gave them the true story." Gene Klein complained to the *San Diego Union*, "Ed Garvey . . . has overpromised so much, he can't deliver."

Ed Garvey wasn't surprised at being vilified. He had taken this into account when developing his own tactics and he stayed in the background and let union President Gene Upshaw issue most of the union statements. "They don't care about you," Upshaw said of the management council. "We're replaceable parts." Garvey himself pointed out how much better prepared the union was now than it had been in 1974. "The input from players is better than before, our staff is large and experienced enough to handle essential contacts in a union so spread out, and we've worked carefully . . . to communicate our need for assistance to the entire labor community. And the key point is, we have the right issue. All the players can see how much is involved. . . . They can see a percentage of the gross will help virtually every player. If it means strike, it means strike. We're not going to get it unless the owners believe the players will strike. No one gives up money or power for the fun of it."

When the strike began, the shutdown was complete and would remain that way for fifty-seven days. "It was the first time the players recognized the union as a viable force," one of its former officers claimed, "an organization you could take seriously. It was the first time the union went after wages. . . . [N]ow was the time to do it."

The strength of the union's solid front grew out of two parallel and mutually reinforcing attitudes: First, and most important, was a righteous sense of being underpaid. Baseball and basketball generated some $610,000 per player per year and the NFL generated $476,000. Baseball had an average salary of $240,000, basketball, $215,000, and football, $95,000. The union claimed that the owners made an average gross profit of $5 million, making the owner more valuable than all his players put together. Ed Garvey had no problem generating agreement among the players that the disproportion was intolerable.

He had also succeeded in selling his notion of percentage of the gross. Such a mechanism would, the union claimed, make the owners spend twice as much on salaries. Those calculations were based on fifty-five percent for the players, the level Garvey was currently demanding as an absolute minimum. Garvey's proposal also included a complex system of incentives for individual and team performance. "We are fighting socialism with socialism," he pointed out. "What else can we do?"

The League's response to Garvey's demand for a piece of the action was that it was "alien to American business," according to management council negotiator Jack Donlan. "It would turn over control of the business to the players. . . . [P]ro football is the most successful of all sports entertainment businesses because of the business decisions made by the owners over the years, and the owners don't want to give up the right to make those decisions." Management was prepared to negotiate over money but not over power. According to Donlan, in 1981, some forty-eight percent of football's gross had been allocated to "player costs, which includes salaries and other benefits," but Garvey's fifty-five percent demand was for salaries alone. Donlan's strategy was to turn the negotiations away from structure and toward money. Management's final offer was a package of immediate payments and salary level pledges it valued at $1.6 billion over its five-year term.

Ed Garvey and the union negotiators rejected the offer the same day it was made. "I am convinced they're offering $1.6 billion," Garvey explained, "about as much as I'm convinced there is a tooth fairy." Garvey's counteroffer was to drop fifty-five percent of the gross in exchange for a $1.6 billion payment over four years into a player's compensation fund administered by the union. The management council rejected the offer and talks broke off on September 17.

The strike began after the League's third regular season game and negotiations resumed on September 26, the first Sunday without a game. What followed was a long series of starts and stops without much discernible progress at all. There was no shortage of animosity in the process.

The union bargaining team was always no less than six: Garvey, Upshaw, three other players, and another attorney. When negotiations began, the other attorney refused to shake hands with Donlan and the management team. Garvey, Donlan remembered, "was the same as in 1974. He was always putting a show on for the players, always trying to put the owners on the defensive." At one point, the two sides sat across the table from each other in absolute silence for more than an hour. At another, Garvey and management council aide Vince Lombardi Jr. ended up almost jaw-to-jaw yelling at each other. The yelling quickly turned to threats of physical violence. Then Gene Upshaw, six foot five and 265 pounds, intervened. "Hey, Vince," he thundered in Lombardi's direction, "if you're looking for some action, here it is." At that point, threats of bodily harm ceased. "If Lombardi ever hit Upshaw," Garvey joked, "and Upshaw found out about it, Vince would be in trouble."

Donlan found negotiating with Garvey as frustrating a venture as he had ever been in. Usually, Donlan pointed out, labor negotiators keep their real position to the last. "[Garvey] was very predictable," Donald explained. "The things he said were the things he kept saying. We kept waiting for his real position and it turned out to be the first one. He talked a lot about his membership, but he decides what the union wants and then sells it to them. I said to him over and over, 'Ed, we can't afford your promises.' "

Garvey was frustrated as well, particularly at the continued absence of any owners from the bargaining table. Finally, in response to Garvey's complaints, Donlan arranged a secret meeting of Garvey and the management council executive committee but Garvey didn't show up. The meeting was eventually held and the management council executive committee told Garvey that Donlan spoke for them and to negotiate with him. In the meantime, the owners also kept the pressure on. "I would say that if the union persists in its demands for a wage scale," Chuck Sullivan told *The New York Times*, "it will leave us no option but to seriously consider shutting down" for the entirety of the 1982 season. Sullivan also noted that many owners wanted to open up training camp and put together new teams out of scabs and NFLPA defectors. "No matter what time we schedule a meeting," management council Vice-Chairman Leonard Tose complained to the Associated Press, "they're at least an hour late. . . . Many times they have rejected our proposal without reading it. These meetings have lasted as short as three minutes. . . . I can say without fear of contradiction that the players have been misled, lied to, subjected to distorted information continuously by their own union leadership."

The League's solid public front toward Garvey had only one serious defector: Al Davis. He thought the management approach all wrong and said so. "The idea should not be to defeat the players," he complained. "To my way of thinking, that's not the way to approach the problem. The players are the game. We own it, but they play it."

Rozelle, of course, was powerless to intervene in the discussion. Because of his position as "the commissioner of all of football," Rozelle could only join negotiations as an impartial intermediary, a role, as Davis no doubt knew, the union would never permit him. Rozelle tried nonetheless, approaching Ed Garvey and Gene Upshaw privately during October.

"From all I can gather," Rozelle told the two union men, "the owners are never going to accept percentage of the gross. I just want to tell you that. . . . Right or wrong, I'm telling you, I don't think they'll ever accept it." Rozelle also told them, "I hope to be an escape valve and anytime I can help, please use me."

According to Rozelle, Garvey responded, "The only way we see your involvement is in negotiating on behalf of the owners."

"They have Jack Donlan for that," Rozelle pointed out. Garvey just shrugged.

According to Hugh Culverhouse, "Rozelle stayed in daily

contact with the owners" and, according to Leonard Tose, "attended meetings of the management council and there were occasions when he helped modify a position." But Rozelle could do nothing on a commissioner's traditional scale. That powerlessness was yet another diminishment at a time when he needed a victory fairly badly. "I couldn't do much during the strike," Rozelle admitted. "I was just frustrated along with everyone else."

Ed Garvey's most significant problem as the strike wore on was keeping his membership together behind percentage of the gross and a union wage scale. "It is our legal right to bargain over wages," he insisted. However, Garvey's support was diminishing as the absence of a strike fund began to be felt. Their malaise was accentuated by the very public collapse of one of Garvey's schemes to supplement the strikers' finances by staging their own football games. Their first effort was held on October 17. While the NFLPA claimed to have sold more than 8,700 tickets, the Associated Press estimated the crowd at 2,500. The projected nineteen-game series never materialized, and the rest of the games were soon dropped as pointless.

The League was, of course, well aware of the pressures on Garvey. "Garvey had told the players the owners would fold after two games," Jack Donlan claimed. "After that, his position had to weaken." On the sixth straight Sunday without an NFL game, the NFLPA summoned all its player reps for what would prove to be the final extended round of bargaining. That same day, the NFL made what it described as a "$1.28 billion," four-year offer. The offer was rejected by the union, but described as a "possible basis for future discussions." By November 4, the League had made its "best offer"—$1.313 billion over four years plus a $60,000 bonus for every veteran as soon as an agreement was settled upon. At that point, according to Dan Rooney, "everyone thought the strike would end . . . but the NFL made a mistake." The mistake was the League's attitude toward the union's desire for a formal gesture that established their right to negotiate wages. Garvey had now abandoned fifty-five percent of the gross, but the NFL refused to allow him some face-saving. On November 5, negotiations collapsed and management walked out.

"Garvey didn't know how to solve the situation he'd gotten himself into," Donlan explained. "He wanted to meet to be able to hold off the players. Our strategy was to have no meetings. When he couldn't get meetings, Garvey called Rozelle and was shut off. He also called individual owners and was shut off there. We put Garvey under pressure and he couldn't hold off the players anymore." The freeze out lasted more than a week, during which time the League mailed copies of its final offer to all players for their "informal discussion." Four days later, players on the New Orleans Saints, Cincinnati Bengals, Los Angeles Rams, and Houston Oilers all voted to accept the League's offer by overwhelming margins. "The rank and file," Dan Rooney noted, "was ready to cave in."

By November 12, Garvey was in somewhat desperate straits as well. He called his one "friend" among the owners, Dan Rooney, to commiserate. "Ed was down," Rooney remembered, "real down and upset. He kept saying the thing was blown. . . . We both kept asking 'What can we do?' Wasn't there someone we could get to mediate?" The name both Rooney and Garvey came up with was Paul Martha, a former player who now worked in the front office of Eddie DeBartolo's 49ers. Rooney and Garvey talked with Martha, then they talked with the rest of the management council and on November 14, negotiations were reopened. Even Garvey soon admitted "progress is being made."

That first day's negotiations were nonetheless rocky, but on the following morning, Garvey, Upshaw, Donlan, Rooney, and Martha all met and finally reached a tentative agreement. That evening, the owners met to ratify it. "Nobody did any handsprings," Art Modell noted of the owners' vote, "and there was no elation. But nobody voted against it either."

On November 17, *The New York Times* ran "Strike Is Ended in Pro Football; Games Sunday" on its front page. "The contract," the "impartial" Pete Rozelle explained, "contains no major changes from our last offer."

The outcome was nothing for Garvey to brag about. "Garvey had a terrible cold and it was obvious he'd just had it," one of the assembled player reps remembered. "The strike collapsed from the top down." Having set out to get fifty-five percent of the gross and the right to act as the sole bargaining agent for players, paying salaries out of a collective fund according to a seniority scale, Garvey had settled for an owners' guarantee to spend $1.6 billion over four years on players' salaries, including $60 million in "money now" bonuses for ending the strike. There would be no collective fund, but there would be minimum salary levels that went up with seniority and the union had won the right to approve the agents who negotiated players' individ-

ual contracts. The $1.6 billion was indeed the same the owners
had offered before the strike began.

"The strike was a complete failure," one player rep noted.
"If we'd kept the old agreement, we would have been better
off."

26
"Pete Is Losing His Fastball"

Though the League "won," there was little for Pete Rozelle to
celebrate when the strike finally ended. He tried to contain the
damage, patching together a schedule for the remaining six
weeks of football season, but as the League limped into 1983, it
was obvious that its accumulated damage was on a scale far
beyond anyone's immediate control.

In dollars and cents, all sectors of the football business showed
heavy debits. The fifteen hundred players lost $72 million in
wages. Employees at football stadia lost $4.5 million and con-
cessionaires lost $17 million. Overall business in NFL cities was
down by $110 million and surrounding municipalities lost some
$11 million in taxes and rent. The twenty-eight owners lost a
total of $240 million in television and gate revenues. While the
owners' losses may have been a worthwhile investment that,
according to *Sports Illustrated*, "preserved their way of life for
half a decade," their losses nonetheless had to be covered with
borrowed money that would have to be repaid with interest.
Though football players would continue to draw the lowest
average salaries in professional sports, salaries would go up and
take the price of doing business with them.

The League was also faced with a legacy of labor ill will that
would be slow to disappear. The NFLPA had trouble digesting
the crow they'd been forced to eat. Faced with the final deal, the
union's player reps had voted nineteen to six to put the deal to a
membership vote and go back to work, but only three of them
recommended acceptance. The Detroit Lions' players boycotted
their first day of practice and the New England Patriots wanted
to call their own wildcat strike. "I noted how the players kept
their distance from me when I went out to practice," Art Modell

observed. "None of them even acknowledged I was there. I guess many of them are angry and bitter."

An even worse legacy, from Rozelle's perspective, was the residual ill will among the League's audience—an attitude that showed up in reduced attendance and reduced television ratings as well. Rozelle had been warning the League about this danger since 1977. After half a decade of lawsuits and the worst labor war in its history, there was now little doubt that the NFL was first and foremost a business, and much of the mystique Rozelle had spent two decades building crumbled in a heap at his feet.

The commissioner's image sustained significant damage as well. "Rozelle was a loser in this strike," *Sports Illustrated* observed. "The world had come to look on him as some kind of savior. He wasn't."

On top of that, Rozelle's embarrassing powerlessness was only deepened by the strike's impact. When he got back to Washington in late November 1982 to revive the League's efforts there, he got a chilly reception. There were no antitrust exemptions available. Rozelle remembered, "If the strike had been forty days instead of fifty-seven days, there might still have been time to do something in 1982. There was a lot of support, but as it was, even when the strike was over, the response was not euphoria. By then everyone had been beaten to death with it. Instead of a positive reaction, the attitude was, 'It's finally over, so to hell with them for a while.' " By early 1983, the League was abandoning its quest for a sports bill. "It just doesn't seem worthwhile doing now," Rozelle explained.

Pete Rozelle's last hope of dislodging Al Davis and saving League Think rested with the appeals court. In the meantime, *LAMCC v. NFL* was the law and Rozelle, by his own description, was surrounded on all sides by legal minefields and unable to act. In his terminology, "anarchy" now had the firm upper hand and, for the first time in more than two decades, there was nothing the commissioner could do about it.

Small consolation for Rozelle and the League in 1983 was the fact that Garvey was a casualty of the strike as well. By January 1983, several clubs' players had voted to oust Garvey. Most also asked for an outside audit of the union's books. According to Garvey's most recent financial report, the NFLPA finished 1982 with assets of minus $962,000. Some of the dissidents placed the union's debts at closer to $2 million. Garvey denied the union was in financial trouble. "Running a union is not like running a business," he explained. "You build up to negotiations and spend what you have to [in order to] carry on negotiations effectively. . . . There's no danger of going into bankruptcy. Unions don't do that." Garvey also downplayed the dissent. "This sounds like a big problem, but it isn't," he said.

The showdown came in February, when the union's player reps met in Florida. The leader of Garvey's opposition there was Keith Fahnhorst, of the San Francisco 49ers. Fahnhorst, a veteran of the abortive 1981 rising against Garvey, was successful in bringing Garvey down immediately. "As we got close to the meeting," Fahnhorst remembered. "I saw we didn't have the votes. Then, when I walked into the meeting, I saw Garvey's wife was there and I knew Garvey's people were pulling out all the stops. . . . Garvey had decided he wasn't going to stay on, but he didn't want to be fired. . . . Some of his opponents voted for him because of that." The official vote split two to one in Garvey's favor but afterward, according to Fahnhorst, "Garvey was real subdued and quiet. He realized he was finished. He couldn't hide things anymore."

In June, Ed Garvey made his resignation official. "He feels that he has finished his business with the players association, and his mind is made up," one of Garvey's friends explained to *The New York Times*. "Ed hopes to move through the mainstream of Democratic politics in Wisconsin and wants to be a congressman. He must move before he is too old. His present job is a one-way street."

The NFLPA's new executive director was Gene Upshaw. "It's reconstruction sort of like after the Civil War," Upshaw explained. "I think we need a change in philosophy in our approach. When people think of the National Football League Players Association, it doesn't rank up there with some of the most credible organizations in the country. I want our image changed." Once Garvey was gone, according to Keith Fahnhorst, it became popular to refer to him around NFLPA circles as "that bastard."

Garvey's departure was the only piece of good news Pete Rozelle would have to report in 1983. The careful structure he had crafted was collapsing around his commissionership. "It is all coming home to roost," Ed Garvey observed. "Rozelle, Tex Schramm, and Art Modell have run the League and the League has to pay the price of their rigidity. The Davis case cost at least $9 million in legal fees and they may have to pay $50 million in damages and all Rozelle has succeeded in doing is making Al Davis the most powerful man in sports. As one owner told me during the strike, 'Pete is losing his fastball.' . . . I suspect his days are numbered. He's just taken one body blow after another.''

While the strike was a landmark of financial devastation, the defeat in L.A. changed the very rules on which the business was built. By the time the NFL 1983 annual meeting convened on March 20, the full impact of what Al Davis had wrought was beginning to sink in.

Hugh Culverhouse worried that "the Davis suit strikes at the crux of the League's ability to govern itself." Tex Schramm called it "a destabilization. . . . If anybody can do what they feel they must, then there's no League." Art Modell called "the Davis litigation" a "debilitating process, particularly for Pete." If sustained on appeal, it would surely lead to "a form of anarchy." All admitted that it left Rozelle's commissionership in severe flux. "There has been a significant erosion of authority," Modell noted. "The important thing for Pete now is to bring the rank and file of ownership back into line so they act as a single unit. His powers will disappear without that."

The challenge Modell posed was no mean trick. The commissioner's powers to enforce agreement were at a low ebb. The eight years leading up to the current disorder had indelibly altered the character of the League he would have to persuade once again to agree. "In the old days," Steve Rosenbloom remembered, "during the fifties, ownership wasn't so ego-oriented. They were mostly football guys who weren't all that impressed with themselves. They didn't get involved in it for the money and they'd had the experience of trying to keep the League from going under. . . . Football was what they enjoyed doing and they saw themselves as providing a team for their city. These days. . . . It has unraveled to the point that the owner is egotistical and self-centered and thinks only of money. The people making the decisions now are all lawyers, business people, and accountants."

Rosenbloom was at the 1983 meeting and the transformation made a deep impression on him. "I was outside the meeting room," he remembered, "and the doors opened and the first fifteen guys to come out I had never seen before. They were all lawyers and accountants. At first, I thought I had the wrong room."

For Pete Rozelle, the last three years had been one long, caustic fight in which he lost and lost and then lost again. "He looked terrible," one friend said of him at the time. "He was nervous. The whole thing with Davis had gotten to him in a very personal way. He was letting his mishaps dominate his life.'' Meantime, Rozelle had little choice but to hang on while bad went to worse.

27
"A Whole League of Al Davises"

Pete Rozelle tried to dress up the annual report he delivered, but the material he had to work with was slim by his usual standards. Television ratings were down "marginally" from the record year of 1981. Super Bowl XVII, pitting Joe Robbie's Dolphins against Jack Kent Cooke's Redskins, had nonetheless been "the second highest rated live TV program of all time." As a consequence, now all of the top ten highest rated live programs in history were NFL broadcasts.

The commissioner's recitation did little to lift the League's grim mood. It hardly seemed possible that only the year before the same group had thought themselves the owners of a goose that laid golden eggs. Everyone was worried about money, and the bills had only just begun to come in. Of particular concern was the United States Football League, the NFL's freshly minted competitor.

A week earlier, the USFL had kicked off its premier season with franchises in Los Angeles, Oakland, Tampa, Denver, Detroit, Philadelphia, Boston, Birmingham, Phoenix, Memphis, Chicago, and New Jersey. By then, it was obvious that the original notion of leaving the "big time" to the NFL and operating as a frugal spring feeder league had been abandoned. "We're a whole league of Al Davises," General Manager Bruce Allen of the new Chicago Blitz warned. "Most of our guys had been promised NFL expansion franchises but had never received them. Most of our people are just as rich as the NFL owners, if not richer, but our guys are hungry. Hungry and imaginative."

While the USFL would not compete directly with the NFL for audience, or for television ratings, it would compete for players. The bidding war began over the most glamorous of incoming college players and soon widened to the NFL's established talent. The effect was to do for the players everything the NFLPA had failed to and then some. Over the next year, several NFL teams would more than double their expenditures on players' salaries and many franchises were driven into the red by the escalation.

"The USFL," Art Modell warned, ". . . [has] attacked our system and we've got to defend ourselves. . . . We must protect ourselves and maintain our competitive stance."

Just how to do so, of course, was another problem altogether. For the League actually to consult about how best to cope with its competition might well be in violation of the Sherman Act. Instead, the USFL war would be fought owner by owner, as each saw fit, becoming yet another force sucking power away from Rozelle's commissionership. It also provided the commissioner with yet another of his worst dreams come true. This time the perpetrator was Eddie DeBartolo, the League's youngest member.

Now starting his sixth year in the League, the thirty-eight-year-old DeBartolo was less than a regular at NFL meetings. On March 22, however, Eddie himself was an item on the executive session agenda. Apparently his father, Mr. D, was about to purchase the Pittsburgh expansion franchise in the USFL. "It's a smash at the guts of the League," a source in the NFL offices argued. "It would violate a sensible conflict of interest agreement. Even worse than the Al Davis case, this invasion of a long-established territory could, down the road, cause a franchise war." But the League had to tread on thin legal ice. Whether it could enforce its own cross-ownership rule was very much up in the air.

For the DeBartolos, buying into the USFL in Mr. D's name was a logical step. "We're going to continue to concentrate on sports," DeBartolo Sr. had pointed out, "and make it a major division of our company. Sports in this country will get greater and greater." Pittsburgh was also the focus of much of that DeBartolo Corp. development. In addition to the hockey franchise, they also owned the indoor soccer franchise, the Civic Arena, and cable TV for much of the Pittsburgh metropolitan area. That family expansionism can hardly have come as a surprise to the NFL in 1983. In 1980, Mr. D had purchased the Chicago White Sox professional baseball franchise in the name of his daughter, only to have the takeover blocked, much to Pete Rozelle's relief, by baseball Commissioner Bowie Kuhn. Unofficially, the *San Francisco Examiner* noted, Kuhn's "real reason" was "the suspicion of a Mafia connection." Eddie considered the allegation nonsense. "I suppose it's a stereotype that Italians who are successful just can't overcome," he complained.

Pete Rozelle had heard rumors of the family's new spring football interest several months before the 1983 annual meeting; "I first learned about it in the newspaper," he said. The rest of the League's owners learned what the DeBartolos were up to the same way and, according to Rozelle, "expressed considerable concern."

On March 22, the League demanded an explanation. At this point, Mr. D had already signed a USFL letter of intent, and Martha explained that entry into the USFL was "a business decision." The DeBartolos wanted the spring team so a "sports package" including its hockey, soccer, and USFL football holdings could be sold on its cable television network in greater Pittsburgh. Martha pointed out that the family would consider "either buying into the USFL . . . or divesting itself of its interest in the 49ers." One owner remembered that Eddie himself said he was going to talk to his father about it, but couldn't control what his father did. "Eddie did assure us that he wants to resolve this," Rozelle commented to *The New York Times*, ". . . he will probably tell his father that the conflict puts him in an embarrassing conflict arrangement, at least in the opinion of the other teams in the NFL."

On March 22, all the League could do was wait and see what Eddie's father said.

"Wait and see" was the watchword of the 1983 annual meeting. Immediately after the DeBartolo discussion ended, the League went into "privileged" executive session to hear a report on *LAMCC v. NFL,* where the attorneys' advice was in essence the same. A number of the country's finest lawyers had participated in putting together the League's appeal brief and had produced a document in which they had great confidence. A decision could be expected sometime toward the end of the year. In the meantime, however, the League might very well be receiving more bad news. Court was in session in L.A. and the jury was hearing evidence on the damage portion of their verdict.

The bad news was finally delivered twenty-one days after the annual meeting adjourned. The jury found that the NFL had damaged Al Davis by some $11.5 million and the LAMCC by some $4.9 million by delaying Davis's move south for two years. Because of the antitrust violation, those damages would be automatically tripled. The total bill was almost $50 million in damages. On top of that, the League would also have to pay another $10 million in the plaintiffs' accumulated legal fees. It was, one NFL source noted, the first time Pete Rozelle had ever cost the League money.

The League immediately appealed the damages and began work on yet another brief.

28
Stabilizing Leonard

Life in the NFL continued, and in Philadelphia, that life still centered on Leonard Tose. By spring 1983, Tose was once again in deep financial trouble and everybody in Philadelphia knew it.

The financing Chuck Sullivan had found for Tose in 1978 had apparently stabilized his finances for little more than two years. By July 1980, Tose was looking for more personal borrowing and arranged a $400,000 loan from Tampa owner Hugh Culverhouse. By October 1982, Tose had to go back to the well again. This time, Culverhouse guaranteed a $3 million personal loan for Tose, and between March 1982 and April 1983, the Eagles also borrowed $7 million from Crocker Bank and another $4 million from the management council's strike fund. Although both Culverhouse loans were in apparent violation of the NFL's constitutional provision banning any loans by one member to another, the League took no action. "If it is a violation," Jay Moyer pointed out, ". . . it would amount to a technical violation that didn't cause any harm to anyone." Both transactions were consummated with the full knowledge of the commissioner and the League's finance committee. Rozelle himself claimed to have "ignored" the apparent conflict "because of Tose's promise to refinance in a short period." Tose noted that Culverhouse had taken a fee for his assistance.

A myriad of indulgences were responsible for Tose's financial shortfall, but one stood out. Casino gambling was now legal in nearby Atlantic City, and the temptation proved too much. In 1982, his wagering flared to an all-time high. According to *The Philadelphia Inquirer*, "it was not unusual for Tose to win or lose $500,000 in one night." His favorite game was blackjack, at which he was known to wager as much as $70,000 on a single hand. "He's probably one of the worst blackjack players I've ever seen," a casino source confided. Nonetheless, Tose acquired a reputation for paying his gambling debts quickly and remaining "unflappable," even when he lost. "He was a sweetheart to deal with," another casino source pointed out. "He paid us like he was a man with no worries."

An evening in April 1982, not long after Tose learned of the League's upcoming television bonanza, was typical of his nocturnal odyssey at the tables. According to the records of one Atlantic City casino cited by *The Philadelphia Inquirer*, at 12:45 A.M. Tose signed a marker and borrowed $25,000. At 12:53, he signed for another $25,000. At 1:00 A.M., he borrowed $50,000 more, then borrowed yet another $50,000 just three minutes later. At 1:30, he added $15,000; at 1:31, $35,000; at 1:35, another $50,000. By 3:07 A.M., Tose had switched tables and borrowed another $50,000. By 3:30, he had borrowed yet $100,000 more. Before he finally left as the sun was coming up, Leonard Tose had lost some $400,000, not counting whatever money he'd brought along to start with. In November, according to reports by a Philadelphia radio station, not long after the settlement of the strike, Tose had hopped over to Atlantic City for a night and lost more than $1 million at an assortment of casinos.

When Tose was in one of his betting frenzies, people would come from all over the casino to watch. "The whole world saw him," a source told the *Inquirer*. "You could tell he loved the attention, the allure . . . it was awesome." One casino eventually began to discourage Tose from gambling there because it was afraid it would be accused of taking advantage of him. "He became a kind of loaded cigar and we just didn't need that," a casino official explained. "He had constant losses." By January 1983, rumors depicted Tose as having at least $2 million in outstanding casino debts.

By the end of January, Pete Rozelle felt obliged to comment. "I don't know what I'll say to him," he explained. Rozelle did not plan to tell Tose to stop gambling, rather just to ask, "Why cause trouble for yourself, the Eagles, and the League?"

In the meantime, Leonard Tose publicly denied his financial difficulties.

"I don't have any financial trouble. Not from gambling. Not from the strike. Honest to God."

Despite his denials, that January Tose took dramatic steps to reorganize his principal asset, the Philadelphia Eagles. He also began a quiet, behind-the-scenes search for a buyer to bail him out. Both moves were spearheaded by Tose's daughter from his first marriage, Susan Fletcher. An attorney, she was considered a tough litigator and was described by *Philadelphia Magazine* as "attractive," "small," and "fiery." On January 12, the Eagles announced that Fletcher was being brought on as a vice-president and house counsel. By then, Tose's private financial crunch was such that he was trying to sell part of his personal luxury box in Veterans Stadium to several casino operators in order to raise some quick cash.

Susan Fletcher said her father wanted to "take some time off and give me more responsibility in the day-to-day operation." Further, she added, "I think that I have all the skills that are necessary and the energy and enthusiasm. I have a business background. . . ." Tose personally confirmed that he intended to leave her the team in his will. "Of course I want to leave it to her," he explained. "What does every Jewish father want?" Fletcher later explained, "I am here to make this team as fiscally sound as possible. That's why I do what I do."

The advent of Susan Fletcher caused some confusion in Philadelphia, and most of it centered around of Jimmy Murray, whom Tose had often referred to as "my adopted son," and who previously had been designated to control the franchise after Tose's death. Many of Murray's responsibilities also seemed to overlap with those just given Fletcher. Also Murray, who had been general manager for more than a decade, had become a popular local figure. Said the *Philadelphia Daily News*, "As GM, he set the tone for the classiest, most civic-minded front office in this or any other city. . . . Murray gave heart to a tin woodsman of a franchise." In January, Tose tried to reassure Philadelphia about Murray's fate. "Jimmy will always be a big part of the team," he explained.

In the meantime, Susan Fletcher had taken over the Eagles' front office. "What you had here when I took over," she explained, "was an old organization where everybody was somebody's best friend. There had been very little movement for years, and I think any organization needs new blood." Fletcher instituted a time clock, tightened expense accounts, and had all the club's executives write job descriptions. Using those, she began to fire people. One of the things she discovered in the process was that many were covered by ten-year contracts given out by Murray two years earlier. "No NFL employees outside of coaches have contracts like that," one Eagles source pointed out. "Susan got upset at the idea of so many people in the organization locked into multiyear deals. Leonard accepted it, but she doesn't like cronyism.'' By the middle of March, rumors of the housecleaning had reached the public and again, questions were raised about Murray's status. This time, Susan Fletcher did the reassuring. ''I think he will be back as general manager,'' she said. ''I think Jimmy Murray is very happy with the situation here. I think it's been a very tough couple of years for Jimmy. We told him to take some well-deserved time off and relax and get himself physically in much better shape, because he's had a very trying year.''

In fact, Fletcher had already fired Murray thirteen days earlier. ''It was like a punch in the heart to me,'' Tose said of firing his best friend. ''I couldn't believe it. I'll tell you this, honestly and truthfully—if it weren't for Susan, I would have sold at that point. I would have sold for anything, it wouldn't have mattered. I was so disillusioned and heartsick that I didn't want to come back to my office again. That's not being dramatic. That's being truthful.'' Philadelphia at large wouldn't learn about Murray's firing for another two months. When the word got out, Tose said he had been ''disappointed'' by the Eagles' financial excesses under Murray and the fact that ''he wasn't able to graciously accept Susan.'' By the time Murray's fate became news, he had taken his contract to Rozelle for arbitration. Rozelle upheld the document and ordered the Eagles to pay it off in full.

On March 19, while Philadelphia was still assuming Murray had just taken ''some well-deserved time off,'' Leonard Tose and his daughter flew to the 1983 annual meeting. ''It's a rough road for a woman in sports,'' Tose observed of the League's reaction. ''Women have it tough in any business—it's a chauvinistic world—and that prevails especially in this one. The membership as a whole was nice to Susan. Some can't change, but fuck them.''

In early April, Leonard Tose finally had a meeting with the commissioner about his gambling problem. ''There's nothing against it,'' Rozelle pointed out. ''It's legal. Players can do it, owners can do it, but I talked to Leonard about how when it reaches the point where this publicity could be embarrassing to you or the club, then it becomes a different problem. He tended to agree with me and said, 'I'm just not going to do it any-more.' '' With that, the subject was dropped altogether.

Not long after meeting with Rozelle, Tose also succeeded in stabilizing his personal finances by refinancing. In April, he borrowed another $5 million from Kidde Company, and agreed to pay the entire sum by January 1984. Should the sum not be forthcoming, Kidde had the right to force the team's sale. One reason such a deadline was acceptable to Tose in April 1983 was that under his current game plan, he would have sold the franchise long before the Kidde loan came due. It was an option, of course, that Tose had long rejected. "After all the fucking problems I went through to get this team," he once pointed out, "after all the fucking charges, all the fucking plots, all the problems with the fucking banks, my fucking broads, my fucking ex-wife, my kids. . . . Now I am finally in a position where I can relax and I'm going to sell the team? No fucking way." Nonetheless, Susan Fletcher had been working that option out since she'd come on the job. By May, she had made significant progress.

The first concrete offer Fletcher turned up was from Ed Snider, owner of the Philadelphia Flyers hockey franchise. In addition to assuming some $33 million in Eagles' bank debt and longterm contractual obligations, Snider offered to guarantee Tose an $8 million income over eight years and $650,000 a year for the rest of his life after that. In total, the offer was valued at $52 million. It also contained a provision allowing Fletcher to buy twenty percent of the franchise and giving her a ten-year contract to manage the Eagles' business affairs. On June 6, the details of the pact had been hammered out, and Snider left thinking he'd made a "handshake deal" to join the NFL. A final meeting was scheduled for June 17.

Unbeknownst to Ed Snider, however, there was another potential buyer maneuvering in the wings: a five-person syndicate. The five included Louis Guida, a Merrill Lynch executive and racehorse owner; Ira Lampert, another racehorse owner and a senior partner in a New York accounting firm; and Dr. Julius Newman and his wife, Sandra. Dr. Newman, plastic surgeon, had redone Susan Fletcher's nose and Sandra Newman was an attorney and Susan Fletcher's "best friend." The fifth member of the syndicate was Fletcher herself. The other members of the syndicate agreed to loan Fletcher the money with which to buy twenty percent of the franchise. In addition, she would be hired as the team's general manager at no less than $125,000 a year and was guaranteed ten percent of the team's net profits.

Susan Fletcher began negotiations on her father's behalf on June 13, four days before her scheduled meeting with Snider. "I'd like to sell the Eagles to you," Fletcher told them. Then she described the offer Snider had made in some detail and discussed how to structure an alternative bid. The offer, as finalized, would include taking on $33 million in team debts and lending Tose $9.1 million to settle his personal debts. The money would have to be repaid by his estate after his death. Tose would continue to hold a title with the franchise and represent it at NFL gatherings until his death as well. In addition, he would be paid consulting fees. The offer's total value to Tose was placed at $42.1 million.

On June 17, the day she had originally been scheduled to meet with Snider in pursuit of his $52 million offer, Susan Fletcher instead joined the rest of her syndicate in Sandra Newman's limousine and drove out to Longport, New Jersey, where Tose was renting a summer home. They carried with them a draft document described as a "memorandum of understanding." Not an actual sale agreement, it was an agreement to negotiate a sale agreement based on the terms it included. As the day was later reconstructed by The Philadelphia Inquirer, Tose greeted the group and immediately suggested opening some Dom Pérignon champagne he had in the icebox. Tose, Louis Guida later testified, just wanted to sign the papers and "get on with the celebration." Fletcher, however, insisted that her father read the papers before signing them.

Donning his glasses, Tose went through the memorandum, asking questions and suggesting alterations. At the section specifying payment of $100,000 cash immediately and $200,000 by July 1, Tose told Guida that he had a $296,000 interest payment due the same day and asked that the second payment be raised to $300,000. Guida agreed. The draft document also called for Tose to be paid $250,000 a year from year five onward. "I can't live on that," Tose pointed out. He wanted $400,000 and again, Guida, on behalf of the syndicate, agreed. The draft's original "no binding effect" paragraph, giving Tose a way out if he changed his mind, had been scratched out. Tose initialed the deletion and told Guida he could understand why it had been made. According to Guida, Tose told him, "If I was in your shoes, I'd want it the same way. Frankly, I've been trying to sell this team for six months . . . and I want it binding as much as you do." When he was finished reading, Leonard Tose signed the last page of the memorandum, then opened the champagne, and the group celebrated. Before the syndicate left, Tose distributed Philadelphia Eagles cuff links and necklaces among them. "The minute I met you," he told Guida in parting, "I knew we had a deal. You're my kind of guy."

Negotiations toward a final sale document continued until June 28 and then suddenly fell apart. On that day, Fletcher said, "He has a better offer from Ed Snider." The Snider offer, of course, had already been rejected by Fletcher herself some two weeks earlier.

On July 1, all the syndicate's members except Susan Fletcher filed suit against Tose, contending their memorandum of understanding was binding and had been violated. Tose himself claimed that parts of the memorandum he signed had been illegible and that he had never considered it binding. He called the memorandum only a "first step" in the negotiating process. "I never envisioned giving up control," he claimed. "They shoved it under my face and said, 'Sign it, sign it.' It was like a kangaroo court. Everyone was surrounding me saying it's not binding, it's not this, it's not that. I told them I couldn't read the damn thing. It wasn't legible. I read parts of it and there were some changes I made after I signed it. It was certainly a vigilante group."

A source in the NFL office told the *Inquirer* shortly after the "vigilante group" filed suit that even if the syndicate won, they were in violation of the League's fifty-one percent ownership requirement and hence, stood only a "one thousand to one" chance of being approved.

On September 20, the parties agreed to settle their differences. Tose would retain uncontested ownership of the Eagles in exchange for an immediate cash payment to Guida, Lambert, and the Newmans, of $1.75 million. Tose admitted that he borrowed the money, but would not say from where. "I didn't have it in my cellar," he pointed out. Back in the saddle, Tose would also find a loan to pay off Kidde and even further secure his hold on NFL membership. Susan Fletcher, having been given a proper Tose introduction to the business of football, returned to her job at the Eagles somewhat chastized and would continue to run the franchise's daily financial operations for the duration of her father's tenure.

"At this point," Pete Rozelle observed once Tose's obligations to Kidde had been met, "I am satisfied Leonard has stabilized his finances."

29
Ugly Days in Cleveland

Art Modell, the owner who in 1977 declared the NFL had "strong feelings" for Leonard Tose and wanted to see him "succeed," said little about the Philadelphian's difficulties in 1982 and 1983. Modell now had his own very pressing concerns with which to occupy himself in Cleveland. It had been a bad year for Art Modell as well. The purchase of Cleveland Stadium Corp. was now out of the back room and onto the front page and Modell's reputation suffered severely in the process. "Modell Enters Fight for Integrity," *The* [Cleveland] *Plain Dealer* declared. With his own civic good name suddenly up for grabs and the League under constant attack as well, Modell got no respite.

Modell's "fight for integrity" had begun on March 17, 1982, the day after the Browns purchased Cleveland Stadium Corp. and got Modell out of debt. That day Cleveland, heretofore operating under the assumption Art Modell owned the Cleveland Browns all by himself, suddenly learned that he had a partner of considerable proportions—Robert Gries, scion of one of the city's oldest, most respected, and well-heeled families—and, even worse, that Gries claimed that Modell had been cheating him. The accusations came in *Gries Sports Enterprises v. Cleveland Browns*. In order to make a personal $4.8 million killing, Gries charged, Modell had led the Browns to pay $6 million for an enterprise with a book value of no more than $385,000. "We're aiming to protect the financial viability of the Browns," Gries announced, "and we're aiming to protect our interests as forty-three percent owner of the Browns."

Before flying off to the 1982 annual meeting, Modell told *The Plain Dealer* the suit was "totally frivolous, unwarranted, and without foundation." The purchase of Cleveland Stadium Corp. had been legitimate Browns business, he claimed, and "the terms of this transaction have been determined by independent appraisers to be more than fair and reasonable." The charges infuriated Modell but, in truth, the shit had only just begun to hit the fan.

Gries was serious and dogged about his pursuit of the Gries family's ownership rights. Modell learned Gries was making plans to attend the next NFL meeting in June and when Gries showed up uninvited at the Browns' press preview of their (annual highlights film) on May 5, Modell's anger and irritation escalated another notch.

Dear Bob, [Art Modell wrote Gries the following day in a letter that later showed up in court]

I consider your uninvited attendance at our highlight film press preview last night to be the most impudent of your actions to date. Functions such as that are sponsored to enhance the Browns' public relations and to foster camaraderie and staff morale. Your name was very intentionally excluded from the invitation list precisely because of the chilling and negative impact that your presence had. You have chosen to create an adversary relationship and to publicize it to the hilt. Surely you cannot be so insensitive to human relations not to have known full well the impact of your actions. I have no idea what your motivations are and, frankly, don't care. You have laid down the gauntlet in court and we are fully prepared to meet and prevail in that challenge. In fact, I welcome the opportunity.

However, I will not allow the diversion of your legal actions to detract from the successful operation of this football team. Staff and media functions are just that, and are by invitation only. They are not stockholders' or directors' meetings. Whatever your rights in those capacities, they do not include the right to be where you are not invited. . . . From this point forward, I will insist that you do not attend any staff, media, or team activities unless invited, and will enforce my authority to do so if it becomes necessary.

In addition, I have learned through counsel that you plan to attend the NFL meeting in June. As a shareholder and director, you have no legal right to do so. . . . I fully intend to enforce my exclusive contractual right to conduct and manage all relations with the NFL on behalf of the Browns. You therefore are not to attend this or any other NFL meeting.

Very truly yours,
Art

Gries responded to Modell's letter as soon as he received it on May 7.

Dear Art,

Despite my firsthand experience with your quick temper and your insistence on always being in total command, it was more in sadness than in anger that I read your letter of May 6. Surely you are not suggesting that I, as an officer, director, and a forty-three percent owner of the Browns, had no right to attend the media party of May 5. . . .

I totally reject your suggestion that my presence had a "chilling and negative impact" on those present. Perhaps I had that effect on you, and on some of those who are dominated by you, but it had no such effect on others, especially the media. . . . Or are you perhaps suggesting that my very presence serves as a reminder of the fact that you are not the sole owner of the Browns, that as majority shareholder you owe me a duty of fairness and that you have made it necessary for me to enforce that duty in court. Nor is there justification in suggesting . . . that it was I who created the adversary relationship. . . . To the contrary, we both know that I tried for four months to avoid the step which you forced upon me. . . . It was you who slammed the door, not me.

I can understand your personal discomfort over press reports of the litigation. But you are not the Cleveland Browns, a team the Gries family helped to found, and which we nurtured and supported over thirty-seven years. Your embarrassment over the suit should not be confused with the image of the team which I have not tarnished one iota. . . . Faced with your actions, I intend to protect my interests and those of my family and those of the Browns. I intend to fulfill my responsibility as a director and as an owner. I expect to be present at such team functions as I deem appropriate in the fulfillment of those duties. Any unwarranted attempt on your part to block me . . . will be met with such necessary, proper, and lawful measures as are called for under the circumstances. . . .

I do, indeed, plan to attend the NFL meetings in June and thereafter, just as other owners and part-owners are entitled to do. I have no intention of encroaching on your right to speak for and act on behalf of the Browns. But I also have a right to be there. . . .

Very truly yours,
Bob

Each man sent a copy of his letter to Pete Rozelle and sought a ruling on the dispute. Rozelle allowed Gries to attend the social functions at all NFL gatherings, but none of the business sessions. Gries's first such attendance was in June 1982, and he continued to attend all meetings that followed, shadowing Modell on what had heretofore been Modell's exclusive turf.

On June 11, Gries filed *Robert D. Gries and Gries Sports Enterprises v. Arthur B. Modell,* subsequently labeled "Gries II." This suit charged that Modell had violated a 1965 agreement with Gries to hold regular meetings of the Browns board of directors. Modell responded that the 1965 agreement was "unenforceable" because the Browns were registered as a corporation in Delaware and, under Delaware law, shareholder agreements could not last longer than ten years. "I do not understand what the man is talking about, nor, more importantly, do I understand his motives," Modell bridled. From that point on, Robert Gries says, he was specifically excluded from all activities of the Cleveland Browns.

Unintimidated, Gries filed "Gries III" on October 29, 1982, challenging Modell's conduct as president of the Browns in four new ways. The first was Gries's charge that Modell had let the option on his previous contract as Browns president lapse, then negotiated a new arrangement with himself for more than triple the pay and an increased bonus. Gries alleged that Modell now received "as much money as the heads of businesses one hundred times larger" than the Browns. Gries also complained about Modell's "lack of accountability for expenses paid by the Browns," his "autocratic one-man control of the Browns, disregarding corporate procedures," and his "abuse of power in attempting to bar our family . . . from virtually all contact with the Browns organization."

"If Modell seemed upset at Gries I," *The Plain Dealer* noted, "and exasperated at Gries II, he was downright furious this time." Modell immediately called a press conference in his attorney's office and appeared noticeably "red-faced and angry." He described Gries's new charges as "outrageous" and "irresponsible and scandalous . . . I have received the same $60,000 base salary for twenty-one years . . . which, by the way, places me at the bottom thirty percent of all NFL *players.* I have no apology that the board of directors saw fit to give me my first raise in twenty-one years. I do not need Gries to approve my business expenses. . . . The record is clear. My personal and professional conduct during twenty-one years of Browns' ownership has been unblemished. Gries has no moral or legal right to question that record. I do not understand Gries's motivations, but I can tell you, he will be held responsible for damaging the Browns organization and the Modell name."

These latest charges came at an embarrassing moment for Modell. The ongoing strike had hurt the Browns as much or more than any franchise in the League. Just as Gries had warned, the Stadium Corp. purchase was a millstone around its neck in the face of labor war. Now with more debt than ever, the Browns also had a piece not only of the League's strike losses, but those of the concessionaires and stadium authorities as well. On November 11, Modell announced that all front-office employees of the Browns and Stadium Corp. would henceforth work half the hours at half the pay, a reduction that would "continue indefinitely until our future can be more clearly defined."

Even with the strike over, the pressure continued on Modell. The Browns were in the January playoffs and he flew to L.A. for a game with Al Davis's Raiders. When the flight arrived in southern California, Modell collapsed and was taken to the hospital, where the doctors concluded his collapse had been due to "fatigue, lack of oxygen on the plane, and a reaction to high blood pressure medication." While Modell was in the hospital, the Browns lost to the Raiders, twenty-seven to ten.

Back in Cleveland again, Modell immediately donned his hat as Stadium Corp. president and reentered a long-standing and acrimonious set of negotiations with the Cleveland Indians baseball franchise, his other principal tenant. Gabe Paul, the baseball club's general manager, had been demanding a significantly better deal for several years and Modell had been pleading poverty. The combination had already produced considerable friction.

By April 1983, when the Indians' lease was just eight months from expiration, the talks were stalemated. On the 21st, Modell presented a dramatic offer to the city that he hoped would break the logjam. To satisfy the Indians' constant harping at him, he was prepared to withdraw Stadium Corp. from the lease picture altogether, turn the stadium back over to Cleveland, and let the Indians and the city find some agreement. In exchange, Modell wanted $10.1 million for the improvements Stadium Corp. had installed, plus the right to lease back the stadium's luxury boxes, the principal such improvement, from the city for $1.25 million a year. He would also commit the football franchise to extend its current lease to match any agreement Cleveland and the Indians could work out. One of the proposition's major advantages to Modell was that it would likely thwart Gries I, then making its way slowly toward a 1984 trial. The mayor turned Modell's offer down, saying the city had better uses for its $10 million.

On April 26, the Indians made their own move to break the stalemate and filed *Cleveland Indians Company v. Cleveland Stadium Corp. and Servomation Corp*. The suit alleged that Stadium Corp. had cheated the Indians on concession revenues to the tune of $1.25 million. They also demanded that Stadium Corp. and Servomation open their books to an outside audit.

The lease did indeed require Stadium Corp. to open its books, but Modell balked at allowing Servomation's books to be examined as well. "It is a sham and a disgrace," he thundered, "that the Indians, with only months remaining on a ten-year lease, should file this frivolous lawsuit . . . purely and simply as a negotiating ploy." Cleveland Stadium Corp. immediately informed the Indians that no more negotiations would take place until the suit had been dropped and the Indians issued a public apology. In a later deposition, Gabe Paul conceded that privately he referred to Modell as a "crook" and Modell called him a "no good, lousy son of a bitch."

Modell stood his ground but, by the beginning of June, he often looked flushed and less than well. He was still a civic heavyweight in Cleveland, and he still moved easily in the city's upper circles and met his political and social obligations faithfully, however exhausted he might be. On June 6, former Secretary of State Henry Kissinger stopped in Cleveland for a speech and Modell took him to the airport. Afterward, Modell felt a tightness in his chest, but it went away shortly.

Then on June 10, the Indians filed a second suit, *Cleveland Indians Company v. Cleveland Stadium Corp. and Cleveland Browns, Inc.*, claiming that their landlord's refusal to negotiate violated the Sherman Act and asked that he be forced to do so. "A disgraceful performance," Modell fumed, "bush league." It was the fifth lawsuit against the owner of the Cleveland Browns in the last fifteen months.

That evening, Art Modell and his wife, Pat, attended a black tie event in the city and then returned to their suburban mansion. Modell complained of indigestion and was unable to sleep. By the time the sun was coming up, his indigestion had turned into a "viselike pressure" in his chest. Finally, his wife rushed him to the hospital and an EKG determined that he was in the midst of a massive heart attack. After the quadruple bypass operation that followed, he suffered a pulmonary failure and was rushed back to surgery to correct several complications. Art Modell survived the second operation and spent the rest of the summer regaining his strength. Meantime, the battle over his good name was put on hold.

30
"Tell Me the Company You Keep . . ."

The last meeting of the NFL Art Modell attended before his heart attack was held outside of Tampa in May. Again, the topic of greatest interest was Eddie DeBartolo and his father. Mr. D's ownership of the new USFL Pittsburgh Maulers was now an established fact and Modell was one of those most put out by the arrangement. "It's a disgrace," he fumed, ". . . But what can we do about it? Everyone is gunshy of litigation now and it's not clear we have any legal powers to force either DeBartolo to divest. It's a perfect example of what has happened to us. . . . This never would have happened years ago and we have Al Davis to thank that it's happening now."

The League's response was to continue to act as though it did have powers with which to handle Eddie and Mr. D. "I'm concerned," Pete Rozelle admitted. "The clubs feel that there is a clear-cut conflict of interests. I can't say what the clubs might do. The range of possibilities, . . . is to disqualify him from votes by asking him to leave the room, all the way up to attempting to throw him out of the League. . . ."

The option presented to the League by Paul Martha, Eddie's employee, was that the NFL and USFL jointly agree to rules that would prohibit Eddie's franchise and Mr. D's franchise from owning the negotiating rights to the same players. "I think the two commissioners are going to have to talk about this," he explained, and "the executive committees of the two leagues are going to have to get together and try to reach some sort of accommodation." That option was, of course, anathema to the NFL. "We have no intention of sitting down with the USFL," Rozelle declared. "We'll make our own rules."

In the discussion on May 25, sentiment ran high against Eddie

DeBartolo. "He's a spoiled rich kid," one owner groused. "He doesn't know his ass from second base."

Eddie himself was adamant and unworried. "The USFL team in Pittsburgh is the responsibility of Edward DeBartolo Sr.," he pointed out to the *Sun Francisco Examiner,* "I have nothing to do with it. I'm Eddie Jr. I own the 49ers. That's the only team I care about. . . . I don't care what Pete Rozelle thinks. . . . If they couldn't do anything to Al Davis, then they aren't going to do anything to me."

On May 25, Pete Rozelle appointed a three-man committee, "to study conflicts that might result from members of the same family owning controlling interests in competing professional football leagues." Alike in form and purpose to the fact-finding committee he had sent after Al Davis in 1980, this committee was given more time in which to do their work; the commissioner said that "the committee would be asked to submit a report within sixty days." In fact, it would be October before any report was available.

If the commissioner was looking for omens on the value of perseverance that summer, he could have found one on June 29, when the crowning touch was put on Old Billy Sullivan's dogged rise to football power in New England. The occasion was a celebration of the remodeling of Schaeffer Stadium. It had cost some $18 million altogether and was, Billy remembered, "a family affair." Chuck had raised the money, Billy Jr. had handled the contractor, and Billy's daughter Nancy had decorated the new luxury boxes. Perhaps the most noticeable alteration in Schaeffer Stadium was its name. The Schaeffer Brewing Company, which owned advertising rights in the structure, had sold its rights back to the Sullivans. They, in turn, had resold them to Budweiser beer and Budweiser wanted a change. The brewer's suggestion, according to Billy, was "William Sullivan Stadium." Billy would have nothing to do with it, insisting a simple "Sullivan Stadium" was enough. On June 29, "Sullivan Stadium" was unveiled in fifteen-foot-tall letters over the stadium entry.

The ceremony was a luncheon for several thousand at the new Stadium Club restaurant. A brass plaque featuring a bust of Old Billy had been attached to the structure and, in the distance, a brand new enormous DiamondVision scoreboard flashed a highlight film of the family's franchise in action. "The inmates at Walpole [State Prison] were evidently the only people not included on Billy Sullivan's guest list," the *Boston Herald* noted. "Tuxedoed waiters shuffled through the milling crowd bearing trays laden with crab claws, shrimp, lamb chops, and [B]loody Marys, which they tried not to spill into the sea of white suits. It looked like a sort of cross between a Roman orgy and one of those mass ceremonies the Moonies periodically hold in Yankee Stadium.''

The program featured sportscaster Howard Cosell as master of ceremonies. Cosell lauded ''the contributions made to the progress of our society'' made by his ''old friend'' Billy and introduced the dignitaries seated up by the dais. Then came Old Billy, whose remarks were, in the *Herald*'s estimation, ''miraculously brief, consuming a record eleven minutes and one second.'' He thanked Budweiser. ''We're delighted with this arrangement,'' Billy observed. ''My grandmother, God rest her soul, once said, 'Tell me the company you keep and I'll tell you what you are.' The King of Beers is awfully good company to keep.'' Billy called the stadium and its new name, ''an impossible dream type of thing. Some people hang around pool rooms and some people hang around churches and some hang around taverns, but I've always kind of hung around stadiums.'' Afterward, the crowd mingled to the serenading of the Boston Pops orchestra. Billy circulated, pumping hands, slapping backs, and beaming.

Perhaps the most remembered incident from Sullivan's stadium bash was Howard Cosell's introduction of Georgia Frontiere among the dignitaries. Georgia, Cosell confessed, was someone for whom he had long had a ''naked lust.'' He then called the owner of the L.A. Rams to the mike and gave her a wet and long-winded kiss on the lips. When Cosell turned to the audience, looking, according to the *Herald,* as though he ''thought he was the first man ever to do it to the woman,'' the crowd laughed.

Georgia took it all in good fun. Sullivan's celebration was her kind of NFL event. She had long since tired of the League's seemingly endless meetings and usually sent a hired hand to take her place. It was no doubt a welcome relief for her to have something to celebrate. On the field, her Rams had slipped badly from the standards set in C.R.'s day and Georgia took the blame. ''Current Management Has Presided Over a Major Collapse,'' the *Los Angeles Times* pointed out. ''It went from first class to just garbage,'' an NFL executive agreed. One obvious explanation for the collapse was Georgia's continued insistence on acting as her own general manager. ''She actually believes she can go one-on-one with people like Al Davis and Tex Schramm,'' a source close to the Rams told the *Times*, ''and hold her own. . . . You're dealing with someone whose perception is not reality.''

By February 1983, the criticism had driven Mrs. Frontiere to name a new head coach to whom she planned to turn over all football responsibilities. It was a ''new'' Georgia at the press conference announcing the change. First, she was on time, and second, she took the blame herself. Asked if all the negative publicity was bothering her, Georgia answered, ''Not really. I can't say it didn't enter my mind. I'd have to be stupid to say that. . . [P]erhaps we deserved some of the negative publicity. Perhaps I tried to do too much myself.'' With that, Georgia withdrew into the background to wait for her team to come back.

Georgia Frontiere also waited on *LAMCC v. NFL,* which she viewed as a way to get back at Al Davis—an opportunity she no doubt wanted more than ever. Her life was still shadowed by the case and the reverberations of the deposition fights of 1980 were still a quite active practical fact. Though the ticket scalping allegations made by Al Davis and Harold Guiver that year had played no subsequent role in the trial, they had not been lost on the Internal Revenue Service. Since December 1980, an IRS investigation centered on ''circumstances involving the sale of 1980 Super Bowl tickets'' and evidenced an apparent curiosity about Jack Catain, the man who had put the arm on Harold Guiver on behalf of an unknown third party.

In spring 1983, that investigation gained new life when two new witnesses surfaced. Both men were associates of Catain's and both claimed to have taken large blocks of Rams' Super Bowl tickets to ticket agencies and resold them for as much as six times their face value. IRS accountants conducted an audit of the Rams' books, looking to confirm or deny ''allegations that there may have been hundreds of thousands of dollars in unreported income from the illegal sale of tickets.'' Georgia's attorney denied any significance to the audit. ''The IRS looks at the Rams all the time,'' he contended.

The IRS was looking at more than just the Rams' books; during the summer of 1983 they interviewed Steve Rosenbloom. ''They were concerned about Georgia and Dominic,'' Steve recalled. ''Since I was gone during all that, there wasn't much I could tell them. I wasn't surprised they were asking, though. I was hearing about it out on the street. It was handled real sloppily. They might as well have taken an ad in the paper.'' The IRS also called on Rozelle and a number of other owners. ''They mainly wanted to know how many tickets each club got,'' Rozelle remembered. According to one NFL source, several owners and franchise employees were also subpoenaed to give secret testimony. Yet another probe at the same time was being conducted by the Justice Department, "focusing on the role organized crime figures may have played in the alleged ticket scalping scheme."

Whether or not all those federal agents would turn up anything was, like much about NFL in the summer of 1983, just another case of wait and see.

31
Raider Ethic: Attack, Fear, Pressure

Gene Klein also carried considerable baggage from the *LAMCC v. NFL* proceedings as well, though in a wholly different way. For him, it remained more a personal obsession than a legal threat.

Al Davis was by no means popular inside the League, but many had by now adopted a grudging but passive acceptance of his presence, at least until they learned what the appeals court had to say. Gene Klein, however, still wanted Davis's scalp in the worst way. "He's an egomaniac," Klein raged about his nemesis. "He loves to bitch and complain and throw smokescreens. He loves to hear himself talk and tries to get the spotlight at our meetings. . . . The son of a bitch has been trying to take power ever since I've been in the League."

By 1983, Gene Klein had sold his mansion in L.A., now Al Davis's hometown, and moved full-time to San Diego County. Klein's estate, a four-hundred-acre horse farm, had a front yard decorated with sculptures by Miro, Moore, Rickey, and Hepworth. Most of the ranch was reserved for Klein's growing passion: the buying, breeding, and racing of Thoroughbreds. "There are pressures in everything," Klein told the *San Diego Union*, "running a football team, having a racing stable, but I think the pressures I've surrounded myself with now are good pressures. There's excitement, but it's good excitement. I don't have to worry about 8,000 employees, 40,000 stockholders, and here I am living out in the country, breathing the fresh air . . .''

"Good pressure" or not, Gene Klein was much more vulnerable to it than he had been. His heart was still fragile from his 1981 attack and, in late spring 1983, Klein was reminded of that medical fact while out for his daily walk along the nearby county road. Often Klein would see no one in the entire course of his walk. Had that been true on the walk in question, it might have been Gene Klein's last. Topping a rise, Klein remembered, "I suddenly felt severe chest pains." Klein recognized the sensation and immediately sat on a rock by the road, hoping the pain would go away. At that moment, a Mercedes came along the road and stopped. Klein opened the passenger door. The driver had a stethoscope around his neck.

"Are you a doctor?" Klein asked. "I'm in trouble."

"Yes, Mr. Klein," his neighbor the physician answered. Klein got in and the doctor drove him to the hospital. The heart attack was contained and he was released after observation. No surgery was required.

Few knew of Klein's second heart attack. There were certainly no signs of either convalescence or retirement. During the summer of 1983, he fought a major battle with the USFL. Klein had been one of the first League members to confront the USFL's potential challenge. Threatening to move his franchise to Tulsa, Oklahoma, should the USFL come to town, Klein had helped persuade the San Diego City Council to vote to bar any USFL franchise from use of the Chargers' home field. His summer fight had actually commenced in April, when the Chargers used their first pick in the NFL draft to choose a running back from the University of Arkansas, Gary Anderson. Anderson was represented by Houston agent Jerry Argovitz, who told his client that the Chargers had offered a three-year contract worth $830,000. He also said someone from the USFL would be in Houston the next day to make another offer. Argovitz did not tell Anderson that Argovitz himself had been awarded the Houston USFL franchise more than a month earlier.

The USFL representative who talked to Anderson was John Bassett, the Toronto millionaire who was the only World Football League veteran who had come back for another try with the USFL. Bassett owned the Tampa Bandits and offered the young running back $1.375 million over four years. While Bassett waited, Argovitz then called the Chargers' general manager, John Sanders, with a "final" proposal—$975,000 over three years. Sanders, ignorant that Bassett had even made contact, refused Argovitz. Gary Anderson then made a handshake deal to

be in Tampa on May 9 to sign a contract. Meantime, Argovitz
sent Anderson to his mother's house in Columbia, Missouri, and
told him not to answer the phone. When Charger officials were
subsequently unable to reach their first-round pick, they called
Argovitz and the agent said he had no idea where Anderson was.
Klein then ordered Sanders to "send out a dragnet," spending
some $30,000 on unsuccessful attempts to locate their future
star. When Anderson surfaced in Tampa on the scheduled date
and signed a USFL contract with Bassett, Klein was furious.
"It's not over yet," Klein vowed. "There was no good-faith
bargaining whatsoever between us and Anderson. . . . One day
Gary Anderson is going to wake up and realize what Mr. Argovitz
did to him and Mr. Argovitz is going to be in for one sizable
lawsuit."

Round two of Klein's summer fight featured exactly the
lawsuit he had predicted. Anderson was befriended shortly after
his USFL signing by Lloyd Wells, a former scout for the Kansas
City Chiefs. In mid-July, Anderson signed a contract naming
Wells as his new agent, despite the fact that Wells had negotiated only one contract in his life. Wells immediately contacted
the Chargers and Gene Klein loaned the agent $5000 with which
to fly his client to southern California. Klein subsequently loaned
Wells $25,000 more. All the loans were unsecured, without
interest, and of no specified duration. On August 3, Anderson's
attorney filed suit against Argovitz, Bassett, and the Tampa Bay
Bandits and asked for a temporary restraining order to prevent
the USFL from interfering with Anderson's dealings with the
Chargers. That evening, Anderson and Wells were back in San
Diego, where the running back signed a series of four one-year
contracts worth $1.5 million. On August 12, a Houston judge
lectured the Chargers for having "financed" Anderson's "cause"
and found no evidence that "Argovitz or anyone else entered
into a conspiracy against Gary Anderson." The highlight of the
court hearing had come when Anderson's attorney revealed that
his client, having earned 82 units toward the 142 required for a
college degree, nonetheless "cannot read" and had no ability to
understand any of the documents he had signed. Once the judge
ruled, Anderson returned to Tampa and the USFL, ending Gene
Klein's summer battle.

The defeat did little to diminish Klein's pugnaciousness. By
October, he was in another skirmish, this time with Al Davis, his
target of choice. Al Davis had himself been back in court again
in May. The case was *City of Oakland v. Oakland Raiders*,

Oakland's attempt to seize Davis's franchise under the California eminent domain statutes. Oakland was trying a unique legal argument. Under California law, intangible property could be condemned in the same manner as more tangible items like real estate, if the city could demonstrate a bona fide "public use." The public use in Oakland's argument was, in essence, the identity of the city itself. "I know of nothing else in the city that is more important to Oakland than the Oakland Raiders," Mayor Lionel Wilson testified. "Everywhere I went . . . all I could get out of people was 'Are we going to be able to keep our Raiders?' . . . It covered all ages. It covered all racial lines. It covered all economic lines, the lame, the sick, the disabled."

The Raiders' counterargument had four principal facets. The first was that Oakland's attempt was an abuse of any real notion of public use. "This is how the Nazis collected art treasures," Mel Durslag noted. The second was that any such public ownership was an overt violation of the NFL constitution. Third was that Davis's team was in fact part of a single national network, not a part of Oakland, and as such, out of the city's jurisdiction.

"The Raiders have been taking different positions in different courts," one League attorney complained. "The L.A. Coliseum argued that this is an exquisite public use and they won that before Pregerson. They then go up to northern California and say there's no public purpose. In L.A., we said we were a . . . single entity . . . They said, 'We're just the Raiders and we're competitors of these people. It's Al Davis's team and he can move it just like the gas station.' Then they went up to Salinas a few months later and said, 'Take the Raiders?' How can the city of Oakland take the Raiders? . . . We're part of an interlocking web which is nationwide, the National Football League. The Raiders are inseparable from the rest of the League."

To no one's surprise, Davis's fourth argument was that the attempt to condemn his property was a conspiracy between Oakland and Rozelle's NFL. "The National Football League and the city of Oakland were in bed together," one of Davis's attorneys argued.

"In a perfect world," Jay Moyer, Rozelle's in-house counsel, admitted, "eminent domain is not something the League would look at with kindness. However, we do not live in a perfect world."

"The Raiders really drew us into that testimony by going to court," Moyer later explained, "and throwing the League's constitution up as a defense. We found it the supreme irony, that the Raiders of all people would hide behind the League, but they did so. . . . Part of our problem was the recognition that the power of eminent domain in any jurisdiction is a pretty damn fundamental sovereign power and we thought it was dangerous at best for any element of the NFL to go to court taking that kind of position. We thought that it was certainly possible that as a result of that a court could say, 'To hell with your private associations and your constitution. Your constitution can't override the law of the land.''

To solidify their conspiracy argument, the Raiders called a surprise witness to end their case. The witness was Joseph Alioto, Al Davis's attorney. Alioto testified that despite the League's claim to having had no knowledge whatsoever of Oakland's intentions to file this suit, his brother-in-law, Chuck Sullivan, had warned him of what Oakland was going to do before the suit was even drawn up. ''Eminent domain is an awesome power,'' Alioto told the press, ''and it was sprung on us very quickly. It is obvious Pete Rozelle is still working with Oakland officials. It's a strange brand of socialism.''

On July 22, the judge ruled in favor of the Raiders. Oakland appealed, but it was yet another Davis victory in the meantime. ''To be corny,'' Alioto observed afterward, ''I think the American flag flies proudly over Salinas today. It's a great day, not only for the Raiders, but for the American dream and free enterprise.''

By then, the L.A. Raiders preseason training camp had opened, and Davis was up there, watching films, observing practices, and working the phone in search of the one or two players he thought he needed to go back to the Super Bowl. Outside of court now, he was inaccessible except by invitation. On July 26, C. W. Nevius from the *San Francisco Chronicle* managed to arrange an interview. Davis picked the reporter up that evening and drove him to a local restaurant in a long black Cadillac, complete with telephone. ''The owner [of the restaurant],'' the reporter remembered, ''leaped to his feet to shake hands and the waitress giggled nervously. Davis's table was ready. It is next to the door, so he can watch everyone come and go. On the table were a pitcher of water and a black telephone.'' Davis looked ''tired'' and mentioned that his doctors had told him to take a couple of weeks off to get away from it all, but he doubted whether that would be possible. Since Davis's ''dislike of tape recorders is legendary,'' the reporter took notes by hand.

Was Davis worried about the USFL? ''It's like putting in ten

McDonalds," he pointed out. "It's easy to do when the time is right. The question is whether they will survive or prosper. I wish them luck. At least it will get our commissioner off the social circuit." Had his attitude toward Rozelle changed at all? "I never have respected him," Davis pointed out. "I've seen him flirt with the truth too often. But that's not important. I beat him. . . . The commissioner thought settlement would be a defeat. I have often said if there was some way he could win and we could settle, we'd do it. I don't begrudge them doing what they wanted . . . but I think they should have negotiated instead of litigated."

While the two were talking, the *Chronicle* reporter noted, "more than once Davis called attention to the reaction of other diners. He is a distinctive figure, dressed in white pants and black and white pullover with a Raider badge on the chest. No one asked for an autograph, but several people stared and did double takes. It pleased him no end."

"See," Davis chided, "and you say people hate me so much."

Did he have any apologies to make to Oakland?

"What do I have to apologize for?" Davis asked. "My conscience is totally clear."

As Al Davis and the reporter were leaving the restaurant, Davis had a question of his own. "Do people ever ask you what I'm like?" he inquired.

"All the time," the reporter answered. "All the time."

By then, of course, Davis was perhaps the most recognizable owner in the NFL. Both his persona and that of his team had become synonymous with a very particular approach. "Attack, fear, pressure," Davis summarized the Raider ethic. "You say you can stop us. Prove it."

The strategy was illustrated once again in October, when Davis locked horns with Klein and the commissioner. The incident grew out of Davis's unceasing search for talent. He had his eye on Mike Haynes, an all-pro who had sat out the season thus far because of a salary dispute with his employer, Billy Sullivan's Patriots. Haynes wanted $1.5 million over three years and the Patriots were looking for a trade. Patrick Sullivan, the Patriots' GM, wanted a first- and third-round pick in the next collegiate draft in exchange for negotiating rights to Haynes and would not come off his price, as hard as Davis tried to budge him. The two were still dickering at 4:00 P.M. Eastern Standard Time on October 11, the League's deadline after which no trades could be made. Several minutes after 4:30 P.M., they settled.

Davis would get Haynes and the Patriots would get the first and third picks they wanted.

In the meantime, Gene Klein had called Patrick Sullivan at 4:30 P.M. to see if the deal had been consummated and Sullivan told him it hadn't been. When Klein finally learned that the trade had been made, he immediately protested to Rozelle and asked him to void the deal because it had been made after the trading deadline had passed. Rozelle agreed with Klein and voided the trade. Al Davis would not back off. "We asked for an extension," he insisted. Davis also pointed out that Haynes's agent was now about to meet with the USFL. "It would be insane not to allow this trade," he argued, "and let Haynes go to the other league."

In less than two weeks, Mike Haynes filed suit under the Sherman Act in L.A., claiming Rozelle had blocked the deal with an "arbitrary and capricious" trading deadline. In addition to seeking an injunction to let the trade proceed, the suit asked $5 million in damages and charged that Rozelle had used the trading deadline as part of a vendetta against Davis for his "past dealings with the NFL." In addition to the League, Pete Rozelle and Gene Klein were named as individual defendants. The League gave in and settled the case exactly as Davis and Haynes wanted it. Gene Klein was now zero to two for the year and Al Davis's winning streak continued.

32
Superstadium Stalemates

The Superstadium Game that had thrust Al Davis into the foreground of the football business had abated during the trial portion of *LAMCC v. NFL,* but by the fall of 1983 was once again flourishing throughout the League.

In Miami, Joe Robbie had finished off 1982 by helping defeat another city of Miami–sponsored referendum for refurbishing the Orange Bowl. In the course of it, Robbie accused Miami Mayor Maurice Ferre of "hurting, rather than helping, the chance of keeping professional football in Miami." Robbie wanted a new stadium and threatened to leave Miami to get it. "Mr. Robbie is bluffing," Ferre insisted. "He will not leave a major franchise [location]. I will do all I can to get him to stay." By the fall of 1983, the city of Miami was preparing yet another such ballot proposal, again to Robbie's intense objections. In September 1983, Robbie announced that the Dolphins would leave the Orange Bowl when their lease expired in 1986, and if a new stadium wasn't built in the meantime, he would leave for another city.

In Baltimore, Robert Irsay had spent 1982 in on-again, off-again negotiations aimed toward a longterm lease that would activate the state legislature's $22 million renovation financing for Memorial Stadium. Though Irsay continued to refuse to sign any kind of longterm agreement, he also steadfastly maintained he had no desire to move elsewhere. Few believed him. "He hates the city, he hates the state, and he hates the governor," one source close to Irsay explained before the League's defeat in *LAMCC v. NFL.* ". . . He's waiting to see the outcome of the Davis case. If the courts let Davis move, then Irsay won't be far behind," the source said.

Phoenix was the first on the list of Irsay's possibilities for 1982 and 1983, followed closely by Indianapolis. In Arizona, one Phoenix source pointed out, ". . . We intend to get some NFL team here before too long." In Indianapolis, 1982 had been opened with groundbreaking on a sixty-three-thousand-seat en-

541

closed stadium called the Hoosier Dome. Scheduled for completion in 1984, it would cost some $65 million to build, complete
with luxury boxes. As yet, the Hoosier Dome had no football
tenant.

Robert Irsay continued to insist that he was staying put throughout 1983, the last year of his short-term agreement with Baltimore. "The Colts could move tomorrow," Irsay pointed out on
June 3, "if they wanted to. . . . When Al Davis moved, we could
have moved. We are not moving. We didn't move. We're not
moving. . . . I could stand on my head, but I don't think that's
going to help. The proof is that I haven't moved. . . . The other
thing is, the Colts and the people here will never get in a
situation such as the gentleman [Al Davis], I won't mention
names, who picked up his candy store. That is not the way my
family and I've been living all my life. As I told you before,
we're here to stay unless you throw us out."

The most visible of 1983's Super Stadium Games was played in
New York City by Leon Hess of the Jets. Since beginning to
attend NFL meetings the year before, Hess had made both
friends and enemies among his fellow owners. "He's very competent," one of Hess's admirers noted, "a very shrewd businessman. He's piss poor with his team, but I like and respect him."
One of his detractors said, "He's an arrogant son of a bitch.
He's only come to about three meetings and he doesn't know
what he's talking about. He's become one of Rozelle's staunchest
backers." His detractors suggested that Hess's "sucking up to the
commissioner" was motivated by his plans for New York, though
it is not at all clear he needed the commissioner's help to pull off
what he had in mind.

Hess's latest round with New York City and Mayor Ed Koch
had entered the preliminary stage in 1980. While the Jets' lease
at the city-owned Shea Stadium did not expire until the end of
1983, the city was already eager for negotiations to begin. Hess,
with his "obsession for neatness," was known to be troubled by
the difficulties involved in keeping Shea looking "attractive"
and to have already had some discussions about moving to
Giants Stadium in the Meadowlands. "I haven't made up my
mind what we'll do," Hess told *The New York Times*. "I've
made no commitment either way. But the more the mayor and
the governor go public with this, the more I'm going to dig in."

On February 25, 1983, Mayor Koch received a letter from
Hess, addressed "Dear Ed." He gave the city until March 15 to
submit a proposal to him for remodeling Shea. By that same

date, Hess informed the mayor, New Jersey would have submitted its lease proposal to him as well. Hess rejected Koch's suggestion that the city's corporation counsel, F.A.O. Schwarz Jr., should personally tour Shea with Hess to get a sense of what the Jets owner wanted. "I appreciate and consider it regrettable," Hess continued, "that you are not personally familiar with the physical and operational problems at Shea during games so that you could familiarize Mr. Schwarz with the subject, since during your five years in office you attended only one Jets game, in the company of Governor [Hugh] Carey, and then only stayed for a brief period."

On March 14, Koch outlined what the city was prepared to do. The proposal, worth an estimated $43 million, called for the addition of ten thousand new seats, plus luxury boxes. "A first class stadium used by first class teams is good for this city," Koch wrote. "We look forward to working with you for many years."

Leon Hess answered in April. He complained that the city's proposal lacked "specific information" about when the improvements would be made and demanded more "specific assurances" that the city actually had the money to make it happen. Even with New York's improvements, New Jersey's offer yielded the Jets about $2 million more gross a year, not counting parking and concessions. Hess was also attracted to New Jersey by the fact that New York's lease still left the Jets a secondary tenant to the baseball Mets. The Mets were now much "friendlier" and sympathetic toward the Jets, but that made little difference in the football club's bottom line. The Mets, as number one tenant, still received all concession and parking income from Shea year-round, including proceeds from the sale of Jets' programs.

By July, the city and Hess had yet to meet for face-to-face negotiations, and Koch was worried. "It is important," he pleaded, "that you or your designee start work with us on implementation. . . . Let me say again," the mayor continued, "that New Yorkers in general—and I in particular—very much want you to stay. . . . New York City will not ever be without an NFL team and the Jets are our favorites." Koch closed the letter with a handwritten "Hope to see you soon."

He didn't. Instead, the two men continued to exchange letters through August and into September, but made no discernible progress. Koch was beginning to panic. On September 9, he wrote "The key is that we meet and meet soon." Koch added another handwritten postscript under his signature. "Honest,

Leon,'' the mayor wrote, ''I'm beginning to love football—and the Jets are number 1.''

On September 12, Leon Hess and Ed Koch finally talked briefly on the phone. According to sources in the mayor's office, Hess was angry over the condition of Shea and made his anger felt. He told Koch he would announce his decision about where to play after the Shea lease expired next January. ''The mayor was rebuffed,'' one of his aides noted.

The following day, Koch wrote another letter. ''I was very disappointed in our telephone conversation yesterday,'' the mayor began. He went on to note that he still had not received a copy of New Jersey's offer and he still had not met face-to-face with Hess himself. ''Are you willing to meet,'' Koch demanded, ''or must we begin to explore other options toward our aim of having first class facilities for all major league sports in the city?''

The city had not received New Jersey's offer, Hess answered, because the city was supposed to have a representative in Hess's office on March 15 when its proposal was submitted and ''neither you nor any representative attended at my office.'' As for meeting face-to-face, Hess claimed he had decided against it because the mayor had released to the public information about the Shea lease. That, Hess noted, ''prompted my refusal to meet with you thereafter.''

Koch made little attempt to hide New York City's irritation. ''I cannot simply wait around for you to announce your decision at the end of January,'' Koch wrote. ''The issue of where a sports team plays is a matter of concern to the public. Cities should not be abandoned for suburbia. Given the profits that you made in the city and the even greater profits you can make in the future, I do not believe that you should analyze the issue with a green eyeshade. . . . Please give me a call. As you know, many of my calls have gone unanswered.''

On September 26, Leon Hess and Ed Koch met face-to-face for the first and last time. Hess, Koch remembered, ''talked about Donald Grant a lot and also about dirty bathrooms.'' According to Koch, Hess also said, ''No matter what you do, we will not stay in Shea.'' On September 28, Koch called a press conference and announced that negotiations had broken down and that the Jets would be playing in New Jersey once this football season was over. Hess said nothing and could not be reached for comment.

On October 5, the NFL met in New York and Hess reported on his negotiations with New York City and the New Jersey

Sports Authority. No permission to relocate was asked and no votes demanded. The following day, Hess dispatched his last letter to Koch. The mayor's announcement had "forced the issue," he explained, and since Shea was "unsuitable," he was moving to New Jersey.

New York City immediately appealed to Pete Rozelle for help and got none. "We went to bat for Oakland," Rozelle complained, "and it could cost the League $50 million. It's probably moot whether we have any opinion at all about a club moving."

That being the case, the Big Apple quickly announced plans to lure another NFL team inside the New York city limits. The two most obvious candidates were Joe Robbie and Robert Irsay. Joe Robbie had no comment, and Robert Irsay had two different responses. "I don't rule out any move," he told the *New York Post*. "At the same time, I don't rule any move in." He was more blunt with *The* [Baltimore] *Sun*. "I hate New York and you can quote me on that."

The closest thing to a positive response New York received was from Joseph Alioto, Al Davis's attorney. Alioto informed an aide to Governor Hugh Carey that in the "unlikely" circumstance that the courts should bar the Raiders from L.A., his boss would be willing to consider Shea as a possibility.

By November, New York officials were admitting they did not "expect" any football team to move into Shea in the "forseeable future." The *Times* lamented, "City Unable to Find New Football Team." The refrain was by now a familiar one.

33
All in the Family

The October 5 League meeting in New York City at which Leon Hess made his report about New Jersey had been preoccupied with other issues. First was the DeBartolo situation, the most serious challenge to the commissioner and the League since the *LAMCC v. NFL* decision.

Pete Rozelle convened the meeting in much better personal shape than he'd been in six months earlier. His depression had apparently run its course. The process culminated in early September with the death of his father, Ray Rozelle. Ray Rozelle's death seemed to focus Pete's disappointment in a very specific grief and the effect was cathartic. "He's happier and healthier now," one of the commissioner's friends noted. "He doesn't let things get so personal anymore. . . . He's come to terms with what's happened. He understands you can't let mishaps dominate your life. Pete's cheery and confident again."

The light that had appeared at the end of the commissioner's personal tunnel was not, however, yet reflected in his professional life. *LAMCC v. NFL*, still in the court of appeals, continued to cast a long shadow over League Think. Rozelle wanted very badly to have confidence in the appeals process, and the longer it lasted, the more his confidence seemed to grow. He considered the League's arguments sound and now that the personal sting had gone out of his L.A. defeat, it was easier to believe those arguments would hold sway, and he thought the League's chances on appeal were "good."

In October, however, reality beckoned in the form of the DeBartolos, with whom Rozelle had to deal right away. The Parins Committee's report was ready and was presented to the entire League. To no one's surprise, it concluded that the concern over "conflicts of interest that might result from Edward DeBartolo Jr. and Edward DeBartolo Sr. owning teams in competing football leagues" was justified. How could the two of them not look out for each other in a business they were now both in?

Rozelle himself did not speak on the question at the October 5 meeting, but his feelings were no secret. By now, the vocabulary had become familiar. "Anarchy could develop," he had warned, "and one indication of it that we've never had before is the DeBartolo situation. For example, you always have litigation between competing leagues. We've had it already between San Diego and Tampa over Gary Anderson. In the history of two-league competition in professional football, . . . it always develops litigation. . . . It's just automatic. That places a terrible burden on Eddie to act against his father." At the same time, Rozelle did his best to cast his opposition in a sympathetic tone. "It's a tough situation for Eddie," the commissioner pointed out to the San Francisco press. "It's not a thrill for him to go through this, obviously."

The DeBartolo position was presented on October 5 by Eddie and the family's attorney, Carmine Policy. Eddie made no secret of his frustration. "I think the owners are trying to make a decision based on fiction," he complained. "The facts are that I own my team and my father owns his team and never the twain shall meet. . . . Look, I'm competitive in business and in football. And that means I intend to be competitive against any other football team, including the Pittsburgh Maulers. . . . I can't even comprehend what they mean by conflict of interest. I haven't even discussed the legal positions or ramifications. I just think it's all very absurd and I know I'm within my rights." Carmine Policy framed the dispute as an unfortunate misunderstanding. "Eddie likes the NFL. He is not a rebel. . . . He does not want to be part of, or in any way interact with, the USFL, but he loves his father. I think what he'll try to do . . . is to try to get his father to disengage himself from the USFL."

The DeBartolo arguments made little headway with the rest of the League. Among the most vehement opponents of the DeBartolos' situation was Al Davis. "We've got these rules," he argued, "and we have to live up to them." At that, Gene Klein "laid into him" for being a fine one to talk. If it weren't for Davis, the League wouldn't be in this fix. But all the League besides Eddie DeBartolo felt the same way. The fact that his father's USFL franchise was located in Pittsburgh, home of the NFL's beloved Art Rooney, only added to many owners' feelings. It was no secret Rooney was very displeased. "Mr. Rooney can't believe that DeBartolo would come in his own backyard with a team from the league we're at war with," a source close to the Rooneys explained, "especially after Mr. Rooney endorsed the DeBartolos when they wanted to buy the 49ers. Anyone with a brain in his head can see the conflict. Who are they kidding?"

"I don't want to make this thing a bloody mess," Eddie pleaded. "I just want to run the 49ers. I want to operate this franchise independent of my family's business . . . and if everybody leaves me alone, everything will be fine. . . . I just don't feel as though I'm doing anything wrong." Eddie's plea fell on apparently deaf ears and he walked out of the meeting room, refusing all comment to the reporters gathered in the hotel's lobby.

After DeBartolo walked out, the rest of the League took steps to deal with their latest hot potato. The possible penalties, Rozelle pointed out again, ranged from nothing to forcing Eddie to divest his team and leave the NFL altogether. By twenty-seven to zero vote, the League then passed a resolution.

RESOLVED, that if the commissioner finds that the ownership of the 49ers has either violated the constitution and
bylaws or is engaged in conduct detrimental to the welfare
of the League, the commissioner is authorized to develop
and implement appropriate remedial actions or discipline
within the League itself . . . to eliminate the prospect of
continuing damage to League interests.

In effect, the owners tossed the dilemma into Rozelle's lap.
Rozelle did his best to toss at least part of it back. "There's
always the fear of legal action," he pointed out. "The owners
will have to decide for themselves whether this is an important
enough issue to take a stand on."

After the October 5 meeting had adjourned, Eddie DeBartolo
quite angrily put his finger on what had everyone else in the
League worried. "They don't like it?" Eddie blustered. That's the
way it is. Nobody's going to take this team away from me,
including the League. Because, I tell you, the League can't
afford the lawsuit. I can. Enough of this bullshit about conflict of
interest. That's ridiculous. They can't afford a lawsuit because
I'll bury them."

That warning wasn't lost on Pete Rozelle. Though he had
promised that DeBartolo would be summoned to his office for a
hearing within thirty days, no such hearing was ever held.
Instead, the commissioner decided to back off and continue
waiting for the appeals court to effect his rescue.

34
"Just Win, Baby, Just Win!"

While the Sherman Act continued to enforce a vacuum at the
core of the NFL, the football business itself had turned an
invisible corner and become something markedly different from
the institution Pete Rozelle had made his name dominating.
Rozelle's job was secure, but the era he had personified was on
its last legs, even while he waited. Super Bowl XVIII, held in
January 1984, was, in several ways, emblematic of the transformation that had overtaken League Think.

First, Tampa was by far the smallest city and smallest stadium ever to host a Super Bowl. That it did was thanks to Hugh Culverhouse. "It was a plum for Culverhouse," one owner said of the site, "pure and simple. He'd earned it." Most of the League now ranked the Tampa owner as the equal in influence to Tex Schramm and Art Modell, hitherto Rozelle's chief lieutenants. In the spring of 1983, Culverhouse was named the new chairman of the management council executive committee, replacing Chuck Sullivan. He was already finance committee chairman and had begun a significant restructuring of the League's internal fiscal practices. He had created a standardized mechanism for handling deferred contract payments and, by 1984, was devising a formula for sharing revenues from luxury boxes. Culverhouse, the management council's Jack Donlan noted, ". . . has the ability to identify the problem early, analyze it, and try to see about getting a solution." Donlan also observed that Culverhouse was "very effective at getting his way."

Indeed, Culverhouse seemed to pop up behind the scenes just about everywhere. He had commissioned the computer software a number of the clubs used to manage their money and consulted with a number more about tax matters. He had also participated in the sale of the 49ers and the Denver Broncos, acted as executor of Carroll Rosenbloom's estate, helped Georgia Frontiere reorganize the Rams, and bailed Leonard Tose out by guaranteeing one of his loans. Though a staunch Rozelle partisan, Culverhouse's rise was also an indication of how much the foundation of the football business had shifted. "Sure it's changed," Tex Schramm admitted, "it's not as much fun. . . . It's become so big and complex and lawyers, accountants, and courts are so much a part of it now . . . [and] now our problems are more created from within than without." Culverhouse, half attorney and half accountant, was the mechanic of football's new age. Where Schramm had risen by understanding the game and preaching professionalism, and Modell had risen by appreciating the League's fraternity and preaching all for one, one for all, Culverhouse rose by understanding litigation and preaching liquidity. This new technocracy made football a very different business from the one Rozelle was used to.

The second way the Super Bowl staged in Culverhouse's hometown reflected the League's shifting larger picture was in the participant representing the National Conference. Jack Kent Cooke's Washington Redskins, the defending NFL champions, were the first half of the Super Bowl billing. Cooke himself was emblematic of the new opposition to Rozelle that had grown up over the last year. Rozelle had always faced opposition here and there over a specific issue, but never had it been so generalized or so attached to his leadership per se. Art Modell described the disaffected as "a group who don't think favorably of the League office," rather than an actual "opposition." Whatever their description, by the end of 1983, their number was fast reaching eight—the critical mass that would allow them veto power under the NFL's three-quarter vote rules.

Cooke was often listed at the head of this group. He was not an NFL insider, rarely attending meetings personally, but he was rich and successful—and still pissed off at Rozelle. His "family bitterness" toward the commissioner's wife was an ongoing resentment. In addition, Cooke still smarted from his forced divestiture and made no secret that he was in the market for a baseball team to bring to Washington, D.C. He also objected to the way Rozelle spent the League's money.

Joining Cooke in that attitude were Al Davis, of course; Joe Robbie, who still smarted from the events leading up to *NASL v. NFL* and thought the League had overreached itself in *LAMCC v. NFL;* Eddie DeBartolo; and Leonard Tose, who was upset at the money Rozelle had cost them, tired of being lectured to, and eager to get on Davis's good side while the getting was good. In addition to those five, there were at least four "floaters." Those included Lamar Hunt, who, one of his fellow owners noted, "was conservative and penurious and found the legal expenses Rozelle had run up appalling"; Ed McCaskey, who had inherited the Chicago Bears and was reportedly obsessed with the bottom line; Paul Brown of the Cincinnati Bengals, who had long hated Art Modell and was glad to go against him when he could; and Ralph Wilson, who was a friend of both Pete Rozelle and Mel Durslag and consequently, according to one NFL observer, "played it both ways."

The minority had two principal bones of contention with Rozelle in early 1984: First was the League office's lack of fiscal accountability and the size of its budget. The only information the League received about its operations was a rough financial breakdown that included no details about the actual cash flow. In all, Rozelle's jurisdiction accounted for "total cash disbursements" of $17,942,000. A number considered the expenses bloated. "If any owner wants to see the books," Culverhouse suggested, "they can come up and see them. . . . We have nothing to hide. I don't know any business that publishes line-by-line items.''

The minority's other objection was Rozelle's contract, drawn up in 1982 by Culverhouse, Gene Klein, and Leon Hess. Most owners had little idea what it provided. "The owners aren't allowed to look at it," Tose complained. "I've never seen a copy. Letting that get by is just stupidity on the part of the owners." By January 1984, Cooke was quite privately leading a chorus of demands that the contract be made available for their inspection.

Publicly, Cooke was content to keep his mouth shut and play the role of visiting mogul appropriate to a Super Bowl owner. Now worth a fortune estimated by *Forbes* at $600 million, Cooke could easily afford to do so. For the Tampa Super Bowl, he chartered a Boeing 747 airliner and footed the transportation and hotel bills of more than one hundred personal guests. Cooke was enjoying himself immensely. "I'd say the satisfaction I have had from the Redskins transcends by far the satisfaction I've had in total from all the other teams I've owned," he gushed to *The Washington Post*. "It's fantastic." Going into Super Bowl XVIII, his Redskins were favored to win, but no one expected it to be easy.

Cooke's opponent from the American Conference was the third and by far most visible reflection of the League's larger change in Tampa that January. With the NFL at yet another critical juncture, Al Davis and his Raiders were back in the Super Bowl once again. The difference was that now they were representing L.A. for the first time.

If League Think's partisans could take any solace from Davis being in L.A., it was that his relationship with the Coliseum there was still informal and tenuous and that the local following for his team was still problematic. By January 1984, he and the LAMCC had still signed no binding lease despite having been landlord and tenant for almost two years. "There is no pressure on Davis," the *San Francisco Chronicle* observed. "If he doesn't sign, what are they going to do in Los Angeles—kick him out? They need Davis more than he needs them.''

The terms Davis had to live with in the meantime were not, of course, hurting him. "No final agreement has been executed yet," Robertson pointed out, "because we still owe Al Davis $4 million under the terms of the last agreement. He put out a hell of a lot of money moving, establishing offices, putting together a practice field and a local staff, and fighting this litigation. Until he gets the money coming to him, he's not going to finalize a deal.'' A source close to Mayor Tom Bradley agreed with Robertson. "Los Angeles has no complaints,'' the source explained. "If anyone does, it's Al Davis. L.A. never kept its agreement. Kenny Hahn told Al Davis the day before the Raiders moved, 'If you come down here, I'll . . . deliver a $2 million check.' Al Davis still hasn't got the money. What happened is we got a guy down here and then broke all our promises. . . . Al Davis doesn't owe anybody here anything.''

Of much more concern to Davis was his team's attendance in their new home. During the strike year, the Raiders established an eight to one record as compared to Georgia Frontiere's two to seven Rams, and drew an average game day attendance of fifty-three thousand, about half the Coliseum's capacity. In 1983, they slipped backward. The cancellations, the *Los Angeles Times* noted, were largely because the Raiders "distributed them poorly and bungled seat assignments so badly that they infuriated thousands of their customers. . . . Coliseum officials said there was one stretch when they were getting as many as five hundred complaints daily. The Raiders blamed the mess on a computer foul up. . . . Executive assistant Al LoCasale . . . had to be hospitalized with exhaustion in the midst of the ticket rush, and Davis was so upset by the ticket snafu that LoCasale was almost fired.''

In response, Davis threw himself into marketing. The Raiders adopted a new motto: "Commitment to Excellence.'' The slogan, accompanied by a Raider logo, was displayed in silver and black on billboards and the sides of buses all over Greater L.A. When he reached the Super Bowl, Davis also bought up billboard space all around Tampa and did the same thing.

Al Davis still placed his ultimate marketing faith in the team itself. Winning football teams would draw crowds, sooner or later, and it was as simple as that. Despite his attendance trouble, Davis didn't bother to hire a franchise public relations man. "I just want to win,'' Davis said. The Raiders did just that, going twelve to four and crushing their two playoff opponents. They did so with the usual Raider attitude. "In 1983,'' Al LoCasale observed to *Sports Illustrated,* "our team battled not only opponents on the field, but a powerful combination of the NFL's propaganda machine, the federal courts, the state courts, the halls of Congress. I can assure you their campaign to prevent the Los Angeles Raiders from being the world champion Los

Angeles Raiders will not go unchallenged. Our goal is the same in the courts or on the field.'' Being underdogs in Super Bowl XVIII suited the Raider personality to a T.

Al Davis, the architect of that personality, played the mogul role in Tampa on a scale that matched Jack Kent Cooke. He, too, chartered an airliner for his guests, who included actor James Garner, singer Frank Sinatra, and actress Jane Fonda. While Cooke spent the week in Tampa partying, however, Davis worked, going over films, lifting weights, and secluding himself from the press. His confidence was apparent to everyone he met. Uncharacteristically, he predicted to his friends that the Raiders would win and win big.

The biggest media event of that week was the commissioner's press conference on January 20. There, in front of at least three hundred reporters, he answered questions about the state of the League. It did not take long for *LAMCC v. NFL* to be raised. ''While the case on the Coast is on appeal,'' the commissioner noted, ''. . . we have nothing to say about franchise shifts.''

The most asked question, Rozelle pointed out, ''is how I'll feel about possibly giving the trophy to Al.'' It was, of course, a question he was now quite used to. ''As far as Al is concerned, I have great admiration for his work developing a fine football team. I can set aside the fact Al is responsible for five pieces of litigation against the League. I have no problem presenting the trophy to Al.''

On Super Bowl Sunday, Davis could be seen during the last half hour before kickoff down on the stadium floor dressed in a long black leather jacket and dark glasses, shaking hands with each of his players. Then he left for the press box to watch the contest by himself. At halftime, his team led twenty-one to three. With 8:51 left to play in the final quarter, the lead was thirty-eight to nine. Davis shook both fists in the air. ''That's it,'' he exulted.

In the locker room, he and Rozelle faced the television lights together. ''Davis,'' Rozelle remembered, ''was hyper. He was more caught up in the emotion of it all than I'd ever seen him.'' Nervously, the Raiders owner kept popping his jaw, as though trying to unplug his ears.

''Congratulations, Al,'' Rozelle said as he handed over the championship trophy. Then, as he'd promised the press earlier in the week, Rozelle shook his nemesis's hand.

''Thank you, Mr. Commissioner,'' Davis offered. Then he began a disjointed but intense monologue, at one point noting,

"This is a great credit to an organization after all the outrageous things the League has done to it."

Off camera, the Raiders' players cheered. Davis responded immediately. Looking past the TV lights toward the sound, he raised a fist and sounded the call to arms of football's new age. "Just win, baby," Davis shouted. "Just win."

Thirty-five days later, the Ninth Circuit Court of Appeals upheld the verdict in *LAMCC v. NFL* by a vote of two to one. The League appealed to the Supreme Court but the Supreme Court refused to hear the case. Pete Rozelle's wait was over. Al Davis had won it all.

PART FIVE

EX POST FACTO

1
Invisible Owners

The advent of football's new age cut across the League's members in different ways.

Texas Schramm managed to land on his feet, though as a League man, Tex considered the new state of affairs an abomination. "There's no structure at all," Schramm reiterated. "Sports leagues must be able to make rules and structures to live by. You take that away and there's no league." Despite his friendship with Al Davis, Schramm had fought on the League side throughout the three-year battle just completed. Of the second trial of *LAMCC v. NFL*, Joe Alioto noted, "Schramm even ran the NFL show. Rozelle . . . moved toward the background and Tex sat in the front row." In the end, it only meant Schramm shared in the diminishment of his friend. The two were still good friends, although not, Rozelle admitted, in as close touch as they'd once been. Tex was still a powerful figure, but few rated him the second most powerful in the League anymore. A "football man" par excellence, his skills were no longer so central to the business. "Anarchy" had moved the action elsewhere.

As 1983 became 1984, the "instability" about which Pete Rozelle had warned over and over again seemed to be symbolized within the Dallas franchise, once the model of League Think ownership. The way Clint Murchison had sat back and let Tex Schramm run things was a central piece of the commissioner's carefully crafted iconography, as was the fact that there had been no changes in the organizational end of the Cowboys since they'd come into the League in 1960 at the same meeting at which Pete Rozelle had begun his commissionership. Stability, as everyone now knew, had a shelf life and, in Dallas, time had caught up with Clint Murchison. "America's team" was for sale.

What eventually put the Cowboys on the block was the death of Clint Murchison's brother John in 1979. John and Clint had managed their inheritance jointly through a partnership agreement that required the surviving brother to liquidate the company. Liquidation posed severe difficulties for Clint. The brothers had made [heavy use] of borrowed money and their own reputation for wealth. "For years," *Newsweek* noted, "a Murchison signature was considered as bankable as a proven oilfield." Extended as the brothers were, liquidation might very well bring the whole structure down before its estimated total value of some $260 million could be extracted. That vulnerability was enhanced when rising interest rates began to put a number of the real estate ventures in trouble.

Clint attempted to hold off executing the partnership agreement as long as he could but, in 1981, his nephew, John Murchison Jr., filed suit contesting the way Clint was managing the family assets. Among other things, Clint and John Sr. had apparently pledged as collateral the assets of trusts set up by their father for his grandchildren. That suit was settled with a payment to John Jr. of some $20 to 30 million. Later, aides to John Jr. would brag they'd forced Clint to sell the Cowboys.

That was not, of course, the official reason given for the Cowboys sale when the possibility was first admitted by Tex Schramm in November 1983. Few people could imagine that Murchison could possibly be prey to financial problems. The stated reason for selling the Cowboys was Clint's health. In 1982, he had begun losing his sense of balance, forcing him to use a cane and then confining him to a wheelchair. The cause was a degenerative brain disease that also attacked his powers of speech. While it did not affect his ability to think, by November 1983 he was unable to stand or speak in anything more than a laborious effort to make a few words come out.

On November 14, Tex Schramm confirmed that the franchise might be sold. "It's just in the initial discussion stage," he said, adding, the next day, "we do not have time constraints and we don't want to rush into anything. On the other hand, if exactly the right people come by, there will be no reason for us to delay the proceedings."

The announcement was the biggest news in Dallas. Nowhere was an NFL franchise more central to a city's sense of itself. Hosting "America's team" was perhaps the city's most cherished claim to fame. Those who dared oppose the Cowboys' wholesome image, W. A. Criswell, pastor of the local First Baptist Church, declared, were "the same bunch" who support "socialists, liberals, communists, pinkos, Ted Kennedy, Washington, and Moscow." Anyone who worried that the Cowboys might deteriorate, however, was no doubt comforted to learn that the sale itself would be managed by Tex Schramm, the same man who'd built the club from day one. "I'm going to try and find people that fit the parameters Clint is looking for," Schramm explained. "Obviously the final decision will be the Murchisons'. The Murchison family wants the present organization to continue without disruption. There are two things I want to be very specific about, number one is I am not part of any group, and number two is I am not seeking to form any group. If the new ownership felt it would be beneficial to include me, I'm prepared to do anything to keep the organization functioning as it is. I fully hope to remain with the team."

Tex Schramm, of course, had good reason to "fully hope." In fact, continuation of Schramm's contract in which he was granted exclusive control of all football operations was a condition of any potential sale. By December 14, he had opened the franchise's books to "five or six" groups of potential investors whom he had screened carefully. Said to be at the top of that list were a combine headed by Dallas businessmen Vance Miller and W. O. Bankston. Bankston, a friend of Schramm's, said that should he and Miller purchase the club, "Tex knows that we'd stay out of the way and let him run it." In January, Schramm submitted Miller and Bankston's names to Rozelle's office for investigation. "They are the only names at the present time to be submitted, but they are not the only ones that will be," Tex explained. Despite that disclaimer, speculation that Miller and Bankston were first in line was additionally fueled when the two men flew to Tampa to watch Super Bowl XVIII from Tex Schramm's box. Miller especially seemed convinced. "As far as the price goes," he told the *Dallas Times Herald*, "we've reached an agreement. Right now I'd say I'm feeling pretty positive about the deal. We need to get the lawyers from both sides together, and we need to get the approval of the NFL owners. . . . But I feel we have the blessings of the Cowboys." Tex Schramm, embodiment of the Cowboys, refused all comment.

Within a week, Miller's confidence seemed something of an overstatement. There was talk about a new name that had popped up: H. R. "Bum" Bright, oilman and chairman of the Texas A&M University board of regents. Though he was well known in Texas money circles, Bright's only brush with national notoriety had been as a signatory of the inflammatory "Welcome Mr. Kennedy" ad in the Dallas papers on the morning President John F. Kennedy was assassinated. "I contribute to conservatives and right-wing causes," Bright explained, "always have and still do.'' Tex Schramm would say only that Bright was ''one of the people I've talked to. I'm not saying anything more beyond that point.'' During February, Bright's name was also submitted to the League for checking, along with at least one other. While this bidding war went on behind the scenes, Clint Murchison was, as usual, invisible.

At the end of January, he appeared in public as Cowboys owner for the last time. The occasion was a dinner in his honor. While Clint sat listening in his wheelchair, unable to say anything himself, Tex Schramm gave him much of the credit for the Cowboys' success. ''A lot of people have said that Clint's greatest contribution was staying out of the way. Well, that isn't true. His contribution was his support and counsel.'' At the time, it was thought Schramm would finalize a sale within a month and said whatever transaction was made would be presented to the NFL's annual meeting for approval during the week of March 19.

On March 19, Schramm submitted Bright's name to the League's executive session. The part of his report that drew the most attention was the price tag. Bright's consortium would pay $80 million to Murchison—almost twice what had been paid for any franchise in NFL history. While there was no doubt an immediate urge among the members to confirm that their franchises were indeed worth that much, to do so would require violating their own rules. Schramm had surmounted the problems posed by the fifty-one percent provision of the commissioner's ownership policy by, in essence, ignoring it. Bright would own only seventeen percent. Two other partners would own fifteen percent apiece, another ten percent, another five percent, and the rest split between a half-dozen or so others. To compensate for having no majority owner, the group had designated a managing partner, much as the L.A. Raiders partnership worked. The managing partner with absolute control of the franchise's League operations was Texas Schramm, in for three percent.

In the course of trying to make the sale, Rozelle remembered, ''Tex found that people of means didn't want to have control over the franchise. They didn't want their peers either to think that they were bad businessmen, paying that much money for a football team, or didn't want their peers to think they'd done it for the self-aggrandizement. It was the first time we'd experienced that. All of the potential purchasers had wanted Tex to run it.'' Both Rozelle and Culverhouse recommended acceptance. ''It was a change from existing League policy,'' Schramm admitted, "but the quality and substance of the individuals concerned was very attractive and made it acceptable to the commissioner and other members of the League."

"Aren't we eroding the constitution?" Leonard Tose complained.

"Yes we are," Leon Hess agreed.

Nonetheless, the Cowboys sale was passed twenty-four to zero. No one wanted to turn down either $60 million or Tex Schramm, and in NFL Year One After Davis, all things were indeed now possible.

Most of the money Clint Murchison received from the sale was taken almost immediately by creditors. After that, Clint's fortunes continued to plummet. "It's as if someone found out the emperor had no clothes," one of his friends lamented. That discovery prompted a run on Clint's assets that resembled a stampede. By the end of 1984, banks and financial houses were lined up in court seeking foreclosure on what they said Murchison owed them. "Clint's problems to a great extent are like that of any bank in the U.S.," one of his partners pointed out to *The Wall Street Journal*. "If everybody wants their [sic] money today, they can't do it." Despite Clint's extreme difficulties with speech, one of Murchison's friends noted in early 1985, "he is on the phone around the clock and he is very determined that everybody get paid."

The Dallas Cowboys, first of Murchison's assets to be jettisoned, were unaffected by the crash. Nothing but the name at the top had changed and even that was still misleading. It was now Tex Schramm's franchise more than ever. "If you think Clint Murchison was an invisible owner," Bum Bright explained, "my group and I are going to be even more invisible." The announcement surprised no one, but Texas Schramm least of all.

2
The Bane of the Baltimore Colts

To the surprise of almost no one, Robert Irsay was the first member of the League to take full advantage of the victory Al Davis had won. He did so with typical Irsay flair.

At the time of the Tampa Super Bowl, Irsay had indeed been conducting secret negotiations in Phoenix. The Arizona principals were Anthony Nicoli, a wealthy Phoenix businessman, and Arizona Governor Bruce Babbitt. In the course of one "visit," Nicoli told Irsay he wanted to buy the Colts and move them to Phoenix. Irsay's first response was to say the franchise would cost $50 million. Later in January, Nicoli remembered, "he wasn't prepared to release one hundred percent of the club. He would entertain very seriously to sell me forty-nine percent. . . . The problem was, I wasn't interested in forty-nine percent. So I said, 'Let me stop negotiating for myself and put on a hat as a citizen for the people of the Valley of the Sun. Let's bring the team to Phoenix in 1984.' "

Nicoli left Chicago with a list of instructions from Irsay. He was to find temporary office space for the Colts, a suitable practice field, arrange a meeting with Arizona State University officials to discuss using their stadium until a new one could be built, and arrange a meeting with Governor Babbitt, legislative leaders, university officials, and local business leaders. Irsay also had told Nicoli to reserve five giant Mayflower Moving and Storage vans for use in his eventual move. Irsay wanted vans from outside of Maryland and said his plan was to leave Baltimore in the middle of the night and announce it after the fact. It was arranged that Irsay would fly to the meetings Nicoli had set up on the Tuesday after the Super Bowl. It was originally thought it would take that long to carry out Irsay's instructions but Nicoli was faster than that. Irsay responded, "Let's do it during the week of the Super Bowl. So much attention is on that that people won't know what we're doing."

The meetings were moved up to Thursday of Super Bowl week. That morning, Irsay called from Las Vegas, canceled the meetings and rescheduled them for Friday afternoon. Nicoli agreed. At 5:00 A.M. Friday morning, Robert Irsay was awake in his Las Vegas hotel room, watching television, and saw a news report that he was scheduled to be in Phoenix to meet with the governor later that afternoon. At 5:30 A.M., Irsay's attorney called Nicoli and told him there was a "security leak" and the deal was on hold. Nicoli asked him to think it over and call him back. He and the attorney talked three more times on the phone that morning. "The last time he called, he said, 'We'll get back to you,' " Nicoli pointed out the next day. "I haven't heard from him since."

By then, Irsay's Jet Star was warming up at the Las Vegas airport, taking on enough fuel to get him to Baltimore. At 7:30 P.M., Irsay's plane taxied to a stop and he bounded into the terminal to be greeted by Mayor Donald Schaeffer and a swarm of reporters. "My name's Irsay," he said to the mayor. "How do you do?" Robert Irsay and Donald Schaeffer then stepped over to a bank of microphones and met the press. The first question was from an AP reporter, but Irsay didn't like the man and refused to answer. "Let the mayor have a chance, will ya?" Irsay snapped.

"There was a story," Schaeffer opened, "that said Robert Irsay is in Arizona. . . . I've told everyone that you told me if you were going to move the team, you'd tell me personally."

"Let me," Irsay broke in. He was at his most belligerent and waved his hands angrily. "We'll get this over real fast. I haven't been in Arizona. I haven't been in zero. I've been in three, four places where I got plenty machines, my own companies. I haven't been in Phoenix. I give you my word of honor. I'm a good Catholic. I haven't been in Arizona. Where the hell did this all come from? Who started this? . . . I didn't have any meetings planned. I don't know where this comes from. Don Schaeffer is my friend."

"You say the Arizona governor's a liar?" the AP reporter asked.

"I don't want to talk to you," Irsay snapped.

"Is there any thought about moving the Baltimore Colts to Arizona?" another reporter asked.

"I don't know where all this comes from," Irsay complained again. "Now, somebody started this. I don't know who did it. We are negotiating [with Baltimore]. . . . Now, why would I want to go to Arizona? . . . I have not any intention to move the goddamn team. If I did, I would tell you about it. . . . I flew a lot of miles today. That's my plane out there. And that bird burns a lot of fuel. I come over to tell you I don't know what the hell this is about. . . . If you love the Colts, why don't you treat me right? . . . You want me here, why do you hang me? Why do you hang me for? . . . I flew over here just to answer you guys. I don't know what the hell you're doing here. . . ."

"Why did you come to Baltimore tonight?" a reporter asked again.

"Because jerks like you, jerks like you put things in the paper that I'm moving to Phoenix."

When the press conference was over and he and Schaeffer had met privately, Irsay flew off for parts unknown, probably Chicago, where he lived. "He's one of the most interesting men I've ever met," Mayor Schaeffer noted. "I am encouraged. I really am. I don't think he's made a deal [elsewhere] . . . I think he would have told us.''

Within a month, Robert Irsay was back in serious negotiations, this time with Indianapolis. On February 27, *The Indianapolis Star* announced, "Deal to Move Colts Here at 'Decision Stage.' " Indianapolis, negotiating through Mayor William Hudnut, had already offered Irsay a package that included free rent in the brand new Hoosier Dome, the building of an accompanying practice facility, and a large loan to Irsay at an annual interest rate of eight percent. By March 2, negotiations were reported to have reached the point where only Irsay's signature was needed.

That same day, the NFL convened a special meeting in Chicago. When Irsay showed up, he was mobbed by the press. Pushing his way through the crowd, Irsay grunted "No information," and then disappeared behind closed doors. Inside, Pete Rozelle told the press afterward "Mr. Irsay said he has not made up his mind what he wants to do. He acknowledged the discussions that he's had with other cities and that there is a possibility he would move, but he stressed he had no firm commitment from anybody." Rozelle later explained that "We had to leave it in his hands because of the judgment in L.A." All the League could ask of Irsay was that he make his decision by April 1, one of the owners confirmed, so that the League's 1984 schedule could be drawn up.

Irsay would meet the League's deadline, but March was a busy month for him. On March 3, Irsay was again talking with Phoenix. "It's hard to figure out," Indianapolis's Mayor Hudnut admitted. "I don't know what's going on." Irsay's communications with Phoenix were scheduled to culminate in a meeting at Caesars Palace in Las Vegas on March 14 at which a new offer would be made. When word of the meeting leaked out, however, the meeting was canceled. Instead, Phoenix officials were told that Irsay was flying elsewhere. He flew to nearby Bakersfield, California, and on March 15, a five-man Phoenix delegation headed by Governor Babbitt flew up by private plane and met him there. Babbitt later refused all comment on the meeting.

Indianapolis was still mystified. The final papers they'd drawn up in a great rush for March 2 remained unsigned on Robert Irsay's desk. "Nobody here had heard anything," a source there explained. "Irsay's lawyer lived with these guys for two weeks and now it's like it all didn't happen."

Baltimore, more accustomed to Irsay, continued to plug along while all this was going on. On March 12, Donald Schaeffer and

Governor Hughes made a revised offer to match those of Phoenix and Indianapolis. When the NFL met for its annual meeting on March 19, Irsay sent his twenty-five-year-old son, Jimmy, to represent him. Jimmy had recently been named the franchise's general manager and was, at this point, perhaps Robert Irsay's only public defender. "I see him as a sensitive person," Jimmy said. "He comes from a tough background—the Bucktown section of Chicago and the Marines—and I think that has shaped his personality. He's had to fight for everything he's got. He's a simple man in that he appreciates the little things and family pleasures. . . . When people really get to know him, I think they'll find he's a sensitive, generous person." For example, Jimmy was fond of pointing to an incident that happened after a Colt victory in 1979, when Jimmy, home from college, was eating dinner with his folks. "All of a sudden," Jimmy remembered, "Dad got up from the table and left. He went across the street to an ice cream store, made a deal with the manager, and put on the guy's hat and took the ice cream scoop and invited every kid to come in off the street and have free ice cream. It must have cost him four hundred dollars. That's a side of him others don't see."

At the annual meeting, all Rozelle could do was to remind Jimmy that the League had to know where his father's franchise was going to play next season by April 1. By then, Irsay had three offers to choose from. Then, on March 28, Phoenix withdrew its offer, saying it could no longer wait for Irsay to make up his mind. By that time the Maryland legislature was hurriedly working on a law that would permit the Colts to be seized under eminent domain. Later that evening, Robert Irsay chose Indianapolis.

In the darkness of the early morning hours of March 29, moving vans were loaded with all the Colts' records and equipment and sent west. When they were long gone across the Maryland state line, Indianapolis Mayor William Hudnut announced the Colts were coming to town. "We are going to welcome them with open arms," he beamed. Hudnut's Baltimore counterpart, Donald Schaeffer, voiced only disgust. "That's the final humiliation," he noted.

Colts General Manager Jimmy Irsay composed a song to celebrate the occasion, which he later helped record in a rendition he described as "very Bruce Springsteen-like." It was called "Hoosier Heartland":

Daddy called me up on the telephone.
"Son, is there anybody listening? Are you alone?
It's goin' down tonight around 9 P.M.
The trucks are on their way as soon as I say when."

Well, the trucks pulled up to Baltimore.
The people 'round there didn't want us no more.
So we packed up our bags and drove out of town.
And 12 hours later we were Indy bound.

Well, the Colts we had it tough a couple of years,
Just a lot of empty seats.
Lord, there was no one to cheer.
But we heard about a place that had a big white dome.
And it didn't take long for us to find a new home.

Hoosier Heartland, that's where we do roam.
Hoosier Heartland, gettin' down in the Hoosier Dome.
Hoosier Heartland, and the Indy Colts have found their home.

While the Colts' move provoked a storm of criticism throughout the country, Al Davis, the man who had opened the door Irsay walked through, claimed it didn't bother him. "I have no misgivings," he explained. "This is America and industries can move. But the difference is that Baltimore made an honest effort to keep the Colts. I gave Oakland the best operation in football—and it wouldn't even give me $11 million in stadium improvements. The League will use this to say, 'We told you so,' but they could have stopped it if they wanted to."

Rozelle, of course, claimed exactly the opposite. "I talked to Irsay," the commissioner explained. "He knew that our rules on franchise moves have been suspended because of the Oakland situation. We just weren't in a position to stop him." While Rozelle did place the blame with *LAMCC v. NFL*, as Davis predicted, he was careful to distinguish Irsay from his predecessor. "As far as the League is concerned," Rozelle pointed out, "Bob hasn't caused trouble. At meetings, he goes along with the majority on things. He's very supportive of staying together and operating as a League. He was really self-conscious about going to Indianapolis. He didn't want to move like Al Davis. He wanted to have a vote. He told me he didn't want to be viewed as an Al Davis."

On April 2, 1984, some seventeen thousand local residents

showed up at the Hoosier Dome to welcome Robert Irsay officially to town. At the accompanying press conference, Irsay was blunt. "It's not your ball team," he warned Indianapolis. "It's mine and my family's ball team and I paid for it and I earned it." The line drew applause from Indianapolis's reporters.

On January 4, 1985, shortly after the close of his first season in Indianapolis, Robert Irsay was driving his car through the north side of Chicago when unknown assailants fired two gunshots through his window. Irsay was unhurt. Reporters seeking more information about the shooting located Robert Irsay's eighty-two-year-old mother. She knew nothing about it and claimed she had not seen her son in thirty-five years. "I got a big heartache," Mrs. Irsay told United Press. "After I put him through school, he goes and marries that Polish girl, I forget her name already. I pay five thousand dollars for the wedding. He's the devil on earth." By June 1985, "that Polish girl," Mrs. Harriet Irsay, had come around to her mother-in-law's point of view and filed for divorce. The precipitating event came when Mrs. Irsay, vacationing alone at the couple's home in Bal Harbour, Florida, called back to their home in Illinois and spoke with her maid. Mrs. Irsay then learned that her husband had, without announcement, taken up with a widow twenty years younger than herself. "All his clothes were gone," Harriet told *People*. "He [even] took the fifty-five-gallon fish tank we kept behind the bar. Did he think I was going to take it out on the fish?"

Instead, Harriet Irsay sued for divorce, demanding, among other assets, the Indianapolis Colts. Her husband, she alleged, was, in *People*'s words, "a drunkard and a compulsive gambler." Harriet Irsay also claimed he had used Colts funds to buy himself a $1 million home in Indiana and had done "a lousy job" of running the football franchise. "All the time Bob was scheming to move the Colts," she complained, "he was also scheming to get rid of me."

3
Joe Robbie's Dream Come True

The second most visible Superstadium Game in the opening months of the League's Year One A.D. was played by Joe Robbie in Miami. Rather than utilize the Davis precedent, however, Robbie took his own singular approach.

On January 27, the Miami City Commission had put a $55 million bond to redo the Orange Bowl on the city's March 13 municipal ballot. But Joe Robbie still wanted nothing to do with a refurbished Orange Bowl. Instead, he stayed home and launched a daring counterstrategy. He planned to build his own $90 million, seventy-two-thousand-seat football stadium for the Dolphins when their lease ran out after the 1986 season. The city of Miami described the announcement as nothing more than a pre-election ploy. "He's made promises and promises," Mayor Maurice Ferre observed, "but not delivered. If he can do it, he should get a prize as sugar daddy of the year."

Four days later, Robbie announced he had arranged for a site. It was on the edge of Dade County in a sandy, barren track. It was currently owned by one Emil Morton, who also agreed to sell Robbie and "partners to be named later" 142 adjacent acres for "an undisclosed sum." There Robbie intended to develop "a hotel, shopping, and entertainment complex." Another 130 acres would be sold by Morton to "an unnamed New England group of investors" where an "amphitheater and restaurant complex" would be constructed.

Robbie also claimed to have found a way to pay for it all. "We have disclosed our financial projects to at least seven investment bankers," he explained. "We have received written financial proposals. We are confident that we will obtain financial commitments within weeks, hopefully days, to provide construction money and permanent financing based upon our target goals in marketing luxury suites and preferred seats in loge areas." Joe Robbie's plan was to lease luxury boxes and the stadium's best seats in advance of construction.

If those announcements were not sufficient to kill the city of

Miami's bond issue, Robbie put the finishing touches on his obstructionism with a last minute pre-election letter to Miami's forty-two thousand season ticket holders. In it, Joe Robbie urged "all season ticket holders, all fans, and all supporters of the Miami Dolphins to join with all other oppressed taxpayers to vote no on the bond issue. City Hall intends to rule or ruin the Miami Dolphins. They threaten to damage or destroy our financial base in this community unless we consent to be held prisoners in the Orange Bowl. We will not be intimidated. We will not be shoved around. We will continue to campaign for a modern, new stadium for our fans rather than have $55 million of taxpayers' dollars poured down a gopher hole to repair a half-century-old, archaic football museum.''

"He's doing what I call the 'Robbie rhumba,' '' Mayor Ferre taunted in response. "You move to the left, you move to the right, you go in a circle and stay in the same place. I am more convinced than ever that Joe Robbie basically doesn't want anything to happen.''

Nonetheless, the "Robbie rhumba'' worked. On March 13, Miami voters rejected the Orange Bowl bonds by a two to one margin. Robbie described the vote as a "resounding defeat'' for City Hall and told the *Miami Herald* he was "gratified.'' The renovation, he noted, had been a plan to "torpedo'' his new Dolphin Stadium. Now that it was defeated, he could get about the business of making his dream a reality.

Joe Robbie took charge of marketing that dream himself. What Robbie had to sell was a seventy-three-thousand-seat stadium with sixteen thousand parking spaces, a tier of "luxury club seats,'' and 234 "executive suites'' in ten-, twelve-, or sixteen-seat configurations. These luxury boxes were all to be "air-conditioned and fully furnished with a choice of three decorator designs . . . [featuring] plush carpeting, lounge furniture, refrigerator and icemaker, lockable liquor cabinet, closed circuit television, and optional telephone connections. Food and beverages will be catered to the suites upon request.'' First, of course, the boxes had to be sold.

Joe Robbie could think of no better way to kick off his sales campaign than to announce that his stadium's inaugural season would be culminated with hosting the January 1988 Super Bowl. He took his case to the rest of the League at their Washington, D.C., meeting on May 25, 1984. One of the items on the agenda was the selection of Super Bowl sites for 1987 and 1988. Both years proved to be tough battles. For 1988, contenders were

Gene Klein's home field in San Diego, and Robbie's projected Dolphins Stadium. In both cases, the owners were unable to reach the necessary three-quarters majority and had to suspend the three-quarters rule in order to decide. The vote on the 1987 site took thirteen ballots before Pasadena beat out Philadelphia. The site for 1988 required eight ballots until Robbie lost a vote and San Diego was selected. Robbie denied it was a setback when he lost. "The Super Bowl would have been a splendid event to have in the stadium's first year," he noted, "but since it didn't occur, I'm going home to sell boxes and build the stadium. It doesn't alter or interrupt our plans."

For the rest of 1984, Joe Robbie was first and foremost a salesman and kept busy at it. He claimed to be doing a land office business. He had already sold twenty-nine of his luxury boxes and had commitments for twice that many. Robbie also evinced high hopes for future sales. "The unusual thing," he explained, "is we haven't started getting orders yet from the law firms, the accounting firms, the major corporations and civic groups that we figure will form the nucleus of our sales. Our sales have come from many people we don't even know. A conservative estimate is that we'll double our figures within the next two weeks."

Joe Robbie's goal was lease sale deposits of $9 million, the capital required to trigger his construction financing. At the "Meet the Dolphins" breakfast on July 6, Robbie gave a typical performance. There, the *Herald* reported, "the estimated 725 aqua-and-orange-dressed fans heard encouraging words about the new season from Coach Don Shula. . . . Autographs were available from the relatively few players on hand. . . . But the morning belonged to Robbie, the owner, who came armed with a six-minute film about the stadium he wants to build. . . . No matter that fans' boisterous cheering at the appearance of game highlights at times obliterated the voiceover. . . . Stadium pamphlets were placed on every table. Stacks of twenty-three-page contracts were out in the lobby. Robbie was in high gear. . . . By the time he yielded the microphone some twenty minutes later, he was talking to a receptive crowd about building 'the finest stadium in America.' " Robbie claimed to be twenty-five percent of the way to his goal already. On July 29, he announced he had reached thirty-three percent. "We're so close to something so important," he claimed, "I would never let up for a moment for fear it might slip away." On October 8, he told the *Herald* he was "within a hair of the halfway mark," and noted,

"The money . . . is coming in at a steady, if not overwhelming pace. I told Jack Kent Cooke about this and he said, 'You mean to tell me you're charging sixty-five thousand dollars a year? Who the hell would ever pay that?' Well, I'm here to tell you those sell first. The top-priced boxes and loge seats are nearly gone."

By January 9, 1985, Joe Robbie's subscriptions were at seventy-two percent and still rising. It was close enough to his goal to convince what was described as a ["consortium of bankers"] to back the stadium's construction financing. Joe Robbie called a press conference. "This is a signal day in the history of the Miami Dolphins," he trumpeted. "We can now announce the stadium will be built. . . . The dream is coming into the field of reality."

On March 17, at the 1985 annual meeting in Phoenix, the League awarded the as yet unconstructed Dolphins Stadium the January 1989 Super Bowl. Thanks to Joe Robbie, Joe Robbie's dream had come true.

4
Eddie and the New Rules

If anyone in the League doubted that NFL business was running by new rules in Year One, they had only to look to the [resolution] of the "DeBartolo situation" announced by the commissioner at the 1984 annual meeting in Honolulu. Pete Rozelle explained that "rather than have a formal hearing, [the DeBartolos] would prefer to recognize that . . . the conflict of interest was created. And for that reason, they would like to volunteer steps that they should take to lessen the conflict that exists between Eddie's owning the 49ers and his father the Pittsburgh Maulers."

What that resulted in was a three-page letter from Eddie to the commissioner. "In truth," the *San Francisco Examiner* observed, "DeBartolo Jr.'s letter does little more than mildly address points of concern brought up by the League's conflict of interest committee. . . . It is three pages of elusiveness. . . . Rozelle accepted it for the League—without even calling for a vote of the other owners—because it was the NFL, not the 49ers, who needed to surrender."

What Eddie specifically agreed to do was withdraw the 49ers from the scouting combine they shared with several other teams, not sign any Pittsburgh Mauler players, not attend NFL discussions of the USFL, and not participate on any NFL committees. In effect, Eddie DeBartolo agreed to say that the commissioner had won and the commissioner agreed to drop the issue for good.

With that, the League could stop, at least for the moment, fighting among themselves and get on to fighting the USFL, what it really had in mind that March. By then, the NFL had lost some forty-eight of its own players and seventeen highly sought college players to its challenger. "The situation was reminiscent of the first year of the late, unlamented World Football League," the *San Francisco Chronicle* noted, but "that has all changed. Now the situation is reminiscent of the last couple years of the AFL-NFL war. The USFL is going after established NFL players, especially quarterbacks, and it is all-out war." A good portion of the League was eager to commit itself to that war. "We have a lot of guys who have the means to fight back," Leonard Tose pointed out. "You certainly have Leon Hess, who according to *Fortune* magazine is worth $500 million. You have Bill Ford, who owns most of the stock in Ford Motor. You certainly have Lamar Hunt, who's got a billion dollars. I believe the Maras are ready to fight."

As a League, however, they still had to tread lightly around the Sherman Act. On March 22, the commissioner appointed a six-man "planning committee." Al Davis called it a "watchdog" committee. Among its assignments was to study "how League finances could be affected by the USFL."

"It's not a go-to-war committee," Rozelle cautioned. "We just want to take an overall look at our future." In fact, the committee was quite the opposite. The goal was to make sure owners didn't throw the League's salary structure totally out of whack in their impatience to crush the USFL. Its membership included three general managers and three owners—Lamar Hunt, Ed McCaskey, and Wellington Mara. All three were known to feel that the best way to deal with the USFL was to let it spend itself to death.

If restraint was in fact their mission, the committee's job was by no means easy. The bidding war had long since begun and eventually reached a point beyond anything ever experienced in the history of the football business. At the end of it, NFLPA would claim that their share of the NFL's gross had risen well past the fifty-five percent Ed Garvey had been unable to win. Joe

Robbie gave his starting nose tackle $515,000 a year to stay. Hugh Culverhouse's starting quarterback, making $180,000 a year in Tampa, jumped to the other league for $400,000. The USFL offered William Clay Ford's best running back $3.5 million over four years and the Lions matched it with $4.5 million over five years. The apex of the process was reached when the USFL's L.A. franchise paid a college senior a $2.5 million bonus to sign a contract that would pay him $1 million for the four seasons it lasted and then pay him a total of $30 million in deferred payments between the years 1990 and 2027.

Ironically, the leader of the NFL's every-man-for-himself signing blitz against the USFL was Eddie DeBartolo. By the end of 1984, he had given his quarterback a raise to $1.1 million a year and his best wide receiver $550,000 a year. His best defensive back was given a new $2.3 million four-year contract and his first choice in the 1984 draft signed for $2 million over four years. Eddie was also one of the first to use his own inside information and announce that the NFL was winning the war. "There are [USFL] teams losing $12 million and $8 million," he claimed in July 1984. "I don't think the USFL can make it."

DeBartolo's enthusiasm for the fight won him no fans on the commissioner's planning committee. "San Francisco is doing more harm than the USFL in escalating salaries," one of its members complained. "The philosophy of a lot of clubs is win at any cost, and clubs that have that philosophy escalate salaries and bring other clubs to their level. So everybody gets in the red quicker than if everybody would just run things in a prudent manner." During the early fall, the planning committee convened a series of regional owners' meetings about the escalation. At the League meetings in October, the planning commission reported that at current rates, the League would lose $90 million collectively by 1986. "DeBartolo himself lost $10 million," Gene Klein complained. "It was madness. We were losing money for no reason. We didn't have to match the USFL. There was a great deal of bitterness over what some of our owners have done."

However, the competition was certainly having its desired effect on the other league. After the completion of its second spring-summer season, the USFL Boston franchise had moved twice, its Washington franchise, three times. Oklahoma merged with Arizona and Detroit with Oakland. "NFL teams may switch towns to make more money," *Sports Illustrated* noted, "but in the USFL you switch towns to keep breathing." One of the casualties was Edward DeBartolo Sr.'s Pittsburgh Maulers, who dissolved before the USFL's third season. Much to the NFL's relief, Mr. D was out of the football business and henceforth, Eddie DeBartolo went his way and the USFL its—just as Eddie claimed he had wanted it in the first place.

For the USFL, the downward spiral only continued. In October, the new league announced that after its 1985 season, it would no longer stage its games in the spring and summer, but starting in 1986 would play in the fall, head to head with the League. During the switch, the USFL would go dormant everywhere except the courtroom. Filed in 1984, *USFL v. NFL* charged the League with "monopolizing and conspiring to control the business of major league professional football." The three television networks were listed as "involuntary co-conspirators." It would come to trial in May 1986.

Meantime, Eddie DeBartolo had acquired a taste for the maverick's role. His pet peeve soon became the commissioner's ownership policy, which he wanted altered to permit him to vest ownership of the 49ers in DeBartolo Corp. Doing so would allow him to write any of the franchise's losses off against his father's corporate tax bill. Eddie raised the issue at the League's 1985 annual meeting, but it went nowhere.

In the meantime, Eddie also played a quick round of the Superstadium Game with the city of San Francisco. He wanted $30 million worth of improvements in the city's Candlestick Park and it was basically no contest. When he ran into political difficulties over the issue, Eddie knew just what to say. "Maybe we'll have to get somebody else to negotiate for us," he offered, "like Al Davis." DeBartolo got his $30 million in improvements shortly thereafter.

For Eddie, playing the game by its new rules came easily.

5

Getting Out While the Getting's Good

The owner who had the greatest difficulty accepting the new order of things was Gene Klein. Unwilling to live with the League's defeat as the last word, Klein opened Year One by filing his own lawsuit against Al Davis, hoping to find at least personal revenge.

Filed on January 30, 1984, *Gene Klein v. Oakland Raiders Ltd., Allen Davis, and John Does I through XX, inclusive* charged Davis with "malicious prosecution" for having named Klein an individual defendant in *LAMCC v. NFL*. Klein asked $3 million in actual damages and $30 million in punitive damages. Davis, Klein alleged, had made the charges "without probable cause" and in a "wilfull, wanton, malicious, vexatious, and oppressive" manner. As a result, Klein had "suffered loss of goodwill, loss of reputation, humiliation, injury to his health, strength, and activity," and had been caused "great mental, physical, and nervous pain and suffering," including, "but not limited to, plaintiff suffering a heart attack when testifying in the underlying action to defend himself from said malicious charges."

Al Davis called the action "frivolous and a sham" and filed a countersuit in March, *Los Angeles Raiders Ltd. v. Eugene Klein,* charging "malicious abuse of the court process." Davis and his franchise alleged that "if Klein's claimed loss of health and business opportunities and feigned emotional distress can ridiculously be attributed to an event, there are numerous events, rather than the Los Angeles Raiders trial" which caused Klein's distress. Davis listed six: "1. a large fine levied [in 1974] against Klein by Commissioner Rozelle for drug-related activities; 2. a [1983] national television program which gave details of Klein's association with notorious underworld figures; 3. a well-known [1962] California civil case which found Klein guilty of malicious prosecution . . . ; 4. a [1976] lawsuit by Barron Hilton and other minority partners against Klein for mismanagement . . . ; 5. the [1983] $60 million damages award against the Chargers and other NFL teams for antitrust violation . . . ; 6. the numerous altercations that Klein has had with the city of San Diego, former Chargers coaches, players, administrators, and owners while Klein served as the Chargers' executive head.''

Davis's countersuit was eventually dismissed and Klein's original action was scheduled for trial in September 1986. By then, Klein was long since out of the football business. He first told Rozelle of his intentions privately while at the 1984 annual meeting. "It was because of the stress," Rozelle remembered. "He was really torn but he said he could buy a box in the stadium and watch as a fan and make his horses his avocation." Klein himself doubted "I would ever have gotten out of football if it hadn't been for that second heart attack." Klein called a press conference on March 23 and explained that he would [entertain bids] for his controlling interest in the franchise. "[I]f someone wants to be in the NFL and wants to acquire the San Diego franchise," he told the press, "I would, for very personal reasons, have to give it consideration."

Gene Klein's ambiguity was fairly quickly resolved. On July 5, 1984, Dallas developer Carl Summers Jr. offered him a reported $40 million for his fifty-six percent interest, setting a value on the whole franchise of some $72 million—$10 million more than America's team had sold for some four months earlier. Klein accepted immediately and notified his minority partners. The partners had a month to exercise their right of first refusal and match any offer for Klein's share. Among those partners in the summer of 1984 was one Alex Spanos, a wealthy developer from Stockton, California. At 11:00 A.M. on the last day of July, Spanos notified Klein that he was exercising his right.

Rozelle was visiting at Klein's home on the day Spanos called and was quick to praise the departing Klein. "He was always thinking League," Rozelle told the *San Diego Union*. "I think he was a major influence on the National Football League, always very constructive." Art Modell also chimed in from Cleveland. Praising Klein's contribution on the television committee, Modell claimed "he also offered a moderating influence in our League meetings when they got heated and spirited. . . . Gene always had the ability to calm the disputants and bring about a peaceful resolution to whatever problem we were facing. He was always an NFL man, and I can't say that about all the owners in the League."

The only public objections to Klein's leaving were raised, ironically enough, by Al Davis. He objected that there were "legal impediments" to the sale "at this time." "No bond has been posted in the federal case [*LAMCC v. NFL*]," Davis pointed out. "Klein as an owner is vulnerable for the damages. We want to be sure that the franchise is not in hock." Davis hinted he might file suit to stop the transaction, but nothing came of either his objections or the hint.

On August 3, Gene Klein introduced Alex Spanos to the San Diego press as the new owner of the Chargers and said his own very quick good-byes. For Gene Klein, Year One was time to get out while the getting was still good.

6
Aloha to the Old Guard

The Old Guard entered football's new age considerably diminished in both number and influence. Of the owners who predated Pete Rozelle, Halas was dead, as was Carroll Rosenbloom. Only the Maras and Rooneys upheld the old traditions. Both had supported Rozelle throughout the Davis fight and continued to do so. In Year One, both were quite openly worried about what was going on.

"The situation now is getting harder and harder on the Old Guard," Wellington Mara observed sadly. "We're people who use football for our primary income and we're getting crowded like the corner grocery faced with a supermarket across the street. Greater capitalization is required. I don't know how to cope with the rise in salaries, the rise in operating expenses. The new owners now are people who've been successful in other areas. They don't depend on football for money. Many of the great fortunes have now come to the game. They're better at business than the founding fathers, but when someone isn't concerned with the bottom line at the end of the year, it sets the salary standards for all the others."

Art Rooney felt much the same way. "The NFL had a constitution that started with the start of the League," he pointed out. "When the NFL lived by the constitution, it prospered. We never sued each other. But that's the whole world now. What Davis did won't make it easier and this could just be the start of things. A lot of the new people haven't lived with the constitution. It's a wholly different game. It's the way of life nowadays. I hope Commissioner Rozelle stays a long time. Pete used excellent judgment. His judgment has been just about perfect. It's a lot tougher to handle twenty-eight guys than eleven. Pete is very honest and calls them as they should be called. He's very fair. Through Rozelle, we made the NFL the strongest of major league sports.''

Art's son Dan was equally adamant in continuing to back the commissioner. "Rozelle approached the Davis problem with the idea it was a problem against the League," Dan Rooney explained. "After all the court cases . . . [h]e still tried to treat Davis fairly. If it were me, I'd be tougher on Davis. The commissioner's job is Pete's as long as he wants it . . . but the problem is, how long does he want it? If he can't operate, why put up with it? All these outside forces affecting the game are difficult to fathom. The biggest thing we have to do now is protect our game.''

For Dan Rooney, Year One was as good a time as any to start all over again. "Judgments have to be made about what's best for the game. That might mean decreasing TV, that might mean paying less because it's not good for the game to lose money. We're entering the most critical point in our history. TV's not going to bail us out. We've reached the limit other than inflation. We have to be more businesslike. Ownership is so important and so is how people get voted in. We have to have the courage to say no to new owners. . . . I think there is a potential of the trusteeship role being lost. The game is at a crossroads. In the current situation, the economics are skewed, people are near the choking point. We need to find a new structure of ownership intelligently. An antitrust exemption would help, but we don't have to have it. A lot of our antitrust problems are internal. Owners isolate themselves now. . . . Then at least you're involved. As it is, people don't even come to the meetings anymore. . . . Our problem is all twenty-eight of us never sit down together. We have to have goodwill, understanding, and courage by owners to make the decisions that have to be made.''

In Year One, however, it was not at all clear how many others were still listening to Dan Rooney.

7
Hunt's Bottom Line

Lamar Hunt was another figure whom the previous decade had significantly diminished. Once the boy wonder of the football business, Hunt now carried little weight at all inside the League. He was still "personally close to the owners from the old AFL days," especially Billy Sullivan, and had hewed to the League court position against Davis faithfully. Nonetheless, *NASL v. NFL* and the ownership policy fight leading up to it had left him outside the lines of heavy influence. He still retained his holdings in the NASL, the Chicago Bulls, and the WCT tennis tour, as well as his NFL Kansas City Chiefs, but his personal involvement in the sports business had been reduced significantly. "I made the mistake of getting involved in too many things," Lamar admitted. Still a regular at NFL meetings, he was nonetheless spending the majority of his sports energy as of Year One on the WCT.

Lamar Hunt was also suffering from a less severe but nonetheless formidable bout with the same financial disease that had afflicted Clint Murchison's Texas-based empire. The affliction had been acquired through his brothers Herbert and Bunker. During the early 1970s, his two older brothers had begun buying up large amounts of silver bullion and silver futures contracts and by 1975 were flying immense amounts of it to a stockpile in Europe. From 1976 to 1979, Bunker and Herbert reduced their buying and concentrated on finding a partner with sufficient capital to make a corner on the world silver market possible. On July 1, 1979, they formed a partnership with two Saudi sheikhs called International Metal Investments. When the Hunts made their run for a corner, International Metal Investments would purchase some $900 million worth of silver to match the $450 million Bunker and Herbert had already collected.

By fall 1979, all that buying had the desired effect and began to drive the price of silver up, from $8 an ounce to $17.88 by October 1. After that, the price began to spiral even further upward. By December 31, it reached $34.45 and Bunker, Herbert, and the Saudis controlled 220 million ounces now worth $7.57 billion. In part, the Hunts had continued to enlarge their stake by involving their younger brother, Lamar. Eventually Lamar pledged himself for some $300 million worth of the brothers' escalating obligations. Since most of Lamar's silver was bought on margin and the price was rising, he had been able to secure that holding with only an immediate $15 million investment. Several sources later claimed Lamar did so because he was tired of being ragged by his brothers for missing out on the big silver killing.

By January 17, 1980, the high water mark of $50 an ounce was reached. Since 90 million ounces of the Hunts' bubble were future contracts deliverable in March 1980, all of those who had opposed the Hunt move and bought short faced possible bankruptcy. Among those in that position were a number of members of the New York COMEX exchange, on which much of the brothers' silver trading was done. On January 21, COMEX ordered that all trading in silver be halted. On January 22, silver had fallen to $34. On March 14, it was down to $21, reducing the value of the Hunt and Saudi investment by more than $2 billion in the space of a month. During that same month, Lamar had to borrow $50 million to cover his own now burgeoning margin calls.

On March 25, 1980, Bunker wired a three-word message to Lamar. It read, "Shut it down." At March rates, the three brothers were losing $4,687.50 per second, and at the end of March, the Hunts had combined debts of some $1.75 billion. "Word that the Hunts were strapped," *Fortune* reported, "sparked fears of Wall Street bankruptcies and talks of national financial calamity." To allay those fears, the Hunts paid off their most significant creditor, and the Federal Reserve Board put together a consortium of banks to make the Hunts a ten-year, $1.1 billion loan.

Since then, the brothers had spent much of their financial energy trying to reduce that debt. The interest alone ran at $220 million a year. To secure that bailout, the three brothers had been forced to post even their personal property as collateral. For Lamar, that included his Rolex watch and his NFL franchise. By 1985, the brothers still had 59 million ounces of silver stashed in a Delaware bank, now worth $5.80 an ounce—and Lamar's football franchise was still in hock.

Though hardly broke, Lamar emerged from the experience seared and it showed in the narrowness of the posture he brought to the NFL's Year One. "The League has to take steps so that the business will remain financially successful," he warned. "We cannot let costs get out of hand. Professional football will not continue to grow. Most stadiums are already full. TV ratings only have so far they can grow. We just can't continue our previous growth and there's not a lot of room left for expansion. We're at a saturation point from the standpoint of logical growth. The battle now will be to keep the relative position the NFL has. The single most important thing we have to deal with is to take the steps necessary to keep this business on a sound business basis." For Lamar Hunt, the bottom line was the bottom line—especially now.

8
End of a Hell of a Run

New age or not, the football business still had a "Philadelphia problem" personified by Leonard Tose. The year 1984 had begun on an upbeat note for the Eagles owner. On January 30, he announced that he had met the deadline on his Kidde Corp. loan and paid back the entire $6.8 million. "Everything has been worked out," he explained, without having to sell his franchise. "I still own ninety-nine percent of the Eagles and I intend to own the club as long as I live."

But as Year One began, even Leonard Tose evinced financial worry. During the 1983 season, Leaguewide paid attendance had not regained the pre strike record levels of 1980 and 1981. In Philadelphia, long an attendance leader, the dip in season ticket renewals during the first months of 1984 was glaring. Tose's answer to the dilemma was what he called "promotion." It was a solution he recommended to the whole League. "If they'll get off their ass at 410 Park Avenue," he complained, "this deterioration will stop. It's no longer automatic to fill the stadium and the biggest thing in our business is to fill the stadiums."

In late March, Tose even participated in the Eagles' promotion, appearing personally to help plug flagging season ticket sales at one of the working class hangouts that were the backbone of the franchise's Sunday afternoon crowds. Tose, his recently acquired fourth wife, Julia, and some of his accompanying staff distributed team pictures, media guides, and Eagles stickers. Tose also bought a round of drinks for all seventy people in the bar. "When I was active in the trucking business," he noted, "I used to do this kind of thing almost every day at one of the terminals." Tose was apparently a big hit. "I think Leonard Tose is a gentleman," one patron observed. "He bought everybody in the place a drink." Before Tose left, the crowd performed a spontaneous Eagles cheer. "I'll drink to that," the ebullient Leonard Tose responded. "I'll drink to anything."

Tose's crack at Rozelle's office about promotion was not an exception. One obvious difference Year One meant for Leonard Tose was a change in his expressed attitude toward the commissioner. "He performs the miracle of making our League cohesive," Tose said in 1983. In 1984, his line was altogether different. "Rozelle's a compromiser," Tose bitched. "I don't think much of him and I don't care who knows it." Tose's disillusionment with Rozelle had been growing for a while and a number of reasons could be advanced. The most pecuniary of those was that his Eagles had been the one NFL franchise not specifically named as a defendant in *LAMCC v. NFL*. At the time, Tose's absence was a device to avoid the trap the NFL had tried to set for Joe Alioto. Now it meant that Tose had a way of escaping his $3 million worth of possible damages from the case and he was preparing to refuse to pay his share of the assessment whenever the damages were finalized in the appeals court.

Escaping that $3 million bill was of particular importance since Tose was still running downhill in front of a financial snowball. The 1982 strike had cost the Eagles $8 million in losses; his daughter Susan Fletcher's office reorganization had cost him $2.5 million; his abortive 1983 sale had cost him another $1.75 million. On top of that were his gambling losses, which Tose himself claimed to be unable to quantify. By the fall of 1984, his bankers at Crocker Bank were getting antsy about the $18 million owed them by the Eagles and the $12 million owed by Tose himself. Tose had been attempting to find a minority partner in the meantime to pump in some fresh cash, but by October, had gotten nowhere. His remaining option was to use Year One to his best advantage.

For several months, Leonard Tose and Susan Fletcher had been engaged in secret back-burner discussions with Canadian real estate developer James Monahan. Monahan was interested in buying a minority share if the Eagles would move to Arizona as a condition of the deal.

The Phoenix Metropolitan Sports Foundation, charged with bringing professional football to the Valley of the Sun, would say through its chairman only that "another situation is coming about involving an NFL franchise that is interested in relocating in Phoenix. It's a club—one that's in a stable situation—that no one would guess. There could be something happening shortly, but nobody wants to say anything until the end of the season for obvious reasons." At the time, Tose's total debts were reported to be over $40 million. When pressed on whether or not her father was going to sell an interest significant enough to cause the franchise to move, Fletcher responded: "Who the hell knows. I don't know what life's going to bring."

By December, however, *The New York Times* reported that Crocker Bank "was making it abundantly clear" that "it wanted Tose to make good on his loans." Rumors about an Eagles move were now all over Philadelphia and Philadelphia's new black mayor, W. Wilson Goode, met with Tose four times to check them out. "Mr. Tose said to me . . . that he had no plans to move the team," Goode reported. On December 10, however, Tose hedged somewhat and let his PR man talk for him. "Mr. Tose is considering a move to Phoenix," the spokesman noted, "but nothing has been signed and no final decision has been made. There is nothing more I can tell you."

When Leonard Tose emerged momentarily from his seclusion three days later to get a haircut at the local barbershop, he was booed by other patrons as he left. By then, Mayor Goode had begun working frantically to put together a counteroffer. "I'd be delighted if he works something out," Tose claimed. "I'm not talking about matching the Phoenix offer. I'm talking about survival." The personal antipathy that had erupted toward Tose in Philadelphia as soon as news got out had apparently shaken him somewhat. "I guess it's a natural reaction," he admitted. "I didn't foresee it, but it doesn't really surprise me. . . . I don't feel very happy. I don't feel very good. I've heard the stories—'Keep the team and kill Tose.' " In his actual discussions with Goode, Tose would say only that there was a "50/50 chance" the team would stay. "I believe that the deal in Phoenix can reach a conclusion at any time," Mayor Goode warned.

So, of course, did Phoenix. There, the actual move was expected to be announced on December 17. The deal had already been cut and agreed to. Only the signing was left. Monahan would buy twenty-five percent of the team for $30 million and some sources even claimed Tose had already received part of the cash. In addition, the Eagles would be marketed in Arizona by leasing seats in addition to selling tickets, each seat costing $3000 for ten years. "It's a rich community," Tose later observed. "I could have had $50 million in my pocket and kept the team in the family forever."

The other development cutting across Tose's path to Phoenix came from the League. After calling a special League meeting to discuss Tose's situation, Rozelle made a calculated gamble and filed suit in Philadelphia Federal District Court. "What began as a trickle in the wake of the Raiders case in California," a spokesman for the commissioner's office explained, "now threatens to become a flood if the Eagles leave the country's fourth largest market. Such a move would abandon a community that has supported its team superbly for more than half a century." The lawsuit asked that Tose be forced to "recognize contractual obligations to Philadelphia" and prevented from leaving without League permission. The suit also asked the court to declare ahead of time that "the NFL would not be violating any antitrust laws if the Eagles were forced to comply" with League regulations. While the suit offered little difference from the unsuccessful *LAMCC v. NFL,* the commissioner's calculation was based on a shrewd perception that Tose's shaky finances would make fighting a suit beyond his means. "I think they thought they had a defense," Mayor Goode said of Tose and the Eagles, "but I don't think he had the time."

While Tose was faced with this roadblock, Philadelphia was offering a loan of $43 million it had arranged for Tose with local banks. Tose had consistently refused the proposal because the banks wanted, as in 1977, to take away his financial control. On Saturday, December 15, the logjam was broken by Rozelle, who informed Tose that the NFL was willing to consider "cooperation" in finding Tose the money he needed. Any approval, of course, would depend on the Eagles remaining in Philadelphia. From that point on, discussions between Tose and Goode shifted to the possibilities for a new lease. When, late on Saturday night, Goode offered a deal that would increase the Eagles' annual revenues by $2 to $4 million, Tose accepted and signed an agreement to keep the Eagles at home. According to Tose, it was the invocation of Philadelphia patriotism by his wife and daughter that finally swayed him. "They told me," Tose remembered, " 'You can't move the team to Phoenix, it belongs here.' And I couldn't do it to Philadelphia. The people here have treated me well. They have supported me.'' As for the NFL's reported loan offer, Rozelle was vague. "It's a sensitive situation,'' he noted.

In the meantime, Tose insisted he had never led Phoenix to believe he was moving there and that he owed them no explanation. Tose said he intended to call Monahan "in the next few days and tell him what I did.'' Monahan, of course, already knew from reading the papers and was outraged. "That son of a bitch,'' Monahan fumed. "I'm furious. I'm disappointed. I'm mad as hell. He used somebody before and he used me this time.'' Leonard Tose's Year One had yielded yet another former or would-be partner who now hated him.

It did not, however, solve his financial problems. "The jackals are still on my heels,'' the Eagles owner shrugged, "and will be until I die.'' The League meeting on December 18 did not loan Tose any money. Instead, Rozelle appointed a three-man committee "to help find a way to refinance the Eagles.'' The committee took its time with what was a "complicated situation.'' One of the complications in Tose's dilemma was that Chuck Sullivan had reportedly acted as personal guarantor of Crocker's $12 million, again in contravention to the constitution.

While the committee took its time, the pressures on Tose became acute. No Philadelphia bank would lend him anything without the right to control the franchise, and by February 3, 1985, according to *The New York Times*, Crocker Bank had refused to extend his loans, which were due in full by January 1986. In addition, the bank was concerned about the Eagles' declining net worth and gave Tose six weeks in which to demonstrate he was capable of retiring the loans in full or face foreclosure. Tose was now cornered and the League's committee did nothing.

His other options exhausted, Tose took the step he had struggled to avoid for sixteen years. On March 6, it was revealed Tose had made an agreement to sell his entire ninety-nine percent interest to Norman Braman, a south Florida businessman who was a native of West Chester, Pennsylvania. The gross value of the deal was estimated at "more than $70 million.'' Pete Rozelle commented that he "felt sorry'' for Tose, because he knew he "so desperately'' wanted to stay in the League. "Leonard Tose has a lot of friends in the League who are sorry that he won't be part of the League anymore,'' the commissioner observed. "By the same token, the League has been concerned about the stability of the club. If everything checks out, the owners won't have to spend any more time on those financial problems."

Tose himself claimed to be relieved. "I'm delighted," he said. "Nobody believes me when I tell them, but selling the team is like lifting a pack off my back. I had a hell of a run for sixteen years. Hey, listen, as a kid, I was a truck driver. My father couldn't read or write. He started a trucking company with a horse and wagon. I've had a hell of a run."

9
A Scalper Gets Scalped

After Leonard Tose sold out, taking Susan Fletcher with him, the only woman who remained sitting in the NFL's inner circles was Georgia Frontiere. Georgia's Year One began on both up and down notes.

The up note was the performance of her team. Despite banners in the Anaheim stands like "Thanks, Georgia, Now the Whole World Is Laughing at Us," the Rams rebounded from their disastrous two-win strike season to a record of nine and seven and made the playoffs for the first time since 1981. After winning their first playoff game, Mrs. Frontiere's team began 1984 with a game against Cooke's Redskins in the National Conference semifinals. Georgia was enormously pleased by the turnaround and called a team meeting for the morning of the Redskins game. When her players had gathered, Georgia thanked them all and said she wanted to give them a present. Next to her was a table piled high with Cabbage Patch Kids, that season's hottest children's toy. Each player was given one before filing onto the bus. When they got off the bus at Washington's R.F.K. Stadium, the Rams made their way through the swarms of rabid Redskins fans, clutching their dolls under their arms. The Rams lost, fifty-one to seven. They were a playoff team nonetheless, and would stay that way during 1984 and 1985.

The down note was the ongoing investigation by an L.A. grand jury of ticket scalping. Among those called to testify in the fall of 1983 was Don Klosterman, who was waiting for his contract with the Rams to run out before taking over the new L.A.

Express franchise in the USFL. According to a source close to the investigation, the grand jury had asked Klosterman whether it was possible that five thousand tickets to the 1980 Super Bowl had been scalped and Klosterman had reportedly answered "right number, wrong year."

In December, 1983, the Frontieres walked into the strangest twist of all in the saga of the ticket scalping inquiry. This episode featured one H. Daniel Whitman and two men named Cohen. Whitman, part owner of exclusive Cyrano's restaurant on Sunset Strip and the Christiana Inn of South Lake Tahoe, was described by the *Los Angeles Herald Examiner* as "a longtime friend of Dominic Frontiere." The first Cohen was Raymond Cohen, who had been in the hands of the grand jury since April and had a lot to talk about. This Cohen told federal authorities that Whitman had introduced him to Dominic Frontiere and that Frontiere was in turn "the source of several thousand tickets" for the 1980 Super Bowl. Those tickets had been sold at some six times their value and, according to Cohen as reported in the *Los Angeles Times*, the money returned to Dominic, who allegedly had made no report of the transaction on his tax returns. Raymond Cohen was also scheduled to testify in an unrelated counterfeiting case against Jack Catain, the man who'd threatened Harold Guiver and Don Klosterman back in 1980. The second Cohen's name was Robert, and he was an old friend of Whitman's. Later, Whitman's lawyer would also characterize Robert Cohen in court as "a small-time criminal who wanted to improve his standing in the underworld . . . hoped to get a better connection for both his cocaine trade and addiction, and wanted to prove to other criminals that he was able to have people murdered."

The drama began in fall 1983, when Whitman told his friend Robert Cohen that he needed someone killed. The someone was Raymond Cohen, who, Whitman told Robert, had to die because he was informing on several "heavyweights out of Chicago." In November 1983, Robert approached someone he knew and offered five thousand dollars worth of cocaine in exchange for Raymond's murder. The man he approached, however, was an FBI informant and, at that point, government investigators began to work their way back up the chain. FBI agents used a Hollywood makeup artist to phony a bullet hole in Raymond Cohen's forehead, took a picture of the "body," and had their informant give it to Robert Cohen and secretly tape their conversation about the deed that was supposed to have taken place on November 15. On December 2, authorities confronted Robert and he quickly turned informant himself. The next step was for Robert Cohen to strap on a secret tape recorder and meet with Whitman and tell him Raymond Cohen was dead. The government agents' apparent hope was that Whitman could in turn be made to implicate Jack Catain.

As it turned out, Whitman did less than that. "For whatever it's worth," he told the wired-up Robert Cohen, "if it means anything to you, let me just tell you that what was done was sanctioned." Cohen assumed the sanction had come from "organized crime," but Whitman never said who. "Remember one thing," Whitman continued, "that when you do a favor, you're owed a favor. . . . You're owed one. . . . I can reach high. . . . You get some idea of where I can go if I have to." The conversation eventually changed to the man Whitman thought was dead and the informing he had done. Whitman noted that "I'm going to get myself killed if I testify, if I tell them anything about what I know." Whitman admitted to Robert Cohen that he had been approached by federal agents himself earlier in the year. "I said, 'You want to talk to me about Dan Whitman, sit down, I'll tell you everything you want to know,' " Whitman remembered. " 'You want to talk about Ray Cohen, Jack Catain, Dominic Frontiere . . . I don't want to talk to you guys about it.' "

H. Daniel Whitman was arrested on December 7 and charged with soliciting a homicide. At the time of his arrest, the owner of Cyrano's Restaurant was driving a stolen Mercedes-Benz and carrying a .22 caliber pistol. A U.S. Secret Service agent later testified that once in custody, Whitman had informed him that Jack Catain "was aware that Raymond Cohen was to be killed," but Whitman later denied saying any such thing. Whitman also specifically told investigators that Dominic Frontiere had no involvement in the murder whatsoever. When Whitman was arraigned on December 9, his attorney told the judge that he had already received "calls from two presidents of banks, and the head of a major film studio" offering to help his client make bail.

Whitman pled not guilty and was tried and convicted in March 1984. During his trial, the *Los Angeles Times* noted, "it was stated for the first time publicly that Dominic Frontiere, husband of the Los Angeles Rams owner, is a subject of the investigation into whether people who may have profited from the scalping failed to report the income for tax purposes." Dominic responded to the allegation through his attorney. "It is untrue," the attorney bristled, and suggested the informant was lying. The Rams, on the other hand, had "provided an accounting to the government of virtually all of the Super Bowl tickets" from 1980. Only two hundred out of twenty-eight thousand had been untraceable. Dominic, he explained, "is very upset that these allegations have been made and believes the reason that they stay alive is that he is a celebrity in the community." Apart from that, neither Mr. nor Mrs. Frontiere had anything to say about H. Daniel Whitman or either of the Cohens.

On June 19, 1986, Dominic Frontiere was indicted for making false statements on his 1980 tax return, making false statements to IRS investigators, and "corruptly endeavoring to obstruct an Internal Revenue Service investigation." The three felony counts carried total maximum sentences of eighteen years in prison and $20,000 in fines. Among other things, the indictment alleged that Frontiere failed to report hundreds of thousands of dollars from the resale of tickets to the 1980 Super Bowl.

10
Going Out at the Top

The Sullivans found Year One discomforting. Old Billy had made no secret whose side he was on in *LAMCC v. NFL*. He found losing to Al Davis a bitter pill to swallow, and remained a Rozelle partisan even when the issue was long since decided. He was also disturbed by the business's new economics. "The biggest problem in our game," Billy observed, "is that we have quite a number of people who inherited wealth and have never had to worry where the next slice of bread is coming from. Nothing in this world says you can't use your head, but we, as a League, haven't had much practice at it. Somewhere we have to look in the mirror and say who's at fault for this. The answer is the owners."

For Chuck, the discomfort was more intense. Year One was the year it was revealed that he did not possess the Midas touch. After a spectacular rise to influence in the football business, Chuck decided to expand into rock 'n' roll and significantly overreached himself. For Chuck, it must have felt like a natural progression. He had promoted concerts in college and organized Bob Hope tours as a captain stationed in Thailand during the Vietnam War. After buying the newly named Sullivan Stadium in Foxboro, he began staging shows there that featured the likes of David Bowie and the group, The Police. In spring 1984, he was looking to book the hottest proposed tour of the summer, the Jackson Family Victory Tour, featuring teen idol Michael Jackson. Sullivan learned that the tour's original promotion arrangement had fallen through and the Jacksons were looking for a new promoter for the tour itself. "Chuck went out to L.A. to talk about the stadium," one of the other Sullivans remembered. "The next thing I knew . . . he was going for the whole banana. I could hardly believe it."

To secure "the whole banana," Chuck Sullivan leaped into a bidding war with some of the more experienced tour promoters in the business. Chuck Sullivan's Stadium Management Corp., a music business unknown, was named promoter of the tour that was expected to gross $70 or $80 million, at least twice the previous rock 'n' roll record. The deal he'd cut gave the Jacksons 83.44 percent of "gross potential ticket proceeds" and Sullivan 16.56 percent. The Jacksons' cut was some twenty-five percent above the industry standard. In addition, "gross potential ticket proceeds" meant they would be paid as though every seat in the house were filled, whether it was or not. Most of the expenses were Sullivan's and he also had to guarantee his stars at least $36.6 million, to be paid in advance. To make the down payment of $12.5 million, he put Sullivan Stadium up as collateral for a bank loan. The remaining $24.1 million was due within two weeks of the opening concert, scheduled for July 6.

Chuck used the NFL meeting in May 1984 to start putting the stops on his tour together. Doing so, was, of course, a music industry first. No one in rock 'n' roll had yet tried the football approach. From Sullivan's perspective, it was also a natural progression. He, too, had a seller's market and a product that would put any place it stopped on the map. The Jacksons were at that moment the hottest thing in music and Chuck was convinced that the frenzy of anticipation for their Victory Tour would provide leverage sufficient to make stadiums put themselves out to book a date. His terms were anything but modest. "If we had given in to Chuck's demands," one stadium manager noted, "we would have lost $300,000."

An example of Sullivan's rock 'n' roll cum football approach was his negotiation with Philadelphia over the city's JFK Stadium. He wanted the city to furnish free hotel rooms for the tour's entire work force, provide free use of the stadium, and forego any of its usual cut of concessions sold at the Jacksons' events—a subsidy in the neighborhood of $400,000. Chuck argued that having the Jacksons in town would generate business well worth the price. Philadelphia found the argument hard to swallow, but other locations were quicker to deal. Lamar Hunt's Arrowhead Stadium in Kansas City got the tour's opening dates by agreeing to a flat fee of $100,000 for three concerts, rather than its usual twelve percent. Jacksonville landed the tour's third stop by agreeing to provide $445,000 worth of goods and services gratis. There were also, however, omens of the disaster to come. Perhaps the most embarrassing of those was the refusal of the Foxboro city fathers, upset by disorderly conduct at previous Sullivan concerts, to issue a permit allowing a Jackson event to be held in the stadium that had been hocked to make the whole Victory Tour possible.

In truth, Chuck Sullivan had made several significant miscalculations. The first was over just how far his NFL-style approach to stadiums would carry him. It wore thin early, created several public relations disasters, and he was soon paying much closer to standard rates and losing money accordingly. The second miscalculation was over the Jacksons' box office staying power. The world's hottest item in June was just another traveling rock 'n' roll extravaganza by August and old news not long after that. Their concerts were not automatic sellouts, tickets cost $28 apiece, and Sullivan had to pay the Jacksons sell-out rates even if he had tickets left over. The third miscalculation was over just how much money something like the Victory Tour ate up as it went along. Just drawing up the Jacksons' contract cost $400,000 in legal fees. Sullivan's insurance premiums ran another $500,000. He also had to cover the standard expenses of electricity, production, ticket takers, ushers, and catering. His payroll included, under the terms of the Jacksons' contract, an "ambiance director," paid to provide "homey touches" to the $40,000 traveling parlor in which the group sat before and after shows, as well as some 250 other employees. At each stop, Sullivan had to erect and then tear down a 365-ton stage one third the size of a football field. To move the operation required more than thirty highway trailer rigs. From the start, overhead expenses ran in the neighborhood of $1 million a week, far beyond what Chuck had counted on.

Sullivan begged out of the $24 million he still owed on the Jacksons' advance. Instead, the arrangement was renegotiated so that the Jacksons' share was reduced to seventy-five percent of "gross potential sales" and the advance was dropped. Having projected earnings of as much as $14 million in June, Chuck had reduced his projection to $3 million by August. By October, when the Jacksons reached Toronto after some thirty appearances elsewhere, the numbers looked even worse. By then, according to the *San Francisco Chronicle*, some fifty thousand tickets had gone unsold. After the last Toronto show, Chuck Sullivan renegotiated the "gross potential sales" into "actual sales." The Jacksons agreed to work on that basis henceforth, but insisted on being paid some $600,000 for previously unsold tickets. Chuck agreed. "The bottom line," he announced, "is that if everything works out well, the profit for Stadium Management Corp. will be about $500,000."

But everything did not work out well. By the time the Victory Tour reached Vancouver and Los Angeles, the last two stops, the extravaganza was a financial shambles. Sullivan and his stars were dealing through intermediaries and Sullivan claimed between $4 and $6 million of red ink. On November 28, Sullivan stopped payment on a $1.9 million check he had given the Jacksons and checked into a cardiac care hospital to recover from a mild heart attack. In order to save the final L.A. performance, Sullivan left his hospital bed to renegotiate, trading the $1.9 million for a bigger piece of the proceeds from the three L.A. dates. Sullivan got the concession but it didn't help much. The Jacksons finished their twenty-city, fifty-five engagement migration in a soggy December rain in Dodger Stadium, playing to conspicuous blocks of empty seats interspersed with an audience that "barely applauded" when they came on stage.

When Year One drew to a close, Chuck's expansion into music promotion had cost Stadium Management Corp. a reported $13 million. League members who were acquainted with the details of Chuck's rock 'n' roll bellyflop were less surprised than others when Old Billy let the word out during the 1985 season that Stadium Management Corp. and the Patriots were both on the market. The Sullivans' reported asking price was $100 million for the package—$99,975,000 more than it had cost Billy to get into the business in the first place.

That there was still some Sullivan magic left was apparent in his team's fortunes once word of a possible sale got out. The Patriots had not played for any kind of title since 1963, but in

1985 their eleven to five regular season earned a wild card berth in the playoffs. They then beat the Jets, the Raiders, and the Dolphins in succession and won a trip to Super Bowl XX in New Orleans, their first Super Bowl ever. The performance maximized the Sullivans' franchise value, but, even more important to Billy was the satisfaction. Most satisfying of all was the win over Al Davis's Raiders. Significant underdogs, Sullivan's team had delivered a twenty-seven to twenty thrashing to the architect of football's new age and the Sullivans found it hard to restrain themselves. Pat Sullivan, the franchise's general manager and Billy's youngest son, roamed the sidelines during the game, shouting insults at the Raiders players. After the Patriots victory, Pat got into an epithet match with Howie Long, a Raiders tackle, and grabbed the man's face mask. When Matt Milley, a nearby Raiders linebacker, saw the move, he swatted Sullivan across the head with his helmet, opening a gash over Pat's eyebrow. The scuffle was all over the front pages the next day.

"I didn't know him," Long claimed. "He said, 'Let me tell you who I am.' I said, 'Wait a sec, big guy. . . . I faked like I was going to hit him, just to see him jump. I'm not going to let a classless, silver-spooned, nonworking son of a bitch like that tell me anything. For me, it's God, Al Davis, and my wife, not necessarily in that order. Sullivan doesn't sign my checks. He's the jellyfish of Foxboro. Anytime he wants to lock it up in a closet and waive all legal rules, he can give me a ring. I'm listed."

"We have our pride, too," Patrick Sullivan noted. Old Billy endorsed his son's attitude. "Guys like Davis," he sneered, "I don't want any part of them. I like the term 'Fighting Irish.' If you fight one of us, you fight us all." Nor could Billy resist taking a parting shot. "Commitment to Excellence?" he crowed, "I like Commitment to Integrity better." Having come in at the bottom, the Sullivans could now go out at the top.

11

A "Good Name" Gets Beat

For Art Modell, football's new age began right where he'd left off before his heart attack.

By 1984, the first round of Modell's desperate struggle to defend his "good name" was already working its way through the appeals courts. This was Gries II, the suit charging that Modell had violated the agreement made with Gries about representation on the Browns board. The common pleas court had ruled in Gries's favor, but, the Ohio Appeals Court had reversed the decision. The Ohio Supreme Court later reversed the appeals court and, finally, in 1985, the U.S. Supreme Court refused to hear the case, in effect upholding the plaintiff, Robert Gries.

Everyone understood, however, that Gries II was more annoyance than anything else. Gries I, challenging the legality of the sale of Cleveland Stadium Corp., was a much greater danger. When Year One began, it was scheduled for trial in June. In the meantime, both Cleveland Stadium Corp. and Robert Gries had to be dealt with.

On the stadium front, Modell continued to try to slip out from under the aging structure he had set out to refurbish a decade earlier. He became a leading proponent for a proposal to build a new $150 million domed stadium on the Cleveland waterfront. "In my twenty-three years in Cleveland, I haven't seen any project that has the dynamics of this one. I'm convinced that it can turn the city around. . . . This dome could give Cleveland the opportunity to launch itself into the twenty-first century."

By March, the Dome had become a bond proposal on the May 1984 Cuyahoga County ballot and a campaign had been launched. "Now is the time to build the dome," one of the "vote yes" brochures argued. "Right now. It says, Greater Cleveland is on the way back. And it says, we're back to stay. We're tired of losing jobs and losing hope. We're finally working together and that's the beginning of real pride and real progress." Art Modell endorsed the measure and said he would commit the Browns to play in the new dome as long as two conditions were met. The first was that the city "make Cleveland Stadium Corp. whole" by paying it $12 million for the work it had done on the existing Cleveland Stadium. The second condition was "that the operator of the domed stadium be from the private sector, that it not be run by a governmental body. If the city knew how to run a stadium," he pointed out, "I wouldn't be in the stadium business to begin with." Modell admitted that his Stadium Corp. was the "logical prospect" to run the new stadium, but claimed he would support it even if it wasn't his to run.

The [Cleveland] *Plain Dealer* columnist Jim Parker greeted Modell's endorsement with a now jaundiced eye. "This Art Modell is one class act. As busy as he is . . . he finds the time to lend his 'unqualified support' to efforts to construct a property tax financed, $150 million domed stadium in downtown Cleveland. Unqualified, Modell says, so long as a couple conditions— otherwise known as qualifications—are met. Modell wants somebody to reimburse him for the $12 million in capital improvements he says his Stadium Corp. has put into the city-owned stadium and he wants his new domed playground operated by the private sector. . . . Who do you think Modell has in mind when he talks about the private sector? . . . This is not a bad deal, not too shabby at all. Modell picks up $12 million [and] moves his herd into some fully carpeted digs, courtesy of property owners and renters who pay their landlords' property tax." On May 8, Greater Cleveland voters rejected Modell's dome idea by a margin of two to one.

Art Modell was equally unsuccessful at trying to shake his shadow, Robert Gries. The two knocked sparks off each other again on day one of Year One. Earlier Modell had publicly claimed he was "proud" of the franchise's record. "I'm embarrassed by the record over the last ten years," Gries responded. "Modell's chief lieutenant wrote a letter to Rozelle," Gries remembered, "saying that I should be fined for criticizing a fellow owner publicly. . . . I said I had shown great restraint and that it was not the same as a direct criticism to comment on the team's record. Nothing was ever done about it."

It seemed Robert Gries was blemishing Art Modell's reputation in every direction he turned and on that level, it was a relief for Modell finally to face off with his adversary when *Gries Sports Enterprises v. Cleveland Browns* came to trial in June 1984. Both men were reported to have spent more than $1 million apiece on legal fees. Gries paid his own and Modell's were charged to the Browns, meaning Gries paid for forty-three percent. The trial lasted some two months, virtually all of it spent dissecting the two-year-old transaction that Modell had used to pay off his burgeoning debts. Even if the judge ruled in his favor, he was still losing every day in the courtroom as his less than impressive finances were dragged into the open for all of Cleveland to see.

"Did you ever have a problem raising a million dollars for anything?" Modell was asked under oath.

"No," he answered.

Both Modell and Gries were in the courtroom virtually every day of the trial but the two did not exchange words, passing each other silently in the hallway outside. Modell kept a proud front, but it seemed he was in trouble. On August 2, the judge issued a strongly worded letter telling Modell to settle the dispute by August 30 or else. If that settlement didn't occur, the court would void the Stadium Corp. sale. He suggested Modell separate the Strongsville land and the hotel note from the rest of the deal. Modell, however, would have nothing to do with it, calling the judge's letter "beyond comprehension." A source close to the case described the ruling as "just another nail in the coffin of Art Modell's ownership."

That nail was driven home on August 30. Since no settlement had been reached, the judge entered his final judgment. "Defendants have failed to prove $6 million was a fair price," he observed. "The deal benefited only Modell, rather than serving the best interests of the Browns." The court ordered Modell to pay back the $6 million to the Browns plus interest calculated from March 1982. He also intended to appoint an accountant to determine if the Browns had lost any other money as a consequence of the Stadium Corp. acquisition. If they had, Modell would have to pay that as well.

Modell's attorneys immediately appealed the decision and got a stay of the judge's order. In the meantime, Modell's reputation in Cleveland had taken a significant beating. When Ronald Reagan visited the city during the last days before his November 1984 reelection, Modell was one of the dignitaries on the platform at his appearance. When Modell was introduced to the crowd, he was greeted with boos.

On April 25, 1985, the Ohio Court of Appeals reversed the lower court, ruling that the court was in no position to second-guess a corporate board. This time Robert Gries appealed. For his part, Art Modell stopped short of claiming vindication. "This thing has been beaten to a pulp already,'' he offered. ''I'll let the decision of the court speak for itself.'' New age or not, Art Modell still had a long way to go in making his ''good name'' whole.

•

12
Davis Overplays his Hand

Year One was, of course, Al Davis's year.

It surprised no one when he proved a less than magnanimous winner. ''Rozelle needs to go to work and get out of the courtroom,'' Davis slashed upon receiving the news that his victory was complete, ''get out of Congress, get off the tennis courts, get out of the race tracks, get out of the social circles, get out of his vendettas, and be the commissioner again for the League. I'm sure the National Football League has greatness in the future, even though the last five years have been a downer. . . . If during the last five years Pete Rozelle had channeled all the energies . . . [and] money that was spent on the Raiders' case into promoting the League, we'd have a tremendous climate for professional football.''

By this time, the *Los Angeles Times* observed, ''no football fan in America needs to be told who Al Davis is.'' His *LAMCC v. NFL* victory had set the Davis legend in concrete.

''If Al Davis had decided he wanted to be president,'' the man who gave him his first college coaching job observed, ''he could have done it. He's that brilliant.''

''I think Al Davis has the serial number of the unknown soldier,'' an NFL coach commented.

''Sure I like to win,'' Davis said of himself, ''and I do have this belief and commitment to excellence. Achievement is important to me. . . . If some say I'm hard-nosed, yeah, I am . . . I just hope that someday this team would be recognized, if it isn't already, as the greatest team of all time in any sport.'' Davis also dismissed all the commissioner's talk about anarchy. ''As Rozelle always does when he's defeated in court and he can't get his way,'' Davis claimed, ''he predicts doom, anarchy, free agency, all the words that are used to create fear in the minds of people, when in reality it's not true.''

Davis felt that the football business was changing and his move to L.A. had been no more than a response to that change. "I foresaw that in the eighties no longer would it be hard work and intelligence," he observed, "but another factor was coming into professional sports that would determine who wins—economics. . . . I don't think that I'm any different than most other owners. I really don't. It's just that my life is professional football. Most of them, their lives are independent businesses and things like that." Al Davis had no doubt that he would end up on top. "I've always been on top ever since I was a kid," he pointed out. "What most people call problems I would call something we've got to solve, something we've got to get a solution to and take care of in the normal course of business. Not respond to it as a special case. I treat problems as normal.''

The League's diehards still hoped that the problems Davis had in L.A. would not prove as tractable as he anticipated. The first of those was the continued absence of a lease with the Coliseum. As 1984 began, the Raiders' negotiations with the LAMCC remained stalemated. The impasse began to dissipate when Bill Robertson was reappointed to the LAMCC in June 1984, this time by Mayor Tom Bradley. Robertson quickly pointed out that the Raiders had "kept their moral obligations" by moving south on their own and argued that "they are looking for us to keep our contract." At issue specifically was a $6.7 million "loan" due to Davis that a number of commissioners described as a "gift" because of its extraordinarily favorable terms.

On November 15, the LAMCC put that issue to rest by agreeing to make the payment. According to one source close to the negotiations, Davis's negotiating posture "greatly improved" once the payment was made. On December 9, he finally signed a ten-year lease with three five-year options. According to Robertson, its terms were "basically the same as the memorandum of agreement" first signed in March 1980.

Lease or not, there was still a question as to whether Davis could draw enough fans in his new hometown to make the move worthwhile. "Once the court case was resolved," Tex Schramm noted, "the Raiders are like any other franchise. They're new in town and they have no longterm following. The Raiders image may not work in L.A." That hope, too, was quashed in no uncertain fashion during the 1984 season. On November 4, Davis's franchise set an NFL regular season single game revenue record, selling 92,469 tickets to a game with the Denver Broncos. Averaging over 70,000 in attendance for each of its eight home games, the Raiders also set a single season revenue record, grossing some $10 million. Hopes that Davis's grip on L.A. would slip of its own accord were dead by 1985.

In their place, two last-ditch options remained. The first was Rozelle's favorite. According to this scenario, the damage award from *LAMCC v. NFL*, which the League was still appealing, would finally be ruled upon. At that point, the decision could be rejoined to the damages and appealed again to the Supreme Court, which could then rule in the League's favor and thwart Davis in a dramatic last stand. However, few League members were prepared to place any more hope in legal rescue. Many more hoped that, instead, Davis could be induced to settle the damages before they were finalized, reducing the League's financial obligation significantly. Throughout the process of appealing the damages, the award was growing by leaps and bounds. The legal expenses of Davis and the LAMCC, for which the League was one hundred percent liable, were expanding daily, and the award itself was subject to ten percent interest. By the time the League gathered for its 1985 annual meeting, the figure had reached somewhere between $70 and $80 million. "By our calculations," one owner pointed out, "if the courts grant the damages requested, we stand to lose $2.5 to $3 million per team. We are hoping to get that figure below $2 million. These aren't the best of times in this League, you know."

Considerable tension surrounded that hope at the 1985 annual meeting when Davis took the floor to address the rest of the League. "I told them all the things I had talked about for five years," Davis explained. "That they tried to beat me, that they're still trying to beat me, but nothing is going to change the fact that I'm in L.A." He also pointed out what he had won for all of them along the way. Because of his move, franchises' leverage in the Superstadium Game had made a quantum leap and that made everyone more money. Instead of thanking him, Davis complained, they did the opposite. Davis considered his speech "tough talk" and warned that the League was "waving swords at windmills" by continuing to pursue him. "There are more important issues to address," he insisted, and "this thing should be put to bed as soon as possible."

The meeting at which Davis spoke was, by all accounts, a tense scene. "There was so much bitterness in the room at times," one of those present noted, "it's hard to believe these guys can run their other businesses one way, in an orderly fashion, and run the League like this.'' Bitterness was the NFL's new dominant mode. "He has left a lot of open wounds," one NFL executive explained, "and even if we settle for less out of court, I doubt anybody will consider it a magnanimous gesture by Al.'' Each day that passed with the *LAMCC v. NFL* judgment outstanding cost the League another fifteen thousand dollars.

"So what's the bottom line, Al?" one owner finally demanded of Davis. "Can we get this thing settled?" Davis answered that he thought that is exactly what ought to be discussed. In response, the assembled League gave Al Davis a standing ovation.

Alex Spanos, the new owner of the San Diego Chargers, spoke for the new pro-Davis sentiment. "After all," Spanos pointed out, "we have already lost the case, so let's clean up the rest of it as soon as possible. You know the man is outstanding in this business. I think he's the best there is. . . . He's been right all along in many cases. . . . I, for one, would prefer to be his ally rather than his adversary. It's hard enough to beat him on the field. We don't need the rest of this too.''

The conditions Davis placed on his offer to discuss settlement were that the League respond within seventy-two hours and that Rozelle be directly involved. Rozelle insisted that another owner be involved as well; he wanted no part of conversations with Davis that didn't include a witness. The witness chosen was John Nordstrom of the Seattle Seahawks. During the last two days of the annual meeting, Rozelle, Davis, and Nordstrom met briefly on two occasions. "It's difficult to characterize the discussions at this point," Rozelle said, "other than to say there will be further talks.''

That there had been talks at all was, of course, historic. After ten years of skirmishing and five years of outright war, it was the first time Davis and Rozelle had ever discussed a formula for settling Davis's differences with the League. It must have been a satisfying moment for Davis. He now had the upper hand and the commissioner had to come to him in pursuit of terms. It was a heady position, and what happened next, one NFL insider remembered, was that Davis "overplayed his hand.''

After the annual meeting adjourned, Rozelle, Nordstrom, and Davis had a conference call. Davis, Rozelle remembered, "threw down the gauntlet in a strident way." His offer was also, in financial terms, much less than his fellow owners had hoped for.

"He wanted to settle at ninety-two cents on the dollar," Rozelle explained. "John Nordstrom and I informed the clubs that we couldn't recommend it. There was no interest by the clubs in the offer. It just wasn't a settlement worth considering. The most common response was, 'That's not settlement, that's capitulation.' " By April 1985, the discussions about settlement had ended and both sides resumed their wait for a ruling on the damages.

None of it changed Al Davis's attitude about Pete Rozelle one wit. The commissioner, Davis observed, was still "scurrilous" and "a fraud."

On June 16, 1986, the Federal Appeals Court returned the Raiders' *LAMCC v. NFL* damage judgment, ruling it excessive in light of the financial "windfall" provided the franchise by its move from Oakland to Los Angeles. It was Al Davis's first loss in ten years. "Obviously I don't feel good," Davis noted. "We would have liked to have won."

13
The Beat Goes On

Pete Rozelle did not simply roll over in the face of the football business's new age, but there was little he could do save try to salvage whatever status and power remained to him. The commissioner's Year One both began and ended on the defensive and Year Two would be no different.

The opening defense of 1984 was in response to the irritated faction championed by Jack Kent Cooke. *The Boston Globe* described it as "the most serious challenge Rozelle has had in his twenty-four years in office." At Super Bowl XVIII in January, Cooke claimed fifteen owners were "upset" with the way Rozelle had run things. Spurred on by the League's declining economics, Cooke's group blamed Rozelle for the L.A. damage judgment hanging over their heads and, like Carroll Rosenbloom years earlier, complained about how much of their money the commissioner's office was spending. The Tampa Super Bowl had only exacerbated their anger. There, Rozelle's office had spent $500,000 on a party for the press and the commissioner's hotel suite cost $1500 a night. Adding further to the owners' heat was the fact that Rozelle was now finishing the second year of a new ten-year contract and, except for the three-man committee who had awarded it to him, none of the men paying his salary even knew what it was.

However, the Cooke rebellion served only to demonstrate how entrenched in office Rozelle was. In truth, Cooke had ten votes at best to unseat Rozelle, and the League's constitution required at least twenty-one votes in order for the commissioner to be dismissed. Rozelle was in no danger of losing his job. He was, however, quite obviously losing his control. The sole victory of Cooke's rebellion symbolized as much. It took place at the March meeting in Chicago. At that meeting, the clamor to know what Rozelle's contract contained could no longer be ignored. Being kept in the dark, the dissident minority complained, was an example of the commissioner "blatantly showing arrogance and power." Leon Hess, chairman of the committee that had negotiated that contract, read it to the group. According to a knowledgeable NFL source, it specified that Rozelle would receive $700,000 a year in salary and another $25,000 a year in deferred income. Once Hess was finished with the recitation, there was little else the Cooke dissidents could do but stand back and watch the commissioner struggle against the tide.

By the end of Year One, examples of Rozelle's less than successful flailings were piling up: Irsay left for Indianapolis, Eddie DeBartolo faced the League down, the football business's economics began going berserk, and Al Davis further entrenched himself in L.A. In the arena of franchise movement, Rozelle's new impotence was most apparent. Irsay was, of course, only the beginning. Leonard Tose's flirtation with Phoenix came next. Rozelle understood there were only more such flirtations in the wings and, in most, the commissioner might well lack the kind of leverage he had over Tose. In response, he attempted to shore up what remained of his position.

The shoring up took the form of a new League policy on franchise movement, promulgated in an attempt to at least partially replace the outlawed Section 4.3. In it, the League committed itself for the first time to a concrete list of procedures and standards that had to be followed if a franchise wished to change home turfs. Rozelle distributed it to his employers on December 21. It was, of course, a step Al Davis had been calling for since 1978. Specifically, the new doctrine required all franchises to file a "statement of reasons" by January 15 of the year in which they intended to move. The reasons had to include comparisons

of the franchise's home revenues with League averages, ticket
sales projections, information on the new site, and a description
of the effects on other teams' travel expenses and the like.
Included with the statement had to be a copy of the franchise's
existing lease, audited financial statements for the preceding four
years, a financial analysis of the new lease, and a projection of
profits and losses for the next three years in the new location.

A spokesman for the commissioner described the new policy
to *The New York Times* as one which "basically reaffirms the
approach the NFL has always taken." Coming when it did, this
new policy was "taking what the League feels is a proper course
in handling an issue about which there is no consensus, on either a
judicial or a legislative level." In fact, it was a somewhat galling
act for Rozelle and one in which he had little faith. Rather than
reducing the League's legal vulnerability, he worried it would
only open up a multitude of further legal dilemmas. The policy,
he pointed out, was only voluntary and "could easily be challenged" by any owner bent on going to court.

His doubts were confirmed less than a month after the policy
was promulgated. In January 1985, two franchises gave official
notification that Rozelle's promulgation was unacceptable and
would be ignored. One of the franchises was the New Orleans
Saints, owned by John Mecom. Mecom was in the process of
trying to sell the club and wanted the latitude to extract the
highest possible bid, either through forcing a renegotiation with
his Superdome landlords or selling the franchise to another city.
This potential challenge was short-lived and was resolved within
two months when Mecom sold the franchise to a New Orleans
auto dealer, Tom Benson, for $65 million.

The other challenge that confirmed Rozelle's doubts was not
so easily resolved. It came from Billy Bidwill's St. Louis Cardinals. Bidwill's attorneys had been the first to file a letter of
exception with the commissioner's office and to claim their
rights under *LAMCC v. NFL*. The letter created an ironic juxta-
position. Bidwill owned the only franchise in the Rozelle era to
transfer under the outlawed Section 4.3 and Bidwill had also
served on the fact-finding committee that had investigated Al
Davis's proposed move to L. A. and found it wanting. "He was
on the committee that said I shouldn't move," Davis pointed out
with a certain satisfaction, "but in recent weeks he has come up
to me and said he shouldn't have done what he did. Now he
realizes what I went through." Bidwill's move was prompted by
his own Superstadium Game with St. Louis. Busch Stadium, the

Cardinals' home field, had the second smallest capacity in the
NFL, the franchise had the League's second lowest average
attendance, and the fourth lowest season ticket sales. Bidwill
wanted the city to build him a new eighty-thousand-seat stadium
in the suburbs and the city wasn't going for it. As a consequence, Bidwill had begun discussions with both New York City
and Phoenix about moving the Cardinals to either of those cities.

Those discussions lasted through 1985 without resolution, but
the situation escalated anyway when, at the end of Year Two,
Busch Stadium sued Bidwill to prevent him from breaking his
St. Louis lease. That in turn led to Bidwill announcing he was
suing the League to prevent it from enforcing Rozelle's new
policy and to insure that the *LAMCC v. NFL* precedent was
applied to the Cardinals, should they choose to move. By then,
of course, Rozelle's disillusionment with his own policy had
been significantly enlarged. "I implemented specific procedures
in response to the appeals court decision in the Davis case," he
explained, "but I really felt it was just a license to litigate.
Bidwill's suit was the first example." In the old days, Rozelle
could have handled a relative nonentity like Bidwill with a
minimum of effort.

The old days, however, were long since dead in the NFL,
even on TV. The commissioner who could do no wrong now
seemed snakebit whichever direction he turned. Not only had his
leverage evaporated, so had the video bonanza which had generated it. The news on the television front was perhaps the worst of
football's new age. The League was suddenly proving significantly less marketable. The "slippage" had begun in 1983, the
first full season after the disastrous 1982 strike, when instead of
climbing back to 1981 levels, ratings sank. Those most upset by
the drop were, of course, the advertisers who were paying the
networks between $220,000 and $370,000 a minute. To help
ease the networks' burden, Rozelle unilaterally enlarged the ad
space available on League broadcasts from twenty-four minutes a
game to twenty-five. "There were no negotiations about it,"
Rozelle remembered. "I just gave it to them."

Nonetheless, the deterioration only continued in 1984. Super
Bowl XIX drew more than 110 million viewers and Super Bowl
XX drew 120 million, but the regular season was an ongoing
disaster for the broadcasters who had bet $2 billion over five
years that the ratings would go up instead of down. Even when
the ratings improved in 1985, advertisers continued to shy away.
"Each week during the 1985 NFL season," *Sports Illustrated*

reported, "network ad salesmen held what became known as Friday afternoon fire sales. Like an airline selling standby seats at discount before a departure, the networks booked unsold commercial spots below their full price rates. Some commercial time was sold for less than 1983 and 1984 prices."

By the time 1986 began, the NFL, once a goose that laid golden eggs, was a network money-loser. Because of the exorbitant terms of the rights contract they had signed in 1982 and under which they had only one more year to broadcast, the 1985 NFL season cost CBS and NBC some $15 million each in red ink while ABC lost at least $25 million. The NFL's advertising revenue base had diminished considerably, thanks to the plethora of other football games now available on cable and pay-for-view television. Worse still, the NFL's demography—an audience of males between the ages of nineteen and forty-nine—had decreased in value. Where once potential NFL viewers had bought almost all the nation's automobiles, for example, now at least half those cars were purchased by women. Whether Rozelle could get another $2 billion, five-year deal was suddenly very much up for grabs. The networks claimed any increase was out of the question.

One effect of the flattening of the League's video future was to close off yet another of Rozelle's dwindling number of options. Having lost the power base he had built with the escalation of television, he would not be able to regain it the same way. The saturation point had been reached and Pete Rozelle would have to turn in another direction if he were ever to put League Think back together. The direction he chose, however, was also familiar. From the beginning of Year One, the commissioner had begun commuting to Washington, D.C., in hopes of reviving the breakout strategy that had failed in 1981 and 1982. By April 1984, Congress was again, at Rozelle's urging, considering a professional sports team community protection act, proposing at least partial NFL exemption from the antitrust laws.

The 1984 version of the legislation had a very familiar look at first. It allowed the League to control franchise movement without interference from the Sherman Act and made such control retroactive to cover both the Raiders and the Colts. As in 1981 and 1982, however, this retroactive element made passage impossible. With or without retroactivity, the renewed effort to break out made it readily apparent that Rozelle had lost his influence over the legislative process as well. By the time the 1984 Sports Community Protection Act was reported out of the

Senate Commerce Committee, it had assumed a form that the League couldn't stomach. The revised bill set up legal requirements for future team moves and established a three-member arbitration board, on which the NFL had only one seat, to rule on all such moves. The proposal, a spokesman for Rozelle noted in announcing the League's opposition, "is a quick-fix solution to a complex problem. It will complicate, not clarify, the question of sports franchise locations, which already is subject to conflicting states' and federal law."

Rozelle's once magic congressional touch succeeded only in keeping something worse off the books during 1984. In his 1985 lobbying campaign, the commissioner dropped retroactivity once and for all and made it clear he was prepared to barter. In this instance, the quid pro quo was NFL expansion by two, if and when the League's Sherman Act status was "clarified." While the offer was tempting, no such legislation was passed during 1985.

When 1986 began, however, the commissioner had managed to get "five or six senators" interested in what he called "a compromise bill." This legislation would subject the League to various criteria for the consideration of moves but give the League back the right to approve or disapprove by three-quarters vote. It also established their right to share their television money by three-quarters vote and the right to approve all new owners. Robert Dole of Kansas, Senate majority leader, was prepared to bring the bill to the floor, but was stymied by the threat of a filibuster led by Senator Albert Gore Jr. of Tennessee. Gore's position was that expansion by two was insufficient and any exemption ought to net at least expansion by six.

"The NFL is rushing Congress to grant blanket antitrust exemptions," Gore argued, "that would give the League unprecedented power to control the marketplace. Fans want to watch football, but a majority of owners would rather play Monopoly. . . . In fact, [this legislation] would give the League even greater leverage to ignore loyal fans and shun market forces. Although it would please current owners, nothing would be done about the shortage of franchises that brought on the rush of team moves in the first place. . . . Never before has the NFL asked for so much running room. In the past, the League tempered its antitrust requests by agreeing to add new teams. . . . Yet in the years since the [AFL] merger, the NFL has expanded by only two teams—Tampa Bay and Seattle. There has been no expansion for ten years. So many cities are hungry for pro football that they have launched a bidding war to lure away established teams. . . . Instead of meeting the demand for more teams, the League seeks antitrust exemptions to give itself control over team movement and all team revenues. . . . This time they are privately promising to stop any more team moves. Senators from states that already have teams are understandably eager to secure such promises. But the underlying problem is the scarcity of teams and the only real answer is expansion.''

Faced with Gore's roadblock, Rozelle simply stood his ground. Citing "all the unknowns on the part of the owners," specifically the upcoming labor and television negotiations, Rozelle rejected the idea of six new franchises out of hand. "There is no way to expand on that basis," he declared. With that, stalemate once again descended on the commissioner's congressional front.

Pete Rozelle still pursued his agenda doggedly, but behind his brave front, football's new age was tinged with a deep weariness. "This job," he admitted in November 1984, "is not as much fun as it once was." There was little to break the omnipresent sense of collapse and disorder and even less in the way of good news. The best of it was personal. On January 26, 1985, the first day of his twenty-sixth year as commissioner, the Pro Football Hall of Fame's panel of judges selected Rozelle for induction.

Rozelle and the four former players inducted with him brought the total of men so honored to 128. Most were players or coaches but among the League's own past honorees were Bert Bell, the man Rozelle succeeded; George Halas and George Preston Marshall, the two men he'd had to face down to get control when still the "boy czar"; Art Rooney, the resident NFL saint and still Rozelle's staunchest backer; and Lamar Hunt, who'd been inducted in 1972 as an honor to the old AFL, the most successful competitor in the NFL's history. Rozelle himself called the induction itself "a big moment."

August 3 was typically muggy in Canton, Ohio, and the inductees were each introduced to the crowd gathered round the hall's front steps by a presenter of their choice. Rozelle selected Tex Schramm. The ceremony began with an invocation by the Reverend Peggy Ecia of Canton's Unity Church. Next, Schramm presented his old friend Pete Rozelle. Speaking of the selection of Rozelle at the Kenilworth Hotel in 1960, Schramm observed that "they probably didn't know it at the time, [but] they probably made one of the most important and wisest decisions that they could have made. Because . . . they selected a man for the times. A man that was prepared to lead [the NFL] through a new era and that man was thirty-three-year-old Pete Rozelle. We are now twenty-six years later honoring that man. But when he was selected, few people realized what they had obtained as their leader. . . . They had obtained a man of tremendous intelligence, foresight, patience, preparation, tenacity, a will to win, and a sense of class and he imparted that through the League and he also had the background to make it work because he was young and had grown with the new giant, television. . . . He handled all the threats to the integrity of the game and he handled them with dignity. He went through the pains of growth because no sport experienced the growth that the NFL did in the past twenty-five years. . . . From the very beginning he said, I don't care what it is, what it takes, we are going to do it with class and with style. . . . He had the foresight. . . . So you have a man here that you are honoring very properly. A man that is very deserving. A man who has stood very tall and who you will look upon for many, many years when you think about the NFL. Probably the greatest commissioner the sport has ever had, the commissioner of the NFL, Alvin Ray Pete Rozelle.''

The crowd greeted the commissioner affectionately. Looking out at them, Rozelle was "surprised at how many of my friends and relatives from California had come. It was a time of a lot of memories. I reflected on all the changes and thought about the seriousness of it all.''

Little of that reflection came out in Rozelle's speech. "The commissioner's job, of course, is very unique,'' he observed. "You are hired by the owners, but you are called upon to make decisions that affect them. You can't please everyone, every time. . . . You simply have to do what you think in your judgment is in the best interest of the game. . . . I feel very fortunate to have always worked at what I love. I don't go out and stamp things on an assembly line. I was blessed. I was always able to work in sports, particularly the National Football League. I can only say that I feel very happy, proud, and so grateful to be here today.''

Once again, the crowd responded warmly. The applause was genuine. No one had the bad manners to spoil the moment by pointing out that the honor amounted to a consolation prize.

EPILOGUE

By 1987, Year Three of the After Davis era of the National Football League, where the League was coming from still remained more apparent than where it was going. The one constant factor was that Pete Rozelle remained in charge of damage control and on this front, seemed to have at least momentarily stemmed the tide of disintegration. He did so by finally winning a case in court.

The case in question was the Sherman Act suit brought against the NFL by the United States Football League, heard in Manhattan Federal Court during the summer of 1986. The potential consequences of a loss were enormous. If the USFL was awarded the $1.5 billion in trebled damages it sought, the NFL was faced with either shelling out $53 million per franchise or cutting a deal to settle the claim, undoubtedly by allowing the upstart league to merge with it. The threat brought 27 of the owners together in what Rozelle described as "considerable harmony." The one outside was, of course, Al Davis. Instead of joining the common front, Davis testified for the USFL. "Davis," Rozelle remembered, "told us what he was going to say and that, if we crossed him, he would hurt us even more." Instead, "the USFL shot itself in the foot" and, "Davis's testifying for the USFL seriously eroded his position in the League."

The USFL's failure became apparent in July, 1986 when the jury returned its verdict. While finding that the NFL was indeed a monopoly as defined by the Sherman Act, it awarded the USFL no relief and damages of only $1. In effect, the verdict killed the USFL's last chance to survive and left the NFL once again without a competitor in the professional football business. Rozelle was understandably ecstatic. "It was probably the high point of my business life," he exclaimed. "With the verdict we're finally out of a terrible morass of 10 or 12 years of litigation."

Out, perhaps, but certainly not free of. The USFL decision did nothing to reduce the League's vulnerability to the Sherman Act and nothing to alter the precedents set by Al Davis. "I don't think anyone's going to lay off their lawyer right now,'' one NFL insider observed. ''We've got a lot of rough water in front of us and who knows what these guys will do if they get it in their heads to do it. It still only takes one guy to throw the whole thing out of whack.''

Nobody had to ask who the one guy was. While the fact that Al Davis had won was now beyond dispute, the rest of the League at least had the satisfaction in the fall of 1986 of seeing Davis pay some heavy prices of his own. It was an exceedingly bad fall for Al Davis. In the football season, his team collapsed down the stretch and missed the Super Bowl playoffs. Many football commentators linked the Raiders' problems with the inattention enforced by Davis's long run of legal distractions. Certainly those distractions continued that fall. While Rozelle might have escaped the ''terrible morass'' of litigation, Davis was still in it up to his ears. That fall's version was *Klein v. Davis* and it marked the point where Davis's long run of legal victories died, much to everyone's surprise. At the opening of the trial, the odds in Las Vegas were that Gene Klein's chances were no better than 50 to 1.

The lawsuit was Klein's parting shot in the world of football he'd inhabited for most of two decades. Otherwise, his shift to the horseracing world was complete. Earlier that year, his horse, Tank's Prospect, had won the Preakness Stakes, and he arrived in the San Diego courtroom on a winning streak. He left the same way. The jury agreed with Klein's argument that Davis's malicious prosecution was responsible for Klein's 1981 heart attack and awarded $10 million in compensatory and punitive damages, later reduced on appeal. ''Al Davis has always been a bully,'' Klein crowed, ''and he found out that this was one kid he couldn't bully.'' While no one could have been more satisfied than Gene Klein at the judgment, Rozelle and the rest of the League no doubt did their share of celebrating as well. Coupled with the Appeals Court's earlier ruling returning the damages of *LAMCC v. NFL* to a lower court for reduction, Al Davis was facing a possible loss of some tens of millions of dollars.

As satisfying as all those potential financial losses were to those who wanted Davis pulled up short, they did nothing to affect the changes he had wrought in the NFL. Anyone who doubted that had only to look at Billy Bidwill in St. Louis. He continued to demand a new stadium from the city on the most advantageous of terms and promised to move elsewhere if he didn't get it. That he could was a given.

Just what the League could do under the After Davis legal standards was still up for grabs when it met in Kaanapali, Hawaii during March for its 1987 Annual Meeting. Ironically, the critical issues on its agenda were identical to those in 1974, when this story began.

The first was the League's new television contract. For the first time in memory, Rozelle and Art Modell, the reigning television committee, did not start negotiations with the networks until after the Super Bowl. Their apparent strategy was to dangle at least part of the NFL package to possible subscription cable outlets. In the meantime, the networks were laying off employees and buckling down to self-enforced economy measures.

The new age of NFL television dawned on the ides of March when Rozelle gave his television committee report. The package, including spinning off a few games to ESPN cable, reduced each franchise's broadcast revenues by some $500,000 a year and would last only 3 years. There was, nonetheless, general agreement that the Commissioner had been lucky to get that. "We all know what the real world is now," Art Modell explained. "The days of the quantum leaps in revenues may have ended."

—*San Francisco Chronicle*, 3/16/87

The second issue dominating the League's financial future was on the labor front. The contract negotiated with the NFLPA during the 1982 strike would expire before training camps opened in the summer and the post-Garvey era of labor negotiations had already begun. Under new Director Gene Upshaw, the union's principal position had two primary characteristics. The first was an unGarveylike desire to keep negotiations out of the newspapers. The second was an insistence on the repeal of Garvey's most notable concession, the abandonment of the free agency won a decade earlier in *Mackey v. NFL*. That repeal was the union's number one issue. For their part, the owners made it clear that free agency was every bit as unacceptable to them now as it had been when first raised in 1974. Nonetheless, they would have to either come up with financial incentives sufficient to change the union's mind or face the possibility of another strike, not unlike the disaster of 1982. Win, lose, or draw, the outcome could only cost the League more money than it wanted to pay.

The third issue on the NFL's 1987 agenda was, for the first

time since 1974, expansion. In the summer of 1986, Rozelle announced that he would be appointing an expansion committee to "proceed cautiously" with an expansion "by two" some time in the near future, once the television and labor contracts had been finalized. However approached, this slicing of a shrinking economic pie in two more pieces was guaranteed to be a painful and divisive process. At least six cities would be contesting for the anticipated franchises, two of them former NFL members, and choosing between them would likely add to the acrimony, as would trying to decide what to charge for these new memberships. Lawsuits by those left disgruntled were a strong possibility, paving the way for yet another legal morass not unlike the one Rozelle had just escaped.

Despite all those dilemmas, Pete Rozelle, the man for whom the previous era had been named, remained determinedly optimistic. That optimism was all the more striking given his own admitted lame duck status. His contract as Commissioner was scheduled to run out in 1991 when he reached age sixty-five and in the summer of 1986 he had announced that he would "definitely not serve" beyond its expiration and might very well leave even earlier. "I want to get the League back in at least reasonable condition before I leave," he explained. "That may be in two years. I'll see." His strategy for doing so was familiar. "Now," he announced when the USFL was defeated, "we can go forward and create more harmony and togetherness."

That, as Rozelle knew better than anyone, was much easier said than done.

CHAPTER NOTES

The chapter notes that follow list the principal sources I have used in writing this book. They are by no means exhaustive but are intended to give the reader a general overview of my research.

1/1.

NFL minutes, 2/25/74, 3/20/72, 3/24/72, 4/2/73. • NFL constitution and bylaws.

INTERVIEWS:
Gene Klein, 9/14/83. • Pete Rozelle, 6/5, 6/6/84. • Leonard Tose, 10/3/84. • Jack Kent Cooke, 9/27/83. • Tex Schramm, 9/15/83. • Lamar Hunt, 9/22/83. • Art Modell, 9/14/83. • Bill McPhail, 9/7/84. • 2 NFL executives, confidential.

TESTIMONY:
Edward Bennett Williams, *NASL v. NFL*, 4/7/80. • *Official NFL Record and Fact Book*. New York: Workman Publishing Company, 1985. • Noll, Roger [ed.], *Government and the Sports Business*, Brookings Institute, 1974. • *The New York Times Magazine*, 1/15/84. • *Sports Illustrated*, 1/6/64. • *Christian Century*, 4/5/72. • *Esquire*, 11/72. • *Time*, 4/5/82. • *The New York Times*, 7/20/73.

1/2.

INTERVIEWS:
Pete Rozelle, 8/9/83, 8/25/83, 10/17/83, 6/6/84. • Tex Schramm, 9/15/83. • Wellington Mara, 10/17/84. • Ken Macker, 9/26/83. • Bill McPhail, 9/13/83.

TESTIMONY:
Pete Rozelle, *LAMCC v. NFL*, 4/2/82.

SPEECHES:
Pete Rozelle, 1985 Hall of Fame Enshrinement Program. •

Tex Schramm, 1985 Hall of Fame Enshrinement Program. •
NFL Record and Fact Book. • *Sports Illustrated,* 1/6/64. •
The [Baltimore] *Sun,* 10/13/59.

1/3.

INTERVIEWS:
  Pete Rozelle, 8/9/83, 6/5/84. • Dan Rooney, 9/19/83. • La-
mar Hunt, 9/20/84. • Bill McPhail, 9/23/83. • NFL owner,
confidential.
TESTIMONY:
  Pete Roselle, *LAMCC v. NFL,* 4/5/82, *NASL v. NFL,*
4/16/80, 4/21/80, Hearings before the Subcommittee on
Monopolies and Commercial Law, U.S. Congress, 10/14/75,
Hearings before the House Select Committee on Profes-
sional Sports, U.S. Congress, 6/23/76.
DEPOSITIONS:
  Pete Rozelle, *LAMCC v. NFL,* 8/27/80. • *NFL Record and
Fact Book.* • Noll, *Government and the Sports Business.* •
Rozelle, Pete, "NFL TV History," *New York Times,* 9/2/79.
• *The New York Times Magazine,* 1/15/84. • *Sports Illustrated,*
1/6/64. • *The New York Times,* 4/18/82.

1/4.

INTERVIEWS:
  Pete Rozelle, 8/9/83, 8/25/83, 6/5/84, 6/11/84. • Bill McPhail,
9/23/83, 9/7/84. • 6 friends of Pete Rozelle, confidential. •
NFL executive, confidential. • Rozelle critic, confidential.

1/5.

INTERVIEWS:
  Gene Klein, 9/16/83, 9/14/84. • Lamar Hunt, 9/22/83. •
Leonard Tose, 9/23/83. • Art Modell, 9/14/83, 11/9/84. • Tex
Schramm, 9/18/84. • Billy Sullivan, 10/19/84. • Pete Rozelle,
6/5/84.
TESTIMONY:
  Art Modell, *Gries Sports Enterprises v. Cleveland Browns,*
7/12/84. • Edward Bennett Williams, *NASL v. NFL,* 4/7/80. •

Pete Rozelle, Hearings before the Committee of the Judiciary, U.S. Senate, 8/16/82. • Theodore Kheel, Hearings before the Subcommittee on Labor-Management Relations, U.S. Congress, 10/2/75.

DEPOSITIONS:

Al Davis, *LAMCC v. NFL*, 3/4/81. • Arthur Anderson & Co., *National Football League Management Council, Member Clubs of the National Football League—Pro Forma Combined Statement of Income for the 1973 Playing Season.* • Arthur Anderson & Co., *NFL Management Council, Member Clubs of the National Football League—Pro Forma Combined Statement of Income for 1974 Playing Season.* • Noll, *Government and the Sports Business.* • *Esquire,* 11/21/78. • *Fortune,* 3/73. • *Time,* 9/6/71. • *Popular Mechanics,* 11/73. • *U.S. News and World Report,* 4/12/74. • [Cleveland] *Plain Dealer,* 9/18/66. • *Philadelphia Inquirer,* 9/6/70. • *Miami Herald,* 7/8/76.

1/6.

INTERVIEWS:

Tex Schramm, 9/18/84. • Lamar Hunt, 9/20/84. • Pete Rozelle, 6/5/84. • Joe Alioto, 2/1/85. • NFL owner, confidential. • 2 NFL executives, confidential. • Chipman, Donald, et al. *The Dallas Cowboys and the NFL,* University of Oklahoma Press, 1970. • *Sports Illustrated,* 6/20/66 • *Dallas Morning News,* 11/14/83, 11/16/83, 11/20/83. • *Dallas Times Herald,* 1/28/84 • *Kansas City Times,* 4/1/75.

1/7.

NFL Record and Fact Book. • Chipman, *The Dallas Cowboys and the NFL.* • *Esquire,* 9/72. • *Dallas Times Herald,* 5/25/75. • *Dallas Morning News,* 6/17/81.

1/8.

INTERVIEWS:

Art Modell, 9/14/83, 11/9/84. • Pete Rozelle, 6/11/84. • Robert Gries, 10/11/84, 10/12/84. • NFL executive, confidential. • NFL sportswriter, confidential.

TESTIMONY:
Art Modell, *Gries Sports Enterprises v. Cleveland Browns,*
7/12/84. • Robert Gries, *Gries Sports Enterprises v. Cleveland Browns,* 6/20/84. • Cleveland Browns press release,
4/78. • *Akron Beacon Journal,* 1/16/83, 1/17/83. • [Cleveland]
Plain Dealer, 3/24/61, 9/18/66, 9/4/82. • *Cleveland Press,*
6/1/68. • *Austin Statesman,* 5/19/39.

1/9.

INTERVIEWS:
Robert Gries, 10/11/84, 10/12/84. • NFL executive, confidential.
TESTIMONY:
Art Modell, *Gries Sports Enterprises v. Cleveland Browns,*
6/18/84, 7/12/84. *NASL v. NFL,* 4/23/80. • *Point of View,*
11/2/74. • [Cleveland] *Plain Dealer,* 8/23/72, 12/3/72, 2/4/73,
2/27/73, 3/8/73, 3/11/73, 5/10/73, 7/7/73, 7/13/73. • *Cleveland Press,* 8/24/72, 5/8/73.

1/10.

INTERVIEWS:
Steve Rosenbloom, 9/21/84, 10/11/84. • Wellington Mara,
10/17/84. • Gene Klein, 9/14/84. • Tex Schramm, 9/18/84. •
Pete Rozelle, 6/6/84. • Ed Garvey, 9/24/83.
DEPOSITIONS:
Al Davis, *LAMCC v. NFL,* 3/4/81. • Pete Rozelle, *LAMCC v.
NFL,* 10/11/79. • Pack, Robert, *Edward Bennett Williams for
the Defense,* Harper and Row, 1983. • Parrish, Bernie, *They
Call It a Game,* Dial Press, 1971. • *Forbes,* 9/13/82. •
Esquire, 11/21/78. • *Sports Illustrated,* 1/6/64. • NFL press
release, 7/16/63. • [Baltimore] *Sun,* 4/20/62, 10/28/62, 11/22/66,
12/16/66. • *Los Angeles Times,* 4/4/79, 9/25/79, 1/26/83. •
Los Angeles Herald Examiner, 4/3/79.

1/11.

INTERVIEWS:
Steve Rosenbloom, 9/21/84, 10/11/84. • Art Modell, 11/9/84.
DEPOSITIONS:
Pete Rozelle, *LAMCC v. NFL,* 8/27/80. • Chipman, *The*

Dallas Cowboys and the NFL. • *Sports Illustrated,* 8/14/72. • *Esquire,* 11/21/78. • [Baltimore] *Sun,* 10/28/62, 3/18/71, 7/14/72. • [Baltimore] *News-American,* 4/1/82. • *Los Angeles Times,* 2/27/80.

1/12.

INTERVIEWS:
Steve Rosenbloom, 9/21/84. • Tex Schramm, 9/18/84. • Lamar Hunt, 9/20/84. • Gene Klein, 9/14/84. • former LAMCC member, confidential.
DEPOSITIONS:
Pete Rozelle, *LAMCC v. NFL,* 10/11/79. • Al Davis, *LAMCC v. NFL,* 3/14/80. • *Esquire,* 11/21/78. • *Los Angeles Times,* 8/30/73, 11/26/73, 1/11/74, 1/17/74, 2/12/74, 10/3/79. • [Baltimore] *Sun,* 10/28/62, 10/5/72, 5/1/73.

1/13.

INTERVIEWS:
Steve Rosenbloom, 9/21/84. • Wellington Mara, 10/17/84. • Gene Klein, 9/14/84. • Wayne Valley, 9/25/84. • George Ross, 10/11/84. • NFL owner, confidential. • NFL executive, confidential.
DEPOSITIONS:
Al Davis, *LAMCC v. NFL,* 11/25/80, 3/4/81, *Barrero v. Davis,* 11/1/73. • Mandell, Arnold, *The Nightmare Season,* Random House, 1976. • *Sport,* 1/81. • *Look,* 11/18/69. • *Saturday Evening Post,* 11/75. • *Sports Illustrated,* 11/4/63, 11/15/65. • *The New York Times Magazine,* 12/13/81. • [Oakland] *Tribune,* 12/21/44, 11/6/46, 2/8/49, 11/17/55, 11/28/56, 3/15/60, 9/8/60, 11/13/60, 2/21/62, 1/6/77.

1/14.

INTERVIEWS:
Tex Schramm, 9/18/84. • Wayne Valley, 9/25/84. • George Ross, 10/11/84.
TESTIMONY:
Al Davis, *Coggins v. New England Patriots,* 5/12/82.

DEPOSITIONS:
  Al Davis, *Valley v. Davis*, 8/23/73, *LAMCC v. NFL*, 11/25/80,
  3/4/81. • Chipman, *The Dallas Cowboys and the NFL*. •
  Sports Illustrated, 11/15/65, 8/29/66. • *Saturday Evening Post*,
  11/75. • *Look*, 11/18/69. • *The New York Times Magazine*,
  12/13/81. • [Oakland] *Tribune*, 8/11/66, 3/23/69. • *The New
  York Times*, 4/27/69.

1/15.

INTERVIEWS:
  Tex Schramm, 9/18/84. • Art Modell, 11/9/84. • Pete Rozelle,
  6/7/84. • Steve Rosenbloom, 9/21/84. • Wayne Valley, 9/25/84.
  • Jim Kensil, 6/7/84. • Jay Moyer, 6/7/84. • George Ross,
  10/11/84. • NFL owner, confidential.
DEPOSITIONS:
  Al Davis, *LAMCC v. NFL*, 3/14/80, 11/25/80, *Valley v. Davis*,
  8/23/73. • Pete Rozelle, *LAMCC v. NFL*, 8/27/80. • *The New
  York Times Magazine*, 11/13/81. • *Look*, 11/18/69. • *The New
  York Times*, 4/23/83. • [Oakland] *Tribune*, 3/19/72.

1/16.

INTERVIEWS:
  Gene Klein, 9/14/84. • Steve Rosenbloom, 9/21/84. • 3 NFL
  owners, confidential. • NFL attorney, confidential. • Mandell,
  The Nightmare Season. • *Forbes*, 11/15/68. • *Home*, 9/25/75.
  • *Business Week*, 10/13/73. • [San Diego] *Tribune*, 1/13/72,
  9/23/81. • *San Diego Union*, 2/24/72, 7/2/74, 8/2/74. • *Los
  Angeles Times*, 3/21/74. • *Wall Street Journal*, 12/4/70.

1/17.

  NFL minutes, 6/26/73.
INTERVIEWS:
  Pete Rozelle, 6/6/84. • Gene Klein, 9/14/84. • Mandell, *The
  Nightmare Season*. • Parrish, *They Call It a Game*. • *Psychology Today*, 6/75. • NFL press release, 4/26/74. • *Los Angeles
  Times*, 3/21/74. • [Oakland] *Tribune*, 7/8/75.

1/18.

NFL minutes, 2/25/74.
INTERVIEWS:
Pete Rozelle, 6/25/83, 6/5/84, 6/7/84. • Dan Rooney, 10/4/84.
• Lamar Hunt, 9/20/84. • Wellington Mara, 10/17/84. • Gene
Klein, 9/14/84. • Ed Garvey, 12/3/84. • Sherman Antitrust
Act, Section 1. • Supreme Court Reports, *Federal Baseball
Club v. National League*, 5/29/22. • Supreme Court Reports,
Radovich v. NFL, 2/25/57. • Federal Supplement, *Mackey v.
NFL*, 12/29/75. • Noll, *Government and the Sports Business*.
• *The New York Times*, 2/17/74, 2/22/74.

1/19.

NFL minutes, 2/26/74. • NFL constitution and bylaws.
INTERVIEWS:
Wellington Mara, 10/17/84. • 3 NFL owners, confidential. •
NFL executive, confidential.
TESTIMONY:
Chuck Sullivan, *NASL v. NFL*, 4/22/80.
DEPOSITIONS:
Pete Rozelle, *LAMCC v. NFL*, 10/11/79. • *Sports Illustrated*,
9/25/72. • *Newsweek*, 9/6/71. • *Time*, 9/6/71. • *The New York
Times*, 8/27/71, 8/28/71, 1/18/74, 2/28/74, 3/14/76.

1/20.

NFL minutes, 2/28/74.
INTERVIEWS:
Steve Rosenbloom, 10/11/84. • 2 NFL owners, confidential. •
NFL executive, confidential. • Colts Game Program, 9/30/73.
• [Baltimore] *Sun*, 7/13/72, 9/17/72, 10/21/72, 10/14/73,
9/18/79, 2/16/84, 3/4/84. • [Baltimore] *News-American*, 7/14/72,
8/4/72. • *Indianapolis Star*, 6/17/84.

1/21.

NFL minutes, 3/20/67, 5/1/71. • NFL, Report of Special
Committee on Membership Rules and Ownership Policy, Sec-

tion 3(f), 5/15/70. • NFL, Confidential Memorandum to Members of the National Football League, 2/18/71. • Agreement of AFL and NFL, Section 4(m), 12/1/66.

TESTIMONY:
Pete Rozelle, *NASL v. NFL*, 4/16/80, 4/17/80, 4/21/80. • Edward Bennett Williams, *NASL v. NFL*, 4/7/80. • Lamar Hunt, *NASL v. NFL*, 4/2/80. • Joe Robbie, *NASL v. NFL*, 4/9/80. • Bill Bidwill, *NASL y. NFL*, 4/22/80. • Art Modell, *NASL v. NFL*, 4/23/80. • National Basketball Association, *Official Guide*, 1968–69.

1/22.

NFL minutes, 5/25/72.

INTERVIEWS:
Pete Rozelle, 6/6/84. • Tex Schramm, 9/18/84. • NFL owner, confidential. • NFL executive, confidential.

TESTIMONY:
Edward Bennett Williams, *NASL v. NFL*, 4/7/80. • Lamar Hunt, *NASL v. NFL*, 4/3/80. • Joc Robbie, *NASL v. NFL*, 4/9/80. • Leonard Tose, *NASL v. NFL*, 4/22/80.

1/23.

INTERVIEWS:
Lamar Hunt, 9/20/84. • Pete Rozelle, 6/6/84.

TESTIMONY:
Lamar Hunt, *NASL v. NFL*, 4/2/80. • Chipman, *The Dallas Cowboys and the NFL*. • *Texas Monthly*, 4/78. • *Forbes*, 10/1/84. • *Pro*, 10/84. • *Kansas City Times*, 9/1/84. • *Kansas City Star*, 8/8/82.

1/24.

INTERVIEWS:
Lamar Hunt, 9/20/84. • Steve Rosenbloom, 9/21/84. • 3 NFL owners, confidential.

TESTIMONY:
Lamar Hunt, *NASL v. NFL*, 4/2/80, 4/3/80. • Edward Bennett Williams, *NASL v. NFL*, 4/7/80. • Pete Rozelle, *NASL v.*

NFL, 4/17/80. • letter, Lamar Hunt to Pete Rozelle, 10/16/67.
• letter, Lamar Hunt to Pete Rozelle, undated. • letter, Lamar
Hunt to Wendell Cherry, 10/8/73. • letter, Lou Spadia to
Lamar Hunt, 11/73. • letter, Lamar Hunt to Pete Rozelle,
11/12/73. • letter, Pete Rozelle to Lamar Hunt, 11/19/73. •
letter, Lamar Hunt to Pete Rozelle, 2/74. • note, Pete Rozelle
to Lamar Hunt, 8/11/72. • *Texas Monthly*, 4/78. • *Sports
Illustrated*, 9/3/73. • *Kansas City Star*, 8/8/82. • [Baltimore]
Sun, 9/2/79.

1/25.

INTERVIEWS:
3 NFL owners, confidential.
TESTIMONY:
Leonard Tose, *NASL v. NFL*, 4/22/80. • Pete Rozelle, *NASL
v. NFL*, 4/16/80, *LAMCC v. NFL*, 4/6/82. • *Philadelphia*,
8/70. • [Philadelphia] *Bulletin*, 6/9/70, 5/4/72, 12/3/72. •
Philadelphia Daily News, 3/11/69, 7/1/72. • *Philadelphia
Inquirer*, 5/14/70, 6/8/70, 6/11/70, 6/12/70, 5/3/72.

1/26.

NFL minutes, 2/25/72.
INTERVIEWS:
Leonard Tose, 10/3/84. • 3 NFL owners, confidential. • NFL
executive, confidential.
TESTIMONY:
Leonard Tose, *NASL v. NFL*, 4/22/80. • NFL, *Official Record
Manual*, 1983. • *Philadelphia Inquirer*, 6/3/71, 8/8/71,
12/16/71, 2/9/72, 7/15/72. • *Philadelphia Daily News*, 6/23/71,
8/2/71, 2/10/72, 2/16/72, 10/4/72. • [Philadelphia] *Bulletin*,
8/9/71, 2/9/72, 10/3/72, 12/3/72. • Jack Anderson column,
San Francisco Chronicle, 6/12/70.

1/27.

INTERVIEWS:
Billy Sullivan, 10/19/84. • Bob Marr, 1/22/85. • Leonard
Tose, 10/3/84. • NFL owner, confidential.

TESTIMONY:
   Chuck Sullivan, *NASL v. NFL*, 4/22/80. • Pete Rozelle, *Coggins v. New England Patriots*, 5/6/82.
DEPOSITION:
   Pete Rozelle, *LAMCC v. NFL*, 8/28/80. • *Boston Globe*, 1/27/70, 3/5/70, 3/22/70, 5/27/70, 9/19/70, 9/24/70. • *Boston Herald*, 5/26/70, 12/9/76, 12/31/78, 7/9/79, 6/15/80. • *Patriot Ledger*, 8/3/71.

1/28.

INTERVIEWS:
   Billy Sullivan, 10/19/84. • Bob Marr, 1/22/85. • 2 NFL owners, confidential.
TESTIMONY:
   Billy Sullivan, Hearings before Select Committee on Professional Sports, U.S. Congress, 6/23/76, *Coggins v. New England Patriots*, 5/3/82, 5/10/82. • NFL, *Official Record Manual*, 1983. • *Boston Globe*, 1/18/74, 3/21/74, 4/7/74, 3/21/82. • *Boston Herald*, 5/26/70, 12/3/70, 3/27/74, 4/3/74, 6/5/80.

1/29.

INTERVIEWS:
   Pete Rozelle, 6/11/84. • George Ross, 10/11/84. • NFL owner, confidential. • NFL executive, confidential.
TESTIMONY:
   Joe Robbie, *NASL v. NFL*, 4/9/80.
DEPOSITIONS:
   Al Davis, *LAMCC v. NFL*, 11/25/80. • Miami Dolphins, *Press Yearbook*, 1967. • Miami Dolphin Game Program, 11/27/66. • *Sports Illustrated*, 8/8/66, 12/15/69. • *Miami Herald*, 5/16/69. • *Palm Beach Post Times*, 12/17/72.

1/30.

INTERVIEWS:
   Pete Rozelle, 6/6/84.
TESTIMONY:
   Joe Robbie, *NASL v. NFL*, 4/9/80. • Chuck Sullivan, *NASL v.*

NFL, 4/22/80. • Shula, Don, *The Winning Edge*, Dutton, 1973. • *Sports Illustrated*, 12/15/69, 11/9/70, 7/27/81. • *Miami News*, 9/10/71, 12/11/75.

1/31.

TESTIMONY:
Edward Bennett Williams, *NASL v. NFL*, 4/7/80. • Lamar Hunt, *NASL v. NFL*, 4/2/80. • petition for temporary conservatorship, George Preston Marshall, 12/12/63. • Pack, *Edward Bennett Williams for the Defense*. • *Washington Monthly*, 6/78. • *American Lawyer*, 5/85. • *The New York Times*, 10/25/83.

1/32.

TESTIMONY:
Edward Bennett Williams, *NASL v. NFL*, 4/7/80. • Pete Rozelle, *NASL v. NFL*, 4/16/80. • Pack, *Edward Bennett Williams for the Defense*. • *The Washingtonian*, 9/82. • *Forbes*, 9/13/82. • *San Francisco Chronicle*, 1/6/84.

1/33.

NFL minutes, 4/2/73, 2/25/74.
INTERVIEWS:
Pete Rozelle, 6/5/84. • Steve Rosenbloom, 9/21/84. • Leonard Tose, 10/3/84. • Dan Rooney, 10/4/84. • Tex Schramm, 9/18/84. • Jay Moyer, 6/5/84. • *Sports Illustrated*, 10/23/72, 12/1/75. • *The New York Times Magazine*, 1/12/75.

1/34.

National Football League constitution and bylaws.
INTERVIEWS:
Dan Rooney, 10/4/84. • Pete Rozelle, 6/5/84. • Stanford Research Institute, *Socioeconomic Information on Candidate Areas for NFL Franchises*, 1973.

1/35.

NFL minutes, 2/25/74.
INTERVIEWS:
Pete Rozelle, 9/25/83, 6/5/84. • Dan Rooney, 9/19/83, 10/4/84.
• Art Rooney, 9/16/83. • Leonard Tose, 10/3/84. • 2 NFL
owners, confidential. • Kowet, Don, *The Rich Who Own
Sports*, Random House, 1971. • *Fortune*, 11/68. • *Nation's
Business*, 9/80. • *The New York Times*, 9/5/74.

1/36.

NFL minutes, 2/27/74.
INTERVIEWS:
NFL owner, confidential. • NFL executive, confidential. •
[Baltimore] *Sun*, 3/1/74.

2/1.

INTERVIEWS:
Ed Garvey, 12/3/84. • Pete Rozelle, 6/5/84. • Keith Fahnhorst,
12/6/84. • Bob Moore, 2/8/85.
TESTIMONY:
Joe Robbie, *NASL v. NFL*, 4/9/80. • Ed Garvey, Hearings
before the Subcommittee on Labor, U.S. Senate, 10/31/77. •
Sargent Karch, Oversight Hearings on National Football League
Labor-management Dispute, U.S. Congress, 9/29/75. • NFLPA
Demands, 3/16/74. • Statement by Wellington Mara, 4/4/74.
• Statement by Management Council, 4/4/74. • *Sports
Illustrated*, 3/22/71. • *Business Week*, 8/8/70. • *Newsweek*,
8/3/70. • *Ebony*, 11/70. • *The New York Times*, 8/2/70,
8/3/70, 8/4/70.

2/2.

INTERVIEWS:
Pete Rozelle, 6/5/84. • *Sports Illustrated*, 4/15/74. • *Time*,
4/15/74. • *The New York Times Magazine*, 1/12/75. • *Fortune*,
9/74. • *Newsweek*, 4/15/74.

2/3.

INTERVIEWS:
Billy Sullivan, 10/19/84. • Chuck Sullivan, 10/17/84. • Bob
Marr, 1/22/85. • Sullivan acquaintance, confidential. • *Fortune*,
8/20/84. • *Boston Globe*, 3/21/74, 4/10/74. • *Boston Herald*,
4/10/74.

2/4.

NFL minutes, 4/23/74, 4/24/74, 6/4/74.
INTERVIEWS:
Dan Rooney, 10/4/84. • Pete Rozelle, 6/5/84. • Gene Klein,
9/14/84. • Tex Schramm, 9/18/84. • Bob Marr, 1/22/85.
TESTIMONY:
Joe Robbie, Hearings before Select Committee on Profes-
sional Sports, U.S. Congress, 6/23/76. • Pete Rozelle, *LAMCC
v. NFL*, 4/5/82.
DEPOSITIONS:
Pete Rozelle, *LAMCC v. NFL*, 8/27/80. • Stanford, *Socioeco-
nomic Information on Candidate Areas.* • *Seattle Post-
Intelligencer*, 4/25/74, 4/26/74. • *St. Petersburg Times*, 4/25/74.
• *San Diego Union*, 6/5/74.

2/5.

INTERVIEWS:
Billy Sullivan, 10/19/84. • Chuck Sullivan, 10/16/84. • Pete
Rozelle, 6/5/84. • Bob Marr, 1/22/85.
TESTIMONY:
Pete Rozelle, *NASL v. NFL*, 4/16/80, 4/22/80, *Coggins v.
New England Patriots*, 4/7/82. • LaSalle National Bank, Billy
Sullivan Financial Workup, 10/28/75. • Rhode Island Hospital
Trust National Bank, Billy Sullivan Credit Workup, 11/3/75.
• NFL press release, 12/5/74. • *Boston Globe*, 6/2/74. •
Seattle Times, 10/29/74.

2/6.

INTERVIEWS:

Ed Garvey, 12/3/84. • Wellington Mara, 10/17/84. • Gene
Klein, 9/14/84. • Sargent Karch, 10/17/84.

TESTIMONY:

Ed Garvey, Hearings before Subcommittee on Monopolies,
U.S. Congress, 10/14/75. • Oversight Hearings on National
Football League Labor-Management Dispute, 9/29/75. • Leon-
ard Lindquist, Oversight Hearings on National Football League
Labor-Management Dispute, 9/29/75. • *The New York Times,*
5/26/74, 7/1/74, 7/4/74, 7/11/74, 7/16/74, 7/18/74, 7/21/74,
7/29/74, 8/5/74, 8/7/74, 8/12/74, 9/14/74, 9/15/74, 11/15/74.
• *Los Angeles Times,* 7/16/74.

2/7.

DEPOSITIONS:

Pete Rozelle, *LAMCC v. NFL,* 8/27/80. • NFL, *Official Record Manual,* 1983. • *Sports Illustrated,* 7/22/74, 8/19/74,
10/7/74. • *Time,* 8/26/74, 11/4/74. • [Baltimore] *Sun,* 10/20/72,
10/21/72, 8/13/73, 11/13/73, 11/14/73, 5/3/74, 9/30/74, 10/3/74,
11/28/74, 3/4/84. • [Baltimore] *News-American,* 12/16/73,
12/21/75.

2/8.

NFL minutes, 10/30/74.

INTERVIEWS:

Hugh Culverhouse, 9/18/83. • Pete Rozelle, 6/5/84, 6/11/84.
• Steve Rosenbloom, 9/21/84, 10/11/84. • Tex Schramm,
9/18/84. • Dan Rooney, 10/4/84. • Bob Marr, 1/22/85. • 3
NFL owners, confidential. • NFL source, confidential. •
Culverhouse associate, confidential. • Source close to Rams
sale, confidential.

TESTIMONY:

Al Davis, *Coggins v. New England Patriots,* 5/12/82. • Pete
Rozelle, *NASL v. NFL,* 4/16/80, 4/21/80. • Leonard Tose,
NASL v. NFL, 4/22/80. • letter, Wayne Field to Pete Rozelle,
10/28/74. • letter, Pete Rozelle to Lloyd Nordstrom, 11/13/74.
• Complaint, *Culverhouse v. Los Angeles Rams,* 7/6/72. •
Florida Trend, 9/78. • Associated Press, 10/29/74. • *Tacoma
News Tribune,* 10/29/74. • *Tampa Tribune Times,* 12/3/74. •
Bradenton Herald, 8/20/78. • *Seattle Post-Intelligencer,* 11/1/74.
• *St. Petersburg Times,* 12/8/74.

2/9.

INTERVIEWS:
Robert Gries, 10/11/84, 10/12/84.
TESTIMONY:
Art Modell, *Gries Sports Enterprises v. Cleveland Browns,*
6/18/84, 7/12/84. • Robert Gries, *Gries Sports Enterprises v.
Cleveland Browns,* 6/20/84. • letter, Anthony G. Gulotta to
Art Modell, 2/26/74. • *Akron Beacon Journal,* 1/16/83.

2/10.

NFL minutes, 3/17/75.
INTERVIEWS:
Ed Garvey, 12/3/84.
TESTIMONY:
Ed Garvey, Inquiry Into Professional Sports, U.S. Congress,
6/23/76. • NFLPA, *Labor Organization Annual Report,* De-
partment of Labor, 12/1/73 to 11/30/74. • *Sports Illustrated,*
5/1/72, 4/21/75. • *The New York Times Magazine,* 1/12/75.

2/11.

INTERVIEWS:
Pete Rozelle, 6/5/84, 6/7/84. • Wayne Valley, 9/25/84. •
Lamar Hunt, 9/20/84. • Gene Klein, 9/14/84. • Dan Rooney,
10/4/84. • Tex Schramm, 9/18/84. • Leonard Tose, 10/3/84.
• Art Modell, 11/9/84. • Jay Moyer, 6/5/84. • George Ross,
10/11/84. • Davis associate, confidential.
DEPOSITIONS:
Al Davis, *LAMCC v. NFL,* 11/25/80, 3/4/81. • *Business
Week,* 6/9/75. • *Overdrive,* 9/74. • [Oakland] *Tribune,* 5/20/75,
6/1/75, 6/4/75, 6/5/75, 6/6/75, 6/12/75, 6/13/75, 12/23/75,
5/25/78. • [New York] *Daily News,* 3/9/80, 3/11/80. • *Miami
Herald,* 7/27/78. • *Chicago Tribune,* 5/31/83. • *San Diego
Union,* 11/25/75, 12/20/75. • *San Jose Mercury,* 12/25/75.

2/12.

NFL minutes, 6/24/75, 6/25/75.

INTERVIEWS:
 Billy Sullivan, 10/19/84. • Bob Marr, 1/22/85.
TESTIMONY:
 Edward Bennett Williams, *NASL v. NFL*, 4/7/80. • Lamar
 Hunt, *NASL v. NFL*, 4/2/80. • Demand note, William Sullivan/
 LaSalle National Bank, 11/7/75. • *Boston Globe*, 8/1/75. •
 Boston Herald, 7/31/75.

2/13.

INTERVIEWS:
 Pete Rozelle, 9/25/83, 6/6/84. • Steve Rosenbloom, 9/21/84.
 • Mel Durslag, 10/18/84. • NFL owner, confidential.
TESTIMONY:
 Pete Rozelle, Hearings before the Subcommittee on Monopo-
 lies, 10/14/75. • NFL, *Official Record Manual, 1983.* • *Sports
 Illustrated*, 9/30/74. • *Los Angeles Times*, 7/14/75, 7/26/75,
 7/30/75, 7/31/75, 8/1/75, 8/2/75, 8/6/76, 10/3/79.

2/14.

INTERVIEWS:
 Pete Rozelle, 6/5/84.
TESTIMONY:
 Leonard Lindquist, Oversight Hearings on National Football
 League Labor-Management Dispute, U.S. Congress, 9/29/75.
 • letter, Chris Hemmeter to Pete Rozelle, 10/22/75. • file
 memo, Jay Moyer, 10/16/75. • *Sports Illustrated*, 12/1/75.

2/15.

 NFL minutes, 11/4/75.
INTERVIEWS:
 Chuck Sullivan, 10/17/84. • Bob Marr, 1/22/85. • Pete Rozelle,
 6/11/84.
TESTIMONY:
 Chuck Sullivan, *NASL v. NFL*, 4/22/80. • Billy Sullivan,
 Coggins v. New England Patriots, 5/4/82. • Pete Rozelle,
 Coggins v. New England Patriots, 5/6/82. • letter, Peter
 Toulmin, Rhode Island Hospital Trust National Bank, to Chuck

Sullivan, 11/4/75. • letter, Pete Rozelle to LaSalle National Bank, 11/7/75. • proxy, Mary Sullivan to Billy Sullivan, 11/6/75. • Financial workup, LaSalle National Bank, William Sullivan, 11/7/75. • Memorandum of Closing, LaSalle National Bank and William Sullivan, 11/7/75. • Credit risk offering, Rhode Island Hospital Trust National Bank, William Sullivan, 11/3/75. • *Boston Globe,* 11/11/75.

2/16.

NFL minutes, 11/6/75.
INTERVIEWS:
Leonard Tose, 10/3/84. • Steve Rosenbloom, 10/11/84. • Gene Klein, 9/14/84. • Wellington Mara, 10/17/84. • Bob Marr, 1/22/85. • Pete Rozelle, 6/6/84. • Art Modell, 11/9/84. • Bill McPhail, 9/23/83. • NFL owner, confidential. • *The New York Times,* 1/30/83.

2/17.

NFL minutes, 1/9/76, 1/10/76, 3/18/76.
INTERVIEWS:
Ed Garvey, 12/3/84. • Pete Rozelle, 6/7/84. • Jim Kensil, 6/7/84.
TESTIMONY:
Pete Rozelle, *Coggins v. New England Patriots,* 5/6/82, *NASL v. NFL,* 4/16/80, 4/17/80. • Lamar Hunt, *NASL v. NFL,* 4/2/80. • *Mackey v. NFL,* 407 Federal Supplement 1000 (1975).

2/18.

NFL minutes, 3/15/76, 6/16/76.
INTERVIEWS:
Jay Moyer, 6/6/84.
TESTIMONY:
Pete Rozelle, *NASL v. NFL,* 4/16/80, 4/17/80. • Joe Robbie, *NASL v. NFL,* 4/9/80. • Leonard Tose, *NASL v. NFL,* 4/22/80. • Lamar Hunt, *NASL v. NFL,* 4/3/80. • Edward Bennett Williams, *NASL v. NFL,* 4/7/80.

2/19.

NFL minutes, 3/16/76.
INTERVIEWS:
Pete Rozelle, 6/5/84. • Tex Schramm, 9/18/84.
TESTIMONY:
Pete Rozelle, *LAMCC v. NFL*, 4/5/82. • Associated Press, 5/29/84. • [Baltimore] *Sun*, 3/31/76, 6/15/79. • [Baltimore] *News-American*, 6/17/79. • *Indianapolis News*, 2/17/77.

2/20.

NFL minutes, 3/15/76.
INTERVIEWS:
Pete Rozelle, 6/6/84. • Gene Klein, 9/14/84. • Steve Rosenbloom, 9/21/84. • Art Modell, 11/9/84. • 2 NFL executives, confidential. • NFL, *Official Record Manual*, 1983. • *The New York Times*, 12/25/75.

2/21.

INTERVIEWS:
Robert Gries, 10/12/84.
TESTIMONY:
Art Modell, *Gries Sports Enterprises v. Cleveland Browns*, 6/18/84, 7/12/84, *NASL v. NFL*, 4/23/80. • Robert Gries, *Gries Sports Enterprises v. Cleveland Browns*, 6/20/84. • *Point of View*, 3/27/82. • *Cleveland*, 1974. • [Cleveland] *Plain Dealer*, 7/71, 2/22/77. • *Cleveland Press*, 9/2/72. •

2/22.

memo, Rhode Island Hospital Trust National Bank, R. B. Baxter, re: William A. Sullivan and New England Patriots Football Club, Inc., undated. • memo, Bruce L. Dahltorp, LaSalle National Bank, to William Powers, Rhode Island Hospital Trust National Bank, re: February 20, 1976, meeting on New England Patriots, undated. • memo, Rhode Island Hospital Trust National Bank, P. N. Toulin to A. M. Anderson, re: Patriots loan, 2/12/76. • letter, Joseph H. B. Edwards to John S. Shapira, 8/19/76. • *Boston Globe*, 3/21/82.

2/23.

INTERVIEWS:
Gene Klein, 9/14/84. • Pete Rozelle, 6/11/84. • Mandell, *The Nightmare Season*. • *San Diego Union*, 2/17/76, 3/12/76, 3/13/76, 3/26/76, 12/28/79. • [San Diego] *Tribune*, 3/15/76, 6/8/77, 6/30/77, 1/29/80, 9/23/81. • *Los Angeles Times*, 3/21/74, 3/27/76, 10/6/76. • *Seattle Post-Intelligencer*, 7/11/74.

2/24.

NFL minutes, 3/18/76.
INTERVIEWS:
Dan Rooney, 10/4/84. • Wellington Mara, 10/17/84. • Pete Rozelle, 6/6/84. • Steve Rosenbloom, 9/21/84. • Bob Moore, 2/8/85.
TESTIMONY:
Pete Rozelle, Inquiry into Professional Sports, U.S. Congress, 6/23/76. • Ed Garvey, Inquiry into Professional Sports, U.S. Congress, 6/23/76. • *The New York Times*, 3/19/76, 8/30/76.

2/25.

INTERVIEWS:
Dan Rooney, 10/4/84. • Pete Rozelle, 6/7/84. • Art Modell, 11/9/84. • George Ross, 10/11/84. • Bob Moore, 2/8/85. • Davis employee, confidential.
DEPOSITIONS:
Al Davis, *LAMCC v. NFL*, 11/25/80, 3/4/81. • *Sports Illustrated*, 12/2/74, 8/1/77. • [Oakland] *Tribune*, 4/4/75, 9/13/76, 9/15/76, 9/26/76, 10/6/76, 12/16/76. • *San Francisco Chronicle*, 4/12/75, 4/21/76. • *The New York Times*, 3/19/76.

2/26.

INTERVIEWS:
Steve Rosenbloom, 9/21/84. • Pete Rozelle, 6/6/84. • Bill Robertson, 9/6/84.
DEPOSITIONS:
Al Davis, *LAMCC v. NFL*, 3/4/81. • Georgia Rosenbloom Frontiere, *LAMCC v. NFL*, 9/4/80. • Pete Schabarum, *LAMCC*

v. NFL, 12/19/80. • Don Klosterman, *LAMCC v. NFL*, 1/14/80.
• Los Angeles Coliseum, suite brochure, 1976. • *Los Angeles
Times*, 4/20/76, 10/1/76.

2/27.

INTERVIEWS:

Wellington Mara, 10/17/84. • Pete Rozelle, 6/6/84. • Dan
Rooney, 10/4/84. • *Mackey v. NFL, Federal Reporter*, 543 F.
2d 606 (1976). • NFLPA, *Labor Organization Annual Report*,
Department of Labor, 12/1/75 to 11/30/76. • *Sports Illustrated*,
3/7/77. • United Press International, 2/16/85. • *The New York
Times*, 3/6/77. • *Los Angeles Times*, 3/31/77.

2/28.

letter, Association of Industries of Massachusetts to the Honor-
able Michael Dukakis, 8/13/76. • letter, Securities and Exchange
Commission to F. Douglas Cochrane, re: New England Patriots
Football Club, Inc., 9/17/76. • letter, Alfonso Puyama to New
England Patriots, undated. • letter, Clifford F. Miller to New
England Patriots, 11/23/76. • letter, Joseph H. B. Edwards to
Douglas Cochrane, 8/20/76. • letter, LaSalle National Bank to
William H. Sullivan Jr., 9/19/76. • letter, LaSalle National Bank
to William Sullivan, 11/5/76. • handwritten note, Rhode Island
Hospital Trust National Bank, "Attitude Change," undated. •
memo, Rhode Island Hospital Trust National Bank, P. N.
Toulmin, 7/14/76. • memo, Rhode Island Hospital Trust National
Bank, P. N. Toulmin and R. B. Baxter, 6/21/76. • memo, Rhode
Island Hospital Trust National Bank, Gordon T. Neal to William
P. J. Powers, re: New England Patriots, 7/30/76. • memo,
Rhode Island Hospital Trust National Bank, G. T. Neale to H.
S. Woodbridge Jr., 9/9/76. • memo "for the record," Rhode
Island Hospital Trust National Bank, re: New England Patriots
loans, 10/8/76. • memo, Rhode Island Hospital Trust National
Bank, re: New England Patriots/Billy Sullivan, 10/29/76. • memo,
Rhode Island Hospital Trust National Bank, H. S. Woodbridge
Jr. to W. P. J. Powers, re: New England Patriots, 11/22/76. •
Boston Globe, 11/3/74, 8/25/76, 12/5/76, 12/9/76, 3/21/82. •
Boston Herald, 3/9/74, 12/9/76.

2/29.

NFL minutes, 3/16/76.
DEPOSITIONS:
Al Davis, *LAMCC v. NFL*, 11/25/80. • NFL, *Official Record Manual*, 1983. • *Newsweek*, 1/10/77, 1/24/77. • *Time*, 1/10/77. • *Sports Illustrated*, 1/17/77. • [Oakland] *Tribune*, 1/10/77.

3/1.

NFL minutes, 3/28/77, 3/31/77, 4/1/77, 6/15/77.
INTERVIEWS:
Gene Klein, 9/16/83. • Tex Schramm, 9/15/83. • Pete Rozelle, 8/25/83, 6/7/84. • Wayne Valley, 9/25/84. • George Ross, 10/11/84. • NFL owner, confidential. • 3 Davis friends, confidential.
DEPOSITIONS:
Al Davis, *LAMCC v. NFL*, 3/14/80. • Tex Schramm, *LAMCC v. NFL*, 8/22/80. • press release, Leonard Tose, 12/2/76. • *Sport*, 9/79. • *Inside Sports*, cited *San Francisco Chronicle*, 6/19/81. • [Oakland] *Tribune*, 1/10/77.

3/2.

NFL minutes, 3/28/77.
INTERVIEWS:
Wayne Valley, 9/25/84. • Pete Rozelle, 8/25/83. • Art Modell, 11/9/84. • Steve Rosenbloom, 9/21/84. • 3 NFL owners, confidential.
TESTIMONY:
Pete Rozelle, *NASL v. NFL*, 4/21/80. • Al Davis, *Coggins v. New England Patriots*, 5/12/82.
DEPOSITIONS:
Al Davis, *LAMCC v. NFL*, 11/25/80. • letter, Robert J. Schrieber to NFL, 3/8/77. • letter, Pete Rozelle to Edward J. DeBartolo Sr. and Edward J. DeBartolo Jr., 3/11/77. • *Sports Illustrated*, 4/18/77. • *Business Week*, 10/11/76. • *Forbes*, 9/13/82. • *San Francisco Examiner*, 4/5/77, 5/6/83, 3/20/84. • *San Francisco Chronicle*, 3/15/77. • *Los Angeles Times*, 4/2/77. • [Baltimore] *Sun*, 1/21/77.

3/3.

INTERVIEWS:
NFL owner, confidential. • *City of New York v. New York Jets Football Club, Inc.*, et al, 394 NY 2d 799. • *Fortune*, 1/70. • *The New York Times*, 5/26/68, 8/7/68, 1/20/74, 3/20/74, 4/10/76, 2/2/77, 2/4/77, 2/11/77, 2/12/77, 2/15/77, 2/16/77, 2/18/77, 2/19/77, 2/20/77, 3/17/77, 3/18/77, 5/27/77, 3/3/81.

3/4.

NFL, *Official Record Manual*, 1983. • *Miami News*, 2/3/76, 7/8/76, 8/23/77. • *Miami Herald*, 1/21/76. • *The New York Times*, 2/16/76. • *Minneapolis Tribune*, 5/13/74, 7/14/74. • *Minneapolis Star*, 2/6/76, 3/21/76, 5/11/77, 7/27/77. • *St. Paul News American*, 2/28/75. • [Baltimore] *News-American*, 9/26/77. • *Indianapolis Star*, 4/2/84.

3/5.

TESTIMONY:
Leonard Tose, *Tose v. First Pennsylvania*, 6/25/80. • Sidney Forstater, *Tose v. First Pennsylvania*, 6/17/80. • John Bunting, *Tose v. First Pennsylvania*, 6/11/80. • Edwin Rome, *Tose v. First Pennsylvania*, 6/18/80. • Gerald Hays, *Tose v. First Pennsylvania*, 6/5/80. • Dick Vermeil, *Tose v. First Pennsylvania*, 6/16/80. • F. Anthony Newton, *Tose v. First Pennsylvania*, 6/10/80. • letter, Herb Barness to Leonard Tose, 9/76. • memo, Gerald Hays, 3/24/77. • Associated Press, 8/11/77. • *Philadelphia Inquirer*, 6/12/77, 8/7/77, 8/10/77, 6/20/80. • [Philadelphia] *Bulletin*, 8/10/77. • *Philadelphia Daily News*, 8/10/77, 8/11/77.

3/6.

INTERVIEWS:
Pete Rozelle, 6/7/84. • Gene Klein, 9/14/84. • Jay Moyer, 6/7/84.
DEPOSITIONS:
Al Davis, *LAMCC v. NFL*, 3/14/80. • *Sports Illustrated*,

8/1/77. • [Oakland] *Tribune*, 7/12/77, 7/19/77, 7/21/77, 7/22/77, 7/23/77. • *San Francisco Chronicle*, 3/11/80.

3/7.

NFL minutes, 10/13/77.

INTERVIEWS:
Pete Rozelle, 6/11/84. • Bob Moore, 2/8/85. • 3 NFL owners, confidential. • NFL observer, confidential.

TESTIMONY:
Pete Rozelle, *Coggins v. New England Patriots*, 5/6/82. • Billy Sullivan, *Coggins v. New England Patriots*, 5/4/82. • Al Davis, *Coggins v. New England Patriots*, 5/12/82. • *Florida Trend*, 9/78.

3/8.

INTERVIEWS:
Pete Rozelle, 6/6/84. • Steve Rosenbloom, 9/21/84.

DEPOSITIONS:
Al Davis, *LAMCC v. NFL*, 11/25/80. • James Kenyon, *LAMCC v. NFL*. • Stanford, *Socioeconomic Information on Candidate Areas*. • *Los Angeles Times*, 1/26/78, 1/27/78, 2/17/78, 8/9/78.

3/9.

INTERVIEWS:
Leonard Tose, 10/3/84. • Pete Rozelle, 6/11/84. • Billy Sullivan, 10/19/84. • Gene Klein, 9/14/84.

TESTIMONY:
Pete Rozelle, *LAMCC v. NFL*, 4/6/82. • Chuck Sullivan, *NASL v. NFL*, 4/22/80. • Billy Sullivan, *Coggins v. New England Patriots*, 5/4/82. • Roger Hillas, *Tose v. First Pennsylvania*, 6/20/80. • Alex Krege, *Tose v. First Pennsylvania*, 6/10/80.

DEPOSITIONS:
Pete Rozelle, *LAMCC v. NFL*, 8/28/80. • *Philadelphia Journal*, 2/1/78, 2/8/78. • *Philadelphia Daily News*, 1/17/78, 2/10/78. • *Philadelphia Inquirer*, 2/1/78, 2/10/78. • [Philadelphia] *Bulletin*, 2/10/78. • Associated Press, 2/2/78. • *Boston Herald*, 9/1/78.

3/10.

NFL minutes, 3/16/78.
INTERVIEWS:
Pete Rozelle, 6/6/84. • Bob Moore, 2/8/85. • Jay Moyer, 6/7/84.
TESTIMONY:
Ed Garvey, Hearings before Subcommittee on Labor, U.S. Senate, 10/31/77. • Joe Robbie, *NASL v. NFL*, 4/9/80. • Chuck Sullivan, *NASL v. NFL*, 4/22/80. • Leonard Tose, *NASL v. NFL*, 4/22/80. • Pete Rozelle, *NASL v. NFL*, 4/17/80. • NFLPA, *Labor Organization Annual Report*, Department of Labor, 12/1/76 to 11/30/77. • NFLPA, *Labor Organization Annual Report*, Department of Labor, 12/1/75 to 11/30/76. • NFLPA, *Labor Organization Annual Report*, Department of Labor, 12/1/77 to 11/30/78. • Associated Press, 7/30/77. • *Miami Herald*, 5/15/77, 7/30/77, 8/2/77. • *Miami News*, 8/25/77. • *Philadelphia Inquirer*, 8/12/77.

3/11.

NFL minutes, 3/16/78.
INTERVIEWS:
Steve Rosenbloom, 9/21/84. • Art Modell, 11/9/84.
TESTIMONY:
Pete Rozelle, *NASL v. NFL*, 4/16/80, 4/21/80. • Leonard Tose, *NASL v. NFL*, 4/22/80. • Lamar Hunt, *NASL v. NFL*, 4/2/80, 4/3/80. • Chuck Sullivan, *NASL v. NFL*, 4/22/80. • Art Modell, *NASL v. NFL*, 4/23/80.
DEPOSITIONS:
Max Winter, cited *NASL v. NFL*, 4/22/80. • letter, Lamar Hunt to Pete Rozelle, 3/8/77. • notes, Robert Schulman, 3/16/78. • *San Francisco Chronicle*, 1/6/84. • *Cleveland Press*, 12/8/77.

3/12.

INTERVIEWS:
Bill Robertson, 9/6/84, 12/4/84.
TESTIMONY:
Pete Rozelle, *NASL v. NFL*, 4/21/80. • Lamar Hunt, *NASL v.*

NFL, 4/2/80. • Bill Robertson, *LAMCC v. NFL,* 4/6/82. • James Kenyon, *LAMCC v. NFL,* 4/1/82.

DEPOSITIONS:
Al Davis, *LAMCC v. NFL,* 3/4/81. • Bill Robertson, *LAMCC v. NFL,* 6/8/79, 10/9/80. • Pete Rozelle, *LAMCC v. NFL,* 8/27/80. • letter, Anaheim Stadium Associates to city of Anaheim, 4/17/78. • letter, William O. Talley to Lawrence N. Strenger, 5/1/78. • letter, Gerald Blakely to Carroll Rosenbloom, 5/31/78. • *Los Angeles Times,* 2/22/78, 3/30/78, 4/28/78.

3/13.

INTERVIEWS:
Joe Alioto, 2/1/85. • NFL owner, confidential. • *Tose v. First Pennsylvania Bank,* 492 F Supp 246 (1980). • *Radovich v. NFL,* 362 US 445 1L ed 2d 456, 77 S Ct 390. • *Kapp v. NFL,* 390 Fed Supp 73 (1974). • *Philadelphia,* 10/83. • Philadelphia Eagles press release, 5/5/78. • Associated Press, 4/19/78. • United Press International, 3/31/82. • *Philadelphia Inquirer,* 4/19/78, 4/20/78, 5/10/78, 6/8/78, 3/28/79, 6/20/79. • *Philadelphia Daily News,* 5/6/78. • *San Francisco Chronicle,* 3/11/80. • *Boston Globe,* 4/25/76.

3/14.

NFL minutes, 6/7/78.
INTERVIEWS:
Tex Schramm, 9/18/84.
TESTIMONY:
Pete Rozelle, *NASL v. NFL,* 4/16/80, 4/21/80. • Joe Robbie, *NASL v. NFL,* 4/9/80. • Edward Bennett Williams, *NASL v. NFL,* 4/7/80. • Leonard Tose, *NASL v. NFL,* 4/22/80. • Lamar Hunt, *NASL v. NFL,* 4/2/80. • Art Modell, *NASL v. NFL,* 4/23/80. • Chuck Sullivan, *NASL v. NFL,* 4/22/80. • notes, Don Weiss, 6/7/78.

3/15.

INTERVIEWS:
Bill Robertson, 9/6/84, 1/24/85. • Pete Rozelle, 6/6/84. • Bradley adviser, confidential.

TESTIMONY:
  Bill Robertson, *LAMCC v. NFL,* 4/6/82. • Pete Rozelle, *LAMCC v. NFL,* 4/1/82, 4/2/82, 4/6/82.
DEPOSITIONS:
  Bill Robertson, *LAMCC v. NFL,* 10/9/80. • Pete Rozelle, *LAMCC v. NFL,* 8/28/80. • letter, Bill Robertson to Peter Schabarum, 7/26/78. • letter, Bill Robertson to Carroll Rosenbloom, 7/17/78. • letter, Pete Rozelle to Kenny Hahn, 8/15/78. • memo, J. Kenyon to J. Hines, re: Ram Deal/ Anaheim, 7/10/78. • telegram, Kenneth Hahn to Pete Rozelle, 7/24/78. • *Los Angeles Times,* 7/26/78.

3/16.

NFL constitution and bylaws. • NASL minutes, 8/28/78.
INTERVIEWS:
  Pete Rozelle, 6/6/84. • Lamar Hunt, 9/20/84.
TESTIMONY:
  Pete Rozelle, *NASL v. NFL,* 4/16/80, 4/17/80, 4/21/80. • Lamar Hunt, *NASL v. NFL,* 4/2/80. • Joe Robbie, *NASL v. NFL,* 4/9/80. • Edward Bennett Williams, *NASL v. NFL,* 4/7/80. • Leonard Tose, *NASL v. NFL,* 4/22/80. • memo, Pete Rozelle to NFL Executive Committee, 6/28/78. • *NASL v. NFL,* 505 F Supp 639 (1980). • *Kansas City Star,* 7/17/78.

3/17.

In both this chapter and the following one, I have re-created the NFL's Chicago meeting through the use of a number of different sources. In some cases, I have combined statements made at different points in time inside a single set of quotation marks, but only to amplify a point made on several different occasions and not to alter the thrust of the statement. • NFL minutes, 10/4/78.
INTERVIEWS:
  Steve Rosenbloom, 9/21/84, 10/11/84. • Wellington Mara, 10/17/84. • Joe Robbie, 9/27/83. • Gene Klein, 9/14/84.
TESTIMONY:
  Pete Rozelle, *LAMCC v. NFL,* 4/1/82, 4/5/82. • Bill Robertson, *LAMCC v. NFL,* 4/6/82.

DEPOSITIONS:
Al Davis, *LAMCC v. NFL*, 3/14/80, 11/25/80, 3/4/81. • Pete Rozelle, *LAMCC v. NFL*, 10/11/79, 8/27/80, 8/28/80. • Gene Klein, *LAMCC v. NFL*, 9/17/80 • Ralph Wilson, *LAMCC v. NFL*, 12/4/80. • Art Modell, *LAMCC v. NFL*, 9/24/80. • Robert Schulman, cited *LAMCC v. NFL*, 4/1/82. • notes, Robert Schulman, 10/4/78.

3/18.

See note Chapter 3/17.
NFL minutes, 10/5/78.
INTERVIEWS:
Pete Rozelle, 6/6/84. • Steve Rosenbloom, 9/21/84. • Leonard Tose, 10/3/84. • Gene Klein, 9/14/84. • Jay Moyer, 6/6/84.
TESTIMONY:
Bill Robertson, *LAMCC v. NFL*, 4/6/82. • Pete Rozelle, *LAMCC v. NFL*, 4/1/82, 4/5/82.
DEPOSITIONS:
Al Davis, *LAMCC v. NFL*, 3/14/80, 11/25/80. • Pete Rozelle, *LAMCC v. NFL*, 8/27/80, 8/28/80. • Ralph Wilson, *LAMCC v. NFL*, 12/4/80. • Robert Schulman, cited *LAMCC v. NFL*, 4/1/82. • report, Jim Kensil, cited *LAMCC v. NFL*, 4/5/82. • notes, Robert Schulman, 10/5/78.

3/19.

NFL minutes, 1/29/79.
INTERVIEWS:
Bill Robertson, 9/6/84, 1/24/85. • Gene Klein, 9/14/84. • Mel Durslag, 10/1/84.
TESTIMONY:
Bill Robertson, *LAMCC v. NFL*, 4/6/82.
DEPOSITIONS:
Al Davis, *LAMCC v. NFL*, 11/25/80, 3/4/81. • Bill Robertson, *LAMCC v. NFL*, 6/8/79. • Ralph Wilson, *LAMCC v. NFL*, 12/4/80. • *Los Angeles Herald Examiner*, 7/26/78, 7/27/78, 8/2/78. • [Oakland] *Tribune*, 1/18/79.

3/20.

NFL minutes, 1/28/79.
INTERVIEWS:
Leonard Tose, 10/3/84.
TESTIMONY:
Leonard Tose, *NASL v. NFL*, 4/22/80. • Jimmy Murray, *Tose v. First Pennsylvania Bank*, 6/23/80. • *Philadelphia*, 10/83. • *Philadelphia Inquirer*, 11/20/78, 12/24/78, 1/18/81, 5/23/83. • *Philadelphia Daily News*, 1/4/80, 1/18/81. • [Philadelphia] *Bulletin*, 9/10/79. • [San Diego] *Tribune*, 8/13/83.

3/21.

NFL minutes, 3/14/79, 3/15/79.
INTERVIEWS:
Pete Rozelle, 6/11/84. • Bill Robertson, 9/6/84.
TESTIMONY:
Pete Rozelle, *LAMCC v. NFL*, 4/5/82. • Bill Robertson, *LAMCC v. NFL*, 4/6/82.
DEPOSITIONS:
Bill Robertson, *LAMCC v. NFL*, 6/8/79. • letter, Robert Bush to James Hardy, 1/24/79. • *Miami Dolphins Ltd. v. City of Miami*, Fla. App., 374 So. 2d 1156, 9/18/79. • *Miami Herald*, 3/17/79, 3/18/79. • *Los Angeles Times*, 3/13/79. • [Baltimore] *Sun*, 1/27/79, 1/28/79, 1/29/79, 1/30/79. • *Minneapolis Tribune*, 2/8/79, 3/14/79.

3/22.

NFL minutes, 6/6/79.
INTERVIEWS:
Steve Rosenbloom, 9/21/84, 10/11/84. • Pete Rozelle, 6/6/84. • Gene Klein, 9/14/84. • Source close to Rosenblooms, confidential. • NFL source, confidential. • NFL, Tribute to Carroll Rosenbloom. • *Los Angeles Times*, 4/12/79, 4/13/79, 5/8/79. • *Los Angeles Herald Examiner*, 4/3/79. • [Baltimore] *Sun*, 4/3/79. • *Miami Herald*, 4/3/79.

3/23.

INTERVIEWS:

George Ross, 10/11/84. • L.A. source, confidential.

DEPOSITIONS:
Al Davis, *LAMCC v. NFL*, 11/25/80, 3/4/81. • Bill Robertson, *LAMCC v. NFL*, 6/9/79, 10/9/80. • Georgia Rosenbloom Frontiere, *LAMCC v. NFL*, 9/4/80. • Al LoCasale, *LAMCC v. NFL*, 2/27/81. • John Madden, *LAMCC v. NFL*, 2/25/81. • *Minneapolis Star*, 4/30/79, 5/22/79. • *Minneapolis Tribune*, 5/14/79, 5/19/79, 5/22/79.

3/24.

NFL minutes, 6/5/79, 6/6/79, 3/13/80.

INTERVIEWS:
Pete Rozelle, 6/6/84. • Jack Kent Cooke, 9/27/83. • Art Modell, 11/9/84. • Gene Klein, 9/14/84. • Cooke friend, confidential.

TESTIMONY:
Edward Bennett Williams, *NASL v. NFL*, 4/7/80. • Pete Rozelle, *NASL v. NFL*, 4/17/80. • *The Washingtonian*, 9/82. • *Los Angeles Times*, 5/30/79. • *The New York Times*, 5/30/79. • *Washington Post*, 8/3/79.

3/25.

INTERVIEWS:
Steve Rosenbloom, 9/21/84, 10/11/84. • Pete Rozelle, 6/11/84.

TESTIMONY:
Pete Rozelle, *LAMCC v. NFL*, 4/5/82.

DEPOSITIONS:
Georgia Rosenbloom Frontiere, *LAMCC v. NFL*, 9/4/80. • Dominic Frontiere, *LAMCC v. NFL*, 2/13/81. • Pete Rozelle, *LAMCC v. NFL*, 8/28/80. • Mel Irwin, *LAMCC v. NFL*, 10/8/80, 10/23/80. • memo, Georgia Rosenbloom to the staff of the Rams, 8/6/79. • Georgia Rosenbloom Frontiere, "The Future Is Suddenly Now." • *Sport*, 10/80. • *Los Angeles Times*, 4/4/79, 8/17/79, 10/3/79, 1/26/81. • [Baltimore] *Sun*, 12/9/79. • New York News Service in *Washington Post*.

3/26.

INTERVIEWS:

Bill Robertson, 1/24/85. • George Ross, 10/11/84. • Los Angeles attorney, confidential. • Source close to L.A. negotiations, confidential.

DEPOSITIONS:
Al Davis, *LAMCC v. NFL,* 11/25/80. • Bill Robertson, *LAMCC v. NFL,* 10/9/80. • Pete Rozelle, *LAMCC v. NFL,* 10/11/79, 8/28/80. • letter, Bill Robertson to Football Search Committee, 9/19/79. • *The New York Times Magazine,* 12/13/81. • [Oakland] *Tribune,* 8/13/79, 9/10/79, 9/11/79, 10/25/79, 10/27/79, 10/30/79, 11/2/79. • *San Francisco Chronicle,* 4/7/80, 1/22/81. • *Los Angeles Times,* 3/14/80.

3/27.

INTERVIEWS:
Pete Rozelle, 6/11/84. • Gene Klein, 9/14/84.

DEPOSITIONS:
Pete Rozelle, *LAMCC v. NFL,* 10/11/79. • Associated Press, 6/11/79, 9/22/79. • [Baltimore] *Sun,* 6/12/79, 6/13/79, 8/9/79, 8/10/79, 8/11/79, 8/16/79, 8/17/79, 8/18/79, 8/30/79, 9/2/79, 9/27/79, 9/28/79, 10/16/79, 10/17/79, 10/27/79, 10/29/79, 10/31/79, 11/1/79, 11/2/79, 11/4/79, 12/4/79, 3/4/84. • [Baltimore] *News-American,* 8/10/79, 8/17/79, 9/27/79.

3/28.

INTERVIEWS:
Pete Rozelle, 8/25/83, 6/7/84. • NFL source, confidential.

TESTIMONY:
Pete Rozelle, *LAMCC v. NFL,* 4/5/82, 4/6/82.

DEPOSITIONS:
Al Davis, *LAMCC v. NFL,* 11/25/80, 3/4/81. • Pete Rozelle, *LAMCC v. NFL,* 8/28/80. • Georgia Rosenbloom Frontiere, *LAMCC v. NFL,* 9/4/80. • Dominic Frontiere, *LAMCC v. NFL,* 2/13/81. • Mel Irwin, *LAMCC v. NFL,* 10/8/80.

AFFIDAVITS: • James Hardy, *LAMCC v. NFL,* 1/8/80. • *Hayward Daily Review,* 1/3/80. • [Oakland] *Tribune,* 12/23/79. • *Los Angeles Times,* 12/17/79.

3/29.

INTERVIEWS:
Pete Rozelle, 8/25/83, 6/7/84. • Bill Robertson, 9/6/84. • Jim Kensil, 6/7/84. • Mel Durslag, 10/1/84.
TESTIMONY:
Pete Rozelle, *LAMCC v. NFL*, 4/2/82, 4/6/82.
DEPOSITIONS:
Al Davis, *LAMCC v. NFL*, 3/14/80, 11/25/80, 3/4/81. • Pete Rozelle, *LAMCC v. NFL*, 8/28/80. • Bill Robertson, *LAMCC v. NFL*, 10/9/80.
AFFIDAVITS: • Bill Robertson, *LAMCC v. NFL*, 3/20/80. • letter, Pete Rozelle to Al Davis, 1/10/80. • [Oakland] *Tribune*, 1/5/80, 1/9/80, 1/11/80, 1/12/80, 1/13/80, 1/15/80, 1/18/80, 1/20/80. • *Los Angeles Times*, 1/16/80, 1/19/80. • *Los Angeles Herald Examiner*, 1/17/80.

3/30.

NFL minutes, 10/31/79.
INTERVIEWS:
Steve Rosenbloom, 10/11/84. • Don Klosterman, 9/27/83. • Pete Rozelle, 6/11/84.
DEPOSITIONS:
Mel Irwin, *LAMCC v. NFL*, 10/23/80. • Dominic Frontiere, *LAMCC v. NFL*, 2/13/81. • Don Klosterman, *LAMCC v. NFL*, 11/4/80. • Georgia Rosenbloom Frontiere, *LAMCC v. NFL*, 9/4/80. • Pete Rozelle, *LAMCC v. NFL*, 8/28/80. • Harold Guiver, *LAMCC v. NFL*, 10/14/80. • Al Davis, *LAMCC v. NFL*, 11/25/80. • letter, Harold Guiver to Georgia Rosenbloom, 11/13/79. • letter, Harold Guiver to Georgia Rosenbloom, 1/28/80. • handwritten note, Harold B. Guiver, 10/24/79. • Los Angeles Rams, *Media Guide*, 1978, 1979. • *Time*, 1/28/80. • *Washington Post*, 1/80. • *Miami Herald*, 9/19/79. • *The New York Times*, 6/12/78.

3/31.

INTERVIEWS:
Pete Rozelle, 8/9/83. • Bill Robertson, 1/24/85. • Davis source, confidential.
TESTIMONY:
Pete Rozelle, *LAMCC v. NFL*, 4/5/82. • Bill Robertson, *LAMCC v. NFL*, 4/6/82.

DEPOSITIONS:
   Al Davis, *LAMCC v. NFL*, 3/14/80, 3/4/81. • Bill Robertson, *LAMCC v. NFL*, 10/9/80. • Mel Irwin, *LAMCC v. NFL*, 10/23/80.
AFFIDAVITS: • Al Davis, *LAMCC v. NFL*, 3/18/80. • Los Angeles Rams phone records, cited *LAMCC v. NFL*, 4/6/82. • *LAMCC v. NFL, California Reporter*, Volume 26, Number 52. • [Oakland] *Tribune*, 1/25/80, 1/30/80, 2/3/80, 2/4/80. • *Los Angeles Times*, 1/25/80, 3/5/80. • *Los Angeles Herald Examiner*, 1/24/80.

4/1.

   NFL minutes, 3/3/80.
INTERVIEWS:
   Pete Rozelle, 6/7/84.
TESTIMONY:
   Pete Rozelle, *LAMCC v. NFL*, 4/2/82, 4/5/82.
DEPOSITIONS:
   Al Davis, *LAMCC v. NFL*, 11/25/80. • Pete Rozelle, *LAMCC v. NFL*, 8/27/80. • Art Modell, *LAMCC v. NFL*, 9/24/80.
AFFIDAVITS:
   Al Davis, *LAMCC v. NFL*, 3/18/80. • [Oakland] *Tribune*, 3/2/80. • *San Francisco Examiner*, 3/3/80. • *Los Angeles Times*, 3/4/80.

4/2.

INTERVIEWS:
   Art Modell, 9/14/83, 11/9/84. • Bill Robertson, 9/6/84. • Stephen Reinhardt, 10/9/84.
TESTIMONY:
   Art Modell, *Gries Sports Enterprises v. Cleveland Browns*, 6/18/84, 7/12/84, *NASL v. NFL*, 4/23/80. • Pete Rozelle, *LAMCC v. NFL*, 4/2/82, 4/5/82, 4/6/82.
DEPOSITIONS:
   Al Davis, *LAMCC v. NFL*, 11/25/80. • Art Modell, *LAMCC v. NFL*, 9/24/80. • Pete Rozelle, *LAMCC v. NFL*, 8/27/80. • telegram, Al Davis to Pete Rozelle, 3/6/80. • *Akron Beacon Journal*, 1/18/83. • [Cleveland] *Plain Dealer*, 3/4/77, 9/26/78, 11/30/79, 1/13/81. • *Cleveland Press*, 3/27/80. • [Oakland] *Tribune*, 3/7/80, 3/8/80.

4/3.

NFL minutes, 3/10/80.

INTERVIEWS:
Gene Klein, 9/14/80. • Leonard Tose, 10/3/84. • Joe Robbie, 9/27/83.

TESTIMONY:
Pete Rozelle, *LAMCC v. NFL*, 4/2/82, 4/6/82.

DEPOSITIONS:
Al Davis, *LAMCC v. NFL*, 11/25/80. • Pete Rozelle, *LAMCC v. NFL*, 8/27/80. • *Sports Illustrated*, 3/24/80.

4/4.

INTERVIEWS:
Tex Schramm, 9/15/83, 9/18/84. • Stephen Reinhardt, 10/9/84. • L.A. source, confidential.

TESTIMONY:
Bill Robertson, *LAMCC v. NFL*, 4/6/82. • Pete Rozelle, *LAMCC v. NFL*, 4/2/82.

AFFIDAVITS: • Yvonne Burke, *LAMCC v. NFL*, 3/18/80. • letter, John Larsen to Al Davis, 3/3/80. • memo, Harry Hufford to Board of Supervisors, 2/26/80. • motion, Baxter Ward to Board of Supervisors, 2/26/80. • *LAMCC v. NFL, Federal Register*, Volume 26, Number 52, 12/24/82. • *Sports Illustrated*, 3/24/80. • *Los Angeles Times*, 3/18/80. • [Oakland] *Tribune*, 3/26/80.

4/5.

INTERVIEWS:
Pete Rozelle, 6/6/84.

TESTIMONY:
Lamar Hunt, *NASL v. NFL*, 4/2/80, 4/3/80. • Edward Bennett Williams, *NASL v. NFL*, 4/7/80. • Joe Robbie, *NASL v. NFL*, 4/9/80. • Pete Rozelle, *NASL v. NFL*, 4/16/80, 4/17/80, 4/21/80, 4/22/80. • Leonard Tose, *NASL v. NFL*, 4/22/80. • Chuck Sullivan, *NASL v. NFL*, 4/22/80. • Art Modell, *NASL v. NFL*, 4/23/80. • *NASL v. NFL*, 505 F Supp 659 (1980). • *NASL v. NFL*, 670 F. 2d 1249 (1982). • *Texas Monthly*, 4/78.

4/6.

TESTIMONY:
Leonard Tose, *NASL v. NFL,* 4/22/80, *Tose v. First Pennsylvania Bank,* 6/24/80, 6/25/80, 6/26/80. • *NFL Record and Fact Book.* • *Tose v. First Pennsylvania Bank,*492 F Supp 246 (1980). • *Philadelphia Inquirer,* 4/5/80, 6/25/80, 6/27/80, 7/1/80. • [Philadelphia] *Bulletin,* 1/22/81. • *Philadelphia Daily News,* 1/4/80.

4/7.

INTERVIEWS:
Gene Klein, 9/14/84. • Pete Rozelle, 8/9/83, 6/11/84. • Joe Alioto, 2/1/85. • Jay Moyer, 6/6/84, 6/7/84. • Bill McPhail, 9/23/83.
DEPOSITIONS:
Al Davis, *LAMCC v. NFL,* 3/14/80, 11/25/80. • Gene Klein, *LAMCC v. NFL,* 9/17/80. • [San Diego] *Tribune,* 2/14/80. • *San Diego Union,* 2/15/80. • [Oakland] *Tribune,* 10/25/79. • *Los Angeles Times,* 3/3/80.

4/8.

INTERVIEWS:
Steve Rosenbloom, 9/21/84. • Pete Rozelle, 6/11/84. • NFL owner, confidential. • NFL source, confidential.
DEPOSITIONS:
Al Davis, *LAMCC v. NFL,* 11/25/80, 3/4/81. • Pete Rozelle, *LAMCC v. NFL,* 8/28/80. • Dominic Frontiere, *LAMCC v. NFL,* 2/13/81. • Bill Robertson, *LAMCC v. NFL,* 10/9/80. • Mel Irwin, *LAMCC v. NFL,* 10/8/80, 10/23/80. • Harold Guiver, *LAMCC v. NFL,* 10/14/80. • speech, Georgia Rosenbloom Frontiere, 4/15/84. • Georgia Rosenbloom Frontiere, "Cynics and Critics," *Los Angeles Times,* 9/4/81. • *TV Guide,* 12/17/83. • *Los Angeles Times,* 4/7/80, 7/22/80, 8/7/80, 9/25/80, 10/30/80, 12/11/80, 4/19/81, 12/18/81. • *Los Angeles Herald Examiner,* 3/20/81. • *Florida Ledger,* 9/17/81. • *Miami Herald,* 12/26/80.

4/9.

DEPOSITIONS:
Al Davis, *LAMCC v. NFL*, 11/25/80. • *Sports Illustrated*, 1/6/81, 1/19/81, 2/2/81. • *Los Angeles Times*, 1/9/81, 1/24/81, 1/29/81. • *Los Angeles Herald Examiner*, 1/5/81. • *Philadelphia Daily News*, 1/8/81. • [Oakland] *Tribune*, 1/16/81.

4/10.

INTERVIEWS:
Robert Gries, 10/12/84.
TESTIMONY:
Art Modell, *Gries Sports Enterprises v. Cleveland Browns*, 6/18/84, 7/12/84. • William Huffman, *Gries Sports Enterprises v. Cleveland Browns*, 6/19/84. • *Sporting News*, 12/6/80. • [Cleveland] *Plain Dealer*, 5/23/82.

4/11.

TESTIMONY:
Art Modell, *NASL v. NFL*, 4/23/80. • letter, Robert Irsay to Colts ticket holders, 1/16/81. • *Playboy*, 8/81. • [Baltimore] *Sun*, 9/16/79, 9/18/79, 3/1/80, 4/4/80, 4/10/80, 5/24/80, 12/19/80, 1/3/81, 1/24/81, 2/11/81, 6/9/81, 6/11/81, 7/15/81, 9/3/81, 11/20/81. • [Baltimore] *News-American*, 11/12/78, 12/22/80. • *Washington Post*, 2/26/80.

4/12.

INTERVIEWS:
Joe Robbie, 9/27/83. • Tex Schramm, 9/15/83. • Pete Rozelle, 6/7/84. • Bill Robertson, 9/6/84, 1/24/85. • Jay Moyer, 6/7/84. • L.A. source, confidential. • *Los Angeles Times*, 1/14/81, 2/7/81, 3/17/81. • *Los Angeles Herald Examiner*, 4/6/81. • *San Francisco Chronicle*, 3/18/81, 5/9/81.

4/13.

In this, and the following two chapters that re-create the first trial of *LAMCC v. NFL*, I have used both the testimony as taken in the trial itself and the trial coverage of the following newspapers: *Los Angeles Times, San Diego Union, San Francisco Chronicle,* [Oakland] *Tribune.* In addition I have also used the following:
INTERVIEWS:
Pete Rozelle, 6/7/84. • Gene Klein, 9/14/84. • Jay Moyer, 6/7/84. • *LAMCC v. NFL, Federal Reporter,* Volume 26, Number 52, 12/24/82. • *The New York Times,* 1/30/83.

4/14.

See note 4/13.
INTERVIEWS:
Federal Court source, confidential. • Georgia Frontiere, "Courting a Sport," *Los Angeles Times,* 9/4/81. • *Riverside Press Enterprise,* 6/9/81. • [Baltimore] *Sun,* 6/10/81.

4/15.

See note 4/13.
INTERVIEWS:
Leonard Tose, 10/3/84. • Jay Moyer, 6/7/84. • NFL source, confidential.
TESTIMONY:
Art Modell, *Gries Sports Enterprises v. Cleveland Browns,* 7/12/84. • [Cleveland] *Plain Dealer,* 7/10/81, 8/16/81.

4/16.

INTERVIEWS:
Ed Garvey, 12/3/84. • Jack Donlan, 10/17/84. • Bob Moore, 2/8/85. • Keith Fahnhorst, 12/6/84.
DEPOSITIONS:
Al Davis, *LAMCC v. NFL,* 11/25/80. • NFLPA, *Labor Organization Annual Report,* Department of Labor, 12/1/78 to 11/30/79, 12/1/77 to 11/30/78, 12/1/76 to 11/30/77. • NFLPA, *The Audible,* 1/82. • NFLPA, *Report to Members,* 9/81. • [Cleveland] *Plain Dealer,* 9/11/81.

4/17.

INTERVIEWS:
Robert Gries, 10/12/84.
TESTIMONY:
Art Modell, *Gries Sports Enterprises v. Cleveland Browns,* 6/18/84, 7/12/84. • Robert Gries, *Gries Sports Enterprises v. Cleveland Browns,* 6/20/84. • Jay C. Hall, *Gries Sports Enterprises v. Cleveland Browns,* 6/19/84. • William Huffman, *Gries Sports Enterprises v. Cleveland Browns,* 6/19/84.

4/18.

INTERVIEWS:
Art Modell, 11/9/84. • Bill Robertson, 9/6/84, 1/24/85. • Stephen Reinhardt, 10/9/84. • Mel Durslag, 10/1/84. • L.A. source, confidential. • 2 negotiations sources, confidential. • Participant, confidential. • *Los Angeles Times,* 9/27/81, 9/28/81, 9/30/81. • [Cleveland] *Plain Dealer,* 3/28/82.

4/19.

INTERVIEWS:
Billy Sullivan, 10/19/84. • Bob Marr, 1/22/85. • Jack Donlan, 10/17/84. • Source at Miami meetings, confidential • NFLPA, Bargaining Demands, 2/82. • United Press, 3/31/82. • *Fortune,* 8/20/84. • *Boston Globe,* 7/26/81, 7/28/81, 8/13/81, 11/6/81. • *Boston Herald,* 4/1/81, 8/4/81. • *The New York Times,* 2/17/82, 2/19/82.

4/20.

INTERVIEWS:
Steve Rosenbloom, 9/21/84. • Paul Tagliabue, 6/7/84. • Ben Zelenko, 9/5/83.
TESTIMONY:
Pete Rozelle, Hearings before the Subcommittee on Monopolies, U.S. Congress, 12/10/81. • NFLPA, *The Audible,* 1/82. • *Memphis Commercial Appeal,* 1/22/82. • *The New York Times,* 2/19/82, 3/26/82. • *Los Angeles Times,* 3/19/82.

4/21.

INTERVIEWS:
  Robert Gries, 10/12/84.
TESTIMONY:
  Art Modell, *Gries Sports Enterprises v. Cleveland Browns,*
  6/18/84, 7/12/84. • Robert Gries, *Gries Sports Enterprises v.
  Cleveland Browns,* 6/20/84. • William Huffman, *Gries Sports
  Enterprises v. Cleveland Browns,* 6/19/84. • [Cleveland] *Plain
  Dealer,* 3/28/82.

4/22.

  NFL minutes, 3/22/82.
INTERVIEWS:
  Pete Rozelle, 6/5/84. • Gene Klein, 9/14/84. • Leonard Tose,
  10/3/84. • Contract source, confidential.
TESTIMONY:
  Pete Rozelle, Hearings before the Subcommittee on Monopo-
  lies, U.S. Congress, 12/10/81, *LAMCC v. NFL,* 4/2/82. • Art
  Modell, *Gries Sports Enterprises v. Cleveland Browns,* 7/12/84.
DEPOSITIONS:
  Al Davis, *LAMCC v. NFL,* 3/4/81. • *Sports Illustrated,* 3/29/82.
  • *San Francisco Examiner,* 3/12/80. • [Cleveland] *Plain Dealer,*
  5/29/82.

4/23.

INTERVIEWS:
  Art Modell, 9/14/83. • Pete Rozelle, 6/7/84. • Jay Moyer,
  6/7/84. • NFL source, confidential. • *Sport,* 8/82. • [Cleveland]
  Plain Dealer, 5/8/82. • *The New York Times,* 1/30/83. • *Los
  Angeles Times,* 3/30/82, 4/2/82, 4/7/82, 4/22/82, 5/8/82. •
  [Oakland] *Tribune,* 5/10/82.

4/24.

INTERVIEWS:
  Pete Rozelle, 6/7/84. • Leonard Tose, 10/3/84.
TESTIMONY:

Pete Rozelle, Hearings before the Judiciary Committee, U.S. Senate, 8/16/82. • Al Davis, Hearings before the Judiciary Committee, U.S. Senate, 9/20/82. • Ed Garvey, Hearings before the Judiciary Committee, U.S. Senate, 8/16/82. • Bill Robertson, Hearings before the Judiciary Committee, U.S. Senate, 8/16/82. • *Los Angeles Times*, 5/22/82, 8/12/82.

4/25.

INTERVIEWS:

Leonard Tose, 9/20/83, 10/3/84. • Dan Rooney, 10/4/84. • Pete Rozelle, 8/9/83, 6/6/84. • Hugh Culverhouse, 9/19/83. • Jack Donlan, 10/17/84. • Bob Moore, 2/8/85. • Keith Fahnhorst, 12/6/84. • NFLPA, flyer, undated. • NFLPA, *Because We Are the Game.* • *Time*, 10/4/82. • *Sports Illustrated*, 2/1/82, 9/27/82. • *U.S. News and World Report*, 9/6/82. • Associated Press, 11/9/82. • *The New York Times*, 9/9/82, 10/1/82, 10/9/82, 10/10/82, 10/18/82, 11/1/82, 11/5/82, 11/7/82, 11/8/82, 11/15/82, 11/17/82, 11/19/82. • *San Diego Union*, 10/28/82. • *St. Petersburg Times*, 11/9/82.

4/26.

INTERVIEWS:

Pete Rozelle, 8/9/83, 6/7/84. • Gene Klein, 9/14/84. • Chuck Sullivan, 10/17/84. • Lamar Hunt, 9/22/83. • Hugh Culverhouse, 9/19/83. • Tex Schramm, 9/14/83. • Art Modell, 9/14/83. • Steve Rosenbloom, 9/21/84. • Ed Garvey, 9/24/83. • Keith Fahnhorst, 12/6/84. • Rozelle friend, confidential. • NFLPA, *Labor Organization Annual Report*, Department of Labor, 12/1/82 to 11/30/83. • *Sports Illustrated*, 11/29/82. • *Macleans*, 11/29/82. • *The New York Times*, 12/7/82, 1/9/83, 6/7/83. • *San Francisco Chronicle*, 9/14/83.

4/27.

NFL minutes, 3/21/83, 3/22/83.

INTERVIEWS:

Dan Rooney, 10/4/84. • Pete Rozelle, 8/25/83, 6/11/84. • Gene Klein, 9/14/84. • NFL source, confidential. • *Phila-*

delphia, 10/83. • [Cleveland] *Plain Dealer*, 3/20/83. • *San Francisco Examiner*, 5/6/83. • *The New York Times*, 3/23/83. • *Los Angeles Times*, 4/14/83.

4/28.

NFL minutes, 3/22/83.
INTERVIEWS:
Leonard Tose, 10/3/84. • Art Modell, 11/9/84. • Pete Rozelle, 8/9/83, 6/11/84. • NFL source, confidential. • *Sports Illustrated*, 9/19/83. • *Philadelphia*, 83. • Associated Press, 1/12/83, 7/21/83, 9/21/83, 11/21/83. • *Philadelphia Inquirer*, 1/5/83, 1/29/83, 5/22/83, 5/23/83, 7/10/83, 7/13/83, 7/17/83, 8/7/83. • *Philadelphia Daily News*, 11/22/83.

4/29.

INTERVIEWS:
Art Modell, 11/9/84. • Pete Rozelle, 6/11/84. • Robert Gries, 10/12/84.
DEPOSITIONS:
Gabe Paul, *Cleveland Indians v. Cleveland Stadium Corp.*, 1/20/84. • letter, Art Modell to Robert Gries, 5/6/82. • letter, Robert Gries to Art Modell, 5/7/82. • letter, Art Modell to Gabe Paul, 1/20/82. • [Cleveland] *Plain Dealer*, 3/18/82, 6/10/82, 10/30/82, 11/13/82, 4/21/83, 4/27/83, 5/3/83, 6/12/83, 9/4/83. • *Cleveland Press*, 3/18/82.

4/30.

NFL minutes, 5/25/83.
INTERVIEWS:
Art Modell, 9/14/83. • Pete Rozelle, 8/25/83, 6/11/84. • Billy Sullivan, 10/19/84. • Steve Rosenbloom, 9/21/84. • Leonard Tose, 10/3/84. • NFL owner, confidential. • NFL source, confidential. • *The New York Times*, 5/25/83. • *San Francisco Examiner*, 9/7/83. • *Boston Herald*, 2/21/83, 6/30/83. • *Boston Globe*, 6/30/83. • *Los Angeles Times*, 12/6/82, 3/13/83. • *Riverside Press Enterprise*, 12/19/80. • *Palm Springs Desert Sun*, 10/8/83.

4/31.

INTERVIEWS:
Gene Klein, 9/14/84. • Paul Tagliabue, 6/7/84. • Jay Moyer,
6/7/84. • *Sports Illustrated*, 8/29/83, 9/5/84. • *San Diego
Union*, 1/15/83, 10/13/83, 12/10/83. • [San Diego] *Tribune*,
11/9/83. • *The New York Times*, 6/26/83. • *San Francisco
Chronicle*, 6/1/83, 6/24/83, 6/28/83, 7/27/83. • *San Francisco
Examiner*, 6/18/83, 7/22/83, 10/12/83. • [Oakland] *Tribune*,
5/83, 6/1/83, 7/22/83. • *Los Angeles Times*, 10/27/83.

4/32.

NFL minutes, 10/5/83
INTERVIEWS:
2 NFL owners, confidential. • *Miami News*, 12/13/82, 12/14/82.
• *Miami Herald*, 9/1/83. • [Baltimore] *Sun*, 8/22/82, 6/3/83,
9/2/83, 9/28/83. • *Indianapolis Star*, 1/13/82. • *New York
Post*, 9/29/83. • *The New York Times*, 9/18/80, 12/5/80,
9/14/83, 9/29/83, 11/23/83, 2/5/85.

4/33.

NFL minutes, 10/5/83.
INTERVIEWS:
Pete Rozelle, 8/9/83, 8/25/83, 6/11/84. • Gene Klein, 9/14/84.
• Art Modell, 10/9/83. • Rozelle friend, confidential. • *San
Francisco Chronicle*, 10/5/83, 10/6/83, 10/7/83. • *Peninsula
Times Tribune*, 10/6/83, 1/9/84.

4/34.

INTERVIEWS:
Pete Rozelle, 6/7/84. • Tex Schramm, 9/18/84. • Art Modell,
9/14/83. • Joe Robbie, 9/27/83. • Leonard Tose, 10/3/84. •
Bill Robertson, 9/6/84. • 2 NFL owners, confidential. • NFL
source, confidential. • Bradley source, confidential. • NFL
observer, confidential. • NFL insider, confidential. • author's
notes, Rozelle press conference, 1/20/84. • *Sports Illustrated*,
9/5/84. • *Forbes*, 10/1/84. • *The New York Times*, 1/15/84. •

Dallas Morning News, 12/14/83. • *Washington Post,* 1/23/84. • *San Francisco Chronicle,* 10/3/83, 10/27/83, 11/29/83, 1/24/84. • *Los Angeles Times,* 2/3/83. • *Peninsula Times Tribune,* 1/22/84, 2/28/84. • *Tampa Tribune,* 1/23/84.

5/1.

INTERVIEWS:

Tex Schramm, 9/18/84. • Pete Rozelle, 6/11/84. • Leonard Tose, 10/3/84. • Joe Alioto, 2/1/84. • *Newsweek,* 9/3/84. • *Forbes,* 9/13/82. • *Dallas Times Herald,* 11/15/83, 1/14/84, 1/22/84, 1/28/84, 3/3/84, 3/17/84. • *Dallas Morning News,* 11/14/83, 11/15/83, 12/14/83, 1/8/84, 1/18/84, 2/25/84, 3/10/84. • *San Francisco Chronicle,* 4/18/84. • *Washington Post,* 3/20/84. • *The New York Times,* 3/5/85. • *The Wall Street Journal,* 1/22/85.

5/2.

INTERVIEWS:

Pete Rozelle, 6/11/84. • Gene Klein, 9/14/84. • transcript, Robert Irsay press conference, 1/20/84, recorded by [Baltimore] *Sun.* • Jimmy Irsay, "Hoosier Heartland," *Sports Illustrated,* 11/19/84. • *Newsweek,* 4/9/84. • *Sporting News,* 1/21/85. • *People,* 1/86. • [Baltimore] *Sun,* 1/20/84, 1/21/84, 1/22/84, 3/2/84, 3/16/84. • [Baltimore] *News-American,* 1/21/84, 3/3/84, 3/15/84. • *Indianapolis Star,* 3/12/84, 3/31/84, 4/1/84. • *Indianapolis News,* 4/2/84. • *San Jose Mercury,* 3/21/84, 3/22/84. • *Washington Post,* 3/30/84, 4/8/84.

5/3.

INTERVIEWS:

Billy Sullivan, 10/19/84. • *Game Day,* 11/11/84. • *Miami News,* 1/27/84, 3/2/84, 3/6/84, 11/28/84. • *Miami Herald,* 3/6/84, 3/10/84, 3/14/84, 5/25/84, 6/23/84, 7/7/84, 7/29/84, 10/8/84, 11/15/84, 1/9/85. • *San Francisco Examiner,* 3/17/85.

5/4.

INTERVIEWS:
Gene Klein, 9/14/84. • *Sports Illustrated,* 1/16/84, 2/25/85. •
Forbes, 11/5/84. • *San Francisco Magazine,* 3/84. • *San
Francisco Examiner,* 3/10/84, 3/19/84, 3/20/84, 3/23/84,
3/27/84, 10/24/84, 12/9/84. • *San Francisco Chronicle,* 1/11/84,
7/23/84, 12/2/84. • *San Jose Mercury,* 3/6/84, 3/16/84. • *The
New York Times,* 3/23/84, 4/30/84, 10/18/84.

5/5.

INTERVIEWS:
Gene Klein, 9/14/84. • Pete Rozelle, 6/11/84, 2/18/86. •
complaint, *Klein v. Davis,* 1/30/84. • *San Diego Union,*
3/23/84, 7/31/84, 8/1/84, 8/3/84, 8/28/84. • [Oakland] *Tribune,*
3/23/84.

5/6.

INTERVIEWS:
Wellington Mara, 10/17/84. • Art Rooney, 9/16/83. • Dan
Rooney, 9/19/83, 10/4/84.

5/7.

INTERVIEWS:
Lamar Hunt, 9/22/83, 9/20/84. • Hearings, Committee on
Government Operations, Subcommittee on Commerce, U.S.
Congress, *Silver Prices and the Adequacy of Federal Actions
in the Marketplace, 1977–80,* 3/31 to 5/22/80. • Commodity
Futures Trading Commission, *Report on Recent Developments
in the Futures Market,* 1980. • *Fortune,* 4/1/85. • *Forbes,*
10/1/84. • *Newsweek,* 3/11/85.

5/8.

INTERVIEWS:
Leonard Tose, 9/20/83, 10/3/84. • *NFL Record and Fact
Book.* • Associated Press, 1/30/84. • *Philadelphia Inquirer,*
3/27/84. • *The New York Times,* 12/17/84, 12/30/84, 2/3/85,

3/6/85, 3/9/85, 3/11/85, 4/7/85. • *Phoenix Gazette*, 11/8/84. • *San Francisco Examiner*, 12/11/84, 12/14/84. • *San Francisco Chronicle*, 11/13/84, 12/13/84, 12/15/84, 12/17/84, 12/18/84.

5/9.

INTERVIEWS:
Source close to investigation, confidential. • Source close to Georgia Frontiere, confidential. • Rams source, confidential. • *TV Guide*, 12/17/83. • *Los Angeles Times*, 12/9/83, 12/23/83, 3/1/84, 3/9/84, 3/10/84, 3/21/84. • *Los Angeles Herald Examiner*, 12/9/83, 12/10/83. • *The New York Times*, 12/10/83.

5/10.

INTERVIEWS:
Billy Sullivan, 10/19/84. • Chuck Sullivan, 10/16/84. • *Fortune*, 8/20/84. • *Sports Illustrated*, 1/13/86. • CBS News, 1/13/86. • *USA Today*, 1/13/86. • *San Francisco Chronicle*, 10/28/84, 12/10/84, 1/6/86. • *San Francisco Examiner*, 6/30/84, 10/23/85. • *Los Angeles Times*, 11/30/84, 12/5/84.

5/11.

INTERVIEWS:
Art Modell, 11/9/84. • Robert Gries, 10/12/84, 10/24/84.
TESTIMONY:
Art Modell, *Gries Sports Enterprises v. Cleveland Browns*, 7/12/84. • brochure, Vote Yes on Issue 1. • [Cleveland] *Plain Dealer*, 3/16/83, 12/2/83, 1/7/84, 3/16/84, 3/17/84, 5/9/84, 8/3/84, 8/31/84, 4/26/85, 7/2/85. • *Akron Beacon Journal*, 7/4/84, 7/16/84, 8/3/84.

5/12.

INTERVIEWS:
Tex Schramm, 9/18/84. • Pete Rozelle, 2/18/86. • Bill Robertson, 1/24/85. • NFL source, confidential. • Davis associ-

ate, confidential. • Associated Press, 11/7/84. • *Los Angeles Times*, 9/17/84, 11/15/84, 11/25/84, 11/30/84, 12/9/84. • *The New York Times*, 3/17/85. • *San Francisco Chronicle*, 3/23/84. • *San Francisco Examiner*, 1/15/84, 12/19/84, 3/17/85.

5/13.

INTERVIEWS:
Pete Rozelle, 6/5/84, 2/18/86. • NFL source, confidential. • invocation, Hall of Fame Enshrinement, 8/3/85. • speech, Tex Schramm, Hall of Fame Enshrinement, 8/3/85. • speech, Pete Rozelle, Hall of Fame Enshrinement, 8/3/85. • *NFL Record and Fact Book*. • A. C. Neilsen and Co., cited *The New York Times*, 10/25/84. • *Sports Illustrated*, 2/24/86. • *Boston Globe*, 2/2/84. • *San Francisco Examiner*, 2/21/84, 6/13/84, 11/25/84. • *San Francisco Chronicle*, 1/27/85, 2/19/85. • *San Jose Mercury*, 4/28/84, 6/14/84. • [Oakland] *Tribune*, 11/6/84. • *Washington Post*, 1/21/85. • *The New York Times*, 11/23/83, 10/25/84, 12/30/84, 1/19/85, 3/17/85, 1/19/86.

Index

BANTAM
SHOP~AT~HOME
C·A·T·A·L·O·G

Special Offer
Buy a Bantam Book
for only 50¢.

Now you can have Bantam's catalog filled with hundreds of titles plus take advantage of our unique and exciting bonus book offer. A special offer which gives you the opportunity to purchase a Bantam book for only 50¢. Here's how!

By ordering any five books at the regular price per order, you can also choose any other single book listed (up to a $5.95 value) for just 50¢. Some restrictions do apply, but for further details why not send for Bantam's catalog of titles today!

Just send us your name and address and we will send you a catalog!
